FASCISM IN GERMANY

*How Hitler Destroyed the World's
Most Powerful Labour Movement*

by Robert Black

CONTENTS

Volume I   Page

Introduction   I

Chapter 1   The Roots of German Reaction   1

         2   Marx and Engels on the German Question:
             Bonapartism and the Bismarckian Legacy   26

         3   'Blood and Iron': The Politics of German
             Heavy Industry   51

         4   The Heroic Age of German Labour   69

         5   The Imperialist Crucible   97

         6   The First Seeds are Sown   142

         7   The First Betrayals: Social Democracy
             in War and Revolution   168

         8   The Political Economy of National
             Socialism   191

         9   Hitler: The Formative Years   224

        10   No Man's Land   246

        11   NSDAP   285

        12   Italy: The First Warning   324

        13   From Kapp to Munich: Genesis of a
             Strategy   367

        14   Big Business Rationalises   423

        15   Hitler Rebuilds   461

        16   United Front from below   493

        17   The World Crisis and the Fall of Mueller   546

Volume II

Chapter 18   September 14, 1930   593

        19   'Toleration'   633

        20   Hitler's Road to Harzburg   653

        21   'Red Unions'   703

        22   Stalin over Germany: From Rapallo
             to Red Referendum   735

        23   The 18th Brumaire of Franz von Papen   787

        24   The Last Chance   844

CONTENTS (continued)

			Page
Chapter	25	National Concentration	880
	26	Capital and Labour in the Third Reich	963

APPENDICES

I	German Fascism and The Historians	1003
II	Social Democracy on the German Catastrophe	1020
III	History Falsified	1029
IV	Germany and the Fourth International	1070

Author's Postscript	1138

| Bibliography and Index | 1140 |

INTRODUCTION

Trotsky once described Hitler's triumph as 'the greatest defeat of the proletariat in the history of the world'.

And despite forty years more of imperialist wars, betrayed revolutions and ultra-rightest coups, we have no reason to revise this judgement. In the brief period between Hitler's terror election 'victory' of March 5, 1933, and July 24, when Nazi Germany was officially declared a one party state, the world's most powerful, disciplined, wealthy and politically cultured labour movement had been reduced to rubble. To grasp the sheer physical magnitude of this defeat, it is necessary to take an inventory of the assets assembled with such sacrifice and devotion by the German working class over three quarters of a century which were pillaged by the Nazi looters.

On the eve of Hitler's victory, the Social Democratic Party published no fewer than 196 daily newspapers, 18 weeklies and one monthly theoretical journal. The German Trade Union Federation, allied with but officially independent of the SPD, also published numerous journals for its various affiliated unions. And with a membership of approximately five million workers, they commanded an entire parallel apparatus alongside that of the Social Democrats. Then there was the German Communist Party, whose membership at the end of 1932 was, at about 350,000, one third of the SPD's. The Communist Party apart from publishing nearly a score of daily papers, produced several weeklies and its own theoretical journal. And it too had its own trade union organisation, the Red Trade Union Opposition, which at its peak claimed about 320,000 workers. So allowing for the inevitable overlapping of membership in these organisations, we still have a compact and centrally directed proletarian army of some six million troops, who at election times with clockwork regularity gathered around themselves a further six to seven million voters. Indeed, in the last free parliamentary elections of November 12, 1933, the combined Communist-Social Democratic vote exceeded by nearly 1.5 million that of the Nazis. Yet the Nazis won!

Clearly we will have to seek for the secret of Hitler's success, not on the plane of parliamentary vote catching, nor even in the field of efficient party organisation and discipline, for here the German labour movement was more than a match for the motley columns who marched for a thousand and one motives behind the Nazi banner.

The answer lies in political strategy. Hitler, despite all the obvious contradictions within his movement, knew what he wanted and how to get it. The great tragedy of the German working class was that its leaders, without intending to, made his victory certain. The immense proletarian army that they commanded was ready to fight and, if necessary, to die in order that fascism should not triumph in Germany as it had in Italy ten years previously. Numerous groups of workers throughout Germany had proved this, both before and after the Nazi seizure of power in bloody battles with the Nazis in defence of working class meetings, demonstrations and party premises. The Nazi battalions, though led in the main by world war veterans and Free Corps Officers, were composed almost entirely of third rate human material — what Trotsky contemptuously termed 'human dust'.

What gave them the resolve to attack the citadels of the German working class was not just the tacit — and sometimes open — support of the police, though this was undoubtedly an important factor in transforming cowards into heroes.

Vacillation, confusion, demoralisation and downright treachery at the summits of the proletarian general staff — this more than anything else cemented the SA rabble with a murdered pimp as its martyred saint into an all-conquering avalanche of brown gangsters. Their true mettle became clear for all to see when, little more than a year after their orgy of pillage and plunder on the debris of the German labour movement, Hitler dispatched their leaders to eternity without so much as a protest or murmur from the ranks of this now four-million strong swaggering horde. In both cases; Hitler's essentially middle class army proved itself incapable of playing an independent political role. When the Nazi leaders — acting in close collaboration with the heads of industry, finance and the armed forces — gave the order to attack, they attacked. The very scope and impact of their enemies' defeat gave to the Nazi petty bourgeois the illusion that the victory — and the spoils — were all his own.

Disabused of this fantasy by the continued and even greatly enhanced power of the trusts, banks and landowners, these millions of frustrated Nazi 'plebeians' were utterly incapable of converting their rage into action. They were, apart from the privileged elements syphoned off into the Nazi bureaucracy, the discarded cannon fodder of monopoly capitalism's counter-revolutionary army. They were only to be given arms again in 1939, when Hitler had found fresh fields to conquer and plunder. And once again, the brown-shirted warrior returned from battle — if he was fortunate enough to survive — empty handed. Again the spoils fell to the same giant trusts that had financed Hitler's march to power. For the first three years of the war, their investment in national socialism proved to be the most lucrative in the entire history of German capitalism.

All too numerous are those who believe that because the German middle class earned little but kicks in the teeth, and bullets in the brain in return for its services to German big business, then never again will the forces be found to rally a mass movement against the organisations of the working class. Pathetic delusion! As if political movements — and least of all fascist ones — evolved on the lines of abstract reason and formal logic. The example of Italy is before us all. There, even after 22 years of fascist rule, and the untold destruction and misery it brought to the Italian people as a result of Mussolini's participation in Hitler's crusade against Bolshevism and the western 'plutocracies', fascism is once again raising its head, attracting hundreds of thousands, even millions to its banner of militant anti-communism and open right-wing dictatorship. Only fools or traitors can point to the numerically large Italian labour movement now and claim that it will never succumb, never permit another 'March on Rome'. We do not doubt for one moment the militant anti-fascist temper and resolve of the rank and file Italian trade unionist, socialist party or communist party worker. But just as surely as night follows day — and the Italian workers endured nearly a quarter of a century of political night — the 'peaceful road to socialism' policies of the Italian Stalinists, centrists and reformists will, unless countered and exposed as suicidal to the entire working class, lead to a new and unimaginably more ferocious reign of terror descending on the Italian proletariat.

Neither is this threat confined to Italy; in Britain the growth of ultra-rightest tendencies inside the Tory party around Enoch Powell and the Monday Club, not to speak of the considerable increase in the membership and activities of the National Front, are but the surface phenomena of a far deeper shift inside sections of the middle class and backward, unorganised workers and youth towards reactionary solutions to their problems.

At a certain stage in the development of the economic and political crisis in this country, these currents could be given organised form, and large forces mobilised by big business, as they were in Germany and Italy, as a battering ram against the labour movement. The main factor militating against such a turn

of events today is not a devotion to parliamentary democracy on
the part of either the Tories or their monopoly capitalist
supporters.

The present Conservative government — these lines were
written in June 1973 — has, despite its militantly anti-union programme, still found it possible to exploit the supine cowardice
and class collaborationist policies of the trade union bureaucracy.

While the TUC is still able to offer this collaboration, and
proves itself able to sell it to sizeable sections of the working
class as preferable to other, more militant lines of action, the
ruling class has no need of a mass fascist movement.

Nor can fascist movements be manufactured overnight by
mass propaganda. Like crucial strategic shifts in the ruling class,
they are generated by powerful objective forces and events, international as well as national. Clearly, if fascism were simply
something hatched up in boardrooms and barracks, then there
would be very little to stop the bourgeoisie attempting to introduce its methods of rule whenever they felt the circuitous ones
of parliamentary democracy irksome.*

Incidentally, this is what distinguishes fascism from military
Bonapartist forms of dictatorship, i.e. Greece. Fascism begins
its bloody work after entrenching itself in power by means of a
combination of manoeuverings at the summits of the state and the
methods of civil war on the streets. Its main combat troops are
not professional soldiers, but disoriented petty-bourgeois and
declassed workers and youth, driven crazy to the point of blind-
ness by the crisis of capitalism; so crazy and blind in fact that
they will follow anyone, however 'mad' (and many were the
politicians and political journalists who called Hitler that!), who
seems to offer them a clear cut and swift solution to the crisis
that is tormenting them.

No one can predict with any reasonable hope of accuracy the
time scale or sequence of events which could precipitate a massive
break up in the present two party political system. But the elements of such a change are already visible in the rapid growth of
the Liberal vote on a catch-all programme which, according to
informed sources within the party itself, is attracting former con-

---

* Not to speak of the enormous resistance that such an unprepared coup would
encounter amongst the working class. Viz. the examples of the Franco uprising in
Spain, which was not linked to any mass fascist movement and the Kapp putsch in
Germany. The prospects of immediate success for a militarist-type putsch are
obviously far greater where the working class is either poorly organised or numerically small, as in the case of the Greek military coup of April 1967. But even here,
the treacherous leadership of the Stalinists, placidly awaiting the long-promised
parliamentary elections that were to open the road to a democratic Greece, was
decisive.

servative voters who are looking for a leader well to the right of Edward Heath.

This work does not pretend to deal with this problem, vital though it is for the future of the British Labour movement. Neither does *Fascism in Germany* intend in any way to supplant the many and brilliant writings of Leon Trotsky on the rise of national socialism and the policies which facilitated its victory. Rather it seeks to place in the hands of the reader something that is not available in any other book in the English language — a thoroughly documented analysis, not only of German fascism itself, but its political antecedents dating from the failure of the 1848 revolution, through the era of Bismarckian Bonapartism up to the outbreak of the First World War.

It also undertakes a detailed survey of the political trends and tensions present throughout the Weimar Republic, and which had their brutal and tragic climax in the victory of National Socialism. The many-sided and still controversial question of the relationship of big business with German fascism, naturally occupies a prominent place in this work, and here again, the reader will encounter documentary evidence and material not readily accessible elsewhere. Finally — and from the point of view of the author — most important of all, there is the problem of the German workers' movement itself. Here an attempt is made to supplement the critique of its leadership undertaken by Trotsky during the last three years of the Weimar Republic, and to relate this in turn to the impact of the rise of Stalinism in the Soviet Union.

It is the author's considered opinion that Soviet foreign policy — and here of course, we are referring exclusively to Stalin and his Bonapartist clique — played a vital, indeed decisive role in the rise to power of German fascism. Naturally, a charge of this nature and dimension is hard to substantiate without access to materials that by their very nature, have either been long ago dispatched to the incinerator, or are inaccessible to the genuine student of Soviet history. Thus the case rests to a certain extent on circumstantial evidence. It is up to those who still hold a brief for counter-revolutionary Stalinism to refute these charges. And they are far less fantastic today, when viewed in the light of the Kremlin's recently kindled friendship for Fascist Spain, Colonels' Greece and the right wing military regime in Indonesia, which has approximately one million communist corpses to its credit. Nor should we belittle the political significance of similar policies pursued by Maoist China or its supporters in Albania. China now recognises General Franco as the legitimate ruler of Spain, while keeping the entire Chinese people in a state of total ignorance as to how he came to hold this position. Meanwhile, those militant upholders of the Stalin myth, the Hoxha clique, have on more than one occasion handed back to the Greek police pro-Moscow communists who have sought political asylum in 'communist' Albania. (It should also be noted that Bulgaria has performed a similar service for the Greek junta, only in this case the unfortunate victims of this act of 'proletarian internationalism' were pro-Peking Stalinists.

All these acts of treachery, revolting though they are, have as their precedent the collaboration by Stalin with the rulers of Nazi Germany, both in the first months of Hitler's victory, when his power was by no means secure, and during the period of the Nazi-Soviet Pact.

That is why this work concerns itself with these — for some at any rate — embarassing historical questions. They take on a new relevance within the context of the Kremlin's accelerated tempo of collaboration with the leaders of world Imperialism, and Peking's desperate attempts to outbid Moscow in slavish devotion to the status quo. A leopard cannot change its spots, and a Stalinist bureaucracy remains a Stalinist bureaucracy, counter-revolutionary through and through and prepared to commit any betrayal of the International working class in order to defend its own material and political privileges.

It is the hope of the author that this book will alert its readers — and he trusts that they will be found principally in the most politically conscious sections of the working class movement — to the real class meaning of fascism, and more than this, to indicate how it can be fought and defeated.

As far as is possible, the 'dramatis personae' in this book will speak for themselves. Industrialists, bankers, Junkers, labour bureaucrats and Stalinist functionaries, Comintern officials and Reichstag deputies, Nazi agitators and political wirepullers — their voices will be heard in this book. Where they speak with several voices — as was more often than not the case — then that too will become clear by use of the same method.

The reader may well be bemused by the space devoted to a critique of other accounts of National Socialism. In fact, any attempt to write a scientific history of German Fascism without challenging those who in one way or another, and for one motive or another, have distorted and even repressed that history, would be simply an academic exercise. For these historians and sociologists, just as much as for Stalinists and reformists, a history of German fascism must have an element of an alibi. The liberal, while horrified at what he sees in the Nazi death camps, recoils from the notion that this could in any way be the product of capitalism. Certain wicked and greedy businessmen (who are usually presented as being, at the same time, political babes in arms) may well have greased Hitler's path to power, and even crossed his palm with gold, but capitalism as a system cannot and must not be indicted for the unspeakable crime of Auschwitz. For the implications of such an admission are too awful to contemplate.

Then along comes the Stalinist, who can of course (when he is not currently engaged in inveigling sections of the ruling class into a 'broad alliance' for the defence of 'peace and democracy') undertake a far more serious class analysis of fascism. He can even trace — as did the veteran British Stalinist, R. Palme Dutt, in his 1934 work *Fascism and Social Revolution* the relationship between the betrayals of Social Democracy from 1914 to 1933 and the eventual victory of Hitler.

But precisely at this point, when the reader should ask himself: "Since the reformists are congenitally unable to mobilise the workers to fight fascism, why could not the communists do the job?" Dutt and his fellow Stalinist historians have to stop. Their relationship to Stalinism, past as well as present, drives them to distort the real relationship of forces in Germany, and in the end, to put the blame for the victory of the Nazis on the working class themselves. Social Democratic commentators on German Fascism simply supplement the distortions of the Stalinists. They can write with great facility — and on occasions with formal correctness — on the ultra-left policies of the German Communist Party, on how it substituted abuse for analysis by labelling Social Democrats as 'social fascists' and how it split the working class by refusing, under any conditions, to enter a united front with the reformist workers' organisations.

This was one of the great crimes of 'Third Period' Stalinism, that it gave the reformists the totally undeserved opportunity to criticise purported communist policies from a seemingly Marxist standpoint.

It enabled — as it still does to this day — reformism to divert attention away from its own complicity in the defeat of the German working class. Stalinism and reformism batten on each other in the realm of history as much as in the field of day to day political struggle. The exposure of this silent, but nevertheless very real collaboration is therefore a necessary part of the overall fight to defeat both these political tendencies. The author also considers it politically correct to take issue with organisations which while claiming to base themselves on Trotsky's writings, theory and general principles, have, in the author's opinion, departed from them in so far as they relate to the problem of fascism. Of course, this revision of Trotsky's analysis of Fascism and the policies which he insisted should be adopted to combat it has gone much further in some organisations than others.

VIII   *FASCISM IN GERMANY*

But unless there is a full and unfettered discussion within the ranks of the workers' movement on this question, the very right to discuss anything at all may well be put in jeopardy; above all else, the movement demands theoretical clarity.

Finally, a word of thanks to all those who helped make the publication of this book possible: to those who lent money with no certainty of seeing it returned, to the Weiner Library, whose staff gave me invaluable advice and assistance in my quest for elusive documents, to my wife Karen for meticulously checking the text at every stage in the book's preparation, to my dear daughter Katharine, who on more occasions than I care to remember, reluctantly but dutifully refrained from helping me type the copy and finally to my father, Bill, from whom I first learned what socialism was, and who in ill-health and at the age of 70, unstintingly undertook the arduous task of translating vast tracts of the most unGoethelike German into perfect English prose. My thanks to them all. I hope they find their efforts and sacrifices worthwhile.

Robert Black, June 28, 1973.

Chapter 1
THE ROOTS OF GERMAN REACTION

England, and later France, were the only nations to enjoy the relative historical luxury of a thoroughgoing bourgeois-demo-cratic revolution. For behind Cromwell and Robespierre there stood not a modern industrial proletariat, already taking its first steps towards political and organisational independence, but an amorphous plebeian mass which, because of its social and political heterogeneity, could the more easily be harnessed to the goals of an emergent bourgeoisie in its struggle against the nobility. This is not to deny that the revolutions of 1640-49 and 1789-94 projected a 'proletarian' wing with its own utopian-communist programme — we have the examples before us of Winstanley and the Diggers, of Babeuf and his 'Conspiracy of the Equals', proving that even the classic bourgeois revolutions contained within them the embryo of the modern proletarian movement and the socialist revolution.

Why, the reader might well ask, the pre-occupation with France and England when the nation under discussion is Germany? The answer is quite simple. The modern class struggle is fought out under economic conditions dominated by a world-wide system — imperialism. But the classes — and this applies with particular force to Western and Central Europe — do battle on a national terrain steeped in the traditions, forms of thought, organisation and political culture generated by conflicts reaching back to the very dawn of capitalist society. Whether conscious of it or not, the combatants of the class war under imperialism, while responding to modern economic, social, and political demands, pressures and crises, do so in a way which has been moulded to a considerable degree by the struggles of their ancestors. As Marx put it:

> Men make their own history, but they do not make it just as they please: they do not make it under circumstances directly encountered, given from the past. The tradition of all the dead generations weighs like a nightmare on the brain of the living. And just when they seem engaged in revolutionising themselves and things, in creating some-thing that has never yet existed, precisely in such periods of revolu-tionary crisis they anxiously borrow from them names, battle cries

and costumes in order to present the new scene of history in this time-honoured disguise and this borrowed language. [1.]

Though financed, supported and armed by modern monopoly capitalism, enforcing its dictatorship through the most up-to-date techniques of propaganda, repression and mass mobilisation, and waging its wars with a truly formidable combination of military precision and political audacity, German fascism marched to power brandishing the symbols of ancient Aryan tribes, shrieking the curses of medieval pogromists and proclaiming the pagan myths of 'blood and soil'. The eastwards drive of German imperialism shrouded itself in the cloak and visor of the Teutonic Knights. From beginning to end, the counter-revolution of German finance capital decked itself out in the garb of the Dark Ages.

So the emergence (as distinct from victory) of national socialism cannot be explained purely in terms of the 1929 economic crisis, nor by the inflation of 1923. Nor is it enough to refer to the failures of leadership on the part of the SPD from 1914 onwards, or the KPD in the post 1918 period. These are factors which, to a greater or lesser extent, contributed to the triumph of German fascism in 1933. They also help to explain why national socialism found favourable conditions both politically and economically for winning the leadership of the middle class in the period immediately prior to its seizure of power. But they are in no way adequate in unearthing the *origins* of the social forces which predisposed the German petty-bourgeoisie to the programme of fascist counter-revolution. Nor do they tell us anything about the precise forms which Hitler's bloody crusade against Marxism and the workers' movement took. Yet without such a study in depth of German fascism, without a dimension which begins with the assembly of the major classes of German capitalist society in the period of the bourgeois revolution, a history of national socialism must of necessity confine itself either to banal generalities about the 1929 crisis or the sophistries of 'cultural determinism'. *

These 'explanations' of German fascism — the 'general' and those that focus almost exclusively on the 'particular' — are the reverse sides of the same non-dialectical coin.

---

* Exponents of the latter theory, which tends to regard the triumph of national socialism as an inevitable outgrowth of cultural patterns and derived political structures developed in Prussian-dominated Imperial Germany, are not confined to bourgeois sociology. Thus the Hungarian Stalinist George Lukacs has argued that the German bourgeoisie was not so much a prime mover in the assumption of power by Hitler (a claim flatly refuted by all the historical evidence) as an unwitting agent in an irresistable historical process, and finds in one of Thomas Mann's novels *(Mario)* 'all the kinds of helplessness with which the German bourgeois faces the hypnotic power of fascism'. (G. Lukacs: *Essays on Thomas Mann*, p.37, London, 1963.)

So too must we dismiss those superficial accounts which treat national socialism as the creation of individual leaders or skilful propaganda. The most gifted leader, agitator or propagandist — and the Nazi party certainly had its share of these — must still strike a chord in the hearts of the masses before they can stand at the head of a movement numbering millions. The seed requires fertile soil and the necessary amounts of sunshine and rain. Thus the Nazi counter-revolution not only required a political camouflage to mobilise its petty-bourgeois and lumpen-proletarian battering-ram against the entrenched organisations of the German working class. The whole course of German history determined the form this onslaught took. The prime issue therefore is one of method, of analysis and synthesis, of delineation between form and content, between general and particular, between the subjective and the objective:

> The difference between subjectivism (scepticism, sophistry, etc.) and dialectics.... is that in (objective) dialectics the difference between the relative and absolute is itself relative. For objective dialectics there is an absolute *within* the relative. For subjectivism and sophistry the relative is only relative and excludes the absolute ... (In objective dialectics) the opposites (the individual is opposed to the universal) are identical: the individual exists only in the connection that leads to the universal. The universal exists only in the individual and through the individual.... [2]

So in laying bare those historical forces which nurtured national socialism, we seek to throw fresh light on the possible — indeed probable — forms that counter-revolution might, given the opportunity, assume here in Britain. Not in the sense that German and British fascism will share many common points of social origin — the absence of a peasantry and artisan class in Britain suggests that mass movements of reaction will find other points of support than they did in Germany and to a lesser degree, in Italy. No, the point is not to hunt for superficial historical parallels. Rather we should bear in mind Lenin's proposition that within every relative we can discern an absolute, that in probing German fascism to its deepest roots we can develop methodological concepts and tools of analysis which will enable us better to equip the workers' movement in this country for the inevitable struggle against those who seek its destruction.*

---

* The old Engels made precisely this point, although from another angle, in a letter to Conrad Schmidt, a leader of the German Social Democratic Party:

  'In general, the word "materialistic" serves many of the younger writers in Germany as a mere phrase with which anything and everything is labelled without further study,... they stick on this label and then consider the question disposed of. But our conception of history is above all a guide to study, not a lever for construction after the manner of the Hegelian. All history must be studied afresh, the conditions of existence of the different formations of society must be examined individually before the attempt is made to deduce from them

This now brings us to the problem of the relationship between national socialism and the aborted bourgeois-democratic revolutions of 1848.

The ironies, paradoxes and tragedies of German history over the last 150 years only become intelligible when viewed within the larger context of the combined yet uneven development of capitalism in both its imperialist and pre-imperialist epochs. Indeed, Engels held that one of the two main causes of Germany's failure to emerge as a unified, modern state in the 16th century was the sudden shifting of the focus of European trade away from its traditional routes through Germany towards the maritime powers in the West. The discovery of the New World disrupted an entire network of commercial, social and political relations in Central Europe, draining the confidence of the German people and throwing the previously rich and politically aroused burghers into utter disarray. Lutheranism quickly lost its revolutionary cutting edge and evolved a quietist character which was to play a pernicious role in German politics for the next four centuries. The bourgeois-Protestant reformation was destined to find its truly democratic and plebeian expression in the 'Lunatiks' of Cromwell's revolutionary army, the Ironsides.

The defeat of Germany's first attempt to carry through the bourgeois-democratic revolution doomed its people to more than a century of fratricidal conflicts as the catspaw of contending religious and dynastic factions, a decline which culminated in the Thirty Years War in which at least a third of the German population died and its meagre economic resources were pillaged or laid waste.

The only victors proved to be the petty and greater nobility and clergy. Unlike the burghers, peasants, artisans and workers, they had much to gain from a weak and divided Germany, torn by religious dissension and shattered into several hundred political fragments. The downward plunging curve of German history after the defeat of the 1525 Peasants' revolt without doubt sapped the political fibre of the German bourgeoisie and kindled within it that trait of extreme conservatism and craving for an all-powerful protector which reached its malignant zenith under the regimes of Bismarck and Hitler.

Here we must warn against any tendency to adopt a 'unilinear' view of German history. Each nation, it almost goes without saying, has internal driving forces, which develop characteristics and

the political, civil-law, philosophic, religious, etc., views corresponding to them... too many of the younger Germans simply make use of the phrase historical materialism... only in order to get their own relatively scanty historical knowledge... constructed into a neat system as quickly as possible...'
(London, August 5, 1890, in *Marx-Engels Selected Correspondence*, pp.494-495, Moscow, n.d.)

peculiarities which constitute precisely the concept of 'nation'. But the nations, and the classes which their boundaries encompass, are also the unique products of a much larger process of crystallisation and fermentation which, since the earliest phases of human history, has not only transcended national and continental barriers, but helped shape them. To return to our first methodological principle, 'the individual exists only in the connection that leads to the universal. The universal exists only in the individual and through the individual.'

So to understand the many vivid contrasts in the course of German, French and English history, it is necessary not only to familiarise oneself with internal developments, but their mutual interaction and penetration, as parts of a unified yet divided and contradictory whole. Concretely, in what ways did the multifarious layers of Germany's and Europe's past prepare the political soil for the seeds of fascist counter-revolution?

Let us take as our starting point a remark made by Nazi Propaganda Minister Joseph Göbbels during a broadcast speech on April 1, 1933, when he declared in all seriousness that with the formation of the Hitler dictatorship, 'the year 1789 is hereby eradicated from history'.*

The German bourgeoisie — and here we are speaking principally of its dominant industrial and banking segments — in 1933 found itself compelled to place in power a party and regime which stridently proclaimed its total repudiation of the bourgeois revolution! And yet beneath this paradox there is concealed a class logic which lies at the core of fascism. In order to retain power in periods of profound social, economic and political upheaval, in order to divide and destroy those class forces which threaten not only its profits but its very right to rule, the bourgeoisie has to declare war on all those ideals which it used in an earlier epoch to rally the people against feudalism, and those institutions with which it both buttressed and popularised its own rule. This is one of the universal aspects of fascism, one which can be detected in every particular national case. But the precise form and course of this reaction by a pro-fascist bourgeoisie

---

* Nazi and anti-semitic diatribes against the French revolution are legion. For example, that infamous forgery *Protocols of the Learned Elders of Zion* has the arche-typical 'Jewish conspirator' reveal that it was 'wholly the work of our hands'. *(Protocols,* p.25, London 1960) And the quack Nazi 'philosopher' Alfred Rosenberg who first encountered the 'Protocols' whilst a student in Moscow at the time of the 1917 Revolution, divided his racially-inspired hatred equally between the Jacobins - 'raving philistines, vain demagogues and... hyenas of political battlefield who rob the abandoned of their belongings' and the Bolsheviks - 'Tartarized sub-humans (who) murdered anyone who by his tall form and confident gait could be suspected of being a master'. (A. Rosenberg *The Myth of the Twentieth Century* in *Alfred Rosenberg: Selected Political Writings,* pp. 78-79, London 1970.)

against its own democratic-revolutionary past will vary widely according to both circumstances and history. In Germany, it was greatly conditioned both by the success of the French Revolution and the miserable fiasco of its own, not only in the 16th century, but far more important, in that of 1848-49. Trotsky aptly summed up the essential difference between the German and French bourgeoisie when he wrote the latter:

> succeeded in bringing off its Great Revolution. Its consciousness was the consciousness of society and nothing could become established as an institution without first passing through its consciousness as an aim, as a problem of political creation. It often resorted to theatrical poses in order to hide from itself the limitations of its own bourgeois world — but it marched forward.

This bourgeois class confidence and aggression contrasted with that of the German capitalist class, which

> from the very start, did not "make" the revolution, but dissociated itself from it. Its consciousness rose against the objective conditions for its own domination. The revolution could only be carried out not by it but against it. Democratic institutions represented to its mind not an aim to fight for but a menace to its welfare. [3]

Great social and political upheavals mould all their participants, whether victor or vanquished, hero or traitor. Those industrialists and bankers who made their counter-revolutionary compact with Hitler in the last years of the Weimar Republic were acting as the heirs of a reactionary tradition reaching back to the very birth of German capitalism.

Enthusiasm for the ideals of the French Revolution — democratic republican government and a world ruled by reason — was to be found not in the propertied strata of the German bourgeoisie nor indeed its associated political circles, but among philosophers, musicians and writers. The young Beethoven (born 1770) was profoundly moved and artistically inspired by the political cataclysm across the Rhine from his native Bonn. At a time when fainter hearts were recoiling from the Jacobin 'reign of terror' the composer had written in the autograph of a friend:

> I am not wicked — fiery blood
> Is all my malice and my crime is youth.
> To help wherever one can
> Love liberty above all things
> Never deny the truth
> Even at the foot of the throne. [4]

Consciously a revolutionary in music, he readily identified with all those struggling to liberate mankind from the fetters of the past. His third symphony, the *Eroica,* which marks the explosive transition from Beethoven's youthful and more conventional First Period to the full maturity of his Second, was initially dedicated to Napoleon, whom the composer hero-worshipped as the liberator of Europe. But when Napoleon crowned himself as Emperor, Beethoven's rage knew no bounds. Tearing out the dedication page, he declared: 'So he is no more than a common mortal! Now too, he will tread underfoot all the rights of man, indulge only his ambitions, now he will think himself superior to all men, become a tyrant.' [5]

And although ambivalent in his attitude to the political methods of the Jacobins, Germany's great writer Johann von Goethe undoubtedly sympathised with many of their goals, and looked forward to the day when they would be realised in his own country:

> I have no fear that Germany will not become one, for our good roads and our future railways will play their part. Above all, may it be the one in mutual love, may it always be one against the foreign foe. May it be one, so that the German thaler and the German groschen have the same value everywhere in the nation, so that my travelling bag can pass unopened through all the thirty-six states. May it be one, so that the municipal passport of a citizen of Weimar is not treated by the frontier officials of some great neighbouring state as invalid...

Furthermore, may Germany be one in weights and measures, in trade and business and in a hundred similar things... [6]

Here one cannot help but detect an emphasis on those goals closest to the heart of the German bourgeoisie. Economic unity and nationalist fervour have crowded out those other essential elements of the classic bourgeois revolution which Goethe followed so closely in France: political freedom, equality before the law and staunchly republican government. In this respect, both Hegel and Kant, Germany's most outstanding philosophers, were Goethe's superiors.

The ageing Kant (born 1724), though opposed in principle to violent revolution, perceived in the struggle against French despotism and the solidarity it evoked throughout the civilised world proof 'that the human race... will henceforth improve without any more total reversals'. [7]

And Kant went further than this. He fervently hoped the French revolution would establish new political and moral principles which could be emulated by all mankind:

> For the occurance in question is too momentous, too intimately interwoven with the interests of humanity and too widespread in its influence upon all parts of the world for nations not to be reminded of it when favourable circumstances present themselves, and to rise up and make renewed attempts of the same kind as before. [8]

Who can doubt that Kant had Germany most of all in mind when he advised his readers to prepare themselves for 'favourable circumstances'. This much must be granted the Koenigsberg philosopher — that he recognised the categorical imperative of the bourgeois revolution.

Hegel would seem an exception to this progressive trend, but this in fact is only partially true. While in his later years recon-

ciled to the Prussian state bureaucracy as the political vehicle for
the earthly rule of reason (at least in its Germanic form)* he too
had been stirred to the depths of his being by the unprecedented
historical drama of the French Revolution and the military ex-
ploits of Napoleon.

The latter's conjuncture with the pinnacle of his own philosophical development was as dramatic as it was symbolic.

Whilst staying in Jena, Hegel had just completed the final
draft of his monumental *The Phenomenology of Mind* when
Napoleon's armies entered the Thuringian city in their triumphant
march across Europe. Hegel's work had ended with the following
lines:

> 'History intellectually comprehended forms the recollection and the
> Golgotha of absolute Spirit, the reality, the truth, the certainty of
> its throne, without which it were lifeless, solitary and alone.

Barely had the ink dried on the page when the author caught
a glimpse of Napoleon himself,

> the soul of the world, riding through the town on a reconnaissance.
> It is indeed a wonderful sensation to see, concentrated in a point, sit-
> ting on a horse, an individual who overturns the world and masters. [9]

Here indeed was the world spirit, living flesh and blood,
challenging and overturning all those social and political relations
which Hegel lashed with such fiery eloquence in his *Phenomenology*. And it must have surely been with his own German bourgeoisie in mind that he wrote, in his chapter on 'Lordship and
Bondage', that

> it is solely by risking life that freedom is obtained; only thus is it
> tried and proved that the essential nature of self-consciousness is not
> bare existence... is not its mere absorption in the expanse of life...

---

* Thus Hegel writes, in his *Philosophy of Right* (1820)':
  'The development of the state to constitutional monarchy is the achievement of
  the modern world, a world in which the substantial Idea has won the definite
  form of subjectivity. The history of this inner deepening of the world mind...
  the history of this genuine formation of ethical life is the content of the whole
  course of history.
  (W. Hegel, *The Philosophy of Right*, p.176, London 1962)
That he had a bourgeois monarchy in mind when he wrote these lines is evident from
the many attacks on feudal economic and political institutions which can be found
in this work, i.e. in the section on 'Alienation of Property', where Hegel writes:
  'Examples of the alienation of personality are slavery, serfdom, disqualification
  from holding property... and so forth...' (Ibid., p.53)
And elsewhere, he repudiates the religious institutions and relations generated by
feudalism:
  'It is in the nature of the case that a slave has an absolute right to free himself
  and that if anyone has prostituted his ethical life by hiring himself to thieve and
  murder... everyone has a warrant to repudiate this contract. The same is the case
  if I hire my religious feelings to a priest who is my confessor. for such an inward
  matter a man has to settle with himself alone...' Ibid, p.241)
The analogy between murders and thieves and catholic priests was not, for the
Hegel the Lutheran, an accidental one!

The individual, who has not staked his life may, no doubt, be recognised as a Person; but he has not attained the truth of this recognition as
an independent self-consciousness. [10]

Scorn for passivity in the face of great events found not only a
philosophical expression. Exasperated by the utter political impotency of the German princes, Hegel wrote shortly after his
confrontation with Napoleon:

The great teacher of constitutional law sits in Paris... The German
princes have not yet grasped the concept of free monarchy, nor have
attempted to realise it.

And he drew the sober conclusion that, as a consequence,
'Napoleon will have to organise all this'. [11]

Certainly at this stage in his philosophical development,
Hegel placed the modernisation of Germany above any narrow
national pride. And although a devout Lutheran, his thoroughly
bourgeois outlook enabled him to praise the French anti-
clerical and materialist school of philosophy, the Enlightenment,
which 'heroically and with splendid genius, with warmth and
fire, with spirit and with courage (maintained) that a man's own
self, the human spirit, is the source from which is derived all
that is to be respected by him'.

This 'fantacism of abstract thought', which in its purest
political form expressed itself in the rule of the Jacobins, Hegel
contrasted sadly with the conduct of his fellow-countrymen:

We Germans were passive at first with regard to the existing state of
affairs, we endured it: in the second place, when that state of affairs
was overthrown, we were just as passive: it was overthrown by the
efforts of others, we let it be taken away from us, we suffered it all
to happen. [12]

For Hegel, unlike so many German politicians of the period,
had grasped the great truth that a thoroughgoing revolution
functions like a broom, sweeping away all the accumulated
backwardness and superstitions of previous epochs. Through
its revolution,

the French nation has been liberated from many institutions which
the human spirit had outgrown like baby shoes, and which weighed
on it, as they still do on others, as fetters devoid of spirit: and the
individual has taken off the fear of death... This is what gives the
French the great strength they are demonstrating against others. [13]

And when the worthy burghers of his native Wurttemberg
did eventually gather at Frankfurt to draw up and enact a
German constitution, Hegel was rightly contemptuous of their
puny, half-hearted efforts:

What we see in the behaviour of the Estates summoned in Wurttemberg is precisely the opposite of what started twenty-five years ago
in a neighbouring realm (i.e. the Revolution in France) and what at
the time re-echoed in all heads, namely, that in a political con-

stitution nothing should be recognised as valid unless its recognition accorded with the right of reason. [14]

It can be seen from these extracts alone that more than any other German thinker prior to Marx, Hegel was involved to the point of obsession with the problem of his nation's political backwardness. Time and again he found himself asking the question, why did the French 'pass over from the theoretical to the practical, while the Germans contented themselves with theoretical abstractions'? [15] Personifying as he did the pinnacle of German — and indeed all — bourgeois thought, Hegel evolved a solution consistent with his entire objective idealist system. German unity had been delayed, and a rational form of government conducive to capitalist development thereby frustrated, 'because the formal principle of philosophy in Germany encounters a concrete real World in which Spirit finds inward satisfaction and in which conscience is at rest'. German 'revolutions' were from Luther on, inner revolutions of the spirit:

> In Germany the enlightenment was conducted in the interests of theology: in France it immediately took up a position of hostility to the Church. [16]

Further than this essentially idealist explanation — containing nevertheless profound insights into the paradoxes of German history — Hegel could not go. He saw world history as the materialisation in time of the absolute idea, and was therefore driven to the conclusion that differences in the material and political circumstances of the European nations were but detours and skirmishes in the march of the world spirit to its final realisation in Hegel's own philosophical system — and the Prussian monarchy! *

It fell to the young Marx, steeped in the Hegelian philosophical tradition, but already seeking to liberate its rational 'kernel' from

---

* Johann Fichte, a follower of Kant, was the third great German idealist philosopher to be caught up by the French Revolution and driven to formulate a political, economic, social and constitutional programme for the bourgeoisie. Thus in his *The Science of Rights* (1796) Fichte seeks, very much in the Kantian tradition, to devise a German constitution with the aid of 'pure reason' alone. Certainly the most radical of the three, Fichte laid down specific situations where the people had the right to overthrow their rulers when they deviated from the dictates of pure reason. The people had this right because they were 'in fact and law, the highest power and the source of all power; responsible only to God'. He also made plans for a body of 'elders', the 'Ephorate', which would check on the activities of the government, and be empowered to bring a charge of treason against it should the government, in its eyes, be guilty of breaking the spirit and letter of the constitution. And here Fichte, like the Jacobin offspring of the Enlightenment, understood that even the power of pure reason had its limits:

> 'It is... one of the chief aims of a rational constitution to provide that when the people are called together in convention by the Ephorate, larger masses of people shall congregate in different places, ready to quench any possible resistance on the part of the government.'

(J. Fichte, *The Science of Rights*, p.261, London, 1970)

its idealist 'husk', to begin the task of placing the 'German problem' in its true material setting and, more than this, to evolve a
progressive practical solution.

We have already noted that Hegel, despairing of any viable
political initiative for German unity from the burghers and
princes, and unable, because of his very firm views on the rights
of private property, to welcome a 'plebeian' movement for
German emancipation, ended his days as the official state philosopher of the Hohenzollerns.

Following Hegel, Marx recognised 'that the real life embryo
of the German nation has grown so far inside its *cranium,* 'that
'in politics the Germans *thought* what other nations did'. [17] And
also like Hegel, Marx was sceptical of the 'will to power' of the
German bourgeoisie. But here their ways parted. Marx turned
his back on his own class, and his face towards the emergent
German proletariat: *

> In Germany emancipation from the Middle Ages is possible only as
> emancipation from the partial victories over the Middle Ages as well. *
> In Germany no kind of bondage can be shattered without every kind
> of bondage being shattered. The fundamental Germany cannot re-
> volutionise without revolutionising from the foundation. The emanci-
> pation of the German is the emancipation of man. The head of this
> emancipation is philosophy, its heart is the proletariat. Philosophy
> (and here Marx is referring to that of Hegel) cannot be made a reality
> without the abolition of the proletariat, the proletariat being made a
> reality. When all the inner requisites are fulfilled the day of German
> resurrection will be proclaimed by the crowing of the cock of Gaul. [18]

Four years after these lines were written, the German bourgeoisie was, for the third time, compelled by the force of events
to supplement its 'weapon of criticism' with what Marx aptly
termed 'the criticism of the weapon'. For in political and social.
as opposed to intellectual revolutions, 'material force must be
overthrown by material force'. [19]

A detailed history of the 1848 revolution lies outside the scope
of this book. However certain of its phases and unique features
must be touched on in order to place the rise of German imperialism and the political strategy of the modern German bourgeoisie in its correct historical perspective.

As Marx had prophesied, the bulk of the bourgeoisie spurned
consistent republicanism like the plague. Its political spokesmen
in the Frankfurt Assembly (which, as it turned out, proved no
more effective than its forerunner of 1815) would venture no
further than a call for the establishment of an all-German constitutional monarchy, based on a franchise limited to the pro-

---

* i.e. the half-hearted and belated reforms introduced in the wake of the French
Revolution when popular support had to be rallied against Napoleon's invading
armies.

pertied classes. Yet this timid demand was advanced while the Prussian monarchy was reeling from its military defeat at the hands of the Berlin workers and artisans in the great uprising of March 18-19. And within days of this initial success, the revolt had spread even to the villages, the backbone of old Prussia, with peasants seizing land wherever it was left undefended by its old owners.

Cromwell's Independents and Robespierre's Jacobins both leaned on the plebeian movements beneath them to settle accounts with the *ancien regime*. Without the Levellers and the Parisian *sans culottes* there would have been neither a 1649 nor a 1793. This is not to say that the English and French bourgeoisie entered such an alliance willingly or without misgivings. But the revolutionary front endured long enough to ensure the defeat of its common foes. The guillotining of the Herbertistes and Thermidor followed the fall of feudal power, just as in England, Cromwell's brutal repression of the Diggers and the most radical of the Levellers was undertaken after the execution of Charles I.

Treading in the footsteps of their ancestors of 1525, the German bourgeoisie retreated from their own revolution with every forward step of the plebeian masses. The sources of their fears were two-fold. Uppermost in their minds was undoubtedly an ever-present dread that the upsurge against feudal rule would not stop short at the boundaries of bourgeois political rights and property. Thus one 'democratic' spokesman — Paul Pfizer of Wurttemberg — warned:

> Every demand to abolish existing feudal dues and revoke rights which have until now been recognised by the state... to break down by a stroke of the pen the distinction between right and wrong must be rejected. For we know that from the destruction of ledgers and registers (these were being burned with great relish by the oppressed and land-hungry peasants) of landed holdings is but one step to the destruction of mortgage records and promissory notes, and from the destruction of promissory notes it is again but one step to the division of property or a common ownership of goods.

Pfizer's shrewd, if reactionary, class instinct differed but little from that of General Ireton who during the famous debate at Putney in the Autumn of 1647 with Colonel Rainborough and other Leveller radicals, countered their claim for a voice in the government of England by arguing that:

> since you cannot plead to it by anything but the law of nature, or for anything but for the end of better being, and since that better being is not certain, and what is more, destructive to another; upon these grounds if you so, paramount to all constitutions hold up this Law of Nature, I would fain have any man show me their bounds, where you will end, and why you should not take away all property. [20]

But Ireton stayed his hand for more than a year, allying himself with his Putney antagonists to carry through the purging of Parliament and so clearing the political road for the trial and execution of the King. In Germany, far from the bourgeoisie seeking the removal (let alone execution) of their main enemy, the King of Prussia, they besought him to annoint himself the constitutional ruler of a united Germany. The cringing reformers of Frankfurt received the reply they deserved. Frederick William IV informed them that such a crown could be accepted only from the German princes. It was not the German bourgeoisie's to give. And furthermore, if such a state did come into being, it would stand not under their ineffectual protection, but that of 'the Prussian sword'. But before the Frankfurt leaders could grovel at the feet of the Prussian junkers, they had to create the necessary conditions for their own defeat. This they did under the lash of titanic battles fought out across the length and breadth of Europe, from Hungary in the East and Sicily in the South to Norway and Finland in the North and Spain, France and England in the West. Germany (with Austria) was the vortex of a revolutionary whirlpool, and this fact, readily appreciated by all those involved in the unfolding drama, raised the already acute social and political tensions to fever pitch. And once again, France was the catalyst in transforming revolution into counter-revolution. Each of the 1848 revolutions began as a movement of the entire people against absolute monarchy and the many other residues of feudal rule, economic as well as political. This seeming unanimity of purpose was soon shattered by the unfolding of even more compelling contradictions between the various classes and leaderships of the revolutionary camp. And nowhere was this process of differentiation more rapid, clearcut and violent than in France, where the great traditions of 1789 and 1830 lent the collisions between the classes an explosive quality they lacked in nations with a weaker revolutionary and democratic tradition. Events in France were therefore followed — as far as the rudimentary communications systems of the time allowed — with great avidity by the more conscious sections of every class. Nowhere was this more true than in Germany, a country which had not experienced a truly popular uprising of the people for more than three centuries. Each class looked to Paris for a mirror to the future of its own development and strategy.

And the great lesson was not long in coming. On June 22, 1848, the Paris proletariat, provoked beyond endurance by the repressive measures of the newly-entrenched bourgeoisie and the temporising of its own leaders, staged the first working class insurrection against the rule of capital in human history. 'It was a fight for the preservation or annihilation of the bourgeois order. The veil that shrouded the republic was torn asunder.'[21]

The impact of this defeat reverberated from Frankfurt to Berlin. The scale and ferocity of the conflict rapidly convinced the German bourgeoisie, already in the process of damping down the revolutionary fires in their own country, that their main enemy was not the Prussian monarchy and the lesser kings and princes but the plebeian movement stirring into life and political consciousness beneath them. True, the plebeians were not spear-headed, as had been the case in Paris, by a large and compact industrial working class steeped in the tradition and well versed in the art of insurrection. The retarded industrial development of Germany — itself partly a consequence of past failures to consumate the national-democratic revolution — ensured that in 1848, a weak German bourgeoisie faced an equally weak, numerically speaking, proletariat. The major proportion of the mass movement was comprised in its early stages of artisans, with the most radical elements being drawn from the apprentices and journeymen. But it was more a question of quality than quantity.

The mere presence of an incipient proletarian movement on the extreme left of the democratic camp was sufficient to alert the Frankfurt parliamentarians to the dangers of another 1525. The savage battles in Paris convinced them that a bargain must be struck by all men of property in the face of this new and terrible foe, even if it meant repeating German history a third time by strangling the democratic revolution:

> It became evident to everyone that this was the great decisive battle which would, if the insurrection were victorious, deluge the whole continent with renewed revolutions, or, if it was suppressed, bring about an at least momentary restoration of counter-revolutionary rule. The proletarians of Paris were defeated, decimated... And immediately, all over Europe, the new and old Conservatives and counter-revolutionaries raised their heads with an effrontery that showed how well they understood the importance of the event. [22]

Treachery on the part of the upper bourgeoisie, and utter incompetence or cowardice within the petty-bourgeois democrats and republicans forced the German working class and those sections of the plebeian movement allied with it to strike out along its own political road. Theoretically, the first blows for the independence of the German proletariat from all other classes had been struck several months before the outbreak of the Berlin uprising with the completion and publication of that foundation stone of the modern revolutionary movement — the *Communist Manifesto* of Marx and Engels. In its closing section, the two authors made the following recommendation for the conduct of the working class in the bourgeois revolution which they knew to be imminent:

> In Germany they (i.e. the Communists) fight with the bourgeoisie

wherever it acts in a revolutionary way, against the absolute monarchy, the feudal squirearchy and the petty-bourgeoisie. But they never cease, for a single instant, to instil into the working class the clearest possible recognition of the hostile antagonism between bourgeoisie and proletariat, in order that the German workers may straightway use, as so many weapons against the bourgeoisie, the social and political conditions that the bourgeoisie must necessarily introduce along with its supremacy, and in order that, after the fall of the reactionary classes in Germany, the fight against the bourgeoisie itself may immediately begin. [23]

It is clear from this passage that Marx and Engels expected the German bourgeoisie, supported 'by a much more developed proletariat than that of England in the seventeenth century and of France in the eighteenth' [24] to defeat its feudal enemies. And they made this assumption without any illusions about the political capacities or enthusiasm for struggle on the part of the German burgher. Marx and Engels also believed that because of the relative preponderance of the working class in comparison with France and England at the time of their bourgeois revolutions, the national-democratic uprising in Germany 'will be but the prelude to an immediately following proletarian revolution'. [25]

The events of the next few months proved this optimistic prognosis to be ill-founded. But the core of the perspective was sound, and has, despite its revisionist and Stalinist traducers, remained the bedrock of all revolutionary working class strategy and tactics up the present day. That is, the working class, as the sole force capable of overturning all social systems based on private property in the means of production, must at all costs maintain its total political and organisational independence if it is to carry out this task. *

In the Revolution of 1848, sheer necessity, and not adherence to previously elaborated principles or strategy, compelled the German proletariat to make its first bid for political independence. The circumstances under which this took place had a particularly important bearing, not only on the future development of the workers' movement, but on relations between all the classes of German society.

---

* With the German experience fresh in their minds, the authors of the *Manifesto* enriched this principle in their *Address of the Central Committee to the Communist League (of Germany)*, Written in March 1850, the *Address* scolded the leaders of the German workers' movement for allowing it to come 'completely under the domination and leadership of the petty-bourgeois democrats'. Instead of which the proletariat should have 'marched together with them against the faction which it aims at overthrowing', and 'opposed them in everything whereby they seek to consolidate their position in their own interests'. In all future revolutions which found either bourgeois or petty-bourgeois parties allied, however fleetingly, with the proletariat, Marx and Engels warned that unless the workers established 'an independent secret and public organisation of the workers' party alongside of the official democrats', they would inevitably 'lose its whole independent position and once more sink down

Working class disenchantment with the Revolution's bourgeois leaders began to turn to anger when the Frankfurt Assembly agreed to exclude the property-less classes from the franchise. The true face of German liberalism was already becoming visible at a time when the workers were rightly regarding themselves as the real backbone of the revolution after their heroic fighting in the streets of Berlin in the March days.

Nor did the only threat to the revolution come from those bourgeois leaders seeking a compromise with the reaction. Contradictory political and social currents were also at work among all those intermediary layers between the big bourgeois and the industrial proletariat, from the richest of guild Masters to the poorest of peasants.

For over the previous decade, Germany's ancient structure of trade and craft guilds, organised in the strict traditional hierarchy of Master, journeymen and apprentices, had been subjected to increasingly bitter competition from large-scale production methods. Capitalist production, though still accounting for a relatively small proportion of Germany's national product (it should be remembered that Germany was still an overwhelmingly agricultural nation) had taken firm root in both textiles and mining, and had begun to spread its tentacles into other preserves of the medieval guilds. The Krupp dynasty had already established its first Essen factory 21 years previously, while in Berlin, the Borsig engineering works had been operating for ten years when its workers took to the streets to overthrow the Prussian monarchy. (By one of history's ironies, both firms were destined to figure in a later era of violent class struggle as prominent supporters and financiers of National Socialism.)

This deep-seated antagonism between the pre-capitalist guilds, which were organised on corporative, and not competitive principles, and the modern industrial and financial bourgeoisie differed in every essential from the struggle between the proletariat and the capitalist class. Unlike the working class, which at the time of the revolution numbered about 700,000, the far more numerous guild artisans saw in the upheavals of 1848 their opportunity to arrest the wheel of history and, if possible, set it

to being an appendage of official bourgeois democracy'. Neither was political independence enough. In a period of revolutionary ferment, the working class must seek to secure and retain arms, forming its own proletarian (i.e. Red) army and military command. Under this banner of intransigent opposition to all other class interests and political movements, Marx and Engels summoned the German working class to prepare, in the next revolutionary upheaval, for their own emancipation and not to serve as cannon fodder for their bourgeois 'allies':

'Their battle cry must be: The Revolution in Permanence'.

(K. Marx and F. Engels, *Address of the Central Committee to the Communist League*, in Ibid., pp.106-117)

trundling back to a supposedly idyllic past. In so far as the guilds acted as a coherent force, they tended to regard the bourgeoisie, and not the princes and kings of feudal Germany, as their chief enemies. When under the leadership of their masters, artisans pressed for the restoration of the old but now threatened guild privileges and with them, state restriction on the development of capitalist industry and commerce, theirs was an 'anti-capitalism' that looked back longingly — and hopelessly — to the Germany of the middle ages.

It had absolutely nothing in common with the anti-capitalism of the emerging industrial working class. In the 1848 revolution, the bourgeoisie embodied the miserable present, the guilds the romantic but irretrievably distant past, and the proletariat all the hopes for a socialist future.

The impact of the revolution on the guilds has, though this may not be readily appreciated, a special significance for our study of the historical roots of German fascism. One of the most potent appeals of National Socialism among the German petty-bourgeois — and here we are referring mainly to either self-employed or small, independent producers or traders — was its virulent 'anti-capitalist' propaganda, especially when directed at banking capital or joint stock industrial enterprises. Can it possibly be that the Nazis *themselves* injected this reactionary anti-capitalism into those millions of Germans tenaciously clinging to their status as independent — even if often semi-pauperised — property owners and producers?

Surely we must probe back into Germany's past, to a period when pre-capitalist layers of the population first engendered this fear and hatred of the big bourgeoisie, adapting their already established corporatist ideology and programme to explain and counter this new threat to their existence.

And because the bourgeois revolution provides the key to understanding so much of a nation's subsequent history, we must also look to 1848 for the origin of that classic petty-bourgeois fascist notion which lumps together the industrial proletarian and the capitalist as enemies of all that is decent and healthy in the body politic. For here we are dealing with ideological and social 'residues' which while lying dormant for long periods of relative class peace, can be capable of rearing their heads and seizing hold of millions in moments of great economic crisis and political stress.

In short, the betrayal of the revolution by the German bourgeoisie helped provide the raw political material which eight decades and more later, the Nazi demagogues worked up into a machine of counter-revolution to rescue this self-same bourgeoisie. Such is the 'irony of history'!

The guilds, it should always be remembered, were more than simply economic organisations. They were woven into the very fabric of pre-capitalist German society. With their strict and highly ritualised rules of membership and codes of conduct, they were rightly regarded as pillars of stability by the rulers of feudal Germany. Their corporative ideology, which stressed the supposed (and generally accepted) harmony of interest between a master and his servants, penetrated deeply into the consciousness of all guild members, and re-inforced by the church, percolated down through every level of the population. So although powerful economic forces were at work undermining the old predominance of the guild system and its medieval outlook, the entrenched forces of resistance were also strong, buttressed by literally centuries of backwardness. And once it struck, the counter-revolution gave them added nourishment.

But even in the Revolution's early days, guild leaders were anxiously pressing their own 'anti-capitalist' but essentially reactionary views. The *Open Letter* of the Leipzig Masters of April 1848 expressed the growing concern of guild masters throughout Germany that their further economic decline would lead not only to the triumph of their hated capitalist rivals, but eventually, to the establishment of communism. The guild system was lauded as the backbone of not only the family and Christian morality, but political stability. The Leipzig Masters roundly denounced the 'French' principle of free trade and economic competition, demanding instead that the entire German nation should be organised on guild or 'corporative' lines. The *Open Letter* — a truly significant historical document — ended by condemning liberal-inspired proposals for the 'emancipation of the Jews' whom the Masters, entirely in keeping with both Germany's feudal past and fascist future, depicted as the 'greatest enemy' of the artisan and small property owner.

The guild masters found themselves battling on two fronts. On the one hand, they fought for economic survival against the political representatives of industrial and banking capital which, as the preceeding example suggests, they tended to equate with the Jews; and on the other, the proletariat, whose struggle for democratic freedoms and, amongst its more advanced layers, for socialism, they saw as a challenge to the very foundation of the guild system.

Acutely aware of these threats, the Masters were quick to organise on a national as well as local scale to combat them. The Master-dominated Hamburg Artisan Congress in June adopted a declaration, condemning competition and calling on the Frankfurt Assembly to include the abolition of free trade in its projected German constitution. * The guild masters also kept a wary eye open for suspected trouble makers in their own ranks. At the next guild Congress, which opened in Frankfurt a month later, attempts were made to exclude journeymen from the hall. One speaker, apparently labouring under the delusion that he was scolding unruly apprentices in his own workshop, suggested to the unwanted intruders that they should 'go quietly home and await written news, consoled in the expectation that the Masters would look after their interests'.

The Masters concern for the welfare of their servants was well-founded. Journeymen and apprentices had fought shoulder to shoulder with the industrial proletariat in the March days, and had imbibed more than a little of their militant republicanism and radical social outlook. It was this which gave them their new found confidence to challenge their Masters. But their demands were still couched in the archaic language of the guilds, and were aimed at the reform, rather than the abolition of the system. They would probably have found very little to criticise in the opening address of the chairman at Frankfurt, who defiantly declared:

> We may be sure that speculation and usury will oppose us with all their resources, for what is at stake is their domination over industriousness. Yet the German handicraftsman has come of age, and he will no longer endure the yoke of slavery imposed by the money interests.

We must pause here to note the astonishing similarity between the anti-capitalism of the guilds and the 'national socialism' of Gottfried Feder, who drafted the economic section of the Nazi Party's founding programme. Very much in the style of the Frankfurt Artisans, point number 11 demanded the "abolition of incomes unearned by work" and the "abolition of the thraldom (i.e. slavery) of interest." Point number 18 called for "ruthless war upon all those whose activities are injurious to the common interests" including under this heading "usurers, profiteers, etc." whose sins were to be "punished with death." Elsewhere, in a work expanding on the main planks in the Nazi platform, Feder declared quite unambiguously that "the abolition of the Thraldom of Interest" was "the Kernel of National Socialism."[26] Yet this is precisely the slogan which the guild masters employed to rally their servants behind a programme of backward-looking utopian anti-capitalism and against an industrial working class seeking to break the back of feudal rule and thus releasing Germany from the fetters of the past. Even as early as 1848, the ideology and organisations of the guilds were serving as tools of

---

* Whatever other issues the Frankfurt Parliamentarians might be expected to compromise on, this one was excluded. Earlier government legislation repealing many of the old laws protecting the guilds had helped prise open the doors baring the road to Germany's industrial expansion. Between 1825 and 1850, pig iron production had leapt by 500% while coal output had tripled. Even the most passionately worded appeals were powerless in the face of this upsurge.

reaction, though in this instance their wielders were not the bourgeoisie but the rulers of pre-capitalist Germany.

And as was the case with those millions of deluded pettybourgeois followers of National Socialism before 1933, the guild master — and indeed many a journeyman and even apprentice — interwove their fear of big capitalism with a contempt for the industrial working class.

The first threatened him with economic strangulation from above, the latter with revolt and expropriation from below. A class thrown into panic by what it takes to be its impending doom can quite readily lump its real and imagined enemies together and depict them as it sees them in the distorting mirror of its own bewildered consciousness. Thus a petition drawn up by the artisans of Bielfeld complained bitterly that "recent times have wounded the artisans deeply, the limitless freedom of industry, the production of handicraft goods in factories, the superior power of capital which enslaves the artisan, threatens to destroy the position which the artisans have held up to now and to make them into a proletariat, will-less tools in the hands of the capitalists."

And the proletarianisation of the artisans would not merely be a disaster for the guilds, but for all Germany, as upon the guild "rests the actual power of the cities: it is the core of the state. It is called to end the great schism which separates the propertyless from the property owners... it stands between, the scales of justice in its hand." Far from siding with the proletariat, into whose ranks many artisans feared they might be thrust, the guilds harboured a deeply-felt contempt for those it termed "the propertyless." The entire guild tradition militated against such an orientation, and it was one that could only be shattered through decisive victory in the struggle against the entire structure of feudal reaction.* The leaders of the 1848 revolution rendered this impossible. The lower ranks of the guilds were thus driven back into the clutches of their exploiters, only in rare cases fighting their way towards a lasting alliance with the industrial proletariat and a perspective oriented towards the future. Repudiation and even open hatred of all forms of class struggle were endemic to the

---

*   In sharp contrast with England, where the shell of the old guilds, their economic and political power eroded by the Cromwellian Revolution and the industrial revolution which followed, became encrusted on the first independent organisation of skilled workers, notably printers.

The guild socialism of Fabian radicals like G.D.H. Cole can therefore not be compared in any sense with the Nazi "guild socialism" of Feder and company, for theirs was a "socialism" that presupposed the wholesale destruction of the working class movement and the establishment of a state based —in form alone — on the medieval corporation or guild.

Hence the term, which has become identified with the   Italian species of fascism, "corporate state."

guilds' self-appointed role as arbiter between the various strata of German society, and the masters therefore looked with grave disquiet upon all those economic policies which threatened to disturb the social equilibrium in favour of the proletariat.

We see this clearly in a petition submitted by the artisans of Prussia. It voiced alarm that Prussia's recent rapid industrial growth had "called forth so great a number of proletarians through the freedom of trade that in fact the Prussian State does not know how it is to satisfy them even slightly."

Historians of National Socialism often stress those facets of its ideology and propaganda which, on the surface at least, seem to militate against the role, ascribed to Fascism by Marxists, of a bulwark of capitalism. Thus they point to the 'ruralism' of Nazi leaders such as Walter Darre (Hitler's Minister of Agriculture) Himmler and Rosenberg as proof of this tendency, ignoring the fact that their deep-seated mistrust of large cities and romanticised view of country life is itself a petty-bourgeois fear of the organised proletariat, mediated and refracted through the particular forms of consciousness inherited by the modern German middle classes from their guild ancestors.

And in so far as Nazi ruralism and anti-industrialism helped mobilise the petty-bourgeoisie of town and country alike against the workers' movement, — and there is ample evidence at hand to prove that it did — this apparent historical throwback, far from colliding with the strategic plans of German monopoly capitalism, actually supplemented them. We shall have cause to return to this theme more than once, but here it is sufficient to stress that the role played by political 'residues' in the rise of National Socialism is unique to Germany only in form. As regards content, fascism possesses a universal character, battening as it does on all that is backward in human consciousness and demagogically combining with it a seemingly radical programme of demands aimed at the most depressed and politically immature sections of the population.

Nazi agitators were only able to make the absurd synthesis of Marxism and economic liberalism seem plausible to their petty-bourgeois audiences because this fantasy — the 'Jewish conspiracy' of 'international loan capital' and 'international Marxism' had, in a less developed form it is true — gripped a numerically large and politically important section of the German nation in the period of the 1848 revolution. Subsequent chapters will trace the development of this reactionary anti-capitalism, how it became saturated with an equally potent tradition of anti-semitism, and how, at every crucial stage of German history, the ruling classes fostered and exploited this counter-revolutionary ideology to further their imperialist aims abroad and their anti-working class strategy at home.

But first we must complete our balance sheet of the 1848 Revolution. On the debit side, we must record the Revolution's defeat, in so far as its goal of a united, democratic German republic was frustrated by the timidity, cowardice and even downright treachery of the leadership which gathered at Frankfurt. They debated while dynastic Prussia armed itself. And we must add to this the consequent reactionary modes of consciousness which were either generated or strengthened by the dashing of countless hopes for a brighter future. Every profound social upheaval — irrespective of its outcome — brings about equally profound shifts in the thinking of those who, at whatever level of awareness, take part in them. This process is at its most intense in periods of revolution, when every established idea and institution is subjected to the closest scrutiny and fiercest criticism. So it was in the England of 1640-49, the France of 1789-94, and the Germany of 1525 and 1848. But in raising the masses to this fever pitch of moral and political passion, the Revolution also poses and creates problems which it cannot possible solve:

> Revolution is impossible without the participation of the masses. This participation is in its turn possible only in the event that the oppressed connect their hopes for a better future with the slogan of revolution. In this sense the hopes engendered by the revolution are always exaggerated... from these same conditions comes one of the most important and moreover one of the most common elements of the counter-revolution... The disillusionment of these masses, their return to routine and to futility is as much an integral part of the post-revolutionary period as the passage into the camp of "law and order" of those "satisfied" classes or layers of classes, who have participated in the revolution.[27]

Trotsky is here writing specifically about the political and social basis of the Stalinist bureaucratic counter-revolution in the Soviet Union, but his remarks about the process known as *Thermidor* (after the anti-Jacobin reaction in the French Revolution), are equally valid for the period of counter-revolution which sets in after a successful bourgeois-democratic revolution.

But what are we to say of the political aftermath of a revolution which, after carrying all before it, fails ignominiously; and, if, together with the peasants revolt, we include the feeble post-Napoleonic attempts at political and economic union (the Wurttemberg Estates and the *Zollverein*) fails not once but thrice?

In this case, the masses do not even enjoy the vicarious thrill of victory. The very notion of revolution becomes discredited where and when its erstwhile advocates capitulate miserably, as they did in Germany before the Prussian sabre. The revolution's defeat affected different classes in different ways. It certainly gave new life to the guilds, by thrusting those they exploited back into the shadows of the past. But it also forced the German working class out along the road of independent political organisation and action. This we must put on the credit side of the revolution's balance sheet. Beginning with the Mainz print workers' congress in June,* the most advanced elements of the proletariat began to develop their own programme in conflict with the demands of both the guild masters and their own employers.

The climax of the workers' struggle for political independence came in August, at a time when the bourgeoisie was in full-scale retreat before the gathering forces of counter-revolution in Prussia. Consciously inspired by the example of English Chartism (the movement had just reached the zenith of its power, and was about to plunge into headlong decline) the organisers of the Berlin Workers' Congress declared that the delegates should have as their sole aim "the expression of the material interest of the working classes," and would seek to draw up a "social people's charter of Germany."

Prominent in the charter were demands for the right to work, state care of the sick and aged, public education, progressive income and inheritance taxes, legal limits on hours of work and finally, the abolition of feudal land taxes, a demand which made explicit working class solidarity with the cause of the oppressed rural population. This socially advanced programme was worlds apart from the demands being formulated at that time by the guild Masters. Indeed as if to underline the point, the convenors of the Congress declared in their "Appeal to the German Workers" that it had been summoned explicitly "in opposition to the Masters' Congress" (this being the Masters' Congress in Frankfurt).

Under attack from Junker, bourgeois and Master alike, the workers' leaders were making a determined bid to win allies from among the lower ranks of the artisans in the towns and the peasants in the countryside. But in both cases, their efforts met with failure. The German proletariat simply lacked the political experience and social weight to achieve such an enormous task. Although containing within it the embryo of a future powerful workers' movement, the revolution was essentially bourgeois in both content and goals, and it stood or fell according to the calibre of the leadership the bourgeoisie gave it. But even here, there was a positive side to things. The course of the German Revolution provided Marx and Engels, as active participants with ready-made laboratory conditions to test out, modify, enrich and codify their scientific theory of class struggle. And it not only enabled Marx and Engels to draw conclusions of a general nature

* As is so often the case, print workers were the pioneers of an independent workers' movement in Germany.

concerning bourgeois revolutions and the role of communists within them, but compelled them to examine even more closely those political features which were unique to Germany.

These are the two opposites which emerged out of the defeat of the 1848 Revolution. At one pole, the initial steps of the German proletariat along the road of political and organisational independence, and with it, an added material impulse to the development of Marxism; and at the opposite pole, the strengthening of the ideology and mass basis of reaction.

From 1848 to 1933, German history is at its core a history of the clash of these polar opposites, their conflict being driven to a brutal and tragic climax both by their own mutually contradictory nature and a series of varied and powerful external impulses which ranged from the First World War and the Russian Revolution to the rise of Stalinism and the Wall Street crash.

This is why a real history of German Fascism must begin with the year 1848.

REFERENCES FOR CHAPTER ONE

[1] K. Marx: *The Eighteenth Brumaire of Louis Bonaparte. Marx-Engels Selected Works* Vol. I, p.247, Moscow, 1962.

[2] V. Lenin: *Philosophical Notebooks. Collected Works,* Fourth Edition, Vol. 38, pp.360-361, Moscow 1961.

[3] L. Trotsky: *Results and Prospects* (1906) p.188, London, 1962.

[4] L. van Beethoven: *Letters, Journals and Conversations,* pp.22-23, London, 1951.

[5] Ibid, p.47.

[6] Conversation with Johann Eckermann, October 23, 1828.

[7] E. Kant: *The Contest of Faculties,* 1798.

[8] Ibid.

[9] Letter to F.I. Niethammer, Jena, October 13, 1806.

[10] G. Hegel: *The Phenomenology of Mind,* p.233, London, 1961.

[11] Letter to F.I. Niethammer, Bamburg, August 29, 1807.

[12] G. Hegel: *Lectures on the History of Philosophy,* Vol. iii, pp.390-391, London, 1955.

[13] Letter to C.G. Zellmann, Jena, January 23, 1807.

[14] G. Hegel: *The Wurttemberg Estates* 1815-1816. Hegel added the scathing comment that the Estates, like the returned French *emigres,* had 'forgotten nothing and learnt nothing. They seem to have slept through the last twenty five years, possibly the richest that world history has...'

[15] G. Hegel: *The Philosophy of History,* p.444, London, 1956.

[16] Ibid.

[17] K. Marx: *Contribution to the Critique of Hegel's Philosophy of Right* (1844) in Marx and Engels *On Religion,* p.44, Moscow, 1957.

[18] Ibid, p.58.

[19] Ibid, p.50.

[20] *Puritanisam and Liberty,* Edited by A.S.P. Woodhouse, p.58, London, 1965.

[21] K. Marx: *The Class Struggles in France* in *Marx-Engels Selected Works,* Vol. I, p.160, Moscow, 1962.

[22] K. Marx: *Revolution and Counter-Revolution,* p.70, London, 1952.
(Engels is now generally recognised to be the author of this series of articles on the course of the German and Austrian revolutions of 1848)

[23] K. Marx and F. Engels: *The Communist Manifesto. Marx Engels Selected Works,* Vol. I, pp.64-65.

[24] Ibid, p.65.

[25] Ibid, p.65.

[26] G. Feder: *Hitler's Official Programme,* p.44. (1934 edition)

[27] L. Trotsky: Extract from his Diary, November 26, 1926. Published in *Workers International News,* October-November, 1942.

26

Chapter Two
MARX AND ENGELS ON THE GERMAN QUESTION: BONAPARTISM AND THE BISMARCKIAN LEGACY

The recapture of Berlin by monarchist forces in October 1848, and the final defeat of the republican forces in the spring of 1849, set the stage for the piecemeal unification of Germany under the hegemony of Prussian Junkerdom—the so called Bismarckian 'revolution from above.' This, the transition of Germany from the brief period in which it attempted a plebeian solution to its problems of backwardness and fragmentation, to the dictatorship of 'blood and iron' occupied a central place in the theoretical, historical and political writings of both Marx and Engels.

And in attempting to lay bare the social and economic forces beneath the governmental forms in Germany, they evolved concepts which are of enormous value in grappling with the theoretical problems posed by the rise of fascism during the last years of the Weimar Republic.

For if Marx and Engels, as committed proletarian revolutionaries, were to map out a realistic road of struggle for the German working class, they were obliged to fill out their general theoretical abstractions on the basic laws of motion of capitalism and the role, nature and origin of the state, with a concrete, historical content; and to apply them to the living and contradictory reality of post-1848, Prussia-dominated Germany. Thus we return once more to the central problem of method, which in its turn revolves around the antagonistic yet unified relationship between the abstract and the concrete, the general and the particular, between theory and practice. Marx said this about the method he was seeking to apply in his study of previous schools of political economy:

> The economists of the 17th century . . . always started out with the living aggregate: population, nation, state, several states, etc, but in the end they invariably arrived by means of analysis at certain leading abstract general principles such as division of labour, money value, etc. As soon as these separate elements had been: more or less established by abstract reasoning, there arose the systems of political economy which start from simple conceptions such as labour, division of labour, exchange value and world market. The latter is manifestly the scientifically correct method. The concrete is concrete because it is a combina-

tion of many determinations, i.e. a unity of diverse elements. In our thoughts it therefore appears as a process of synthesis, as a result, and not as a starting point and, therefore, also the starting point of observation and conception. By the former method the complete conception passes into an abstract definition; by the latter the abstract definitions lead to the reproduction of the concrete subject in the course of reasoning.[1]

Thus an abstraction, while being an opposite of concrete reality from which it is distilled, is at the very same time an integral part of this reality, and serves to illuminate it to the degree that this relationship—one of the mutual interpenetration of opposites—is understood.

Applied to history and politics, this methodological principle demands of the investigator that, in applying his abstract concepts to the problems of a particular nation, he takes care to avoid the twin pitfalls of either failing to explain why the development of nation 'A' differs so radically from that of nations 'B' and 'C'—and in so doing simply remains at the level of abstraction—or becomes so immersed in the concrete and the particular that he obscures the workings of those general laws which govern the development of society as a whole.

The many writings of Marx and Engels on Germany are exemplars of how to surmount this double obstacle.

On the plane of pure theory, after 1848 there emerged an ever-widening gap between the schema presented in the *Communist Manifesto* of an aggressive and confident bourgeoisie seizing the machinery of state power and re-fashioning the world in its own image, and the living, if pitiful reality of a Germany, where the bourgeoisie had voluntarily surrendered the state power to the Prussian aristocracy and yet, despite this, entered upon an epoch of unprecedented industrial and technological expansion.

Marx himself was acutely aware of this contradiction, for in the wake of the Berlin counter-revolution, he attempted to concretise the general propositions in the *Manifesto* about the historical role of the bourgeoisie by drawing attention to the uneven way in which the bourgeois revolution had unfolded in the various major European nations. In the Germany of 1848, the bourgeoisie

> was hurled to the height of state power . . . not in the manner it desired, by a peaceful bargain with the crown, but by a revolution. It was to defend not its own interests but the interests of the people, versus the crown, that is, against itself, for a popular movement had paved the way for the bourgeoisie . . . hence the ecstatic fondness of the German and especially the Prussian bourgeoisie for constitutional monarchy.[2]

The great English and French bourgeois revolutions also

passed through phases where advocates of a constitutional
monarchy held the upper hand amongst the leadership of the
revolution. But in both cases, when repeated attempts at compromise had failed, the most resolute wing of the bourgeoisie
were pushed by the plebeians along the road of republicanism.
This transition was marked in England by Cromwell's victory
over the Presbyterians in the period of the second civil war,
and in France, by the expulsion of the Girondins from the Convention in June 1793. Marx was therefore correct in saying
that, in both these revolutions, 'the bourgeoisie was the class
that really formed the van of the movement' and that even
when the plebeians clashed with the bourgeoisie,

> they fought only for the realisation of the interests of the
> bourgeoisie, even if not in the fashion of the bourgeoisie, The whole
> French terrorism was nothing but a plebeian manner of settling
> accounts with the enemies of the bourgeoisie . . .[3]

This was the universal character of the two revolutions.
They 'were not English and French revolutions; they were
revolutions of a European pattern. They were not the victory
of a definite class of society over the old political order; they
were the proclamation of political order for the new European
society'. 1789 and 1648 heralded

> the victory of the bourgeoisie over feudal property, of nationality
> over provincialism, of competition over the guild, of partition over
> primogeniture, of the owner of the land over the domination of
> the owner by the land, of enlightenment over superstitition, of the
> family over the family name, of industry over heroic laziness, of
> civil law over medieval privilege . . . [4]

It is at this point that Marx modifies and concretises the
perspective which, with Engels, he evolved a year earlier in
relation to Germany. Then, he had anticipated that the
approaching bourgeois revolution would be more thorough
going than either the English or the French because of
Germany's more advanced state of industrialisation. Now, in
the light of the living experience of the revolution, Marx
quickly saw that events had taken an opposite course for
precisely that reason:

> The German bourgeoisie had developed so slothfully, cravenly
> and slowly that at the moment when it menacingly faced
> feudalism and absolutism it saw itself menacingly faced by the
> proletariat and all those factions of the burghers whose interests
> and ideas were akin to those of the proletariat. And it saw
> inimically arrayed not only a class behind it but all of Europe
> before it.[5]

Marx concludes this short article on the German Revolution
with a savage onslaught on the class which betrayed it, branding it with such epithets as could only come from one who had

only recently severed the political umbilical cord with this self-same German bourgeoisie:

> no energy in any respect, plagiarism in every respect; common because it lacked originality, original in its commonness, dickering with its own desires, without initiative, without faith in itself, without faith in the people, without a world history calling; an execrable old man, who saw himself doomed to guide and deflect the first youthful impulses of a robust people in its own senile interests—sans eyes, sans ears, sans teeth, sans everything—such was the Prussian bourgeoisie that found itself at the helm of the Prussian state after the March Revolution. [6]

It is competely legitimate to ask: but did not the political supineness of this class invalidate one of the most fundamental propositions of historical materialism? Did not the failure of the German bourgeoisie to rise to the abstract or generalised norms ascribed to it in the *Communist Manifesto* overthrow the entire theoretical basis from which Marx and Engels had derived this norm? This was possibly the first, but most certainly not the last, occasion on which this problem was to confront the revolutionary movement. Trotsky had to deal with it in his last theoretical struggle, against the Shachtman-Burnham opposition in the American Socialist Workers' Party. They declared that the Stalin-Hitler pact of August 1939 offered proof that the USSR had so degenerated from the 'abstract norm' of a healthy workers' state that Marxists were no longer obliged to defend it against the attacks of imperialism. Trotsky replied in the following way:

> In the question of the social character of the USSR, mistakes commonly flow . . . from replacing the historical fact with the programmatic norm. Concrete fact departs from the norm. This does not signify, however, that it has overthrown the norm; on the contrary, it has reaffirmed it, from the negative side . . . The contradiction between concrete fact and the norm constrains us not to reject the norm but, on the contrary, to fight for it by means of the revolutionary road . . . we do not say: "Everything is lost. We must begin all over again." We clearly indicate those elements of the workers' state which at the given stage can be salvaged, preserved and further developed. [7]

And this—with the important proviso that Marx was concerned with the degeneration of a bourgeoisie, and Trotsky with the bureaucratic decline of a state established by a proletarian revolution—was precisely the methodological approach of Marx and Engels to post-1848 Germany. They did not permit their political perspectives to be distorted 'by opposing a good programmatic norm to a miserable, mean and even repugnant reality',[8] no more than Trotsky did the 'bureaucratic collectivists' with their cynical references to the USSR as a 'counter-revolutionary workers' state'. The German bourgeoisie—not

the generalised, abstract and supra-national bourgeoisie of the
Communist Manifesto, but the one subjected to Marx's wither-
ing contempt after its betrayal of the March Revolution—
still remained a bourgeoisie. All its political sins did not negate
its historical role as the vehicle in Germany of a revolutionary
mode of production. The political failings of the German
capitalist class certainly undermined its ability to carry
through this task in the way that the French and English
bourgeoisies had done before it, but this did not mean at all
that Germany's economy would go into decline as a result of
the defeat of the 1848 revolution.

What the set back of 1848 did mean was that the economic
development of the bourgeoisie in Germany would now take on
forms not previously experienced by the class, and that, in
turn, this would create new political forms arising on the
foundations of this unique combination of social and
economic forces. Again we must stress: the deviation of
Germany from the classic 'European' norm in no way invali-
dates that norm, it dialectically complements it, just as the
June insurrection of the Parisian workers entered into and
helped shape the course of the revolution across the Rhine.
Historical materialism does not 'provide the answers'; it is a
theoretical and methodological key—and an inexact one at
that—for unlocking the doors which conceal the mysteries of
the past and forces which have gone to shaping the present.

For it would be the height of anti-Marxism to suppose that
Marx and Engels either took their world outlook and method
ready-made from the pinnacles of bourgeois culture (i.e. German
idealist philosophy, French utopian socialism and English
political economy) without recasting it in a new mould, or that
they were confronted with no problems or experiences which
demanded its amendment and enrichment. Opponents of
Marxism seize on this ever-present contradiction between
abstraction and reality to challenge the need for any form of
theory. Trotsky answered these sceptics by taking their
arguments to their logical conclusion:

> Inasmuch as the economic basis determines events in the super-
> structure not immediately; inasmuch as the mere class characteris-
> ation of the state is not enough to solve the practical tasks,
> therefore . . . therefore we can get along without examining
> economics and the class nature of the state . . . But why stop
> there? Since the law of labour value determines prices not
> "directly" and not "immediately"; since the laws of natural
> selection determine not "directly" and not "immediately" the
> birth of a suckling pig; since the laws of gravity determine not
> "directly" and not "immediately" the tumble of a drunken police-
> man down a flight of stairs, therefore . . . let us leave Marx, Dar-

win, Newton and all the other lovers of "abstractions" to collect
dust on a shelf. This is nothing less than the solemn burial of
science for, after all, the entire course of the development of the
sciences proceeds from "direct" and "immediate" causes to the
more remote, and profoundness from multiple varieties and
kaleidoscopic events—to the unity of the driving forces. [9]

Trotsky was compelled, by the unfavourable course of events
in the Soviet Union after 1923, to explain the contradiction
between the Bolshevik 'norm' of 1917 and the bureaucratised
reality of a Stalin-ruled USSR. Marx and Engels, also working
in conditions of political reaction after the defeat of a whole
series of European revolutions, likewise were confronted with
similar theoretical and political problems in Germany. At
first, the course of German development was unclear. The
Prussian nobility, the real power behind the Hohenzollern
throne, in turn rested on the rich farmers or Junkers of the
East. This class of landowners stood in a highly contradictory
relationship to the German industrial bourgeoisie. Many of
them, while imbibing the values and political outlook of the
Prussian monarchy, were at the same time highly competitive
and profit conscious producers and exporters of rye and wheat.
There was therefore the possibility of a 'bloc' with the defeated
industrial bourgeoisie in which the Junkers continued to hold
the main levers of state power through their control of the army
and government bureaucracy, while permitting and even
encouraging the industrialists and bankers to expand Germany's
economic wealth in such a way that would not undermine the
predominance of the old ruling elites.

Of course, such a combination could not unfold immediately
in the wake of the revolution, no more than it could be from
the very outset a consciously evolved strategy on the part of
its major participants.

The 'pact of steel and rye' as the bloc between the Ruhr and
East Prussia became known in the last years of Bismarckian
Germany, only came to fruition after a long process of
improvisation and adaptation.

Indeed, in the wake of the defeated revolution, when the
Junkers were seeking every possible means to batten down the
political hatches on a still-restless proletariat, Bismarck tended
to side with those who preferred an economically stunted
Germany to one which, alongside a flourishing industry, would
be at the mercy of a large and radical proletariat:

> Factories enrich the individual, but they also breed a mass of
> proletarians, a mass of undernourished workers who are a menace
> to the state because of the insecurity of their livelihood. Handi-
> craftsmen, on the other hand, constitute the backbone of the
> burgher class, of an element whose survival is essential to a healthy

national life . . . It is true that industrial freedom may offer the public man advantages. It produces inexpensive goods. But to this inexpensiveness the misery and sorrow of the artisan are poisonously bound, and I believe that the inexpensive garments from the clothing shop may after all lie uneasily on our backs, when those who make them must despair of earning their daily bread honestly . . .'[10]

Not that the young Bismarck had any real sympathy for the plight of the German artisan, threatened with ruin by the onward march of industrialisation. The future 'Iron Chancellor' was, in his characteristically shrewd fashion, casting around for points of support for the Junker regime to balance against the emergent bourgeoisie and industrial working class. And the pro-Junker economist Hermann Wagener argued very much along the same lines when he declared in the Prussian legislature:

> I believe that the events of the years 1848 and 1849 have taught us that the artisan class desires not political but social improvements. If we want to wean the artisans from the political theory of subversion, then we can do so only by improving their social condition in accordance with the proper theory.

Advocates of such a policy clearly had the sympathetic ears of ruling government circles, because in the year that followed the defeat of the revolution, most anti-guild legislation enacted in the previous period of economic liberalism was reversed. And while government edicts could at most retard the tempo of Germany's industrialisation, it certainly did much to create a political climate of support for Junker rule amongst those either organised in, or influenced by the guilds.

And it without doubt engendered, after years of traumatic uncertainties, the utterly false hope that the artisan would be permitted to perform this role of 'backbone' of the Prussian state into the indefinite future. The shattering of this illusion in the period of imperialism and post world war economic crisis unleashed a ferocious despair within this economically impotent, but numerically large class, and provided fascism with just the disoriented social material it required to hurl against the organisation of the German proletariat. The role— and art—of national socialism lay in setting in motion on behalf of monopoly capital precisely those classes which it dooms to economic strangulation. The basis for this petty-bourgeois 'backlash' had been created in the period of deep political reaction after the defeat of the 1848 Revolution. So, too, had the seeds been sown in the same social classes of deep contempt for the most modest forms of democracy and individual freedom. These had been demagogically lumped together with capitalist free trade, and denounced by the Junkers as an alien importation from France. This strategy, directed as much against the bourgeoisie as the proletariat, drew heavily on the historical fact that bourgeois democracy and economic reform had been brought to Germany on the bayonets of Napoleon's army, and that for this reason, had provoked hostility in quarters which might, in other circumstances, have been sympathetic to the ideals of the French Revolution. But because of the already-discussed uneven development of the bourgeois revolution in Europe, its concrete juxtaposition led to the national cause becoming identified with political reaction in Germany, and support for democracy with treason. In France, ironically, the reverse was the case. Patriotism and 1789 became interwoven to such an extent in the French body politic that the bourgeoisie was able, through the leaders of French socialism and syndicalism, to march the proletariat off to the trenches without the slightest organised resistance from within the ranks of the French labour movement.

Unevenness *and* combination—here is one of the most vital keys to grasping the contradictory development of European, and especially German history. We have repeatedly stressed the unique role of the guilds in providing Junker reaction with a counter-weight to the working class and bourgeoisie. But, in the case of England, the artisans played a leading part in spearheading Chartism. They were to be found, not in the ranks of the reaction, or even as sympathisers of the London-based moderates, those who followed Lovett's philosophy and political strategy of 'moral force.'

In complete contradiction to the majority of their German counterparts, they fought as partisans of the most militant, 'physical force' wing of Chartism, under the leadership of its northern leader, Feargus O'Connor. And this can only partly be explained by their different economic circumstances. It is true that the power of the guilds had long been in decline since the onset of the industrial revolution nearly a century before, and that the consequent process of the separation of the individual artisan from his own instruments of production was nearer completion. These factors would help to account for the English artisan's readiness to identify his own cause with that of the industrial proletariat. But we must also take into consideration the question of political tradition which also played such an important part in the behaviour of the German guilds during 1848. Two centuries before Chartism reached its apogee, feudal institutions had been dealt a death blow by the military and political defeat of the Stuart monarchy. This single act did more to cleanse England of rural and guild idiocies than any amount of radical pamphleteering and agita-

tion. The millions strong supporters of Chartism trod, however
dimly they perceived it, in the footsteps of their victorious
revolutionary ancestors. This is what gave them their great
strength, and this is what the German revolutionaries lacked.
The role of tradition in politics can never be given too much
attention, and this applies as much to movements of reaction as
to those with a revolutionary goal. Prussia's ruling Junker caste,
once under the astute leadership of Bismarck, based itself on
a very real, if distortedly perceived, tradition of reaction in
Germany which reached back over three centuries to the epoch
of Luther. And within this Junker-bureaucratic-monarchist
shell, the bourgeoisie was still able to develop Germany's
productive forces at an unprecedented tempo. Far from relaps-
ing into a rural European backwater, those German states
organised in the 'Zollverein' or customs union, enjoyed over
the decade which followed the bourgeoisie's political defeat a
threefold increase in pig iron production, and an even greater
expansion in coal mining. Already the basic outlines of the
German economy—and its bourgeoisie—were becoming well-
defined. And Junkers like Bismarck who had in the immediate
post-revolutionary period tended to look askance at these
developments, began to revise their opinions.

It was one thing to lecture the German bourgeoisie on the
moral necessity of paying through the nose for their Sunday
finery, but something entirely different when it came to
equipping an army for war. The Prussian sword—or rather
cannon—could hardly see the light of day in a dingy guild
master's workshop. Prussia's wars of German unification could
only be fought with weapons forged in the furnaces of Krupp,
Stinnes and Mannesmann.

This thought may well have lurked at the back of the mind
of the future victor at Sedowa and Sedan when he confided to
Hermann Wagener in 1853 that his faith in the efficacy of the
guilds was being undermined:

> . . . we are spared none of the disadvantages which it brings, that
> is, excessive prices for manufactured articles (including, presumably,
> those offensive "inexpensive garments from clothing shops"),
> indifference to customers and therefore careless workmanship,
> long delays on orders, late beginning, early stopping, and pro-
> tracted lunch hours when work is done at home, little choice in
> ready-made wares, backwardness in technical training, and many
> other deficiencies . . . [11]

Repudiation of the guilds, save as a demagogic ploy to
retain their political loyalty, drove Junkerdom willy-nilly
towards an alliance with the industrial and financial bourgeoisie. The content of this combination with its implications
for the German labour movement engrossed Marx and

especially Engels for the next two decades.

After four years of Bismarck's rule (he was appointed Chancellor in 1862) Engels undertook an important, if partial, revision of their conception of the European bourgeoisie as enunciated in the *Communist Manifesto*.

> It is becoming ever clearer to me that the bourgeoisie has not the stuff in it for ruling directly itself, and that therefore where there is no oligarchy, as there is in England, to take over, for good pay, the manning of the state and society in the interests of the bourgeoisie, a Bonapartist semi-dictatorship is the *normal form*. It upholds the big material interests of the bourgeoisie even against the will of the bourgeoisie, but allows the bourgeoisie no share in the power of government. The dictatorship in its turn is forced against its will to adopt these material interests of the bourgeoisie as its own. [12]—emphasis added.

As a species of state power, Bonapartism derives its name from the military dictatorship established by Napoleon Bonaparte after his coup of November 9, 1799, this being the 18th Brumaire of the year VIII by the French revolutionary calendar. It brought to a close a decade of political conflict and social tension in which the state power had oscillated—often violently—between a multiplicity of parties, factions and individual leaders. The exhaustion of the plebeians, and the yearning of the big bourgeoisie for political stability to enjoy the fruits of victory created the conditions for the entry of the army, with Napoleon as its most illustrious and politically astute leader, as the supreme arbiter of the nation. His rear consolidated and made secure from either fresh revolutions or attempts at feudal restoration, Napoleon felt free to embark on his wars of conquest. Marx and Engels were the first to see that within certain historically conditioned limits, the original Bonapartist model could be employed to unravel the complexities of later episodes in European history where state forms deviated sharply from the classic bourgeois-democratic 'norm'. And this was to prove the case not only with France, where Bonapartism reappeared in the guise of Napoleon's nephew Louis, but in Bismarckian Germany.*

This is the first occasion, to the author's knowledge, on which either Marx or Engels sought to explain the unique political development of Germany by reference to Bonapartism. However, the one-sided, politically stunted evolution of the

---

*Marx's immortal study of this second edition of French Bonapartism, *The Eighteenth Brumaire of Louis Bonaparte* and his complementary work *The Class Struggles in France* are absolutely essential reading for an understanding of Bismarckian Germany, not to speak of the role of the semi and full Bonapartist regimes of Brüning, von Papen and Schleicher which preceeded Hitler's assumption of power in January 1933.

German bourgeoisie had been commented on by Engels some
seven years earlier, in his review of Marx's *Contribution to
the Critique of Political Economy*, where he points out that the
defeat of 1848 forced the capitalist class to concentrate its
energies along lines most directly related to productive
techniques:

> . . . Germany . . . applied itself with quite extraordinary energy
> to the natural sciences, in accordance with the immense bour-
> geois development setting in after 1848; with the coming into
> fashion of these sciences, in which the speculative trend had never
> achieved anything of real importance, the old metaphysical mode
> of thinking . . . gained ground rapidly. Hegel was forgotten and a
> new materialism arose in the natural sciences; it differed in
> principle very little from the materialism of the 18th century
> . . . [13]

This passage is highly significant in that it once again refines
earlier formulations made by Marx and Engels on the bourgeois revolution in Germany. After its defeat, Marx's initial
reaction was to denounce the German bourgeoisie as incapable
of *any* progressive work—'sans eyes, sans ears, sans teeth,
sans everything'—and yet here is Engels, ten years later, writing
of 'the immense bourgeois developments setting in after 1848',
which included important advances in the field of natural
science.

A large part of the problem lay not with the German
bourgeoisie, but with their half–protectors, half–tormentors,
the Prussian Junkers. This class was particularly well suited
to its role of mediator between rising industrial capitalism and
the old, declining rural Germany, as it had much in common
with both. Long before the 1848 revolution, it had begun to
adapt the forms of feudal tenure and peasant bondage to a
market economy, and after 1848 showed an equal capacity
for directing Germany's industrial and financial bourgeoisie
into channels which aggrandised its own power and made
possible the realisation of its dynastic and military goals.

In inheriting the social and political situation bequeathed to
him by the defeat of 1848 (Bismarck had been among the
revolution's most fanatical enemies) the 'Iron Chancellor'
exploited this unique balance of class forces to the maximum.
And here the limitations of historical analogies become all too
obvious, since the two periods of Bonapartist rule in France
arose on bourgeois state foundations, and under conditions
where the role of feudal residues, either in the form of a
politically active aristocracy or monarchist peasantry, was
virtually non-existent. German Bonapartism followed the
defeat of the bourgeois revolution, and herein lies its unique
feature, one which posed so many political problems for both

Marx and Engels. Engels especially, since Marx throughout this period, though of course active in the work of the First International, was deeply involved in the production of his *Das Kapital,* and tended to leave to Engels the task of following the day-to-day events and broader political trends in Germany.*

Thus, of Bismarck's early attempts to secure his domestic rear before undertaking his wars of German unification, he writes:

> Politically, Bismarck will be compelled to rely on the bourgeoisie, because he needs them against the Princes . . . as soon as he wants to secure from parliament the conditions necessary for central governmental power, he will have to make concessions to the bourgeois. And the natural course of events will compel him or his successors to appeal to the bourgeoisie again and again. This means that even if for the moment Bismarck does not make more concessions, than he absolutely must, he will nevertheless be driven more and more into a bourgeois direction . . .[14]

But Bismarck proved to be a driver of hard bargains— harder even than Engels had anticipated. He still believed that because of the bourgeoisie's indispensable economic role in Prussia's unification of Germany, its parliamentary leaders would exploit their strong position by extracting political concessions from the Junkers. In fact, nothing of the kind happened. They were permitted to cheer Bismarck's military victories—after all, they had supplied the arms that alone made them possible. Neither could they complain of their share in the loot. Bismarck's wars were the making of many an industrial fortune, and many were the firms launched on the proceeds of French war reparations, which amounted to the astronomical sum of five milliard francs. But as for a share in the guidance of the sacred Prussian State—never.

Nevertheless, Engels had grasped an essential element of Bismarck's strategy. In dealing with the petty-minded princes, whose particularist tradition and outlook made the cause of German unity anathema for them, Bismarck most certainly did lean for support on the more 'national minded' bourgeoisie. But leaning did not—at this stage at least—necessarily involve sharing. For Bismarck also had his answer ready for those amongst the bourgeoisie who might exploit this alliance to their own advantage. This consummate tactician did not hesitate to lean, however fleetingly, even on the German proletariat if this ruse could have the effect of bringing the more adventurous

---

*In fact this had been the case for some time. It was Engels who wrote a history of both the German revolutions: his 'The Peasant War in Germany' (1850) and 'Revolution and Counter-Revolution' (1852). But these must be balanced by Marx's brilliant and profound studies of French revolutionary history.

elements of the bourgeoisie to order.

Certainly at this time, the bourgeoisie was beginning to flex its rather flabby political muscles. 1867 saw the foundation of the National Liberal Party, a right wing breakaway from the more democratically oriented Progressives, and it was this party, based on the coal and iron interests of the Ruhr and Germany's other industrial regions, which allied itself with Bismarck in the latter's struggle for a strong central state overruling both provincial and religious particularism.

(This coalescence of the Prussian Protestant bourgeoisie with Bismarck resulted, three years later, in the formation of the exclusively Catholic Centre Party, which at once identified itself politically with provincial centres of resistance to rule from Prussian Berlin. Thus the religious question—yet another historical 'residue' from the defeat of the 16th century revolution—became a further element in the Bonapartist structure of German politics. In this sense too it differed from both varieties of French Bonapartism.)

Bismarck had the measure of his bourgeois allies-cum-opponents from the very outset of his political career. He well understood their inbred fear of thorough going democracy, and their distaste for any reliance on the poor of town and country. This was one of the central political lessons of 1848. Bismarck now applied it in his Bonapartist strategy after the victory over France. It was he, and not the timid bourgeois democrats, who introduced manhood suffrage, converting it into a bulwark of Junker rule.*

Bismarck had been attempting to convert the Prussian king to this policy for some time before the adoption of the German constitution in 1871. In 1866, he confided to Kaiser William I that he believed that far from undermining the foundations of the Prussian monarchy as many Junkers feared, it would 'raise the king high up on a rock which the waters of revolution would never touch . . .'

Engels undertook a lengthy study of these problems of German politics in his uncompleted work, *The Role of Force in History*, written in the winter of 1888-89. But he also touched on them in his voluminous correspondence with Marx, and his 1874 Preface to *The Peasant War in Germany*.

Here we find him recoiling in disgust from the pusillanimous conduct of the German bourgeoisie in the newly-created Reichstag:

---

*While making sure that in his own Prussia, the cornerstone of the new Germany, the votes of the propertied classes outweighed the far more numerous votes of the workers and rural poor. This was the infamous system of the Prussian 'Three Tier Franchise', only demolished by the Revolution of November 1918.

I do not want to blame the poor National-Liberals in the Chamber more than they deserve. I know they have been left in the lurch by those who stand behind them, by the mass of the bourgeoisie. This mass does not want to rule. It has 1848 still in its bones. [14]

Engels explained this previously unknown phenomenon in the following way:

> It is the misfortune of the German bourgeoisie to have arrived too late, as is the favourite German manner. The period of its florescence occurs at a time when the bourgeoisie of the other Western European countries is already politically in decline. In England, the bourgeoisie could get its real representative, Bright (a leading advocate of free trade), into the government only by an extension of the franchise . . . In France, where the bourgeoisie as such, as a class in its entirety, held power for only two years, 1849 and 1850, under the republic, it was able to continue its social existence only by abdicating its political power to Louis Bonaparte and the army. And on account of this enormously increased interaction of the three most advanced European countries, it is today no longer possible for the bourgeoisie to settle down to a comfortable political rule when this rule has already outlived its usefulness in England and France.

Engels, employing the concept of uneven and combined development,* then reaches the nub of his argument:

> It is a peculiarity of precisely the bourgeoisie, in contrast to all former ruling classes, that there is a turning point in its development after which every further increase in its agencies of power, hence primarily its capitals, only tends to incapacitate it more and more for political rule. *Behind the big bourgeois stand the proletarians* . . . at a certain point—which need not be reached everywhere at the same time or at the same stage of development— it (the bourgeoisie) begins to notice that this, its proletarian double, is outgrowing it. From that moment on, it loses the strength required for exclusive political rule, it looks around for allies, with whom it shares its rule, or to whom it cedes the whole of its rule, as circumstances may require. In Germany, this turning point

---

*This passage alone renders absurd Stalin's claim that it was Lenin who 'discovered' the 'law of uneven development' (J. Stalin: *The Social-Democratic Deviation in our Party*, being a report delivered to the 15th Conference of the CPSU, November 1, 1926, published in Stalin, *Collected Works*, Vol 8, p.261, Moscow 1954). In defending his nationalist and reformist theory of 'socialism in one country', against the attacks of Trotsky, Stalin was obliged to declare as 'no longer correct' the unequivocal statement by Engels in his *Principles of Communism* (1847) that the socialist revolution could not triumph in a single country. Stalin argued that uneven development was unique to the monopolist, imperialist stage of capitalism, and that therefore, 'in these conditions the old formula of Engels becomes incorrect and must inevitably be replaced by another formula, one that affirms the possibility of the victory of socialism in one country'. (Ibid., p.261). How much sympathy Lenin had for this 'formula' can be seen from the comprehensive selection of Lenin's writings and speeches on world revolution reproduced in the author's *Stalinism in Britain* pp.41-50. (London 1970.)

came for the bourgeoisie as early as 1848. [15]

Then we have, dating from a year earlier, Engels' equally perceptive analysis of the 'social' side of Bismarck's Bonapartism, namely, his flirtations with the so-called 'state socialism'. To those social reformers who argued that the Bismarck regime could solve the 'social question' because it did not rest directly on any single exploiting class, Engels replied:

> That is the language of reactionaries . . . the state as it exists in Germany is . . . the necessary product of the social basis out of which it has developed . . . there exists side by side with a landowning aristocracy, which is still powerful, a comparatively young and extremely cowardly bourgeoisie, which up to the present has not won either direct political domination, as in France, or more or less indirect domination, as in England. [16]

Engels then points out how the growth of the industrial proletariat introduced a third prop into the Bonapartist state structure:

> Side by side with these two classes . . . there exists a rapidly increasing proletariat which is intellectually highly developed and which is becoming more and more organised every day. We therefore find here, alongside of the basic condition of the old absolute monarchy—an equilibrium between the landed aristocracy and the bourgeoisie*—the basic condition of modern Bonapartism—an equilibrium between the bourgeoisie and the proletariat. But both in the old absolute monarchy and in the modern Bonapartist monarchy the real governmental authority lies in the hands of a special caste of army officers and state officials. In Prussia this caste is replenished partly from its own ranks, partly from the lesser primogenitary (hereditary) aristocracy, more rarely from the higher aristocracy, and least of all from the bourgeoisie. The independence of this caste, which appears to occupy a position outside and, so to speak, above society, gives the state the semblance of independence in relation to society. [17]

Here Engels at last concretises in relation to Germany the general theory of the state which both he and Marx had been evolving over the previous 20 years. It was by no means the rule for the bourgeoisie to exercise direct state power, in the sense of holding all or most of the key governmental and departmental posts in a particular country where the capitalist mode of production had become dominant. In fact Engels could only point to France—and for brief period of two years at that—where the entire bourgeoisie had held the reins of state power firmly in its own hands. In every other case, capitalist

---

*The classic form of Bonapartism under the absolute monarchy evolved first in England under the Tudors, which leaned for support alternately or even simultaneously upon the old aristocracy and the rising commercial classes, and later, in France under the Bourbons.

class rule had been, to one degree or another, exercised by proxy, had been mediated either through a faction of the bourgeoisie itself, or through a caste selected and trained for this task from other social classes. This caste, which has as its sole or central task the exercising of direct state power can be drawn from the most varied layers of society, according to both immediate circumstance and political tradition.

In Bismarck's Germany, it was the Junkers who provided this governing stratum, thus at the same time extending the historical life of a class that would otherwise have ossified and withered away as an economic anachronism. They did not simply and mechanically occupy a political vacuum that the bourgeoisie was unable to fill. They actively fought to defend their role as the sole wielders of state and military power. The Junkers sensed that, in post 1848 Germany, they had no other right to existence save as this.

And it is no mere coincidence that Germany—only on this occasion Hitler's Germany—provides us with the reverse case of a bourgeoisie being ruled not 'from above', by the landed aristocracy, but 'from below' by the petty-bourgeois Nazi leadership. Invoking the aid of other classes or layers of classes to ward off the threat of proletarian revolution—for such was the basis of its pact with both Bismarck and Hitler— is therefore very much an integral part of the political make up of the German bourgeoisie. And we may, with the reservations that are necessary with all such parallels, also point to the early days and months of the German Republic as proof that this same bourgeoisie was even prepared to delegate power to the leaders of its old enemy, the Social Democrats, if that was the only means of averting the socialist revolution.

None of these cases is unique to Germany. Marx shows in his *Eighteenth Brumaire* how Louis Bonaparte's coup d'etat of December 2, 1851 became possible through the mobilisation of the 'lumpenproletariat' against the institutions of bourgeois parliamentary democracy, and also how once firmly in power, Louis Bonaparte secured the mass support of the French peasantry by exploiting the heroic aura around the name of his dead uncle:

> The French bourgeoisie balked at the domination of the working proletariat; it had brought the lumpen proletariat to domination, with the chief of the Society of December 10 at the head . . . A bunch of blokes push their way forward into the court, into the ministries, to the head of the administration and the army, a crowd of the best of whom it must be said that no one knows whence he comes, a noisy, disreputable, rapacious boheme that crawls into galooned coats with the same grotesque dignity as the high dignitaries of Soulouque.[18]

The political rule of the monarch, the aristocrat, the labour bureaucrat, the gutter—or even the priest—these are some of the forms which the dictatorship of capital can assume at various periods of its rise and decline. In fact, as a general rule, it is true to say that the greater the political crisis facing the bourgeoisie, the more ready it will be to cede its power to these strata, and the more necessary it becomes for other social groups to screen the bourgeoisie's own rule. And the tenacity with which these governing castes defend the rule of capital hinges to a large degree on the extent of their own stake-material as well as 'moral'-in the existing system.

Hence the acquiescence of the German bourgeoisie in the penetration of their own elites by the top Nazi cliques, and their readiness to accept a considerable degree of graft and self-aggrandisement by the upper circles of the party leadership and bureaucracy. It was not, as some historians claim, 'protection money' but more a means of ensuring Nazi loyalty to their own class goals and interests by integrating them into the capitalist system of property ownership. Leaders such as Goering, Hitler and Goebbels became capitalists in their own right, as did many hundreds of lesser party officials beneath them.

Engels noted this process of fusion and mutual interpene-tration of classes in Bismarckian Germany. Industrialists aped the mores and manners of the aristocracy, and hunted titles that would prefix their surname with the almost holy 'von;' while on the other hand, 'the nobility, who have been industrialists for a long time as manufacturers of beet sugar and distillers of brandy, have long left the old respectable days behind and their names now swell the lists of directors of all sorts of sound and unsound joint-stock companies . . .'[19] This process of the 'bourgeoisification' of an aristocracy had of course been noted by Marx and Engels in the case of Britain, but here it took place on a solidly capitalist state foundation, and under conditions where the bourgeoisie was not lacking in either political experience or aggression.

In Germany, despite the impression created by Engels of the two classes meeting in mid-stream, the political initiative remained with the Junkers, for the reasons already alluded to. Engels was quite correct when he insisted that 'the transition from the absolute monarchy to the Bonapartist monarchy is in full swing', but more than a little over-optimistic when he added 'with the next big business and industrial crisis not only will the present swindle collapse* but the old Prussian state as well'.[20]

---

*Engles refers here to the involvement of the more avaricious layers of the government bureaucracy in dubious stock exchange dealings.

This he acknowledged in a note to the 1887 edition of the work in question, where he stated that the bourgeois-Junker alliance had remained intact chiefly by virtue of 'fear of the proletariat, which has grown tremendously in numbers and class consciousness since 1872'. Nevertheless, Engels' hatred for the Junker caste, which stifled German politics and gravely hindered the unfolding of an open struggle between the bourgeoisie and the proletariat, often led him either to exaggerate the tempo of its political demise, or detect oppositional trends within the German bourgeoisie where there were none. For example, in 1886 he wrote to August Bebel, joint founder with Wilhelm Liebknecht of the German Social Democratic Party, that he had again detected signs 'that the German bourgeois was once more being compelled to do his political duty, to oppose the present system, so that at long last there will be some progress again'.[21]

Bebel had the doleful duty of reporting that this was not so, and that in fact the bourgeoisie remained loyal almost to a man behind Bismarck's programme of anti-socialist persecution.*

Not that Engels had any illusions in the possibility of a bourgeois political renaissance in Germany. Far from it. Rather he understood that in the context of Bismarckian Germany, there was absolutely no likelihood of a successful proletarian bid for power**. So while consolidating its own positions and preparing for a future period when the struggle for power was on the agenda, the German workers' movement searched for chinks in the armour of its enemy. Engels considered a fully bourgeois government not only inevitable but, as far as the political education of the German working class was concerned, necessary:

> Our turn can only come when the bourgeois and and petty-bourgeois parties have openly and in practice proved their inability to govern.[22]

How could Engels have anticipated that 32 years later, when this situation did arise, the main instrument in handing state power back to the bourgeoisie would be the now utterly degenerated party of Bebel?

---

*This was of course the period of Bismarck's anti-socialist law, which ran from 1878 to 1890. It secured the eager support of the National Liberals in the Reichstag.

**In the 1884 Reichstag elections, the outlawed SPD secured 549,990 votes and 12 deputies, Bismarck's parliamentary allies, the Conservatives, 861,063 votes and 78 deputies, the right-wing 'Reichspartei' 387,687 votes and 78 deputies, the National Liberals 997,033 and 51, the Progressives 1,092,895 and 74, and the Centre Party, 1,282,006 votes and 99 deputies.

The balance of power as refracted through the parliamentary prism was overwhelmingly tilted against the SPD, and the party leaders adjusted their tactics accordingly.

Engels never lived to see even the most theatrical of revolts by the German bourgeoisie against its Junker overlords. Bismarck's decision in the mid 1880's to go over to an aggressive colonial policy, coupled with his support for protectionism, cemented the 'pact of steel and rye'. In turn, it hardened their united resolve to ward off at all costs the threat posed by the irresistable growth of Social Democracy. To a certain extent, this clearly minimised the Bonapartist manoeuvres which the regime could undertake, as the two warring factions based on private property were now beginning to sink their differences. There still remained, however, the 'proletarian' card, and on occasions Bismarck—and even the young William II—were not averse to playing it. It was not so much the content of Bismarck's social policy that was significant—the reforms were in themselves trifling and did very little to alleviate the plight of the proletariat—but the political thinking behind them:

> . . . if legislation in the economic field since 1866 has not been even more to the interests of the bourgeoisie than has actually been the case, whose fault is that? The bourgeoisie itself is chiefly responsible, first because it is too cowardly to press its own demands energetically, and secondly because it resists every concession if the latter simultaneously provides the menacing proletariat with new weapons. And if the political power, that is, Bismarck, is attempting to organise its own bodyguard proletariat to keep the political activity of the bourgeoisie in check, what else is that if not a necessary and quite familiar Bonapartist recipe which pledges the state to nothing more, as far as the workers are concerned, than a few benevolent phrases and at the utmost to a minimum of state assistance for building societies a la Bonaparte? [23]

Engels undertakes his most thorough going analysis of Bismarck's policy in *The Role of Force in History*, a work which makes extensive use of analogies between Bonapartist France and Prussia dominated Germany:

> Bismarck is Louis Napoleon translated from the French adventurist Pretender to the Throne into the Prussian Junker squire and German cadet officer.

But he scored over his French counterpart in that he was not only 'a man of great practical understanding and immense cunning' but a statesman capable of restraining his ambition within the limits of what was realisable..Unlike so many would-be Bonapartes, he spurned adventures, and when the going was hard 'his willpower never deserted him. Rather was it the case that it was often suddenly translated into open brutality.'[24] And this, stresses Engels, 'was the secret of his success. All the ruling classes in Germany, Junkers and bourgeois alike, had so lost all traces of energy, spinelessness had become so much the custom in "educated" Germany, that the one man amongst them who still had the willpower thereby became their greatest personality and a tyrant over them.'[25]

So how, then, are we to describe the Germany of Prince Otto von Bismarck, and how should we evaluate the political legacy bequeathed to the bourgeoisie he both ruled for and over? Confronted by the contradictory and still-evolving phenomenon of Stalinist Russia, Trotsky found that the Soviet Union could not be accurately depicted in a phrase. In his *Revolution Betrayed* (1937) he found it necessary to devote more than half a page to the apparently simple task of defining the Soviet state and economy. To those who demanded a clear cut 'yes-no' formula, Trotsky replied:

> Sociological problems would certainly be simpler, if social phenomena had always a finished character. There is nothing more dangerous, however, than to throw out of reality, for the sake of logical completeness, elements which today violate your scheme and tomorrow may wholly overturn it. [26]

And despite their occasional lapses into unfounded optimism —which always had as its basis an irrepressible revolutionary spirit, and not any lack of scientific objectivity, Marx and Engels employed precisely this method in their analysis of Germany. Engels always approached the Germany of Bismarck as a contradictory whole (which in turn was part of a greater whole) whose development was determined by the perpetual conflict between its antagonistic parts. The real theoretical complexities which arose in the case of Germany (reflected in the extreme hazardous nature of any predictions concerning its future political development) were due to the superimposing of one historical epoch, together with its constituent classes, institutions and ideologies, over another, rather than the new driving out the old. Thus the three-fold nature of Bismarckian Bonapartism, and the two-fronted war which each class waged against the others—Junkers against bourgeois and proletariat, proletariat against Junkers and bourgeoisie, and bourgeoisie against Junker and proletariat.

Like Trotsky, who was grappling with an entirely new historical process—the degeneration of the first successful workers' revolution, and the political usurpation of the proletariat by a ruthless and rapacious bureaucracy, Marx and Engels could have legitimately claimed that in Junker Germany, they were faced with 'dynamic social formations which have no precedent and have no analogies'.[27]

But that did not deter either Trotsky or Engels and Marx from searching for them. France, the nation where the class battles were 'fought to finish', so rich in its violent political oscillations from revolution to counter-revolution and back again, provided the best available models from which to work. In the case of Trotsky's analysis of the Soviet Union, he sought a historical parallel for the degeneration of the October Revolution in the period of bourgeois reaction which followed the overthrow of the 'Committee of Public Safety' headed by Robespierre and Saint Juste. They were guillotined on July 27, 1794,—the ninth Thermidor by the revolutionary calendar— and it is this month which has given its name to the process of reaction which sets in after the period when a revolution is in the ascendent and then reaches its peak of radicalism.

Trotsky transposed this 'model' to the Soviet Union of the period immediately following the end of the civil war, the illness and death of Lenin and the aborting of the 1923 revolutionary situation in Germany.

But while making the all-important distinction between the predominant property forms in Napoleonic France and the Soviet Union, he depicted as the Russian equivalent of Thermidor the restoration of bourgeois property forms, whereas in the case of France, the fall of the Jacobins did not mark the beginning of a reversion to feudalism, but the consolidation of the newly established state on political lines more amenable to the big bourgeoisie. Thus for a time Trotsky was tending to equate a *social* counter-revolution in Russia (i.e. the overthrow of the proletariat as the ruling class, and the restoration of capitalist forms of property ownership) with a *political* counter-revolution in France, where power shifted between segments of the bourgeoisie (in this case from the middle bourgeoisie and its petty-bourgeois allies) into the hands of the biggest capitalists and bankers. Every shift in power under the Thermidorians, the Directorate and finally Napoleon himself took place upon the capitalist property relations established in the course of the first years of the revolution.

The flaws in this analogy soon became evident to Trotsky, and he revised it in 1935, when he wrote:

> We can and must admit that the analogy of Thermidor served to becloud rather than clarify the question . . . In the internal controversies of the Russian and the international Opposition we conditionally understood by Thermidor, the first stage of the bourgeois counter-revolution, aimed against the social basis of the workers' state . . . the historical analogy became invested with a purely conditional, and not realistic character, and this comes into ever increasing contradiction with the demands for an analysis of the most recent evolution of the Soviet state.[28]

For if Stalin had assumed the mantle of a Soviet Bonaparte,

and 'since there has been no Soviet "Thermidor"* as yet,
whence could Bonapartism have arisen?'[29] By 'radically revising'
his analogy, Trotsky was able to come to the conclusion that
the real 'Thermidor', a political reaction corresponding to the
anti-Jacobin coup of July 1794, was already more than 10
years old:

> The smashing of the Left Opposition implied in the most direct
> and immediate sense the transfer of power from the hands of the
> revolutionary vanguard into the hands of the more conservative
> elements among the bureaucracy and the upper crust of the
> working class. The year 1924—that was the beginning of the Soviet
> Thermidor. [30]

This brief survey of Trotsky's employment and re-evaluation
of the 'Thermidorian' and 'Bonapartist' episodes of the
French and Russian Revolutions is by no means a diversion
from our main theme, as it may indeed appear at first sight.
Trotsky paid such close attention to the complexities of Soviet
reality, amending and revising his concepts and conclusions
where and when the facts demanded it, because he was constantly seeking a correct political orientation for the Left
Opposition, and after 1933, the Fourth International. That is
why he could not remain content with bald abstractions and
and banal generalities, with categories that allowed for only a
clear cut black or white, a yes or no. Along this methodological
line lay the path to capitulation either to Stalinism (i.e. totally
identifying the Stalinist bureaucracy with the progressive
nationalised property relations on which it rests) or capitulation
to imperialism i.e. since Stalin has strangled the last remnants of
Soviet democracy, the USSR is no longer a workers' state
and therefore should not be defended against imperialism**).

Now this was precisely the motive which guided Marx and
Engels in their theoretical work on the German question. At
stake was the future of the SPD and with it, the outcome of
the struggle for socialism not only in Germany but throughout
the continent of Europe. Any tendency to ignore the concrete
and highly peculiar state forms and social structures engendered
by Germany's past development could have either thrown the
working class into the arms of the bourgeoisie in an unprincipled bloc against the Junkers, or led to the equally suicidal
course of allowing the proletariat to serve as a bargaining
counter in Bismarck's Bonapartist manoeuvres with the
bourgeoisie.

---

*This is, Thermidor as conceived under the old and faulty schema, in which it
represented a capitalist restoration.
**This is the position held by the 'International Socialism' group, which publishes
the weekly *Socialist Worker*.

Both these strategies were canvassed and even employed during the lifetime of Engels. Thus a section of the SPD leadership sought to placate the wrath of the German bourgeoisie during the initial period of Bismarck's anti-socialist laws by playing down the party's proletarian basis and programme, and emphasising in its stead the necessity of winning 'the so-called upper strata of society'. This opportunist trend occasioned an angry rebuff from both Marx and Engels in their famous *Circular Letter* to the SPD leadership.

But Marx and Engels were equally opposed to the type of backstairs dealing engaged in by Ferdinand Lassalle—one of the great pioneers of the German labour movement—with Bismarck on the basis of their mutual hostility to the bourgeoisie. Lassalle also had illusions in the socialist character of Bismarck's programme of social reform, a mistake which flowed from his idealisation of the Prussian state. Their negotiations—cut short by Lassalle's tragic death in a duel in 1864—revolved around a deal whereby Lassalle would attempt to rally the workers behind Bismarck's policy of a Prussian-dominated greater Germany, while in return, the Chancellor would introduce manhood suffrage and a programme of social legislation protecting the workers against the profit hungry German bourgeoisie.

And one of Engels' last disputes with the leadership of the German party arose over this same vexed question of the nature of the German state and the attitude the working class should adopt to the more liberal elements among the bourgeoisie and petty-bourgeoisie.

Engels strongly objected to the use of the phrase 'one reactionary mass' to describe all the other political parties in Germany. This term, which appeared in the draft of the SPD's 1891 Erfurt Programme (it was excluded from the final version) Engels considered to be 'extremely one-sided . . . and hence entirely wrong in the apodictically absolute form in which alone it rings true'. [31] And very much in the same way as Trotsky warned against regarding the Soviet Union of the middle 1930's as a finished social formation, Engels went on:

> Wrong because it enunciates an *historical tendency* correct in itself as an *accomplished fact*. The moment the social revolution starts all other parties appear to be a reactionary mass vis-a-vis us. Possibly they already are such, have lost all capacity for any progressive action whatsoever, although not necessarily. so. But at the *present moment* we cannot say so . . . [32]

So right up to the end, Engels refused to state categorically that the German bourgeoisie had exhausted its meagre revolutionary energies:

Even in Germany, conditions may arise under which the left (bourgeois) parties, despite their miserableness, may be forced to sweep away part of the colossal anti-bourgeois, bureaucratic and feudal rubbish that is still lying there. And in that event they are simply no reactionary mass.[33]*

So much for the peculiarities on Bismarckian Germany, which if we wished to paraphrase a formulation employed by Trotsky to describe the Soviet Union, could be termed variously a 'Junkerised bourgeois state' or a 'bourgeoisified Junker state' according to its stage of evolution.

The impact of the Bismarck era on the consciousness of. Germany's main classes, and the ways in which it influenced the political strategy of the bourgeoisie under the Weimar Republic, will be constantly recurring themes in this work.

*Yet only a year later, Engels was to concede the point, if not the method employed to argue it. In a letter to Paul Lafargue, he noted that 'in France too, Lassalle's "one single, compact reactionary mass', the coalition of all the anti-socialist parties, is beginning to form. In Germany we have had that for years . . . The whole of official history in Germany, apart from the very heterogeneous camarilla which surrounds young Wilhelm and leads him a dance, is made on the one hand, by socialist action which causes all the bourgeois parties to merge into one large party of straightforward resistance and, on the other, by the play of the divergent interests within these parties themselves, which drives them apart from each other. Reichstag legislation is nothing but the product, the outcome of the conflict of these two opposing trends of which the secondary, the tendency to split up, grows weaker and weaker . . .' (F. Engels to Paul Lafargue, London, May 19, 1892, in *Frederick Engels, Paul Lafargue and Laura Lafargue, Correspondence,* Vol. III, p.173, Moscow nd.)

Here Engels still speaks of a 'tendency' and not a completed, cut and dried state of affairs. And this, the method, is what is most important.

REFERENCES FOR CHAPTER TWO

[1] K. Marx: *Grundrisse,* edited by D. McLellan, pp.34-35, London, 1971.
[2] K. Marx: *The Bourgeoisie and the Counter-Revolution* (Cologne, December 11, 1849) in *Marx-Engels Selected Works,* Vol. I, p.66.
[3] Ibid., p.67
[4] Ibid., pp.67-68
[5] Ibid , pp.68-69
[6] Ibid., p.69
[7] L. Trotsky: *The USSR in War,* published in *In Defence of Marxism,* p.3, London 1966
[8] L. Trotsky: *Again and Once More Again on the Nature of the USSR* in ibid. p.30
[9] *From a Scratch—To the Danger of Gangrene* in ibid., pp.146-147
[10] Speech to Prussian Parliament, October 18, 1849
[11] Letter to H. Wagener, Frankfurt, April 27, 1853
[12] F. Engels: letters to K. Marx, April 13, 1866, *Marx-Engels Selected Correspondence,* p.214, Moscow, nd
[13] F. Engels: Review of K. Marx, *A Contribution to the Critique of Political Economy* in *Das Volk,* August 6, 1859
[14] F. Engels: Preface, *The Peasant War in Germany,* p.18, Moscow 1956
[15] Ibid., pp.21-22
[16] F. Engels: *The Housing Question* (1872-1873) in *Marx-Engels Selected Works,* Vol. I, p.605
[17] Ibid., p.605
[18] K. Marx: *The Eighteenth Brumaire of Louis Bonaparte,* in ibid., pp.330-343
[19] F. Engels, ibid., p.606
[20] Ibid., p.606
[21] Letter to A. Bebel, September 13, 1886
[22] Ibid.
[23] F. Engels: *The Housing Question,* ibid., pp.606-607
[24] F. Engels: *The Role of Force in History* (1887-88) pp.56-57
[25] Ibid., p.57
[26] L. Trotsky: *The Revolution Betrayed,* p.255, London 1967
[27] Ibid., p.255
[28] L. Trotsky: *The Workers' State and the Question of Thermidore and Bonapartism* (1935), p.41, London 1968
[29] Ibid., p.48
[30] Ibid., p.49
[31] F. Engels to K. Kautsky, London, October 14, 1891, in *Marx-Engels Selected Correspondence,* p.514
[32] Ibid., p.514
[33] Ibid., p.514

Chapter Three
'BLOOD AND IRON':
THE POLITICS OF GERMAN HEAVY INDUSTRY

Lenin once said that politics were 'concentrated economics'. Not that he believed there was a mechanical, automatic or unmediated relationship between economics and politics, or that political structures could not at certain times play an important role in shaping economic events. We only have to recall the economic consequences of the English and French Revolutions, and compare them with the negative example of Germany in 1525, 1815 and 1848, to appreciate that the calibre of a class's political leadership in a revolutionary situation can have economic repercussions over a much longer period of time. But we should also remember that these variations in the political make-up of the European bourgeoises were themselves a product of their uneven and combined economic development over the preceeding epoch. So, after sifting through all the mediations and processes of reciprocal action and mutual interpenetration, we are obliged to return to one of the most basic of Marxist propositions—the primacy of economics. And it is in the economic structure of the German bourgeoisie that we shall find at least some of the factors which shaped its reactionary political outlook.

First some statistics, for they speak louder and more clearly than can any words about the transformation of the rural, small town Germany of princedoms and guilds into a nation which in a matter of 40 years, rivalled England as the 'workshop of the world'. In 1815, 73.5% of the Prussian population lived in the countryside. And in Germany's 12 largest towns dwelt only double the number of people inhabiting Paris. Even as late as 1846, when industrialisation had begun to accelerate in several regions, the percentage of persons officially classified as rural had declined by a mere 1.5%. Meanwhile, in France, and of course above all in Britain, an enormous exodus from the countryside into the towns—many of them relatively new—was in full swing. Germany's industrial revolution only really began as those of France and England were drawing to a close. Much has been said and written about Germany's late arrival as an industrial nation, and the economic advantages which accrued to its bourgeoisie as a result of its own tardy maturation. German industry culled from the largely empirical evolution of English technology all that it required to make the Ruhr, greater Berlin, Saxony and Hamburg the most feared rivals of the Black Country, Lancashire, South Wales and Liverpool. How effectively it did so can be gauged from the following indexes of industrial growth:

Year		1871	1910
	million tons		
Pig Iron		1.5	14.8
Iron Ore		5.3	28.7
Steel (1880)		1.5	13.1
Coal		37.9	279.0

never has there been a comparable industrial upsurge in the entire entire history of capitalism! English expansion over the same period, formidable though it was, never approached such a giddy tempo:

Pig Iron		7.8	10.1
Steel		3.7	7.6
Coal		118.0	268.7

In coal and steel—the economic language not only of heavy industry, but of the machines of war—Germany was, by 1910, the master of Europe. The same process was at work in other fields. Thus in 1861, Germany's miniscule machine production industry employed only 51,000 workers. Yet by the turn of the century, this branch of the labour force had multiplied twenty-fold. Here too, planning and plagiarism played their part, with Bismarck's emphasis on industrial espionage and technical training in the education of the young. Neither were transport and communications permitted to respond to the expansion of industry in a pragmatic, planless and exaggerated way, as had earlier been the case in England. State investment in and control over Germany's rail network flowed not only from Prussian conceptions of an economy oriented towards war, but also from the industrial requirements of the bourgeoisie itself. The English railway slump of 1848, bringing in its wake a series of spectacular bankruptcies, underlined the speculative nature of much railway investment. Far better to leave this risky field clear for state intervention and investment, and reap the rewards which a centrally organised and non-profit making railway system had to offer for the industrialist and manu-facturer. The Junkers proved themselves to be as efficient railway pioneers and managers as they had army officers and state bureaucrats. During a period when the expansion of the

English railway system had already begun to slow up, the length of Germany's network increased from 16,560 kilometres in 1871 to 60,521 in 1912. Likewise with shipping; before her industrial boom, Germany—and here we are speaking principally of Prussia—had been an exporter of cereals and an importer of machinery and other industrial products. After 1871, and with the rapid shift in population balance from the countryside to the towns, from agriculture to industry, Germany became an industrial exporter and importer of foods and raw materials. In 1873, only 38% of German exports were finished goods, while on the eve of the First World War, this percentage had nearly doubled. Germany's enormously enhanced ties with the world market both as an importer and exporter created a vast demand for merchant shipping, one that could not initially be met by its domestic ship builders. Soon however, the North Sea yards of Hamburg, Bremen and Kiel were launching some of the world's fastest, strongest and largest merchant vessels. In 1871, the newly founded German Empire inherited from its constituent states a puny merchant fleet of 147 ships with a gross tonnage of 82,000. By 1914, German ships ploughed the oceans' trade routes in a fleet of 2,000 vessels weighing 4.4 million tons.

In the 20 years between 1880 and 1900, Germany had in effect overhauled both France and Britain as an exporter nation, and stood second only to that other titanic 'late arrival' the United States. Yet all these achievements, truly astounding not only in their quantity and tempo, but also in scope and quality, were accomplished in a period when the German industrial and financial bourgeoisie were almost totally excluded from the summits of political power. The most tempestuous epoch of capitalist development had been paralleled by an equally unprecedented epoch of political emasculation on the part of this very same bourgeoisie! Yet when we look closer at the relationship which evolved between the capitalist class and state power, we see that in a certain sense, it had little need or incentive to compete with the Junkers for government office. Despite and even against his own subjective feelings, Bismarck, stage by stage, carried out its economic programme. And while he did so, those sections of the bourgeoisie who identified themselves politically with the National Liberals had no compelling motives to break with him because of his high-handed and even contemptuous political methods. They adapted to and even to a certain extent absorbed the feudal residues of Junker rule, while carving out for themselves a position of European economic and technological supremacy. It redounded to the German bourgeoisie's advantage that its energies and individual talents were concentrated towards that one single goal rather than being simultaneously dispersed in several directions. The philistinism and apparant political backwardness of the German capitalist class under the Empire are only one side of its development, and should be seen as the dialectial complement to its truly monumental industrial fanaticism. This class, politically crushed and apparantly demoralised after 1848, nevertheless clung on to several important economic conquests which it made during the revolution. The Frankfurt of 1848 not only witnessed the ludicrous spectacle of the bourgeoisie's parliamentarians fiddling while Prussia loaded its cannons but the foundation of Germany's modern banking system, which in its turn provided much of the funds for the expansion of industry after 1871. Though he would have been loath to admit it, Bismarck had as much need of the House of Rothschild as of the Prussian Officer Corps. Without a modern industry, no cannons and no shells. And without a Rothschild or Gustav von Mevissen, * . no capital for modern industry. Both in an historical and economic sense, German capitalism began its forwards leap with massive accumulation of money capital, the 'abstract' form of capital as opposed to industrial capital in the form of raw materials, machines etc. In this, it was typically 'German'. 1849, the year of the great reaction, also saw the formation of Germany's first joint stock mining company, the 'Kolner Bergwerksverein'. This revolutionary type of capitalist organisation was soon rapidly extending to other branches of heavy industry, including steel and machine manufacturing. Closely allied to the joint stock company, upon whose foundation would shortly be erected the trust, and to a large · extent initiating it, were a series of new industrially oriented banks: the Disconto-Gesellschaft (1851) the Darmstadter (1853) the Berlin Hadelsgesellschaft (1856), the Deutsche Bank (1870) and finally the Dresdner (1872). With the exception of the Dresdner, these banks, the financial giants not only of Bismarck's Germany but Hitler's Third Reich, *were founded prior to the formation of the Empire in 1871.* They provided the indispensable springboard both for the growth of monopoly capitalism in the last decade of the 19th century, and subsequently, that of German imperialism itself. How false then is the oft-encountered view, which in turn is frequently based on a one-sided and shallow reading of the writings of Marx and Engels on Germany, of a German bourgeoisie devoid of any overall class strategy or political

---

*von Mevissen was the founder of the Cologne A. Schaaffhausensche Bankverein. Set up in 1848, it subsequently received Prussian government backing for its policy of promoting industrial development and innovation.

programme. In the later years of imperial Germany, it became evident that reliance on mediating agencies such as the ruling Junker caste was an integral part of its political strategy, and not, as some have claimed, a substitute for it.

In 1862, Bismarck shocked all but the most intransigent members of the Prussian parliament when he made his first speech as the kingdom's new Chancellor. His brutal words may have outraged liberal conventions and democratic sensibilities, but they became a programme around which the entire industrial bourgeoisie was soon to rally:

> Germany looks not to Prussia's liberalism, but to her force . . . The great decisions of the day will not be settled by resolutions and majority votes—that was the lesson of 1848—but by iron and blood.

Iron and blood: if ever the history of a class could be summed up in that brief aphorism, it was that of the German bourgeoisie. How little Bismarck cared for the niceties of parliamentary majority rule can be gleaned from the contrast between the formal balance of party forces in the Reichstag and the composition of his own administration. In the founding Reichstag elections of 1871, the bourgeois parties—National Liberals and Progressives—sent 171 deputies into a 397 seat chamber. Ranged against them were Bismarck's closest allies, the Conservatives, with only 57 deputies, and the Reichspartei, with 67. The Catholic Centre could also be relied upon to casts its 63 mandates against the Protestant-Prussian bloc, giving the potential bourgeois opposition a theoretical majority in the first Reichstag of at least 110 over the Bismarck bloc. Yet the 'Iron Chancellor' reigned supreme, suffering only one serious parliamentary reverse in his 28 years of office.* The simple fact was that despite its rapidly accumulating economic wealth and technological prowess, the German bourgeoisie had utterly failed to acquire the most rudimentary forms of statecraft, without which a class cannot successfully hold the reins of power. Thus there could exist an enormous, and for considerable periods of time unbridgeable gap between a bourgeoisie's economic vitality and its possibility of translating this into the language of direct state power. Contrast Germany's development with that of England, where Tudor Bonapartism permitted the leaders of the merchant bourgeoisie, allied with sections of the new aristocracy, to acquire considerable experience in influencing and even shaping governmental policies. This they did not only in repeated clashes with the royal power in Parliament, but through the evolution of a series of religious reform movements and by exercising control over

---

*This defeat arose over Bismarck's bid in 1890 to renew and strengthen his notorious anti-socialist legislation, first introduced in 1878. Bismarck staked his continued tenure of office on it, and lost.

their own economic institutions. The German bourgeoisie enjoyed no such rich tradition of internal self government, let alone one of courageously challenging the institutions and representatives of absolutism. The economic decline of the 16th century, the relapse into semi-barbarism which followed the 30 Years War, paralleled by the evolution of the 'Germanic' form of Protestantism, Lutheranism (which on the bones of the slain anabaptist peasant revolutionaries, and in vivid contrast to its French and English varieties, rapidly revealed a facility for adapting the language of religious revolt to the rigidly dictatorial structures of feudal Germany) all now became negative factors in the bourgeoisie's struggle for governmental power. The result, as we have already had occasion to stress more than once, was a unique species of state power based on a tacit and ever-fluctuating compromise between two distinct classes; the very nature of which forced them to fuse with one another:

> The abolition of feudalism, expressed positively, means the establishment of bourgeois conditions. As the privileges of the nobility fall, legislation becomes more and more bourgeois. And here we come to the crux of the relation of the German bourgeoisie to the government . . . the government is *compelled* to introduce these slow and petty reforms. As against the bourgeoisie, however, it protrays each of these small concessions as a *sacrifice* made to the bourgeoisie, as a concession wrung from the crown with the greatest difficulty, and for which the bourgeoisie ought in return to concede something to the government. And the bourgeoisie, though the true state of affairs is fairly clear to them, allow themselves to be fooled. This is the origin of the tacit agreement which is the mute basis of all Reichstag and Chamber debates in Berlin: on the one hand, the government reforms the laws at a snail's pace in the interests of the bourgeoisie, removes the feudal obstacles to industry as well as those which arose from the multiplicity of small states, establishes uniform coinage, weights and measures, freedom of occupation. etc, puts Germany's labour power at the unrestricted disposal of capital by granting freedom of movement, and favours trade and swindling. On the other hand, the bourgeoisie leaves all actual political power in the hands of the government, votes taxes, loans and soldiers, and helps to frame all new reform laws in such a way that the old police power over undesirable characters remains in full force and effect. The bourgeoisie buys its gradual social emancipation at the price of immediate renunciation of its own political power. Naturally the chief motive which makes such an agreement acceptable to the bourgeoisie is not fear of the government but fear of the proletariat.

The wretched conduct of the bourgeoisie in Bismarck's Reichstag drove many voters away from the National Liberals towards the more democratically inclined (but still not consistently republican) Progressives, generally regarded as the legitimate inheritors of the 1848 tradition. In the 1881 elections, their verbal opposition to Bismarck's persecution of the Social Democrats swelled the Progressive's votes to nearly 1.2 million, as compared with little more than 600,000 three years previously. Meanwhile, the National Liberals, who had dutifully toed the Bismarck line, lost heavily, falling from 1.3 million votes and 99 deputies to 746,000 votes and a mere 47 deputies. Undoubtedly, a big segment of Progressive support came from workers who had yet to identify their class interests with the Marxist-influenced SPD, but who were determinedly opposed to the fundamentals of Bismarck's anti-democratic regime, * Even though the National Liberals were later able to regain much of the ground lost during this period, they never succeeded in re-establishing their position as the largest parliamentary party. Bismarck's gamble on manhood suffrage had paid off handsomely. The bourgeoisie, faced by the ever-rising tide of social democracy, pulled in its blunted political horns and delegated the arduous and time consuming task of policing the German working class to the Junker bureaucracy. But in doing so, it never for one moment abdicated the struggle for supremacy in its own domain—the factory, mine or mill. Here, at the physical point of extraction of surplus value from the proletariat, the class war was waged with true Prussian thoroughness and without a trace of the compromise that characterised industry's relations with Bismarck. The factory politics' of the leaders of German heavy industry as they evolved under Bismarck, provides us with many insights into the crucial alliance forged between Hitler and the coal, steel and chemical kings in the last years of the Weimar Republic. The firm of Krupps** by its very nature drew close to the Junker state power, as its main business was the manufacture of weapons of war. Its reactionary pedigree had been established during the 1848 revolution at a time when the owners of several other similar enterprises were, however briefly and hesitatingly, drawn into the movement for democratic reform. Alfred Krupp summarily dismissed any of his

---

*The German working class sent but two deputies into the 1871 Reichstag-August Bebel and Wilhelm Leibknecht. Then, with the exception of the first two elections under Bismarck's anti-socialist legislation, the SPD climbed steadily: 124,000 in 1871, 352,000 in 1874, 493,000 in 1877, 437,000 in 1878, 312,000 in 1881, 550,000 in 1884, 763,000 in 1887, and after 12 years of unrelenting state persecution, an astounding 1.4 million in 1890.
** The then head of the Krupp dynasty, Gustav von Krupp, von Bohlen und Halbach, is usually quite incorrectly depicted as being strongly opposed to the Nazis right up to the formation of the Hitler government in January 1933. In fact, there is formidable evidence that the Nazi leadership had begun negotiations with the firm of Krupps as early as the summer of 1931. This question will be dealt with in much greater detail at a later stage.

workers whom he suspected of democratic sympathies, instructing his management to keep revolutionary agitators out of his
Essen plant by the crude but effective method of shutting the
factory gates for the duration of the upheaval. Krupps
employees were marched in strict Prussian formation from the
workers quarters in the town to the factory gates in the
morning, and back again at night, for fear that despite their
employer's every precaution, the revolutionary contagion might
infect his traditionally loyal work-force. Foremen at the plant
were told to ensure their charges were kept busy throughout
the day so as, in the words of Alfred Krupp himself, to 'keep
them out of mischief'. Krupp's loyalty was well-rewarded by
the Junkers, who never really forgave those bourgeois who
flirted with the 'alien' ideologies of republicanism and
parliamentary democracy. Bismarck himself maintained close
personal and political relations with the Krupps, first visiting
the Essen works in October 1864, when he discussed with Alfred
his future plans for Prussian foreign policy. The Krupp dynasty
also evolved its own brand of 'corporative' ideology, much
of which reappeared in the guise of the national socialist
'works community' of Dr. Robert Ley and company. 'The goal
of work shall be the general welfare' was one of Alfred Krupp's
pet homilies, and he saw to it that it was inculcated into his entire
labour force. * 1872, one year after the establishment of the
German Empire, saw the appearance of Krupp's *General
Regulations*, being a code of labour, social and political
discipline for the Krupp work force not one wit less
dictatorial than any imposed by a German government prior
to victory of the Nazis. Bismarck's anti-socialist laws were mild
in comparison. Following a miners strike which hit Krupp's
own collieries in the July of 1872, Alfred Krupp instructed his
subordinates that 'neither now nor at any future time' should a
former striker 'be taken on at our works, however shorthanded
we may be'. Krupp had also been outraged—like all good
'national' Germans—by the courageous stand of the two SPD
deputies Bebel and Liebknecht in the Prussian parliament
against Bismarck's annexation of Alsace and Lorraine. Then
came the Paris Commune, electrifying the most advanced
German workers and rousing their class enemies to a white
heat of terror and fury. When the first ripples from these titanic

---

*In a letter to Kaiser Wilhelm I, Alfred Krupp describes his concern as 'a national
workshop' whose factories were 'in a certain degree inseperable from the conception of the growth and importance of the state, and consequently indispensable'. Although Alfred had good cause to stress the 'national' character of his
undertaking—he was petitioning the Kaiser for state assistance after the
collapse of the speculative boom in 1873—this is, nevertheless, an accurate picture
of the intimate relationship which had evolved between the 'Cannon king' and the
men of 'blood and iron'.

events lapped against the Krupp fortress, its sole proprietor struck back savagely: 'When a strike appears to be imminent in any clique, I shall come there at once' he warned the Krupp management. '. . . then we shall see about settling the lot. I intend to act quite ruthlessly, for there is, as I see it, no other possible course.' And then he added, omminously, 'What does not bend can break'.[2] Krupp then immediately dispatched to everyone of his 16,000 workers the new *General Regulations*. They are historic for several reasons, not least because they provided both ideas and even slogans which the Nazis later adopted as their own:

> 'The full force of authority must be used to suppress disloyalty and conspiracy. Those who commit unworthy acts must never be permitted to feel safe, must never escape public disgrace. Good, like wickedness, should be examined through a microscope Even as a seed bears fruit in direct ratio to the nourishment or poison it is given, so it is from the spirit that an act, benign or evil, arises.'[3]

Krupp demanded of his work force (or 'followers', as the Nazi labour code was later to describe them) 'full and undivided energy', 'loyalty', love of 'good order' and freedom from what the *General Regulations* called 'all prejudicial influences'.[4] Strikes, or any other form of resistance by the workers were to be regarded and punished as acts of treason towards the firm. Any worker adjudged guilty of such heinous crimes was "never again to become a member of the concern'. The *Regulations* also took care to exclude from Krupp's employ all workers suspected of previous union activity or sympathies, for they stipulated that 'no person known to have taken part in troublemaking of a similar kind elsewhere may be given employment in the firm.'[5]

Such an all-embracing regime, which seeks not only to discipline the worker outwardly in the actual labour process, but also to control and regiment his innermost political thoughts, required a full-time staff of spies and informers. And Krupp set about creating one. Their instructions were to maintain:

> a constant quiet observation of the spirit of our workers, so that we cannot miss the beginning of any ferment anywhere; and I must demand that if the cleverest and best workman or foreman even looks as though he wants to raise objections, or belongs to one of those unions, he shall be dismissed as quickly as practicable, without consideration of whether he can be spared.

Even Krupp's much vaunted standards of workmanship were therefore to be sacrificed in the struggle to root out what Alfred once called the 'devilished seed' of social democracy. But in vain. The huge industrial concentrations of the Ruhr region were a fertile breeding ground for political radicalism

and militant trade unionism, and though at first held back by
both Bismarck's anti-socialist laws and the strong grip of
'social' catholicism in this predominately catholic area, the
SPD began to break down the barriers erected against it by
Krupp and the other leaders of heavy industry and mining.
Despairing of ever cleansing his workers' minds of 'prejudicial
influences', Alfred Krupp wrote some 15 years later: 'I wish
somebody with great gifts would start a counter-revolution for
the best of the people — with flying columns, labour battalions
of young men.' Little wonder that all the Nazi leaders, from
those closest to big business like Funk and Goering, to the
self-styled radicals such as Feder and Gobbels, not only
carefully eschewed all demogogic attacks on Krupp, but went
out of their way to praise the firm's traditions and style of
management. * For it had given National Socialism something
far more valuable than cash for election campaigns. It had
helped provide them with a programme of political, social and
economic counter-revolution. It is worth bearing in mind a
certain phrase which occurs in the Krupp *General Regulations*,
for it not only became a slogan of German heavy industry,
but found its explicit recognition and implementation in the
'Labour Front' of Dr. Robert Ley. Krupp's letter to his
workers advised them that if they disliked his new regime,
they had better leave his employ, 'the sooner the better'. He
was, he stressed, determined *'to be and remain master in my
own house'.*[6] Let us now jump over the intervening 61 years to
the Spring of 1933. The Nazis have on May 2, seized the
assets and premises of the entire German trade union
movement, and arrested its leaders. Gustav Krupp, the son of
Alfred, a fanatical enthusiast of Hitler's anti-labour policies,

---

*Thus Feder, in his official commentary on the Nazi Party programme of 1920,
writes: 'The true employer must be a man of moral worth. His task is to discover
the real economic needs of the people . . . He must keep his costs as low as
possible in order to get his goods out on to the market, must maintain both the
quality and quantity of his output, and must pay his employees well, so that they
may be able to purchase goods freely; and he must always be thinking of
improvements of his plant and his methods of trading. If he puts these things
first in his business, he is "supplying the necessaries of life" in the best, highest
sense, and his profits will come of themselves without his making them his first
objective. The finest and most universally known example of this kind of manufacturer is Henry Ford. There are other names in our own heavy industries which
stand equally high-Krupp, Kirdorf, Abbe, Mannesmann, Siemens and many more.'
(G. Feder: *Hitler's Official Programme*, pp.84-85.) Ford's place in the Nazi
pantheon had little or nothing to do with his pioneering in methods of assembly
line production. Ford was not only the most rabid of American union-busting
bosses—he only recognised the UAW in 1940—but also an avowed anti-semite,
and it was on this basis that the early Nazi movement approached him for funds
shortly after the fiasco of the Munich Putsch. Kirdorf, the coal king, was an early
supporter and financier of the Nazi party, while Mannesmann's backing came at
a later stage.

has already made haste to introduce Nazi methods into his own plants. And as head of the former 'German Federation of Industry' he will shortly take his place as head of the new regime's Provisional Supreme Economic Council. Robert Ley, butcher of the trade unions, steps forward and declares his party's economic programme fulfilled. Employers (now, in Nazi parlance, 'Leaders') were at last restored to their place as 'natural leaders' of the factory. 'Many employers' Dr. Ley recalled, 'have for years had to call for the "master in the house". *Now they are once again to be the "master in the house"* . . .' Alfred Krupp had taken his posthumous revenge on those feared and hated 'poisoners' of the Essen workers. The 'flying columns'—the SA and the SS—had triumphed where even Alfred Krupp's plant police and Bismarck's repressive legislation had failed. After a siege lasting more than half a century, the fortress of German labour was reduced to rubble. For Krupp had been one of the most outspoken and active supporters of Bismarck's bid to strangle the Marxist movement in its infancy. Parallel with the Berlin government's nationwide campaign to extirpate the Social Democratic hydra, Alfred Krupp stepped up his own private war against the workers of Essen. Potential employees were obliged to give an oath of personal loyalty to their employer. If they submitted to this unprecedented act of self-abasement, they were, on engagement, subjected to a non-stop barrage of directives and harangues from Alfred Krupp on their alleged slothfulness, greed and other moral deficiencies. On one occasion he informed his workers:

> I expect and demand complete trust, refuse to entertain any unjustifiable claims, and will continue to remedy all legitimate grievances, but hereby invite all persons who are not satisfied with these conditions to hand in their notices, rather than wait for me to dismiss them . . .

And in a fit of pique after losing a local election battle against a pacifist-inclined and SPD-backed Catholic candidate, he ordered that all known or suspected Social Democrats be dismissed from his plants:

> The next time I go through the works I want to feel at home and I would rather see the place empty than find some fellow with venom in his heart (sic!), such as every Social Democrat is . . .

It could be argued that the case of Krupp is not typical of the German bourgeoisie as a whole, and that is of course perfectly correct.* But then, since this class, like all bourgeoisies, comprised itself of many economic, political and social groupings,

---

*Unlike many German employers, Alfred Krupp was not a supporter of the National Liberals. He identified himself with the pro-Bismarck Conservatives.

no single firm, family dynasty or individual capitalist could in this sense serve as an example for the entire class. We are not searching for arithmetical averages or means, but for the *political core* of that class which, under the stress of Germany's and the world's most profound economic crisis, turned to Fascism as a means of averting disaster. In this historical sense, the example of Krupps is of enormous significance. Neither is it an isolated one. The Ruhr concerns of the Stumm, Stinnes, Kirdorf and Thyssen families certainly rivalled that of Krupp in their authoritarian attitude towards trade unions and socialism, even if perhaps they did not share its intimacy with Berlin. Together with the big banks, these firms comprised the hub of German heavy industry around which revolved not only the entire economy of Germany but its very existence as a nation. Therefore it is to the political make-up of this numerically insignificant, . but economically preponderant grouping that we must turn if we wish to establish an historical continuity between the Empire of Bismarck and Wilhelm II and the Third Reich of Hitler. Karl freiherr von Stumm-Halberg, proprietor of a massive Saar-based iron and steel empire, held political and social views which in their form and mode of expression, owed more to feudalism than modern industrial capitalism. Yet in content, they were but a projection of this all-consuming drive by the leaders of German heavy industry to be 'masters in their house', and had absolutely nothing to do with any yearning for an idyllic and regimented pastoral past. The homilies of Krupp and Stumm were delivered amidst the smokestack forests and slag heap hills of the world's most concentrated industrial complex. Von Stumm used to summon all his workers to regular meetings, at which he would harangue them on the evils of democracy, trade unionism and socialism. One such speech, delivered in 1889, catches well the flavour of this 'Junkerised' industrial serfdom:

> . . . in the Stumm kingdom, as our enemies sarcastically call our community, only one will prevails, and that is the will of his Majesty the King of Prussia . . . Wherever we look authority is maintained in the case of need by penalities, imposed on those who do not submit to necessary authority . . . If an industrial enterprise is to flourish it must be organised in a military, not parliamentary fashion . . . Just as military discipline includes all the members of any army from the field marshall down to the youngest recruit and all take the field against the enemy united when the king calls them, so do the members of the Neunkirch Factory stand together as one man when it is a matter of combatting our competitors as well as the dark forces of revolution . . . Any decline in the authority of employers . . . appears to me to be the more dangerous since in the long run it will confine itself to those sections of the population which are under discussion here. Once

the worker has overthrown the authority of the employer, if he
no longer submits to it, if he simply ridicules him when he intends
to punish him . . . then authority in other fields, in state and
church, will follow very soon. But if this happens, if authority is
destroyed all along the line in all branches of business . . . then it
will not be long before it is undermined even there where it is
most necessary, in the army . . . I should not remain at your head
one moment longer if I were to replace my personal relationship
with each of you by negotiations with an organisation of workers
under outside leadership. Such a relationship with, as it were, a
foreign power, would violate my moral sense of duty and my
christian convictions.*

Now what is most interesting about this speech is not the
highly 'teutonic' conceptions of loyalty and discipline, but the
amazing degree of *bourgeois* class consciousness that they
overlay. Von Stumm perceived that the crystallisation of any
independent working class organisation and the development of
the least political awareness in the proletariat placed in jeopardy
not only the stability of his own 'Kingdom', but the Empire
of his sovereign. The 'front line' of the Second Reich ran
right through the blast furnaces of Essen and Neunkirch.

Striking too is the resemblance between von Stumm's notion
of the 'works community' which he shared with Alfred Krupp,
and that of the Nazis. In both cases, the driving force of the
capitalist mode of production, the quest for profit through the
extraction of surplus value from living human labour
power, is shrouded and in fact concealed from the politically
naive by a web of non-economic values, many of them being
ideological 'residues' from Germany's feudal and guild past,
and overlaiden with the militarised conceptions of government
evolved by the Junkers. The goal of von Stumm's production
is nothing so vulgar and 'materialistic' as personal profit, no
more than his ruthless repression of all dissident views reflects
any desire for personal power. Each member of the factory
community has his allotted place, and a duty to perform it to
the best of his—unequal—capacities. Neither did this regimentation cease when the worker left the gates of the Stumm
kingdom behind him at night:

An employer who is indifferent to how his worker behaves outside
his factory is not living up to his most important duties, I could

---

*The Stumm tradition lived on long after the death of Karl in 1901. His son,
F. von Stumm, was a vehement supporter of the Third Reich, and a raging
anti-semite to boot. He also undertook reconnaissance missions on behalf of
Nazi diplomats while on business trips, as can be seen from the following extract
from a letter to the Nazi ambassador in London, Herbert von Dirksen, written
after Stumm's visit to Britain:
    'About Sir N. S. S. I should like to add that he is thoroughly pro-Franco and
thoroughly anti-semitic. He has a soft spot for us and is at least objective . . .'
(*Dirksen Papers*, Vo. II, p.202. Moscow, 1948.)

name a whole series of actions by workers outside the factory
which I regard it as an absolute duty of an employer fully
conscious of his moral task to prevent . . . Every master and
worker must behave even outside his work in such a manner as to
bring honour to the firm of the brothers Stumm; they should be
aware their private life is constantly supervised by their superiors.

Here too, Stumm, Krupp and several other leaders of German
heavy industry were already indicating, allbeit in somewhat
archaic language and style, the road later taken by the Nazi
'Labour Front' to its goal of the total atomization of the
German working class. For like the Jesuits, Stumm and Ley
both desired 'the whole man'. * Stumm naturally indignantly
repudiated charges that it was a class regime which ruled in
his kingdom:

> we all belong to one estate, and that is the honourable estate of
> blacksmiths . . . This fiction of the existence of a fourth estate in
> contrast to property the three 'estates' of pre-revolutionary France
> had been the aristocracy, the clergy and the bourgeoisie—all based
> on private property—is also the basis of the insidious attempts to
> organise the workers against their employers and to place them
> under the leadership of people who lack any knowledge of their
> conditions, such as wages, hours, etc . . .

Stumm shared with Krupp an intransigent hostility to trade
unionism, which, as we have already seen, he regarded as
the agent of 'a foreign power,' much as his King, Wilhelm II,
depicted the Social Democrats as 'vagabonds without a
country', 'a gang of traitors' who did not 'deserve the name of
Germans'. This was also, as is well known, a constant theme of
Nazi propaganda directed against the leaders of the German
labour movement. And we are far from exhausting our inventory
of what, for want of a better term, we shall call 'proto-Nazi'
employers. In fact, in the person of Emil Kirdorf, the Westphalian coal magnate, we have at the same time an industrialist
cast in the Stumm-Krupp mould, being a fanatical opponent of
trade unionism and socialism, and also one of the key figures
in Hitler's strategy to win the adherence of heavy industry to
the Nazi cause. Kirdorf's long reign as one of the barons of the
Rhine-Westphalian coal basin spanned both the era of Bis-

---

*Cf. the statement by Nazi Front chief Robert Ley, that 'we begin with the child
when he is three years old. As soon as he begins to think he gets a little flag
put in his hand; then follows the school, the Hitler youth, the SA and military
training. We don't let him go; and when adolescence is past, then comes the
Labour Front, which takes him again and does not let him go till he dies, whether ne
likes it or not'. Elsewhere Ley wrote that a worker escaped the Third Reich
only in his sleep: 'There are no more private citizens. The time is past when any-
body could or could not do what he pleased'. Ley's organisation even calculated
the number of non-working and non-sleeping hours the average worker
'enjoyed' in a year, and then attempted to fill them via the 'Strength through Joy'
movement. All these techniques originated with the 'social' employers of German
heavy industry.

marck's anti-socialist laws and the early years of the Nazi Third Reich. His views on trade unions are therefore invested with a double significance. As was the case with Alfred Krupp, nothing enraged him so much as the supreme act of proletarian insubordination—a strike. A wave of stoppages in his coal fields provoked this onslaught from Kirdorf at the 1905 Mannheim conference of the Association for Social Policy:

> It is regrettable that our workpeople are able to change their positions at any time. An undertaking can only prosper if it has a stationary band of workers. I do not ask that legislation should come to our help, but that we must reserve to ourselves the right to take measures to check this frequent change of employment. The proposal has been made that all workpeople should be compelled to join organisations and that employers should be required to negotiate with these organisations. For myself, I would remark that I refuse to negotiate with any organisation whatever.

Kirdorf even refused to treat with the Catholic unions, which were set up in direct opposition to those under the leadership of the SPD:

> While the Social Democratic organisations at least say openly at what they are aiming—viz, the subversion of the present social order, the Christian unions fight under a false flag. They know well that the subversion desired by the Social Democrats cannot be brought about, so they seek to place capitalism under the domination of the clergy.

And for good measure, Kirdorf also criticised the Berlin government for its half-baked attempts to introduce a programme of social reforms and factory legislation: 'I regret, too, that the State intereferes at all in labour relationships.' It was, of course, a different matter when some 28 years later the state, under the leadership of his Nazi allies, intervened on the side of the employer against the trade unions! Barbarism in fact lay very close to the surface of German heavy industry. At a time when large sections of British capitalism were being compelled to retreat from their previous position of intransigent opposition to factory legislation, the steel and coal kings of Germany were not merely standing firm, but taking the offensive. The Rhine iron producers banded together in 1873 in the 'Centralverband deutscher Industrieller' precisely to block all attempts at social reform by the Bismarck government. It opposed restrictions on the exploitation of child labour with the altruistic argument that 'it seems to be more reasonable to set children to work at pleasant jobs and let them make money (sic!) than to allow them to go idle and become wild.* Similarly a ban on night work for women

---

*Contrast this lofty, 'non materialistic' justification for child labour with unashamed claims by English manufacturers that Factory Acts shortening the

was denounced in the name of 'liberty of the people to work
whenever they want to'. This intransigent attitude was not
confined to the Ruhr, though this region undoubtedly contributed more than its fair share of anti-labour warriors.
Everywhere that large-scale industry had arisen, there were to
be found the spokesmen and practitioners of unremitting class
warfare against the proletariat. In 1907, the director of the
principal Saxon employers' organisation declared at its annual
conference that:

> the military state of Germany owes the supremacy of its industry
> in the world market to the discipline asserted in its factories. The
> authority of the employer is a precious possession, to defend
> which is our most immediate duty. We shall never yield when it
> is a question of a test of power on the part of the workman,
> where the authority of the employer might be menaced.

And then, as if to mitigate, or rather justify, the harshness of
this policy, he proceeded to use the same 'corporatist' ideology
so favoured by Stumm and Krupp, and later plagiarised by
Dr Ley:

> For this authority is not merely the possession of the individual,
> *it is a common good*. Modern economic development has brought
> to the front the estate of the industrialists, who have superseded
> the old feudal landed proprietors as employers. Upon the
> efficiency of the industrialists depend the nation's power and
> progress. It is the duty of the industrialists not merely to provide
> the increasing millions of the population with a livelihood, but it
> must *primarily* wage war against subversive endeavours in every
> form. Our battle against the trade unions is at the same time a
> battle against Social Democracy. (Emphases added.)

The same view was expressed by the most powerful of the
pre-Weimar employers organisations, the Central Union of
German Industrialists, which in a policy statement on labour-
capital relations declared:

> The conclusion of wages agreements between employers'
> organisations and the organisations of the workers is altogether
> injurious to German industry and its prosperous development.
> The agreements not only deprive the individual employers of the
> liberty of deciding independently as to the employment of their
> workpeople and the fixing of wages . . . but they inevitably bring
> the work people under the domination of the labour organisations.
> The agreements* are, according to the conviction of the Central
> Union, fully confirmed by the experience of England and the
> United States, serious obstacles in the way of the progress of
> German industry in technical matters and in organisation.

---

working day for juveniles would rob them of their profits. Thus 'Senior's "Last
Hour" ', immortalised by Karl Marx in Volume I of *Capital* (pp.224-230).
*The agreements referred to are those which were, at the turn of the century,
sponsored by the Government between employers and trade unions.

How can we explain this organic tendency of German heavy industry towards political and social reaction? Is it a purely German or 'Prussian' phenomenon, a product of a prolonged economic liason with and political dependence on the East Elbian Junkers? Surely not, for the magnates of coal and steel have been traditionally aligned with extreme right wing political not only throughout Europe, but also in the United States and Japan. This general and for imperialism, universal, trend can only arise on the foundations of the nature of heavy industry itself, its irresistible drive towards concentration and mono-polisation, its ever present concern to keep at maximum production the vast fixed capital installations which are unique to heavy industry. The very nature of large-scale iron and steel production, with its continuous processes and delicate chemical combinations, also places a premium on a work force which is disciplined to the rhythms of the production cycle and which will not be prone to strikes and other interruptions of an 'external' nature. With this in mind, we can well appreciate the oft-expressed desire of the leaders of German heavy industry for a work force which would, willingly or otherwise, subordinate itself entirely to the dictates of the employer. The high organic composition of capital in the 'heavy' industries—i.e. the ratio between capital expended on means of production and on labour power (wages) also means that the employer finds the vast bulk of his capital costs do not lend themselves to reduction. Unless he has already secured the advantages of 'vertical integration'* he will be compelled to pay the market price for all his constant capital. Thus enormous pressure is brought to bear on variable capital, as the only element in a heavy industrialist's costs which can, given a suitable political and economic climate, be attacked with any prospect of success. The leaders of German heavy industry may not, necessarily, have seen the problem in this clinical light in the period under discussion, but it was undoubtedly one of the most powerful factors driving them to seek a confrontation with the labour movement To these factors we must, of course, add the well-known, but often vulgarly interpreted relationship between heavy industry and militarism. A desire for government arms contracts is obviously an important motive amongst industrialists for supporting movements and regimes which

---

*Germany pioneered this type of industrial organisation, which involved a concern extending 'vertically' by absorbing those enterprises which either supplied it with raw materials, or purchased its own product. Kirdorf was a leading advocate of the vertical monopoly: 'All economic development necessarily leads to integrated undertakings, for a company can only prosper permanently when, besides manufacturing finished goods, it also produces its own raw materials'.

will, because of their imperialist orientation undertake extensive armaments programmes. But the mistake is sometimes made of deducing from this that imperialist war is little more than the outcome of a conspiracy on the part of the arms manufacturers and those industries allied with them. Rather we should seek the origins of political reaction in the overall relationships engendered by the rise of heavy industry. Small wonder that a German commentator on the Wilhelmian industrial scene noted that:

> the decisive battles of German politics will be fought neither on the Neckar (Baden) nor on the Isar (Bavaria) but in the district of the Elbe (Prussia). For in North Germany capitalism has attained the gigantic expression which is characteristic of the world market; there classes oppose each other so nearly and so roughly that one disputant can look into the white of his enemy's eye: there amiability long ago disappeared from politics.

Yes, Munich witnessed the birth of the 'National Socialist German Workers Party', but to the north, in the heartland of not merely Germany, but all Europe there smouldered and raged the class forces which were to raise it to the pinnacles of state power.

REFERENCES FOR CHAPTER THREE
[1] F. Engels: Preface to *The Peasant War in Germany,* pp.29-30.
[2] Quoted in W. Manchester: *The Arms of Krupp,* p.178, London, 1969.
[3] A. Krupp: *General Regulations,* September 9, 1872.
[4] Ibid.
[5] Ibid.
[6] Ibid.

Chapter Four
THE HEROIC AGE OF GERMAN LABOUR

Thus far we have focused on those social, economic and political factors, international as well as national, which contributed to the formation and development of the political consciousness of the propertied classes in Germany. We have also sought to show how these forms of consciousness comprised an alloy of many elements, which in turn were the complex outcome of a whole series of interwoven historical processes and events dating back, in effect, to the very dawn of the modern era. Finally, the trajectory of these developments was projected towards the future rise of fascism, and some of the constituent elements of its programme and ideology located, even if in an embryonic form, in post 1848, Bismarckian Germany.* Now it is necessary to analyse and synthesise developments at the other pole, that of the German proletariat. For here too we shall discover that tradition played its full part in the shaping of the present and the future, and that the life and death struggles of the infant German labour movement against its Junker, bourgeois and petty-bourgeois enemies came to overshadow so many of the class battles under the Weimar Republic. And here it must be said without any reservations that the reaction, personified by Adolf Hitler, absorbed the lessons of this period far more tellingly than any leader of German Social Democracy.

Initial attempts to found a stable working class movement in

* Fascism is, of course, first and foremost a movement of imperialist reaction and counter-revolution, and can only rise to maturity in an epoch where the threat of proletarian revolution has become an actuality. The movements led by Hitler and Mussolini were unthinkable in the Germany of Bismarck or William II. But this by no means negates the fact that even at this early date the deep-going shifts in petty-bourgeois consciousness, partly reflected in the activities of anti-semitic and pseudo-socialist demogogues, were the first stages of a process which culminated in the formation and development of the Nazi party. Even more important were the parallel developments among the leaders of heavy industry, which were discussed in the previous chapter. What makes fascism so potent, and therefore so dangerous, is that it is not simply an artificial creation of a clique of reactionary businessmen, but the product of a long historical process. Only when this is understood can it be effectively combatted.

Germany proved short lived. The defeat of 1848 cast its long shadow over the working class. Its most radical elements found refuge in the camp of bourgeois left liberalism, while others, temporarily disillusioned with politics, emigrated to the New World.* But these workers, who had lived and fought in the crucible of revolution, and had witnessed at first hand the fruits of the bourgeoisie's cowardice, could never be reconciled to a long sojourn in the parties of petty-bourgeois democracy. Unlike England, where the working class underwent a protracted and convoluted experience of supporting two openly bourgeois parties, the Liberals and the Conservatives, before striking out along an independent political path, the German working class was driven to a split from Liberalism in little more than a decade. And the manner in which this was done was very different from the route taken by workers in England. There, the impetus to form a class party came from an attack on the trade unions, whose leaders had, traditionally given their electoral support to the Liberals. And these unions had a history in some cases reaching back to the middle of the 19th century and even earlier. How different from Germany, where it was workers and intellectuals influenced by various schools of socialist thought who broke from Liberalism to found first an independent political party, and only then, a trade union movement. The contrasting series of steps whereby the German and English working classes established their organisational and political independence** from all other classes and parties is of enormous importance for comprehending the subsequent histories of both nations. And precisely because the German labour movement originated in the development of diffuse and divergent schools of socialism, and not in the economic organisations of the class, which by their very nature embrace workers of all political views, it was from its very inception confronted by profound theoretical problems. Contrary to what the dictates of 'common sense' might suggest, this gave the movement its one great strength, and even though compromises over principle and programme were sometimes effected to achieve organisational unity, the German working

---

* Many were destined in later years to play a significant part in pioneering the American socialist movement.

**This is not to say that the vast majority of workers in England and Germany had broken free from the grip of bourgeois ideology. As Lenin pointed out in his famous polemic against the Russian 'Economist' school, which advanced a schema of spontaneous working class development towards and into socialist consciousness, 'trade union consciousness is bourgeois consciousness'. And, as first conceived by its founders, the Labour Party was little else but the political party of the trade unions. This is not to deny that it also contained another element pregnant with revolutionary implications—the groping of the working class towards political power.

class of necessity became drawn into these doctrinal disputes, and as a result, underwent a political education unrivalled by any other proletariat. And here too, just as was the case with their class enemies, the development of the German working class was profoundly influenced by the combined and uneven development of capitalism. Engels observed that the German workers enjoyed two enormous advantages over their class brothers in the rest of Europe:

> Firstly they belong to the most theoretical people of Europe and they have retained that sense of theory which the so-called "educated classes" have almost completely lost. Without German philosophy, which preceeded it, particularly that of Hegel, German scientific socialism . . . would never have come into being*. Without a sense of theory among the workers, this scientific socialism would never have entered their flesh and blood as much as is the case. [1]

This instinctive feel for theory Engels contrasted with 'the indifference towards all theory' which he had encountered at first hand in the English labour movement. It was a powerful retarding factor in its development, 'in spite of the splendid organisation of the individual unions.'[2] And the second advantage was that

> Chronologically speaking, the Germans were about the last to come into the workers movement' and for this reason were able to climb to the political heights attained by German social democracy by 'resting on the shoulders of Saint-Simon, Fourier and Owen . . . it has developed on the shoulders of the English and French movements . . . it was able to utilize their dearly bought experience . . Without the precedent of the English trade unions and French workers' political struggles, without the gigantic impulse given especially by the Paris Commune, where would we be now?[3]

The modern German workers' movement dates from the year 1863. The brilliant but erratic dramatist and Hegelian philosopher Ferdinand Lassalle attracted a small group of workers around him after they had been denied full membership of the Progressive Party's National Association. Later that year, on May 23, 1863, these workers founded, under the rigidly centralised personal leadership of Lassalle, the General German Workers Union. Based on the Saxon city of Leipzig, its declared aim was the achievement of universal suffrage and the establishment of socialism through direct action by the state.* Lassalle's idealisation of the state, his view of it as an

---

* Hegelian philosophy was itself a product of the uneven, or one-sided development, of the German bourgeoisie (see Chapter One).
* This emphasis on 'State Socialism', as opposed to the achievement of socialism by the independent revolutionary action of the working class itself, was enshrined in the Lassallian *Workers' Programme*, which declared:
'Thus the purpose of the state is to bring about the positive unfolding and

organisation above classes and existing purely for purposes of rational government and 'cultural progress', he undoubtedly owed to his uncritical assimilation of the Hegelian heritage. This was the central issue dividing Lassalle from Marx. It was not, as some biographers of the latter suggest, a clash of personalities or a question of political rivalry and prestige. Both men were constructed on too grand a scale for such petty concerns. Lassalle's Hegelian theory of the state was destined to lead him astray also in the field of political tactics and strategy. Burning with hatred for the German bourgeoisie, which he saw as not just the principal, but the only enemy of the working class, Lassalle allowed himself to be trapped into making an alliance with Bismarck on the questions of national unity and universal suffrage. When the affair become known after Lassalle's death, it did great harm to the young workers' movement in Germany, for it enabled its bourgeois and petty-bourgeois opponents to portray Social Democracy as an agent of feudal reaction. All the biting invective hurled against Lassalle by Marx and Engels was therefore fully justified, as the essence of all their theoretical work was directed towards establishing the political premise of the socialist revolution—the complete independence of the working class from all other classes, together with an intransigent opposition to all the state machinery of class oppression.* The other wing of the movement was founded by Wilhelm Liebknecht a revolutionary student of 1848, and August Bebel, a wood turner by trade. Their organisation, the League of German Workers' Clubs, also dates from 1863, but did not sever its umbilical cord with

progressive development of man's nature, in other words, to realise the human purpose.' Elsewhere he wrote that 'the task and purpose of the state consists exactly in its facilitating and mediating the great cultural progress of humanity . . . That is why its exists; it has always served, and always had to serve, this very purpose.'

* Yet Lassalle's futile death in a fuel deeply grieved Marx and Engels. The bitter words they had exchanged were exclusively about how best to fight and defeat the class enemy. Marx and Engels now saluted him as a fallen comrade:

'No matter what Lassalle may have been personally, and from a literary and scientific standpoint, politically he was certainly one of the finest brains in Germany . . . it hits one hard to see how Germany is destroying all the more or less capable men of the extreme party. What joy there will be amongst the manu-facturers and the Progressive swine after all. Lassalle was the only man in Germany of whom they were afraid.' (Engels to Marx, September 3, 1864.) To which Marx replied:

'Lassalle's misfortune has been worrying me damnably during the last few days. After all, he was one of the old guard and an enemy of our enemies . . .' (Marx to Engels, September 7, 1864). Perhaps it is significant that neither of these letters, which bring out the warm, human side of their authors, is in the current Moscow edition of the Marx-Engels *Selected Corespondence.* These qualities, and not the cynical ersatz version presented in pictures of Stalin hugging little children at the height of his bloodpurge, have been rare commodities in the Soviet Union for many decades.

liberalism until 1866, when Liebknecht and Bebel broke their loose association with the German People's Party to create their working class-based Saxon People's Party. And it took another two years of fierce internal struggles with the more backward political elements in the party to finally launch the Social Democratic Labour Party in the south German town of Eisenach, from which they derived their popular soubriquet of 'Eisenachers' to distinguish them from Lassalle's movement, which was now under the leadership of Johann von Schweitzer. The new party, though it differed on many important points from the Lassallians, was also far from complete agreement with Marx and Engels, a state of affairs which became glaringly obvious when merger moves between the two movements were consumated by the unity Congress at Gotha in 1875. The criticisms made by Marx of the Gotha Programme have more than an historical interest, as they underlined theoretical and political weaknesses in the new German Party which were never truly mastered, and which played a central part in its degeneration in the years immediately preceeding the First World War. If we have to single out two issues around which the capitulation of German Social Democracy in 1914 revolved, then they would be the attitude of its leadership to working class internationalism and the capitalist state—precisely those questions which Marx considered to be either watered down or distorted in the unification programme.*

Thus Marx took issue with the fifth point of the Erfurt Programme, which couched its internationalism in all too feeble terms:

> Lassalle, in opposition to the *Communist Manifesto* and to all earlier socialism, conceived the workers' movement from the narrowest national standpoint. It is altogether self-evident that, to be able to fight at all, the working class must organise itself at home as a class and that its own country is the immediate arena of its struggle. In so far its class struggle is national, not in substance, but, as the *Communist Manifesto* says, "in form". But the "framework of the present day national state", for instance, the German Empire, is itself in its turn economically "within the framework of the world market ... of the [world] system of states..."[4]

What Marx is insisting here, against the Lassallians especially, is that there can be no 'socialism in one country', that the very international nature of capitalist economy and world political relations presupposes an international struggle by the working class to take state power and begin the construction of

---

* Marx challenged cloudy and false formulations on the nature and difference between bourgeois and communist conceptions of 'right' in relation to the distribution of the produce of labour. Here the Lassallian heritage made itself felt most strongly, as it did with the well-known formulation in the programme that in relation to the proletariat, 'all other classes are only one reactionary mass.'

socialism. By implicitly rejecting thoroughgoing internationalism, the Programme was placing at risk the fighting unity of the entire European working class:

> And to what does the German workers' party reduce its internationalism? To the consciousness that the result of its efforts will be "the international brotherhood of peoples"—a phrase borrowed from the bourgeois League of Peace and Freedom, which is intended to pass as equivalent to the international brotherhood of the working classes in the joint struggle against the ruling classes and their governments. Not a word, therefore, about the international functions of the German working class! [5]

And these functions were, and remained, onerous indeed. It was the German proletariat, whose first struggles for political and social emancipation had pumped blood into the Hegelian schemas of the youthful Marx and Engels, which gave the initial impetus for the writing of the landmark in socialist literature, the 'Communist Manifesto'. Also it was the German working class, whose best elements were brought together in the Lassallian and Eisenacher movements, which comprised the politically most strategic and theoretically advanced detachment of the First (Workingmen's) International. And when the International went into decline and liquidation after the defeat of the Paris Commune, it was the German movement which stood firmest against the anarchist attack on Marxism. Neither was it an accident that the SPD later provided the biggest and theoretically most weighty battalions of the Second International after its foundation in 1889. The dominant position of German industry and arms in the period of the Second International's prime compelled the German working class to take up a position of leadership within the international movement, and this it held right up to the outbreak of war in 1914. Strategically, speaking there could be no successful socialist revolution anywhere in Europe without the active solidarity of the German working class. This Marx understood only too well, having still fresh in his memory the recent tragic defeat of the Paris Commune, drowned in the blood of thousands of Paris workers under the protective and approving gaze of Bismarck's Prussian general staff.

Therefore to fulfil its international obligation, the German working class had to be broken from all forms of nationalism, however refined and however much dressed up in the language of democracy and even socialism. This was a task only a small minority of the SPD leadership took up in earnest, as the drift towards chauvinism in the imperialist epoch was to testify. Marx was equally biting in his criticism of the programme's section devoted to democratic demands. He poured scorn on the notion, derived as much from the Eisenach as the Lassallian wing of the party, of a 'free state'. Such a vague, non-class formulation in effect served to obscure the repressive functions of any state, be it feudal, capitalist or the state power established after a victorious workers' revolution:

> The German workers' party — at least if it adopts the programme — shows that its socialist ideas are not even skin-deep; in that, instead of treating existing society (and this holds good for any future one) as the *basis* of the existing state . . . it treats the state rather as an independent entity that possesses its own intellectual, ethical and libertarian basis. [6]

Thus, far from idealising the state, the task of German socialists was to prepare for its overthrow, and the creation of the new state power based on socialist, and not capitalist property relations:

> 'Between capitalist and communist society lies the period of the revolutionary transformation of the one into the other. There corresponds to this also a political transition period in which the state can be nothing but *the revolutionary dictatorship of the proletariat.* [7]

Marx and Engels, while being frank to the point of bluntness with the leaders responsible for the adoption of the Gotha programme, never abused their position of political and theoretical authority to bludgeon Bebel, Liebknecht and Bracke into unthinkingly and uncritically accepting their proposed revisions of the draft. The German movement was an autonomous one, and both Marx and Engels saw their role in relation to it as one of comradely critics and advisers. Their greatest concern was that in their desire to abolish the 12 year old organisational cleavage in the German workers' movement Eisenachers would conclude a rotten compromise with the Lassalians over vital programmatic issues. Far better, wrote Engels to Wilhelm Bracke, that the Eisenachers 'should simply have concluded an agreement for action against the common enemy'.[8] But by trading programmatic points with the Lassallians, 'one sets up before the whole world landmarks by which it measures the level of the Party movement . . . One knows that the mere fact of unification is satisfying to the workers, but it is a mistake to believe that this momentary success is not bought at too high a price' Engels made the same point even more forcefully in a letter to Bebel. After reiterating Marx's criticism of the 'free people's state', which he called 'pure nonsense'.* Engels warned that the adoption of such a programme would mean

---

* This notion of the 'free people's state' is by no means a Lassallian or Eisenacher preserve. It has been resurrected by Soviet Stalinism in the guise of Khrushchev's celebrated 'state of the whole people'. No Stalinist ever succeeded in explaining away the all-too-obvious contradiction between the state as an instrument of class rule and its survival in a country where all the people allegedly ruled.

Marx and I can *never* give our adherence to the *new* party established on this basis, and shall have very seriously to consider what our attitude towards it—in public as well—should be . . . you will realise . . . that this programme marks a turning point which may very easily compel us to refuse any and every responsibility for the party which recognises it. [10]

In the event, Marx and Engels were not driven to a public break from the new German party. Not because they were reconciled to its programme, but because within three years, the course of the class struggle in Germany took such a sharp turn that a whole new set of problems and disputes were created both inside the SPD and between the newly founded party and Marx and Engels in England. The new situation was, of course, Bismarck's determined bid to crush the German labour movement. Bismarck's decision to outlaw the SPD and its allied organisations, although implemented in 1878, had been made much earlier. The first serious repressions began in the wake of Prussia's victorious war against France, when Bebel, Liebknecht and other leaders of the infant workers' movement were jailed on the Chancellor's orders for opposing his annexation of Alsace and Lorraine. Every other party, from the Progressives through the National Liberals to the Conservatives, unleashed an unprecedented barrage of chauvinst invective against the social democrats, and both Liebknecht and Bebel were subsequently re-arrested after serving their four month jail term, and tried for treason at Leipzig in March 1872. This time, the sentence was two years, for intervening between the two verdicts was not only the Reichstag elections of 1871, where the party of Bebel and Liebknecht succeeded in returning them as deputies, but also the Paris Commune. Its impact on the propertied classes in Germany was truly traumatic, far more so even than the Paris June uprising of 1848. What made the Commune even more horrific in the eyes of Germany's rulers was the unequivocal support given to the heroic Parisian proletariat by the leaders of the German workers movement. Bismarck himself subsequently recalled that he saw the Commune as 'a flash of light: from that moment I saw the social democrats as an enemy against whom state and society must arm themselves'. All the old fears of a possible working class revolution now surfaced again after lying dormant since the defeat of 1848. The years of political reaction had masked the emergence of a powerful industrial working class in the main cities of west and central Germany and both Junkers and bourgeoisie suddenly realised that here, in Berlin, Leipzig and Essen they stood on alien soil.* The coming together of the two wings of the socialist

* This had been instinctively understood by Bismarck from very early on in his

movement in 1875, together with their respective trade union organisations, heightened apprehensions that the revolution was drawing near. It is easy to see now that these fears were unfounded, and that the development of the German proletariat into a class numerically and politically capable of seizing state power had barely begun. *In this sense,* the class consciousness of both bourgeoisie and Junkers was false. But this is hardly the point, since propertied, exploiting classes are always, to one degree or another, motivated by false consciousness, and are organically incapable of seeing things and relations as they really are. Their false consciousness is indeed one of the most powerful factors in sustaining their rule in defiance of all but the most powerful and correctly led challenges from the working class. The conviction that the bourgeoisie (and even more so, the Junkers) represented doomed modes of production was hardly calculated to give it the class confidence required to combat the threat of expropriation! Instead the German ruling classes saw every movement of the proletariat towards its emancipation, however modest, through counter-revolutionary spectacles. The experiences of 1525, 1789, 1815 and 1848 had become so fully absorbed into the consciousness of the bourgeoisie, and had so sapped the political confidence and skill necessary to undertake an 'English' policy of compromise and maneouvre with the leaders of the working class, that it demanded and supported measures which were from a 'rational' point of view, quite excessive.* But the class struggle does not proceed according to the dictates of Kantian pure reason, but through the clash of material forces as they are mediated through the consciousness of those who participate in the conflict. As Engels expressed it:

> Ideology is a process accomplished by the so-called thinker consciously, it is true, but with a false consciousness. The real forces impelling him remain unknown to him, otherwise it simply would not be an ideological process. Hence he imagines false or seeming motive forces. Because it is a process of thought he derives its form as well as its content from pure thought, either his own or that of his

political career. In 1852, he vehemently denied 'that the true Prussian people' lived in the cities. If the city were ever to revolt again, the true Prussians would know how to make them obey, even though it had to erase them from the earth.

This revealing remark also gives us an insight into the political and historical pedigree of Nazi ruralism. And in the year of this anti-socialist legislation, Bismarck described the working class as 'that menacing band of robbers with whom we share our largest towns . . .'

* There is a certain parallel between Bismarck's anti-socialist laws and the anti-trade union Combination Acts passed by the English Parliament in 1799. Both were responses by the ruling classes to the rise of organised labour, and both were related indirectly to revolutionary events in France. But the German labour movement was already being influenced by Marxism, and was largely based on a modern industrial proletariat.

predecessor. He works with mere thought material, which he accepts without examination as the product of thought, and does not investigate further for a more remote source independent of thought: indeed, this is a matter of course to him, because, as all action is *mediated* by thought, it appears to him to be ultimately based on thought.[11]

Thus individuals and even entire classes can be driven into actions not as a direct reflex of a real and clearly comprehended economic, social or political stimulus, but at varying degrees of a tangent to these material forces. To say otherwise is to believe that all human beings act at all times with a total consciousness of what they are doing. 'Over-reaction' to an imagined or exaggerated threat is as much a part of history as the 'underreaction' by classes or individuals to warnings of dangers that were all too real.* All are moments in a total process of class struggle, in which between its polar opposites there are ranged out an infinite series of shadings in constant motion and conflict. Bismarck's war on the German labour movement can be understood in no other way, for though it ended in humiliating defeat and resignation for the Junker of iron and blood, it established a precedent on which others were later to build with devasting success.

Evidence that Bismarck had been preparing his blow against the social democrats ever since the Commune is to be found in a letter written to him by his old Conservative friend and political adviser, Hermann Wagener. Warning against any hasty attempts to outlaw the socialists, he said:

it seems to me to be an exceedingly dangerous undertaking to wish to combat the Ultramontane** and the Socialist parties at the same time and thereby to drive the Socialists even more irrevocably into the clerical camp. Even though it may be justified and necessary to enforce existing laws energetically and thereby to keep away from the socialist movement foreign elements and all others who are pursuing anti-national goals, nevertheless I regard it as definitely a political mistake to subject the socialist leaders to exceptional laws solely on account of their social aspirations, particularly if one does not, at the same time, do anything to satisfy the justified demands of their supporters.

The debate raged inside both the bourgeoisie and the Junker landowners for several years before a decision was finally arrived

---

* Thus a rationalist could argue that the massacre of the Communards was unnecessary and therefore illogical since the Paris workers had no hope of extending their revolution to the remainder of France.
**A reference to the Catholic Centre Party, founded in 1870 and strongly opposed to Bismarck's Prussian and Protestant based regime. It drew most of its support from the Catholic regions of the Rhine and Bavaria. Led by the hierarchy and the Catholic bourgeoisie, it drew in its tow the overwhelming majority of Catholic workers, peasants and petty-bourgeoisie, for many years serving as a strong bulwark against the spread of socialist ideas and genuine trade unionism among the Catholic proletariat of the Ruhr.

at, with both classes being split on the issue from top to bottom.Ironically, (but very much in keeping with the German tradition) some of the most vehement opponents of anti-socialist legislation were to be found amongst Bismarck's fellow Junkers. They instinctively (and in some cases quite consciously) felt that too harsh a repression of the workers' movement would destroy the delicate balance between the classes which, under Bismarck, had become a central factor in Junker political strategy and tactics. They also believed that persecution would only strengthen the most radical elements in the movement, and render any compromise between it and the government impossible. This was a view expressed by the monarchist historian and economist, Gustav Schmoller, wo in 1874 wrote his highly polemical *The Social Question and the Prussian State,* setting out his programme for a 'social monarchy'; and the case for a policy of tolerating, and not provoking, the social democrats.

> . . . Social Democracy represents merely the youthful exuberance of the great social movement which we are entering. Our Social Democracy is a little different but it is hardly worse than English Chartism was in its time and I hope that like the latter it will prove to be merely a transitional phase of development . . . The social dangers of the future can only be averted by one means, by the monarchy and the civil service . . . the only neutral elements in the social class war, reconciling themselves to the idea of the liberal state, absorbing into their midst the best elements of parliamentary government and taking a resolute initiative towards a great venture in social reform . . .

This represented what was quite an advanced view for the German bourgeoisie, and it was immediately countered by the highly influential nationalist historian, Heinrich von Treitschke, who in his *Socialism and its Sympathisers* (1874) denounced those who advocated political reform and toleration of socialism as traitors to their own class:

> Envy and greed are the two mighty forces that it (socialism) employs to lift the old world from its hinges; it thrives on the destruction of all ideals . . . The very foundation stones of all community life are endangered by Social Democracy . . . The doctrine of the injustice of society destroys the firm instincts that the worker has about honour, so that fraud and bad and dishonest work are scarcely held to be reprehensible any longer . . .

And in a direct riposte to the 'liberal Gustav Schmoller, von Treitschke went on:

> The learned friends of socialism are in the habit of pointing to the Chartists,* who also began with cosmopolitan dreams but nevertheless in the end learned to accommodate themselves to their country. This overlooks the fact that the English island

---

* Like Schmoller, and indeed many other bourgeois and Junkers, von Treitschke followed the development of the international workers' movement with an eagle eye.

people possessed an age-old resistance which is lacking in our unfinished country open to all foreign influences. It also overlooks the fact that Chartism was in its origins English, whereas German Social Democracy is led by a mob of homeless conspirators. With every passing year Social Democracy has become more antagonistic toward the idea of the national state . . .

The political consequences of Germany's long-delayed national unification were now assuming malignant forms which the bourgeoisie and Junkers employed skillfully to whip up chauvinist hatred against the 'anti-national' leaders of the German working class. As was later the case with the Nazis, Marxism was not attacked before the masses on the grounds that it sought to better the conditions of the workers—quite the contrary, lip service was always paid to this principle—but because of its 'foreign' origin, even though both Marx and Engels were Germans.* Thus von Treitschke, like the counter-revolutionaires of 1848 and before, detected a French element in German social democracy:

> Socialism, therefore, alienates its adherents from the state and from the fatherland and in place of community of love and respect which it destroys it offers them the community of class hatred amongst the lowest classes . . . powerful agitators seek to encourage a boastful class pride . . . No Persian Prince was ever so flattered and fawned upon as "the real people" of Social Democracy. All the contemptible devices of French radicalism in the 1840s are called upon in order to awaken among the masses an arrogance that knows no bounds.

These extracts—and we could provide many more—illustrate perfectly Engels' contention that class interests and actions are mediated through modes of consciousness which the present is constantly inheriting and adapting from the past. The class struggle is therefore fought out under all manner of strange banners and devices—individual liberty, the divine right of kings, the right of 'freeborn men' to choose their own government, the right to work and the rights of property. In Germany, both bourgeoisie and Junkers waged war on the proletariat in the name of the 'nation' and this became, from very early on, the rallying point of all those forces who sought to crush Marxism. It even became the accepted convention to refer to the bourgeoisie, petty bourgeoisie and Junkers as Germany's 'national classes', and the proletariat as 'the international class'.**

Von Treitschke rounded off his diatribe against Marxism with a warning. The social democrats would be suppressed

---

* Naturally, the most extreme anti-socialist resorted to anti-semitism, claiming that Marx's Jewish origins were proof that German socialism was the product of an alien 'race'. This too became a central theme of Nazi agitation against Marxism.

** Hitler followed this usage, especially when addressing meetings of industrialists.

unless they 'submitted themselves to the traditional order of society . . . this demand means, first you must become the opposite of what you are today!' And then he gave an even graver warning to the rulers of Germany. If they 'allowed the masses to become too powerful', and 'if the masses succeed in taking power directly for themselves, then the whole world is turned upside down, state and society are dissolved and rule by force sets in.' Publicists like von Treitschke, who enjoyed an enormous standing amongst bourgeois intellectuals, were closer to the pulse of political life than the moderates. The election returns of 1877 confirmed Bismarck's worst fears. The SPD vote not only held up against this ferocious anti-socialist barrage, but actually increased from 351,000 to 493,000. Now there were 12 Social Democratic deputies, 'aliens', in the Imperial parliament. This electoral success was largely the outcome of the newly united movement's tremendous strides forward in organisation and its dissemination of socialist propaganda and agitation. Before the anti-socialist laws banned all left-wing literature, the SPD published no fewer than 24 journals with some 100,000 regular subscribers, and was now beginning to develop a powerful trade union movement under direct social democratic leadership and control.* It too had a flourishing press, with 16 union journals. The most far-sighted members of the ruling classes could see that this, the education of the most advanced layers of the workers in the basic principles of socialism, was the most serious and permanent challenge to their rule, even though it was a work which could only begin to reap its rewards after long years of patient toil. Bismarck now decided to act before it was too late. Early in 1878, he wrote to a National Liberal Reichstag deputy: 'If I don't want any chickens, then I must smash the eggs.' But first a suitable climate had to be created before the Chancellor could begin to wield his sledge hammer. And it seemed that fate was determined to assist him. On May 11, an unsuccessful attempt was made on the life of William I whilst he was riding in an open carriage along the fashionable Berlin Street, 'Unter den Linden'. The would be assassin turned out to be a plumber, one Max Hoedel, who had only the previous month been expelled from the Leipzig branch of the SPD for embezzling its funds. Bismarck gleefully seized on this coincidence—for that was all it proved to be—to press home his attack in the Reichstag, where he was battling against an obdurate majority which would not endorse his carte blanche for repressions

---

* In the two brief years since their own unity conference at Gotha (May 25, 1875) the trade unions had drawn more than 50,000 workers into their ranks, with the ubiquitous printers well to the fore with 5,500 members.

against the SPD.* On May 20, Bismarck's draft bill outlawing the SPD was presented to the Reichstag, and on the 24th, was rejected by a crushing vote of 251 to 57, with the bourgeois National Liberals split. It seemed as if Bismarck had run into a brick wall. Then, one week after his Reichstag reverse, another gunman fired at the Emperor in the Unter den Linden, inflicting serious wounds. Now Bismarck acted. With patriotic and monarchist sentiment outraged by the two assassination attempts, Bismarck found it a simple matter to direct it against the social democrats, whose views on royalty were only too well known. The shrewd Bismarck also exploited the new political situation to put fresh pressure on the recalcitrant National Liberals, who now ran the risk of being branded with the SPD as 'anti-national'. The new elections, called for July 30, were conducted in an atmosphere of reactionary frenzy. The 'Progressives' made haste to separate themselves from any supposed connection with the despised socialists, while all the major parties vied with one another to appear the most patriotic and loyal to the throne. This was truly a baptism of fire for the young workers' party. It spoke volumes for the heroism devotion and political consciousness of its activists and supporters that the SPD withstood the assault, kicking Bismarck and his 'liberal' allies in the teeth by returning only three fewer deputies to the new Reichstag. The popular vote for the party fell by 10%—a matter of 56,000 votes. In the circumstances, it was an inspiring political victory.** Bismarck smarted for revenge, and he was soon to have it. On October 19, 1878, the new Reichstag, with the far right now greatly strengthened,† passed Bismarck's anti-socialist bill by 221 votes to 149, although the Centre Party and the National

---

* The 1877 elections had distributed the 397 seats thus: Conservatives, 40, Reichspartei 38, National Liberals 128, Progressives 52, Centre 93, Social Democrats 12, others (based on national minorities, and thus opposed to Bismarck) 34. Thus the hard core pro-Bismarck vote was a mere 78 mandates.
** In fact the party had gained ground in its industrial strongholds. In the city districts, the SPD rose from 220,000 to 240,000 on the 1877 elections, while in Berlin, Social Democracy scored an amazing victory over all its opponents, increasing its vote from 31,500 to more than 56,000. This was evidence that while the middle classes gravitated away from the party to the right, the hard core socialist proletariat clung more than ever to the party which defended them against their bourgeois and Junker enemies. Such traditions of loyalty die hard. In the Reichstag terror elections of March 5, 1933, the SPD, already on the verge of a new and far more crushing illegality, polled 7,181,000 votes, a fall of less than 66,000 on the previous elections, held in November 1932, when there was no state-organised anti-socialist terror. The great tragedy lay in that this truly heroic class loyalty was utterly perverted and betrayed by the leaders of the SPD, whose capitulationist policies contrasted so miserably with the courageous example of those who pioneered the party in the teeth of Bismarck's repressions.
† Election returns gave both the Conservatives and the Reichspartei, or 'free Conservatives', an extra 19 seats, while the National Liberals and Progressives,

Liberals succeeded in weakening it somewhat by declining to endorse Bismarck's demand for a total ban on all activity of the SPD, including its participation in elections. This single loophole enabled the SPD to maintain a legal foothold in the Reichstag, where their deputies were protected by parliamentary immunity, and at election times, when the SPD was permitted to campaign for votes along with Germany's legal parties. At this stage, it will be fruitful to compare Bismarck's anti-Marxist strategy with that adopted by Hitler nearly six decades later. Firstly one is struck by the uncanny similarity—indeed, almost indentity—between the highly fortuitous assassination attempts on the Kaiser and the Reichstag Fire of February 27, 1933, which the Nazis exploited to mobilise the middle class masses against the 'red peril' in the elections of March 5. True, in the former case, no links have as yet been established between the two assassination attempts and Bismarck, whereas with the Reichstag fire, the evidence pointing towards Nazi complicity is weighty. But it cannot be denied that both Bismarck and Hitler proved themselves master tacticians in exploiting these incidents to create the political atmosphere in the more backward masses and small propertied classes necessary for an all-out war against the workers' movement. And it is only at this point—the methods employed to destroy the organisations of the proleteriat—that the great divide opens up between Bismarck and Hitler. While Bismarck sought and secured a national mandate to destroy social democracy, from the moment his bill became law, the task of making it effective rested solely in the hands of the Police, the judiciary and the organs of Government rule. Hitler has grasped from quite early on in his political career, and not only from his own experiences, but from examining the history of Bismarck's anti-socialist legislation—that the modern workers' movement, especially in a country like Germany where the proletariat had developed such powerful and disciplined organisations, and where Marxism had become flesh of their flesh, could never be destroyed by pure police methods, or even by the use of the armed forces. And it is possible to see how Hitler evolved his conception of a *mass* counter-revolutionary, intensely nationalistic and at the same time 'socially' oriented movement, from the negative example of Bismarck's 12 year war to extirpate Marxism from the consciousness of the German working class. On paper,

who had been branded by Bismarck and his supporters as allies of social democracy, lost heavily, the former dropping 29 deputies, and the latter, 13. Obviously a large section of the middle class had swung over sharply to the far right under the impact of Bismarck's carefully stage-managed anti-socialist crusade.

Bismarck's new law was truly formidable. Apart from the already referred to loophole of parliamentary and electoral immunity, the SPD and all its allied organisations had quite literally been rendered seditious overnight. Here there was complete indentity of purpose with Hitler's respression of the German workers' movement. The sweep of Bismarck's legislation can be appreciated from the following extracts. Entitled *Law against the Publicly Dangerous Endeavours of Social Democracy*, its clauses were directed against 'societies which aim at the overthrow of the existing political or social order through social democratic, socialistic or communistic endeavours . . .' Clause four gave to the government and its agents the right

> to attend all sessions and meetings (of the organisations in question) to call and conduct membership assemblies, to inspect the books, papers and cash assets, as well as to demand information about the affairs of the society, to forbid the carrying out of resolutions which are apt to further the endeavours (of the said organisations), to transfer to qualified persons the duties of the officers or other leading organs of the society, to take charge of and manage the funds.

And in the case of the officers or membership of such a society resisting such measures, 'the society may be prohibited'. Authority to implement these clauses of the law was vested in the State Police. If the State Police Authority prohibited any society, its 'cash assets, as well as the objects intended for the purposes of the society are to be confiscated . . .'

Those aspects of the law dealing with freedoms of speech, press and assembly were equally harsh:

> Meetings in which social democratic, socialist or communistic endeavours which aim at the overthrow of the existing political or social order are manifested are to be dissolved . . . Public festivities and processions shall be treated the same as meetings . . .

And as for the thriving socialist press:

> Publications in which social democratic . . . endeavours aimed at the overthrown of the existing political and social order are manifested in a manner calculated to endanger the public peace, and particularly the harmony among all classes of the population, are to be prohibited.

The State Police were also responsible for the implementation of these aspects of the law, which in effect, imposed a total censorship on all socialist and trade union publications in Germany. And the law went even further than censorship:

> . . . the publications concerned are to be confiscated wherever found for the purpose of distribution. The confiscation may include the plates and forms used for reproduction, in the case of printed publications in the proper sense, a withdrawal of the set

types from circulation is to be substituted for their seizure, upon the request of the interested parties. After the prohibition is final, the publication, plates, and forms are to be made unusable.

So it was also a question of the physical destruction, as well as seizure of the assets of the workers' movement. Here too, Bismarck was blazing a trail later to be followed with far greater success by the Nazis. Finally the act laid down penalties for breaches of the anti-socialist laws:

> Whoever participates as a member in a prohibited society, or carries on an activity in its interest, is to be punished by a fine of not more than 500 marks or with imprisonment not exceeding three months. The same punishment is to be inflicted on anyone who participates in a prohibited meeting, or who does not depart immediately after the dissolution of a meeting by the police. Imprisonment of not less than one month and not more than one year is to be inflicted on those who participate in a society or assembly as chairman, leaders, monitors, agents, speakers or treasurers, ro who issue invitations to attend the meeting . . . Whoever distributes, continues, or reprints a prohibited publication is to be punished with a fine not exceeding 1,000 marks or with imprisonment not exceeding six months.

All appeals against the infliction of these penalties were to be heard before a special Commission of five members, whose chairman was to be appointed by the Emperor, along with one other member. There was no appeal from this body to a higher court. Such was Bismarck's anti-socialist legislation, the most draconian body of repressive law enacted against the working class by a European state since the English Combination Acts of 1799. Under them, every single independent workers' organisation from the SPD to the trade unions and numerous cultural and educational societies were placed outside the law. 127 periodicals were compelled by the police to cease publication, along with 278 less regular publications. Even seemingly 'innocent' bodies such as workers' singing clubs and theatrical societies were deemed subversive of the social and political order, and forced to close down. Nothing except the party's nine lonely Reichstag deputies remained above the legal surface of German political life. At first, the party was stunned by the sheer suddenness and severity of Bismarck's law. The trade unions either collapsed or dissolved themselves, the SPD press wound itself up or was banned, and, under one of the act's clauses, entire groups of militants were banished from their home towns.* There is considerable evidence to suggest that the vast majority of

---

*These were the three co-authors of the article in question: Hoechberg, Carl Schramm and Eduard Bernstein, the last named being destined to earn eternal notoriety as the pioneer of revisionism.

party members, from the highest to the lowest levels, entered their 12 year period of illegality under the illusion that any ban on their activities would be largely formal. So disoriented were they by the ruthless efficiency of Bismarck's police under the leadership of his Minister of the Interior, Robert von Puttkamer, that an official year book for 1878 jubilantly announced that 'the execution of the Socialist Law is taking a completely successful course'. The enemies of the SPD, its editor reported, were already beginning 'to breathe easier . . .' The next year—1879—saw the party begin to pull itself together. A centre was established in Zurich, conveniently close to the German frontier, where leading social democrats could edit and publish the party's clandestine press and direct the underground movement in Germany itself. Enormously encouraged by the creation of this new centre of resistance to the Bismarck regime, the party's staunchest members and supporters quickly began to re-organise their activities on an illegal basis. These largely revolved around the smuggling of the party press across the Swiss frontier and its distribution throughout the industrial centres of Germany. By 1884, around 9,000 copies of each number of the new party weekly, *Sozialdemokrat*, were reaching workers in Germany by one means or another. Apart from the sheer technical feat of maintaining this circulation under such adverse conditions, the Zurich leadership were able, by means of their regular weekly contact with their comrades in Germany, to sustain the morale and political consciousness of a movement which in the early months of Bismarck's repressions, had seemed on the point of disintegration. Neither should all the credit for this achievement be awarded to the Zurich-based exile leadership. Marx and Engels were both highly critical of some of its members, notably Karl Hoechberg, whose own private journal, the *Jarbuch,* published an article calling for a policy of conciliation towards the 'upper strata of society'. This brought forth the *Circular Letter* of Marx and Engels to the leaders of the SPD, attacking the 'manifesto of the three Zurichers'*. They warned that such views were a direct result of the party's revolutionary perspectives and proletarian basis becoming undermined by the growing influence of bourgeois and petty-bourgeois intellectuals in its ranks. And they issued a warning to Bebel, Liebknecht and Bracke:

For almost 40 years we have stressed the class struggle as the

---

* In the first two months of the Law's operation, the police closed down 17 central trade union committees and 22 local union branches. The SPD avoided this fate only by voluntarily liquidating itself two days before the anti-socialist bill became law.

immediate driving force of history . . . it is therefore impossible for us to co-operate with people who wish to expunge this class struggle from the movement . . . The emancipation of the working classes must be conquered by the working classes themselves. We cannot therefore co-operate with people who openly state that the workers are too uneducated to emancipate themselves and must be freed from above by philanthropic big bourgeois and petty-bourgeois.

And they concluded on this sombre note; one which they had had caused to strike on the occasion of the Gotha unity congress:

If the new party organ adopts a line that corresponds to the views of these gentlemen . . . then nothing remains for us . . . but publicly to declare our opposition to it, and to dissolve the bonds of solidarity with which we have hitherto represented the German party abroad. [12]

The SPD leadership were halted in their tracks, such was the theoretical authority of Marx and Engels within the German movement. But neither had they given the party any 'orders'—that was neither their right, nor their political method. Their shafts struck home, and stung the sound core of the SPD leadership into action against the opportunists. Bebel visited Marx in London, bringing the erring Bernstein with him. After a series of searching discussions, it was agreed that Bernstein should take over the editorship of the party organ, and should work in the closest possible liaison with Bebel and Liebknecht inside Germany.* There, the movement was experiencing a true rebirth. The Hamburg organisation, traditionally a stronghold of German labour, raised its membership to 6,000, while Berlin was not far behind. The first national trial of strength came in 1881, with new elections to the Reichstag. The result was an overwhelming reverse for those parties which had voted for the anti-socialist law three years previously. The returns, with the 1878 figures in brackets, were:

Conservatives	50	(59)
Free Conservatives	28	(57)
National Liberals	47	(99)
Progressives	115	(39)
Centre	100	(94)
SPD	12	(9)
Others	45	(40)

Viewed in purely parliamentary terms, Bismarck's position had become untenable. His majority for the anti-socialist law, based on a combined right-wing vote of 215, had now dwindled to a minority of 125. And even if Bismarck rarely,

---

* As Reichstag deputies enjoying parliamentary immunity, Bebel and Liebknecht were able to operate far more openly than other party members.

if ever, concerned himself with the preservation of parliamentary majorities, he could scarcely afford to ignore the voting returns for the imperial capital, where the Progressives captured all six seats. And he could draw precious little comfort from the decline in the SPD vote*, for this could be put down entirely to the cumulative effect of three years' unremitting government persecution.

And at the next Reichstag elections of 1884, this trend was not only halted but reversed. The SPD vote now leapt to a record high of 550,000, doubling its quota of deputies. It was becoming glaringly obvious to Bismarck's Junker and bourgeois supporters that unless far sterner measures were taken, the social democratic 'eggs' would shortly be hatching out all over industrial Germany. Even more disturbing from their point of view was that this sudden electoral upsurge was immediately followed by an unprecedented wave of purely spontaneous strikes. 1886 saw this movement reach its highest point,** and the government decided that the time had now come to legislate directly against strikes, which had, as a comparatively rare occurance in the German labour movement, been ignored in the laws of 1878. On April 11, less than two weeks before the scheduled renewal of the anti-socialist laws, Puttkamer promulgated a decree outlawing all strikes, linking them directly to the activity of the already banned SPD. Police were authorised to expel strike leaders from the area of the dispute, and to intervene in any stoppage which allegedly contained 'tendencies serving upheaval'. And, in the now immortal words of Puttkamer himself, this could mean any and every strike:

> Behind the large labour movement, which at the present time calculates by means of force and agitation, namely through work stoppages, to bring about an increase in wages, and which draws many branch trades into the same misery, behind every such labour movement lurks the Hydra of violence and anarchy (shouts of "absolutely correct!" from the Right) [13]

But this measure, like its predecessors, was powerless to halt the advance of German labour. The 1887 Reichstag results told their own story. While the pro-Bismarck Right regained

---

* It fell by 125,000 to an all-time low of 312,000.

** Bismarck's surveillance of the international workers movement was greatly intensified and systematised in this period of continent-wide industrial and political unrest. For example, the German ambassador in London sent regular reports on the activities of the English labour movement, then engaged in a bitter struggle for universal suffrage and basic trade union rights. Reports were also received in Berlin of a nationwide strike movement in Belgium in March 1886. The intensity and scope of these strike movements beyond Germany's frontiers did much to exacerbate political tensions in the Reichstag, and certainly played a part in bringing forth Puttkamer's anti-strike decrees. For all the strident nationalism of its rulers, imperial Germany could never escape the disintegrating effect of the international class struggle.

much of its former support (the Conservative-National Liberal bloc or 'cartel' as it became known held 220 seats) the SPD also gained, at the expense of the mushy liberal centre, epitomised by the Progressives. Its vote has now passed the three-quarters of a million mark, and the tempo of its increase revealed no signs of diminishing. What could Bismarck do? He had tried the demagogic manoeuvre of 'State Socialism', which entailed little more than the most moderate programme of social reforms coupled with purely verbal recognition of the 'rights' of labour to minimum standards of living and working conditions. As we have already seen, powerful leaders of German industry together with several important employers' organisations, utterly repudiated these principles in practice. After a brief period of success, candidates claiming to stand for various breeds of 'state' or 'Monarchial Socialism' failed to woo significant sections of the socialist oriented working class away from their allegiance to Social Democracy. The final act in this drama opened with a new strike wave in 1889, whose most violent expression was a near-complete stoppage of Ruhr miners for shorter hours in the May of that year. In a bid to prevent the miners' movement turning towards the SPD for leadership,* the new Emperor Wilhelm II agreed to receive a deputation from the strikers, whose organisational affiliations were entirely Catholic.

The new king was anxious, in the best Bonapartist traditions, to win a reputation for himself as protector of the workers from a rapacious bourgeoise, and saw himself, at least in the early years of his reign, as 'king of the beggars'. But this policy explicitly ruled out any toleration of Social Democracy, a fact which he made abundantly clear to the miners' delegation:

> If . . . any excess be committed against public order and tranquility, or if it should become evident that Social Democrats are connected with the agitation, I shall not be able to take into consideration your wishes with my royal favour; for to me the world Social Democrat is synonymous with enemy of empire and fatherland. If, therefore, I observe that social democratic opinions are concerned in the agitation and incitement to unlawful resistance, I will intervene with unrelenting vigour and bring to bear the full power which I possess and which is great indeed.

The strike ultimately failed to gain any of its objectives, but Wilhelm was shrewd enough to see that unless some of the wind was taken out of the Social Democrats' sails, events

---

* Government fears were, as it turned out, groundless. Approaches had been made by miners to the SPD for financial support, but had been shamefully snubbed on the dogmatic grounds that trade union struggle was of little significance when compared with the political activity of social democracy. Much to his discredit, Bebel turned down the request for aid, and advised the miners' leaders to seek an 'acceptable compromise.' He seemed to overlook the fact that the raw Ruhr miners were striking powerful blows against the same enemy.

would move towards a nationwide, and not localised confrontation between capital and labour, and it would be one
which the cautious SPD leaders would scarcely be able to
ignore. The tactical conflict between Bismarck and his new
king therefore dates from the miners strike, as very rapidly,
the chancellor found himself at odds with Wilhelm's proposals
for legislation to mitigate the incredible harshness of conditions in German industry. Bismarck, while agreeing that
ways had to be found to counter the seemingly unstoppable
rise of socialist influence among the masses, favoured even
stronger repressions. The failure of his own attempts to buy
proletarian support for the Government undoubtedly turned
his thoughts in such a direction, and as the date for the new
Reichstag elections approached (February 20, 1890), he reached
the momentous decision for a convinced monarchist that he
must defy his king. Backed only by his die-hard Conservative
allies, Bismarck refused to accept amendments to the anti-
socialist law which would have had the effect of weakening it.
When the amended bill was finally presented to the full
Reichstag, Bismarck's Conservatives joined with the centre
and Left deputies in voting it down, with only the National
Liberals voting for. This, according to the best informed sources
of the period, was just what the wily old Bismarck wanted.
Now he hoped the SPD leaders would be tempted to stage a
millitant action against the obviously divided ruling classes
and government, perhaps even an insurrection. This would
then provide Bismarck with the long-awaited opportunity to
drown the Marxist 'hydra' in its own blood. Here Bismarck's
own distorted view of social democracy played an important
role in his own downfall. Nothing was further from the minds
of Bebel, Liebknecht and the other SPD leaders than a
revolutionary uprising against the Bismarck regime, and not
only for subjective reasons, but because the relationship of
forces rendered such a development impossible. The German
proletariat was concentrating all its forces towards two
goals, the steady and unspectacular rebuilding of its own
organisations, and the maximum mobilisation of support for
its party candidates at elections. And on February 20, the
results in this sphere can only be described as spectacular!
After nearly 12 years of illegality, police persecution, arrests
and jailings of its leaders and activists, banning of its publications, confiscation of its funds and the daily vilification of its
principles from pulpit, university professorial chair, officers'
mess and company boardroom, the despised 'vagabonds
without a country' emerged from the election as Germany's
largest party, with an incredible 1,427,298 votes.* The magnitude of the party's victory and of Bismarck's humilitation, was

so great that no-one — not Bebel, Liebknecht nor even Engels — either knew precisely what to. do with it or what this triumph implied for the future of the class struggle in Germany. It became an accepted canon of party doctrine that social democracy was invincible, that since the SPD had parried all the blows hurled at it by the formidable iron chancellor, then the movement would inevitably arise, phoenix-like, from the ashes of any future period of persecution. This utopian theory was soon to become intertwined with several other integral strands of what eventually became the SPD's opportunist adaptation to German imperialism. It flowed from the failure of German social democracy to grasp what was implied historically by Bismarck's attempt to destroy the party and trade unions. He failed, not because the task itself was impossible, (as the SPD leaders fondly believed) *but because the attempt was undertaken at the wrong time and with the wrong methods.* Furthermore, German Social Democracy made the fatal error of presuming that the reforms undertaken after the fall of Bismarck represented the beginnings of a change of heart on the part of the ruling classes and their government, this false estimation being reflected in a growing willingness of the SPD Reichstag fraction to amend, rather than oppose outright, proposed government legislation. Electoral combinations with radical bourgeois politicians necessarily flowed from this perspective, and were well under way before the lapsing of the anti-socialist legislation in 1890. We have said that Engels too cannot be regarded as blameless in this regard, and the evidence to uphold this contention is formidable.* In his still controversial introduction to Marx's *The Class Struggles in France*, Engels devotes a passage to the successful struggle of German social democracy against the anti-socialist laws. Correctly pointing out that since the defeat of the Paris Commune in 1871, the centre of gravity of the European workers' movement had shifted to Germany, he then draws political lessons from the defeat of Bismarck which are utterly mistaken:

There is only one means by which the steady rise of the socialist

* By combining against the SPD in run-off ballots, the right wing parties managed to hold down the number of Social democratic Reichstag deputies to 35.

* And not only after 1890. Thus in a dispute within the SPD Reichstag fraction over whether to call for the creation of state assisted farm co-operatives in East Prussia, Engels wrote to Bebel on December 30, 1884, that with guaranteed trade union and political freedoms, such a policy would 'lead gradually to a transition of the total production into co-operative production.' On this occasion, Bebel found himself defending Marxist orthodoxy against one of its two creators, for he replied a year later that 'with this proposal you make a regrettable concession to Lassalleianism.'

fighting forces in Germany could be temporarily halted, and even
thrown back for some time: a clash on a big scale with the military, a blood-letting like that of 1871 in Paris. In the long run that
would also be overcome. To shoot a party which numbers millions
out of existence is too much even for all the magazine rifles of
Europe and America. [14]

Yet Hitler did precisely that! And furthermore, he too studied
closely the experience of Bismarck's anti-socialist laws* and
drew political conclusions that not only differed greatly from
those of Engels, but which proved to be closer to historical
reality. One might argue that Engels could not possibly have
anticipated the political treachery which would make Hitler's
victory possible, or that Engels died in 1895 (the year he wrote
these lines), two full decades before the birth of fascism. But
that is no real answer. Firstly Engels did indeed foresee possible
political errors which could be committed by the SPD leadership on the threshold of a revolutionary situation, and secondly,
Hitler drew his own lesson from Bismarck's struggle against
socialism at least ten years before applying them in practice.
We should not be astonished when we see a leader of the
counter-revolution grasping, however distortedly, or however
reactionary his motives, a fundamental political truth more
quickly and effectively than a leader of the revolution. Instead
this should alert us to the immense perils which can be
obscured from the working class and its leadership by the
rigid employment and repitition of formulas and slogans which
while correct in a certain period and for a certain country,
are, by the emergence of new forces and class relationships,
rendered not only powerless to grasp and change reality, but
even transformed into their opposite, becoming vehicles for
disorienting the most advanced elements of the proletariat.
Such was the 'Old Bolshevism' of the 'democratic dictatorship
of the workers and peasantry,' pitilessly discarded by Lenin
in the Spring of 1917 in the teeth of determined opposition
from among others, Stalin. In the case of post-Bismarckian
Germany, this qualitative leap in Marxist theory was not
carried through with anything like the same severity and
clarity, with devastating results for not only the SPD, but the
entire German, and indeed, European proletariat. But how did
the young Hitler, as an ardent chauvinist, fanatical, anti-Marxist
and vehement Jew-baiter, assess the failure of Bismarck's anti-
socialist crusade? We know, chiefly from his own testimony in
Mein Kampf but also from other evidence, that Hitler first
seriously studied past attempts to destroy Marxism when he
arrived in Munich from Vienna in the May of 1913. What he says
about this period of his life is so important that we reproduce it

---

* So much for the theory that Hitler was a power-hungry madman.

here in its near entirety:

> For the second time I dug into this doctrine of destruction—this time no longer led by the impressions and effects of my daily associations, but directed by the observation of general processes of political life. I again immersed myself in the theoretical literature of this new world*, attempting to achieve clarity concerning its possible effects, and then compared it with the actual phenomena and events it brings about in political, cultural and economic life. Now for the first time I turned my attention to the attempts to master this world plague. I studied Bismarck's Socialist Legislation in its intention, struggle and success. Gradually I obtained a positively granite foundation for my own conviction, so that since that time I have never been forced to undertake a shift in my own inner views on this question. Likewise the relation of Marxism to the Jews was submitted to further thorough examination. Though previously in Vienna, Germany above all had seemed to me an unshakable colossus, now anxious misgivings sometimes entered my mind. I was filled with wrath at German foreign policy and likewise with what seemed to me the incredibly frivolous way in which the most important problem then existing for Germany, Marxism, was treated. It was really beyond me how people could rush so blindly into a danger whose effects, persuant to the Marxists own intention, were bound some day to be monstrous . . . In the years 1913 and 1914 I for the first time in various circles which today in part faithfully support the National Socialist movement expressed the conviction that the question of the future of the German nation was the question of destroying Marxism. [15]

What we should note here is not only the very obvious fact that Bismarck's anti-socialist legislation became a component part of Hitler's counter-revolutionary 'granite foundation' but his perception from quite early on that the survival of German imperialism was, in the long term, incompatible with the existence of a thriving German labour movement. The number of SPD leaders who shared this view—from the other side of the class trenches—could at this time be counted on the fingers of one hand! Hitler's respect for Bismarck was by not means a show of reverence staged to impress the 'national classes', who still idolised him—far from it. The anti-socialist legislation was a recurring, and central theme, in a series of important speeches which he delivered to leaders of German industry and finance at various times during the life of the Weimar Republic. Thus in his speech to the Hamburg '1919 National Club', made on February 28, 1926 before leading right-wing politicians and businessmen of the city, Hitler outlined his view of the causes of Germany's defeat in the First World War, the most important being the existence of the SPD:

* i.e. of Marxism.

On that day when a Marxist movement was allowed to exist
alongside the other political parties the death sentence was passed
on the Reich. . . Already in 1870-71 there was put forward the
Marxist opposition to the national preservation of the Reich at
the end of the then war.* This opposition was ignored as only
three men were involved. Nobody grasped the greater significance
that it was in fact possible for these representatives of a movement to dare to come out against national defence . . . It appeared
to be overcome without danger . . . the success of the war led to
the belief that the ideas of these three men had been defeated . . .
Then there were the so-called election victories of the bourgeois
parties, often resulting in a loss of votes by the Left, but never a
reduction in their support. There was perhaps an exception in the
period of the socialist legislation, which was later dismantled.
They had cut down the number of social democratic supporters,
or so it seemed. Then as soon as the anti-socialist laws were
repealed as unpracticable, these numbers automatically grew
again . . . [16]

In other words, Bismarck had driven the Marxists underground, but he had not broken their will to fight, or severed
their links with the masses. Neither had he succeeded in
counterposing an alternative and combative 'social' ideology
to the programme, principles and theory of the banned party.
Hitler was determined not to make the same mistake. And here
again we must quote at length from Hitler's autobiography
written, it should always be remembered, a full eight years
before his movement seized power:

Any attempt to combat a philosophy with methods of violence
will fail in the end, unless the fight takes the form of an attack
for a new spiritual attitude. Only in the struggle between two
philosophies can the weapon of brutal force, persistently and
ruthlessly applied, lead to a decision for the side it supports.
This remains the reason for the failure of the struggle against
Marxism. This was why Bismarck's socialist legislation finally
failed and had to fail, in spite of everything. Lacking was the
platform of a new philosophy for whose rise the fight could have
been waged. For only the proverbial wisdom of high government
officials will succeed in believing that drivel about so called "state
authority" or "law and order" could form a suitable basis for the
spiritual impetus of a life and death struggle. Such a real
spiritual basis for this struggle was lacking. Bismarck had to en-
trust the execution of his socialist legislation to the judgement and
desires of that institution which itself was a product of Marxist
thinking. By entrusting the fate of his war on the Marxists to the
well-wishing of bourgeoies democracy, the Iron Chancellor set
the wolf to mind the sheep. All this was only the necessary consequence of the absence of a basic new anti-Marxist philosophy
endowed with a stormy will to conquer . . . [17]

---

* The Franco-Prussian War of 1870, opposed by the SPD after the annexation
of Alsace and Lorraine.

Thus, arising out of the negative as well as positive experiences of Bismarck's anti-socialist legislation was the lesson drawn by Hitler that the masses can never be mobilised on behalf of reaction under the banner of defending the status quo. Hence the unavoidable need for slogans and programmes of a 'socialist' and even, when the situation demanded it 'revolutionary' hue. Not that Bismarck had considered such a strategy, and then rejected it in favour of his police-parliamentary methods. The option had not even arisen, save in the appearance of a handful of anti-semitic agitators during the middle period of Bismarck's rule. And these he treated with a truly patrician scorn as contemptible plebeian rabble rousers, little better than the Marxists they claimed to be fighting. Hitler therefore set out three main desiderata of a successful counter-revolutionary movement. It must set out to win broad layers of the masses to its side by employing social demagogy on the broadest and most uninhibited scale; it must not shrink from using the most extreme methods of violence to cow its opponents, and finally, it must spurn the pussy-footing methods of bourgeois parliamentary democracy like the plague. These were the three lessons which Hitler drew from the failure of Bismarck's war against German socialism. They also comprise when allied to an all pervading nationalism, the main components of Nazi political strategy. To use an Hegelian construction, the German social democrats 'negated' Bismarck's anti-socialist laws, and for the next 14 years experienced a period of almost continuous organisational and electoral growth. But since the political and theoretical implications of this 'negation', with all its contradictory elements, were not plumbed to their depths by the leaders of the victorious party a process set in which began to undermine it. In turn, the betrayal of German social democracy in 1914 and 1918-19 enabled reaction to regroup its forces under a new banner, a movement which based itself on the lessons of the Bismarck period, finally 'negated' German social democracy, and with it, the flower of the entire proletariat. This proves the philosophical truth that dialectical development proceeds by regression as well as progression, and that the degree of regression is in its turn not an automatic reflex of social-economic conditions, but also bound up with how deeply the leadership of the workers movement is able to extract from its own experiences and those of others the dangers as well as the revolutionary possibilities created by a defeat of the class enemy. Bismarck's law of 1878 ended up in the Reichstag dustbin* but so, 55 years later, did the SPD. And that, perhaps, is the most important lesson of all.

---

* Attempts to crush German labour did not end with the fall of Bismarck's anti-

REFERENCES FOR CHAPTER FOUR

[1] F. Engels: Preface to *The Peasant War in Germany*, p.32.
[2] Ibid, pp.32-33.
[3] Ibid, p.33.
[4] K. Marx: *Critique of the Gotha Programme* (1875) in *Marx-Engels Selected Works*, Vol. II, p.27.
[5] Ibid, p.27.
[6] Ibid, p.32.
[7] Ibid, pp.32-33.
[8] F. Engels: Letter to W. Bracke, London, May 5, 1875, in Ibid, p.16.
[9] Ibid, p.16.
[10] F. Engels: Letter to A. Bebel, London, March 18-28, 1875, in Ibid, pp.42-43.
[11] F. Engels: Letter to F. Mehring, London, July 14, 1893. *Marx-Engels Selected Correspondence*, p.497.
[12] K. Marx and F. Engels: *Circular Letter*, London, September 17-18, 1879, *Selected Correspondence*, p.395.
[13] Speech in Reichstag debate on The Strike Decree, May 21, 1886.
[14] F. Engels: *Introduction: The Class Struggles in France* (London, March 6, 1895) in *Marx-Engels Selected Works*, Vol. 1, p.136.
[15] A. Hitler: *Mein Kampf*, pp.154-155. (1943 edition).
[16] Translated from Werner Jochman: *Im Kampf um die Macht, Hitlers Rede vor dem Hamburger Nationalklub von 1919*, Frankfurt, 1960.
[17] A. Hitler, ibid, pp.172-173.

socialist legislation. In 1894, Kirdorf and Stumm headed an industrial alliance to secure the passing of their so-called 'Umsturzorlage' or 'anti-revolution' bill. They even succeeded in deposing Chancellor Count Caprivi, whom industry regarded as being too soft on labour, and installing in his place Prince Hohenloe, who supported the bill. And although it failed to win a majority in the Reichstag, the Ruhr barons continued to press for legislation restricting the right to strike. They returned to the offensive three years later, when the support of the Kaiser, they introduced a new bill, the 'Penal Servitude Bill' which in the words of Count Possadowksy, the German Home Secretary, sought to 'give those who are willing to work better protection against the terrorism of strikers and agitators'. Earlier in 1897, none other than the Kaiser, that self-proclaimed 'king of the beggars', declared in a speech that 'the heaviest punishment should be meted out to the man who is audacious enough to hinder his fellow-man from working when he desires to do so'. Shortly after the bill was defeated in the Reichstag, it came to light that the government had accepted a secret donation of 12,000 marks from industry to publish printed propaganda against the trade unions and the right to stroke. Only a massive nationwide counter offensive by the SPD and the trade unions compelled wavering elements in the Reichstag to vote the bill down on its second reading.

Chapter Five
THE IMPERIALIST CRUCIBLE

I employ the word "State"; it is easy to see what I mean — a band of blonde beasts, a race of conquerors and masters organised for war and strong enough to organise in their turn, seizing without qualms in their terrible grip a population that is perhaps enormously superior in numbers but that still lacks cohesion...
(Friedrich Nietzsche: *On the Geneology of Morals.*)

'The political structure ...of monopoly capitalism' Lenin wrote in 1916 'is the change *from* democracy to political reaction'.[1] Corresponding, though not directly, immediately or mechanically, to the transition from free capitalist competition ('Manchester capitalism') to monopoly capitalism dominated by the big trusts and banks, is the trend away from classical liberalism and parliamentary democracy towards authoritarian, extra-parliamentary, militarist, Bonapartist or even fascist forms of rule. Lenin, who made this observation six full years before Mussolini's 'March on Rome', had grasped more clearly than any other contemporary workers' leader the political implications for the international labour movement of the imperialist era ushered in by the war of 1914. And it is the only methodological approach which enables us to discover how and why certain ideological and philosophical trends which began to emerge in the middle and late 19th century subsequently crystallised and fused together in the formation of fascist movements in the three main nations of continental Europe — Italy, France and Germany.

In so doing, we must guard against any tendency to simplify and vulgarise the highly complex skein of dialectical relationships which exists between the economic 'base' and the ideological 'superstructure' of capitalist (or indeed any) society. Several of Engels' last letters warn precisely against this eagerness to explain *every* movement and conflict in the realm of ideas by seeking out — or even inventing — an economic or class origin for such phenomena:

According to the materialist conception of history, the *ultimately* determining element in history is the production and reproduction of real life. More than this, neither Marx nor I have ever asserted. Hence if somebody twists this into saying that the economic element is the *only* determining one, he transforms that proposition into a meaningless, abstract, senseless phrase. The economic situation is the basis, but the various elements of the superstructure — political forms of the class struggle and its results, to wit: constitutions established by the victorious class after a successful battle, etc, juridicial forms, and even the reflexes of all these actual struggles in the brains of the participants, political, juristic, philosophical theories, religious views and their further development into systems of dogmas - also exercise their influence upon the course of the historical struggles, and in many cases preponderate in determining their *form*.[2]

Thus far, we can agree with Engels completely. Unless the importance and origin of form is given its due weight, historical materialism, which is the application of *dialectical* materialism to the study of human history and specifically, the struggle of classes, is vulgarised and reduced to mechanical materialism, to a social variant of Newtonian mechanistic physics. But it is only honest to state that when Engels, in his anxiety to combat the mechanist approach, states that "history is made in such a way that the final result always results from conflicts between many individual wills, of which each in turn has been made what it is by a host of particular conditions of life"[3] he introduces a formulation which can weaken the materialist content of the Marxist historical method. True, the *form* in which classes and nations act is through the medium of the "individual will". But the content is the movement of collective material forces, unified in moments of historical crisis and decision through the medium of parties and leaderships to forge and wield a *collective* will. Without such a transition from the molecular and "individual" in periods of relative tranquillity to the united action of millions in situations of profound tension, revolutions would be impossible.*

What Engels says about this problem is, in some ways, almost indistinguishable from Hegel's "cunning of reason" or the "hidden hand" of Adam Smith:

> Thus there are innumerable intersecting forces, an infinite series of parallelograms of forces which give rise to one resultant - the historical event. This may again itself be viewed as the product of a power which works as a whole *unconsciously* and without volition. For what each individual wills is obstructed by everyone else, and what emerges is something that no one willed..."[4]

---

* More in keeping with the historical materialist method is Bukharin's formulation on the same problem: "Marxism teaches us that the historical process... is a necessity. To deduce political fatalism from this doctrine is absurd, for the simple reason that historic events are taking place not outside of but through the will of the people, through the class struggle... The will of the classes is in every instance determined by given circumstances: in this respect it is not at all "free". However, that will becomes in turn a conditioning factor of the historic process". (N. Bukharin: *Imperialism and World Economy* (1915) p.131, London, 1972.)

By so dwelling on the mediating factor in human action, i.e. the ideological residues and their distillation through the individual consciousness, Engels here almost liquidates class action and class consciousness, though that is obviously completely alien to his purpose.* For the proletarian class struggle, the highest form of human action and consciousness, cannot be reduced to a lower form, that of individual actions and wills, even though on an *arithmetic* plane, the class is the sum total of its component individual parts. Hegel's law of the transformation of quantity into quality, developed by Marx (and Engels!) in a materialist fashion, holds that higher forms of motion cannot be reduced to lower, that they contain new opposites, new forms of conflict and tension which are not present in the old.

The reader will, it is hoped, see the relevance of these remarks, not only in the following discussion of the politics of imperialism, but throughout the remainder of the book.

Lenin never fell into the tempting trap of drawing an absolute parallel between imperialism and political reaction. He spoke and wrote only of tendencies and trends, of an overall, but contradictory and oscillating drive of monopoly capitalism to undermine and overturn the most important democratic victories which had been won, under the leadership of an earlier, pre-imperialist bourgeoisie, against the forces of feudalism. He by no means excluded the possibility that, in a given conjuncture of domestic and international forces, an imperialist bourgeoisie could adapt itself to the forms of parliamentary democracy. Thus against those within the international Marxist movement (and also the Russian Bolshevik Party) who argued that since imperialism suppressed all democratic and national rights, there remained little purpose in struggling for them.* Lenin wrote:

> In general, political democracy is merely one of the possible *forms* of superstructure *above* capitalism (although it is theoretically the normal one for "pure" capitalism). The facts show that both capitalism and imperialism develop within the framework of *any* political form and subordinate them *all*. It is, therefore, a basic theoretical error to speak of the "impracticability" of *one* of the forms and of *one* of the demands of democracy.[4]

In fact, the rise of imperialism took place, in the cases of France and England, in countries where parliamentary and democratic traditions had sunk deep roots into the petty-bourgeois and proletarian masses, and where parliamentary institutions had evolved into the customary vehicle for the resolution of political differences within the possessing classes. Therefore the imperialist-oriented sections of the bourgeoisie were, whether

---

* This tendency Lenin dubbed "Imperialist Economism", after the Russian "Economists" who abjured the political struggle against Tsarism as a diversion from the fight for socialism.

they liked it or not, compelled to take these traditions and institut- ions into account when shaping their own political strategy. Not so in Germany, where as we have already noted, democratic traditions were almost entirely lacking in the big and petty bourgeoisie. Added to this of course was the aristocratic contempt felt by the Prussion Junker caste for anything which remotely smacked of popular rule and wide-ranging democratic liberties. The German bourgeoisie therefore not only found itself politically and psychologically pre-disposed towards a con- sistently anti-democratic imperialist policy at home as well as abroad, it encountered scant resistance to such a course amongst any class of the population save the proletariat.

Britain had its highly vocal bourgeois - and even aristocratic - critics of imperialism and colonialism, and the bourgeoisie learned to live with them. They were minor irritants, and only in the war of 1914-18 did they suffer serious persecution for their views. But in Germany, the picture was entirely different. There, the opposition to imperialism, chauvinism, racialism and militar- ism was confined almost exclusively to those workers organised within the SPD and affiliated bodies such as the trade unions.

So it was inevitable that the main offensive of the emergent imperialist bourgeoisie should be directed against social demo- cracy, the movement led by "aliens" and "traitors". As Germany moved into the imperialist epoch and towards the explosion of 1914, the bourgeoisie was faced with two alternative methods of achieving the same political goal. Either it would have to attempt to reimpose a new and far more rigorous version of Bismarck's anti-socialist laws (and now at a time when the SPD numbered millions amongst its supporters), or seek a rapprochement with the more "moderate" and "nationally minded" elements of its leadership. History tells us that it was the second option which won out in 1914. But this should not be allowed to obscure those political forces and ideas which, while pushed to one side in the period of enforced collaboration with social democracy during the world war,* were not only indicative of ultra-reactionary trends inside the German bourgeoisie, but re-emerged with ten- fold vigour and eventual triumph in the final years of the Weimar Republic. However before examining the origin, function and development of these "proto-fascist" ideologists, it will be necessary to discuss briefly the important changes which were

---

* Even this is not strictly true, for it was the war which greatly accelerated the evolution of ultra-chauvinist and anti-socialist groups and ideologists into fully- blown fascism. Thus the "Fatherland Front", a super-patriotic offshoot from the Conservatives founded by industrialists and military leaders to press for a "victor's peace" in the World War, spawned in its turn the Munich-based "German Workers' Party" of Anton Drexler. It was this tiny sect which Hitler joined in 1919 and sub- sequently transformed into the "National Socialist German Workers' Party".

taking place in the economic base of German society.

Lenin and Bukharin, the two principle theoreticians of the Bolshevik Party prior to 1917, only began a serious and detailed study of imperialism after the outbreak of the First World War, yet their works, together with Rosa Luxemburg's *"The Accumulation of Capital"* (1913) remain the most penetrating and politically valuable contributions in this field. Both emphasised the qualitative changes that had taken place in capitalism during the last quarter of the nineteenth century - the transition from "laisser faire" to monopoly capitalism - and understood this as the bedrock of what Marxists term imperialism. We shall employ the works of Lenin and Bukharin on imperialism to illuminate the many and profound economic transformations which were underway in Germany from the 1870s onward, and how they made themselves felt at every level of society.

Lenin denoted five salient features of imperialism. They were, in their order of chronological appearance:

1: the concentration of production and capital has developed to such a high state that it has created monopolies which play a decisive role in economic life; 2: the merging of bank capital with industrial capital, and the creation, on the basis of this "finance capital", of a financial oligarchy; 3: the export of capital as distinguished from the export of commodities acquires exceptional importance; 4: the formation of international monopolist capitalist associations which share the world among themselves, and 5: the territorial division of the whole world among the biggest capitalist powers is completed.[6]

Elsewhere in the same work, Lenin stresses that imperialism, being the highest stage of capitalism, remains subject to its laws of development and that it is therefore, like the preceding capitalism of free competition, always developing at an uneven tempo, both with regard to rival imperialist states and internally vis a vis the various branches of national economy. This is especially true in the case of Germany which, as we have so often had cause to stress, was the "late arrival" on the stage of European capitalism. The "late developer" learnt his economic and technological lessons from his English and French tutors so well and rapidly that by the turn of the century, Germany was in many ways the best prepared of the major imperialist powers to wage a struggle for continental supremacy. Let us see precisely how swift and thoroughgoing this development was. Beginning with Lenin's first ingredient of imperialism, we see that German capitalism pioneered the large-scale transition from competitive to monopoly capitalism, and that it did so in semi-planned fashion. We are referring of course to the emergence of the "Cartel" system within German industry in the early years of the Empire. The initial impulse towards the creation of cartels was undoubtedly the economic crisis which hit German industry and finance in 1873. The largely speculative boom nourished by the French war indemnity collapsed after two years of feverish stock exchange activity and dubious financial transactions, and the leaders of heavy industry especially sought to protect their markets and profits by entering into agreements with concerns operating in the same sphere. Prices were maintained and markets divided up between the major companies to the exclusion of the less powerful, thus greatly accelerating a trend towards concentration already under way as a result of business bankruptcies. Thus by 1877, 14 such cartels had been formed, embracing the coke, pig iron, sheet steel and potash industries. Agreements to restrict production were also common, as in the case of the Rhenish-Westphalian coal-owners, who when faced with a contraction of demand, jointly cut output by 10%. In this way they hoped to - and largely succeeded in - maintaining existing price levels. These working agreements contained within them the seeds of a more permanent union, since they recognised the advantages of large scale, planned production geared to the maximisation of profits. And so, slowly at first, and at an uneven tempo in each sector of industry, firms already organised in cartels began to merge into integrated monopolies, sometimes as in the case of the Rhenish-Westphalian coal syndicate, through the intermediate stage of a marketing union. This process is reflected statistically in the changing ratio of workers employed in large and small-scale enterprises. Thus in 1882, when the cartel system was in its infancy, the number of workers employed in the manufacturing industry was divided almost evenly between large firms on the one hand (166,500) and firms classified as small and medium on the other (189,500). Twenty five years of capital concentration, cartellisation and monopolisation then greatly undermined the position of the small and medium firm. They now employed 231,500 workers, an absolute increase of a mere 65,000, while the labour force of large-scale manufacturers had swollen more than fourfold to 788,800! Taking German industry overall, 0.9% of firms employed 39.4% of Germany's total work force. Capital concentration was even more intense, with 75% of the nation's industrial energy supply being used by these same 0.9% of firms.

By this time - 1907 - the number of cartels had risen to nearly 500, and had embraced every important sector of economy,* This was the period of the formation and consolidation of the industrial giants which little more than two decades later swung their

---

* It is important to note that German technology was far ahead of other nations in several key branches of industry, notably chemicals and electricity production and traction. Monopoly was here the rule from the very outset. A full decade before the outbreak of war, Germany's electrical industry was dominated by two giants: Siemens and AEG. Concentration in chemicals was also well advanced, en route to its consummation in the I.G. Farben monolith of Nazi infamy'.

enormous economic power and political influence behind Hitler. The same is true of the big banks. Established, as we have seen, in the period of reaction following the defeat of 1848, they very quickly became closely involved in the investment policies of German heavy industry, and used their indispensible role as a financier of industry to secure key positions on the boards of the largest concerns. This is, of course, Lenin's second feature of imperialism, the union of banking and industrial capital. The extent of this fusion can be depicted graphically, as can the degree of dominance which banking capital assumed over industry as a consequence of this process.

(Column A denotes the number of firms where the big banks held a place on the managing board, column B the number of bank directors holding such positions, and column C the branch of trade or industry where the bank in question had its strongest interests.)

Bank	A	B	C
Bank fur Handel und Industrie	93	102	Transport, commerce, metal, mining
Berliner	88	100	Ditto
Commerz und Disconto	32	35	Engineering, commerce
Deutsche	1160	128	Metal, mines
Disconto-Gesellschaft	92	126	Ditto
Dresdner	87	102	Mines, engineering, transport, catering
Nationalbank	96	102	Mines, engineering, commerce
Schaffhausen	94	111	Mines, metal, commerce, trade

Several of these banks were later to fuse, finally comprising the "big six" of German finance, but even here, before 1914, we can see the basic economic structure of German imperialism already solidified. Looking more closely at the interests of the banks, we find that the immensely powerful Deutsche Bank (several of whose directors later helped to finance Hitler's bid for power) held important positions on the boards of Siemens and Halkse (electrical) Nordeutscher Lloyd* (shipping) and Oberschlesiche Kokswerke (coke). Moreover, the Deutsche was banker to the giant Krupps concern. The Berliner Handelsgesellschaft was firmly esconced on the board of Siemens' chief rival, AEG, while the Darmstaedter had important interests in the Luxembourg mining industry.

* Also a supporter of the Nazi cause well before 1933.

Looking even more closely at the structure and leadership of German monopoly capitalism in the immediate pre-1914 period, certain highly interesting and significant factors emerge. Firstly, there was the enormous economic power concentrated, not simply in the hands of a trust or bank, but single individuals. In effect, a tiny group of monopoly capitalists, by virtue of their grip on entire sections of industry and finance, exploited and dominated socially, literally millions of German workers. Thus in the Ruhr, the future backer of National Socialism, the coal magnate Emil Kirdorf through his association with the Discontogesellschaft Bank and fellow tycoon Hugo Stinnes employed either directly or indirectly no less than 69,000 of the region's 354,200 miners. Altogether, only ten banking and industrial families accounted for 89.3% of Ruhr coal output! (These ten also included the future Nazi tycoons Thyssen and Krupp). Looked at from the standpoint of the big banks, who held the purse strings of nearly all the large mining concerns, we see that the Deutsche Bank controlled 20 mines employing 72,600 workers and producing 19.3 million tons per year, out of a total 89.3 million tons. No bank could match the Deutsche's degree of penetration into Ruhr coal mining except the Discontogesellleschaft, whose operations were linked with Stinnes* and Kirdorf.

In the other main branch of Ruhr heavy industry - iron and steel production - the same picture emerges. And even the same names, for here too, Thyssen and Krupp were among the leaders of the trust, together with Stumm, Kirdorf and Stinnes. Taken overall, the nerve centres of German monopoly capitalism - the electrical, chemical, mining and steel industries, together with shipping and banking, were ruled, at the outbreak of the First World War, by no more than 13 groups or trusts. And in their turn, these associations were dominated either by single families, as was the case with Stumm, Stinnes, Krupp and Thyssen, or by the biggest banks. The German economy therefore presented the appearance of an inverted pyramid of a few score monopoly capitalists supporting - or rather seeming to support - an immensely broad and variegated industrial, commercial and agricultural base. This economic tyranny could not but have its repercussions in every facet of Germany's political and social life.

For as regards both the process of monopoly concentration and the fusion of industrial with banking capital, Germany had, by the turn of the century, advanced further along the imperialist path than any of its world rivals. But this immense strength at the industrial base did not find an immediate and direct reflection in

---

* Hugo Stinnes, Germany's largest ever industrial tycoon, was sympathetic to Hitler in the months preceeding his abortive "Munich Futsch" of November 1923. He died in 1926.

the external position of German imperialism. And the main reason for this was once again the uneven nature and tempo of world capitalist development. France and England, Germany's two main continental competitors, had already carved out vast colonial empires many decades before capitalism in these countries began its transition into the monopoly stage.*

Whereas in 1876, the British Empire ruled over 250 million colonial subjects, Germany had yet to even stake a claim for its first overseas possession. Everywhere it turned, German capital came up hard against the already firmly established "zones of influence" of either British, French or Russian imperialism. There could be no question of peaceful or evolutionary development towards a position of European predominance commensurate with its burgeoning economic might. Right from the outset, German capitalism was confronted with the stark alternatives: either prepare for war, or accept the status quo and be slowly ground down by the combined pressure of its French, English and Russian enemies.

It is essential to see how this strategic relationship between the major European capitalist powers accentuated the already powerful trend towards reaction within Germany's possessing classes, and how it found a peculiar echo among wide layers of the petty-bourgeoisie. The German bourgeoisie found itself, as it entered the imperialist epoch, fighting a war on two fronts; against the workers' movement, now emerging triumphant and unscathed from its 12 years of illegality under Bismark's anti-socialist laws, and against its foreign capitalist rivals, France, Britain and, to a lesser extent, the United States. Indeed, the first shots in this war had been fired some years before when after a prolonged and at times bitter debate within ruling political and economic circles, Bismarck agreed to institute legislation to protect German industry from foreign competition. And significantly, this change of heart coincided with Bismarck's equally momentous decision to drop his earlier opposition to colonialism, and come out firmly in favour of fighting for Germany's place in the imperial sun. The great concern felt by the bourgeoisie for Germany's weak international position vis a vis the main colonial powers was expressed very cogently by Friedrich Fabri in his *Bedarf Deutschland der Kolonien?* of 1879:

> Should not the German nation, so seaworthy, so industrially and commercially minded hew a new path on the road of imperialism? We are convinced beyond doubt that the colonial question has become a

---

* Contrary to "vulgar" Marxists, and their equally vulgar critics, Lenin never claimed that *colonialism* was the product of capitalism in its monopoly stage. Marx shows in *Capital* how the seizure and exploitation of the first colonies comprised, together with the domestic expropriation of non-bourgeois propertied classes, the phase of early capitalist development described as "primitive capital accumulation".

matter of life or death for the development of Germany. Colonies will have a salutary effect on our economic situation as well as on our entire economic progress.

And in words which were later to become all too familiar for the peoples of Europe, Fabri went on:

If the new Germany wants to protect its newly won position of power for a long time, it must heed its Kultur-mission, and, above all, delay no longer in the task of renewing the call for colonies.

In the same year, on May 2, 1879, Bismarck addressed the Reichstag on the allied question of protection:

...we are slowly bleeding to death owing to insufficient protection. This process was arrested for a time by the five milliards which we have received from France after the war: otherwise we should have been compelled five years ago to take those steps we are taking today... I see that those countries which possess protection are prospering, and that those countries which possess free trade are decaying. Mighty England, that powerful athlete, stepped out into the open market after she had strengthened her sinews, and said, "who will fight me? I am prepared to meet everybody". But England is slowly returning to protection, and in a few years she will take it up in order to save for herself at least the home market.

Fabri and Bismarck here summed up succinctly the problems facing German capitalism on the eve of the imperialist epoch, and in fact correctly indicated the strategy it later adopted to overcome them. In 1885, Bismarck declared a German 'protectorate' in the East African region subsequently known as Tanganyika, and the bid for empire was on. The industrialists of the National Liberal party and agrarians of the Conservatives submerged their political and economic differences in the imperialist-oriented, and anti-socialist 'pact of steel and rye,' which functioned as a parliamentary 'cartel' for all governments up to the outbreak of the First World War. Unity against the working class movement at home, unity in the struggle for domination abroad — this was the driving force of ruling class politics from the mid 1880s onwards. These important policy shifts made themselves felt at every level of German society, and not least amongst intellectuals most closely linked with the bourgeoisie. For to them fell the task of evolving a theoretical justification for the aggressive and dictatorial course upon which the regime had embarked in all fields of policy.

This development reached its nadir with the *Manifesto of the 93 German Intellectuals*, published on the outbreak of hostilities by leading university professors and scientists in support of German imperialism's war aims.* But the subordination of

---

* Written in the spirit of blind chauvinism which characterised nearly all war-time propaganda, it nevertheless also revealed something unique to German bourgeois intellectuals, a quality which the novelist Thomas Mann once aptly called "power-protected inwardness".   "It is not true that the combat against our so-called

'official' intellectual life and cultural activity to the Second Reich began much earlier, and it leaned heavily in its turn on those reactionary, subjectivist and pessimistic trends which had emerged out of the ruins of the classical Hegelian school. In many cases, these philosophers began by regressing to the position adopted by Kant, that the objective world of 'noumena' was by its very nature unknowable (the thing-in-itself) and that mankind was forever limited in his knowledge to the world of appearances, 'phenomena', which were filtered through from the noumenal world by the subjective categories of mental perception: i.e. causality, quantity, quality, etc.

Now while Kant's philosophy marked a clear step forward from the scepticism of the later English empiricists Berkeley (who held an extreme solipsist* position) and Hume, it was also criticised by Hegel for inconsistency in its establishing an arbitrary limit to human knowledge. The contemporary and follower of Kant, Johann Fichte, gave his philosophy a highly humanistic and radical interpretation, holding that since the world existed only through man's perception of it, then it was within his power, through the exercising of his will, to mould the world as he desired. Here the 'will' played a relatively progressive role, as it was the philosophical refraction of the desire by a historically progressive class to create a modern, rationally governed and united German state. But we can see how this same notion of the will underwent a dramatic transformation in the hands of those philosophers who took part in the anti-Hegelian reaction of the 1840s, a movement that was later given added impetus by the political reaction which followed the defeat of the 1848 re-

militarism is not a combat against our civilisation... Were it not for German militarism, German civilisation would long since have been extirpated'. Its signatories were numbered among Germany's intellectual and cultural elites, and included Emil von Behring, Professor of Medecine, Marburg; Prof. Paul Ehrlich, Frankfurt on Main; Fritz Haber, Professor of Chemistry, Berlin; Ernst Haeckel, Professor of Zoology, Jena; Prof. Adolf von Harnack, General Director of the Royal Library, Berlin; Karl Lamprecht, Professor of History, Leipzig; Max Lieberman, Berlin; Max Planck, Professor of Physics, Berlin; Prof. Max Reinhardt, Director of the German Theatre, Berlin; Wilhelm Roentgen, Professor of Physics, Munich, and Gustav von Schmoller, Professor of National Economy, Berlin.

* Subjective idealism carried to its logical conclusion, namely that the external world exists only in so far as the individual perceives it: "That neither our thoughts, nor passions, nor ideas formed by the imagination, exist without the mind is what everybody will allow. And to me it seems no less evident that the various sensations or ideas imprinted on the Sense... cannot exist otherwise than in a mind perceiving them... For as to what is said of the *absolute* existence of unthinkable things, without any relation to their being perceived that is to me perfectly unintelligible. Their *esse* is *percipi* (being is to be perceived); nor is it possible they should have an existence out of the minds or thinking things which perceive them. It is indeed an opinion strangely prevailing amongst men, that houses mountains, rivers, and in a word all sensible objects, have an existence, natural or real, distinct from their being perceived by the understanding." (G. Berkeley: *Principles of Human Knowledge* (1710) in *Berkeley: Selections*, pp.125-126, New-York, 1957)

volution. The main links in this chain, which in fact reaches from the post-Napoleonic reaction to the ideologues of National Socialism, are Arthur Schopenhauer and Friedrich Nietzsche.

How Schopenhauer became instrumental in evolving an utterly reactionary philosophical and political system out of elements of Kantianism can be seen from his most famous work, *The World as Will and Idea*. Written in 1818 when the philosopher was 30 years of age, it explicitly sets out to undermine the prevailing Hegelian influence in Germany, a fact which Schopenhauer openly acknowledged in the preface to the book's second edition, which he wrote in 1844:

> ...my writing bears the stamp of honesty and openness so distinctly on the face of them, that by this alone they are a glaring contrast to those of three celebrated sophists of the post-Kantian period.*

He roundly condemned Hegelian dialectics as 'bombast and charlatanism', and Hegel himself as an 'intellectual Caliban'. (Caliban, derived from a Shakespearian character, denotes someone who is 'degraded and bestial.) Ironically, it was Schopenhauer's subjectivist antidote to Hegelianism which in a later historical epoch, became an integral strand in the web of that greatest bestiality and degradation known to man, National Socialism.

Central to Schopenhauer's philosophy was the repudiation of an external, material world existing prior to and independently of human consciousness. 'Idea' and 'Will' — these were the driving forces of all development:

> It is palpable contradiction to call the will free, and yet to prescribe laws for it according to which it ought to will... it follows from the point of view of our system that the will is not only free, but almighty. From it proceeds not only its action, but also its world; and as the will is, so does its action and its world become... The will determines itself, and at the same time both its action and its world; for besides it there is nothing, and these are the will itself.[8]

So intuition and instinct, rather than analysis, synthesis and reflection, should serve as modes of thought for confronting and understanding reality:

> ...whoever supposes that the inner nature of the world can in any way, however plausibly disguised, be *historically* comprehended, is infinitely far from a philosophical knowledge of the world... The genuine philosophical consideration of the world, i.e., the consideration that affords us a knowledge of its inner nature, and so leads us beyond the phenomenon, is precisely that method which does not concern itself with the whence, the whither, and the why of the world, but always and everywhere demands only the what, the method which considers things not according to any relation, not as becoming and passing away,... but, on the contrary, just that which remains when all that belongs to the form of knowledge proper... has been abstracted, the

* Hegel, Fichte and Schelling.

inner nature of the world, which always appears unchanged in all the relations, but is itself never subject to them, and has the Ideas of the world as its material object or material.[9]

The breakdown of the Hegelian school led, through the material intervention of the German and international working class, to Marxism. The disintegration of Kant's system on the contrary brought forward all those elements within it that left a door ajar for mysticism and extreme subjectivism, the denial of objective, law-governed processes and the material, social basis of human consciousness. Thus empiricism, however 'rational' in its assumptions and method, does not stand at the opposite pole to subjectivism, but can, in certain conditions, pass over into it. And though the work in question does not treat directly with the political implications of Schopenhauer's philosophy, they nevertheless intrude in a disguised form. In discussing the concept of "freedom of the will", Schopenhauer carefully qualifies it when applied to individual human beings:

> ...we must be aware of the error that the action of the individual definite man is subject to no necessity... The freedom of the will as thing-in-itself... does not extend to the rational animal endowed with individual character, i.e., the person. The person is never free although he is the phenomenon of a free will...[10]

How far have we travelled from the bourgeois-revolutionary ideal of the free, rational autonomous individual in a free and rational society where the interests of each coincide with the interests of all. Schopenhauer's political ideas, which are very clearly derived from his subjectivist philosophy, show how profound was the reaction in German intellectual circles against this bourgeois-democratic Utopia. Here too his main target was Hegel, whom as we have previously observed, was profoundly moved and influenced by the philosophical ideals and government principles of the French revolution. Not reason, but brute force, was the means by which men and nations should be governed. He looked with favour on the doctrine of Machiavelli, which Schopenhauer interpreted thus:

> What you wouldn't like done to yourself, do to others. If you do not want to be put under a foreign yolk, take time by the forlock, and put your neighbour under it himself...[11]

And of the notion that the people had the right to choose their own form of government and control its leaders, he wrote:

> The people, it must be admitted, is sovereign; but it is a sovereign who is always a minor. It must have permanent guardians. And it can never exercise its rights itself, without creating dangers of which no one can forsee the end; especially as, like all minors, it is very apt to become the sport of... what are called demagogues.[12]

This thoroughgoing anti-democratic contempt for the masses runs like a thread through all Schopenhauer's political writings, exemplified by his essay on *Government*, from which these extracts have been taken:

...the great mass of mankind, always and everywhere, cannot do without leaders, guides and counsellors, in one shape or another... their common task is to lead the race, for the greater part is incapable and perverse, through the labyrinth of life... That these guides of the race should be permanently relieved of all bodily labour as well as of all vulgar need and discomfort; nay, that in proportion to their much greater achievements they should necessarily own and enjoy more than the common man, is natural and reasonable. Great merchants should also be included in the same privileged class, whenever they make far-sighted preparations for national needs... It is physical force alone which is capable of securing respect. Now this force ultimately resides in the masses, where it is associated with ignorance, stupidity and injustice. Accordingly the main aim of statesmanship in these difficult circumstances is to put physical force in subjection to mental force — to intellectual superiority, and thus to make it serviceable. But if this aim is not itself accompanied by justice and good intentions, the result of the business, if it succeeds, is that the State so erected consists of knaves and fools, the deceivers and the deceived. That this is the case, is made gradually evident by the progress of intelligence amongst the masses, however much it may be repressed; and it leads to revolution... No doubt it is true that in the machinery of the State the freedom of the press performs the same function as a safety valve in other machin-ery... On the other hand, the freedom of the press may be regarded as a permission to sell poison—poison for the heart and the mind. There is no idea so foolish but that it cannot be put into the heads of the ignor-ant and incapable multitude especially if the idea holds out some prospect of any gain or advantage. And when a man has got hold of any such idea, what is there that he will not do? I am, therefore, very much afraid that the danger of a free press outweighs its utility... A peculiar disadvantage attaching to Republics... is that in this form of government it must be more difficult for men of ability to attain high position and exercise direct political influence than in the case of monarchies. For always and everywhere and under all circumstances there is a conspiracy, or instinctive alliance, against such men on the part of all the stupid, the weak, and the commonplace; they look upon such men as their natural enemies... There is always a numerous host of the stupid and the weak and in a republican constitution it is easy for them to suppress and exlude the men of ability... They are fifty to one; and here all have equal rights at the start. In a monarchy, on the other hand, this natural and universal league of the stupid against those who are possessed of intellectual advantages is a one-sided affair; it exists only from below, for in a monarchy talent and intelli-gence receive a natural advocacy and support from above... intelligence has always under a monarchical government a much better chance against its irreconcilable and ever-present foe, stupidity and the advantage which it gains is very great... In general, the monarchical form of government is that which is natural to man, just as it is natural to bees and ants, to a flight of cranes, a herd of wandering elephants, a pack of wolves seeking prey in common, and many other animals, all of which place one of their number at the head of the business in hand.* Every business in which men engage... must also be subject to the authority of one commander, everywhere it is one will that must lead. Even the animal organism is constructed on a monarchical principle; it is the brain alone which guides and governs, and exercises the hegemony. Although heart, lungs and stomach contribute much more than the continued existence of the whole body, these philistines cannot on that account be allowed to guide and lead. That is a business which belongs solely to the brain; government must proceed from one central point. Even the solar system is monarchical. On the other hand, a republic is as unnatural as it is unfavourable to the higher intellectual life and the arts and the sciences... How would it be possible that, everywhere and at all times we should see many millions of people... become the willing and obedient subjects of one man... unless there were a monarchical instinct in men which drove them to it, as the form of government best suited to them?...[13]

It is hardly surprising therefore that Schopenhauer should declare himself for a monarchical solution to the problem of German national unification:

> ...if Germany is not to meet with the same fate as Italy, it must restore the imperial crown, which was done away with by its arch-enemy, the first Napoleon, and it must restore it as effectively as possible.[14]

Although Schopenhauer died some four years before Bismarck took the helm of the Prussian state, we would be completely justified in regarding him as Germany's first philosopher of 'blood and iron.' And we can go much further, and indicate the many remarkable points of contact between Schopenhauer's reactionary political ideology and that enunciated by Hitler in his semiautobiographical *Mein Kampf*. Hitler's attack on parliamentary democracy, like that of Schopenhauer, had absolutely nothing in common with the Marxist critique of the same political system. Marx and Lenin stressed time and again that bourgeois democracy, while in its time representing an enormous advance on feudal despotism, still denied the working masses real access to the levers of state power. However wide-ranging the political and social concessions which the bourgeoisie might be obliged to make to the working class either in its struggle against feudalism or as a means of buying temporary class peace from the proletariat, bourgeois democracy remains a form of the dictatorship of big capital. This does not, however, lead Marxists to deny the importance of those political social and economic concessions which the proletariat has wrested from the bourgeoisie. On the contrary, they must be defended strenuously, not only for their own sake, but as those fortified proletarian positions within capitalist society which must serve as powerful material and

---

* Scientific tests have shown that schools of dolphins do not have a "leader" but coordinate their movements by means of highly sophisticated and complex sound signals. And this highly democratic animal is renowned both for its high intelligence (in some ways approaching that of man) and its utterly pacific nature.

moral levers for the overturn of capitalist rule.*

Both Hitler and Schopenhauer, along with an entire range of reactionary German ideologists, instinctively grasped this two-sided nature of bourgeois democracy, and denounced it accordingly. They saw it as a potential doorway to revolution, for it conceded the principle first enunciated in the French Revolution, that the masses are sovereign. Of course, with Hitler, the connections between democratic government and the dangers of socialist revolution are made much more explicit, but this is hardly surprising in view of the fact that unlike Schopenhauer, he had witnessed at first hand German social democracy's skilful exploitation of manhood suffrage and the many varied political freedoms which accompany the existence of parliamentary democracy. Thus he writes:

> The Western democracy of today is the forerunner of Marxism without which it would not be thinkable. It provides this world plague with the culture in which its germs can spread.[15]

And here Hitler develops precisely the same line of argument as Schopenhauer to discredit the notion of popular rule, even under capitalism.

> The Jewish doctrine of Marxism rejects the aristocratic principle of Nature and replaces the eternal privilege of power and strength by the mass of numbers and their dead weight. Thus it denies the value of personality in man, contests the significance of nationality and race, and thereby withdraws from humanity the premise of its existence and culture.[16]

This was the classic programme of German reaction - the elite must assert its right to rule over the "dead weight" of the inert masses, whose only task is to work, fight and obey. And Hitler proceeds to elaborate on this theme at some length and with even more vehemence:

> Isn't the very idea of responsibility bound up with the individual? But can an individual directing a government be made practically responsible for actions whose preparation and execution must be set to the account of the will and inclination of a multitude of men ? Or

---

* In the *Communist Manifesto* Marx and Engels make clear that while in Germany communists "fight with the bourgeoisie wherever it acts in a revolutionary way, against the absolute monarchy, the feudal squirearchy, and the petty-bourgeoisie... they never cease, for a single instant, to instil into the working class the clearest possible recognition of the hostile antagonism between bourgeoisie and proletariat, *in order that the German workers may straightaway use, as so many weapons against the bourgeoisie, the social and political conditions that the bourgeoisie must necessarily introduce along with its supremacy, and in order that, after the fall of the reactionary classes in Germany, the fight against the bourgeoisie itself may immediately begin.*" (K. Marx and F. Engels: *Manifesto of the Communist Party*, in *Selected Works*, Vol. I, pp.64-65; (emphasis added). Whether Hitler, Schopenhauer or Nietzsche had ever read these lines is not important. They were well aware of the revolutionary implications of a thoroughgoing struggle for bourgeois democracy in Germany.

will not the task of a leading statesman be seen, not in the birth of a creative idea or plan as such, but rather in the art of making the brilliance of his projects intelligible to a herd of sheep and blockheads, and subsequently begging for their kind approval? Is it the criterion of the statesman that he should possess the art of persuasion in as high degree as that of political intelligence in formulating great policies or decisions? Is the incapacity of a leader shown by the fact that he does not succeed in winning for a certain idea the majority of a mob thrown together by more or less savoury accidents? Indeed, has this mob ever understood an idea before success proclaimed its greatness? Isn't every deed of genius in this world a visible protest of genius against the inertia of the mass?... Mustn't our principle of parliamentary majorities lead to the demolition of any idea of leadership? Does anyone believe that the progress of this world springs from the mind of majorities and not from the brain of individuals... By rejecting the authority of the individual and replacing it by the numbers of some momentary mob, the parliamentary principle of majority rule sins against the basic aristocratic principle of nature...[17]

Here, derived from the philosophic tradition pioneered by Schopenhauer, with its reliance on pseudo-scientific parallels from the world of nature, is a worked-out system of counter-revolution and naked dictatorship over the masses, who are derided variously as "sheep", "blockheads", "mob" and "inert". Hitler's ideal was a regime which paid absolutely no attention to the desires or feelings of the masses, and which put down with ruthless severity any attempt to challenge its authority. Such a system of government Hitler chose to call "truly Germanic democracy" in which once its leader is elected, "there is no majority vote on individual questions, but only the decision of an individual who must answer with his fortune and his life for his choice".[18]

Hitler's views on "genius" are also remarkably similar to those of Schopenhauer, betraying the same contempt for the vast majority of mankind unable to rise to the same heights - or rather sink to the same depths - as the so-called gifted few. This elitism also became the point of departure for Nietzsche's evolution from a highly gifted writer into a bitter foe of democracy and socialism. Schopenhauer says of genius that it distinguishes "the countless millions who use their head only in the service of their belly" and "those very few and rare persons who have the courage to say: No! it is too good for that; my head shall be active only in its own service; it shall try to comprehend the wondrous and varied spectacle of this world, and then reproduce it in some form, whether as art or as literature, that may answer to my character as an individual. These are the truly noble, the real *noblesse** of the world. The others are serfs and go with the soil. Great minds, of which there are scarcely one in a hundred millions, are thus the

* Aristocracy.

lighthouse of humanity; and without them mankind would lose itself in the boundless sea of monstrous error and bewilderment"[19]

On this theme, the equally anti-Hegelian Nietzsche wrote:

> ...the hope is that with the preservation of so many blanks one may also protect a few in whom humanity culminates. Otherwise it makes nonsense at all to preserve so many wretched human beings. The history of the state is the history of the egoism of the masses and of the blind desire to exist; this striving is justified to some extent only in the geniuses, inasmuch as they can thus exist. Individual and collective egoisms struggling against each other - an atomic whirl of egoisms - who would look for aims here? Through the genius something does result from this atomic whirl after all, and how one forms a milder opinion concerning the senselessness of this proceedure...[20]

And here too we find, in an even more explicit and violent form, Schopenhauer's contempt for the masses, which with Nietzsche, who wrote with the example of the Paris Commune present in his mind, assumed the proportions of an all pervading fear of revolution:

> I simply cannot see what one proposed to do with the European worker now that one has made a question of him. He is far too well off not to ask for more and and more, not to ask for more immodestly. In the end, he has numbers on his side. The hope is gone for ever that a modest and self-sufficient kind of man... might develop here as a class... But what was done? Everything to nip in the bud even the pre-condition for this... The worker was qualified for military service, granted the right to organise and to vote: is it any wonder that the worker today experiences his own existence as distressing?... 'If one wants an end, one must also want the means: if one wants slaves, then one is a fool if one educates them to be masters.[21]

What was implicit in Schopenhauer now becomes explicit in his most dedicated follower. The crucial factor in this transition was not the more morbid or unstable personality of Nietzsche, nor even the progressive internal degeneration of a reactionary idealist philosophical school, but rather the intervention of the German and international proletariat as force in its own right. Nietzsche's reaction to the rise of the German workers' movement was, in fact, a brilliant negative verification of the immortal words of Karl Marx written, ironically, in the year of that avowed anti-Hegelian's birth:

> ...theory... becomes a material force as soon as it has gripped the masses... Philosophy cannot be made a reality without the abolition of the proletariat, the proletariat cannot be abolished without the philosophy being made a reality.[22]

Theory had gripped the German working class and raised it from an inarticulate and unorganised mass to a movement, despite the repressions of Bismarck, numbering millions. *This* was the force that Nietzsche, like so many German bourgeois intellectuals feared above all else. The 'will to power' was the will and desire to rule and exploit the proletariat without mercy. Hence Nietzsche's anger with those governments who out of a mistaken sense of political finesse, conceeded to the workers the right to be treated as other citizens. If one teaches a worker how to use a gun, allows him to organise in parties and unions, and then permits him to vote for leaders of his own choice, then the worker is being permitted to forge the weapons which can transform him from a slave into a master. In other words, the bourgeoisie was simply committing class suicide. And this, as we shall see, was the central theme of Hitler's critique of political currents prevailing in the German ruling class in the period prior to the crisis of 1929. We also find in Nietzsche, as in so many of the philosophical antecedents of national socialism, a craving for rigidly hierarchical society based on the now familiar elitist principles of 'genius' and 'will':

> The *order of castes*, the supreme, the dominant law, is merely the sanction of a *natural order*... over which no arbitrariness, no 'modern idea' has any power. In every healthy society there are three types which condition each other and gravitate differently physiologically; each has its own hygiene, its own field of work, its own sense of perfection and mastery. Nature, not Manu*, distinguishes the pre-eminently spiritual ones, those who are pre-eminently strong in muscle and temperament, and those, the third type, who excel neither in one respect nor in the other, the mediocre ones—the last as the great majority, the first as the elite. The highest caste—I call them *the fewest— being perfect, also has the privileges of the fewest: among them, to represent happiness, beauty and graciousness on earth... The most spiritual men, as the strongest,* find their happiness where others would find their destruction: in the labyrinth, in hardness against themselves and others, in experiments; their joy is self-conquest... They rule not because they want to but because they *are*; they are not free to be second. The *second:* they are the guardians of law, those who see to order and security, the noble warriors, and above all the king as the highest formula of warrior, judge, and upholder of the law... The order of castes, the *order of rank*, merely formulates the highest law of life; the separation of the three types is necessary for the preservation of society, to make possible the higher and then the highest types. The *inequality* of rights is the first condition for the existence of any rights at all.[23]**

---

* Hand.

** Here the reader can compare Nietzsche's conception of a society rigidly ordered along hierarchical lines with that of Hitler:

"Organising the broad masses of our people which are today in the international camp into a national people's community does not mean renouncing the defence of justified class interests. *Divergent class and professional interests are not synonymous with class cleavage, but are natural consequences of our economic life. Professional grouping is in no way opposed to a true national community, for the latter consists in the unity of a nation in all those questions which affect this nation*

Nietzsche went further than sketching the outlines and principles of his reactionary utopia, which in several ways was a crude plagiarism of Plato's 'Republic'. It also signposted the road towards the future fascist strategy of securing a basis for their policies and regime in the many-millioned petty-bourgeoisie and aristocracy at the one pole and the industrial proletariat at the other. Nietzsche, as the following extract shows, had begun to grasp one of the essentials of this strategy: namely, that in the era of the masses, the old-style absolutism was utterly unable to repress the rising workers' movement. Thus his already quoted remark that 'in the end', the worker 'has numbers on his side.' Mass must be pitted against mass, and for this, a wide layer of the population must be given either a real or illusory stake in the status quo.

> A culture is a pyramid: it can stand only on a broad base: its presupposition is a strong and soundly consolidated mediocrity. Handicraft, trade, agriculture, *science*, the greatest part of art, the whole quintessence of *professional* activity... the instinct required here would contradict both aristocratism and anarchism.[25]

Standing between the ruling elite, the "aristocrats" of "genius", and the "rabble" - Nietzsche's third caste - is therefore the "soundly consolidated mediocrity" of the petty bourgeoisie, ranging from government officials, professional workers, scientists and artists, to its lowermost reaches: among the artisans, shopkeepers and farmers. It is this class, multifarious in its sub-divisions but capable of great homogeneity in political questions when reaction holds sway, that was to serve as the base of Nietzsche's capitalist "pyramid". And this strategically important counterweight to the menace of the "rabble" must be courted and flattered accordingly, very much after the style of the later fascist demagogues:

> To be a public utility, a wheel, a function, for that one must be destined by nature: it is not *society*, it is the only kind of *happiness* of which the great majority are capable that makes intelligent machines of them. For the mediocre, to be mediocre is their happiness; mastery of one thing, specialisation - a natural instinct.[26]

These supports of the aristocratic apex are happy in their mediocrity - such is the cynical view Nietzsche takes of them. But it would not do to treat them publicly as such:

> It would be completely unworthy of a more profound spirit to consider mediocrity as such an objection. In fact, it is the first necessity if there are to be exceptions: a high culture depends on it. When the exceptional human being treats the mediocre more tenderly than himself and his peers, this is not mere politeness of the heart - it is his simple duty.[27]

as such.' (A. Hitler: *Mein Kampf*, p.339 - emphasis added) So the "national people's community" accepted as "natural" the existence of class divisions. So much for Hitler's "socialism"!

We can better understand the elitist Nietzsche's toleration of "mediocrity" when we turn to his overt expressions of hatred for and fear of socialism which were, as we have already noted, far more clearly articulated than was the case with Schopenhauer, who died three years before the formation of the German socialist movement and eleven years before the Paris Commune:

> Whom do I hate most among the rabble of today? The socialist rabble, the chandala apostles, who undermine the instinct, the pleasure. The workers' sense of satisfaction with his small existence — who make him envious, who teach him revenge. The source of wrong is never unequal rights but the claim of "equal" rights.[28]

At this juncture we should refer to Nietzsche's tendency to lump together and then denounce Christianity with socialism, or what he sometimes calls "anarchism". He saw them as linked ideologies and movements in that they both advocated a world free from violent or repressive social relations*, and espoused the cause of the weak and poor and against the rich and powerful. Both were therefore branded and condemned as spokesmen of the "rabble" and enemies of "genius":

> What is *bad*?... all that is born of weakness, of envy, of revenge. The anarchist and the Christian have the same origin... One may posit a perfect equation between *Christian* and *anarchist*: their aim, their instinct, are directed only toward destruction... [Nietzsche cites as proof of the Christian "instinct toward destruction" the decline and disintegration of the Roman Empire after its rulers embraced the faith]. The Christian and the anarchist: both decadents, both incapable of having any effect other than disintegrating, poisoning, withering, blood-sucking, both the instinct of mortal hatred against everything that stands in greatness, that has duration, that promises life a future.

In fact Nietzsche's critique of Christianity led him directly to his celebrated cult of the 'superman' with his irresistible and utterly amoral 'will to power':

> What is good? Everything that heightens the feeling of power in man, the will to power, power itself. What is bad? Everything that is born of weakness. What is happiness? The feeling that power is *growing*, that resistance is overcome. Not contentedness but more power; not peace but war, not virtue but fitness... The weak and the failures shall perish: first principle of *our* love of man. And they shall be given every possible existence. What is more harmful than any vice? Active pity for all the failures and all the weak: Christianity.

Repudiating the Christian message of the 'meek inheriting the earth' Nietzsche called instead for the creation of a new race of supermen to rule over and exploit the socialist-led 'rabble'.

> what type of man shall be *bred*, shall be *willed,* for being higher in value, worthier of life, more certain of a future? Even in the past this

---

* This is, of course, Nietzsche's, and not the author's, conception of Christianity.

higher type has appeared often—but as an accident, as an exception, never as something *willed*. In fact, this has been the type most dreaded—almost the dreadful—and from dread the opposite type was willed, bred, and attained: the domestic animal, the herd animal, the sick animal—the Christian.[30]

Is this so far removed from the pagan cults of Himmler's SS and the rambling anti-Christian, but equally mystical diatribes of Rosenberg—or indeed, the selective breeding indulged in at Nazi stud farms by blond and blue eyed SS stallions?

And we should also mark well his use of the term 'decadent'* to denote political, philosophical or cultural trends which undermined the rise and rule of the 'superman.' It was taken over, first by Hitler in his attacks on what he termed 'cultural Bolshevism' and then ironically, by the 'Bolshevik' but in reality counter-revolutionary Stalinist bureaucracy to slander modernist cultural tendencies in the Soviet Union or the capitalist world which clashed with the official cannons of 'socialist realism.'

Another target of Nietzsche's invective is the French revolution, with its attendant schools of rationalist and material-ist philosophy. Here his *bete noire* is that ardent champion of 'liberty, equality and fraternity', Jean-Jacques Rousseau, whom he vilified as:

> this first modern man, idealist and rabble** in one person—one who needed moral 'dignity' to be able to stand his own sight, sick with un-bridled self-contempt... I still hate Rousseau in the French Revolution: it is the world-historical expression of this duality of idealist and rabble. The bloody farce which became an aspect of the Revolution, its 'immorality', are of little concern to me what I hate is its Rousseauan *morality*—the so-called 'truths' of the Revolution through which it still works and attracts everything shallow and mediocre. The doctrine of equality! There is no more poisonous poison anywhere...[31]

This total rejection of bourgeois rationalism and humanism nec-essarily led Nietzsche to an equally final rupture with the moral philosophy of Kant, notwithstanding those subjectivist notions which he had, partly via Schopenhauer, inherited from the author of the maxim 'act as though you would create a moral law for all men'. Thus he writes

> Did not Kant find in the French Revolution the transition from the inorganic form of the state to the *organic*? Did he not ask himself

---

* E.g.: "The Christian and the anarchist are both decadents. When the Christian condemns, slanders and besmirches 'the world', his instinct is the same as that which prompts the socialist worker to condemn, slander, and besmirch *society*. The 'last judgment' is the sweet comfort of revenge - the revolution, which the socialist worker also awaits, but conceived a little further off." (F. Nietzsche, *Twilight of the Idols*, in *The Portable Nietzsche*, p.535.)

** In his literary masterpiece *Thus Spoke Zarathustra*, Nietzsche likens "the rabble" to pigs, with "grinning snouts and the thirst of the unclean".

whether there was any event which could be explained only in terms of a moral disposition of mankind, an event which would demonstrate once and for all the "tendency of mankind toward the good"? Kant's answer: "This is the Revolution". The instinct which errs without fail, *anti-nature* as instinct, German decadence as philosophy - *that is Kant!*[32]

And so we could go on, citing example after example of how, in a variety of ways, Nietzsche both anticipated much of the ideology of German fascism, and also helped to shape it. Thus while openly contemptuous of the state of German politics under Bismarck, he nevertheless sang the virtues of "iron and blood" politics, both in relation to domestic affairs, where his demand was for a ruthless dictatorship, and in foreign policy, which he saw as simply a preparation for war. By "freedom" (and what reactionary ideologue or politician has not waged his battles in its name) Nietzsche explicitly meant the freedom of the few to tyrannise the many. This idea runs like a thread through all his major writings and even his private notes:

> ...what is freedom? That one has the will to assume responsibility for oneself. That one maintains the distance which separates us. That one becomes more indifferent to difficulties, hardships, privation, even to life itself. That one is prepared to sacrifice human beings for one's cause, not excluding oneself. Freedom means that the manly instincts which delight in war and victory dominate over other instincts, for example those of "pleasure"...[33]

And elsewhere, he writes: "I welcome all signs that a more manly, a warlike age is about to begin, an age which, above all, will give honour to valor once again".[34] Nietzsche saw the question of war and colonial conquest, as did the English imperialist Cecil Rhodes*, as very much related to the fight against revolution at home:

> Do your ears ring from the pipes of the socialistic pied pipers, who want to make you wanton with mad hopes?... until this waiting turns into hunger and thirst and fever and madness, and finally, the day of the *bestia* triumphans rises in all its glory? Against all this, everyone should think in his heart: sooner emigrate and in savage fresh regions seek to become *master* of the world... but no more of this indecent serfdom, no more of this becoming sour and poisonous and conspiratorial... the workers... should introduce an era of vast swarming out from the European beehive the like of which has never been experienced, and with this act of emigration in the grand manner protest against the

---

* In 1895, Rhodes told his friend, the journalist W. Stead: "I was in the East End of London yesterday and attended a meeting of the unemployed. I listened to wild speeches, which were just a cry for "bread! bread!" and on my way home I pondered over the scene and I became more than ever convinced of the importance of imperialism... My cherished idea is a solution for the social problem, i.e. in order to save the 40 million inhabitants of the United Kingdom from a bloody civil war, we colonial statesmen must acquire new lands to settle the surplus population... If you want to avoid civil war, you must become imperialists" (quoted in V. Lenin: *Imperialism, the Highest Stage of Capitalism, Collected Works*, Vol. 22, pp.256-257).

machine, against capital*, and against the choice with which they are now threatened, of becoming *of necessity* either slaves of the state or slaves of a revolutionary party. Let Europe relieve itself of the fourth part of its inhabitants... What at home began to degenerate into dangerous discontent and criminal tendencies will, once outside, gain a wild and beautiful naturalness, and be called heroism...[35]

We are in no sense arguing that the political ideology evolved by Nietzsche in the Bismarckian era corresponded in every respect either to that of national socialism or indeed, the outlook of the German bourgeoisie. For very much to his credit, Nietzsche went completely against the prevailing anti-semitic trend in reactionary circles by coming out firmly in defence of the Jews. When his sister became involved in the activities of the German anti-semites, he wrote to her:

> Your association with an anti-semitic chief expresses a foreignness to my whole way of life which fills me again with ire or melancholy... It is a matter of honour with me to be absolutely clean and unequivocal in relation to anti-semitism, namely, *opposed* to it, as I am in my writings...[36]

And, in another direction, we can see that his frontal attack on Christianity could alienate him from bourgeois, petty-bourgeois and Junker circles which would otherwise have embraced his political ideas with very few reservations. But here, even here, Nietszche's barbs struck home, for his onslaughts on the pacifist-humanist interpretation of Christianity were partially echoed in the turn of extreme reaction in Germany towards what was euphemistically called "positive Christianity", a creed that adapted itself with the greatest facility to militant chauvinism, militarism, unbridled anti-semitism and even paganism!**

It would be the greatest folly to imagine that the political ideas articulated by Nietzsche were the property only of a small circle of isolated intellectuals. The collapse of genuine liberalism in Germany under Bismarck threw entire generations of students, writers and scientists into the arms of the most extreme reaction, and at precisely a time when the rise of the workers' movement and the growth of colonialist tendencies in Germany's foreign policy were posing political decisions point-blank to all intellectual strata between the proletariat and the big bourgeoisie. The case of Bismarckian Germany's most celebrated historian, Heinrich von Treitschke, is highly instructive here. Treitschke was an utterly committed scholar, being not only a Reichstag deputy but an ardent propagandist in his earlier years for the cause of

---

* Shades of Nazi "ruralism"!

** Point 24 of the founding Nazi Party programme declared its support for "positive Christianity", but did not "bind itself in the matter of creed to any particular confession. It combats the Jewish-materialist spirit within and without us..."

German unity. This was the period of his liberalism, of his opposition to Bismarck's undemocratic and arrogant disdain for parliamentary conventions and proceedures. But since Treitschke was, like so many of his ilk, a nationalist first and foremost, he rapidly made his peace with Bismarck once it became clear that no other force could unify Germany. From this time on, which dates from the mid-1870s, von Treitschke, became a spokesman for the most reactionary elements of the big bourgeoisie, dabbling not only in extreme chauvinism but even anti-semitism. In this sense, he was closer to the pulse of German imperialism than Nietzsche, whose social and political ideas he otherwise shared. Treitschke's onslaught on Marxism, *Socialism and its Sympathisers*, written in 1874, was directed not only against the fledgling workers' movement, but those within the liberal camp who were not prepared to sanction an all-out war of extermination upon it. Universal suffrage was denounced as a sin almost commensurate with that of socialising private property. And he also made the by now familiar claim that "class rule... follows from the nature of society as the contrast between rulers and ruled follows from the nature of the State..." But what predominates is fear of revolution. Awarding the vote to the workers had

immeasurably encouraged the fantastic over-estimation of their own power and their own value among the masses. The irreconcilable contrast between the democratic equality of political suffrage and the necessary aristocratic structure proves to the dissatisfied little man with all possible clarity the social decadence* of the present and makes him a credulous dupe of demagogues... universal suffrage means organised ignorance, the revolt of the soldier against his officer, of the journeyman against his master, of the worker against his employer.

Social democracy, railed Treitschke, consisted of nothing else but "envy and greed". Marxism's "doctrine of the injustice of society destroys the firm instincts that the worker has about honour, so that fraud and bad and dishonest work are scarcely held to be reprehensible any longer..." This is, almost word for word, the credo of Krupp, Stumm *et al,* as is the assertion that

such a crudely materialist doctrine can know no fatherland, can know no respect for the personality of the national state. The idea of nationalism, the moving force of history, in our century, remains incompatible with socialism. Socialism is everywhere in league with unpatriotic cosmopolitanism** and with a weakness of loyalty toward the state.

---

* And again!

** Another term from the vocabulary of reaction later appropriated by Stalinism. As was the case with Treitschke and his nationalist contemporaries, it was used in the immediate post-1945 period in the Soviet Union to denote Jews who were deemed disloyal to the state. The obligatory term was "cosmopolitans without kith or kin", as in the editorial of *Questions of History*, no.2, 1949, entitled *On the Tasks of Soviet*

Trade unionism was singled out as a particularly pernicious enemy of "national" Germany, not least because it excluded employers from membership! Its only aim was to "inflame class hatred to fury, getting people unaccustomed to loyalty during their work, of confusing the masses in their adherence to the law by breaches of contract which occur in every cessation of work..." Now the ascendancy of views such as those canvassed by Treitschke and Nietzsche among wide segments of the upper and middle bourgeoisie in the final quarter of the 19th century was, without the least doubt, related both to economic and political developments within Germany and the heightening of the contradiction already referred to between Germany's industrial strength and its position of relative backwardness as an imperialist power.

1873 marked a turning point and watershed in German rightwing politics. It was not only the year of intensified propaganda against social democracy and demands for its supression, but a year of profound economic crisis for every section of the propertied classes. Beginning in Austria and New York, a banking and industrial crisis spread rapidly to Germany, where it found hordes of Junkers, bourgeois and even petty-bourgeois engaged in an orgy of speculation on the Berlin stock exchange with inflationary money originating in the indemnity levied on France after the defeat of its armies in the war of 1870. Numerous speculative firms collapsed overnight, including real estate, railway, building, banking and brewing companies. Of 50 real estate businesses established in Berlin between 1871 and 1873, only seven survived. The petty-bourgeois would-be-parvenus were thrown into utter disarray by the cruel dashing of all their hopes, and became an easy prey for those with a simple — and traditional — remedy for their distress.* Anti-semitic agitators quickly seized on the involvement of a Jewish financier in the crash - one Henry Bethel Strousberg - to paint a lurid picture of a nation-wide and even international "Jewish conspiracy" to destroy the German

Historians in the Struggle with Manifestations of Bourgeois Ideology, where unabashed great Russian chauvinism is raised to a semi-official cannon of Stalinist ideology:

"A bunch of nationless cosmopolitans have been preaching a national nihilism hostile to our world view... have slandered the great Russian people and have propagated a false assertion about its centuries-old backwardness." Imperialism and Stalinism, though operating from different economic bases, share an intense hatred of internationalism.

* A contemporary report from Austria spoke of the "calamity which overwhelmed the Vienna Bourse... It involved not merely stock-gamblers, but the representatives of every class who had trusted them... and the wild frenzy of the miserable crowd who had assembled when their bubble burst threatened tumult and riot, forcing the bearers of the greatest financial names in the Empire to flee for their lives, compelling the Bourse to temporarily close its doors..." Of the 1,005 joint stock companies formed between 1867 and 1873, more than half folded almost at once.

economy and its industrious burghers. In the uppermost levels of
the bourgeoisie, steps were taken to protect industrial interests
from the worst effects of the crisis by forming cartels and supporting moves in the Reichstag for protectionism. The politically and
economically impotent petty-bourgeois had no such easy access
to the levers of power, and lacked the resources to insulate themselves from the buffetings of a market economy. Neither could the
infant workers' movement hope to attract large numbers of the
middle class and peasantry to its side when it had only just begun
the long and arduous task of organising the industrial proletariat.
So Germany's artisans, ·traders, small businessmen and
professional strata were drawn in their hundreds of thousands
into the trap of those backward-looking, guild oriented solutions
which were prevalent at the time of the 1848 revolution, and
which were consciously fostered by the Junkers as means of
counteracting the political influence of both the bourgeoisie and
the proletariat. Now this same ideology, after slumbering for
more than a decade beneath the surface of German political life,
re-emerged in an entirely new situation, invested with the
viciously sharp cutting edge of anti-semitism.

Let us trace the progression of events from the 1873 crisis. It
was followed in the same year by Bismarck's first speech in
support of protection, and the formation of the first industrial
cartels. Treitschke's already quoted polemic also dates from this
year. Then there ensued a veritable spate of anti-semitic
pamphlets and articles whose central theme was that the Jew,
either in the guise of the banker, money-lender, stock-exchange
manipulator, or workers' leader - was seeking to destroy the
fabric of German society by pitting one class against another. The
prime target of this mythical plot was, of course, the petty-bourgeoisie trapped between the two contending class giants and
threatened with destruction by both. The usurer threatened him
with bankruptcy, the Marxist-led worker with expropriation.
Either way, the argument ran, the middle class was rendered
propertyless and converted into the dreaded and despised
proletarian. 1873 saw the publication of the first of these anti-
Jewish, middle class-oriented tracts, Wilhelm Marr's *The Victory
of Judaism over Teutonism*, which not only coined the term "anti-
semitism" but initiated an infamous *canard* of the Nazi era that
Germany had been converted into a "New Israel" through Jewish
control over its government and press. There then followed in
1874 a book specifically about the crisis of the previous year
entitled *The Stock Exchange and Founding Swindle in Berlin*
by Otto Glakua. Its message, manna to the floundering and
enraged petty-bourgeois speculator with burnt fingers, was that
"Jewish capital" had begun to destroy the middle class, using

liberalism as its political weapon. Other anti-Jewish broadsides from this period included *The Jewish Question* by Eugen Duhring (which claimed that anti-semitism was democratic since it was directed at a minority!), *The Anti-Semitic Catechism* of Theodor Fritsch and, in 1910, Werner Sombart's *The Jews and Capitalism*, which attempted to prove that the Jews pioneered capitalism, and therefore by implication were responsible for its sins. (Sombart's work was later used by the Nazis to embellish their anti-capitalist demagogy). This was also a time for founding anti-Jewish organisations, such as Marr's "Anti-Semitic League" of 1879, which used biblical texts to justify its attacks on Jews, and the Gobineau Society of Ludwig Schemann, named after the French racist ideologist who, it is believed, influenced Hitler and many other Nazi leaders in their evolution towards fanatical hatred of the Jews. But the most significant movement of this period, and one which pointed towards the rise of mass-based counter-revolutionary politics in the imperialist epoch, was Pastor Adolf Stöcker's "Christian Social Party". Stöcker, originally a member of the Conservatives,* enjoyed far-reaching political influence and patronage as Court Chaplain to the Kaiser, and he undoubtedly enjoyed the support of both the monarchy and Bismarck in his initial attempts to woo workers away from the atheistic and internationalist SPD by a clever mixture of anti-capitalist demagogy, anti-semitism and "social" Christianity.

Stöcker—and Bismarck—hoped that the new party would be able to exploit the tremendous difficulties experienced by the SPD as a result of the anti-socialist laws. As it turned out, this strategy, like Bismarck's "State Socialism" proved a total failure, but it did reveal that there was a previously untapped reservoir of support for "social" anti-semitism amongst wide layers of the Germany petty-bourgeoisie. Early in 1880, after repeated attempts to rally the workers of Berlin to the party's banner had failed,** Stöcker dropped all pretences at being a workers' leader and directed his propaganda towards the middle class. A speech from this period warned of the dangers of social democracy in Germany, which he correctly saw as a part of a far larger international revolutionary movement: "Nihilism in the East, the Commune in the West, the whole great revolutionary movement in Germany all show that we in fact are on volcanic ground..."

---

* In early 1880, police reports revealed that less than 20% of this "socialist" party's 1,000 members were workers. They also spoke of "better educated persons" predominating at its public meetings.

** The Conservatives founding programme of 1859 upheld a corporatist view of state and society, opposing what it called "the increasing and destructive Jewish influence in our national life". Note the similarity on this question to point 24 of the Nazi programme.

Such statements were attuned to the nationalist, bitterly anti-Marxist middle class masses of Bismarckian Germany, as was his insistence that, contrary to bourgeois democratic opinion, "social democracy is not just a movement for social reforms... it is a new conception of the world... which once it has taken hold of people prises them away from Christianity, patriotism and German morality... and directs them down a road... which can only lead to an abyss." But it was not enough to attack the workers' movement. The German petty-bourgeoisie, especially those most dependent on the ownership of small property for their livelihood, also feared and detested the power of big business and high finance, and this had to be attacked too if Stöcker's brand of reaction was to win mass support. In the same speech he emphasised that unrest in the working class was not simply the reaction of "evil agitators", but that it was also caused "by the present form of business life, by large industry in combination with free competition, by the alternation of boom and bust". Here we have the age-old yearning of the small producer for the regulated, crisis-free pre-capitalist economy of the guilds. And even though the social and economic conditions which engendered this longing were fast dying away, the mode of consciousness not only lingered but proved itself remarkably adaptable to the political currents of Bismarckian, and subsequently, imperialist Germany.

Yet while functioning as an ideology of capitalism, it necessarily, because of its function as a political diversion for the anti-capitalist petty-bourgeois masses had to take a firm line against the 'excesses' of the big bourgeoisie. Private property must be defended — it was after all the very foundation of middle class existence — but it "carried with it heavy duties, just as wealth carries with it heavy responsibilities. If property abandons the foundations on which it rests... then it is itself conjuring up the dangers of revolt...' Also anticipating the future German fascism, and distinguishing his brand of reaction from that of Treitschke and other advocates of rule by a bourgeois-junker elite, was Stöcker's attempt to steal the clothes of his Marxist opponents by professing a "national" (and therfore utterly spurious) socialism:

> ...the social conception has something to be said for it. For socialism does not mean only the idea of converting all private property into state property, but it contains as well the demand that business life should be made into something social and organic... we can deal with the socialist fantasy of abolishing private property only if we take up very seriously two ideas of socialism. One, to cast economic life in an organic* form and two, to narrow the gap between rich and poor.

Armed with this, for its time, quite sophisticated political demagogy, Stöcker's party, allied with the like-minded "Social

---

* i.e., corporative.

Conservatives", gathered 46,228 votes in Berlin at the Reichstag
elections of 1881. The high point was reached in 1887, with 72,000
votes, and then came the decline of 1890, when Stöcker, now
deprived of much of his previous ruling class support, saw his
party crushed in Berlin by the hated Marxists, who recorded
125,000 votes to his own 34,000. This reverse marked the end of
Stöcker's own political career, but not that of militant anti-
semitism. His pledge, made in 1883, to "offer battle to the Jews
until final victory has been gained" was to be honoured, with
devastating results for all mankind, by his Nazi successors.*

And Stöcker also, despite his fiery anti-capitalist propaganda,
endorsed the same views on work discipline which were con-
currently being advocated by industrial leaders like Krupp,
Stumm and Kirdorf. There was to be "no meddling by the worker
in the technical, financial or economic policy of the enterprise..."
while the employer was to be the "leader" and the workers his
"followers", terms and concepts plagiarised and enforced by Ley's
Labour Front in the Nazi Labour Law of 1934.

Support for Stöcker's ideas reached far beyond his party. In
April 1881, he succeeded in collecting no fewer than 225,000
signatures for an "Anti-semitic Petition" presented to Bismarck
demanding a halt to Jewish immigration from eastern Europe,
their exclusion from teaching and high public office, and a
numerus clausus in schools, universities and the legal profession.
And even more ominously, there were anti-semitic riots and
demonstrations in Berlin and Pommerania, with mobs attacking
synagogues to the chant of "out with the Jews". For the first time
since the middle ages, pogromists ran amok in the streets of
Germany, egged on by a man who enjoyed the confidence of the
highest court and government circles. The long and bloody march
to Auschwitz had begun. Stöcker's reactionary work was carried
on by the Anti-Semite Party, which from a modest 12,000 votes in
1887, rallied 264,000 avowed Jew-baiters to their racialist banner
six years later. The party then lost ground slightly over the next
two elections of 1898 and 1903, only to more than recoup it in the
election of 1912, when 357,000 Germans - mainly artisans,
peasants, shopkeepers and backward, unorganised workers, cast
their votes for a party which boldly proclaimed its intention of
hounding the Jews from public life. Just as in the first months of
the Third Reich, bourgeois Jews sought to deflect this anti-semitic
offensive by proclaiming from the roof tops their loyalty to the
Hohenzollerns, but to little effect. There was scarcely a single
university which did not have its ban on Jewish membership of

* Stöcker was rightly regarded by the Nazis as a pioneer of German fascism, his
memory being celebrated in a biography by Walter Funk which went through several
editions.

student associations, while more than 80% of Wandervogel branches (the mainly petty-bourgeois and highly romantic German youth movement) excluded Jews from their ranks. Our survey of chauvinist and anti-socialist tendencies in Imperial Germany does not end here. Many were the illustrious names of German culture, letters and science who lent their prestige and talents to the cause of extreme reaction, thus helping to render respectable not only militarism and anti-democratic theories, but open racialism. There is the illuminating case of Ernst Haeckel, the celebrated biologist and philosopher whom Lenin, Engels and Plekhanov quoted with approval in polemics against various schools of idealism. But Haeckel's materialism was not enriched by the dialectical method, and as a result, degenerated when applied to social questions, into a most reactionary mystical philosophy. Haeckel's mechanistic outlook led him to utterly negate the active role of human consciousness in historical development, depicting man as a merely transient and passive phenomenon in the totality of the universe. Thus he declared that "the great struggle between the determinist and the indeterminist, between the opponents and the sustainers of the freedom of the will, has ended today, after more than 2000 years, in favour of the determinist". This position is far removed from that of the great Marxist thinkers, who never ceased to stress the dialectical relationship between man and the material world around him. Since man is himself a part of that world - a fragment which being the highest and the most complex product of the process of evolution, is capable of abstract thought through the material organ of the brain — he has the potentiality of discovering through practice the nature of the world outside him, and of changing it in accordance with both natural laws and his own needs. This Haeckel emphatically denied. His was as one-sided a world outlook as that of the subjectivists Schopenhauer and Nietzsche, who erected an entire system on the foundation of the will. And indeed, as is so often the case, these two apparent philosophical extremes merged on the important political questions of the day. Haeckel's rejection of traditional Christianity in the name of science did not lead him to a consistent materialist outlook, but towards a romantic nature worship (pantheism) and the crudest attempts to transpose theories derived from the world of the lower animals to human society* ("Social Darwinism"). How

---

* Just as Schopenhauer and later Hitler, had done. Of mechanical and crude attempts, usually politically motivated, to project Darwin's theory of evolution onto human society, the Italian Marxist pioneer Antonio Labriola wrote: "Darwinism, political and social, has, like an epidemic, for many years invaded the mind of more than one thinker, and many more of the advocates and declaimers of sociology, and it has been reflected as a fashionable habit and a phraseological current even in the

popular this notion was among the German bourgeoisie, currently engaged in a desperate struggle for mastery over both its
internal and external foes is illustrated by the theme set for an
essay competition in 1900. The chosen topic was "What can we
learn from the principles of Darwinism for application to inner
political development and the laws of the State?" The sponsor of
this highly ideological literary event was none other than... Alfred
Krupp! So great was the response from the German intelligentsia
that the essays filled ten large volumes, with the first prize going
to William Schallmayer, a protege of Ernst Haeckel. Some
six years afterwards, Haeckel founded the "Monist League" to
spread his pantheist gospel among German scientists and men of
letters. In politics, it rapidly emerged as a pro-imperialist, anti-
socialist force, employing the language of science to justify the
most blatant dictatorial and racialist views. Haeckel himself once
declared that "woolly haired Negroes are incapable of true inner
culture and of a higher mental development", thereby anticipating
future Nazi "racial science", while the Monist League's vicepresident, Dr. Johannes Unold, justified violence in human
relations in rhetorically asking: "Does not human nature lose its
best character and fall into weakness... when there is general
happiness and a termination of the struggle for existence?" Unold,
who shared Haeckel's elitist prejudices, held that "unlimited
freedom leads to a lack of regard for the minority and the progressive degeneration of the majority." For under democracy, the
"poorest" had power. "Won't they give their approval to those
who charm by their eloquence and win over the masses by
promises." Democracy led to the "exploitation of quality by
quantity, the best by the majority, the fit and the conscientious
by the unfit and the frivolous, the expert by the inexpert, the
prudent by the covetous." Unold was scandalised that the rise of
social democracy in Germany had resulted in a situation where
"the opinion of a 26 year-old labourer can mean as much as that
of a 60 year-old owner of a factory..." The universal franchise had
"restrained and excluded" the political influence of the "educated
and property-owning bourgeoisie, the middle class, which was the
true backbone of every state".

And nothing aroused the ire of German academics more than
the rise of the untutored worker in the historic old cities of
Germany. "Who can justifiably explain" thundered Unold, "that
cities like Munich, Nuremberg and Stuttgart should be represented exclusively by members of the workers' party?"

Haeckel's attacks on socialism and the working class were no

daily language of the politicians." (A. Labriola, *Essays on the Materialist Conception of History*, p.114, New York, 1966.)

less trenchant. In the year of the anti-socialist legislation he poured scorn on the scientific claims of Marxism:

> The equality of individuals which socialism strives after is an impossibility... it stands in fact in irreconcilable contradiction to the inevitable inequality of individuals which actually and everywhere exists... The theory of selection teaches that in human life, as in animal and plant life everywhere... only a small and chosen minority can exist and flourish, while the enormous majority starve and perish miserably and more or less prematurely.*

This last is nothing more nor less than naked justification of imperialism, of "chosen minorities" to conquer and exploit the "enormous majority". And indeed, the German Haeckels and Unolds put their theories into practice as ardent members of numerous patriotic societies, the most important undoubtedly being the Pan-German League. Founded in 1891, it was the most representative and influential of imperial Germany's many nationalist organisations agitating in favour of an aggressive military and colonial policy. (Precursors of the League included the Colonial Society - 1882 - and the Association for German Colonisation - 1884 - fusing in 1887 to form the German Colonial Society). The Pan-Germans not only espoused the cause of all-German unity, a demand which involved the incorporation of all German speaking peoples within a Prussian-dominated "greater Germany", but following this, German imperialist world domination. Just as Nazi domestic political strategy originated in the activities and theories of such racialists as Stocker and anti-Marxist statesman like Bismarck, so too did the Pan-Germans, a thoroughly "respectable" clique of imperialists, father Hitler's foreign policy.**

Leading Pan-Germans included Haeckel of the Monist League, the industrialists Krupp and Kirdorf, Admiral Tirpitz (later a fervent Nazi) and numerous government officials, academics and school teachers. (36% of the League's branch chairmen were school teachers. They were instrumental in poisoning entire generations of petty-bourgeois with the doctrines of racialism and

---

* Haeckel lived just long enough to witness the revolution of November 1918, an event which occasioned the characteristic comment "no one knows the kind of new folly that will be perpetrated by the ordinary German citizen - the least politically educated in the world". Kurt Eisner, murdered leader of the short-lived Bavarian Soviet Republic, was derided as a "Galacian Jew" and "degenerate swindler". Haeckel's last political act before his death in August 1919 was to curse "those damned shop committees". The Nazis closed them down 14 years later.

** Not that the League was indifferent to domestic political questions. From its very foundation, it called for a government ban on Jewish immigration, and under its second President, Heinrich Class, evolved a consistently anti-semitic programme which included demands for the exclusion of Jews from teaching and public offices, and the compulsory display of the Star of David on the masthead of all publications employing Jews in their editorial offices.

militarism). The Bavarian Social Democrat Kurt Eisner was not exaggerating when he wrote in 1914 that

> Behind the programme of the Pan-German League and its manifold branches and daughter associations stand the Land League, the Central League of Industrialists and other employers' associations, a part of the finance capital interests, especially the shipping interests, and finally, an executive of former generals and admirals...

Under its President Heinrich Class, the League moved steadily towards the ultra-chauvinist, racialist right, making a bid for petty-bourgeois support by attacks on "international finance", while taking care to demarcate it from model "national" capitalists like Krupp. Class set out the Pan-German case for a right-wing dictatorship in his book *If I Were the Kaiser,* published in 1912:

> "A powerful leader is necessary who will enforce the steps necessary for our recovery..." This "saviour of the Reich" must be a dictator "who uncompromisingly resists the democratisation of the state". Under this regime, Jews would be treated "without pity". Small wonder that Hitler was later to declare that this work, which anticipated so much of the Nazi programme, "contained everything that was important and necessary for Germany."* The activities of the Pan-Germans were supplemented by a proliferation of societies ostensibly pursuing purely "cultural" causes. Such were the Gobineau Society, founded by the leading Pan-German Ludwig Schemann, and the "Wagner Circle", established by the composer's wife Cosima after his death in 1883. Arthur de Gobineau was the French exponent of racialist ideology who, it is considered by most authorities, enjoyed the greatest influence among German anti-semites, Hitler included. Gobineau's political and philosophical writings were clearly a reaction against the rationalist and humanist traditions of the French Revolution, holding as he did the convictions that:

> the racial question overshadows all other problems of history, that it holds the key to them all, and that the inequality of the races from whose fusion a people is formed is enough to explain the whole course of human destiny... everything great, noble and fruitful in the works of man... derives from a single starting point, is the development of a single germ and the result of a single thought; it belongs to one family alone, the different branches of which have reigned in all the civilised countries of the universe.[37]

Gobineau was, of course, referring to the so-called "white races", of whom pride of place went to the "Germanic race... endowed with all the vitality of the Aryan variety."[38] For unlike France, "a country where the nobility does not exist, where the bourgeoisie is no more preponderant as a political class".[39] Germany remained relatively free from the democratic virus. This cult of the mythical "Aryan", with its emphasis on the "civilising" world mission of the higher "white races", enjoyed an enormous vogue among bourgeois intellectual and artistic circles as Germany entered upon the imperialist phase of its development. Wagner himself in his later years degenerated into a rabid anti-semite and religious mystic, in sharp contrast to the militant socialist who in 1849 charged, musket in hand, to the barricades of revolutionary Dresden. Politically disoriented by the defeat of the revolution, the composer turned his back on the working class, the only force capable of modernising and democratising Germany in a thoroughgoing fashion, and delved deep into his nation's mythical past in a search for artistic and philosophical inspiration. The result was, in the sphere of pure music, often superlative. But in the realm of ideology - and Wagner would never have denied the importance of this side of his work - it was utterly escapist, grist to the cultural mill of those in Germany who sought to embellish the nauseous doctrines of racialism with a veneer of great art. Was it just mere coincidence that Hitler's favourite composer was Wagner, or that even in the pre-1914 period, the circle dedicated to preserving his works and memory became a meeting point for the ideologues of German racialism?*

The most influential among these was undoubtedly Houston Stewart Chamberlain, the Portsmouth-born natural historian and physicist who became enmeshed in the politics of German reaction through his almost religious conversion to the cult of Wagner at the 1882 Bayreuth Festival. He soon settled permanently in Germany, branching out from his activities on behalf of the Wagner Circle to a rabid propagandist of all things German. Nearly all things, we should have said, for it was Kant and Schopenhauer, not Hegel, whom Chamberlain took as his philosophical mentors. From Kant he took his criticism of the "exact sciences". The unknowable nature of the external world, the world of "things-in-themselves", lay beyond reason's reach. If this numenual world was to be grasped at all, then it would be by means of what he called the "world of the eye", or more prosaically, intuition. And so he passed over the Kantian threshold into the subjectivist, mystical world of Schopenhauer and his successors. Chamberlain sought to employ the "world of the eye"** in his main work, *The Foundations of the 19th Century,* which he completed in 1898. It shares with de Gobineau's essay on race the idea that human history is the history of racial struggle, and that

---

* Wagner's contradictory evolution from revolutionary democrat to German mystic and chauvinist is discussed in the thought-provoking essay on the composer by Anatoly Lunacharský, the Soviet Union's first People's Commissar of Education. He makes the telling point that like so many great minds trapped by German reaction, Wagner was a follower of the neo-Kantian Schopenhauer. (A. Lunacharsky: *On Literature and Art*, p.349, Moscow, 1965.)

** Chamberlain coined the term *gestalt* to distinguish his intuitive methods from those of the orthodox scientist.

the German or "Aryan" race is the highest point of this process (Chamberlain was probably the first "scientific" racialist to assert that Christ was not a Jew, but an "Aryan". His hero, Wagner had pointed the way for this ludicrous contention in *Religion and Art,* where the composer declared he was "more than doubtful whether Jesus was a Jew". This issue was of profound importance for those imperialists and racialists seeking to ground their theories in traditional Christian teachings). Chamberlain's intellectual pretensions enhanced the acceptability of his views in ruling class circles. Kaiser Wilhelm II not only read the "Foundations" but distributed it amongst his immediate political and court associates. The two then conducted a voluminous correspondence which ended only in 1923. Long before this, Chamberlain had lost faith in the ability of the Hohenzollern dynasty to fulfil Germany's racial destiny, and in his last years, he became an open supporter, and finally member, of the Nazi party. Hitler, who first met Chamberlain at the 1925 Wagner Bayreuth Festival, paid him the highest possible compliment by attending the latter's funeral in 1927 as the official representative of the Nazi Party. The Nazis recognised their own.

The point therefore being made is that the precursors of national socialism were by no means 'cranks' on the margin of German intellectual or political life, but men at its very centre. And neither is it a question of Germany alone. True these ultra-reactionary and racialist tendencies assumed their most developed form in the country where the problem of national unification had loomed largest, and where the ruling class was faced point blank with the necessity of outright military conflict with the major European capitalist powers if German imperialism was not to be strangled at birth. And nowhere more than in Germany was the working class better organised and politically educated to thwart the reactionary strategy of its enemies. These contradictions, taken together with the entire tradition of counter-revolutionary politics became a forcing house for the growth of anti-semitic, anti-Marxist and imperialist ideology amongst the German middle class. But basically the same process was at work in all the imperialist nations. The form it took depended to a great degree on already-established political, philosophical and cultural patterns. But the content embodied within these diffuse forms was precisely that described by Lenin: away from classical bourgeois democracy and liberalism towards reaction, towards open dictatorial rule over the working class and the waging of imperialist war. And in almost every case, the spokesman for this tendency began by challenging, very much in the manner of Schopenhauer, the rational world outlook developed by the bourgeoisie in its struggle for class hegemony over the forces of feudal and Catholic obscurantism. In other words, intuition is substituted for reason, faith for Knowledge, 'action' for theory. This is already evident in the writings of Schopenhauer, who argued that 'The aim of our life... is a practical one: our actions, not our knowledge, appertain to eternity. The use of the intellect is to guide our actions, and at the same time to hold up the mirror to our will...'[39] This notion, which seems to begin from the obvious proposition that theory is derived from practice, and in the last analysis must therefore be subordinate to it, is carried much further in the philosopher's essay on genius, where he contends that

> if man's grasp of the universal is so deep as to be *intuitive*, and to apply not only to general ideas, but to an individual object by itself, then there arises a knowledge of the *Ideas* in the sense used by Plato. This knowledge is of an aesthetic character; when it is self-active, it rises to genius, and reaches the highest degree of intensity when it becomes philosophic; for then the whole of life and existence as it passes away, the world and all it contains, are grasped in their true nature by an act of intuition, and appear in a form which forces itself upon consciousness as an object of mediation.[40]

With Nietzsche, the role of intuition is even more explicit, being counterposed not only to natural science but the study of history. Man can only act freely when he forgets the past — such is the thesis of Nietzsche:

> Forgetfulness is a property of all action... life in any true sense is absolutely impossible without forgetfulness... there is a degree of sleeplessness, of rumination, of "historical sense", that injures and finally destroys the living thing, be it a man or a people or a system of culture'.[41]*

Nietzsche had sound class motives for opposing any serious and objective study of the past:

> Monumental history loves by false analogy; it entices the brave to rashness, and the enthusiastic to fanaticism by tempting comparisons. Imagine this history in the hands — and head — of a gifted egoist or an inspired scoundrel; kingdoms would be overthrown, princes murdered, war and revolution let loose...[42]

And this, Nietzsche considered, was a special danger in Germany, where the people were inclined to theory and an historical approach towards political problems. Instead, men should be guided and motivated by what the self-appointed theoretician of French syndicalism Georges Sorel called 'myths':

> The unrestrained historical sense, pushed to its logical conclusion, uproots the future, because it destroys illusions and robs existing things of the only atmosphere in which they can live. Historical justice... is therefore a dreadful virtue, because it always undermines and ruins the living thing — its judgment means annihilation... the creative instinct is sapped... the historical audit brings so much to light which is false and absurd, violent and inhuman, that the condition of

---

* Or as Henry Ford, the super pragmatist, put it: "History is bunk."

pious illusion falls to pieces. *And a thing can only live through a pious illusion.*[43] (emphasis added)

And of necessity, this war on historical objectivity on behalf of the philosophy of myth and so-called intuitive knowledge — in other words in defence of the 'big lie', demanded a total renunciation of the Hegelian heritage:

> I believe there has been no dangerous turning point in the progress of German culture in this century that has not been made more dangerous by the enormous and still living influence of the Hegelian philosophy.[44]

In France, where the rationalist tradition was far more deeply embedded in the bourgeoisie, open adherents of subjectivist and intuitionist theories of knowledge were fewer, but not a wit the less vocal and persistent for all that. Their most gifted representative was undoubtedly Henri Bergson, who evolved the notion of the *elan vitale* as the driving force of human evolution. In the case of Bergson, who although conservative in outlook took little interest in politics,* we have a philosopher who epitomises the state of flux in all branches of intellectual and cultural activity predominating in the last years of the 19th century as the old mechanist conceptions of change and reality, in particular those derived from Newtonian physics, began to disintegrate under the weight of fresh scientific inquiry and evidence. Bergson's argument contained a particle of truth: that since the real world was in a constant state of motion, it could not accurately be depicted by even the most sophisticated of representational models or symbols. These remained at best tools of analysis, and not reality itself. But Bergson went further than this. Working from an essentially Kantian position, he came to the conclusion that the wall between human consciousness and reality could only be breached by intuition, by an act of will. The old models of the world and the universe were breaking down — this was most certainly the case. Bergson's answer to this problem was not, like that of Lenin, to view the contradictory development of human knowledge about the world as an eternal process of finer and finer approximations to a reality infinite in both space and time. Instead, a short cut to infinity was proposed, as subjective as the earlier methods had been mechanical and empirical:

'There are things that intelligence alone is able to seek, but

---

* Though Bergson did hold strong and ultra-reactionary views on war which he regarded as a strong antidote to revolution:

"...the only principle capable of neutralising the tendencies of societies to disintegration is a warlike virtue, which may be tinged with mysticism, which mingles no calculation with its religion, which overspreads a great country, which is slowly and reverently evolved out of memories and hopes, out of poetry and love, with faint perfume of every moral beauty under heaven." (H. Bergson: *Two Sources of Morality and Religion,* p.277, New York, 1954.)

which, by itself, it will never find. These instinct alone could find, but it will never seek them' [45] Instinct or intuition was therefore the higher form of understanding, for it could reach, according to Bergson, beyond the shadowy world of phenomenon to the ultimate reality of noumenon:

> We see that the intellect, so skillful in dealing with the inert, is awkward the moment it touches the living. Whether it wants to treat the life of the body or the life of the mind, it proceeds with rigour, the stiffness and brutality of an instrument not designed for such use... We are at ease only in the discontinuous, in the immobile, in the dead. The intellect is characterised by a natural inability to comprehend life. Instinct, on the contrary, is moulded on the very form of life. While intelligence treats everything mechanically, instinct proceeds... organically.[46]

Bergson's subjectivist method hinged on the belief that one can, by an act of will, place oneself "inside" a process, and by so doing, discover total, absolute and perfect truths. The political implications of such a notion are as obvious as they are reactionary. It places in the hands of government leaders a theory to justify their riding ruthlessly over the most elementary democratic wishes of the people, on the grounds that they alone can grasp and interpret the true "will of the people". Ordinary mortals, the "herd" to use Hitler's terminology, are not capable of such intuitive perception and decision-making. The power and right to act reside in the hands of an elite gifted with Bergson's "sixth sense", the inner eye which can penetrate the fog created by the human intellect to the real world of instinct beyond. And it is doubly reactionary because such a method recognises no objective criteria of proof:

> ...an absolute could only be given in an *intuition*, whilst everything else falls within the province of *analysis*. By intuition is meant the kind of *intellectual sympathy* by which one places oneself within an object in order to coincide with what is unique in it and consequently inexpressible.[47]

Bergson had stumbled across the basic flaw in the rationalist and empirical methods, but instead of seeing them as historical moments in the evolution of human consciousness towards a more and more scientific world outlook, an outlook which, with the theoretical work of Marx and Engels, reached its highest point in dialectical materialism as a theory of knowledge, he eclectically combined the most "useful" elements of rationalism and empiricism with his own intuitionist method of perception.*

---

* And here again it must be stressed that Bergson praised Kant as the pioneer in this respect: "He affirmed, against his immediate predecessors, that knowledge is not entirely resolvable into terms of intelligence. He brought back into philosophy - while modifying it and carrying it on to another plane — that essential element of the philosophy of Descartes which had been abandoned by the Cartesians. (i.e., dualism). Thereby he prepared the way for a new philosophy which might have estab-

Bergson counterposed to the objective materialist dialectic of Marxism a subjective and intuitionist dialectic which reconciled opposites in the mind through an act of will, and not by acting on and changing material reality:

> There is hardly any concrete reality which cannot be observed from under two antagonistic concepts. Hence a thesis and an antithesis which endeavour in vain to reconcile logically, for the very simple reason that it is impossible, with concepts and observations taken from outside points of view to make a thing. But from the object, seized by intuition, we pass easily in many cases to the two contrary concepts; and as in that way thesis and antithesis can be seen to spring from reality, we grasp at the same time how it is that the two are opposed and how they are reconciled. [48]

In a future chapter on Italian fascism, we shall seek to show how the reaction to French rationalism led, in the case of Sorel, to theories which directly served the imperialist counter-revolution against the European workers' movement. Here we can see that a perfectly sincere attempt to overcome practical and theoretical problems posed by the inadequacies of mechanical materialism, rationalism and empiricism, because it remained indifferent or even hostile to the Marxist world outlook, passed imperceptibly but inexorably over to extreme mysticism. The end product, when combined with the ideas of the other main subjectivists Nietzsche and Schopenhauer, was a school of philosophy and theory of knowledge which proved itself highly adaptable in a period of intense class and national conflict, to the most reactionary political tendencies. At the base of this development were two related and converging processes - the break-up of the mechanist-rationalist world outlook in the physical and natural sciences, and a profound crisis in bourgeois democracy as colonial rivalries intensified and the proletarian movement began to stake its claim for political power. Naturally, this process did not evolve uniformly in each country, or necessarily penetrate into the same branches of science, the arts and philosophy. But a general trend does emerge. The reaction in each and every case both preceded and anticipated the rise of imperialism as a world system, but followed and flowed from the decline of the bourgeoisie as a revolutionary class. We can see this even in the case of England, where parliamentary traditions had deep roots, a country where only with the Reform Act of 1832 did the industrial and banking bourgeoisie finally succeed in widening its political base by extending the franchise to the urban propertied classes. Yet even as the bourgeoisie was celebrating its victory over the landed aristocracy, a new and far more dangerous enemy was already assembling its forces under the banner of Chartism. It was to this

lished itself in the extra intellectual matter of knowledge by a higher effort of intuition." (H. Bergson: *Creative Evolution*, p.378, London, 1960.)

threat that the political writer and essayist, Thomas Carlyle, addressed himself. His writings, spanning the period beween the rise of the English workers' movement and the dawn of imperialism, contained none of that so-called "Victorian optimism" which is said to be typical of bourgeois thought in that era. Sceptical of democracy, profoundly distrustful of the proletariat, and fanatical in his opposition to what he termed "Mammonism"* Carlyle's thought moved along lines which we have already traced in Germany,** as can be seen from a reading of his *"Lectures on Heroes"* (1840), where he seeks to replace bourgeois democracy by the cult of hero worship. But his most revealing remarks arise in the course of his essays on Chartism and the problems of contemporary English politics. It is here that Carlyle, with a precision that is, in the light of subsequent developments almost uncanny, anticipates the economic programme of national socialism. Firstly there is Carlyle's mystique of work, a concept which the Nazis employed to dupe backward workers and artisans into believing that fascism was a unique, idealist species of socialism that returned to the worker the "dignity of manual labour" without challenging the rights of private property. This was a constant theme of Labour Front and Labour Service propaganda, and we can also see strong elements of this notion in the writings of Carlyle counterposed, as it was with the Nazis, to "Mammonism" or what Feder termed the "thraldom of interest":

> ...there is a perennial nobleness and even sacredness in Work... there is always hope in a man that actually and earnestly works... Work, never so Mammonish, mean, *is* in communication with Nature; the real desire to get work done will itself lead one more and more to truth, to Nature's appointments and regulations, which are truth... Consider how, even in the meanest sorts of labour, the whole soul of man is composed into a real kind of harmony...[49]

The reader can also see here how, very much in the manner of the German pantheists, labour becomes a quest for "harmony" with "nature"†. And here too we find ourselves in the world of instinct

* Worship of money.

** Carlyle was an avid student of German philosophy, especially Schopenhauer. And in his turn, he influenced Nietzsche in the latter's elaboration of the "superman" concept.

† How close the Nazis later came to Carlyle's labour mystique can be seen from a speech by Hitler quoted by "Reich Labour Leader" Muller Brandenburg in an article on *The State Labour Service in Germany*: "...we want the Labour Service to compel every young German to work with his hands at least once and thus to contribute to the progressive development of his people. Above all, we want those Germans who are in sedantry occupations to learn what manual work means, so that they may find understanding and sympathy for those of their comrades whose lives are spent in the fields, tne factory or the workshop... The whole idea underlying the Labour Service is to promote understanding between all classes and thus strengthen the spirit of national solidarity... In our camps, class distinctions are overcome by the facts of experience... we abolish them with the aid of the spade... " (from *Germany Speaks*, pp.193-195, Berlin, 1938.)

and intuition, of pure "action", labour divorced from its economic function as the source of value and profit. And like the petty-bourgeois quack economists of national socialism, Carlyle always depicted labour as struggling to break free from capital in its money form, while remaining intransigently opposed to the socialisation of industrial capital:

> Industry still under bondage to Mammon... is a tragic spectacle... Labour is not a devil, even while encased in Mammonism... The un-redeemed ugliness is that of a slothful people. Show me a people energetically busy; heaving, struggling, all shoulders at the wheel, their heart pulsing, every muscle swelling, with man's energy and will;—I will show you a people of whom a great good is already predictable... By very working they will learn; they have Anteus-like, their foot on Mother Fact: how can they but learn?[50]

Carlyle's panegyric to work as a means of communion with nature, obscured as did Nazi talk of labour as an expression of "national solidarity", the real motive force of capitalist production through all phases of its cycle from money capital, through productive capital to commodity capital. That is, it concealed or rather sought to conceal, the quest for profit and the origin of profit in capitalist production. Stripped of its high flown phrases and mystical language, this is the essence of what we might call "labour romanticism". For despite his alleged heroic and mystical qualities, the worker was, under Carlyle's regime, to be kept firmly in his place. Power was to be wielded exclusively by an "Aristocracy of Talent"[51] to be found chiefly among "captains of industry" - who had the task of "managing" what Carlyle called the "alarming problem of the working classes".[52] Worker and employer were, he argued, parts of an organic whole, and instead of pitting their strengths against each other, should be joined together in the pursuit of "holy" work. Only one detail marred this picture of idyllic harmony - the worker was to be totally subordinated to his employer:

> The leaders of Industry, if Industry is ever to be led, are virtually the Captains of the World; if there be no nobleness in them, there will never be an Arisocracy more... Captains of Industry are the true Fighters, henceforth recognisable as the only true ones...[53]

But nothing so sordid as profit should serve as their goal. Neither should workers seek their own monetary advancement in the form of higher wages. All this was "Mammonism", or what the Nazis called "Jewish-Marxist materialism".

> Love of men cannot be bought by cash payment... You cannot lead a fighting world without having it regimented, chivalried: the thing, in a day, becomes impossible; all men in it, the highest at first, the very lowest at last, discern consciously or by noble instinct, this necessity.[54]

Unless such a relationship between worker and employer was sub-stituted for that of classical "Manchester" laisser faire, which

Carlyle despised, then revolution would certainly ensue:

> ...dark millions of God's human creatures (will) start up in mad Chartisms, impracticable Sacred Months and Manchester Insurrections:- and there is a virtual Industrial Aristocracy as yet only half alive, spell-bound amid money bags and ledgers... no working world, any more than a Fighting World, can be led on without a noble Chivalry of Work, and laws and fixed rules which follow out that... As an anarchic multitude on mere supply and demand, it is becoming inevitable that we dwindle in horrid, suicidal convulsion... will not one French Revolution and Reign of Terror suffice, but must there be two?[55]

Military regimentation embellished by a little "love" and "chivalry" - this was Carlyle's recipe for the "problem of the working classes". For "on the present scheme and principle, work cannot continue. Trades' strikers, Trades' Unions, Chartisms, mutiny, squalor, rage and desperate revolt, growing ever more desperate, will go on their way."[56] It is easy, in the light of historical experience, to dismiss Carlyle as a gifted writer obsessed by the threat of a Chartist-led revolution which never materialised. But that is not the point. Far more significant is that here, in the homeland of liberalism and free trade, in a nation noted for its tradition of compromise, was a publicist feeling his way towards an outlook which in so many ways, forshadowed the political and economic ideology of fascism. Which underlines our contention that several important ingredients of fascism originated in the pre-imperialist phase of capitalism, and then underwent a qualitative transformation under the impact of the intense social, political and economic crises and upheavals engendered by the development of monopoly capitalism. Just as elements of monopoly are present even in the period of free competition, so, in different ways and at varying tempos in each capitalist country, did the ideologists of extreme reaction and chauvinism, of fulminating hatred against socialism and the workers' movement, begin to evolve their theories at a time when bourgeois democracy seemed to be in the ascendent. And just as we saw that the so-called era of optimism contained within it the forces which unleashed the most terrible global slaughter, so the philosophers of optimism and rational, ordered progress were powerless, despite their worship of the power of reason and science, to prevent the rise of the most horrific manifestations of wild subjectivism and barbaric mysticism. The diffuse - and indeed contradictory - elements which eventually comprised the alloy of Fascism were fused in the imperialist crucible.

REFERENCES FOR CHAPTER FIVE

[1] V. Lenin: *A Caricature of Marxism*, (August-October 1916) *Collected Works*, Vol. 23, p.43.
[2] F. Engels: Letter to J. Bloch, London, September 21-22, 1890. *Marx-Engels Selected Correspondence*, p.498.
[3] Ibid, p.499.
[4] Ibid, p.499.
[5] V. Lenin: *The Discussion on Self-Determination Summed Up*, (July 1916). *Collected Works*, Vol. 22, p.266.
[6] V. Lenin: *Imperialism, the Highest Stage of Capitalism*, (Spring, 1916), *Collected Works*, Vol. 22, p.266.
[7] A. Schopenhauer: *The World as Will and Idea*, Preface to Second Edition, Vol. 1, p.xxi, London, 1957.
[8] Ibid, p.351.
[9] Ibid, pp.352-353.
[10] Ibid, p.372.
[11] A. Schopenhauer: '*Government* in *Human Nature*, p.30, London, 1951.
[12] Ibid, p.35.
[13] Ibid, pp.37-42.
[14] Ibid, p.44.
[15] A. Hitler: *Mein Kampf*, p.78.
[16] Ibid, p.65.
[17] Ibid, pp.79-81
[18] Ibid, p.91.
[19] A. Schopenhauer: *On Genius* in *The Art of Literature*, p.83, London, 1951.
[20] F. Nietzsche: *Notes (1873)* in *The Portable Nietzsche*, pp.40-41, New York, 1962.
[21] F. Nietzsche: *Twilight of the Idols* (1888) in ibid, p.545.
[22] K. Marx: *Contribution to the Critique of Hegel's Philosophy of Right* (1844). In K. Marx and F. Engels: *On Religion*, pp.50-58.
[23] F. Nietzsche: *The Anti-Christ* (1888), in ibid, pp.644-646.
[24] Ibid, pp.646-647.
[25] Ibid, p.646.
[26] Ibid, pp.646-647.
[27] Ibid, p.647.
[28] Ibid, p.647.
[29] Ibid, pp.647-648.
[30] Ibid, pp.570-571.
[31] F. Nietzsche: *Twilight of the Idols*, in ibid, pp.552-553.
[32] F. Nietzsche: *The Antichrist*, in ibid, p.578.
[33] F. Nietzsche: *Twilight of the Idols*, in ibid, p.542.
[34] F. Nietzsche: *The Gay Science*, in ibid, p.97.
[35] F. Nietzsche: *The Dawn*, in ibid, pp.90-91.
[36] F. Nietzsche: Letter to his sister, Christmas, 1887, in ibid, pp.456-457.
[37] A. de Gobineau: *Essay on the inequality of the Human Races* (1853-55) in *Selected Political Writings*, pp 41-42, London, 1970.
[37] Ibid, p.170.
[38] A. de Gobineau: *France in 1870*, in ibid, p.208.

[39] A. Schopenhauer: *The Failure of Philosophy* in *Religion: A Dialogue*, pp.80-81, London, 1951.
[40] A . Schopenhauer: *On Genius* in *The Art of Literature*, pp.82-83, London, 1951.
[41] F. Nietzsche: *The Use and Abuse of History*, pp.6-7, New York, 1957.
[42] Ibid, p.16.
[43] Ibid, p.42.
[44] Ibid, p.51.
[45] H. Bergson: *Creative Evolution*, p.159, London, 1960.
[46] Ibid, pp.173-174.
[47] H. Bergson: *An Introduction to Metaphysics*, pp 23-24, New York, 1955.
[48] Ibid, p.38.
[49] T. Carlyle: *Past and Present*, p.223, London, n.d.
[50] Ibid, p.231.
[51] Ibid, p.93.
[52] Ibid, p.280.
[53] Ibid, pp.281-282.
[54] Ibid, p.282.
[55] Ibid, p.283.
[56] Ibid, p.299.

142

Chapter Six
THE FIRST SEEDS ARE SOWN

With the SPD's triumphant emergence from illegality in 1890, the leaders of German social democracy faced a series of political and theoretical problems which were in many ways similar to those which confronted Marx and Engels after the defeat of the 1848 revolutions. In a superficial sense, the historical situations were diametrically opposed. The authors of the *Communist Manifesto*, which predicted for Germany an immediate proletarian revolution, now had to deepen and ground in political economy the brilliant generalisations and insights of their earlier writings. This essential theoretical work, undertaken in the great political trough which lay between the decline of the movements of '48 and the Paris Commune of 1871, was of necessity divorced to a great degree from the day-to-day struggle of the international working class. The central task which Marx and Engels set themselves in this period was to lay bare the basic laws of motion of capitalist production, thereby providing the essential theoretical key to understanding and intervening in the struggle of classes. In 1890, the SPD leaders - and here we can include Engels among their number - stood at the head of a movement numbering more than a million members and supporters. The proletariat was very much in the ascendant, not only in Germany but throughout Europe. Yet precisely this upwards movement tended to obscure the enormous theoretical tasks, and indeed immense political dangers, which this new situation contained. Complacency, passivity, even smugness - these were characteristics which steadily gained the upper hand over the pugnacity and political sharpness that despite occasional backslidings and waverings, set the tone for the party's 12 year fight against the anti-socialist laws. In both cases, the main task was to accomplish the transition to a qualitatively new economic and political situation. Marx, principally with his *Capital*, did precisely this. He recognised that far from standing on the verge of a socialist revolution, Germany was experiencing the birth pangs of modern industrial capitalism. His studies of English capitalism, then the most advanced in the world, convinced him that "the country that is more developed industrially only shows, to the less developed, the image of its own future."[1] This conclusion, which in 1848 he would probably have dismissed as the prediction of an incurable pessimist, necessitated a wholesale re-orientation of revolutionary programme, strategy and tactics. Perspectives were no longer to be reckoned in months or even years, but decades, as he and Engels warned those in the leadership of the German movement who in 1850 were still blithely proclaiming the imminent arrival of a new revolutionary wave:

> The minority replaces critical observation with dogmatism, a material-ist attitude with an idealist one. It regards its own wishes as the driving force of the revolution instead of the real facts of the situation. Whilst we tell the workers that they must go through 15, 20, perhaps even 50 years of war and civil war, not only in order to alter existing con-ditions, but even to make themselves fit to take over political power, you tell them, on the contrary, that they must seize political power at once or abandon all hope.

Yet now, when new developments within German and inter-national capitalism forshadowed these very struggles, almost without exception the SPD leadership remained trapped by its past thinking and experiences, unable to detect what was emerging out of the old *laisser faire* capitalism and then to draw the necessary political conclusions. All around the party, signs were visible of a qualitative shift in ruling class circles and among the middle ranks of the bourgeoisie towards an imperialist orient-ation, expressing itself as much in the language of subjectivist, anti-rational philosophy as in the soaring output of Krupp's gun shops and the North Sea ship yards. Almost mesmerised by the party's spectacular election successes, and the equally impressive growth of members and party resources, the SPD leadership tended to see only the movement's strengths, and allowed these to cloud over its very real - and growing - theoretical deficiencies. And although Engels for one was well aware of this problem, he too allowed himself to be carried way by the post-Bismarckian euphoria which had virtuali, ngulfed the entire leadership. Thus after noting how

> too many of the younger Germans simply make use of the phrase historical materialism.. only in order to get their own relatively scanty historical knowledge... constructed into as neat a system as possible... [he then concludes]... all this will right itself. We are strong enough in Germany to stand a lot. One of the greatest services which the Anti-Socialist Law did us was to free us from the obtrusiveness of the German intellectual who had got himself tinged with socialism. We are now strong enough to digest the German intellectual too, who is giving himself great airs again.[3]

But it was not a simple question of "digestion", but an active and unrelenting struggle against the revision of Marxism by these alien elements, such as had been earlier undertaken by Engels himself in his famous polemic against Duhring, the anti-semitic and idealist university professor who was unaccountably permitted to remain within the SPD for a period of several years. Judged by the evidence of his writings, the old Engels did not measure up to this task, which like that of the post-1848 period, was in essence one of transition, of preparing the party for a leap in its develoment from a movement geared to quantitative growth and peaceful, if periodically sharp, political campaigns, to a mass revolutionary party capable of fighting for state power in an epoch of profound national and international turmoil, revolutionary upheaval and war. In the period of the anti-socialist laws, Engels had warned on more than one occasion that the party could find itself propelled by such events into political situations where it could completely lose its bearings. In 1884, he wrote to Bebel pointing out the dangers implicit in limiting the party's demands to that of bourgeois democracy, ending with this truly remarkable anticipation of the German bourgeoisie's political tactics in the revolution of November 1918:

> ...our sole adversary on the day of the crisis and on the day after the crisis will be *the whole of the reaction which will group around pure democracy*, and this, I think, should not be lost sight of.[4]

Yet lost sight of it was, with even Engels suffering in his last years from blurred vision. We saw how in the criticism of the Gotha unity programme of 1875, Marx and Engels directed their most pungent polemics against the newly-formed party's attitude towards proletarian internationalism and the state. Beginning with the last writings of Engels, there was after 1890 a slow but nevertheless steady retreat from the positions established in 1875, and it was one which met with firm opposition only from a tiny section of the German movement headed by Rosa Luxemburg and; though not on the same plane of theoretical profundity, Karl Liebknecht. The nature and tempo of this decline is well brought out in the international sphere by the party's attitude towards national defence. Here it was simply not enough for the SPD to rehash and embellish everything written by Marx and Engels on this question, if only because without exception these writings pertained to an epoch that knew no imperialism in the sense that Lenin and Bukharin understood it.   Marx died in 1883, when the problem facing socialists was nowhere one of directly preparing to take power, but rather of pursuing policies which while favouring the most rapid development of capitalist social relations, would also defend the interests of the working class and preserve its political independence from all other classes. It was this realistic, as opposed to utopian, conception which governed Engel's approach to the problems of the workers' movement in Germany, where he constantly cautioned against any tendency to ignore potential or actual conflicts between the bourgeoisie and the Junker agrarians. For while the working class remained incapable, for objective historical reasons, of taking power into its own hands, it had no other alternative than to husband and expand its forces until the objective contradictions of a fully-developed capitalist system placed revolution on the order of the day. (This was also the position of the first Russian Marxists in their struggle against the utopian and terroristic Populists, who held that Russia would bypass the capitalist stage of development and proceed directly from feudalism to socialism.) The same conceptions necessarily applied to relations between states. The Leninist tactic of defeatism, of desiring the military defeat of one's "own" bourgeoisie in an imperialist war both as a lesser evil than its victory, and as a means of accelerating the onset of revolution, simply could not have arisen in Marx's day, any more than could have Bolshevism, being the theory and practice of proletarian revolution in the imperialist epoch. Marx had instead to lend his critical support to whichever warring nation he considered to be serving, however unconsciously, feebly, reluctantly or inconsistently, as the vehicle of historical progress. So in the Crimean war, Marx "supported" capitalist England against Tsarist Russia, for despite his loathing of the English bourgeoisie, with its unmerciful exploitation of child and female labour, Marx desired the defeat of Russian despotism, the counter-revolutionary gendarme of continental Europe.* Marx and Engels adopted an identical line in relation to Germany, supporting that country in all its wars which facilitated the achievement of national unification (1864 against Denmark, 1866 against Austria, and 1870 against France). Only when Bismarck began to transgress the limits of the nation state did Marx and Engels raise their voices in protest, as they did following Prussia's annexation of Alsace and Lorraine after the French defeat at Sedan. From this point onwards, they saw as the main danger in Europe a war between Russia, acting as an agent of a revenge-seeking French bourgeoisie, and Germany. And in the event of such a war, Marx and Engels declared they would be unequivocally on the side of Germany, despite its vehemently anti-socialist, Junker-based government. Pre-occupation with this threat from Russia led Engels in particular to employ phrases and formulations which were, to put it mildly, insensitive to the national rights of the Balkan Slavs, whom he tended to regard as mere pawns and tools of Tsarist foreign policy. "The principle of nationalities', Engels wrote in 1866, "is nothing but a Russian invention to destroy Poland. Russia has absorbed the greater part of Poland on the plea of the principle of nationalities."[35] But because the principle had been exploited and

---

* Marx was also a life-long supporter of Ireland's right to independence from England.

perverted by reaction, that did not necessitate its repudiation by revolutionaries, rather its consistent application. The same must be said of Engels' disparaging comments on Slavic peoples incorporated against their will in the Austro-Hungarian empire:

> The · so-called democrats among the Austrian Slavs are either scoundrels or visionaries, and the visionaries are constantly being led by the nose by the scoundrels. To the sentimental slogans offered in the name of the *counter-revolutionary peoples of Europe* we reply that the hatred of Russia was, and still is, the first revolutionary passion of the Germans; and that since the revolution (of 1848) a hatred of the Czechs and Croats has been added... We and the Poles and the Magyars (Hungarians) will only be able to safeguard the revolution through the most determined terror against these Slavic peoples."[6]

This tendency to view German foreign — and sometimes even domestic — policy from the standpoint of relations with Russia remained with Engels until his death in 1895. It was, without doubt, responsible for the articles the SPD leadership cynically exploited in 1914 to justify their support for the Kaiser's imperialist war against France and Russia. They were, they claimed, merely carving out Engels' policy to its logical, if bloody, conclusion. No blame attaches to Engels for this perversion of his work. Where he did certainly err was in failing to detect the first manifestations of imperialism in German economic politics and philosophy. In 1891, at a time when German finance capital had already embarked on a series of colonial adventures in Africa and the Pacific, and when chauvinist writers and anti-semitic demagogues were proclaiming Germany's racial supremacy and god-given right to rule Europe and even the world. Engels still continued to discuss German-Russian relations in the old way, identifying the military defeat of Imperial Germany with the destruction of the SPD. He considered that if in a war with Russia, Germany is beaten, "we will be beaten with her..."[7] That same year, Engels wrote to Bebel just prior to the SPD congress at Erfurt on the same question, once again making the connection — this time far more explicitly — between the fate of Imperialist Germany and German social democracy:

> A war against Germany... would be, above all, a war against the strongest socialist party in Europe. And there would be nothing left for us but to fight with all our might any aggressor who helped Russia. For either we would be defeated, and then the socialist movement in Europe, would be done for for 20 years, or we ourselves must aim to take the helm.[6]

Now what Engels had in mind when he wrote these words of advice was a national uprising against the invader after the example of the Jacobin *levee en masse* of 1793, when revolutionary France took to arms against the coalition of powers seeking to restore the Bourbon monarchy. But Engels was transposing this policy into a considerably changed situation, into a country which had not only completed the 'national' aspects of its bourgeois revolution, but was already actively engaged in repressing the democratic rights of other peoples, from Poland and Alsace-Lorraine to Africa and Oceana. The cloudiness of Engels' formulation, while militant in spirit, left itself open to widely differing interpretations, ranging from unconditional defence of the Kaiser's empire against any invasion, whether from east or west, to a revolutionary bid to seize power and wage a 'plebeian' war against Germany's enemies. As far as most of the party leadership were concerned, there was no doubt whatsoever. Bebel roundly declared at the Erfurt Congress that "if Russia, that bulwark of savagery and barbarism, that enemy of all human culture, were to attack Germany in order to dismember and destroy her — then we are as much, and indeed more concerned than those who lead Germany, and we shall oppose it." No question then of overthrowing the Kaiser and "taking the helm" in order better to defend the fatherland. The job of the SPD was to prove itself more patriotic than its class enemies! There is evidence suggesting that Engels disapproved of such excesses, and not only in the German party. Some two years later he had cause to chide Marx's son-in-law Paul Lafargue for employing the term 'true patriot' to distinguish the French socialist party's national loyalties from those of bourgeois chauvinists. Engels said that the term 'patriot' had "a limited meaning — or else such a vague one, depending on circumstances — that for my part I should never dare to apply that title to myself." Further on in the same letter, he made the revealing admission that the French party was not the only one to have "overshot the mark a little" in this respect for "our worthy Germans have not always been correct, either, in their expressions."[9] His unease was certainly justified, and would have multiplied greatly had he lived to witness the nationalist utterances of the SPD leadership not only at Party congresses, but in the Reichstag itself. Only a few weeks before his death in 1913, Bebel informed the German parliament that "there is not a single person in Germany who would surrender the fatherland to an enemy without a fight. This is particularly true of the Social Democrats." Bebel, who must certainly be numbered amongst the very finest leaders of the German proletariat, never explained how his unashamedly patriotic stand could be reconciled with his justly famed slogan: "Not a man, not a farthing for this system." (This can only mean that had Bebel lived another year, he would have thrown his enormous political influence and prestige behind a policy of support for German imperialism in its war against Russia, France and Britain.) Bebel was particularly sensitive to charges that the party leadership were failing to combat militarism amongst the youth, and when challenged on this issue at the 1906 Party Congress by Karl Liebknecht, who praised the Belgian Socialist Party for its work in this field, Bebel replied:

> It is incomprehensible to me how he can hold up to us as the example of Belgium, a country which signifies nothing, and whose army cannot be compared to Prussian military organisation.

And this was a debate on anti-militarist propaganda!* Bebel's militantly nationalist tone was grist to the mill of opportunist elements in the French Socialist Party, who eagerly cited such speeches as proof of the need to adopt a line of national defence in France against an SPD-backed invasion by Germany. At the party congress in 1907, held at a time when strenuous attempts were being made in the Second International to achieve a united front of all its sections against a possible European war, Bebel again declared himself unconditionally for national defence:

> If we really have to defend our fatherland, then we shall defend it because it is our fatherland, the soil on which we live, whose language we speak, whose customs are our own: because we want to transform this our fatherland, into a country which has no equal in perfection and beauty anywhere on earth.

The goal of a socialist Germany in the indefinite future was therefore employed — seven years before the actual outbreak of war — to justify defence of the Kaiser's Germany of the present. It was as if Bebel and his fellow SPD leaders made a mental distinction between the material Germany exploited and ruled by the Junkers and bourgeoisie, and an ideal, almost mystical Germany which existed outside of space and time, and believed that by defending the former they were also protecting the latter. Bebel's exposition of this notion was certainly eloquent, but it had nothing in common with that celebrated dictum of the *Communist Manifesto* "The working men have no country. We cannot take from them what they have not got."

It would, however, be quite wrong simply to single out Bebel for criticism.** Eduard Bernstein, the pioneer of revisionism, was well to the fore in justifying and embellishing the foreign and even colonial policy of Imperial Germany. In his first broadside against Marxism, published in 1899, he wrote that: "only a conditional right of savages to the land can be recognised, the higher civilisation ultimately can claim higher right."[10] The same Bernstein supported the SPD right wing in its demands for a 'realistic' colonial policy at the 1907 Stuttgart Congress of the Second International with the most cynical sophistries:

---

* Bebel's contemptuous opinion of Belgium and its armed forces were shared by the German High Command, as the first days of the war revealed.

** Since this book is concerned chiefly with Germany, it obviously cannot examine similar and equally reactionary nationalist deviations in the other parties of the International.

All the earth has been taken for colonies, and with the increasing power of the socialist fractions in the different parliaments Socialist responsibility has increased. They must oppose the bourgeois colonial policy, but they cannot wash their hands like Pilate and say, "We will have none of the colonies." To do that would be to deliver the natives over to their exploiters.

Bernstein was more honest when he stated, later in the same speech, that "however much damage the colonies might have caused, our economic life largely depends on them." Equally reactionary views on the military and colonial questions appeared regularly in the SPD press, especially that right-wing preserve, the *Sozialistische Monatshefte*, where in November 1905 Richard Calver wrote:

Today, when Germany is the equal, economically, of England and the United States, and is compelled to take up an attitude towards all questions of world-politics in the interest of its industry, the naval policy of modern industrial states may indeed be severely condemned, but it cannot be expected of one's own country that it should take up an exceptional position which might be fatal. As matters are today the prestige of a State abroad depends on its readiness for war both on sea and land.

Elsewhere Calver recommended — in language utterly alien to the Marxist tradition — that

German socialists should not ignore the fact that our capitalists and employers are compelled to colonise if Germany's economic future is to be secured against competing countries abroad... We see how the enterprise of all other powerful industrial lands... appropriates the globe. Social Democrats cannot expect German enterprise to stay quietly at home and renounce the aims of a world policy. Should not and must not capitalism first bring the world under subjection before a socialistic organisation of economics will be possible?... it follows that capital — including German capital as well — must go forth and subdue the world with the means and weapons which are at its disposal. There will still be ample room for criticism of capitalistic colonial policy.

These amazing lines, justifying to the hilt the rapacious policies and actions of German imperialism were written at a time when Bernsteinian revisionism had been formally ostracised from the SPD, when it was official party policy and practice to solemnly affirm the revolutionary and internationalist principles of German social democracy. What a wretched farce, when out-and-out chauvinists like Calver could sully the columns of the official party press month after month with propaganda which did not merely justify imperialist war, but actually *demanded* it on behalf of "German capital." And presiding over this disgusting spectacle was none other than Karl Kautsky, regarded not only in Germany but throughout Europe as the foremost theoretician of the Second International! But before turning to Kautsky's responsibility for the degeneration of the SPD, we must examine the party's attitude to the question of the state, an issue which bedevilled relations between Marx and Engels and the German movement from its very inception in 1863.

Again we must return to Engels, this time to his introduction to Marx's *The Class Struggles in France*. This essay has a history all of its own. Engels makes a sober analysis of the prospects for a successful street insurrection against the best-equipped armies of the day, and comes to the realistic conclusion that the old-style barricade fighting of 1848 can no longer be conducted with reasonable hope of victory. These lines were eagerly seized on by the SPD leadership when the article was published in *Vorwärts* in March 1895 as Engels' endorsement of the party's rejection of all violent means to achieve its goal. But that was not at all the intention of the author who also appended to this judgment the opinion:

> Does that mean that in future street fighting will no longer play any role? Certainly not. It only means that the conditions since 1848 have become far more unfavourable for civilian fighting and far more favourable for the military. In future, street fighting can, therefore, be victorious only if this disadvantageous situation is compensated by other factors. Accordingly, it will occur more seldom in the beginning of a great revolution than in its further progress, and will have to be undertaken with greater forces.[11]

Precisely these lines, which spoke of future, better organised and wider supported insurrections, were deleted from the article by the *Vorwärts* editor, Wilhelm Liebknecht. Engels was naturally furious, and wrote to Kautsky asking that the whole introduction be published in the SPD theoretical journal, *Neue Zeit*, lest he appear as a "peaceful worshipper of legality at any price!"[12] Engels was never this, and yet there are other sections of this same essay which convey the impression that he had been carried away by the electoral successes of the SPD to such an extent that Engels saw in them not only evidence of the party's growing support in the working class, but a political factor in its own right:

> Its growth proceeds as spontaneously, as steadily, as irresistibly and at the same time as tranquilly as a natural process. All government intervention has proved powerless against it... If it continues in this fashion, by the end of the century we shall conquer the greater part of the middle strata of society, petty-bourgeois and small peasants, and grow into the decisive power in the land, before which all other powers will have to bow, whether they like it or not. To keep this growth going without interruption until it of itself gets beyond the control of the prevailing governmental system... to keep it intact until the decisive day, that is our main task.[13]

Again, as was the case with his letter to Bebel on a possible Russo-German war, Engels combines semi-reformist concepts with revolutionary ones, the idea of peaceful, gradual and irresistable progress towards an unchallengeable parliamentary majority interwoven with the notion of a "decisive day," which, in the discreet language imposed on Engels by the German censors, can only mean revolution. Then there is the formulation concerning the winning of the petty-bourgeoisie to socialism, which is conceived of as an inevitable outcome of the SPD's triumphal parliamentary march, and not as the result of a combative anticapitalist policy which detaches, by virtue of its resoluteness, the middle class masses from their allegiance to the main bourgeois parties. Finally there are the less well known but equally ambiguous statements made by Engels in an interview with the French newspapter *Le Figaro* in 1893, where he predicted:

> The time is drawing near when our Party will be called upon to take over government... Perhaps towards the end of the century you will see this event occur. (Since there was) a constant increase at each election (it would soon lead to at least) half the army (being on the side of the SPD*) On the day when we shall be in the majority, what the French army did by instinct by not firing on the people will be done by our people in a conscious way.[14]

A rationalist, as distinct from a dialectical materialist approach can also be detected in remarks made to the English *Daily Chronicle* about the ease with which the notoriously reactionary German petty-bourgeoisie could be won to the side of the proletariat:

> The small tradesman, crushed out by the big store, the clerk, the artisan... are beginning to feel the pinch of our present capitalist system. And we place a scientific remedy before them, and as they can all read and think for themselves, they soon come round and join our ranks.[15]

In fact, the SPD never made any real headway amongst these layers under the German Empire. Its steadily mounting vote came from new generations and sections of workers freshly won to the socialist cause, and not from a petty-bourgeoisie converted by the "scientific remedies" of Marxism. Here too, the old Engels departs from ideas which he himself developed in an earlier period, for he was, with Marx, the most trenchant critic of the German petty-bourgeoisie, with its inbred philistinism and distaste for even the most modest democratic reforms. Also at variance with the younger Engels is his reply when asked if the SPD hoped to form a government in the near future: "Why not? If the growth

---

* Here Engels was mistaken. It was Government policy to recruit their standing army from non-proletarian, preferably peasant, strata of the population, where socialist sympathies were weakest. On the eve of war only 6.14% of army servicemen came from the large towns, whereas 19.1% of the total German population lived in them. On the other hand, rural-born soldiers made up nearly 65% of the army, while only 42.5% of the population lived in the countryside. Thus even a sizable SPD election majority would not necessarily have resulted in a socialist majority in the army.

of our Party continues at its normal rate we shall have a majority between the years 1900 and 1910."[16] Here the formation of an SPD government is predicated quite unambiguously on the achievement of a parliamentary majority,* which in its turn devolved on a 'normal' growth of the party's vote. Although Engels' predictions went sadly astray — the SPD won only 34.8% of the total poll in the 1912 Reichstag elections, with 4.25 million votes and 110 deputies — this is not really the point. As in questions of German foreign policy, Engels erred in his method, which while capable of illuminating a whole range of political, economic and philosophical problems as few other Marxists could, failed to penetrate to the very depths of the new relations evolving between classes and nations in Europe. The burning necessity of 'rearming' the party theoretically to enable its members to make the transition from the old situation under illegality, to one where the movement was becoming a serious contender for state power, was simply not appreciated either by Engels or the established leaders of the SPD in Germany. And here too we see the same process of combined and uneven development, now working itself out in a highly original — and ironic — way. Germany — the land of Hegel, Marx and Engels — and the SPD, the historical inheritors of the revolutionary legacy of German idealist philosophy, began to lose its place as the theoretical fountainhead of the international workers' movement. Just as the nation's political backwardness had thrust the young German proletariat forward as the sole protagonist of democracy and national unification, the theoretical 'leap' that this development involved was in its turn transformed into its opposite. The movement rested on its laurels — Engels included — and gradually began to adapt to the political status quo. Of course, this process was based upon the rapid growth of a conservative, nationalist, party and trade union bureaucracy —ideas must be nourished and sustained by the sap of material conditions — but in saying this we must not delude ourselves that the degeneration of the SPD has therefore been fully explained.

There exist tendencies towards conservative thinking and bureaucratic practices in the healthiest of revolutionary workers' parties. And it could not be otherwise, because such parties comprise both a unity and a struggle of opposites where the entire membership, at widely differing levels of consciousness, participates to one degree or another in the fight to combat these political and theoretical weaknesses. However, in Germany the

* Yet in 1889 — one year before the fall of the anti-socialist legislation (an event which undoubtedly coloured Engels' strategic and tactical conceptions in the last years of his life) — Engels bluntly declared: "The proletariat cannot conquer its political domination .. without violent revolution." (Letter to G. Trier, London, December 18, 1889, in *Selected Correspondence*, p.492)

party used its strengths to *conceal* its growing weaknesses, while in Russia, principally under the leadership of Lenin, but also in its early period under Plekhanov, the movement employed its strong points to expose, combat and overcome its deficiencies. Compelled to wage the sharpest philosophical and political battles against the Populists, "Legal Marxists," Economists and after 1903, Mensheviks, Ultra-Lefts and 'conciliators', Lenin and the pioneers of Russian Marxism raised the theoretical level of the Russian revolutionary movement from an abyss of backwardness born of centuries of ignorance and oppression to a peak which even the most clear-sighted German Marxists never attained. And they did this by absorbing all that was finest in the international workers' movement:

> Russia achieved Marxism... through the *agony* she experienced in the course of half a century of unparalleled torment and sacrifice, of unparalleled revolutionary heroism, incredible energy, devoted searching, study, practical trial, disappointment, verification, and comparison with European experience. Thanks to the political emigration caused by Tsarism, revolutionary Russia in the second half of the last century, acquired a wealth of international links and excellent information on the forms and theories of the world revolutionary movement, such as no other country possessed.[17]

By contrast, the days of agony for German social democracy were receding into the past. Its leadership, while paying lip service to the heroic traditions of that era, were steadily adapting themselves both theoretically and politically to the peaceful expansion of German capitalism, a growth which permitted sizeable layers of the proletariat to win living standards unthinkable in the early years of the Empire. Instead of waging war against the illusions of these "labour aristocrats" in the viability — or even desirability — of German capitalism, as Lenin had combatted the Economist protagonists of the possibility of spontaneous working class development into socialist consciousness, the SPD bureaucracy was allowed by the top party leadership to adapt to these tendencies. Fearing a conflict with the entrenched trade union apparatus, Kautsky delegated the handling of all tactical and political questions to Bebel, who in his turn sought to balance himself between the SPD Right and Left wings. Thus there evolved a series of unprincipled combinations at almost every level of party activity. Until his death in 1895, Engels was seen as the interpreter of Marxist 'cannon' especially in philosophy and economics, while within Germany, 'theory' was handled by Kautsky and the practical questions by Bebel and Wilhelm Liebknecht. Yet even while Engels lived, this "division of labour" contained dangers which both Trotsky and Lenin later came to recognise, for the main theoretical burden was carried by an exile who in his last years was unable to grasp the transition already well under way from pre-monopoly capitalism to imperialism, foreshadowed in Germany by the growth of the cartel system and the seizure of colonies. Both these processes were, as we have noted, initiated ten full years before the death of Engels, yet they seem to have made little, if any impact on his thinking. Trotsky was fully justified in taking Engels to task for having

> visualised the future course of revolutionary development too much along the straight line. Above all he did not foresee the mighty capitalist boom which set in immediately after his death and which lasted up to the eve of the imperialist war. It was precisely in the course of these 15 years of economic full bloodedness that the complete degeneration of the leading circles of the labour movement took place. This degeneration was fully revealed during the war and, in the last analysis, it led to the infamous capitulation to national socialism.*[18]

So we are completely justified in concerning ourselves with the problems of German social democracy prior to 1914, for it was in this period that the traitors of 1933 experienced their formative years and underwent their political training. And we are equally justified in seeking to contrast this process of degeneration, whose hallmark was theoretical compromise, with the struggle for revolutionary leadership — firmly grounded in revolutionary theory — waged by Lenin in the Russian workers' movement. Lenin, like Trotsky, was not uncritical of Engels' last writings, especially on the question of war. Although more guarded than Trotsky (he never voiced these differences publicly) his private correspondence and notebooks contain remarks which are either direct or implied criticisms of Engels. Beginning in the Autumn of 1916, Lenin conducted a lengthy correspondence with his old friend Inessa Armand on the seemingly abstruse question of the periodisation of imperialism. Seemingly, because Armand claimed that imperialism had already become a predominant trend in world capitalism before the death of Engels, and that consequently, he shared, to however small an extent, the blame of the SPD leadership for failing to re-orient the German working class on the question of national defence. Looking only at Lenin's replies (Armand's letters are reputedly under lock and key in some Moscow vault), it becomes clear that Lenin was hard pressed to defend Engels against this charge. He nevertheless upheld him on the question of a possible war between Russia and Germany:

> In 1891, the German Social democrats' really should have defended their fatherland in a war against Boulanger** and Alexander III. This would have been a peculiar variety of a national war.[19]

---

* Trotsky is of course in no sense implying that Engels was responsible for this degeneration, simply that he failed to detect its beginnings, which is another question.

** A military contender for the Presidency of France. His plebeian-based, intensely nationalist movement had collapsed a full year before Engels wrote the article under discussion. Thus Lenin's argument in this respect does not stand up, hinging as it

This reply clearly did not satisfy the insistent Inessa, for we find Lenin still trying to convince her a month later with the bold assertion that "in 1891 no imperialism existed *at all*" and that therefore, "there was no imperialist war, therefore could not be, on the part of Germany."[20] Finally, Lenin concedes, after several more exchanges, that Engels had possibly failed to detect the new political forms which were emerging in the last years of his life. Further than this Lenin would not go. But in his *Notebooks on Imperialism* compiled mainly in the First World War, we find him making critical remarks in the margin of Engels' pamphlet *Can Europe Disarm?*, published in 1893. Despite his almost reverential attitude toward the life-long comrade and friend of Marx, Lenin could not refrain from quizzical annotations in passages where Engels revealed a truly rationalist belief in the possibility of "a gradual reduction of the term of service by international agreement", when he stated "I maintain disarmament, and thereby the guarantee of peace, is possible" and that Germany had the "power and vocation" to achieve it.[21] An uncritical and unthinking acceptance of the Marxist heritage was utterly alien to Trotsky, Lenin, Plekhanov and Luxemburg. How different with Kautsky, who in seeking to defend Marxism from its opponents, degenerated into a custodian of "orthodoxy," a populariser of Marxism who was, in the words of Trotsky, "never a man of action, never a revolutionist, or an heir to the spirit of Marx and Engels."[22] We can see the truth of this judgment in Kautsky's role in two great theoretical controversies which burst upon the international movement in the first decade of the 20th century.

The first, and far more well-known, concerned Bernstein's attempt to adjust the SPD's formally revolutionary theory and programme to its increasingly reformist practice. Kautsky, the recognised leading theoretician of German social democracy, was at first extremely reluctant to cross swords with Engels' literary executor, even when Bernstein was quite openly departing from and challenging both Engels and Marx on every basic question of Marxist political strategy, tactics, programme and philosophy. In 1898, *Die Neue Zeit* published an article by Bernstein pointing out — with some justification — that the SPD was concealing its reformist activity beneath a facade of revolutionary phrases, and it was high time the party acknowledged this publicly. Excluding the younger generation of Lefts personified by Rosa Luxemburg, Bernstein's onslaught on revolutionary Marxism only aroused genuine anger and concern in the Russian movement. Plekhanov, not Kautsky or Bebel, was the first to hit back in print, and even

does on the existence of an anti-German alliance of two ultra right-wing dictatorships.

then, Kautsky submitted him to the same indignity as the older Liebknecht had inflicted on Engels — that of censoring those sections of his article which were sharpest in their criticisms of Bernstein. Plekhanov had originally hoped to persuade Kautsky to spearhead the counter-attack, and to this purpose wrote to him on May 20, 1898:

> If Bernstein is right in his critical endeavours, one may ask what remains of the philosophical and socialist ideas of our teachers? What remains of socialism? and in truth, one would have to reply: not very much!

Unable to understand Kautsky's aloofness from what Plekhanov rightly saw as a life and death battle for the future of the revolutionary movement, he bluntly asked him:

> Can you be in agreement with Bernstein? It would be too painful for me to believe that. If not, why do you not answer? It is you who are attacked... yes, we are going through a crisis, and this crisis is making me suffer very much.

In fact, Plekhanov's half-rhetorical question was far nearer the mark than he would have suspected, for once combat with the revisionists had been joined it emerged that Kautsky did indeed share much common ground with those whom he had been reluctantly compelled to do battle. Kautsky felt himself on firm ground when rebutting Bernstein's reformist perspectives, which the latter summed up in his well-known aphorism: "To me that which is generally called the ultimate aim of socialism is nothing, but the movement is everything."[22] Crushing majorities were amassed at a succession of SPD congresses in support of resolutions declaring Bernstein's theories incompatible with social democracy, yet when the dust had settled, revisionism emerged stronger and more entrenched than ever. The answer lies only partly in the immense preponderance of the conservative party and trade union machine in determining day-to-day policies and activities of the movement. It undoubtedly both nourished and responded to Bernstein's revision of Marxism, as did the growing band of bourgeois intellectuals who flocked to the party's banner once it became a major force in German political and cultural life. Neither was it a simple matter of Kautsky being able, single-handed or with the support of the party Left, to stem the rising flood of opportunism. This was a product of deep-going, objective processes in both the German and international economy, an ideological refraction of the material privileges which a relatively broad layer of the most skilled workers had secured for themselves in the period of pre-1914 capitalist expansion. Only the most profound and violent convulsions could — and in fact did — undermine the reactionary role of the social democratic bureaucracy and the social stratum upon which it rested. The great political treason committed by

Kautsky was his utter failure to penetrate to the core the methodological roots of Bernstein's revisionism, to show how his political programme of capitulation to German imperialism flowed from his philosophical rejection of dialectical materialism and his reversion to the subjective idealism of the neo-Kantians.

Bernstein ended his *Evolutionary Socialism* with the recommendation that the socialist movement should no longer base itself on the materialistic world outlook of Marxism, but the morality of Kant:

> A class which is aspiring needs a sound morale and must suffer no deterioration. Whether it sets out for itself an ideal ultimate aim is of secondary importance if it pursues with energy its proximate aims... And this in mind, I... resorted to the spirit of the great Königsberg philosopher, the critic of pure reason, against the cant* which sought to get a hold of the working class movement and to which the Hegelian dialectic offers a comfortable refuge. I did this in the conviction that social democracy required à Kant who should judge the received opinion, and examine it critically with deep acuteness, who should show where its apparent materialism is the highest — and is therefore the most easily misleading — ideology, and warn it that contempt of the ideal, the magnifying of material factors until they become omnipotent forces of evolution, is a self-deception...[24]

All Bernstein's previous — and subsequent — attacks on Marxism paled before this bid to drag the German workers' movement back, not only to a pre-Marxist, but even pre-Hegelian philosophical foundation. In doing so, he acted in concert with all those ideologues of German reaction from Schopenhauer to Nietzsche who recoiled from the revolutionary implications of the Hegelian dialectic and constructed out of Kant's subjective theory of knowledge a series of apologias for mysticism and in the last analysis, political reaction. But amazingly, Kautsky regarded Bernstein's Kantianism as the least objectionable feature of his revisionist system. Evidently Kautsky saw nothing revolting in this humbug preaching a higher morality to the German working class while at the same time denying the right of land ownership to "savages." Plekhanov, whose knowledge of German philosophy dwarfed that of any leading German social democrat save Franz Mehring, wrote once more to Kautsky imploring him to open the pages of the SPD theoretical journal to a discussion on philosophy. And when the editor of *Die Neue Zeit* lamely replied that only a handful of readers could hope to follow what Kautsky regarded as an esoteric debate, Plekhanov made the admirable retort: "It is essential to *force* the readers to interest themselves in philosophy... *it is the science of sciences.*" Such an aggressive approach was utterly alien to the increasingly complacent Kautsky. The idea of actually disturbing, provoking and even

* A deliberate play on words.

angering one's readers in order to raise their level of political consciousness shocked him deeply. Undismayed by Kautsky's coolness, Plekhanov directly addressed the SPD *Die Neue Zeit* in the same querulous tones:

> I am always and always will defend the outlook of Marx and Engels with passion and conviction, and if some readers shrug their shoulders over the fact that I am so heated in a polemic, which concerns the most important questions of human knowledge and at the same time touches upon the most essential interests of the working class... then I say, shrugging my shoulders in turn: *so much the worse for such readers*

The great tragedy was that ultimately, it was not the slothful readers of *Die Neue Zeit* who paid the supreme penalty for their disinterest in philosophy, but the entire German proletariat. As Kautsky sowed, so the Weimar leaders of German social democracy — Müller, Wels, Severing, Braun and Leipart — reaped. Their harvest was a bitter and bloody one. Kautsky's apologetic reply to the demand by Plekhanov that he wage war on Bernstein's philosophical idealism was not merely a confession of theoretical bankruptcy but downright treachery to both the German and international working class:

> I must openly declare that neo-Kantianism disturbs me least of all. I have never been strong on philosophy, and although I stand entirely on the point of view of dialectical materialism still I think that the economic and historical viewpoint of Marx and Engels is in the last resort compatible with neo-Kantianism. If Bernstein was moulting only in this respect, it would not disturb me in the least.

Kautsky, the great populariser, was also the great vulgariser. He broke down what he took to be Marxism into a series of propositions on different fields of human activity and natural processes — much in the way now done by sociologists specialising in "Marxism," overlooking their unified origin in a materialist world outlook. So it was quite possible on this eclectic basis, to find what appeared to be common ground between certain views of idealists and the practical sides of the socialist movement. The divergences deepen precisely when the ground is shifted from "concrete political tasks"* to the seemingly rarified atmosphere of

---

* Max Shachtman, co-leader with James Burnham of the middle-class based opposition in the American Socialist Workers Party in 1939-1940, used this formulation to blur over their profound differences with dialectical materialism. They argued against Trotsky that agreement on "concrete" questions transcended such differences. Both subsequently left the SWP, Burnham joining the extreme right wing of anti-communist publicists, Shachtman becoming a "State Department socialist." Shortly before his clash with Trotsky, Shachtman wrote an article for the SWP journal *New International* where he used a formulation whose spirit, if not wording, had much in common with Kautsky's reply to Plekhanov: "...nor has anyone yet demonstrated that agreement or disagreement on the more abstract doctrines of dialectical materialism necessarily affects today's and tomorrow's concrete political issues — and political parties, programmes and struggles are based

method, theory of knowledge, and philosophy. So it was with Marx and Engels in their rupture from the young Hegelians, Trotsky in his fight against Stalin's metaphysical theory of "socialism in one country," and so it should have been, but was not, in Kautsky's polemic with Bernsteinian revisionism.

Only in the Russian movement was the theoretical battle fought with the gloves off, first by Plekhanov, and then, following his decline into Menshevism and eventual support for the First World War, by Lenin. And it was a struggle which transcended national frontiers and rode rough-shod over smugness, prestige and backwardness. The fighting was at its most intense, and the knives at their sharpest, precisely in the domain of the highest abstractions. In Lenin's *Philosophical Notebooks,* compiled during the war, we see why this was so:

> Hegel is completely right as opposed to Kant. Through proceeding from the concrete to the abstract — provided it is correct... does not get away from the truth; but comes closer to it... all scientific (correct, serious, not absurd) abstractions reflect nature more deeply, truly and completely. From living perception to abstract thought, *and from this to practice,* — such is the dialectical path of the cognition of *truth,* of the cognition of objective reality.[25]

The first salvoes of the October Revolution were not fired by the cruiser *Aurora* at the Winter Palace, but by Plekhanov and Lenin at the traducers of dialectical materialism! And Lenin did not suddenly come to the conclusion in 1914 that philosophy was all-important for the political struggle, nor even in the days of the struggle against Bernstein, when in his classic pamphlet on the trade union question *What is to be Done?* he made his famous declaration that "without revolutionary theory there can be no revolutionary movement." We find him, at the very outset of his political career as a professional revolutionary, seeking to probe political problems and differences to their philosophical roots, as in his long article, written in 1894 at the age of 24, *What the "Friends of the People" are, and how they fight the Social Democrats.* In this youthful *tour de force,* Lenin already reveals a deep understanding of the Marxist classics, and employs it to counter the attack on the dialectical method then being launched by a section of the liberal Russian intelligentsia.

But he was far from being the Lenin of the *Philosophical Notebooks.* In the initial phase of the struggle against Bernstein, Lenin was content to lend his uncritical support to Kautsky, as can be seen from his review of the latter's *Bernstein and the Social*

---

on such concrete issues." And Burnham, who later advocated "preventative" nuclear war on the Soviet Union, shared with Bernstein both his aversion to Hegel, whom he once described as "the century-dead arch muddler of human thought" and, before his final defection to the far-right, the belief that "socialism is a moral ideal, which reflective men choose deliberately by a moral act."

Democratic Programme, which Lenin drafted, but never published, in 1899. However, he soon struck a different note from Kautsky, who was concerned simply to re-state, and not enrich, the theory and principles pioneered by Marx and Engels. For Lenin, this was not enough:

> To defend such a theory, which to the best of your knowledge you consider to be true, against unfounded attacks and attempts to corrupt it is not to imply that you are an enemy of *all* criticism. We do not regard Marx's theory as something completed and inviolable; on the contrary, we are convinced that it has only laid the foundation stone of the science which socialists *must* develop in all directions if they wish to keep pace with life...[26]

So much for Lenin the "dogmatist"! From the turn of the century, Lenin increasingly saw and combatted opportunism in the Russian movement as an integral part of a wider offensive against revolutionary Marxism. The Russian Economists, Bernstein's revisionism and the openly reformist practices of English trade union leaders were all reflections and expressions of an international tendency which arose in response to the pressure, mediated through the radical petty-bourgeoisie and the labour aristocracy, exerted by imperialism on the workers' movement. The struggle against revisionism was therefore the theoretical expression of the struggle between classes, a fight not simply for correct formulations, important though these were, but for the destiny of the workers' movement and an integral part of the preparation for the revolutionary overthrow of capitalism. This urgency, this sense of the life-and-death nature of the theoretical struggle, was precisely that element in Kautsky's political make up which was lacking: "His character, like his thought, lacked audacity and sweep, without which revolutionary politics is impossible..."[27] Lenin, who for nearly two decades regarded himself as a pupil of Kautsky, was in this respect his polar opposite. He entered the fray bent on determining the inner forces of a problem, process or controversy, all the time gathering the forces in and around the Bolshevik Party for one single purpose — revolution. It was on this basis that he fought out his prolonged philosophical struggle within the Bolshevik faction against a tendency which, under the leadership of Alexander Bogdanov, sought to update Marxism by importing into it concepts derived mainly from modern physics, but also from the writings of various neo-Kantian philosophers. This new attempt to revise the dialectical materialist foundations of the Marxist world outlook, to replace it with a subjectivist theory of knowledge which harked back to the solipsism of Bishop Berkeley, arose in the conditions of pessimism created by the crushing of the 1905 revolution. Mysticism in its various guises gripped wide sections of intellectuals who had either been sympathetic towards or committed supporters of Marxism in the previous period when the workers' movement had been in the ascendent. In the Bolshevik party, they eclectically combined the general propositions of Marxism about the class struggle and economics with a theory of knowledge which denied, after the manner of Kant's "thing-in-itself" the possibility of cognising the world outside human consciousness; and even in extreme cases, in the tradition of the English sceptic David Hume, whether one could say with certainty that there was anything which lay beyond the data recorded by our senses. And here we find ourselves on familiar philosophical territory, that of the German subjectivist school which after rejecting Hegel, returned to Kant and eventually degenerated into the mystical power-worship and anti-socialist pathology of Nietzsche. The same Kantianism also succeeded — albeit in another guise — in penetrating into the very heart of the German workers movement, and in Russia, Lenin found himself fighting the same philosophical opponents, this time dressed up in the garb of *Empirio-Criticism.** The result — after several years of intensive study — was his *Materialism and Empirio Criticism*, published in 1909 as a broadside against all those who were bending to the most reactionary philosophical theories yet evolved — namely the schools of subjectivism and mysticism. And for this very reason — not for its style and fierceness of polemic — the book has been more abused than almost any other in Marxist literature. Most of all its critics baulk at Lenin's concluding statement that

> one must not fail to see in the struggle of parties in philosophy a struggle which in the last analysis reflects the tendencies and ideology of the antagonistic classes in modern society... the contending parties are essentially... materialism and idealism. The latter is merely a subtle, refined form of idealism, which stands fully armed, commands vast organisations and steadily continues to exercise influence on the masses, turning the slightest vacillation in philosophical thought to its own advantage.[28]

Lenin could have been writing about the SPD! For here, reluctance to combat revisionism philosophically led in the first great historical test of the party to its utter capitulation to precisely those forces which had been seeking the movement's annihilation for more than half a century. Neither was this confined to the struggle against Bernstein. Kautsky also revealed a profound reluctance to become involved in the Russian party controversy between Lenin and Plekhanov as partisans of dialectical materialism and the Bolshevik "Machists."** (Not that Lenin

* The name given to his philosophy by the German follower of Spinoza, Richard Avenarius, who unwittingly provided the Bogdanov group with many of its anti-Marxist notions.

denigrated the work of non-Marxist or even idealist scientists in their own specialised fields. In his last article on philosophical questions, written in 1922, he stressed the importance of following every trend in modern science and philosophy, pointing out "that the sharp upheaval which modern natural science is undergoing very often gives rise to reactionary philosophical schools... Unless, therefore, the problems raised by the recent revolution in natural science are followed, and natural sciences are enlisted in the work of a philosophical journal, militant materialism can be neither militant nor materialism"[29] Ignoring this work — work that Kautsky considered irrelevent to the prosecution of the class struggle — necessarily led to reactionary ideologists and philosophers interpreting the findings of modern science in an idealist fashion, what Lenin called "clutching at the skirts of Einstein," even though the pioneer of relativity theory was "not making any active attack on the foundations of materialism.")

Asked to comment on the dispute currently raging inside the Russian Marxist movement Kautsky stated — for the record — the he was himself a dialectical materialist, adding that "Marx proclaimed no philosophy, but the end of philosophy." As in the debate with Bernstein, Kautsky went out of his way to emphasise that philosophical differences, however profound, could co-exist with complete agreement on programme and indeed, on Marx's proposition that social consciousness is determined by social being. Marxism was thus debased from a general world outlook and theory of knowledge into a theory concerned solely with society; in other words, historical "materialism" without dialectical materialism*

> Whether this conception (that of the social determinants of consciousness) is based on 18th century materialism, or on Dietzgen's dialectical materialism, is not at all the same for the clarity of our *thought*; but it is a question that is entirely inconsequential for the clarity and unity of our *party*. Individual comrades may study this as private people, as they may the question of electrons or Weissmann's law of heredity; the *party* should be spared this.[30]

Kautsky not only spoke for himself when he wrote these truly philistine lines, but an entire layer within the party and trade union bureaucracy who feared thoroughgoing theoretical and philosophical conflicts as much as an elemental movement of the masses which they could not control and guide into constitutional channels. Theoretical and organisational ossification went hand in hand, producing the reformist adaptation to German imperial-

** After Ernst Mach, the physicist whose neo-Kantian interpretations of discoveries made by modern science were used by the Bogdanov group to bolster their own subjectivist theory of knowledge.

* The same position is now held by the French phenomenologist Jean-Paul Sartre, and was, before his recent death, by the Hungarian Stalinist Georg Lukacs.

ism which was revealed for the whole world to see on August 4, 1914, when the entire SPD Reichstag fraction voted for the Kaiser's war credits. So great was the class hatred of the overwhelming majority of bourgeois political commentators that they were blinded to this process at work within German social democracy. But it did not escape the most astute minds among the enemies of Marxism, notably the sociologist Max Weber. In some ways, he saw even more clearly than Lenin and Trotsky how far the SPD had deviated in practice from the revolutionary principles to which it subscribed, and what attitude the majority of its leaders would adopt when faced with a great political crisis.* Although a founder member of the Pan German League — he later resigned in protest against its tendency to favour agrarian interests in preference to those of the industrial and banking bourgeoisie — Weber never allowed his partisan class position to prevent him from making a serious study of Marxism and the activities of those who claimed to be Marxists. In this sense, he was far ahead of his time in Germany, where only in 1914 did significant (and then by no means all) sections of the bourgeois intelligentsia reluctantly concede that the SPD had discarded at least some of its revolutionary rhetoric and was on the road to becoming "national." Weber was saying this as early as 1906, when in commenting on the SPD's Mannheim Congress of that year, he wrote:

> I should like to invite our German princes on to the platform at the Mannheim party conference, just to show them how Russian socialists, sitting there as spectators, were horrified at the spectacle of this party! They had really believed it to be revolutionary... but now only the smug innkeeper face, the physiognomy of the petty-bourgeois, caught the eye... I think that no prince would continue to fear this party which has no real source of power, whose political impotence is manifest even today for all to see who choose to see.

But few at that early date chose to see. In vain, Weber addressed the liberal "Society for Social Politics" the following year, imploring bourgeoisie and government to adopt a new policy of encouraging the "realistic" and "national" wing of the party to play an active, if subordinate role in the various institutions of

* As early as 1905, the year when the first Russian revolution drove the entire SPD leadership to the left, compelling it to adopt resolutions endorsing the mass political strike as a means of achieving reforms in the Prussian electoral system (it was still based on the "three tier" class franchise of Bismarck's day) a prominent trade union leader defiantly wrote:
"What a change in our judgment of tactical questions has been produced by the continued practical and economic activity of the labouring masses... No negotiations with the employer, no contact with the bourgeois! That was the old slogan and the old tactic, meanwhile we have got away from it. The steadily increasing responsiblity of the trade union leaders has forced a new tactic. One negotiates with the employer, utilizes the state conciliation apparatus and — horror — tries to awaken understanding in the ministries for the demands of the workers."

political life:

> If the contradictions between the material interests of the professional
> politicians on the one hand and the revolutionary ideology on the
> other could develop freely, if one would no longer throw the Social
> Democrats out of the veterans' associations, if one admits them into
> church administrations, from which one expels them nowadays, then
> for the first time serious internal problems would arise for the party.
> Then it would be shown not that Social Democracy is conquering city
> and state, but, on the contrary, that the state is conquering Social
> Democracy.

And it is evident from these amazingly astute observations that
Weber was working towards a policy of splitting the SPD, of
winning its "professional politicians" or more accurately, bureaucrats, to a programme of open reformism and defence of the nation state, at the same time isolating as far as possible those who
still clung to the party's "revolutionary ideology." Presumably em-
barrassed by this all-too-accurate characterisation of the party's
leadership Kautsky never replied to Weber's critique of German
social democracy, any more than he took seriously the political
implications of those philosophical tendencies hostile to
dialectical materialism. Neither did he or any other SPD
theoretician make a serious analysis of Weber's sociology, which
originated and evolved as an alternative theory of social development and theory of knowledge to that of historical and dialectical
materialism. And because Kautsky's indifference towards the
reactionary nature and role of Kantianism led him to turn a·blind
eye to its advocates within the SPD, he was utterly unprepared to
combat its influence in the various branches of bourgeois thought
and natural sciences. For while singing the praises of a supposed
rationality in modern bourgeois politics, (a rationality mediated
through a rigidly organised bureaucracy) Weber nevertheless like
the neo-Kantian Schopenhauer and also Nietzsche, allowed the
forces of irrationality, or intuition and instinct, to invade the
world of morality:

> Here we reach the frontiers of human reason, and we enter a totally
> new world, where quite a different part of our mind pronounces
> judgment about things, and everyone knows that its judgments,
> though not based on reasons, are as certain and clear as any logical
> conclusion at which reason may arrive.[31]

However much the devotees of Weber* may be outraged by the
idea, this dichotemy between the rigidly rational functioning of
the machinery of government and industry, which Weber saw as
the heritage of what he called the "Protestant ethic," and the
highly subjective and irrational basis of "moral" actions, is perfectly compatible with the SS bureaucrats, equipped with horse

---

* Who included, during the period of E.P. Thompson's editorship, a group of
sociologists around the journal *New Left Review*.

whips, gas chambers, card indexes and ledgers, systematically organising the destrution of an entire people and then converting its human remains and material possessions into lamp shades, fertilizers, soap and a credit account with the Reichsbank amounting to RM. 178,745,960.59. Weber saw as one of his main political tasks the weaning of the German proletariat from internationalism, without at the same time openly challenging its adherence to socialism. Once again, the SPD leadership seemed, on all the available evidence, to be blind to the dangers implicit in this policy. One of Weber's most enthusiastic and far-sighted supporters in this undertaking was Friedrich Naumann. Both bemoaned the political immaturity of the German bourgeoisie, yet shrank before the alternative of a Germany ruled by the proletariat. Neither did they relish Germany's continued domination by the Junker caste, which they saw as the surest means of alienating the worker and peasant masses from a policy of national defence. The only possible alternative, they both contended, was a "power state" pursuing social policies which while defending the existing system of property relations, created a wider popular basis for the regime. In short, it was a combination of the old Bismarckian Bonaparism with elements of something new — a "social" nationalism, with the emphasis strongly on the latter. This is how Naumann, one of the moving spirits behind the "Society for Social Politics," described it in an article written in 1895:

> Is he (Weber) not right? Of what use is the best social policy if the Cossacks are coming. Whoever wants to concern himself with internal policy must first secure people, fatherland and frontiers, he must first consolidate national power. Here is the weakest point of the SPD; we need a socialism which is administrable, capable of making a better policy than hitherto. Such a socialism still does not exist. *Such a socialism must be national.*

We are not condemning the SPD leadership, and principally Kautsky, for their failing to be political clairvoyants, for failing to detect in the ideas of those who were wooing the right wing of their party the embryo of a counter-revolutionary movement which arose several decades later. That would be an unjust and absurd charge. Kautsky's great betrayal, one that led to his support for the Kaiser's armies, was his neglect of the ideological struggle against those who, whether from seemingly "liberal" positions, or from the extreme chauvinist and anti-semitic right, were working towards the destruction of the workers' movement in Germany. All Kautsky's great erudition in historical and economic questions, and his defence of the SPD programme against its reformist critics, were undermined and in the end reduced to zero by this major weakness, which in its turn, became the Achilles heel of the entire party. He never mastered the art and science, so essential for a great theoretician and workers' leader, of making the transition from one form of activity to another, of raising, in line with the requirements of a new epoch, the ceiling of his own theoretical work and with it that of the entire party. It was a passive acceptance of Marxism, an acceptance which while even recognising that all change is the product of the conflict of opposites, remained on the level of what Hegel termed "intelligent reflection," which "consists in the understanding and enunciating of contradictions," but "does not express the concept of things and their relations, and has only determinations of imagination for material and content." This method of cognition and analysis Hegel contrasted with "thinking reason" which

> sharpens the blunt difference of variety, the mere manifold of imagination, into essential differences, that is, opposition. The manifold entities acquire activity and liveliness in relation to one another only when driven on the sharp point of contradiction: thence they draw negativity, which is the inherent pulsation of self-movement and liveliness.[32]

Lenin, in a notation on this passage, observed: "Ordinary imagination grasps difference and contradiction, but not the transition from one to the other, this however is the most important..."[33] Had Kautsky pursued his revisionist quarry with the passion that must be the basis of all revolutionary activity he would not only have unearthed the manifold and complex relations which had evolved between opportunism within the SPD and the major ideological trends outside it, but in so doing, to use Hegel's expression, would have driven the entire party to "the sharp point of contradiction," the point at which the transition begins from "intelligent reflection" to where "thinking reason" grasps reality in all its "activity and liveliness," "pulsation and self-movement." Such a struggle does not of course take place in a vacuum, it develops not only on the basis of the experiences of leaders but of millions, and cannot provide advance guarantees of revolutionary success. The driving force for the theoretical struggle must be the objective movement of class forces, but in turn it can play a vital part in their future development, as witnessed in a positive sense by the October Revolution, which without Lenin's 20 years of unremitting struggle for theoretical clarity would have been impossible; and in a negative fashion, by the tragic experience of Germany, not merely in 1914 and again in 1918, but 1933. The revenge exacted by history for theoretical negligence is savage indeed.

REFERENCES FOR CHAPTER SIX

[1] K. Marx: *Capital*, Vol. I, pp.8-9, Moscow, 1959.
[2] K. Marx: *Neue Rheinische Revue*, November 1850.
[3] F. Engels: Letter to C. Schmidt, London, October 27, 1890. *Selected Correspondence* p.497.
[4] F. Engels: letter to A. Bebel, London, December 11, 1884, ibid. p.457.
[5] Article serialised in the English radical journal *Commonwealth*, whose editors included Marx, Eccarius and Odger.
[6] F. Engels: *Neue Rheinische Zeitung*, February 16-17, 1849.
[7] F. Engels, to F. Sorge, October 24, 1891.
[8] F. Engels to A. Bebel, September 29, 1891.
[9] F. Engels to P. Lafargue, London, June 27, 1893, in *Frederick Engels, Paul and Laura Lafargue Correspondence*, Vol. III, pp.269-273, Moscow, (n.d.)
[10] E. Bernstein: *Evolutionary Socialism*, pp.178-179, New York, 1963.
[11] F. Engels: *Introduction, The Class Struggles in France* by K. Marx. *Marx-Engels Selected Works*, Vol. I, p.133.
[12] F. Engels to K. Kautsky, London, April 1, 1895, *Correspondence*, p.568.
[13] F. Engels: *Introduction*, p.135.
[14] F. Engels: *Correspondence*, Vol. III, p.393.
[15] Ibid, p.399.
[16] Ibid, p.400.
[17] V. Lenin: *Left Wing Communism — An Infantile Disorder* (April-May 1920) in *Collected Works*, Vol. 31, pp.25-26.
[18] L. Trotsky: *Engels' Letters to Kautsky* (October 1935) in *Leon Trotsky on Engels and Kautsky*, p.18, New York, 1969.
[19] V. Lenin to I. Armand, Zurich, November 30, 1916, *Collected Works*, Vol. 35, p.251.
[20] V. Lenin to I. Armand, December 25, 1916, in ibid, p.268.
[21] Quoted in V. Lenin: *Collected Works*, Vol. 39, pp.499-500.
[22] L. Trotsky in ibid, p.5.
[23] E. Bernstein: *Evolutionary Socialism*, p.202.
[24] Ibid, pp.222-223.
[25] V. Lenin: *Conspectus of Hegel's "Science of Logic"* in *Collected Works*, Vol. 38, p.171.
[26] V. Lenin: *Our Programme* (1899) in *Collected Works*, Vol. 4, pp.211-212.
[27] L. Trotsky: *Karl Kautsky* (1938) in ibid, p.26.
[28] V. Lenin: *Materialism and Empirio-Criticism* (1908), in *Collected Works*, Vol. 14, p.358.
[29] V. Lenin: *On the Significance of Militant Materialism*, (March 12, 1922) in *Collected Works*, Vol. 33, pp.232-233.
[30] K. Kautsky: *Der Kampf*, 1909, No.10, p.452.
[31] M. Weber: letter to Emmy Baumgarten, July 5, 1887.
[32] W. Hegel: *Science of Logic*, Vol. II, pp.61-69, London, 1961.
[33] V. Lenin: *Conspectus of Hegel's 'Science of Logic'* in *Collected Works*, Vol. 38, p.143.

Chapter Seven

THE FIRST BETRAYALS:
SOCIAL DEMOCRACY IN WAR AND REVOLUTION

Unless the Kaiser abdicates, the social revolution is inevitable. But I will have none of it. I hate it like sin.
Friedrich Ebert, SPD Chairman, November 7, 1918.

The milestones marking Hitler's victorious march to power are each marked with an historic date in the life of the German proletariat: August 1914, when on the fourth of that month, the entire SPD Reichstag fraction voted its unconditional support to the Kaiser's imperialist war; November 1918, when the SPD leaders, headed by Ebert, entered into a secret pact with the rulers of old Germany to strangle a rising socialist revolution; October 1923, when a vacillating KPD leadership aborted the revolutionary situation which prevailed throughout the summer and early autumn of that year; August 1928, when the Stalinised Communist International embarked at its Sixth World Congress on the suicidal course of branding social democrats as "social fascists" and consequently ruling out any possibility of forming a united front with reformist parties to fight fascism; October 1930, the month when the SPD Reichstag fraction made its fatal decision to "tolerate" the anti-working class semi-Bonapartist Brüning government; August 1931, when on Stalin's orders the KPD aligned itself with the Nazis in their referendum to depose the Prussian SPD government; July 1932, which found both the SPD and KPD powerless to resist Chancellor von Papen's military-backed coup in Prussia; January 1933, when the reformist party and trade union apparatus was employed to prevent the German workers from fighting back against the newly-installed, and still uncertain Nazi-Nationalist coalition; and finally May 1933, when the trade union leaders unashamedly marched with the Nazi "Labour Front" to Hitler's "May Day" rally in Berlin, setting the seal on the ignominious capitulation of the leaders of the German working class to fascist counter-revolution.

It could of course be argued — and in fact has been — that each of these retreats necessarily led to the next, that Hitler's destruction of the German workers' movement was but a logical

outcome of all that went before. Neat and seemingly historical
though this line of reasoning is, it ignores one of the main factors
in German political life throughout this period — the working
class. Had there been on each occasion a leadership with deep
roots in the masses capable of making a stand against these
blunders and betrayals, and of devising revolutionary strategy
and tactics appropriate to the prevailing situation in Germany
and Europe, there is no room for doubt that Hitler's movement
would never have achieved the proportions that it did, let alone
conquer power. For unlike the defeat of the 1525 Peasants' Revolt
and the bourgeois revolution of 1848, we are now dealing with
reverses inflicted on the masses *as a direct consequence of the
inadequacies of their own leadership,* be it social democratic,
centrist or Stalinist. The entire course of the class struggle in
Germany between 1914 and 1933 is the most tragic verification of
Trotsky's assertion, written into the founding programme of the
Fourth International, that "the world political situation as a
whole is chiefly characterised by a historical crisis of the leadership of the proletariat."[1] The dimensions of this crisis only
became fully visible after the bankruptcy of the Stalinist-
dominated Communist International was confirmed by the
monumental defeat of the German proletariat in 1933, but its contours were already discernable in August 1914, when the leading
party of the Second International, no only failed to mount any
serious opposition to the war, but actually threw its massive
political and organisational weight behind the Kaiser's imperialist
war machine. From being avowed enemies of militarism and
capitalist exploitation, the SPD leaders almost without exception
were transformed literally overnight into recruiting sergeants for
the Prussian Officer Corps and strike-breakers for the Thyssens,
Krupps, Stumms, Stinnes and Kirdorfs, the most implacable foes
of the German working class. The magnitude and suddenness of
this unprecedented *volte face* was a traumatic experience even for
those in the international movement who had been the SPD's
sharpest critics. Lenin for one simply refused to believe it had
happened telling his fellow exile and close comrade Grigory
Zinoviev that the issue of *Vorwärts* which carried news of the war
credits vote was a government forgery.* Trotsky, who had spent
several of his exile years working in close collaboration with the
leaders of German and Austrian social democracy, held out less

---

* Zinoviev recalled four years later that he and Lenin had bet on the outcome of the
Reichstag vote. Lenin believed the SPD fraction would not lead an opposition to the
war, but would, to salve their consciences, vote against the war credits. Although
Zinoviev was nearer the mark in predicting an abstention, he frankly conceded that
'neither of us had taken the full measure of the flunkeyism of the social democrats.'
(G. Zinoviev: *Lenin—a speech to the Petrograd Soviet,* September 6, 1918, p.33,
London. 1966.)

hopes for any anti-war stand on their part, even doubting whether
had Bebel lived another year, he would have stood firm against a
rising torrent of chauvinism which engulfed not only the German
petty-bourgeoisie, but the overwhelming majority of the working
class. Nevertheless,

> the telegram telling of the capitulation of the German Social
> Democracy shocked me even more than the declaration of war, in
> spite of the fact that I was far from a naive idealising of German
> socialism... I did not expect the official leaders of the International, in
> case of war, to prove themselves capable of serious revolutionary
> initiative. At the same time, I would not even admit the idea that the
> Social Democracy would simply cower on its belly before a nationalist
> militarism... the vote of August 4 has remained one of the tragic ex-
> periences of my life.[2]

This sense of shock and betrayal was understandable. At the
Stuttgart (1907) Congress of the Socialist International, the SPD
delegation — though not without considerable prodding from
Lenin, Rosa Luxemburg and Martov — voted unanimously for a
resolution which, after analysing the causes of militarism and
national rivalries, ended with the following call:

> If a war threatens to break out, it is the duty of the working class and
> of its parliamentary representatives in the countries involved,
> supported by the consolidating activity of the International Bureau, to
> exert every effort to prevent the outbreak of war by means they con-
> sider most effective... Should war break out none the less, it is their
> duty to intervene in favour of its speedy termination and to do all in
> their power to utilize the economic and political crisis caused by the
> war to rouse the peoples and thereby to hasten the abolition of
> capitalist class rule.[3]

This anti-war position was endorsed by subsequent Congresses at
Copenhagen (1910) and Basle (1912), the latter adopting a
manifesto *On the International Situation* which in the light of
imperialist rivalries in the Balkans, declared:

> The most important task in the International's activities devolves upon
> the working class of Germany, France and England (and that)
> proletarians consider it a crime to fire at each other for the benefit of
> the capitalist profits, the ambition of dynasties, or the greater glory of
> secret diplomatic treaties.[4]

So strongly-worded was it that Lenin, on reading the manifesto
remarked prophetically to Zinoviev "They have given us a large
promissory note; let us see how they will meet it". We recall these
resolutions not out of antiquarian interest but to illustrate one of
the most salient features of social democracy and centrism - their
ability to adopt militant-sounding and even correct policies on the
eve of a crisis while at the same time adapting to social forces
which made capitulation inevitable. This Lenin understood even
before August 4, but not as clearly as Rosa Luxemburg, who had
been engaged in a protracted battle with not only the SPD right

wing, but the Kautsky-Bebel "centre" from as early as 1905. It took Kautsky's refusal to denounce the war to convince Lenin that 'Rosa Luxemburg was right when she wrote, long ago, that Kautsky has the "subservience of a theoretician" — servility, in plainer language, servility to the majority of the party, to opportunism.' Lenin now saw his former teacher as "the main representative of bourgeois corruption in the working class movement."[5] Yet right up to the last days of peace, the SPD maintained what appeared to be a firm anti-war stand. The Austrian ultimatum to Russia was denounced in fire-eating language on July 25, the SPD manifesto directly calling upon all party members and supporters "to express immediately in mass meetings the unshakable will to peace of the class conscious proletariat." It denounced the German bourgeoisie and Junkers "who in peace-time oppress you, despise you, want to see you as cannon-fodder" and concluded with the rallying cry "We don't want war! Down with war! Long live international brotherhood!" As one by one the imperialist powers of Europe began to mobilise, the SPD line began to waver. Now, when it was no longer a question of protest demonstrations against a threat of war initiated by a foreign power's government, but of an actual struggle against one's own imperialist bourgeoisie, all the vacillations which had in the past manifested themselves in the party leadership on the questions of internationalism and the state were qualitatively transformed into factors determining the overall line of the party. On July 31, *Vorwärts* reverted to the old patriotic formulation of Bebel when it declared:

> If the fateful hour strikes the workers will redeem the promise made by their representatives on their behalf. The "unpatriotic crew" will do their duty and will not be surpassed by any of the patriots.

The very next day, the German government declared war on Russia. The imperialist slaughter had begun.

All the evidence suggests that right up to August 4, the German government took the SPD's anti-war propaganda seriously, so much so that the general staff prepared a long list of party and trade union leaders who would be arrested in the event of war.* The irony was that these same party and union leaders were, within a matter of days, to be granted immunity from military service by their would-be captors, on the grounds that their services were more urgently needed at home to boost war production and maintain "social peace." Naturally, those among the party leadership and its 110 strong Reichstag fraction who favoured the policy of national defence used the argument that any other course would mean suicide for the German socialist

---

* Their opposite numbers in France had also taken identical precautions with what proved to be as little justification—the so-called 'carnet B.'

movement. In the words of the centrist Wilhelm Dittmann, who had witnessed patriotic demonstrations by social democratic workers on his way to the fateful fraction meeting on August 3 which committed the party to its pro-war line:

> The Party could not act otherwise. It would rouse a storm of indignation among the men at the front and people at home against the SPD if it did [vote against the credits]. The socialist organisation would be swept clean away by popular resentment.

However true this last statement was, it neither explained nor justified the conduct of the SPD majority who voted for imperialist war. Their motives may indeed have been mixed — a desire to preserve the legality and resources of the German labour movement obviously played no small part in swinging wavering sections of the middle leadership and lower cadres behind the official line, as did an inbred, and on most occasions thoroughly correct reluctance to flout publicly majority decisions of party bodies. This weighed heavily in the thinking of even the anti-militarist activist Karl Liebknecht, who though voting in the Reichstag fraction with 13 other deputies against the proposal to support the war credits, nevertheless, when it came to the actual Reichstag division, submitted to discipline. But what pre-dominated in the minds of those who supported the war was a "national" conception of socialism, that not only the establishment of a socialist government but even the building of a fully developed socialist society could be carried out within the confines of a single nation state.* This had been implicit in much of the party's propaganda from 1890 onwards, and even explicit in the speeches and articles of the extreme right-wing of the party headed by Georg von Vollmar, who 46 years before Stalin came to the utopian conclusion that socialism could be built in one country (only the country was not holy mother Russia but "culture-bearing" Germany). The transition from what Trotsky called the SPD's "legitimate patriotism to their own party" to a conception of "national" socialism and finally, after August 4 1914, to a position of national defence, was a complex process which had its roots not only in the treachery of leaders, but the evolution of an entire stratum of the German working class:

> If we leave aside the hardened bureaucrats, careerists, parliamentary sharpers, and political crooks in general, the social patriotism of the

---

* In setting their sights on the creation of a socialist economy independent of the world division of labour, the SPD leaders were overlooking the principle contra-diction, which provided the impulse towards imperialist war, complemented and intensified the already-existing contradiction between the productive forces developed by capitalism and the social nature of the productive process, and the basis of this process in the private ownership of the means of production. Fascism is an attempt by capitalism to overcome both these contradictions without challenging the domination of capital, while Stalinism, basing itself on the property relations, seeks to maintain the nation state.

rank and file social democrat was derived precisely from the belief in building German socialism. It is impossible to think that hundreds of thousands of rank and file social democrats... wanted to defend the Hohenzollerns or the bourgeoisie. No. They wanted to protect German industry, the German railways and highways, German technology and culture, and especially the organisations of the German working class, as the necessary and sufficient national pre-requisite for socialism.[6]

The great tragedy was that their devotion to the goal of a future socialist Germany was cruelly and cynically exploited by both their class enemies and their own leaders to serve the ends of an all too real imperialist present.

Thus workers read in the German trade union journal *Correspondenzblatt* that

the policy of August 4 accords with the most vital interests of the trade unions; it keeps all foreign invasion at bay, it protects us against the dismemberment of the German lands, against the destruction of flourishing branches of the German economy, and against an adverse outcome of the war, which would saddle us with reparations for decades to come.

The political responsibility for such a line, which undoubtedly found an echo amongst wide layers of trade unionists in the early period of the war at least, lay largely with the Kautsky "centre" which had miseducated entire generations of workers to believe that patriotism and an evasive attitude towards the struggle for power could co-exist with the SPD's formal adherence to socialist internationalism and the Marxist theory of the state. For as the preceding chapter attempts to show, the seeds which ripened into the fruit of August 4 were sown in the period of party expansion which followed the lapsing of the anti-socialist laws in 1890. When confronted by the magnitude of their betrayal, the more sophisticated party leaders attempted to evade their own responsi-bility before the German and international movement — one they had solemnly accepted at a succession of Socialist International congresses — by blaming the working class for a situation which they themselves had helped to create. And we must also look at the capitulation of August 4 from another angle, one which con-cerns our search for the root causes of German fascism. Firstly, the SPD's quite unabashed endorsement of the Kaiser's rapacious imperialist war policy, together with its acceptance of the utterly reactionary idea of "social peace" at home, had the effect of legiti-mising both nationalism and the notion of "national solidarity" among wide strata of the working class, especially those whose class consciousness was at a low level. For years the SPD had pro-claimed, both in its press and at public rallies, the international solidarity of the proletariat and the existence of an unbridgeable chasm between the worker and his exploiter. And workers grew to respect and assimilate these ideas, not only because of their inherent validity, but because they were learnt from a movement which enjoyed an enormous moral as well as political reputation amongst millions of German workers. It was a movement which had fought the redoubtable iron chancellor and won. Its voice deserved a hearing, and its opinions careful and sympathetic consideration. What, therefore, was the German worker to think and do when he saw these self-same leaders tearing up the resolutions of their own party and the International, eating their own revolutionary words and calling upon him, not only in the name of the fatherland, but socialism, to shoulder arms with the bourgeoisie against the invader? Only the most class conscious, dedicated and courageous of proletarians could have hoped to withstand this double pressure of government-induced hysteria and duplicity on the part of his own trusted leaders. August 4 was therefore not only a victory for the Kaiser, who on that day declared that he recognised not parties, but Germans. It was the first step along the road to the even more humiliating capitulation 19 years later, when on May 17, 1933, the SPD Reichstag fraction again voted unanimously in support of the foreign policy of German imperialism. The only difference being that on this august occasion, Hitler, and not the Kaiser, was laying down the line.* The SPD was not to break from the foreign policy of the German bourgeoisie until the party's suppression by the Third Reich on June 22, 1933. Neither was it ever again to advocate the revolutionary overthrow of German capitalism. August 4 was a political rubicon for German social democracy, and despite all the party's twists and turns between November 1918 and the victory of the Nazis, it never retraced its steps. The new political situation created in Germany by the vote of August 4 also had a profound impact on the consciousness of those layers of the workers most closely bound up with the every day life of the party, not to speak of the many thousands of petty and middle ranking officials for whom it provided not only a political programme but a means of livelihood.** Their sudden acceptance into the bosom of the German empire without doubt convinced the vast majority that the old class hatreds would be quietly laid to rest, that the industrial barons and Junkers had seen the error of their ways in waging war on social democracy as a subversive, anti-national

* The SPD fraction took this decision to support Hitler's foreign policy by a vote of 48 to 17. Most of the party's remaining 55 deputies were either in hiding from Hitler's thugs or in jail, though this did not seem to have had any bearing on the outcome of the vote!

** On the eve of war, the SPD owned 90 daily papers and 62 printing offices. The party employed 267 editors, 89 office managers, 273 business officials, 140 administrators, 85 propagandists, 2,640 technicians and 7,589 news agents. Its assets were valued at 21,514,546 marks. The unions employed an even larger full-time staff, and owned assets worth 80 million marks.

force, and finally the conduct of the party's leaders in the hour of the Kaiser's greatest need would be rewarded with a permanent stake in the new Germany which, they fondly hoped, would emerge after a victorious conclusion to the war. "We are defending the fatherland" the right wing SPD leader Philipp Scheidemann told the Reichstag, "in order to conquer it," while a former party leftist, the journalist Konrad Haenisch displayed more sophistication when he wrote:

> What the Junkers are defending is at most the Germany of the past, what the bourgeoisie are defending is the Germany of the present, what we are defending is the Germany of the future.*

Even before the official declaration of war, the trade union leaders, on August 2, pronounced an end to the class struggle, suspending all strikes in progress and withholding strike pay for the duration of hostilities which they now regarded as not only inevitable but desirable. This step had been precipitated by a meeting with Interior Ministry officials the previous day, one of whom assured them:

> We do not think of going after you, provided that you make no difficulties for us, for we are glad to have the great labour organisations which can help the administration in necessary social work.

* Haenisch headed the extreme right wing of the SPD which was openly demanding the fusion of nationalism and socialism. He argued that Germany embodied the revolutionary forces in Europe, and England those of reaction. Hence the need to prosecute not a 'defensive war, as most SPD apologists of imperialism advocated, but a ruthlessly offensive one. The chauvinist ideas of the Haenisch group were propagated in *Die Glocke*, the journal of that other renegade from the SPD left, Alexander Helphand, better known by his pseudonym Parvus.

Another contributor to *Die Glöcke*, Ernst Heilmann, quite frankly declared that 'the idea of a catastrophe of revolution as a means of building a socialist society should be discarded once and for all, and not from a particular day, but as a matter of principle. *To be socialist means being in principle an anti-revolutionary.* The opposite conception is merely a carry-over from the emancipatory struggle of the bourgeoisie, from which we have not yet completely freed our minds.' (*Die Glöcke* No. 20, August 12, 1916) So in the extreme right wing of the SPD flourished tendencies which even repudiated the feeble democratic traditions of the liberal bourgeoisie of '48! Socialism was conceived of more in terms of 'socialising' the worker than the property of the ruling classes: 'Socialism is increasingly realised from day to day because of the growing number of people who do not make their living from private economic activity, or receive wages or salaries from private hands. The worker in a state, municipal or co-operative enterprise is socialised just as is the health insurance doctor or trade union official.' (Ibid) The similarity of these ideas with English Fabianism is obvious. Finally there was Paul Lensch, another right-wing social democrat who sought to lend his party's pro-war policy a radical and even revolutionary tinge. Employing the argument that Germany, as a nation deprived of its imperialist 'rights', represented the forces of change and revolution as against the established and conservative Anglo-Saxon imperialist powers, he claimed Germany's workers should back the war to break England's 'class domination' over world economy. Germany's was a revolutionary war in which 'the rise of this class (i.e. the proletariat) is taking place... amid the thunder of a revolutionary world war, but without the lightning of a revolutionary civil war.' (P. Lensch: *Social Democracy, its End and its Successes,* Leipzig, 1916).

Just as in the early months 'of 1933, the trade union bureaucrats were ahead of the political wing of the movement in seeking an accomodation with the bourgeoisie and its state. The contrast between August 1914, when they were welcomed with open arms by a regime which sought their co-operation, and May 2, 1933, when after marching with the Labour Front in Hitler's Nazi "May Day" rally, their offices were occupied and themselves arrested by picked units of the SA, provides us with a deep insight into the unique role of fascism, a role which demarcates it from all other forms of political reaction. Bismarck repressed social democracy, while preserving the forms of parliamentary democracy and permitting only official state organs to apply his anti-socialist laws. There was no room in Bismarck's anti-Marxist strategy for a plebeian-based terror directed against the workers' movement. Neither can the "class truce" concluded by the leaders of the SPD and the trade unions be compared in any sense to fascism, for it presupposed the continued existence of proletarian-based organisations, even though these were temporarily tied by the class collaborationist policies of their leaders to a line of supporting the domestic and foreign policy of German imperialism. Repressions were carried out — as in the case of Karl Liebknecht and Rosa Luxemburg who were both jailed for their anti-war activities — only against those who attempted to win workers for an alternative policy. And while German arms continued to meet with success, there was but little need for such a harsh regime. However unpalatable it might be to genuine internationalists, the fact remains that in the opening months of the war, the majority of the German working class was, like its counterparts in the other belligerent nations, enthusiastically behind its chauvinist leaders. The depths to which the social democratic and trade union bureaucracy had sunk is made clear in the following extracts from the trade union press of the period:

> We were accustomed to regard war purely from the standpoint of its socially destructive forces... However, the facts have taught us differently. War creates situations which are not socially destructive but to the highest degree socially progressive, situations which awaken social forces in *all classes* of the population to an undreamt of degree, and eliminate anti-social tendencies. At this stage the war is an affair of the whole people and it is calculated to advance the cause of socialism to a degree attained by hardly any other event. People at war must feel socialist and above all act socialist...[7]

> A new age has opened up. In a short space of time the war has made new men of us all. This is equally true of high and low or rich and poor. Solidarity and mutual assistance in bitter and undeserved distress, the principle of action which we have always hammered into the working masses and so often demanded without success from the rich, has become the common principle of a great and capable people, overnight. Socialism wherever we look.[8]

The villainous plans of the dishonourable, bloody and faithless Tsar and his allies, the cunning Japs, the perfidious Britons, the boastful French, the lying Belgians, the thankless Boers, the swaggering Canadians, and the enslaved kidnapped Indians, Zouaves, Niggers and the remaining scum of the earth, have broken against the strong wall set up by the implacable heroism of the German and Austrian troops...[9]

It is almost impossible to credit that these lines, all written in the first months of the war came from the pens of men who had dedicated their lives to defending, even if in a reformist fashion, the interests of the German proletariat. Now this same reformism became a vehicle for inciting chauvinist contempt for the workers of the allied powers, and what is just as significant, an ideology which differed little from that of the so-called "war socialism" of the Prussian general staff. These leaders of German trade unionism presented government regimentation of the economy and labour as giant strides towards socialism simply because these measures had been undertaken by the state and since they involved a certain degree of central planning and control, had encountered initial resistance by certain sections of industry.

The real nature and purpose of government control over industry was made clear in a report, dated December 20, 1915, by Walter Rathenau,* head of the war Raw Materials Department of the German War Office.

> Coercive measures had to be adopted regarding the use of all raw materials in the country. No material must be used arbitrarily, or for luxury... The needs of the army are of paramount importance... "sequestration" does not mean that merchandise is seized by the state but only that it is restricted, that it can no longer be disposed of by the owner at will... The system of war boards is based upon self administration (in private industry) yet that does not signify unrestricted freedom... The boards serve the interests of the public at large; they neither distribute dividends nor apportion profits...

And, despite initial reluctance on the part of certain sectors of industry to work under this new regime (notably the chemical industry) a harmonious partnership was soon established between the state and the major, war-oriented monopolies. They under-

---

* Rathenau was undoubtedly one of the most astute leaders of the German bourgeoisie. A director of the electrical giant AEG, he was constantly faced with the problem of how to deal with the huge concentrations of workers brought together by the growth of monopoly capitalism. In 1911, he revealed his well-grounded fear that the pre-war capitalist boom was in its turn preparing a new crisis pregnant with revolution:

    I see shadows wherever I turn. I see them in the evening when I walk through the noisy streets of Berlin, when I perceive the insolence of our wealth gone mad, when I listen to and discern the emptiness of big-sounding words.' An architect of Weimar's social and economic policy, Rathenau also served the Republic as Foreign Minister, meeting his death at the hand of a band of pro-fascist assassins weeks after concluding in April 1922 the Rappallo Treaty establishing more harmonious relations between Germany and the Soviet Union.

stood that sectional interests and policies had to be subordinated to the overall, longer term requirements of the big bourgeoisie as a whole. It was their war, and they would have to take the steps necessary to win it. The ghost of Lassalle's and Bismarck's "state socialism" had returned to haunt not the bourgeoisie but the German proletariat! Neither did the services of the bureaucracy go unacknowledged by a grateful government. In a communique issued in November 1915, it declared in terms that would have been unthinkable before August 1914 that

> the free trade unions have proved... almost indispensable to the economic and communal life of the nation. They have made numerous valuable suggestions in the military, economic and social fields, part of which were carried out. Their co-operation and advice were placed at the disposal of the military and civil authorities, and were gladly accepted. The gratitude of the nation for the patriotic efforts of organised labour has been frequently expressed by the responsible authorities...

Perhaps the most amazing somersault of all was that performed by Erwin Belger, former General Secretary of the "Imperialist Alliance Against Social Democracy." In his pamphlet, *Social Democracy after the War*, published in 1915, he heaps the most fulsome praise on the party he and his colleagues had previously scourged for its lack of patriotism and revolutionary aspirations. Now he found the SPD leaders' conduct "irreproachable" and "honourable," their vote for the war credits giving him "great joy." Ludwig Frank, the right-wing leader of the Mannheim party organisation, he lauded as a "hero" while Rosa Luxemburg was branded for her anti-war writings in what Belger described as the "bandit party press." Shrewdly sensing that the war-time policy of the party leaders was not simply a tactical adjustment, but a new stage in the party's evolution, he hoped the SPD would openly convert itself into "a purely labour party... a national party," and that "when they reach the point — and it will be reached eventually — of reshaping the entire obsolete Erfurt Programme, let them draw the necessary conclusions, and above all delete the international principles."

Similar views were being expressed by some (though by no means all) sections of the bourgeoisie. A commentator on the war-time policies and attitudes of German employers' organisations noted:

> The employers regard the effects of the war, insofar as they extend to the internal political situation, as predominantly favourable. This applies especially to its effect on the Socialist Party... For the war has led to unity of the nation and had cut the ground from under the most attractive socialist theories... The socialists of the opportunist trend see the war as an economic war. They take the view that the war is imperialist and even defend the right of every nation to imperialism. From that they deduce a community of interests between employers

and workers within the nation, and that line followed consistently, leads to their becoming a radical bourgeois reform party...[10]

As we have already suggested, this viewpoint, for all its prescience on the future evolution of German social democracy, was not shared by the bourgeosie in its entirety. Emil Kirdorf for one fulminated against the prevailing policy of government and industrial collaboration with the social democrats, whom he still regarded as traitors and subversives, despite all their claims to the contrary. Scepticism about the conversion of the SPD to "national" values was also expressed succinctly in the business journal *Deutsche Arbeitgeberzeitung* for August 15, 1915. There, in an article warning against any serious democratic reforms in the German political system after the war, it was asserted that the SPD had still much to achieve in the way of casting off the old traditions of class struggle and internationalism. It would

> above all have to show, after the war as well, whether the process of transformation to which it refers has really become part of its *flesh and blood.* Only if this has been decisively demonstrated for a fairly lengthy period will one be able to say, with due caution, whether some of these changes in Germany's home policy are feasible... the harsh school of war provides us with the strongest possible arguments against further democratisation of our state system.

So we have here two diametrically opposed tactical lines. One — the line that prevailed throughout the war, and for the period of revolutionary upheaval which followed—favoured intimate collaboration with the leaders of the SPD right wing as a means of splitting the working class and establishing a new basis in the masses for capitalist rule. (Endorsement of this tactic in no way implied or involved any conversion on the part of the German bourgeoisie to democracy, even less the slightest sympathy for the social and political aspirations of the working class). Ranged against the liberals were the "hard-liners." They feared that this policy of concessions would be interpreted by the workers as an admission of ruling class weakness, serving not as a diversion from revolution, but rather as the gateway to it. Naturally, both these trends had their echoes in the petty-bourgeoisie, with on one hand, the beginnings of a regroupment in the old liberal camp for a policy of alliance with the SPD right wing against the radical elements of the workers' movement,* and on the extreme right the crystallisation of fanatically anti-Marxist, chauvinist groupings which called for a war unto death against the enemies of the Reich, internal as well as external.** So if the leaders of social

* Max Weber, who personified this trend in the immediate pre-war period, was partly instrumental in founding, at the end of 1918, the Democratic Party (DDP), which stood for a liberal capitalist Germany ruled by a coalition of moderate bourgeois parties and a thoroughly 'reformed' and 'nationalised' SPD.

** The 'Fatherland Front' brought many such individuals and groupings together under the leadership of rabidly chauvinist military leaders and industrialists.

democracy believed their post-August course had disarmed their former enemies — and their entire conduct up to Hitler's victory suggests that they did — they were very much mistaken. What Hitler has to say on the conduct of the SPD in the war period is highly revealing in this respect:
(We should bear in mind that throughout these extracts, Hitler means by "Marxism" the ideology of the official SPD, and not that of the party left wing which opposed the war!)

> [What] angered me was the attitude which they [the authorities] thought fit to take to Marxism. In my eyes, this only proved that they hadn't so much as the faintest idea concerning this pestilence. In all seriousness they seemed to believe that by the assurance that parties were no longer recognised,* they had brought Marxism to understanding and restraint. They failed to understand that here no party was involved, but a doctrine that must lead to the destruction of all humanity... It was an unequalled absurdity to identify the German worker with Marxism in the days of August 1914, in those hours the German worker had made himself free from the embrace of this venomous plague, for otherwise he would never have been able to enter the struggle. The authorities, however, were stupid enough to believe that Marxism had now become "national"... which only shows that in these long years none of these official guides of the state had even taken the trouble to study the essence of this doctrine, for if they had, such an absurdity could scarcely have crept in. Marxism, whose goal is and remains the destruction of all non-Jewish national states, was forced to look on in horror as... the German working class it had ensnared, awakened and from hour to hour began to enter the service of the fatherland with ever increasing rapidity... suddenly the gang of Jewish leaders stood there lonely and foresaken... it was a bad moment for the betrayers of the German working class, but as soon as the leaders recognised the danger which menaced them they... insolently mimicked the national awakening.[11]

On the surface, viewed from the standpoint of formal logic, we have two mutually exclusive positions. Lenin, Trotsky, Luxemburg and all those who followed them in their opposition to the war rightly regarded the SPD leaders as "betrayers of the German working class" — but for their capitulation to chauvinism, and their failure, in the pre-war period, to prepare the party and the entire working class for this crisis. Yet we find Hitler (in company with the chauvinists of the Fatherland Front, to name out one organisation) still depicting the SPD leadership as died-in-the-wool internationalists and revolutionaries, pawns in the hands of a mythical "world Jewish conspiracy" to subjugate and exterminate the "Aryan race". But if we move from the plane of formal logic to that of the real movement of classes in history, the contradiction can be resolved.

---

* An allusion to the already-quoted statement by the Kaiser which he made after the unanimous Reichstag vote granting him his war credits.

We must return to the proposition of Engels that individuals and classes do not perceive their interests in a clear cut way, nor do they necessarily derive their political ideas and programmes purely from problems immediately confronting them. The process of the formation of consciousness is far more subtle, protracted and many-sided. The false notion of a homogeneous bourgeois class consciousness is belied by the controversy which raged inside the German capitalist class over the nature of social democracy, a debate which began some years before the war and which continued right up to its destruction by Hitler in 1933. Writing on this very problem some four years before the outbreak of the war, Lenin noted:

> If the tactics of the bourgeoisie were always uniform, or at least of the same kind, the working class would rapidly learn to reply to them by tactics just as uniform or of the same kind. But, as a matter of fact, in every country the bourgeoisie inevitably devises two systems of rule, two methods of fighting for its interests and of maintaining its domination, and these methods at times succeed each other and at times are interwoven in various combinations. The first of these is the method of force, the method which rejects all concessions to the labour movement, the method of supporting all the old and obsolete institutions, the method of irreconcilably rejecting reforms... The second is the method of "liberalism," of steps toward the development of political rights, towards reforms, concessions, and so forth.[12]

We could add, with the example of war-time Germany very much in mind, that these two trends are by no means confined to the upper reaches of the propertied classes, but penetrate down through the middle bourgeoisie and the professional and intellectual strata to the lowest layers of the petty-bourgeoisie. In doing so, these tactical conceptions undergo all manner of mutations, which derive not only from the particular political and cultural medium through which this process is taking place, but which are even affected by the personalities and prejudices of individuals. Thus the "accidental" is at bottom no more than the unique but nevertheless law-governed interpenetration and working out of a more broad historical process. Hitler's alleged "lunacy" has long been the subject of debate amongst politically-oriented psychologists. Though their findings are useful for filling in some of the details of Hitler's character and in providing possible motives for his raging prejudices against Jews and other minorities, they bring us no nearer the solution of the major theoretical problem which has bedevilled so much of the writing on German fascism: how could someone who for the major part of his early years existed on the "margin" of Austrian and German society, who embraced such an outrageously mystical and distorted ideology, possibly be said to represent the political interests of the German bourgeoisie? The answer lies partly in his comments on the war-time conduct of the SPD, which though

couched in the language of a totally unhinged Jew-baiter and
demented anti-Marxist, so blinded by his hatreds that he could
not see the social democrats were instrumental in aiding the war
effort of German imperialism, contained more than a grain of
political sense when viewed from the long-term strategic interests
of the imperialist bourgeoisie. If Lenin was right when he said
that reaction was the political expression of monopoly capitalism,
then Hitler's refusal to admit that the opportunist SPD deserved a
favoured role in German politics must be viewed as part of his
wider political strategy of destroying every vestige of bourgeois
democracy. He quite correctly saw the SPD as an essential prop
of such a parliamentary system; a system which, since it permitted
workers to organise in parties and unions, yielding to them the
same formal political rights as the bourgeoisie, left the door ajar
for the propagation and implementation of revolutionary ideas.
With this in mind, let us return to Hitler's account of the early war
days:

> ...now the time had come to take steps against the whole treacherous
> brotherhood of these Jewish poisoners of the people. Now was the
> time to deal with them summarily without the slightest consideration
> for any screams and complaints that might arise... It would have been
> the duty of a serious government, now that the German worker had
> found his way back to his nation, to exterminate mercilessly the
> agitators who were misleading the nation. If the best men were dying
> at the front, the least we could do was to wipe out the vermin. Instead
> of this, His Majesty the Kaiser himself stretched out his hand to the
> old criminals, thus sparing the treacherous murderers of the nation
> and giving them a chance to retrieve themselves... While the honest
> ones were dreaming of peace within their borders,* the perjuring
> criminals were organising the revolution.[13]

Hitler only saw subterfuge in the pro-war line of the social
democrats, it is true. But he also understood that while the SPD
was permitted to function legally, the danger of revolution was
that much greater. True, he was completely wrong in believing
that the 1914-18 war could have been prosecuted more effectively
by arresting the SPD leaders and banning all socialist and trade
union organisations — the very organisations which were,
through the nationalist orientation of their leaders, harnessing the
entire German proletariat to the war effort. Such a policy would
have been suicide for the government, as it would certainly have
alienated millions of socialist and trade union workers from the
regime and taught them a bitter lesson in the class basis of the
imperialist war. But looked at from a longer perspective, Hitler's
desire to exploit the nationalism aroused by the war to destroy the
workers' movement contained the germ of the tactics the Nazis

* The 'social peace' (*Burgfrieden*) concluded on the outbreak of war between the
SPD and ADGB leaders on the one side and the government and employers on the
other.

were later to employ in isolating, weakening and then smashing the organisations of the German proletariat. While the First World War could not have been fought in Germany without the active collaboration of Social Democracy, the Second World War could only be waged after its total extirpation. Like Bismarck's bid to strangle the still-youthful party, Hitler's initial notions of how to wage the class war were not immediately applicable, though now the degree of error was to be measured, not in quarter centuries, but a mere decade:

> What then, should have been done? The leaders of the whole movement should have at once been put behind bars, brought to trial, and thus taken off the nation's neck. All the implements of military power should have been ruthlessly used for the extermination of this pestilence. The parties should have been dissolved, the Reichstag brought to its senses, with bayonets if necessary, but, best of all dissolved at once...[14]

These lines were written, it should never be forgotten, around 1924-1925, a full eight years before the Nazi regime acted out this scenario almost to the letter! Let no one say that Hitler was a political madman, that fascism is a species of social pathology, or that national socialism was a product of the "German psyche"!

Precisely the same observations apply to Hitler's seemingly half-demented ravings against the SPD leaders for their conduct in the revolutionary upheaval of November 1918. For once again we are confronted by the problem of reconciling Hitler's passionate diatribes against the reformists with the irrefutable historical fact that these same social democratic leaders were instrumental in rescuing the German bourgeoisie from revolution when even the bourgeoisie itself had begun to give up all hope of survival. By relying on formal logic alone, one can come to the conclusion — as do so many liberal historians — that since both Hitler and the Bolsheviks employed the epithet traitor to describe the SPD leadership, and since both fascism and communism seek to destroy social democracy as a tendency in the workers' movement, then they are, subjective intentions notwithstanding, essentially similar political ideologies.* This type of formalist thinking, which seizes hold of superficial and transitory similarities between opposed phenomena, and then takes this fleeting indentity as proof of an overall convergence, is utterly unable to grasp the real class nature and role of either social democracy, Stalinism, communism or fascism.

---

* Distortions of this type were greatly assisted by the Stalinist theory of 'social fascism,' which because it placed the SPD firmly in the camp of fascist counter-revolution, and even depicted it as the main enemy of the working class, led to tactical alliances being formed with the Nazis, who were of course determined to smash the SPD as the largest single organisation of the German proletariat. Hence the Nazi-KPD block against the Prussian SPD government in the so-called 'Red Referendum' of August 1931.

Let us examine the sequence and inter-relationship of the main events leading up to the establishment of the Ebert government on November 9, and attempt to see how Hitler and his co-thinkers came to the conclusions that far from being mainstays of German capitalism, the SPD leaders were "November criminals."

On October 3, 1918, moves were initiated by the newly-installed Chancellor Prince Max of Baden to sue the allies for peace. With the war in the west clearly lost, the main concern of the High Command and the bourgeoisie was to free their hands to fight the growing menace of revolution at home. But this could not be done without broadening the base of the Imperial government, which though eagerly accepting the support of the social democrats, had steadfastly refused to include their representatives in the cabinet. The SPD press had already prepared the ground for such a step by muting its strident nationalism, which would have been out of place in a party seeking to enter a peace-making cabinet. Even here, the SPD leaders proved to be little more than the obedient echo of the General Staff and the bourgeoisie. On October 20, *Vörwarts* conceded defeat, and on October 28, with the anti-war mood of both workers and front line servicemen running high. began to adopt a pacifist line. Gone were the chauvinist intoxications of August 1914. Now the paper which for four years had summoned its proletarian readers to the trenches declaimed: "Enough of death, not one more man must fall." The very next day, negotiations commenced which ended with two social democrats, Scheidemann as minister without portfolio and trade union leader Otto Bauer as the inevitable minister of labour, being co-opted into Prince Max's cabinet. The alliance between old Germany and the social democracy against the revolution had been forged. But the bourgeoisie and Junkers had to pay a price for the services of the SPD and now, unlike August 1914, when the bulk of the masses were behind the war, their bargaining position was desperately weak. If the opportunists were to deliver the goods, then the masses had to be split and the revolutionary elements, the still-small "Spartacists" led by Luxemburg and Liebknecht, isolated from the less politically advanced workers and servicemen. All this both parties to the deal understood perfectly. But the German proletariat, steeped in a 50 year tradition of socialism and now utterly alienated from a regime for which they had given their blood and sweat, could be induced to follow a non-revolutionary path only if it appeared to be leading to socialism. The example of revolutionary Russia was a constant reminder — if any were needed — that unless the old ruling classes were for the first time prepared to make a series of wide-ranging political and social concessions to the beleaguered social democrats (and therefore, in the final analysis, to the workers who followed them) they would forfeit not only their Prussian class franchise and beloved monarchy, but their infinitely more precious private property. The issue was nearly as stark for the SPD and trade union bureaucracy. Having raised itself on the backs of the labour aristocracy far above the material level of the mass of German workers, it constituted an intensely conservative social caste which having solved its own "social question" now became bitterly hostile to revolution, which it quite correctly feared as a threat to its own social and political privileges,. What emerged from this purely tactical alliance was a clear-cut division of labour. The social democrats' task was to erect a "socialist" façade on the foundations of the old regime, defending the property of the bourgeoisie and junkers while simultaneously, indulging in endless rhetoric about the merits of "socialisation." To facilitate this role, the SPD leaders deemed it essential to secure the abdication of the Kaiser (but not, incredibly, the creation of a republic!), since millions of workers would never accept a government, however radical its pledges, which permitted the Kaiser to remain on his throne. As an SPD deputation expressed it in their crisis talks with Prince Max on November 7, "the Kaiser must abdicate at once or we shall have the revolution."[15] Ebert made it quite clear that unless the SPD ultimatum on the Kaiser was made known to the workers of Berlin that very evening "the whole lot will desert to the Independents."*

The other partner in this counter-revolutionary pact — the leaders of the now threatened bourgeois state — hoped that behind Ebert's "socialist" screen, they could begin to rebuild their temporarily shattered forces. They planned to assemble sufficient politically reliable troops to crush those sections of the working class that had not been deceived by the SPD's false pledges of radical social and political change, or confused by the continual vacillations of the USPD. Thus there was employed a combination of the two trends in bourgeois state policy of which Lenin wrote in 1910 — the "stick" and the "carrot." Events were unfolding just as Engels had anticipated 34 years previously in his letter to Bebel, when he warned him that "our sole adversary on the day of the crisis and on the day after the crisis will be the whole of the reaction which will group around pure democracy." And with the revolution spreading hourly towards the capital

---

* The Independent Social Democratic Party of Germany (USPD) which had split from the SPD early in 1917 over the pro-war policy of the official party. Its right wing included Kautsky and Bernstein, their old battles over revisionism long since forgotten. The UPSD centre was dominated by Hugo Haase, Wilhelm Dittmann and Emil Barth, who committed the fatal blunder of joining the Ebert Cabinet, thereby lending it their prestige among the radical workers. The UPSD Left was led by Rosa Luxemburg, Franz Mehring, Clara Zetkin and Karl Liebknecht who waited until the end of December before separating themselves from the centrists to form the Communist Party of Germany (KPD).

from the North Sea ports via the industrial west and Saxony, the counter-revolutionary plotters had to move with even greater speed and determination. On November 9, Prince Max came to the conclusion that "we can no longer suppress the revolution by force, we can only stifle it." Workers' and soldiers' councils were being elected all over Germany, and would soon be preparing to convene a national congress in Berlin to decide the country's future political and social structure. "Council rule" spelt Bolshevism for Junkers, bourgeois and social democrats alike, so it was necessary, while permitting the councils to function (there was in any case no means of disbanding them violently) to use political methods to prevent a majority emerging within the councils which would opt for a soviet-style system in Germany. So on November 9, the Kaiser's abdication was announced, and Ebert proclaimed as the new Imperial Chancellor. But these two moves, essential though they were for alleviating the crisis, only had the effect of heightening it. Thousands of Berlin workers took to the streets, believing that at last, the socialist republic was at hand. They milled around the steps to the Reichstag building where the SPD leaders were lunching. Learning from a workers' deputation that Karl Liebknecht was about to proclaim the republic at a mass meeting outside the royal palace, Scheidemann rushed to the window and much to Ebert's consternation, launched himself into a demagogic speech which ended with the cry: "The people have won all along the line. Long live the German Republic!"[16] Despite Ebert's fury — he shouted to Scheidemann that he had "no right to proclaim the republic" — their differences were purely tactical. Scheidemann had turned republican not out of conviction but because he "saw the Russian folly" staring him in the face" — supreme authority for the workers' and soldiers' councils." [17] And the SPD leaders were to adopt an even more radical stance over the next few crucial days, a manoeuvre epitomised by their proclamation of November 12, which flatly stated "the government created by the revolution, the policy of which is purely socialist, is setting itself the task of implementing the socialistic programme." Yet such pledges, no less revolutionary in their phraseology than undertakings given in the summer of 1914 to combat the menace of imperialist war, were made against a well-concealed background of collusion with the forces of reaction. It was perhaps the crowning irony of German history that its first parliamentary system of government could only be established under the direct protection of the bayonets of those died-in-the-wool antiparliamentarians the Prussian general staff. On the night of November 9, with countless thousands of workers celebrating the creation of the republic in the streets of Berlin, Chancellor Ebert rang the headquarters of the High Command at Spa on a secret line. At the other end was Lt. General Wilhelm Groener, First Quartermaster-General of the Imperial High Command — hardly a man who could be expected in normal times to sympathise with a social democrat in distress. But these were no ordinary days. The hourly-increasing threat of proletarian revolution made them comrades in arms, just as had the war. Their conversation was terse and to the point, with Chancellor Ebert very much assuming the role of supplicant. Gröner first demanded that Ebert pledge his party to "fighting anarchy" and "restoring order," which Ebert did with great conviction. "Then" Gröner replied, "the High Command will maintain discipline in the Army and bring it peacefully home." In return, Gröner expected the new government "to co-operate with the Officer Corps in the suppression of Bolshevism, and in the maintenance of discipline in the Army."* And so, on the very day which witnessed unprecedented revolutionary scenes and the formation of Germany's first SPD government, there was forged by its head a secret and traitorous pact to prepare the counter-revolution.

All the subsequent crimes committed against the German working class, culminating in the victory of Hitler, flowed from this initial act of perfidy — the formation of Noske's counter-revolutionary cut-throats, the "Free Corps," the liquidation of the workers' and soldiers' councils in favour of a bourgeois parliamentary republic, the murder of Rosa Luxemburg, Karl Liebknecht and countless less celebrated revolutionary fighters, the abandonment of the SPD's solemn pledge to "socialise" heavy industry (thereby giving a fresh and for many, largely unexpected lease of life to the tycoons who later showed their gratitude by aiding Hitler to outlaw Ebert's own party!), the protection and continued employment given to the bitterly anti-socialist officials of the old imperial regime and last, but by no means least, the steadfast refusal of the SPD leaders to ally Germany with the embattled Soviet Union in a proletarian alliance directed against the imperialist west. These were and remain monumental crimes, and no worker should ever forget them. Yet Hitler was still not satisfied. Ebert and company he brands as "miserable and degenerate criminals," while even the Kaiser is depicted as a political dupe, "the first German Emperor to hold out a conciliatory hand to the leaders of Marxism, without suspecting that scoundrels have no honour." He should have realised that "while they still held the imperial hand in theirs, their other hand was reaching for the dagger" and that "there is no making pacts with Jews; there can only be the hard: either—or."[18] In fact it was precisely the formation of the Ebert government which decided

---

* Regular nightly conversations were conducted over the secret line between Ebert and Groener reviewing, in the words of the latter, 'the situation from day to day according to developments.'

Hitler that he had to "go into politics" [19] And why? Because, like countless other reactionary German or Austrian petty-bourgeois, Hitler saw only those sides of social democracy which were, of necessity, sensitive to the pressure and demands of the workers. In August 1914, they justified their pro-war line by depicting it as a war by "revolutionary" Germany against "reactionary" England, by claiming that it was not being fought on behalf of bourgeoisie and Junkers, but to defend the achievements of the German labour movement. Thus there was more than a grain of sense in Hitler's contention that the SPD leaders were posing as loyal patriots. For all their undoubted chauvinism, they remained tied to organisations built and maintained by millions of workers, a relationship which established certain limits to the distance they could travel in company with the bourgeoisie. The bureaucracy in order to preserve its position in the working class, was obliged to maintain a certain political distance between itself and the bourgeoisie even when committing the most revolting betrayals, as on the occasion of the January 1918 anti-war strike of Berlin engineering workers. Ebert later stated quite frankly that he and his fellow SPD leaders "supported" the strike precisely in order to take the movement over and wind it up as quickly as possible. This tactical nuance escaped many reactionaries, who never tired of upbraiding Ebert for what they sincerely considered to be an act of unspeakable treachery. Similarly with Hitler's endless ravings against the "November criminals" Ebert *did* place himself, however reluctantly, at the head of a mass revolutionary movement; Scheidemann *did* attempt to outbid the Spartacist Liebknecht by proclaiming the republic to thronging Berlin workers; the SPD government *was* instrumental in bringing about the abdication of the Kaiser; it *did* pledge itself to socialise Germany industry and introduce a thoroughgoing reform of Germany's semi-feudal political system. And because the social democrats did and said these things, Hitler saw in them the refracted power of the masses. Obsession with the danger of revolution led Hitler to depict not only the SPD and the USPD, but even the KPD, as sharing the same socialist goal:

> In the course of the war a small but ruthlessly dedicated corps had been formed. These later enabled the revolution to take place... when the Independents were formed, the bourgeoisie thought the social democrats were becoming weaker... They forgot that both sections had the same objectives, that the social democrats, the Independents and the Spartacists, the trade unionists and the Russian Bolsheviks all shared the same Marxist world outlook... It was quite wrong for certain circles to be pleased in 1917 that the Marxist movement had split into two sections... both had the same final objective and one of them was only the advanced guard... when the Independent section of the Marxists attacked the citadel, the hitherto majority socialists

would not fail to follow.[20]

Perhaps we are now closer to an understanding of why fascism differs qualitatively from all other methods of bourgeois rule, and above all, why the social democrats found it impossible, despite their craven capitulation to Hitler in 1933, to co-exist peacefully with the Third Reich. Precisely because fascism makes a clean sweep of bourgeois democratic rights and institutions, it must of necessity root out every last vestige, both ideological and organisational, of an independent workers' movement. Neither the SPD's chauvinist conduct in the war nor its collaboration with the forces of reaction afterwards redeemed the party in the eyes of Hitler and his accomplices.* For all their revisionist theories and opportunist practice, the leaders of social democracy stood at the head of massive, proletarian-rooted organisations, and while the SPD and the trade unions were permitted to exist, there always remained the danger for Hitler that a bold lead from the Communists would pull the helm over to the left. The leaders of German social democracy without doubt genuinely believed that by ditching the party's Marxist 'ballast' and undertaking an unlimited period of collaboration and coalition with the bourgeoisie, they had layed forever the ghost of Bismarck's anti-socialist laws. In truth they were digging—in some cases quite literally—their own graves.

---

* Though in unguarded moments even Hitler was prepared to paint certain of the 'November criminals' in colours other than black: 'Amongst the men who became conspicuous during the events of 1918 I draw certain distinctions. Some of them, without having wished it, found themselves dragged into the revolution. Amongst these men was first of all Noske, then Ebert, Scheidemann, Severing, and in Bavaria, Auer.' (*Hitler's Secret Conversations*, p.220, New York, 1953). Praise indeed!

REFERENCES FOR CHAPTER SEVEN.

[1] *The Death Agony of Capitalism and the Tasks of the Fourth International* (1938) p.11, London, 1972.
[2] L. Trotsky: *My Life* (1930) pp.236-237, New York, 1960.
[3] *Internationaler Sozialisten-Kongress zu Stuttgart, 1907,* p.102.
[4] *Ausserordentlicher Interationaler Sozialisten-Kongress zu Basle, 1912,* pp.23-27.
[5] V. Lenin: Letter to A.G. Shlyapnikov, Berne, October 27, 1914, in *Collected Works,* Vol. 35, pp.167-168.
[6] L. Trotsky: *The Draft Programme of the Communist International — A Criticism of Fundamentals* (1928) in *The Third International After Lenin,* p.70, New York, 1957.
[7] *Correspondence of the General Commission of the ADGB,* No. 35, September 5, 1914.
[8] *Metallarbeiter-Zeitung* (organ of the German Metal Workers' Union) November 7, 1914.
[9] *Courier* (organ of the German Transport Workers' Union) October 25, 1914.
[10] *Archiv fuer Sozialwissenschaft und Sozialpolitik* Vol. 41, No. 1, September 1915.
[11] A. Hitler: *Mein Kampf,* pp.167-168.
[12] V. Lenin: *Differences in the European Labour Movement* (December 1910) in *Collected Works,* Vol. 16, p.350.
[13] A. Hitler: ibid, p.169.
[14] Ibid, p.169.
[15] Max, Prince of Baden: *Memoirs,* Vol. II, p.318, London, 1928.
[16] P. Scheidemann: *The Making of New Germany,* Vol. II, p.261, New York, 1929.
[17] Ibid, p.261.
[18] A. Hitler: *Mein Kampf,* p.206.
[19] Ibid, p.206.
[20] A. Hitler: *Im Kampf um die Macht.*

Chapter Eight
THE POLITICAL ECONOMY OF NATIONAL SOCIALISM

Hitler frequently and vehemently denied the primacy of economics and the class struggle in human affairs and history.* Yet together they shaped not only the ideology and programme of national socialism, but determined the rise and fall of its leader, Adolf Hitler. For as Marx and Engels pointed out in their youthful tour de force, *The German Ideology* 'the phantoms formed in the human brain are ...necessarily sublimates of their material life-process, which is empirically verifiable and bound to material premises.'[1] Returning to this problem — the determinates of human consciousness — some 20 years later, Marx insisted that

> just as one does not judge an individual by what he thinks about himself, so one cannot judge such a period [that of the transition from one social and political order to another] by its consciousness, but, on the contrary, this consciousness must be explained from the contradictions of material life, from the conflict existing between the social forces of production and the relations of production.[2]

Such is the task we have set ourselves in seeking to trace the origins of what subsequently became the ideology of national socialism back to the transition in Germany from feudal to capitalist economy in the first instance, and from pre-monopoly to finance monopoly capitalism in the second. So before embarking on the central section of this book, which deals with the principle events leading up to the victory of the Nazis in 1933, we must draw these various strands together and attempt to delineate the main features of what might be termed the 'political

---

*...the state has nothing at all to do with any definite economic conception or development. It is not a collection of economic contracting parties in a definite delimited living space for the fulfilment of economic tasks, but the organisation of a community of physically and psychologically similar living beings for the better facilitation of the maintenance of the species and the achievement of the aim which has been allotted to this species by providence. This and nothing else is the aim and meaning of a State. Economics is only one of the many instruments required for the achievement of this aim . . . Belief in the state-forming and state-preserving power of economics seems especially incomprehensible when it obtains in a country which in all things clearly and penetratingly shows the historic reverse. Prussia. . . demonstrates with marvelous sharpness that not material qualities but ideal virtues alone make possible the formation of a state...(A. Hitler: *Mein Kampf,* pp.150-152)

economy' of national socialism.

This requires a two-tier analysis along the lines indicated by . Marx. We must not only present the conceptions of national socialism as its own originators conceived them, but show how this ideology, with all its anti-capitalist pretensions and invective against bourgeois society and values, nevertheless came to function as a unique species of bourgeois consciousness. Firstly then the Nazi programme as presented in the party's public propaganda.*

One of the most characteristic expositions of Nazi 'anti-capitalism' is the pamphlet *Hitler's Official Programme* written as a commentary on the original 1920 party programme by the one-time Nazi economic 'expert', Gottfried Feder. The following extracts illustrate not only how little Feder's 'socialism' had in common with that of any tendency to be found in the workers' movement, but the way in which Nazi anti-capitalism fastened onto one aspect of capitalist production — interest and credit — (personified by the ubiquitous Jew) thereby abstracting it from every other phase and aspect of the capitalist mode of production:

> The farmer is forced to run into debt and to pay usurious interest for loans, he sinks deeper and deeper under this tyranny, and in the end forfeits house and farm to the moneylender, who is usually a Jew ...The sham state of today, oppressing the working classes and protecting the pirated gains of bankers and stock exchange speculators, is therefore the most reckless private enrichment and the lowest political profiteering ...the power of money, most brutal of all powers, holds absolute sway, and exercises a corrupting and destroying influence on state, nation, morals, drama and literature, and of all moral inponderables ...[3]

And while industrialists are not held to be blameless for this state of affairs, Feder presents them as men led astray by their quest for profit, which results in their being ensnared by the anonymous forces of finance and the stock exchange:

> The industrialists, great or small, have but one end in view — profits; only one desire — credits; only one protest — against taxations: they fear and respect only one thing — the banks: they have only a super-cilious shrug of the shoulders for the national socialist demand for the abolition of the thraldom of interest ...The producers have surrendered to high finance, their greatest enemy. The employers in factories and offices, deeply in debt, have to go content with the barest pittance, for all the profits of labour go into the pockets of the impersonal money power in the form of interest and dividends.[4]

Feder is then able to make the leap, characteristic of all fascist

---

* We shall deal elsewhere with the real Nazi programme as it was unfolded to the leaders of the German economy in a series of meetings between 1926 and 1933. Sufficient to say here that the public face and private dealings of the Nazi leaders were frequently in diametric opposition to each other!

propagandists, of depicting industrial capitalists as honest, if sometimes misled 'producers', exploited and cheated out of the fruits of their toil by parasitic money lenders and dividend-drawers. And he also at this stage introduces that other familiar weapon in the fascist arsenal — the notion of an industrious middle class, 'crushed from above by taxation and interests, menaced from below by the subterranean grumblings of the workers'. The pursuing of 'self-interest' — the employers' in the form of bigger profits, the workers' in the shape of higher wages — is depicted as the source of all evil. The result is a divided nation and 'race', with only the Marxist-cum-stock-exchange Jew the victor.

> Employer against employee, merchant against producer and consumer, landlord against tenant, labourer against farmer, officials against the public, worker against 'bourgeoisie', Church against state; each blindly hitting out at his particular adversary and thinking of his own selfish interests ...No one thinks of his neighbours' welfare, or of his higher duties to the community. A breathless chase after personal gain ...That is the spirit of modern business.[5]

And because Feder equates a worker's struggle for a living wage with his employer's determination to exploit the worker's labour power, he is then able to draw the utterly absurd conclusion that 'Marxists, capitalists and the leaders of public life all worship the same god — individualism. Personal interest is the sole incentive — the advantage of one's own narrow class the sole aim in life.' Instead of fighting each other, employers and workers should be united in battle against their common enemy,

> the capitalistic finance which overshadows the world, and its representative, the Jew. All classes of people have felt the scourge of interest; the tax collector bears heavily on every section of the population — but who dares oppose the supreme power of the Bank and Stock Exchange? ...The devilish principle of falsehood has triumphed over the ordered principle of creative labour ...What do we mean by the 'Thraldom of Interests'? The condition of the nations under the money domination of Jewish high finance. The landowner is subject to his thraldom who has to raise loans to finance his farming operations — loans at such a high interest as almost to eat up the results of his labour ...So is the wage earning middle class, which today is working almost entirely to pay the interest of bank credits ...So is the industrialist, who has laboriously built up his business and turned it in the course of time into a company. He is no longer a free agent, but has to satisfy the greedy board of directors, and the shareholders also, if he does not wish to be squeezed out ...The thraldom of interest is the true expression of the antithesis: 'Capital against Labour, Money against Blood, Exploitation against Creative Work'[6]

The struggle of 'races' is substituted for the struggle of classes, and the fundamental conflict between wage labour and capital dissolved into a purely mythical battle of both labour and

industrial capital against 'Jewish' usury. The bogus nature of
Feder's anti-capitalism is well brought out in his other
commentary on the Nazi Party programme, *Der Deutsche Staat*.
Here the attempt to construct a catch-all programme pledged to
defend the interests of not only the middle class, but workers and
employers, is even more flagrant:

> National socialism recognises private property on principle and gives
> it the protection of the state. The national welfare, however, demands
> that a limit shall be set to the amassing of wealth in the hands of
> individuals ...Within the limits of the obligation of every German to
> work, and the fundamental recognition of private property, every
> German is free to earn his living and to dispose of the results of his
> labour ...All existing businesses which until now have been in the form
> of companies* shall be nationalised ...Usury and profiteering and
> personal enrichment at the expense of and to the injury of the nation
> shall be punished with death.[7]

Even when indulging in such radical-sounding phraseology, the
Nazi leaders almost without exception ensured that their 'anti-
capitalism' remained highly selective. Their definition of capitalism and capitalists made it possible to exonerate some of
Germany's most rapacious and reactionary employers from the
charge of profiteering:

> The true employer, he who is conscious of his high task as an
> economic leader is a very different person. He must be a man of moral
> worth — in the economic sense at least, his task to discover the real
> economic needs of the people ...He must keep his costs as low as he
> can, and lay them out to the best advantage, must keep prices as low as
> possible in order to get his goods on to the market, must maintain
> both the quality and quantity of his output, must pay his employees
> well, so that they may be able to purchase goods freely, and he must
> always be thinking of improvements of his plant and his methods of
> trading. If he puts these things first in his business, he is 'supplying the
> necessaries of life' in the best and highest sense, and his profits will
> come of themselves without his making them his first object. The finest
> and most universally known example of this kind of manufacturer is
> Henry Ford, there are other names in our own heavy industries which
> stand equally high: Krupp, Kirdorf, Abbe, Mannesmann, Siemens,
> and many more.[8]

So after all the high flown, moral toned diatribes against grasping
capitalism and greedy profiteers, the national 'socialist' Feder
ends up by singing the praises of the Ruhr industrial tycoons, the
very men who stood at the head of the entire structure of German
finance capitalism!

Astute propagandists and political tacticians, the Nazi leaders
preferred, even in their wildest demagogic moments, to fire off
verbal salvoes at less formidable targets, ones that also had the
advantage of being far more unpopular among the mass of the

---

* Presumably as distinct from family enterprises of the Krupp-Stumm-Thyssen type.

petty-bourgeoisie, the Nazis' main source of support and recruitment:

> The large retail stores [are] all in the hands of Jews ...the large stores spell ruin to the small shopkeeper ...We regard them as a special form of the capitalistic idea in practical operation, which does not provide necessaries of life, but exists for the purpose of producing huge profits for the shareholders.[9]

Feder's writings, which until his fall from favour after 1933 were taken as authoritative statements on Nazi economic policy, abound with such appeals to the middle class, constantly harping on its simultaneous dislike of large, expecially banking, capital on the one hand and organised labour, ('Marxism') on the other. The end product is a crazy, topsyturvy world in which millionaire bankers (almost never named) are linked with Jewish labour leaders in a conspiracy to subvert the German body politic and plunder the industrious of all classes. The following extract is a typical example of this propaganda, totally unsupported by any facts, and yet capable of gripping literally millions, when all other methods of solving their economic problems seem to have failed:

> Class war as a political principle — this is to preach *hatred* as a guiding principle. 'Expropriation of the expropriator' makes *envy* a principle of economics, and 'socialisation' means striking down personality and leadership and setting up material, the mass, in the place of interest and efficiency ...This pseudo-socialism, born of Marxism, is not founded on common sense ...it is based on the crass individualism and the chaotic structure of society ...Can we be surprised that the social question is not, and cannot be solved by this means, and that the sole response is hatred and the desire for loot? No living state could result from the Marxist Stock Exchange revolt, but only a heap of ruins. Marxism is an obvious capitalistic bogey, capitalistic, because when a society founded on individualism has fallen into chaos, it falls of necessity under the sway of the great financial magnates ...Capitalism and Marxism are one! They grow on the same intellectual base. There is a whole world of difference between them and us, their bitterest opponents. Our whole conception of the construction of society differs from theirs, it is either a class struggle or class selfishness; our supreme law is the general welfare ...They are not inspired by the wish to construct an organic, articulate order, to amalgamate ...the various industrial classes under the high conception of national unity.[10]

The same notions, though with a less 'radical' and 'anti-capitalistic' tinge, run through Hitler's speeches and writings on economic questions.* What they certainly do not lack is a virulent anti-semitism, which for Hitler was the key to all economic wisdom. A speech made on April 12, 1922 employed Feder's device of depicting the Jew in his twin guise of capitalist and

---

* Once again, we make the exception of his private addresses to industrialists, where anti-capitalist demagogy vanishes entirely.

revolutionary:

> Christian capitalism is already as good as destroyed, the international
> Jewish stock exchange capitalist gains in proportion as the other loses
> ground ...[The Jews also act] as 'leaders of the proletariat' ...in this
> capacity you might see the millionaire, the typical respresentative of
> capitalist exploitation, in a culture of the utmost purity ...The same
> Jew who, whether as majority socialist or Independent, led you then
> [in the November Revolution] leads you still, whether as Independent
> or as Communist, whatever he calls himself, is still the same. And just
> as then in the last resort it was not your interests which he champion-
> ed, but the interests of capital which supported him, the interests of his
> race; so now will he never lead you in an attack on his race, an attack
> on capital. On the contrary, he will prevent you from waging war
> against those who are really exploiting you ...It was only the Jews who
> succeeded, through falsifying the social idea and turning it into
> Marxism, not only in divorcing the social idea from the national, but
> in actually representing them as contradictory.

This theme was developed at even greater length and complexity
in another speech on July 28 of the same year. Drawing heavily
on the forged *Protocols of the Elders of Zion,* which had recently
been published for the first time in German, Hitler exposed to his
credulous, mainly petty-bourgeois audience how the Jews went
about their conspiratorial work, fomenting class strife where
there had once been peace and harmony between worker and
employer — or rather guild master and his journeyman and
apprentices:

> The immense industrialisation of the nations meant that great masses
> of workers streamed together in the cities ...Parallel to this ran a
> tendency to turn all labour to money. There was a sprouting of stocks
> and bonds, and little by little the stock exchange began to run our
> whole national economy, and the owners of this institution, then as
> today, were without exception Jews ...By press propaganda and
> educational work, they succeeded in forming the big classical parties.
> Even then, they cleverly formed two or three groups which apparently
> combated one another, but actually hung by the same gold thread
> ...Then Jewry took a step which showed political genius. This
> capitalist people ...found a way to lay hands on the leadership of the
> fourth estate [the proletariat]. The Jew founded the Social Demo-
> cratic, the Communist Movement ...On the Right, he attempted to
> intensify all existing wrongs to such an extent that [the worker]
> ...would be provoked beyond measure ...It was he [the Jew] who
> fostered the idea that the unscrupulous use of all methods in business
> dealings was a matter of course, and by his competition forced others
> to follow suit ...On the Left, he was the common demagogue ...Well he
> knew that, once he taught the workers the international viewpoint as a
> self-evident premise of their existence and their struggle, the national
> intelligentsia would shun the movement ...and ...as soon as the Jews
> declared that property was theft, ...as they departed from the self-
> evident formula that only natural resources can and should be
> common property, but that what a man honourably creates and earns

is his own; from that moment on, the nationally minded economic intelligentsia was again unable to follow ...he ...succeeded ...in influencing the masses to such an extent that the errors of the Left were viewed by people on the Right as the errors of the German workers. While to the German worker the errors of the Right seemed nothing other than the errors of the so-called bourgeoisie ...Only now do we begin to understand the monstrous joke of world history, the irony that stock exchange Jews could become the leaders of a German workers' movement ...While Moses Kohn sits in the directors' meeting, advocating a policy of firmness ...his brother, Isaac Kohn, stands in the factory yard, stirring up the masses: take a good look at them; all they want is to oppress you.

Hitler's anti-semitism was clearly not a simple theory of 'race', but embraced an entire mystical view of history and economics, which, as we shall see, he did not invent himself but eclectically plagiarised from earlier protagonists of an 'anti-capitalist', corporative social structure. Hitler frankly admitted that until he became familiar with the ideas of Feder, whom he first met on joining the Munich-based German Workers' Party' in September 1919, he

> had been unable to recognise with the desired clarity the difference between ...pure capital as the end result of productive labour and a capital whose existence and essence rests exclusively on speculation ...In my eyes Feder's merit consisted in having established with ruthless brutality the speculative and economic character of stock exchange and loan capital, and having exposed its eternal and age-old presupposition, which is interest.[11]

This entirely arbitrary distinction had considerable political advantages for the Nazi's strategy of extending their mass basis by anti-capitalist demagogy while preserving and strengthening their connections with leaders of the German business world, as the following comment makes clear:

> As I listened to Gottfried Feder's first lecture about the 'breaking of interest slavery', I knew at once that this was a theoretical truth which would inevitably be of immense importance for the future of the German people. The sharp separation of stock exchange capital from the national economy offered the possibility of opposing the internationalisation of the German economy without at the same time menacing the foundations of an independent national self-maintenance by a struggle against all capital!...[12]

So there was capital and capital...

We also find in his random comments on economics the same moralist outbursts against money and a highly romaticised nostalgia for Germany's pre-industrial past which were common to nearly all *volkisch* ideologists of this period. Again we can see that this revolt against urban, highly industrialised society dominated by the 'cash nexus' is not so much a fear of large-scale capitalism — even Feder accepted that it was necessary in certain branches of the economy* — but of the huge concentrations of industrial workers brought about by the decline of a guild system of production and the movement of impoverished and expropriated peasants into the towns:

> Proportionally as the peasant class diminished, the mass of the big city proletariat increased more and more, until finally the balance was completely upset. Now the abrupt alternation between rich and poor became really apparent. Abundance and poverty lived so close together that the saddest consequences could and inevitably did arise. Poverty and frequent unemployment began to play havoc with people ...the consequence of this seemed to be political class division ...In proportion as economic life grew to be the dominant mistress of the state, money became the god whom all had to serve and to whom each man had to bow down...[14]

Even a nodding acquaintance with the economic facts of life would seem adequate intellectual equipment to punch holes through the theories of Feder and Hitler. Yet this is hardly the point, for they were shared by men of far higher academic standing, publicists, historians and even economists, who peddled in the guises of scholarship and profundity the Nazi credo that proletarian socialism and the stock-exchange were linked in a conspiracy of global proportions, whose aim was to subvert the existence of the Germanic people. One example will suffice — that of the idealist historian — Oswald Spengler. He was in the process of completing his epic, *The Decline of the West* at about the time Hitler was becoming involved in the activities of Feder's small group, the 'German Workers' Party'. Spengler spells out at some length the fundamental contradiction between his, so-called 'Prussian socialism', and the socialism of the workers' movement:

> Not Marx's theory, but Frederick William's Prussian practice which long preceeded Marx and will yet displace him — the socialism, inwardly akin to the system of old Egypt, that comprehends and cares for permanent economic relations, trains the individual in his duty to the whole, and glorifies hard work as an affirmation of Time and Future.[15]

Spengler's cyclical theory of historical development saw mankind as in the final stages of its approach to 'the last conflict ...in which Civilisation reaches its conclusive form — the conflict between money and blood'[16] And so we are back to Feder, Hitler — and indeed, Carlyle. The forces of 'blood' were to be spearheaded by what Spengler termed a new 'Caesarism' which would, he prophesied, triumph over and destroy the 'dictature of money and

---

* 'It is of course out of the question to run mines, blast furnaces, rolling mills, or shipyards on a small scale, but a 100,000 free and independent master-shoemakers are better than five monster shoe factories'. (G. Feder: *Hitler's Official Programme*, p.90) Under Nazi rule, Feder's beloved guilds were subjected to ruthless periodic 'comb outs' to provide labour for the rapidly expanding armaments industry. By this time, Feder had been pensioned off.

its political weapon, democracy.'[17] He therefore shared with the Nazis and their immediate forerunners their total identification of political democracy with an economy dominated by production for profit; a conception which, as we saw in Chapter One, originated in the struggle of the guilds against the rise of large-scale capitalism and the individualist outlook inspired by the French Revolution of 1789. Spengler's 'socialism' is a highly mystified version of a traditional distaste encountered among wide sections of the German intelligentsia for a society overtly based on monetary values and a class structure manifestly derived from relations of production and not on 'status' or alleged intellectual and moral worth:

> After a long triumph of the world city economy and interests over political creative force, the political side of life manifests itself after all as the stronger of the two. The sword is victorious over the money, the master will subdues the plunder will. If we call these money powers 'capitalism', then we may designate as socialism the will to call into life a mighty politico-economic order that transcends all class interests ...Money is overthrown and abolished only by blood'.[18]

Having made definitions of socialism and capitalism, Spengler is then able to arrive at the conclusion reached by Hitler, Feder and company: namely that the rubric 'money powers' incorporates the 'interest politics of workers' movements ...in that their object is not to overcome the money values, but to possess them.'[19]

Unlike Feder and Hitler who despite their claims to the contrary, were profoundly ignorant of Marxist literature, Spengler did attempt to refute the economic theories of Marx. Value did not originate in human labour power, he argued, but in what Spengler considered to be the genius of industrial leaders:

> as every stream of being consists of a minority of leaders and a huge majority of led, so every sort of economy consists in leader work and executive work [Spengler's term for manual labour] ...The inventor of the steam engine and not its stoker is the determinant.[20]

'Prussian socialism' turns out to be little different from Carlyle's fawning hero-worship of aggressive industrial tycoons. All that is of lasting economic value derives from their activity alone. By a sheer act of will, they can create money — what Spengler calls 'Faustian money':

> Thinking in money generates money — that is the secret of world economy. When an organising magnate writes down a million on paper, that million exists, for the personality as an economic centre vouches for a heightening of the economic energy of his field ...But all the gold pieces in the world would not suffice to invest the actions of the manual labourer with a meaning, and therefore a value, if the famous 'expropriation of the expropriators' were to eliminate the superior capacities from their creations; were this to happen these would become souless, will-less, empty shells.[21]

Spengler's veneration for the leaders of industry naturally is no obstacle to his indulging in the cult (common to most German rightists) of the peasant, who was depicted in *volkisch* and Nazi writings as a bulwark against proletarian revolution and a repository of traditional 'German' values:

> All higher life develops itself on and over a peasantry ...It is, so to say, race-in-itself, plantlike and historyless, producing and using wholly for itself, with an outlook on the world that sweepingly regards every other economic existence as incidental and contemptible...[22]

The enemies of the peasant, were to be found not amongst the class of rich landowners, but in the big city, for Spengler the source of all evil:

> There is little to choose in this respect between Versailles and the Jacobin club, business bosses and trade union leaders, Russian governors and Bolshevists. And in the maturity of democracy the politics of those who have 'got there' is identical, not merely with business, but with speculative business of the dirtiest sort of great-city sort.[23]

And so the stage is set for the arrival of Spengler's 'Caesarism', destined to lay low the world of money and greed, which he artfully links with rationalism and political democracy:

> Everything in order of dynastic tradition and old nobility that has saved itself up for the future, everything that is intrinsically sound enough to be, in Frederick the Great's words, the *servant* — the hard working, self-sacrificing, caring *servant* — of the State ...all this became suddenly the focus of immense life forces. Caesarism *grows* on the soil of Democracy, but its roots thread deeply into the underground of blood tradition ...there now sets in the final battle between Democracy and Caesarism, between the leading forces of dictatorial money-economics and the purely political will-to-order of the Caesars.[24]

This massive, brooding, highly esoteric work, written for the most part in a period of profound social unrest and permanent political tension, ends with a strangely calm confidence that the redeemer is at last at hand, the 'Caesar' who 'approaches with quiet, firm step... We have not the freedom to reach to this or to that, but the freedom to do the necessary or to do nothing'. And he closes with these ominous words: '...a task that historic necessity has set *will* be accomplished with the individual or against him'.[25] Spengler never became a member of the Nazi party* — he distrusted their plebeian methods and style, and had the utmost contempt for their philosophical pretensions. Nevertheless, we can detect a clear affinity with their conceptions of 'socialism', with its emphasis on rigid rank and 'service'. In his more popularly-written *Prussianism and Socialism* (1919) Spengler declared that Germany 'needs hard men ...a class of socialist natural lords ...might, and ever more might ....Socialism as I understand it pre-

* Though he did vote for Hitler in the Presidential elections of 1932.

supposes individual proprietorship with its old-German enjoyment of power and booty ...Everybody is put in his place. There are commands and there is obedience.'* This differs little from the definition of Nazi 'socialism' given by that master of demagogy, Josef Gobbels:

> Socialism is Prussianism. The conception 'Prussiansim' is identical with what we mean by socialism ...Or socialism is that which animated the kings of Prussia, and which reflected itself in the march-step of the Prussian Grenadier regiments; a socialism of duty.

And it is to Germany's past — back in fact to the age of Luther — that we must now turn in our attempts to unravel the secrets of the Nazi 'philosophy of history', and its evolution into a highly individual branch of vulgar bourgeois political economy. Listing the main features of what passes for national socialist political economy, we find the following: an indentification of capitalism with 'loan capital', 'usury', 'international finance capital', 'stock exchange speculation' or joint stock companies; an attitude of moral disapproval towards economic activities conducted, whether by workers or employers, for the purpose of monetary reward rather than 'service' to the 'community'; the notion of a strictly hierarchical society with its ranks based more on economic function that the simple ownership or non-ownership of productive property; and flowing from this, an equally guild-derived or 'corporative' rejection of the class struggle; the counterposing in quasi-religious terms of the 'creative' forces of 'blood and soil' to the parasitic and life-sapping evils of 'pure' money, personified in the Jew; a romantic yearning for a long past 'golden age' when production was based on handicrafts and not mass mechanisation, and was designed to fulfill a need and not create a profit; and finally, an unequivocal defence of private property as the basis of a 'healthy' and 'national' economy. What emerges from this compilation is that none of these economic notions is unique to national socialism. Certainly, the Nazi movement succeeded in exploiting and welding together these irrational prejudices and phantasies into a programme and ideology which exerted an enormous attractive power amongst the German petty-bourgeoisie and peasantry, especially in the two periods of economic crisis of 1922-1923 and 1929-1933. But the potency of these illusions, as we have already stressed more than once,

---

*Cf. the writings of the 'revolutionary conservative' Möller van der Bruck, who while attacking rentiers and money-lenders as parasites, lauded the industrialists as 'creators of values'. He called for a 'German socialism', based on 'the ideas which have issued from the oldest tradition allied to the most frequent conception of the aim to be attained.' It was a 'socialism' of 'organic growth ...hierarchy, membership. Marxism alone professes an international socialism'. Also the anti-semitic economist Werner Sombart, whose *German Socialism* (1934) called for the unification, not abolition of classes. Germany had to be freed from the 'disgusting faith in progress which dominates proletarian socialism...'

cannot be explained purely in terms of these two crises, the first inflationary and the second, deflationary in nature. The prejudices and distortions which comprised the social outlook of the Nazified petty-bourgeoisie had undoubtedly been accumulated over many generations and propagated through an entire spectrum of political, cultural, religious, philosophic, and economic agencies.

Marx and Engels on the Nazi precursors.

Since neither Marx nor Engels lived in the epoch of fascist counter-revolution nor even in the period of national socialism's formative years, we would on immediate reflection hardly expect their writings to illuminate many of the central problems concerned with the origin or role of fascism. Yet this is far from being so. Firstly there is their famous criticism in the *Communist Manifesto* of various schools of non-proletarian 'socialism' prevalent in pre-1848 Germany and Europe. Each of them displayed features which, to one degree or another, were later to be absorbed into national socialism. 'Feudal Socialism' originated in the fear of the landed aristocracy of the emergence of a usurping industrial bourgeoisie, a fear which in order to conceal its own reactionary class interests, took the form of a spirited defence of the industrial working class against its bourgeois exploiters:

> In this way arose Feudal Socialism: half lamentation, half lampoon, half echo of the past, half menace of the future; at times, by its bitter, witty and incisive criticism, striking the bourgeoisie to the very heart's core; but always ludicrous in its effect, through total incapacity to comprehend the march of modern history ...What they upbraid the bourgeoisie with is not so much that it creates a proletariat, as that it creates a revolutionary proletariat. In political practice, therefore, they join in all coercive measures against the working class; and in ordinary life, depite their high falutin phrases, they stop to pick up the golden apples dropped from the tree of industry, and to barter truth, love and honour for traffic in wool, beetroot and potato spirits.[26]

'Feudal Socialism' describes perfectly the ideology and political strategy of the Prussian Junkers*, even though these lines were

---

* The most sophisticated exponent of German 'state socialism' was the Pommeranian landowner, Johann-Karl Rodbertus. Engels likened him to the French utopian, petty-bourgeois socialist Proudhon in that he sought to ameliorate the evils engendered by large scale capitalist production without abolishing their economic foundation — private ownership of the means of production. He devised a scheme whereby workers would be paid wages, not in money, but 'labour certificates', which would be presented to the worker by the employer on the former's completion of a twelve hour working day. These certificates would then entitle him to purchase products equivalent to the value of only four hours labour. The surplus would then be divided between capitalists and landowners. This system differed from that of Proudhon, who in true petty-bourgeois fashion envisaged the free exchange of equal values between independent small producers. Thus he hoped to abolish the

written some years before Bismarck began to borrow heavily from its repertoire in his Bonarpartist manoeuvrings between the German Junkers, bourgeoisie and proletariat. Indeed, it is even accurate down to the Junker's support for Bismarck's anti-socialist laws! Feudal socialism also anticipated the 'social clericalism' of the Junker-based Conservatives, with their programme's emphasis on 'positive Christianity' and a corporative economy:

> As the parson has ever gone hand in hand with the landlord, so has clerical socialism with Feudal Socialism. Nothing is easier than to give Christian asceticism a Socialist tinge...Christian Socialism is but the holy water with which the priest consecrates the heart-burnings of the aristocrat.[27]

The next variant, 'Petty-Bourgeois Socialism', though originating in the same historical period — that of the transition from feudal to capitalist economy — appeals to a different social stratum; not the industrial working class, but the middle class of town and country:

> In countries where modern civilisation has become fully developed, a new class of petty-bourgeois has been formed, fluctuating between proletariat and bourgeoisie and ever renewing itself as a supplementary

'bad' sides of capitalism — degradation of the worker by the machine, exploitation, crises, etc. while retaining its 'good' aspects — private property competition, etc. Which led Marx to comment on Proudhon and his ilk: 'They all want competition without the lethal effects of competition. They all want the impossible, namely, the conditions of bourgeois existence without the necessary consequences of those conditions ...From head to foot M. Proudhon is the philosopher of the petty-bourgeoisie. In an advanced [capitalist] society the petty-bourgeois is necessarily from his very position a socialist on the one side and an economist on the other; that is to say, he is dazed by the magnificence of the big bourgeoisie and has sympathy for the sufferings of the people. He is at once both bourgeois and man of the people...' (K. Marx: Letter to P.V. Annenkov, Brussels, December 28, 1846, in *The Poverty of Philosophy*, pp.190-193, Moscow, n.d.) Marx and Engels regarded these two branches of non-proletarian 'socialism' as especially dangerous for the future of the workers' movement in France and Germany in that they appealed to bourgeois intellectuals inclined towards socialism but reluctant to accept the full implications of the Marxist theory of class struggle. In Germany, followers of Rodbertus (who was himself a monarchist) wrote occasional articles for the SPD press, and were even permitted to become active party members! This enraged Engels and Marx, since this group had joined the SPD with the expressed purpose of weaning the movement away from internationalism and proletarian-based socialism. Marx also devoted considerable sections of *Capital* to a rigorous critical analysis of Rodbertus' theories on rent and surplus value, which, Marx considered, reflected the viewpoint of a capital-starved 'Pommeranian landowner who gets money on tick in order to improve his property and who, for theoretical and practical reasons, only wants to pay the money-lender the "customary interest" ' (K. Marx: *Theories of Surplus Value*, Vol. II, p.158, Moscow, 1968). Rodbertus attempted to counter Marx's critique of capitalist production by claiming that it applied only to 'the present form of capital', but not to the 'pure conception of capital', which like Proudhon's society of independent propertied producers, was free from the blemishes of capitalism as it had evolved in history. This quest for a 'good' or 'pure' capitalism lay at the back of the German petty-bourgeois predeliction for quack remedies to economic problems, and certainly heightened its susceptibility to Nazi 'anti-capitalist' propaganda.

part of the bourgeois society. The individual members of this class, however, are being constantly hurled down into the proletariat by the action of competition, and, as modern industry develops, they even see the moment approaching when they will completely disappear as an independent section of modern society ...this form of Socialism aspires either to restoring the old means of production and of exchange, and with them the old property relations, and the old society, or to cramping the modern means of production and of exchange, within the framework of the old property relations that have been, and were bound to be, exploded by those means. In either case, it is both reactionary and Utopian. Its last words are: corporate guilds for manufacture, patriarchal relations in agriculture.[28]

These were of course the precise demands of the petty-bourgeois oriented Nazi 'guild socialists' under the leadership of Adrian von Renteln's 'Fighting Organisation of the Industrial Middle Class', which after serving to penetrate and Nazify Germany's guild organisations in the period prior to the seizure of power, was wound up as part of Hitler's big-business-inspired campaign against the so-called 'second revolution'.

Just as reactionary was 'German' or 'True' Socialism, which arose in Germany in the pre-1848 period as 'philosophers, would-be-philosophers and *beaux esprits*' attempted to graft the teachings of French socialism, directed against an already well-established ruling bourgeoisie, onto a political movement which had barely begun to challenge the rule of the Prussian landowning aristocracy. This eclecticism — an ever present feature of reactionary politics in Germany — entirely emasculated the revolutionary content of French socialism, which when subsumed under the categories of German idealist philosophy, served instead as a weapon of feudal reaction against those among the bourgeoisie struggling for political and constitutional reforms. The 'True Socialists', who recognised not classes but an abstract 'Human Nature', were political opponents of the liberal German bourgeoisie, railing against its demands for freedom of the press, representative government, and all the other bourgeois democratic rights established by the French revolution. It warned the people 'that they had nothing to gain, and everything to lose, by this bourgeois movement'.[29] Superficially radical in its opposition to the demands of the bourgeoisie, 'True Socialism' served 'the absolute governments, with their following of parsons, professors, country squires and officials ...as a welcome scarecrow against the threatening bourgeoisie'[30] Marx and Engels located the main social basis of this particular variety of 'socialism' in the backwardness of the German petty-bourgeoisie,

> a relic of the sixteenth century, and since then constantly cropping up again under various forms ...To preserve this class is to preserve the existing state of things in Germany. The industrial and political supremacy of the bourgeoisie threatens it with certain destruction; on

the one hand, from the concentration of capital; on the other, from the rise of a revolutionary proletariat ...It proclaimed the German nation to be the model nation, and the German petty Philistine to be the typical man. To every villainous meanness of this model man it gave a hidden, higher character. It went to the extreme length of directly opposing the 'brutally destructive' tendency of Communism, and cf proclaiming its supreme and impartial contempt of all class struggles.[31]

It is a sobering thought that these lines, depicting as they do the salient features of a petty-bourgeois pre-disposed towards fascism, were penned more than 70 years before the foundation of the Hitlerite movement. And elsewhere in the *Manifesto*, Marx and Engels had accurately depicted the potentially reactionary role of this class, even before they witnessed it at first hand in the German revolution of 1848:

> The lower middle classes, the small manufacturer, the shopkeeper, the artisan, the peasant, all these fight against the bourgeoisie, to save from extinction their existence as fractions of the middle class [i.e. the bourgeoisie]. They are therefore not revolutionary, but conservative. Nay more, they are reactionary, for they try to roll back the wheel of history. If by chance they are revolutionary, they are so only in view of their impending transfer into the proletariat, they thus defend not their present, but their future interests, they desert their own standpoint to place themselves at that of the proletariat. The 'dangerous class', the social scum, that passively rotting mass thrown off by the lowest layers of old society, may, here and there, be swept into the movement by proletarian revolution, its conditions of life, however, *prepare it far more for the part of a bribed tool of reactionary intrigue.*[32] (emphasis added)

Of course, we must not fall into the trap of equating the German petty-bourgeoisie of 1848, or even of half a century later, with that of Britain today. The last remnants of pre-capitalist classes — peasants, artisans and similar independent producers — were eliminated more than a century ago by the early development of English capitalism. The British petty-bourgeoisie, a stratum tapering off at each extremity into the proletariat and the medium and big bourgeoisie, is an exclusive creation of capitalism. It has neither a 'pre-capitalist' past nor, therefore, any ideological residues associated with such a history. This is of enormous importance for the future of British politics, as it will greatly influence the forms assumed by a genuine, mass-based fascist movement. Once again therefore we have occasion to emphasise the methodological principle with which we began this study of German fascism: the importance of grasping the unique, concrete refraction of the general and universal by and through the particular and the relative.

Such was the accuracy of their analysis of the petty-bourgeoisie in the *Manifesto* that Marx and Engels did not find it necessary to revise it in their subsequent writings on Germany. In his 1870 Preface to *The Peasant War in Germany*, Engels continued to characterise the German petty-bourgeoisie as politically unstable, as hoping 'to climb, to swindle their way into the big bourgeoisie' and afraid of 'being plunged down into the proletariat. Between fear and hope, they will, during the struggle, save their precious skin, and join the victor when the struggle is over. Such is their nature'.[33] And such, as the history of Stalinist Popular Frontism has proved, it remains.

Engels' comments on the role of the 'lumpenproletariat' are equally far-sighted, not only in view of its subsequent role as one of the main sources of recruitment for the Nazi Storm Troops (SA), but the repeated attempts by the Stalinist KPD leadership to 'capture' this hopelessly disoriented layer by engaging in unprincipled manoeuvres with allegedly 'radical' elements in the

* Cf. the remarks made by Engels in *The Peasant Question in France and Germany* on the rural counterparts of the artisan and small trader: 'This small peasant, just like the small handicraftsman, is ...a toiler who differs from the modern proletarian in that he possesses his instruments of labour; hence a survival of a past mode of production.' And also like the artisan, the rise of large scale capitalist production cuts the economic ground from under the small peasant's feet: 'Taxes, crop failures, divisions of inheritance, and litigations drive one peasant after another into the arms of the usurer ...in brief, our small peasant, like every other survival of a past mode of production, is hopelessly doomed. He is a future proletarian. As such he ought to lend a ready ear to socialist propaganda. But he is prevented from doing so for the time being by his deep-rooted sense of property. The more difficult it is for him to defend his endangered patch of land the more desperately he clings to it, the more he regards the Social Democrats, who speak of transferring landed property to the whole of society, as just as dangerous a foe as the usurer and lawyer...' (F. Engels: *The Peasant Question in France and Germany* in *Selected Works*, Vol. II, pp.422-423.). Engels was obviously no stranger to the canard that Marxism and 'loan capital' were united in their desire to strangle the independent producers of town and country. This article recommends a series of programmatic demands which could serve as a means of countering such propaganda by uniting the proletariat and small peasantry against the big urban and rural exploiters: '...we forsee the inevitable doom of the small peasant ...it is not our mission to hasten it by any interference on our part [and] it is just as evident that when we are in possession of state power we shall not even think of forcibly expropriating the small peasants ...as we shall have to in the case of the big landowners [in vivid contrast with Stalin's policy of enforced collectivisation between 1929 and 1933!]. Our task relative to the small peasant consists, in the first place, in effecting a transition of his private enterprise and private possessions to co-operative ones, not forcibly but by dint of example and the proffer of social assistance for this purpose. And then of course we shall have ample means of showing to the small peasant prospective advantages that must be obvious to him even today'. (Ibid, p.433). Also of interest are Engels' observations on the anti--semitism rife among wide sections of the German peasantry: '...it is not in our interests to win the peasant overnight only to lose him again on the morrow. We have no more use for the peasant as a Party member if he expects us to perpetuate his property in his small holding than for the small handicraftsman who would fain be perpetuated as a master. These people belong to the anti-semites. Let them go to them and let them promise to salvage their small enterprises. Once they learn there what these glittering phrases really amount to and what melodies are fiddled down from the anti-semitic heavens they will realise in ever increasing measure that we who promise less and look for salvation in entirely different quarters are after all more reliable people.'(Ibid, p.433)

SA and NSBO:*

> ...this scum of the depraved elements of the big cities, is the worst of all possible allies. This rabble is absolutely venal ...If the French workers, in every revolution, inscribed on the houses: Mort aux voleurs! Death to thieves! and even shot some, they did it, not out of enthusiasm for property, but because they rightly considered it necessary above all to keep that gang at a distance. Every leader of the workers who uses these scoundrels as guards or relies on them for support proves himself by this action alone a traitor to the movement.[35]

But we must return to our main theme, which is the nature and origin of Nazi 'political economy'. How and why did its specious anti-capitalism become intertwined with a very real anti-semitism? To answer this question, we must retrace our steps to the very dawn of the modern era.

Early Christian doctrine forbade its followers to engage in money-lending for gain.** So by a process of elimination and natural selection, the indispensable role in medieval Europe of usurer fell to the only sizable non-Christian minority culturally and economically capable of fulfilling it — the Jews of the Diaspora. Rejected culturally, socially and religiously by the host nation, the Jews existed and functioned 'like pores'[36] in the fabric of pre-capitalist Europe. Because of their social role as providers of credit, the Jews inevitably became everywhere identified with all the nefarious moral qualities traditionally associated with money: greed, avarice, sharp practice and so on. These prejudices were compounded by the Jews' being treated as outcasts both on account of their alien origin and religion. In every possible way, they were ready-made targets and receptacles for economic, social and political grievances, as is all too evident from much literature of the period, ranging from Chaucer to Marlowe and Shakespeare. But the money-lending Jew, despite his economic importance, was not functioning as a capitalist: 'In pre-capitalist stages of society commerce ruled industry. In modern society the reverse is true.'[37] There was nothing productive about usury. While providing a service — at a price — it simply battened onto already existing relations, forces and levels of production. The most penetrating analysis of 'vulgar'† theories about the relationship between interest-bearing capital and productive capital — the fulcrum of Feder's doctrine — is to be found in Volume III of Marx's *Capital,* and in his little-used *Theories of Surplus Value,*

---

* The Nazi party's 'fifth column' inside the trade unions and factories.

** Nicholas Oresme, Bishop of Lisieux, wrote in 1377 that 'there are three ways ...in which one may make profit from money, apart from its natural use. The first of these is the art of exchange ...the second is usury, and the third is the altering of money. The first is base, the second is bad, and the third is even worse.'

† Marx's term for schools of political economy which begin from superficial impressions of the features of capitalist production, and treat them as fixed, permanent a-historical categories.

where in Volume III he examines in minute detail the historical and economic basis of the spurious socialism which hurls its bolts against 'loan capital' while leaving intact industrial or 'productive' capital. Marx begins with Luther's writings on usury, from which he quotes extensively. Like Feder (though of course in a completely different historical and political context) Luther depicts the money lender as an enemy of all classes of society, as much capable of ruining a 'rich prince' as a 'peasant or a burgher ...a squire or a rich gentleman, ...a rich count' or 'the great merchant'.[38] Marx saw in Luther's colourfully imaged tirades against usury an intuitive grasp of its origin and role. Usurer's capital arises

> through the ruination of the citizens (small townspeople and peasants) the gentry the nobility and the princes. On the one hand, the usurer [who, we should remember, was more often than not in this period — circa 1500 — a Jew] comes into possession of the surplus labour and, *in addition, the conditions of labour,* of plebeians, peasants, members of craft guilds, in short, of small commodity producers who need money in order to make, for example, payments before they convert their commodities into money, and who have to buy certain of their conditions of labour. On the other hand, the usurer appropriates rent from the owners of rent, that is, from the prodigal, pleasure seeking rich.[39]

Thus it is easy to see how every propertied class of German society, where this state of affairs prevailed for far longer than in any other major European nation, evolved its own particular brand of 'anti-capitalism' intertwined in many cases with varying degrees of hatred for the Jews.

The earliest recorded attacks on usury were not only antisemitic in flavour, but couched in mainly religious terms, a tradition which the Nazis exploited to the full.* Economic motives were however clearly paramount with Peter Schwarz, a German burgher, who wrote in 1477 that the persecution of Jews was thoroughly justified:

> They do not suffer innocently, they suffer because of their wickedness, because they cheat people and ruin whole countries by their usury ...That is why they are so persecuted ...There is no people more wicked, more cunning, more avaricious, more independent, more troublesome, more venemous, more wrathful, more deceptive and more ignominious...

More typical of Christian anti-semitism were the opinions of the scholar Johann Reuchlin, for whom the Jews 'every day outraged, blasphemed and sullied God in the person of His son ...They regard us Christians as stupid pagans'; and the theologian Geiler

---

* I believe that I am acting in accordance with the will of the almighty Creator: by defending myself against the Jew, I am fighting for the work of the Lord' (A. Hitler: *Mein Kampf,* p.65).

von Kaiserberg, who asked 'are the Jews then better than the Christians that they should be unwilling to work with their hands? ...To practice usury is not to work but to flay others, while wallowing in idleness.' (This worthy man of God knew full well that Jews were barred from membership of the guilds and denied the right to own land — the two main spheres of productive labour.) Since these attacks on the Jews were launched ostensibly on behalf of the 'productive class' — chiefly artisans and peasants — it is easy to see why and how anti-semitism acquired a pseudo-radical character and populist idiom. In doing so, it provided the richer elements of the propertied class — the Princes, big landowners, merchants, guild masters and the like — with a convenient means of diverting the anger of the oppressed artisans and peasants away from their real exploiters towards a readily identifiable and 'alien' scapegoat — the Jew. Here too, churchmen were well to the fore. 'The learned and the naive, the princes and the peasants', wrote the theologian Johannes Trithan,' are filled with animosity against the usurious Jews, and I approve all legal measures taken to protect the people against such exploitation ...are these people to grow fat with impunity on the labour of peasants and artisans?' Luther proved in his later years to be no exception to this tradition. In fact his political degeneration underlines the well-established truth that at all times and in all places, the prevailing popular attitude towards the Jews is a most reliable political barometer. Prior to the defeat of the 1525 peasants' uprising, Luther had been most stubborn in his defence of the Jews, pointing out to their detractors that it was the Church itself which compelled them to follow the trade of money-lending:

> I advise being considerate to them. So long as we use violence and lies ...so long as we keep them from living and working among us ...and force them to practice usury, how can they come to us ...we must welcome them in friendship, let them live and work with us, and they will be of one heart with us.

This is clearly not the Luther whom Hitler numbered, with Wagner and Frederick the Great, among those 'great warriors' whose 'life and work are followed with admiring gratitude and emotion, and especially in days of gloom ...have the power to raise up broken hearts and despairing souls.'[40] Hitler revered Luther the anti-semite; the Luther who recoiled in horror from the plebeian revolt called forth by his own passionate invective against the tyranny of Rome and its clerical agents in Germany.* We find him in the period of post-1525 reaction moving over

---

* Once the peasants advanced the struggle from a revolt against Roman rule to one against German princes and burghers, and under the leadership of the utopian communist Thomas Munzer, even to challenge the rights of private property, Luther's fury knew no bounds. He called upon the princes and burghers to 'stab,

rapidly to a position of compromise with state authority, be it
Protestant or Roman Catholic, and employing the most
scurrilous slanders against those he had previously defended, the
Jews:

> If I find a Jew to baptize [Luther wrote in 1532] I shall lead him to the
> Elbe bridge, hang a stone around his neck, and push him into the
> water. These dogs mock us and our religion.

Nine years later he wrote his most extended anti-semitic tract,
Against the Jews and their Lies, in which he declared that the Jews

> being foreigners, should possess nothing and what they do possess
> should be ours ...they do not work, none the less, they keep our money
> and our goods, and have become our masters in our own country ...O
> adored Christ ...you have no enemy more venemous, more desperate,
> more bitter, than a true Jew who truly seeks to be a Jew.

Luther's proposals for countering the 'Jewish conspiracy'
included not only his already quoted demand for 'aryanisation' of
Jewish property, but the burning of synagogues, the banning of
Jewish prayers, the confiscation of Jewish books, and their
deportation from German soil. All were carried out some four
centuries later by the Nazis. But even in Luther's day, the support
for his anti-semitic diatribes was such that in Saxony, Brandenburg and Silesia, the 'Jewish question' was 'solved' by the
wholesale expulsion of Jews from these largely Protestant regions
of Germany.

From this time on, anti-semitism, with its strong anti-usurious
undertones, became not a prejudice amongst others, but an entire
system of religious, political, social, cultural and economic
illusions which penetrated into the very marrow of the bones of
the German artisan and peasant classes. And because of his role
as usurer, as a catalyst in the process of ruin of these classes, the
Jew became identified in the petty-bourgeois consciousness with
social change and the various philosophical and political ideas
and institutions which facilitated the break up of the guild and
patriarchal order — democracy, liberalism, republicanism,
rationalism, materialism, free trade, capitalism, socialism and
revolution. All were tarred indiscriminately with the same
'Jewish' brush, heralding the day when Nazi demagogues could
equate 'Jewish' Marxism with 'Jewish' international finance
capital.

Both in England and France, triumphant bourgeois-
democratic revolutions had repealed legislation discriminating
against the Jews. But in Germany, the long period of reaction,

---

knock and strangle them ...just as one must kill a mad dog ...The peasants must have
nothing but chaff. They do not harken to the Word, and are foolish, so they must
harken to the rod and the gun, and that serves them right.' (T. Luther: *Against the
Murderous and Plundering Peasant Hordes,* 1525.)

national disunity and economic stagnation which set in after 1525 stoked up enormous popular frustrations which often found their only outlet in either overt or covert persecution of the Jews. This fact has a special significance for our study, because precisely in this period were evolved the economic conceptions Marx analysed in *Capital* which he described as a 'religion of the vulgar'.[41] The superficial similarity between the economic theories of Luther and Feder are too obvious to require repeating. But their protagonists are separated by nearly four centuries of German and world history. Therefore while the forms of anti-usury in 1530 and 1920 have much in common, their content differs qualitatively. Luther's attacks on usury — 'Jewish' or otherwise — were intended for the ears of pious peasants and artisans, feudal princes and the incipient German bourgeois, the burgher. His polemics were penned in a world witnessing the very dawn of modern capitalism, the rise of an economy whose motive force was not the production of use values, but exchange values for private profit, based upon the exploitation of free labour power. True, like the Nazi propagandists, Luther appealed to contradictory social strata and classes, to guild masters *and* their journeymen, to princes *and* their peasants; and also like the Nazis, was well-versed in the art of exploiting wounded national sentiments. But there the analogy ends. The Nazis peddled their anti-semitic poison and economic nonsense about 'loan capital' and the 'thraldom of interest' in the epoch of imperialist crisis, world wars and revolutions. Their political camouflage served other interests and classes than those of Princes and guild masters, budding burghers and turncoat clergy. Disguised at the heart of Nazi 'political economy' by all its anti-capitalist bluster, was a theory perfectly capable of adjustment to the strategic needs of German monopoly capitalism, and in particular, its dominant, heavy industrial sector. How far the pioneers of the theory appreciated this fact when they first propagated it is hardly the most important question — though one thing is certain. Neither Feder, Hitler nor any other Nazi leader can in any sense be described as subjectively 'honest' socialists who went astray.* What we have to remember is that the Nazi leaders did not devise their economic programme from scratch. We should not mistake their undoubted quackery and prejudice-ridden notions for the fumblings of those striving, with scant intellectual or academic equipment, to establish an entirely new school of economic theory and practice. That may well have been how Feder and his supporters in the party saw their role, but the reality was very different. The founders of the Nazi movement, thoroughgoing

---

* One advocate of this theory — Peter Sedgwick of the International Socialists — is answered in the appendices at the end of this work.

eclectics that they were, could not but help plagiarise the work of previous generations of 'anti-capitalist' and 'national' economists who voiced the aspirations of an industrial bourgeoisie struggling to free itself from the parasitic embrace of more primitive forms of economy where usury dominated production, and not production usury.

This conflict against the 'money power' produced its own unique form of bourgeois 'false consciousness'. The struggle between the productive capitalist and the money lender for the surplus value extracted by the former from human labour power was refracted in a highly distorted fashion in the thinking of the productive or industrial capitalist:

> The form of revenue and the sources of revenue are the *most fetishistic* of the relations of capitalist production. It is their form of existence as it appears on the surface, divorced from the hidden connections and the intermediate connecting links ...The distorted form in which the real inversion is expressed is naturally reproduced in the views of the agents of this mode of production ...the vulgar economists ...translate the concepts, motives, etc., of the representatives of the capitalist mode of production who are held in thrall to this system of production and in whose consciousness only its superficial appearance is reflected. They translate them into a doctrinaire language, but they do so from the standpoint of the ruling section, i.e., the capitalists, and their treatment is therefore not naive and objective, but apologetic.[42]

This is Marx's starting point for his analysis of apologists for industrial capitalism masquerading as socialists waging war on 'loan capital'. The origin of this mode of consciousness lies at the very heart of the process of capitalist production, a cycle which begins and ends with 'capital in its finished form' — interest-bearing capital, which Marx termed 'the perfect fetish'.[43] The 'loan capitalist' or in Nazi parlance the 'usurer' loans capital at a rate of interest to the productive capitalist, who then employs it to extract surplus value from the labour power of his work force. A proportion of this surplus value — determined by the rate of interest agreed between the loaner and the borrower — does not however remain in the pocket of the productive capitalist, but returns to the loan capitalist in the form of interest. Objectively viewed, what takes place is a division of the spoils between two groups of capitalists, but the participants see matters differently. The productive capitalist's opinions are highly coloured by the fact that he sees himself — and even his workers — as the creative factor in the process, and the loan capitalist as a pure parasite. The loan capitalist's money seems to him to possess the mysterious quality of expanding its own value without any effort on the part of its owner, while the productive capitalist earns his profit, and the workers their wages, by mental and physical effort:

> In the form of interest-bearing capital only this function [that of

yielding a definite profit in a definite period of time] remains, without the mediation of either production process or circulation process, memories of the past still remain in capital and profit although because of the divergence of profit from surplus value and the uniform profit yielded by all capitals — that is, the general rate of profit — capital becomes very much obscured, something dark and mysterious.[44]

The more we delve into this remarkably perceptive section, the more insights it provides into the origins and content of Nazi economic theory. Because the industrially-based segment of the capitalist class confronts interest-bearing capital as an opponent, it employs weapons derived from the past to characterise and fight it. Battle is waged in the name of 'creative' labour by 'hand and brain' — a favourite Nazi expression for the unity in production of worker and employer —against unproductive loan capital, which is even designated as capital itself. Capital in its most fetishistic, mystified form as 'pure' capital seemingly able to increase its value at will, is singled out by industrial capitalists as the enemy all 'productive' classes must combine against to defeat:

> It is thus clear why superficial criticism — in exactly the same way as it wants to maintain commodities and combat money — now turns its wisdom and reforming zeal against interest-bearing capital *without touching upon real capitalist production,* but merely attacking one of its consequences. This polemic against interest-bearing capital, undertaken from the standpoint of capitalist production, a *polemic which today parades as 'socialism',* occurs ...as a phase in the development of capital itself, for example, in the seventeenth century, when the industrial capitalist had to assert himself against the old-fashioned usurer who, at that time, still confronted him as a superior power.[45] (emphasis added)

And in Germany, as we have seen, this struggle unfolded within the context of a virulent anti-semitic tradition lending the 'polemic' an anti-Jewish as well as a 'socialist' character. And though this specious 'socialism' shaded over into the petty-bourgeois variety described in the *Communist Manifesto,* a 'socialism' which opposed not only loan capital but industrial capital as a threat to the existence of the small independent producers,* it was in its developed form a creation and servant of large scale, industrial capitalism:

> It is clear that any other kind of division of profit between various kinds of capitalists, that is, increasing the industrial profit by reducing the rate of interest and vice versa, does not affect the essence of capitalist production in any way. The kind of socialism which attacks interest-bearing capital as the 'basic form'** of capital not only remains completely within the bounds of the bourgeois horizon. Insofar as its polemic is not a misconceived attack and criticism prompted by a

* As was the case with Proudhon.
** Cf. the definitions of capital made by Feder and Hitler quoted above.

vague notion and directed against capital itself, though identifying it with one of its derived forms [i.e. petty-bourgeois socialism] it is nothing but a drive, *disguised as socialism,* for the development of bourgeois credit and consequently only expresses the low level of development of the existing conditions in a country where such a polemic can masquerade as socialist and is itself only a theoretical symptom of capitalist development...[40](emphasis added).

Marx also discusses another aspect of this branch of 'vulgar' political economy which later became a feature of the Nazi, and especially the Italian fascist programme — the tendency to stress the community of interest (in reality of course fictitious) between workers and employers vis a vis the 'loan capitalist', the former being grouped under the rubric 'producers'. How this unreal alignment comes about is explained by Marx in the following way:

Whereas ...*interest* and *interest-bearing capital* merely express the contradiction of materialised wealth as against labour, and thereby its existence as *capital* this position is turned upside down in the consciousness of men because, *prima facie,* the *moneyed capitalist* does not appear to have any relations with the wage worker, but only with other capitalists, while these other (productive) capitalists, instead of appearing to be opposition to the wage workers, appear rather as *workers,* in opposition to themselves or to other capitalists considered as mere owners of capital, representing the mere existence of capital ...*Industrial profit,* in contradistinction to *interest,* represents capital in the production process in contradistinction to capital outside the process, capital as a process in contradistinction to capital as property; it therefore represents the capitalist as functioning capitalist, as representative of *working capital* as opposed to the capitalist as mere personification of capital, as mere owner of capital. He thus appears as *working capitalist* in contrast to himself as capitalist, and further, as *worker* in contrast to himself as mere *owner.* Consequently, in so far as any relation between surplus value and the process is still preserved ...this is done precisely in the form in which the very notion of surplus value is negated. *Industrial profit* is resolved into labour, not into *unpaid* labour of other people but into *wage labour,* into wages for the capitalist who in this case is placed into the same category as the wage worker and is merely a more highly paid worker, just as in general wages vary greatly.[47]

In Volume III of *Capital* (namely Part Five, *Division of Profit into Interest and Profit of Enterprise*) these observations are systematised into a lengthy analysis of the various misconceptions and false ideologies which arise under capitalism as a result of the inherently contradictory nature of its mode of production, especially the role played by money as the abstraction of value created by human labour power; a role which in its turn further mystifies by obscuring the origin of profit. The productive capitalist

creates surplus value not because he works as *capitalist* but because he *also* works, regardless of his capacity of capitalist. This portion of surplus value [the portion falling to the productive capitalist after the loan capitalist has taken his cut] is thus no longer surplus value, but its opposite, an equivalent for labour performed. Due to the alienated character of capital, its antithesis to labour, being relegated to a place outside the actual process of exploitation, namely to the interest-bearing capital, this process of exploitation itself appears as a simple labour process in which the functioning capitalist merely performs a different kind of labour than the labourer.[48]

The result in the realm of consciousness is a conception of production which German and Italian* fascism deliberately employed both in their propaganda and economic and social institutions (i.e. Labour Front, Labour Service, 'Works Community' etc.) to dupe the less politically aware sections of the working population that exploitation, profiteering and the class divisions that accompanied them had been overcome. Under the rule of national socialism, all were 'workers of hand and brain', just as in the Italian 'corporate state', all were 'producers':

> ...the labour of exploiting and the exploited labour both appear as identical as labour. The labour of exploiting is just as much labour as exploited labour.[49]

If indeed all were workers — and Nazi propaganda vehemently and incessantly asserted that they were — then there was no need for class organisations, whether they be economic, political or even cultural and sporting. A theory evolved by apologists for capitalism in the period of its ascendency now served, in the period of its crisis, to justify the most ruthless repressions against the workers' movement. But of course, since the Third Reich claimed to be socialist, and its ruling party a 'workers' party, the destruction of the trade unions and the workers' parties had to be presented as a measure carried out *in the interests of the workers,* and accompanied by what was purportedly an equally firm treatment of the employers' organisations:**

> One of the first necessities with which the Hitler Government found itself faced was that of dissolving the organisations that kept alive the antagonism between employers and employees. They were replaced by the German Labour Front — a body comprising employers as well as employees. At the same time, preparations were made for the creation of an entirely new system of social order based on the following principles: the solidarity of all persons working for their living; the idea of leadership; the recognition of the factory, etc., as a

---

* Thus the attempt to present Italy as an exploited 'proletarian' nation waging a national 'class' war against the 'plutocratic' nations.

** This of course was far from being the case. While the Nazis outlawed the trade unions and either murdered or jailed their leaders, the disbanded employers' organisations soon reappeared — often with the same leadership — under new names. For a fuller discussion of this feature of Nazi 'anti-capitalism', see the chapter *Capital and Labour in the Third Reich.*

bond of union, and the ethical conceptions of honour and loyalty. All this preliminary work crystallised in the passing of the Act governing the regulation of national labour, Jan. 20, 1934 ...[its object] is clearly set forth in Article 1 of the Act, according to which employers and employees are required 'to collaborate with one another to promote the objects for which the undertaking has been founded and for the common benefit of the people and the State'. The same principle of solidarity is given expression in Article 2, where it says that the employer — described as the 'leader' of the undertaking, is required to uphold the welfare of employees, whilst the latter are asked [sic!] to show that spirit of loyalty towards the employer which is founded upon the basis of their joint interest in the undertaking.[50]

This was how Robert Ley characterised the ethos allegedly under-lining the activities of his own 'Labour Front'. A similar corporatist theme underlay the propaganda of the allied 'State Labour Service:

...all civilised countries since the coming of the machine age have greatly suffered from the erection of certain social barriers ...populations have been divided into two great classes, bourgeoisie and proletariat. The bourgeoisie adopted, for the most part, a Liberal Capitalism which amounted to a recognition of the principle that 'those who have may do as they please' to which the proletariat replied by asserting that 'possession is theft' ...both these ideas will finally lead to anarchy and Bolshevism.* Germany, because of her historical development and, above all, because of her rapid transition from an agricultural to an industrial country, suffered from class quarrels in their extremist form ...When the Fuehrer attained power, he was faced with the fact that the German people were divided into two sections neither of whom ...could understand the other. Indeed, they were even prepared to fight one another to the death. The Fuehrer and his movement succeeded in achieving the impossible by putting an end to class hatred ...he instructed the Labour Service to be an instrument by which the lack of vision of the bourgeoisie and the class hatred of the proletariat should be counteracted, and a true community of all Germans should be created.[51]

This is the essence of corporatist ideology. It maintains an utterly spurious community of interest between the worker and his employer. But in one sense there is no deception. The creation of such a 'factory', 'works', 'people's' community is stated quite bluntly to follow the complete destruction of all working class organisations. While their former members are 'co-ordinated', to use the Nazi term, within the new state and economic structure, the trade unions are by definition excluded from any role or place in the fascist corporate state. And this applies with just as much force to trade unions dominated by a reformist as by a centrist or even revolutionary leadership. The social democratic AGDB suffered exactly the same fate as the KPD-led trade union

---

* Once again, the claim that free trade, liberal capitalism and proletarian socialism are in collusion.

organisation, the RGO. There was no question of their being allowed to perform, in however humble or craven a posture, the role of bureaucratic policemen on behalf of the Nazis, even though a section of the ADGB leadership pleaded with Hitler in the first weeks of his rule to be permitted to carry out this task under the Third Reich. This gives the lie not only to the ultra-left claim, peddled by the Stalinists between 1928 and 1934, that social democracy is a variety of fascism, but that bona fide workers' organisations, however craven and class collaborationist their leadership, can somehow survive the introduction of corporatism, and even become part of its repressive machinery. Involved in this false presentation of fascism is the notion, based on superficial impressions of corporative ideology and organisation, that the corporate or fascist system rests upon the 'tying' of trade unions to the capitalist state, and that rather than marking the end of all forms of class collaboration as practised by the leaders of social democracy and reformist trade unionism, is indeed a continuation of this collaboration in new guises (Hence the tendency to equate 'collaborationist' with 'corporatist' rather than to point out the all-important difference between them, namely that the former presupposes independent workers' organisations, the latter, their annihilation.) This confusion has even spread to organisations which claim to base themselves on Trotskyist principles. Thus the *Workers Press*, 'Daily Organ of the Central Committee of the Socialist Labour League'* has repeatedly attempted to draw direct parallels between the Tory government's incomes policy and what the *Workers Press* usually terms corporatism. One instance of this suggests how little the SLL leadership appears to have learned either from the history of fascism or Trotsky's many writings on the subject, even though in 1970 they published a sizable selection of them!**

An article taking Transport Workers' leader Jack Jones to task for solidarising himself with the struggle of Spanish workers against fascism while neglecting the fight against the danger of a similar regime in Britain makes the following false comparison between the two countries:

> He [Jones] is now a leading trade union figure in the joint talks with the Tory government who want to make the corporate state legislation embodied in Phases One and Two of the pay laws a permanent feature of capitalist society. *The cardinal feature of Franco's fascism is corporatism — a structure of dictatorship which ties unions to the state and prevents them from making independent decisions.*[52](emphasis added)

---

* At the time of writing, the SLL was in the process of transforming itself into a revolutionary party.

** L. Trotsky: *Germany 1931-32;* New Park Publications, 1970.

One can only be amazed that this article appears in a journal which should be serving to equip theoretically the working class for struggle against any future fascist danger. Firstly, state control of wages is only *one* of the features of corporatism. It also involves — as the examples of Italy (the home of corporatism) Germany and Spain have long since proved — the total *destruction* of trade unionism. Because the Tories now begin to employ some of the weapons in the armoury of fascism, this does not make their government 'corporatist'. If we take state control of wages as the sole, or decisive criterion of fascism, then many other capitalist countries can also be included under this heading; i.e. the United States and West Germany. This false line of reasoning based upon a highly impressionistic, empirical method, recalls the KPD line between 1930 and 1932, which held that the semi-Bonapartist regime of Brüning, and the fully Bonapartist ones of von Papen and Schleicher, were varieties of fascism, as indeed was the preceding government headed by the social democrat Müller. Here too, government control — and cutting — of wages, on this occasion by Presidential decree, was presented as a fully-blown fascist measure. When they did come to power, the Nazis upheld the Brüning and Papen cuts, even extending them, but they did a lot more besides. For to make these cuts effective and safe from the threat of upwards pressure by the working class, the worker's means of fighting — the trade union — had to be torn from his hands. This was the essential distinction between the Hitler regime and the series of Bonapartist governments which both preceded and helped clear the road for it. And it is a distinction which the *Workers Press* has repeatedly overlooked. Equally disturbing is the description of Franco fascism as a system which 'ties the unions to the state and prevents them from making independent decisions'. Is it the position of the SLL that the fascist 'syndicates' in Spain are genuine trade unions, or even 'unions' that have become emasculated by Franco's corporatist legislation? Surely not, for in that case, what precisely are the illegal 'workers' commissions', which daily defy Franco's police terror in their fight to organise and defend the Spanish working class?

While on the one hand, certain TUC leaders are depicted in the *Workers Press* as either conniving at, supporting or even operating an already-existing or emerging corporate system in Britain, the utterly bogus 'unions'; the fascist-dominated vertical syndicates in Spain are not only confused with genuine workers' organisations, but presented as 'unions' restrained from fulfilling the function of representing their members by the actions of a hostile government! For one only speaks of 'tying to the state' and 'prevention from making independent decisions' when and where there exists resistance to such government control. Again, is it the considered opinion of the SLL Central Committee that Franco's fascist syndicates (the bodies the *Workers Press* insists on calling 'unions') are *resisting* state control of their functions, when these functions are precisely to \chain the Spanish workers to their employers and the state?* How alien this idea is to Trotsky's analysis of fascism is clear from his voluminous writings on the subject, from which we need quote only a few lines to prove the point:

> According to Stalin they [Fascism and Social Democracy] are 'twins', not antipodes. Let us assume that the Social Democracy would, without fearing its own workers, want to sell its toleration to Hitler, But Hitler does not need this commodity: he needs not the toleration but the abolition of the Social Democracy. The Hitler government can only accomplish its task by breaking the resistance of the proletariat and by removing all the possible organs of resistance. Therein lies the historical role of fascism ...fascism in no way threatens the bourgeois regime, for the defence of which the Social Democracy exists. But fascism endangers that role which the Social Democracy fulfills in the

---

* As any militant Spanish worker or refugee from the civil war will tell the editor of *Workers Press,* Franco's so-called 'unions' were founded on the corpse of independent trade unionism in Spain. In every region occupied by Franco's fascist armies, the leaders of the workers' organisations were almost without exception shot on the spot, and their members herded at gun-point into the 'syndicates', headed by leaders of the Falange, the Spanish fascist party. How little these syndicates had in common with genuine trade unionism, even of the 'collaborationist' or 'corporatist' variety practised by Jones, Feather and company, can easily be appreciated from the following statement on the aims of the 'vertical syndicates' made by the Falange general secretary Raimundo Fernandez Cuesta, upon the occasion of their official formation in the Spring of 1938. He is at pains to point out that the Spanish version of 'national syndicalism' had even less to do with recognising the claims of the proletariat than Italian 'corporatism'.
'In those countries which the governors have encountered, on coming to power, as in Italy, a class syndicalism that they could not dismantle [this is of course, false, Mussolini exploited only the *forms* of syndicalist organisation in building his corporate system], they have seen themselves forced, as a lesser evil, to convert it into a State syndicalism and afterwards to create supersyndical organs of interconnection and self-discipline in defence of the totalitarian interest in production. Those organs are Corporations. The Corporation then, had a forced basis in class syndicalism. The Vertical Syndicate, on the other hand, is both the point of departure and of arrival. *It does not suppose the previous existence of other syndicates. Broad horizontal [i.e. class] structures do not interfere with it.* It is not an organ of the State, but an instrument at the service of its utilitarian economic policy.' (emphasis added) So not even the founders of Franco's 'unions' (to use the term employed by the *Workers Press)* attempted to depict them, for demagogic reasons, as in any way being class organisations. In fact, as the above quotation proves, they strenuously — and quite justifiably — denied it. This notion is all the more disturbing in that the ultra-opportunist Spanish Stalinist movement under the leadership of Santiago Carrillo has for some time now engaged in the treacherous policy of encouraging workers to 'reform' the fascist vertical syndicates and thus abandon the fight to create their own illegal organs of struggle. If this line is to be applied consistently, then one might have, under the Nazis, worked for similar 'reform' of the Labour Front. Indeed, taking the argument of *Workers Press* to its logical conclusion, since the TUC is 'corporatist' — or at any rate several of its leading members — then Robert Ley could be cast in the role of a German Vic Feather or Jack Jones. Either this, or 'Workers Press' corrects its false analysis of Spanish fascism.

bourgeois regime and the income which the Social Democracy derives from playing this role. Even though the Stalinists forget this side of the matter, the Social Democracy does not for one moment lose sight of the mortal danger with which a victory of fascism threatens *it* — not the bourgeoisie, but it — the social Democracy ...If the Social Democratic leaders do not want to abandon compacts with the bourgeoise, the fascist bourgeoisie does, however, abandon compacts with the Social Democracy ...In the passage of power from Papen to Hitler [this article — *The Only Road* — was written on September 14, 1932] the bourgeoisie will in no way be able to spare the Social Democracy.[53]

Elsewhere in the same article, Trotsky refers quite unambiguously to the 'incompatibility of Social Democracy and fascism'[54], which of course in no way implies that its leaders were, are or ever will be capable of leading the working class in a successful fight against fascism. So it is self-evident that when the SLL seeks — as it has done — to present not only the trade union leadership but that of the Labour and Communist Parties as 'supporters of corporatism',[55] it is substituting radical phraseology for sober Marxist analysis and policies.

The extent and possible causes of the SLL's departure from Trotskyism in this field is the subject of an appendix at the end of this work. It has been raised at some length here in order to stress the enormous importance of a Marxist-based methodological and historical approach to what we have termed the 'political economy' of fascism. Without the theoretical understanding that such an approach helps provide, there can be no successful fight against fascism, either in Britain or anywhere else.

REFERENCES FOR CHAPTER EIGHT

[1] K. Marx and F. Engels: *The German Ideology* (1845-1847), p.38, Moscow, 1964.
[2] K. Marx: *A Contribution to the Critique of Political Economy* (1859), p.21, London, 1971.
[3] G. Feder: *Hitler's Official Programme,* pp.44-45, English Edition, 1934.
[4] Ibid, pp.48-49.
[5] Ibid, p.52.
[6] Ibid, pp.58-59.
[7] Ibid, p.68.
[8] Ibid, pp.84-85.
[9] Ibid, pp.86-87.
[10] Ibid, pp.100-101.
[11] A. Hitler: *Mein Kampf,* pp.209-210.
[12] Ibid, p.213.
[13] Ibid, p.235.
[14] Ibid, p.234.
[15] O. Spengler: *The Decline of the West,* Vol. I, (1918), p.138, London, 1959.
[16] Ibid, Vol. II, p.506.
[17] Ibid, p.506.
[18] Ibid, p.507.
[19] Ibid, p.506.
[20] Ibid, p.493.
[21] Ibid, p.492.
[22] Ibid, p.474.
[23] Ibid, p.476.
[24] Ibid, p.464-465.
[25] Ibid, p.507.
[26] K. Marx and F. Engels: *Manifesto of the Communist Party,* in *Selected Works,* Vol. I, pp.55-56.
[27] Ibid, p.56.
[28] Ibid, pp.56-57.
[29] Ibid, p.59.
[30] Ibid, p.59.
[31] Ibid, pp.59-60.
[32] Ibid, p.44.
[33] F. Engels: Preface: *The Peasant War in Germany,* p.22.
[34] Ibid, p.23.
[35] Ibid, p.23.
[36] K. Marx: *Capital,* Vol. III, p.325.
[37] Ibid, p.325.
[38] Cited in K. Marx: *Theories of Surplus Value,* Vol. III, p.529, London, 1972.
[39] Ibid, p.529.
[40] A. Hitler: Ibid, p.243.
[41] Ibid, p.453.
[42] Ibid, p.543.
[43] Ibid, p.454.
[44] Ibid, pp.454-455.
[45] Ibid, p.456.

[46] Ibid, pp.467-468.
[47] Ibid, pp.477-490.
[48] K. Marx: *Capital*, Vol. III, p.375, Moscow, 1962.
[49] Ibid, p.375.
[50] R. Ley: *Social Policy in the New Germany*, in *Germany Speaks*, pp.159-161, 1938 edition.
[51] Senior Labour Leader Müller-Brandenburg: *The State Labour Service In Germany*, in ibid, p.190.
[52] *What about the Corporatist threat here Mr Jones?* in *Workers Press*, August 14, 1973, p.11.
[53] L. Trotsky: *The Only Road* (September 14, 1932) in *The struggle Against Fascism in Germany*, pp.278-293, New York, 1971.
[54] Ibid, p.288.
[55] Cf. *Corporatism accepted, Workers Press*, June 11, 1973, p.2, and billed subject of a meeting of the Woolwich branch of the SLL-led 'All Trade Unions Alliance': *TUC and Stalinists — supporters of corporatism* in ibid, June 12, 1973, p.11.

A note on the 'Jewish question' in modern Germany

This chapter cannot be complete without at least a brief comment on the changed structure of Jewry in modern Germany. Continued social, economic and political discrimination against the Jews during the rise of capitalism in Germany led to their more well-to-do elements who had previously been engaged in usury being excluded from a prominent role in those sectors of the economy which were expanding most rapidly and were proving themselves the most lucrative. All the advantages which their role as suppliers of credit had secured richer Jews in the pre- and early capitalist epochs now turned into almost insurmountable obstacles. 'Gentile'-owned industrial concerns and finance houses steadily displaced the old Jewish banking families as the 'powers behind the throne' not only in Germany, but throughout Europe (Church teaching on the iniquities of moneylending and profiteering began to make the necessary adjustments). The rise of large-scale, and then monopoly capitalism therefore revolutionised both the internal social structure of Jewry and its relations to society as a whole. According to the Belgian Trotskyist authority on the history of Jewry, Abram Leon*, 'at least 90% of the Jews were agents and merchants at the beginning of the capitalist era'. (A. Leon: *The Jewish Question*, p.180, Mexico, D.F., 1950.) He showed that of an estimated 15,800,000 Jews throughout the world, 36.4% were engaged in industry, as compared with 38.6% in trade, which included transportation and amusements as well as banking. There was a similar shift in the class, as distinct from occupational structure of Jewry. Before the rise of industrial capitalism, the Jews taken as a group were among the richest communities in Europe, due to their role as holders and lenders of the means of exchange. The break-up of pre-capitalist economic relations — itself accelerated by usury — and the rise of monopoly capitalism expropriated and impoverished millions of Jews, thrusting them like their 'gentile' counterparts into the ranks of the modern industrial proletariat. By the first decade of the 20th century, 62% of Jews in Germany were either workers or employees, while the proportions for England, the USA and France were 77, 75 and 48% respectively. While it is clear from these figures that the tendency for the Jews to become proletarianised was directly related to the degree of industrialisation and urbanisation in the countries concerned, the past history of the Jews as a highly cultured and persecuted people greatly influenced both the extent and nature of this process. Inclined toward radicalism by centuries of official and unofficial repressions, even many wealthy Jews looked towards the workers' movement (and before its emergence, radical liberalism and republicanism) as the only force which could cleanse society of racial and religious prejudice. The high proportion of leaders of Jewish origin in the German and international workers' and

---

* A leader of the Belgian resistance, Leon was arrested by the Gestapo in 1943 and after repeated torturing, died in the Dora concentration camp.

revolutionary movement was a natural and inevitable consequence of the persecution of Jewry by feudal and capitalist society. Those sections of Jewry unable to keep a foothold in their traditional spheres of banking and commerce tended to gravitate towards the so-called 'free professions' — though even here barriers were erected against their advancement — and publishing, where Jews achieved prominence in the bourgeois democratic German press. Nazi propaganda eagerly seized on these linked phenomena — the 'over representation' of Jews in the labour movement and the publishing world — as proof of a Jewish take-over of German business and political life. In fact both were due precisely to the centuries-old German tradition of anti-semitism, of which the Nazis were the most systematic and hideous exponents.

A Jewish rebuttal of these charges, published in 1932 by the 'Association to Counter Anti-Semitism', naturally did nothing to abate Nazi attacks on Jews, but at the same time it provided revealing information on who really owned the German economy, and therefore by implication, who really stood to gain from inflaming hatred against the Jews as the personification of 'Jewish world finance':

'Today, capital formation takes place in large industry. Its largest enterprises are almost entirely dominated by non-Jewish interests: Krupp, Vereinigte Stahlwerke, Kloeckner, Stinnes, Siemens, Stumm, Hugenberg, Hapag, Nordlloyd. International connections are concentrated most heavily in those industries in which Jews are without influence or altogether unrepresented: the German-French iron cartel, wooden matches trust, oil trust, potash industry, and shipping conventions are all 'clean of Jews' and so are the international chemical cartel, nylon production and all the other raw material and key industries in which Jews have no influence either as owners or directors ...The ten largest conglomerations of wealth are in the following hands: Ex-Emperor Wilhelm II, Count Albert von Thurn und Taxis, Mrs Bertha Krupp von bohlen und Halbach, Fritz Thyssen, Otto Wolff, Johann Count zu Hohenlohe-Oehringen, Count Maximilian Egon zu Fuestenberg, Count Guidetto Henckel von Donnersmarck, Count Heinrich von Pless, Prince Frederick of Prussia...'

Aryans all! There was just as little substance to the Nazi claim that Weimar was a 'Jewish republic':

'...the 10 post-war cabinets consisted of 237 ministers of whom three — Preuss and twice Rathenau — were Jews and four — Landsberg, Gradnauer and twice Hilferding — of Jewish descent ...In the German provinces the situation is not different: none of the provincial cabinets contain a Jew. The administration is not full of Jews either ...in Prussia, among the twelve chief Presidents, 35 government presidents and 400 provincial counsellors, there is not a single Jew. (*Abwehr-Blatter*, October, 1932.)

Nazi anti-semitism permitted millions of German petty-bourgeois to brandish their fists at 'finance capitalism' only in the form of a Jew. As Trotsky pointed out:

'The Nazis abstract the usurious or banking capital from the modern economic system because it is the spirit of evil; and, as is well known, it is precisely in this sphere that the Jewish bourgeoisie occupies an important position. Bowing down before capitalism as a whole, the petty-bourgeoisie declares war against the evil spirit of gain in the guise of the Polish Jew in a long skirted kaftan and usually without a cent in his pocket. The pogrom becomes the supreme evidence of racial superiority.' (L. Trotsky: *What is National Socialism*, — June 10, 1933 — in ibid, pp.404-405.) And we might add, of the German petty-bourgeoisie's economic impotence.

Chapter Nine
HITLER: THE FORMATIVE YEARS

German fascism was born out of two defeats: that of German imperialism in the world war, and the defeat - or rather betrayal - of the revolution which followed it. Without the humbling of Prussian military might, and the resulting predatory treaties forced on the German nation by the victorious allied powers, there would have been little basis for the chauvinist resentments and smouldering desires for revenge which national socialism exploited so skillfully in its rise to power. And had the proletariat succeeded in its initial bid to create the necessary economic basis for a socialist society in Germany, there would have been no monopolist industrialists and bankers to subsidise Hitler's movement, and a far more favourable foundation established for undermining the hold of reactionary ideas among wide layers of the middle class and peasantry. Imperialist war and social democracy - these were the mid-wives of national socialism. But if we are to sustain the analogy with child birth - and to a certain extent the analogy is a serviceable one - then we must also look back through the process of gestation to that of conception and parentage. We have already examined in detail some, though by no means all, of the political and philosophical ancestors of German fascism, while at the same time seeking the origins and class content of those reactionary schools of political economy which reappeared in a vulgarised and distorted form in the theories of the leading Nazi economist, Feder. There remains, however, the task of tracing the genesis of national socialism through the period of its crystallisation out of the numerous and disparate ideologies and movements which begat it. This, the crucial point of transition, must be paid the closest attention since it reveals precisely that which is unique to fascism - a system of counter-revolution which seeks to destroy the working class movement in its entirety and for all time by mobilising against it those very social layers which stand closest to the proletariat in their conditions of life. This is the service which fascism provides for monopoly capitalism, one which no other reactionary movement - let alone social democracy - can rival. In return for a sizable share of the spoils, and a dominant position in the state, the leaders of fascism pledge themselves to cut out the proletarian cancer. The knife they wield is a sharp one, and sometimes the plebeian hands wielding it thrust at the wrong targets, but the overall result, as the record of big business under Mussolini, Hitler and Franco testifies, has given the monopolist bourgeoisie little to complain of. Thus the two extremes of the process are clearly visible: firstly the traditionalist, religious, monarchist, imperialist, often anti-semitic Right, which for all its claims to a "social" policy, and dis-regard for the material interests of the bourgeoisie, never succeeded in rallying millions of petty-bourgeois to the good fight against the twin evils of godless proletarian socialism and internationalism. Indeed, with the possible exception of Stöcker, this was never its intention. Violence against the workers' move-ment, in the eyes of the "old" Right, was the prerogative of the state. The exemplar of this attitude was Bismarck's legislation against the SPD, which while receiving the enthusiastic backing of the main right-wing parties, was never supplemented by "extra-parliamentary" activities even on the part of social democracy's bitterest enemies. At the opposite pole stands the organised mass terror of the Nazis, which reached its peak in the period between their assumption of power on January 30, 1933, and the destruction of the trade unions on May 2 of the same year. In two months, Hitler achieved something the most reactionary elements of the bourgeoisie had dreamt of for more than half a century, but failed to carry through - the shattering of the German workers' movement. And while no fully satisfactory answer will ever be given to the question of why Hitler, rather than some other equally obscure racialist bigot and fanatical anti-Marxist, was raised from the depths of petty-bourgeois anonymity to the pinnacles of political power, much about the nature of national socialism and those who supported it can be gleaned from the story of Hitler's early years. No less an authority on fascism than Trotsky made the point that while

> there are naturally great objective causes which created the autocratic rule of Hitler,... only dull-witted pedants of "determinism" could deny today the enormous historic role of Hitler. The arrival of Lenin in Petrograd on April 3, 1917, turned the Bolshevik Party in time and enabled the party to lead the revolution to victory.[1]

Hitler's own account of his early years is highly interesting in that it both fills out and confirms the picture of the German—and here we must of course include German speaking subjects of the Austro-Hungarian Empire—nationalist petty-bourgeoisie as it evolved in the last decades of the nineteenth century—the period when the major European powers entered the imperialist phase of their development. Some might find it strange that Austria, rather than Germany, was destined to provide the Third Reich with its Fuehrer. Yet it was precisely in Austria where the national question loomed largest in the thinking of the major bourgeois parties and among their middle class following. This state of affairs was of course the direct historical legacy of the failures of 1848. Then the road had been opened up both in Berlin and Vienna by successful plebeian revolts to unify the German-speaking people in a thoroughgoing democratic and revolutionary fashion. In both cases, the bourgeoisie proved unequal to the task, and the conditions were created for the dynastic restorations and consolidations which sundered the German nation for 90 years. Unity, when it was finally achieved took the form of Hitler's 'Anschluss', the complete negation of German unity as conceived and fought for by the revolutionaries of '48. In this sense too, both Hitler and the movement he led were the malignant products of a defeated revolution. What the masses, betrayed by their leaders, failed to win for themselves 'from below' Hitler (and also Bismarck) distorted and perverted on behalf of the bourgeoisie 'from above'. Despite their many differences the two dictators were both bastard offspring of 1848.

Nationalism loomed large in the childhood of Hitler just as it did with countless other offspring of the Austrian middle class. Of peasant origin. Hitler's father served the Austro-Hungarian empire as customs official, and by all accounts seems to have imbibed all the traditional values and attitudes associated with such a humble post in the state hierarchy. But as a German (rather than a Slavic Hungarian or Czech) his limited political and cultural universe would in all probability have revolved around Prussian Berlin rather than cosmopolitan Vienna. This was most certainly the case with his son Adolf:

> Rummaging through my father's library, I had come across a... popular edition of the Franco-German War of 1870-71... It was not long before the great heroic struggle had become my greatest inner experience... But in another respect as well, this was to assume importance for me. For the first time, though as yet in a confused form, the question was forced upon my consciousness: Was there a difference - and if so what difference - between the Germans who fought these battles and other Germans? Why hadn't Austria taken part in this war... Are we not the same as all other Germans?[2]

Thus the young Hitler - barely into his teens - was already receiving a nationalist imprint upon his dawning social consciousness. This process was intensified at school as he relates with evident pride. His High School teachers at Linz indoctrinated their pupils with a fanatical hatred for all those whose native tongue was not German. The language question became the vehicle for the inculcation of chauvinism amongst middle class youth, who lacked the internationalist outlook which enabled the organised working class to resist this deadly virus:

> As everywhere and always, in every struggle, there were, in this fight

for the language in old Austria, three strata: *the fighters, the lukewarm and the traitors.* This sifting process began at school. For the remarkable fact about the language struggle is that its waves strike hardest perhaps in the school, since it is the seed-bed of the coming generation. It is a struggle for the soul of the child, and to the child its first appeal is addressed: "German boy, do not forget you are a German," and "Little girl, remember that you are to become a German mother."[3]

Hitler also recounts how fierce were the nationalist passions aroused in his fellow pupils by such methods:

> They carry on this struggle in hundreds of forms, in their own way and with their own weapons. They refuse to sing un-German songs. The more anyone tries to alienate them from German heroic grandeur, the wilder becomes their enthusiasm... their ears are amazingly sensitive to un-German teachers... Thus on a small scale they are a faithful reflection of the adults, except that often their convictions are better and more honest... It goes without saying that even then I had become a fanatical "German nationalist", though the term was not identical with our present party concept. This development in me made rapid progress: by the time I was fifteen I understood the difference between dynastic "patriotism" and folkish* "nationalism", and even then I was interested only in the latter.[4]

Again under the impact of his chauvinist teachers, the young Hitler came to identify his nationalist-inspired hatred for the Austro-Hungarian empire with a populist, even revolutionary political outlook, since it was directed against a government and state which were founded on the very negation of the sacred principles of nation and 'race':

> ...it was then that I became a revolutionary. For who could have studied German history under such a teacher** without becoming an enemy of the state which, through its ruling house, exerted so disastrous an influence on the destinies of the nation?... Immense were the burdens which the German people were expected to bear, inconceivable their sacrifices in taxes and blood... What pained us most was the fact that this entire system was morally whitewashed by the alliance with Germany, with the result that the slow extermination of Germanism in the old monarchy was in a certain sense sanctioned by Germany itself.[5]

It is impossible, due to the probably deliberate vagueness of his narrative, to place a precise date on the moment when Hitler first began to conceive of German nationalism in this 'volkisch', as opposed to dynastic sense. However, the year 1904, when Hitler reached the age of 15 is as close as we can get. The year is significant in that it also witnessed the foundation of the organisation which, more than any other, can be justly considered to have spawned the Nazi party. The 'German Workers' Party',

---

* This is the usual English translation of the German "volkisch" which is in reality a far more complex term, conveying a populist flavoured racialism rather than orthodox nationalism.

** Dr. Leopold Pötsch, Hitler's history teacher at the Linz 'Realschule'.

despite its name, was not a creation of the proletariat, but of
German-speaking artisans who were seeking means of maintaining their privileges against the supposed threats of 'slavic'
workers in Bohemia, where the party enjoyed its strongest
influence. This is not to say that the 'German Workers' Party' did
not number industrial workers among its members and
supporters — it certainly did, much to their discredit. But the
prime movers in the creation of this nationalist, plebeian-oriented
movement were artisans and master-craftsmen. Perhaps it is
significant for a clearer understanding of Hitler's early political
development that the party was particularly strong in Linz, where
there had been a considerable migration of Czech workers in the
previous few years. The German Workers' Party programme and
its subsequent evolution indicates how little the movement had in
common with the Austrian labour movement, which was under
the leadership of social democracy. The founding manifesto of
1904 declared the GWP to be a 'liberal national party... fighting
with all its strength against the reactionary tendencies, feudal,
clerical and capitalist privileges as well as all foreign national
tendencies'. It was pledged to combat 'the untenable conditions of
the society of today' and to aiding 'the social rise of the workers'.
These contradictory elements in the programme were soon
resolved. While continuing to pay lip service to the protection of
working class interests, the nationalist basis of the party turned it
in a clearly anti-socialist direction. The 1913 programme
denounced what it called 'the teachings of the Social Democratic
Party Saint Marx', which it deemed 'wrong and of immeasurable
damage to the Germandom of central Europe'. Especially
distasteful was Austrian social democracy's attitude of class
solidarity towards the Slavic workers of the empire. It violated
the GWP's first principle of national solidarity: 'The German
employer took the cheaper Slav workers; but the red organisation
refuses to give the German party veterans the protection to which
they are entitled'. This nationalistic line of argument led directly
to the conclusions which we have already encountered in the
writings of Feder and Hitler: that the Marxist movement 'is led by
Jews and closely allied with the big mobile (i.e. 'international
finance') capitalists'. It is therefore hardly surprising to discover
that the German Workers' Party supplied not only the name but
several of the cadres for the Munich-based movement which
Hitler joined towards the end of 1919. But here we are chiefly concerned with the GWP inasmuch as it serves us as a political
barometer for the nationalist tensions which were developing in
the period of Hitler's formative years, and which on his own
testimony convinced him of the necessity to evolve a populist
racialism that would supplant the 'anti-national' and 'dynastic'

patriotism of the Hapsburg monarchy and Austrian aristocracy. It is also important to bear in mind that Hitler's nationalism initially defined itself negatively, not against the Jews, who were domiciled chiefly in Vienna, but the Slavs, whom he despised as backward and devoid of 'culture'. Neither had the question of Marxism or the workers' movement arisen at this early stage, since his life had thus far been spent either in his tiny Upper Austrian home town of Braunau, or the classrooms of the High School at Linz. Hitler's move to Vienna, where he unsuccessfully sought a place at the city's Academy of Fine Arts, soon added several new dimensions to his developing nationalist outlook:

> In this period my eyes were opened to two menaces of which I had previously scarcely known the names, and whose terrible importance for the existence of the German people I certainly did not understand: Marxism and Jewry... who knows when I would have immersed myself in the doctrines and essence of Marxism if that period had not literally thrust my nose into the problem.[8]

In fact Hitler admits that his first impressions of Austrian social democracy, formed at long distance, were on the whole favourable:

> I was profoundly pleased that it should carry on the struggle for universal suffrage and the secret ballot. For even then my intelligence told me that this must help to weaken the Hapsburg regime which I so hated. Consequently this activity of the Social Democracy was not displeasing to me.[9]

And Hitler also claims he approved of Austrian social democracy's goal of "improving the living conditions of the worker," since that appeared to accord with his own predeliction for a populist-flavoured nationalism. But precisely at this point, the national question, Hitler and social democracy parted company for ever. Their roads led along opposed class paths: "What most repelled me was its hostile attitude towards the struggle for the preservation of Germanism, its disgraceful courting of the Slavic "comrade'..."[10] The manner in which Hitler made his first real contact with social democracy, and the indelible imprint it left on his petty-bourgeois nationalist consciousness, is vividly described in the following passage:

> ...at the age of seventeen the word "Marxism" was as yet little known to me, while "Social Democracy" and socialism seemed to me identical concepts. Here again it required the fist of Fate to open my eyes to this unprecedented betrayal of the peoples. Up to that time I had known the Social Democratic Party only as an onlooker at a few mass demonstrations, without possessing even the slightest insight into the mentality of its adherents or the nature of its doctrine; but now, at one stroke, I came into contact with the products of its education and "philosophy." And in a few months I obtained what might otherwise have required decades: an understanding of a pestilential whore, cloaking herself as social virtue and brotherly love, from which I hope

humanity will rid this earth with the greatest dispatch...[11]

The incident to which Hitler refers is his confrontation with a group of trade union workers on a Vienna construction site:*

> From the very beginning it was none too pleasant. My clothing was still more or less in order, my speech cultivated, and my manner reserved... Perhaps I would not have concerned myself at all with my new environment if on the third or fourth day an event had not taken place which forced me at once to take a position. I was asked to join the organisation. My knowledge of trade union organisation was at that time practically non-existent. I could not have proved that its existence was either beneficial or harmful. When I was told that I had to join, I refused.[12]

Hitler's first sally against the fortress of trade unionism ended—unlike his last—in fiasco:

> At the end of two weeks, I could no longer have joined, even if I had wanted to... no power in the world could have moved me to join an organisation whose members had meanwhile come to appear to me in so unfavourable a light... what I heard was of such a nature as to infuriate me in the extreme. These men rejected everything: the nation as an invention of the 'capitalistic' (how often was I forced to hear this single word!) classes; the fatherland as an instrument of the bourgeoisie for the exploitation of the working class, the authority of law as a means for oppressing the proletariat; the school as an institution for breeding slaves and slaveholders, religion as a means for stultifying the people and making them easier to exploit; morality as a symptom of stupid, sheeplike patience, etc. There was absolutely nothing which was not drawn through the mud of a terrifying depth.[13]

His every ideal challenged, refuted and spat upon, Hitler determined to fortify his own feeble arguments with a study of the enemy's propaganda. The result was ever more heated conflicts, until Hitler was forced to leave the building site or risk being 'thrown off the scaffolding' by his trade union opponents. Nor was this the end of the future fascist's one-man crusade against Marxism:

> I was determined to go to work on another building in spite of my experience... The same old story began anew and ended very much the same as the first time.'[14]

Small wonder that this petty-bourgeois bigot, full of delusions in his own artistic genius, puffed up with a snobbish contempt for those less educated and well-born than himself, and now driven to sully his artist's hands in cement and brick dust, asked the question: 'are these people human, worthy to belong to a great nation?... and added:

> ...if it is answered in the affirmative the struggle for my nationality really ceases to be worth the hardship and sacrifices which the best of us have to make for the sake of such scum; and if it is answered in the

---

* It seems that Hitler had been compelled, in the course of his Bohemian existence in the Austrian capital, to supplement his meagre resources by manual labour.

negative, our nation is pitifully poor in human beings.[15]

As if this trauma was not enough, it was compounded by an even more devastating experience a short time after. Hitler's clashes with trade union workers had made him aware of the real nature of the Austrian and international workers' movement—its foundation on firm class lines, and its adherence—even though more often than not formally—to the principle of international working class solidarity. Far from serving as an unwitting agent in the achievement of Pan German goals, it now became a living and growing threat to all those values and institutions which Hitler and countless other middle class nationalists understood by the term 'Germanism':

> I pondered with anxious concern on the masses of those no longer belonging to their people, and saw them swelling to the proportions of a menacing army.[16]

And that was certainly a justifiable impression. Although founded some 26 years after the SPD, the Austrian Social Democratic Party expanded rapidly in the industrialised regions of the country, and most of all in Vienna. A class-based franchise, much on the lines of the Prussian system, prevented the party from securing the parliamentary representation its votes merited,* but even so, it was feared and hated by the movement's monarchist, clerical and bourgeois enemies. And in the immediate pre-war period, when Hitler witnessed the party's mass activities at first hand, Austrian social democracy was in its most radical phase. This helps us to appreciate more fully the political import for Hitler's subsequent development of the following event:

> With what changed feeling I now gazed at the endless columns of a mass demonstration of Viennese workers that took place one day as they marched four abreast, For nearly two hours I stood there watching with bated breath the gigantic human dragon slowly winding by![17]

Hitler now felt compelled to study the press of the movement responsible for such an awesome parade of proletarian power and solidarity. He came to the conclusion that it was possible to shatter the grip of social democracy on the masses only by emulating what he took to be its methods of organisation and propaganda:

> I now understood the significance of the brutal demand that I read only Red papers, attend only Red meetings, read only Red books, etc. With plastic clarity I saw before my eyes the inevitable result of this doctrine of intolerance... the masses love a commander more than a

---

* In 1896, the Austrian constitution divided voters into five groups: aristocrats, the bourgeoisie (manufacturers, merchants and bankers), town and city tax payers, workers and peasants. The voters in the last two groups, which comprised the over-whelming majority of the population, elected 13 fewer representatives than the numerically insignificant aristocracy!

petitioner and feel inwardly more satisfied by a doctrine, tolerating no other besides itself... *If Social Democracy is opposed by a doctrine of greater truth, but equal brutality of methods, the latter will conquer,* though this may require the bitterest struggle.[18]

And such a doctrine of necessity could not, if it sought to win a foothold in the masses till now regarded as the preserve of social democracy, afford to repudiate openly all the goals embraced by the workers' movement. Stridently 'national' in its aims, the new anti-Marxist ideology had to steal the 'social' clothes of the enemy, while repudiating its class and internationalist basis and principles:

> By my twentieth year I had learned to distinguish between a union as a means of defending the general social rights of the wage-earner, and obtaining better living conditions for him as an individual, and the trade union as an instrument of the party in the political class struggle.[19]

Here is the germ-cell of the 'Labour Front', a 'union' which while paying lip service to the rights of the worker and the obligations of the employer, served as an instrument for binding the proletariat ever more tightly to the requirements of capitalist production, since the very principle of the 'Labour Front' denied to the worker both the right and opportunity to organise as a class independently of and against his exploiters. Labour Frontism, 'corporatism' and 'national syndicalism'—these are the very negations of trade unionism, as the workers of Germany, Italy and Spain have learned at the cost of unprecedented suffering and oppression.

The real nature and object of Hitler's 'national trade unionism' is not immediately apparent from his comments on the trade union question in *Mein Kampf.* For example, he says:

> ...to call the trade-union movement in itself unpatriotic is nonsense and untrue to boot. Rather the contrary is true. If trade union activity strives and succeeds in bettering the lot of a class which is one of the basic supports of the nation, its work is not only not anti-patriotic or seditious, but 'national' in the truest sense of the word. For in this way it helps to create the social premises without which a general national education is unthinkable. It wins the highest merit by eliminating social cankers, attacking intellectual as well as physical infections, and thus helping to contribute to the general health of the body politic. Consequently, the question of their necessity is really superfluous.[20]

And this remained the public position of the Nazis on trade unionism right up to, and even after, their seizure of power.*

---

* 'It is a lie, when the SPD asserts that Hitler is going to smash the trade unions'. *(Nazi Election Leaflet No. 33,* Hamburg, 1932). 'Not that we want to destroy the trade unions. Workers! Your institutions are sacred to us National-Socialists, they are not to be touched. Workers! I give you my word, not only shall we preserve everything that exists, but we are going to extend the protection and the rights of the workers'. *The Day of National Labour.* Proclamation on May 1, 1933. The very next day the 'sacred' unions were abolished!

Herein lies one of the greatest dangers that fascism poses to the workers' movement; it seeks to trap the less politically aware worker, or even those more radical elements disenchanted with the trade union, reformist (or Stalinist) bureaucracy who have yet to find their way to a viable revolutionary alternative leadership. Fascism does so by presenting its 'left' face, its 'social' programme, playing down or even at times neglecting entirely the 'national' and consequently more clearly discernible bourgeois aspects of its policies. How the Nazis accomplished this manoeuvre so essential for their success, and yet so fraught with the constant risk of alienating either the bourgeois or plebeian supporters of fascism, will be discussed at some length in later chapters. Here we are concerned primarily with the origin and evolution of this strategic and tactical conception, which Hitler first began to formulate in his pre-war years spent first in Vienna and then Munich. If we study more closely what Hitler has to say about the nature of his projected 'social' policy, it begins to reveal, despite all his anti-bourgeois invective and cloudiness of language, a pro-capitalist orientation of a special and indeed, unique variety. Firstly, Hitler undertakes his criticism of bourgeois policies which prevailed in pre-1914 Austria and Germany on the foundations of the defence of private property, a position he was to uphold both theoretically and with the utmost physical force to the end of his life.* Thus we find the main target of his barbs to be not the magnates of heavy industry, whom as we have already seen, Hitler regarded as the custodians of 'national' capital, but what he termed the 'political bourgeoisie'—that section of the bourgeoisie which has the task of formulating and carrying out policies on behalf of the entire class. The nature of Hitler's attack on the 'political bourgeoisie' raises some critical points of theory pertaining to the nature of the state and the contradictory and unstable relationships which evolve between a class and its leadership. In one of their earliest major works—*The German Ideology* Marx and Engels traced the origin of the 'political bourgeoisie' to the economic principle of the division of labour which

* The record on this all-important question speaks for itself. Apart from the already-quoted reference to the rights of private property in *Mein Kampf*, we have the following equally unequivocal statements on the same subject made at various stages in Hitler's career: "In contrast to men like Hermann Esser, Hitler never permitted himself to be caught up in such [socialist] demagogy. He declared that as long as private property was recognised as one of the foundations of national life, he would not yield, irrespective of how bad the rulers of various states had been. The NSDAP adopted this point of view." (*Memoirs of Alfred Rosenberg,* p.204, Chicago-New York, 1949). Rosenberg was here relating Hitler's attitude to the referendum organised by the SPD and KPD to secure the expropriation without compensation of the former German princes. At a meeting called in Bamberg on February 14, 1926, to determine Nazi policy towards the referendum, Hitler came out strongly against the party "radicals" headed by the Strasser brothers and Göbbels, who were for back-

manifests itself also in the ruling class as the division of mental and material labour so that inside this class one part appears as the thinkers of the class (its active, conceptive ideologists, who make the perfecting of the illusion of the class about itself their chief source of livelihood) while the others' attitude to these ideas is more passive and receptive, because they are in reality the active members of this class and have less time to make up illusions and ideas about themselves. Within this class this cleavage can even develop into a certain opposition and hostility between the two parts, which, however, in the case of a practical collision, in which the class itself is endangered, automatically comes to nothing.[20]

Written between 1845 and 1846, this work, like the *Communist Manifesto*, contains generalised formulations that subsequent historical events and class battles were to fill out with a richer and more complex content. Thus in Marx's classic historical works, *The Class Struggles in France,* (1850) and *The Eighteenth Brumaire of Louis Bonaparte* (1851-52) we find their

ing the referendum in order to hold and extend Nazi influence amongst the workers.) "Nationalisation, or socialisation... is nothing but dilettantism, not to say Bolshevism... I have never said that all enterprises should be socialised. On the contrary, I have maintained that we might socialise enterprises prejudicial to the nation. Unless they were so guilty, I should consider it a crime to destroy essential elements in our economic life... there is only one economic system, and that is responsibility and authority on the part of directors and executives... That is how it has been for thousands of years, and that is how it will always be" (O. Strasser quoting Hitler in: *Hitler and I,* pp.111-113. This extract is taken from Strasser's account of his two meetings with Hitler on May 21 and 22, 1930, which led to his defection from the Nazis on the grounds that Hitler was "sold to the capitalists".) "Private property cannot be maintained in the age of democracy, it is conceivable only if the people have a sound idea of authority and personality... All the worldly goods which we possess we owe to the struggle of the chosen... It is an impossibility that part of the people recognises private ownership while another part denies it. Such a struggle splits the people. The struggle lasts until one side emerges victor." These remarks, startling both for their frankness and perspicacity, were made to a secret meeting of industrialists and bankers at the Reichstag President's residence on February 20, 1933. Hitler was appealing for financial and political support from big business in the elections scheduled for March 5. (*Nuremberg Document D-203*). "I absolutely insist on protecting private property. It is natural and salutary that the individual should be inspired by the wish to devote a part of the income from his work to the building up and expanding of a family estate. Suppose the estate consists of a factory. I regard it as axiomatic that this factory will be better run by one of the members of the family than it would by a state functionary... In this sense, we must encourage private initiative." (*Hitler's Secret Conversations*, p.294, New York, 1953, being a day-by-day record of Hitler's war-time "conversations" - in reality monologues - with his most intimate party colleagues.) "The creative force not only shapes but also takes what it shapes under its wing and directs it. That is what we generally mean by such phrases as private capital or private property... Therefore the future will not belong, as the Communist holds, to the communist ideal of equality, but on the contrary, the farther humanity moves along the road of evolution, the more individualised achievements will be... The basis for all real higher development, indeed for the future development of all mankind, will therefore be found in the encouragement of private initiative." (Hitler's speech to 100 arms manufacturers, June 26, 1944, quoted in A. Speer: *Inside the Third Reich*, pp.359-360, London, 1970.) Yet we still find historians prepared to take Hitler's "anti-capitalism" seriously!

author tracing in the finest detail and complexity the fluctuating interplay of class, parties, leaders and the state as they respond not only to the imperatives of current economic and social pressures, but ideologies, programmes, illusions and prejudices inherited from the past. And in writing his study of the rise to power of Napoleon's nephew, Marx also seized the opportunity it presented to enrich earlier generalisations made with Engels about the nature of the bourgeois state and bourgeois politicians. The period between the revolution of February 1848 and the coup d'etat of Louis Bonaparte on December 2, 1851 proved that there was nothing "automatic" about the way the productive section of the bourgeoisie resolved its differences with the politicians and journalists who ostensibly represented its interests. Indeed, the rule of both Bonapartes* proved that in order to defend its economic right to exploit the proletariat, the French bourgeoisie had to surrender many of its cherished political rights, and in so doing throw to the wolves its literary and political representatives, who could obviously only function and flourish under a regime which recognised parliamentary democracy and the freedom of the press. What Marx has to say on this subject not only pertains to the form of rule known as Bonapartism, but to fascism, which in a far more thoroughgoing and ruthless manner, also sets itself the goal of saving and defending the bourgeoisie from economic expropriation by the proletariat *by expropriating it politically*:

> The aristocracy of finance... condemned the parliamentary struggle of the party of Order with the executive power as a *disturbance of order*, and celebrated every victory of President over its ostensible representatives as a *victory of order*... The industrial bourgeoisie, too, in its fanaticism for order, was angered by the squabbles of the parliamentary party of Order with the executive power... the struggle to maintain its public interests, its own *class interests*, its *political power*, only troubled and upset it as it was a disturbance of private business... Still more unequivocally than in its falling out with its *parliamentary representatives* the bourgeoisie displayed its wrath against its literary representatives, its own press. The sentences to ruinous fines and shameless terms of imprisonment, on the verdicts of bourgeois juries, for every attack of bourgeois journalists on Bonaparte's usurpationist desires, for every attempt of the press to

---

* It is not strictly accurate to say that Marx and Engels had never considered this problem before 1848. In *The Holy Family* (1844), they noted how Napoleon while understanding that the "modern state" was "based on the unhampered development of bourgeois society, on the free movement of private interest," and undertaking to "recognise and protect that basis," nevertheless "regarded the state as an end in itself and civil life only as its treasurer and his subordinate which must have no will of its own... If he despotically oppressed the liberalism of bourgeois society he showed no more pity for its essential material interests, trade and industry, whenever they conflicted with his political interests. His scorn of industrial business men was the complement to his scorn of ideologists." (K. Marx and F. Engels: *The Holy Family*, p.166, Moscow, 1956)

defend the political rights of the bourgeoisie against the executive power, astonished not merely France, but all Europe. While the *parliamentary party of Order...* declared the political rule of the bourgeoisie to be incompatible with the safety and existence of the bourgeoisie... *the extra-parliamentary mass of the bourgeoisie*, on the other hand, by its servility towards the President, by its vilification of parliament, by its brutal maltreatment of its own press, invited Bonaparte to suppress and annihilate its speaking and writing section, its politicians and its *literati*, its platform and its press, in order that it might then be able to pursue its private affairs with full confidence in the protection of a strong and unrestricted government. It declared unequivocally that it longed to get rid of its own political rule in order to get rid of the troubles and dangers of ruling... Thus the industrial bourgeoisie applauds with servile bravos the coup d'etat of December 2, the annihilation of parliament, the downfall of its own rule... As the executive authority which has made itself an independent power, Bonaparte feels it to be his mission to safeguard "bourgeois order." But the strength of this bourgeois order lies in the middle class [bourgeoise]. He looks on himself, therefore, as the representative of the middle class and issues decrees in this sense. Nevertheless, he is somebody solely due to the fact that he has broken the political power of this middle class and daily breaks it anew. Consequently, he looks on himself as the adversary of the political and literary power of the middle class.[21]

And so we are brought back to the young Hitler, who without doubt saw himself, even in his Vienna days, as a future vanquisher of bourgeois politicians and "literati", even though the methods he would employ differed in many ways from those of Louis Bonaparte.* He had nothing but scorn for what he considered to be their pusillanimous reluctance to wage a war of extermination against Marxism:

Before two years [in Vienna] had passed, the theory as well as the technical methods of Social Democracy were clear to me. I understood the infamous spiritual terror which this movement exerts, particularly in the bourgeoisie, which is neither morally nor mentally equal to such attacks... [Its tactics] will lead to success with almost mathematical certainty unless the opposing side learns to combat poison gas with poison gas. It is our duty to inform all weaklings that this is a question of to be or not to be... Terror at the place of employment, in the factory, in the meeting hall, and on the occasion of mass demonstrations will always be successful unless opposed by equal terror.[22]

With his reference to social democratic or trade union "terror at the place of employment [and] in the factory," Hitler ranges

---

* However they shared Bonaparte's use of corrupted plebeian elements - his so-called Society of December 10, whose members' occupations Marx listed as "vagabonds, discharged soldiers, discharged jailbirds, escaped galley slaves, swindlers, mountebanks, *lazzaroni*, pickpockets, tricksters, gamblers, procurers, brothel keepers, porters, *literati*, organ grinders, rag-pickers, knife-grinders, tinkers, beggars - in short, the whole indefinite disintegrated mass thrown hither and thither, which the French term *la boheme*."

himself quite openly on the side of the bourgeoisie - not its political or literary wing, but the industrial, whom the former by their political ineptitude or cowardice, were abandoning to the Marxist-led masses. And even when, out of demagogic considerations, he finds it expedient to criticise the lack of a "social" attitude on the part of the employers, he still manages to divert his polemic away from the real culprits towards the same "political bourgeoisie":

> Since on innumerable occasions the bourgeoisie has in the clumsiest and most immoral way opposed demands which were justified from the universal point of view... even the most self-respecting worker was driven out of the trade union organisation into (Marxist) political activity. Millions of workers... started out as enemies of the SPD in their innermost soul, but their resistance was overcome in a way which was sometimes utterly insane; that is, when the bourgeois parties adopted a hostile attitude toward every demand of a social character...* Never can our political bourgeoisie make good its sins in this direction, for by resisting all attempts to do away with social abuses, they sowed hatred and seemed to justify even the assertions of the mortal enemies of the entire nation, to the effect that only the SPD represented the interests of working people. Thus... they created the moral basis for the actual existence of the trade unions, the organisation which has always been the most effective pander to the [Marxist] political party... Proportionally as the political bourgeoisie did not understand... the importance of trade union organisation, and resisted it, the Social Democrats took possession of the contested movement. Thus, far-sightedly it created a firm foundation which on several critical occasions has stood up when all other support failed.[23]

So the main - in fact it would seem only - blame for the rise of a Marxist-influenced trade union movement lay with the bourgeois political parties, the so-called "political bourgeoisie." The actual beneficiaries and instigators of this harsh industrial regime - big employers of the Krupp-Stumm-Kirdorf variety - were completely overlooked. And well they might be, for it was here that Hitler sought to win support for his policy of all-out struggle against the workers' movement, a strategy he was in the process of formulating when he wrote these lines. To return to Hitler's early opinions on "political" trade unionism. His Vienna experiences convinced him that under the leadership of the Austrian social democrats, it "had no use except as a battering ram in the class struggle. Its purpose was to cause the collapse of the whole arduously constructed economic edifice by persistent blows, thus, the more easily, after removing its economic foundations, to prepare the same lot for the edifice of the state."[24]

And here too, Hitler was critical of the bourgeoisie's political representatives:

* The Hitler regime's reactions to these same demands will be discussed in the chapter *Capital and Labour in the Third Reich.*

The bourgeois camp was indignant at this obvious insincerity of social democratic tactics, but did not draw from it the slightest inference with regard to their own conduct... Instead of attacking and seizing the enemy's position, the bourgeoisie preferred to let themselves be pressed to the wall and finally had recourse to utterly inadequate makeshifts, which remained ineffectual because they came too late, and moreover were easy to reject because they were too insignificant... like a menacing storm-cloud, the "free trade union" hung even then [i.e. before 1914] over the political horizon and the existence of the individual. It was one of the most frightful instruments of terror against the security and independence of the national economy, the solidity of the state, and personal freedom.[25]

And when Hitler refers to "national economy" and "personal freedom" it is perfectly clear that he has the economy and freedom of the bourgeoisie in mind, for it was against this class that the "frightful instruments of terror" were exclusively directed. If Hitler also felt threatened by the power of the organised working class - and he most certainly did, as his own testimony proves - then that was because, anti-bourgeois rhetoric nothwithstanding, he identified himself with and tied his fortunes to the destiny of this same class, Hitler's anti-semitism likewise flows from his essentially bourgeois world outlook, and in fact can be shown to have its immediate origins not in any family or local tradition, but in his pathological hatred of Marxism.

Hitler's account of how he became an anti-semite shows that far from opposing Marxism for its "Jewish" origins, he came to despise the Jews because of their disproportionate role in the Austrian social democratic movement. Hitler's racialism was a direct product of his ingrained fear of the organised proletariat:

Only a knowledge of the Jews provides the key with which to comprehend the inner, and consequently real, aims of Social Democracy. The erroneous conceptions of the aim and meaning of this party fall from our eyes like veils, once we come to know this people, and from the fog and mist of social phrases rises the leering grimace of Marxism.[26]

That Hitler's anti-Marxism preceded his anti-semitism chronologically as well as mentally is clear from his own testimony. If we are to believe Hitler, his father was not in the least anti-semitic. Indeed, 'in the course of his life he had arrived at more or less cosmopolitan views which, despite his pronounced national sentiments, not only remained intact, but also influenced me to some extent'.[27] Neither did the 'Jewish question' come up with any force at the high school in Linz. There, Hitler even found himself instinctively defending Jews on the rare occasions when a fellow pupil made an anti-semitic comment:

There were few Jews in Linz. In the course of the centuries their outward appearance had become Euopeanised and had taken on a human look [sic!] in fact, I even took them for Germans. The absurdity of this idea did not dawn on me because I saw no distinguishing feature but the strange religion. The fact that they had, as I believed, been persecuted on this account sometimes almost turned my distaste at unfavourable remarks about them into horror. Thus far I did not so much as suspect the existence of an organised opposition to the Jews.[28]

Nationalist prejudices at Linz were, as we have already noted, directed almost exclusively at the Czechs. It was only when Hitler arrived in Vienna that the veil began to fall from his eyes. And even then, the future scourge of European Jewry was slow to learn. The trouble was that despite their "sub-human" character, the Jews looked just like anyone else:

> Notwithstanding that Vienna in those days counted nearly 200,000 Jews among its two million inhabitants, I did not see them... the Jew was still characterised for me by nothing but his religion, and therefore, on grounds of human tolerance, I maintained the tone, particularly that of the Viennese anti-semitic press, seemed to me unworthy of the cultural tradition of a great nation. I was oppressed by the memory of certain occurences in the Middle Ages, which I should not have liked to see repeated [sic!].

Only when Hitler began to concern himself with Viennese political life did anti-semitism begin to intrude into his thinking. Hostile to the liberal-democratic press, which cared little for Hitler's nationalist aspirations, and already deeply disturbed by the power of the even more avowedly 'anti-national' workers' movement, he then made what he considered to be a world-shattering discovery:

> What had to be reckoned heavily against the Jews in my eyes was when I became acquainted with their activity in the press, art, literature and the theatre... It sufficed to look at a billboard, to study the names behind the horrible trash they advertised, to make you hard for a long time to come. This was pestilence, spiritual pestilence, worse than the Black Death of olden times, and the people was being infected with it... The fact that nine tenths of all literary filth, artistic trash, and theatrical idiocy can be set to the account of a people, constituting hardly one hundredth of all the country's inhabitants, could simply not be talked away: it was the plain truth.[30]

So the struggle against the bourgeoisie's "literati" was to be waged with more discrimination than was the case under the rule of the two Bonapartes. And here there was a certain parallel with the bogus war national socialism was later to wage against "capital," personified by the same ubiquitous - and highly convenient - Jew. But it was only when Hitler looked long and hard at the press of his greatest enemy - the workers' movement - that he became a confirmed anti-semite:

> when I learned to look for the Jew in all branches of cultural and artistic life and in its various manifestations, I suddenly encountered him in a place where I would have least expected to find him. When I recognised the Jew as the leader of the Social Democracy, the scales dropped from my eyes, a long soul struggle had reached its conclusion.[31]

In other words, it required a supposed Jewish control over the

affairs of social democracy before Hitler finally accepted as true,
allegations made in anti-semitic papers and pamphlets that the
Jews were the ring-leaders in a vast conspiracy to destroy the
German nation:

> I gradually became aware that the Social Democratic press was
> directed predominantly by Jews; yet I did not attribute any special
> significance to this circumstance, since conditions were exactly the
> same in the other papers. Yet one fact seemed conspicuous: there was
> not one paper with Jews working on it which could have been
> regarded as truly national... I swallowed with disgust and tried to read
> this type of Marxist press production, but my revulsion became so
> unlimited in so doing that I endeavoured to become more closely
> acquainted with the men who manufactured these compendiums of
> knavery. From the publisher down, they were all Jews.[32]

Now the struggle against Jewry could be fought without any
reservations. The Jew was the leader of the proletariat, a
revolutionary. From members of parliament to

> trade union secretaries, the heads of organisations or street agitators...
> the party with whose petty representatives I had been carrying on the
> most violent struggle for months was, as to leadership, almost ex-
> clusively in the hands of a foreign people... to my deep and joyful satis-
> faction I had at last come to the conclusion that the Jew was no
> German.[33]

Neither were original 'discoveries'. We have already noted how
from its inception, the German labour movement was branded by
its Junker and bourgeois enemies as a foreign creation, usually
French. Neither were the Jews regarded by the 'best' circles as true
Germans. They were excluded from membership of professional
associations, student societies, and barred from holding
commissions in the armed forces. Here Hitler was treading on
well-worn ground. But standing on the shoulders—or rather
another part of the anatomies—of the German and Austrian
reactionaries, Hitler unified these two conceptions to forge an
ideology which while utterly devoid of any scientific or historical
foundation proved itself to be an immensely potent force in
rallying the middle class and demoralised unorganised sections of
the working class against the labour movement. This was a crucial
'nodal point' in Hitler's transition from a run-of-the-mill petty
bourgeois nationalist into a fully-fledged counter-revolutionary
leader:

> For me this was the time of the greatest spiritual upheaval I have ever
> had to go through. I had ceased to be a weak-kneed cosmopolitan and
> become an anti-semite. Just once more—and this was the last time—
> fearful, oppressive thoughts came to me in profound anguish... Have
> we an objective right to struggle for our self-preservation or is this
> justified only subjectively within ourselves?

And again it was Hitler's attitude to Marxism that tipped the
scales:

As I delved more deeply into the teachings of Marxism and thus in tranquil clarity submitted the deeds of the Jewish people to contemplation, Fate itself gave me its answer. The Jewish doctrine of Marxism rejects the aristocratic principle of Nature and replaces the eternal privilege of power and strength by the mass of numbers and their dead weight. Thus, it denies the value of personality in man, contests the significance of nationality and race, and thereby withdraws from humanity the premise of its existence and culture... If, with the help of his Marxist creed, the Jew is victorious over the other peoples of the world, his crown will be the funeral wreath of humanity... Eternal Nature inexorably avenges the infringement of her commands. Hence today I believe that I am acting in accordance with the will of the Almighty Creator: by defending myself against the Jew, I am fighting for the work of the Lord.[34]

The main source of Hitler's "information" on the Jewish question appears to have been the Christian Social Party of the Viennese Mayor, Dr. Karl Lüger. Here too, Hitler's conversion from opponent to supporter was protracted:

When I arrived in Vienna... the man and the movement seemed "reactionary" in my eyes. My common sense of justice, however, forced me to change this judgment in proportion as I had occasion to become acquainted with the man and his work; and slowly my fair judgment turned to unconcealed admiration... How many of my basic principles were upset by this change in my attitude toward the Christian Social movement! My views with regard to anti-semitism thus succumbed to the passage of time, and this was my greatest transformation of all![35]

But Hitler learned more than gutter anti-semitism from Lüger's party. For the first time, he saw in its activities and propaganda techniques the possibility of constructing a movement capable of fighting and defeating the Marxists on their own terrain. For in distinct contrast with the Austrian Pan-German movement under the leadership of Georg von Schönerer* (a movement whose nationalist goals Hitler shared) it did not disdain "popular" slogans and tactics to win support for its reactionary policies. Where Hitler differed with Lüger was over the latter's futile struggle to preserve the nationally non-viable Austrian monarchy, instead of which he should have been, in Hitler's judgment, directing all his energies towards the unification of the two German speaking states. What Hitler learned from Lüger's skilfully directed and pitched propaganda was nevertheless crucial in the subsequent development of Nazi political strategy:

* Like Hitler, Schönerer depicted the Jews as fomentors of revolution: "There is no place where we do not see them in league with the forces of rebellion... Our racial anti-semitism is not the result of religious intolerance. Rather, it is the indisputable evidence of a nation's new strength and self-confidence, the firm display of national feeling... every loyal son of his nation must see in anti-semitism the greatest national progress of this century..." (Speech to the Austrian Parliament, April, 1887)

Dr Lüger was the opposite of Schönerer. His thorough knowledge of men enabled him to judge the possible forces correctly, at the same time preserving him from underestimating existing institutions, and perhaps for this very reason taught him to make use of these institutions as instruments for the achievement of his purposes. *He understood only too well that the political fighting power of the upper bourgeoisie at the present time was but slight and inadequate for achieving the victory of a great movement.* He therefore laid the greatest stress in his political activity on winning over *the classes whose existence was threatened and therefore tended to spur rather than paralyse the will to fight.* Likewise he was inclined to make use of all existing institutions in his favour, drawing from these old sources of power the greatest possible profit for his own movement. *Thus he adjusted his new party primarily to the middle class menaced with destruction, and thereby assured himself of a following that was difficult to shake...*[36]

Depicted here are two of the most vital components of Nazi strategy - the exploitation of existing political institutions in order to seize power (and then destroy them!) and the creation of a mass movement of reaction recruited largely from the ranks of the petty-bourgeoisie. Hitler also found Lüger's strategy confirmed by his own experiences in Vienna, since he moved in Bohemian circles frequented by many like himself who had failed to establish themselves as stable members of the petty-bourgeoisie, and yet who feared the drop into the despised proletariat as a fate worse than death:

The environment of my youth consisted of petty-bourgeois circles, hence of a world having very little relation to the purely manual worker... the cleft between this class, which in an economic sense is by no means so brilliantly situated, and the manual worker, is often deeper than we imagine. The reason for this hostility... lies in the fear of a social group, which has but recently raised itself above the level of the manual worker, that it will sink back into the old despised class, or at least become identified with it. To this, in many cases, we must add the repugnant memory of the cultural poverty of this lower class, the frequent vulgarity of its social intercourse; the petty-bourgeois' own position in society, however insignificant it may be, makes any contact with this outgrown stage of life and culture intolerable.[37]

Precisely. And Hitler was able to make this sober and astute analysis of the anti-proletarian predjudices of the lower middle class not simply because he shared them in full measure, rather because he sought to transform them into a political doctrine which later became the means for welding this class into a compact counter-revolutionary force. From his Vienna experiences he gleaned one fundamental political truth - that in the age of mass movements and revolutions, those seeking to counter the proletarian movement could not hope to succeed by addressing appeals to the ruling powers that be. This was the great flaw in the Austrian Pan-German movement:

Theoretically speaking, all the Pan-German's thoughts were correct, but since he [Schönerer] lacked the force and astuteness to transmit his theoretical knowledge to the masses - that is, to put it in a form suited to the receptivity of the broad masses, which is and remains exceedingly limited - all his knowledge was visionary wisdom, and could never become practical reality... he saw only to a limited extent the extraordinary limitation of the will to fight in so-called "bourgeois" circles, due... to their economic position which makes the individual fear to lose too much and thereby holds him in check. And yet... a philosophy can hope for victory only if the broad masses adhere to the new doctrine and declare their readiness to undertake the necessary struggle... Since Schönerer and his followers addressed themselves principally to bourgeois circles, the result was bound to be very feeble and tame.[38]

And it is at this point that Hitler returns to the by now familiar theme of the political failings of the German bourgeoisie. Again, his criticism can in no way be equated with his venomous attacks on Marxism,* even though fascist demagogy usually tries to maintain the utterly false impression that it pursues a middle course between the two great class camps:

Though some people fail to suspect it, the German bourgeoisie, especially in its upper circles, is pacific to the point of positive self-abnegation, where internal affairs of the nation or state are concerned... in times of good government such an attitude makes these classes extremely valuable to the state; but in times of an inferior regime it is positively ruinous, to make possible the waging of any really serious struggle, the Pan-German movement should have above all dedicated itself to winning the masses.[38]

But it could not have done so even if its leaders saw the necessity of such a policy, for like nearly all nationalist politicians of the period, they were totally unsuited to employing the type of wild rabble-rousing and social demagogy needed to set such a movement in motion. Their entire social "breeding" and political outlook and training inhibited them from attempting what would have been a complete *volte face* in their ways of deciding political questions. Hence the need for a new type of politician, a "man of the people," able to speak the language of the disposessed and the frustrated, the bitter, the prejudiced and the confused, and yet holding fast to basic bourgeois principles such as the defence of private property, religion (albeit of a non-denominational variety) and of course, the "nation." While adopting the long term strategic goals of the imperialist as his own, the fascist "plebeian"

* Thus one of many examples runs: "No more than a hyena abandons carrion does a Marxist abandon treason... If at the beginning of the War and during the War twelve or fifteen thousand of these Hebrew corrupters of the people had been held under poison gas... the sacrifice of millions at the front would not have been in vain... On the day when Marxism is smashed in Germany, her fetters will in truth be broken for ever." (A. Hitler: *Mein Kampf*, pp.679-682. As far as poison gas was concerned, Hitler was to achieve his aim more than four hundred fold in the gas chambers of Auschwitz.)

fights for them in his own way, and yields nothing to the "political" bourgeoisie in questions of tactics and methods. Herein lies the basis and origin of the many clashes and even open ruptures which flared up between national socialism and the German ruling class, not only in period of Hitler's rise from obscurity to power, but even afterwards. That is why Hitler's "Vienna period" was perhaps the most crucial of his entire life insofar as it gave a definitive contour to his political outlook and aims, and began to indicate ways and means of fulfilling them:

> I had set foot in this town while still half a boy and I left it [for Munich in Spring 1912 as a man grown quiet and grave. In it I obtained the foundations for a philosophy in general and a political view in particular which later I only needed to supplement in details, but which never left me... I do not know what my attitude toward the Jews, Social Democracy or rather Marxism as a whole, the social question, etc., would be today if at such an early time the pressure of destiny - and my own study - had not built up a basic stock of personal opinions with me.[39]

"...the pressure of destiny..." An apt phrase for the conjuncture and penetration of the many cultural, religious, political, economic and social forces in the person of the young Hitler, forces which began to mould him for his role as the executioner of the German - and international - workers' movement. But there was nothing pre-ordained about this process. As the penniless and unknown Hitler made his way from Vienna to the Bavarian city that was to serve as the fortress of his movement, the German Social Democratic Party was emerging triumphantly from its greatest-ever election victory - 4.25 million votes and a Reichstag delegation of 110 deputies. It was not Hitler's "fist of fate" that enabled him, 21 years on, to lay low this ostensibly invincible Goliath. It was the supine cowardice, vacillations and theoretical decay of its own leadership. This, more than any other single factor, put flesh and blood around the skeleton of Hitler's early political ideas, and transformed the fifth child of an insignificant customs official in an equally insignificant Austrian border town into the dictator of continental Europe. These events became significant for Germany and mankind more by virtue of what others failed to do, than by what Hitler did. But if it is true that fascism is the punishment exacted by history on the proletariat for its failure to carry through the social revolution, then it is necessary to study in some detail the make-up of the jailers, torturers and executioners who carry out the sentence. In this sense, the evolution of Hitler's political ideas is highly instructive, and it is a theme to which we shall return more than once.

REFERENCES FOR CHAPTER NINE

[1] L. Trotsky: *The Class, the Party, the Leadership,* (August 20, 1940) in *The Spanish Revolution (1931-1939),* p.361, New York, 1973.
[2] A. Hitler: *Mein Kampf,* pp.6-7.
[3] Ibid, p.12.
[4] Ibid, pp.12-13.
[5] Ibid, p.15.
[6] Ibid, p.16.
[7] Ibid, p.16.
[8] Ibid, pp.21-37.
[9] Ibid, p.37.
[10] Ibid, p.38.
[11] Ibid, pp.38-39.
[12] Ibid, p.39.
[13] Ibid, pp.39-40.
[14] Ibid, pp.40-41.
[15] Ibid, p.41.
[16] Ibid, p.41.
[17] Ibid, p.41.
[18] Ibid, pp.42-43.
[19] Ibid, p.46.
[20] K. Marx and F. Engels: *The German Ideology,* p.61.
[21] K. Marx *The Eighteenth Brumaire of Louis Bonaparte* in *Selected Works,* Vol. I, pp.318-341.
[22] A. Hitler: Ibid, pp.43-44.
[23] Ibid, pp.45-48.
[24] Ibid, p.46.
[25] Ibid, pp.49-50.
[26] Ibid, p.51.
[27] Ibid, p.51.
[28] Ibid, p.52.
[29] Ibid, p.51.
[30] Ibid, p.52.
[31] Ibid, p.60.
[32] Ibid, p.61.
[33] Ibid, p.61.
[34] Ibid, pp.64-65.

Chapter Ten

NO MAN'S LAND

The Swastika on the helmet of steel
Black-White-Red band*
Is known throughout the land.
Workman, workman, what will become of you
When the Ehrhardt Brigade stands ready for the fight?
The Brigade of Ehrhardt knocks everything to bits.
Woe to you, woe to you, workman, son of a bitch.

(Song of the Captain Hermann Ehrhardt 'Free Corps' Brigade)

The German Reich is a Republic. Political authority emanates from
the people ...Freedom of association for the preservation and promotion of labour and economic conditions is guaranteed to everyone
and all vocations. All agreements and measures attempting to restrict
or restrain this freedom are unlawful. (Articles one and 151 of the
Weimar Consititution)

'Political power' says the *Communist Manifesto* '...is merely the
organised power of one class for oppressing another'.[1] The key
word is organised, for like all the general propositions of
historical materialism, those pertaining to the state must be concretised and filled out through study of the class struggle in
particular periods and countries. We have already noted how,
because of its unique development, the German bourgeoisie
found itself able to exert political influence only indirectly,
mediating its enormous economic power and dominance over the
proletariat through the caste of state bureaucrats and officials
selected from the Prussian squirearchy, the Junkers. The war of
1914-1918 and the ensuing collapse of the Hohenzollern
monarchy did not eliminate this characteristic of the German
bourgeoisie, rather they changed the bases on which the process
of the mediation of state power continued. The war accelerated
two political trends already at work — one, the search for a
means of securing collaboration with the right flank of social
democracy; the other, a drive towards militarisation of political,

* The colours of the overthrown Hohenzollern monarchy.

economic and social life with a consequent subverting of the most basic democratic liberties and rights. But the great irony of the war — and one to which we have already referred more than once — was that these two trends, far from running counter to each other as they had done under Bismarck and were to do later under the Bonapartist regime of von Papen, for a brief period approached though never quite attained, parallel courses.

While SPD leaders and High Command could jointly mobilise the resources of the nation for military victory without disruption from 'below', the latent tensions which always existed between reformist labour and the ruling classes could be smothered quite successfully. In this way, the optical illusion was conjured up in the early months of the war (an illusion Hitler depicted as a permanent reality) that the class struggle had been abolished in Germany. But on each and every occasion when the previously silent masses began to stir and speak, fissures began to open up in this strangest of all united fronts. The arrest and jailing in May 1916 of Karl Liebknecht for his consistent and public stand against the war immediately provoked not only a strike on his behalf by an estimated 60,000 Berlin factory workers, but a deep-going split in the ranks of the SPD. The expulsion of a majority of the Berlin party executive committee's members for supporting the strike helped create the organisational nucleus for the oppositional grouping that a year later formed the Independent Social Democratic Party of Germany (USPD). In turn, as the centrists and Lefts won more support from the war-weary, overworked and poorly-fed working class, the SPD leaders had to engage in a series of left manoeuvres to stem the haemorrhage from their ranks. Ebert, the super-patriot and hater of revolution, even went so far as to order his party officials to endorse the anti-war strike of January 1918* lest it come under the exclusive leadership of the Lefts, and so develop in a revolutionary direction.

The zig-zag course forced on the SPD leaders throughout and after the war exemplifies the Marxist theory of bureaucracy, pioneered by Lenin in his deep-going analysis of the degeneration of the Second International and the initial stages of bureau-cratisation in the Soviet Union, and then enriched by Trotsky in his many and brilliant writings on the nature and role of the Stalinist bureaucracy both as regards the Soviet Union and its impact on the world class struggle through the medium of the Communist International. The SPD and ADGB bureaucracy was not a class, even though like its future counterpart in the Soviet Union, it constantly struggled to secure for itself an independent

---

* Which began as a protest against the rapacious treaty of Brest Litovsk which the Imperial regime had just forced on an almost defenceless revolutionary Russia.

position in German society. Craving respectability in the eyes of the bourgeoisie, aping its manners and style of dress, and raising himself above the mass of proletarians to the standards of life of the stolid German petty-bourgeois, the SPD or ADGB functionary remained, whatever his subjective delusions of grandeur, a paid official of the reformist wing of the German labour movement. His social privileges and conservative outlook suited him admirably for the role of 'labour lieutenant of the bourgeoisie', but only for as long as he continued to draw his salary from the party treasury. Whether in a workers' or capitalist state, the party bureaucrat represents that portion of the workers' movement which has, through a whole range of mediations and agencies, arisen as a response to the corrupting pressure of imperialism on the workers' movement. And because of this contradictory relationship that the bureaucracy has with both imperialism and the working class, it is unable to pursue a clear-cut policy. Its survival depends upon a series of pragmatic improvisations, about-turns and somersaults, all of which have but one aim — the preservation of its own material privileges.

Its organic tendency is to seek to muffle the impact of the clash of classes, for it requires social peace in order to enjoy and extend its privileges. It therefore sees its role as one of buffer between the bourgeoisie and proletariat, and makes many adjustments in the realm of ideology to further this role of mediator, twisting the vocabulary of socialism often out of all recognition as it does so (this was the basic driving force behind Bernstein's attack on revolutionary Marxism, and the many subsequent attempts to blunt the cutting edge of the Marxist dialectic). But the bureaucracy is a buffer with a difference. *It is not an independent social class.* It remains tied to organisations founded, built and financed by the working class and can only hope to go on enjoying the rights and privileges which it has usurped from the proletariat by holding onto a sizable proportion, if not the majority, of those in whose name the bureaucracy claims to speak. Thus while the bureaucracy stands or falls with the rule of capital (for as a mediator in the class war, it must at all costs seek to maintain the rule of the bourgeoisie, and not its overthrow) neither can it sever the umbilical cord which ties it to the organisations whose aim it has perverted. If the bourgeoisie decides to make an end of independent working class organisations — and this is the essence of fascism — then it must also, despite social democracy's many, invaluable services to capitalism in the past, *make an end of the bureaucracy as well.* Herein resides the key to the understanding of one of the greatest and for many, the most perplexing of all ironies of German history: that the party which created the Weimar Constitution and was its most fervent defender, *was also outlawed by it.*

More than any other element of the political 'superstructure', constitutions embody and codify the accumulated illusions and prejudices of men. This is not to say of course that constitutions do not serve as screens for the rule of a single class. But they carry out this function imperfectly, sometimes even to such an extent that the bourgeoisie can be compelled in certain circumstances to tear up its own constitution.* The seemingly absurd spectacle of a bourgeoisie rising up in revolt against its own rule often leads formalistic thinkers to conclude that fascism contains a 'revolutionary' or anti-capitalist element, since it uproots institutions and subverts rights which the bourgeoisie itself has fought for — with varying amounts of energy and success — in the past. We will return to this aspect of fascism again, but it is first necessary to separate out the various forces which brought the Weimar Constitution into being before passing on to those which occasioned its demise. Like all other forms of thought — law, philosophy etc. a constitution is an abstraction of real material relations, both past and present. Engels warned against simplistic thinking in this field when he wrote:

> The economic situation is the basis, but the various elements of the superstructure — political forms of the class struggle and its results, to wit: constitutions established by the victorious class after a successful battle, etc., juridical forms ...also exercise their influence upon the course of the historical struggles and in many cases preponderate in determining their form.[2]

Weimar illustrates this perfectly. Like nearly all constitutions, it issued out of a profound social and political upheaval which either broke up or seriously undermined the previous forms of domination — ideological as well as institutional — through which the bourgeoisie had exerted its dictatorship over the proletariat. But although the Weimar Constitution can justly be described as one of the most systematic expositions and codifications of bourgeois democracy, the German bourgeoisie can hardly be credited with having fought for its introduction. For the most part they viewed its articles proclaiming the sovereignty and rights of the people with the gravest disapproval and apprehension. Therefore in the sense implied by Engels, this class cannot be regarded as 'victorious'. The real victory, such as it was, went to social democracy and those liberal elements closest

---

* Lenin detected this tendency in the Conservative-inspired revolt of the Ulster loyalists under Sir Edward Carson, and wrote about it with great perception in his article *Constitutional Crisis in Britain* (April 10, 1914), where he speaks of Carson's supporters as 'revolutionaries of the right' on account of their readiness to 'tear up the British constitution and British law to shreds.' (*Collected Works,* Vol. 20, p.228). By the same token — and also for their reliance on plebeian forces (Carson leaned on wide layers of the Protestant middle and working classes) — the Nazis can be regarded as 'revolutionaries of the right'.

to them organised in the German Democratic Party (DDP).

But neither could the bourgeoisie actively oppose the reforms proposed by social democracy and subsequently formalised — though by no means consistently implemented — under the Weimar Constitution. With the army crumbling away before its eyes, the ruling class quickly saw that it lacked the material means to suppress the deep-going movement in the masses for democracy, peace and social change. The only alternative to delegating governmental powers to the Ebert leadership was, as we have already seen, a social and not political revolution. This alliance, forged in the heat of imperialist war and the threat of proletarian revolution, was purely one of necessity so far as the dominant sectors of the bourgeoisie were concerned. On the other hand, the leaders of social democracy quite sincerely believed that the pact of November 9 concluded with Gröner and the leaders of old Germany was ushering in an entire era of peaceful and fruitful collaboration between the reformist bureaucracy and the German bourgeoisie. Illusions, as Engels pointed out, can exert a powerful influence on the course of history, especially when they grip not merely leaders, but as they did in Germany, millions.

Weimar also illustrates another tenet of historical materialism; namely that ideas, institutions and the other aspects of the super-structure, no more reflect the material basis of society immediately than they do perfectly. The Weimar Constitution became law in August 1919, yet the conditions which had given rise to it — the enforced alliance between social democracy and the bourgeoisie against the revolution — had already passed away. Certainly the threat of proletarian revolution remained, but its initial thrusts had either been diverted by the creation of the Ebert government or crushed by Free Corps murder squads under the direction of Minister of Defence Gustav Noske. The bourgeoisie, military leaders and of course Germany's old rulers, the Junkers, were by this time already finding Weimar democracy irksome, especially as by the very nature of things, its smooth functioning depended upon the participation of representatives of various workers' organisations at every level of political and economic life. This basic antagonism towards the economic, social and political fruits of the November bloc lay at the heart of all the great crises which shook Weimar to its foundations in the first years of its life,* and which in the end, resulted in its disintegration.

* The most profound were: the military Kapp Putsch of March 1920, which led directly to a general strike and revolutionary struggles in the Ruhr, Saxony and other industrial regions; the 'March Action' of 1921, in which the KPD staged an ill-conceived and adventurist bid to seize power during a sharp strike battle in central Germany; the assassination of DDP Foreign Minister Rathenau in June 1922, which precipitated a one-day general strike, and finally the inflation crisis and the French

And not only was the edifice of Weimar — the most democratic constitution in the world as the SPD leaders often smugly insisted — erected on a rickety political foundation, namely the transitory identity of interests which prevailed in the winter of 1918-1919; it also saw the light of day in a Germany whose economy and currency had been bled white by four years of all-out imperialist war and the predatory reparations exacted by the victorious allies. The social democrats and their liberal allies were seeking to re-enact — this time they hoped successfully — the revolution of 1848 in an epoch and in a country where the ruling classes were becoming ever more hostile to the notions and institutions of democratic government and social reform. The Weimar Constitution, whose authors quite consciously took both the colours and the programme 1848 as their model — arrived a matter of seventy years too late.

Although democratic demands still played an important part in mobilising the masses against capitalist and landlord rule in those countries where feudal institutions and social relations survived, throughout Europe from Britain to Russia, the revolution could only secure basic democratic rights for the mass of the working population by overthrowing, not reforming, the capitalist state and establishing the dictatorship of the proletariat. Thus attempts to force the November revolution into a bourgeois-democratic mould were counter-revolutionary both in intent and result, even though in the course of the struggle, the working class could only be sidetracked by means of a series of social and economic reforms.* That the proletariat secured basic trade union rights and the establishment of a 'welfare state' was entirely due to its own fighting capacity and courage in the early days of November 1918. The tragedy was that these concessions were so paltry in comparison with the enormous sacrifice paid in literally thousands of workers' lives. As far as the leaders of social democracy were concerned, the reforms sufficed to lift them to what they took to be the summits of political power, and as such, they had to be seen to be defending these gains on behalf of those workers who still supported the SPD. But the reforms which became embodied in the Weimar Constitution were viewed differently again by those who had to surrender them. To appreciate the fleeting and unstable nature of what we might term the 'November bloc', we can contrast the initial attitude of leading bourgeois and military circles to the formation of the Ebert government with the shift towards reaction which gathered pace

occupation of the Rhineland, which culminated in the aborted revolutionary situation in the autumn of 1923, and the Hitler putsch a matter of days later.

* The bulk of which were whittled away — with the tacit support of the SPD — under the Bonapartist regimes of Brüning and von Papen.

in these same quarters less than a year after the official proclamation of the Weimar Constitution.

Let us therefore return to the Autumn of 1918 to see precisely how the ruling class, with the aid of social democracy, devised its strategy of exploiting the democratic aspirations of the German masses to head off the socialist revolution. And on this question, the main participants in this counter-revolutionary conspiracy have been most frank. Thus Prince Max of Baden, who handed over the Chancellorship to Ebert on November 9, writes:

> I said to myself that the Revolution was on the point of winning, that it could not be beaten down, but might perhaps be stifled out. Now it is the time to come out with the abdication, with Ebert's Chancellorship, with the appeal to the people to determine its own constitution in a Constituent National Assembly. If Ebert is presented to me as a tribune of the people by the mob, then we shall have the Republic; if Liebknecht is, we shall have Bolshevism as well. But should Ebert be appointed Imperial Chancellor by the Kaiser at the moment of abdication ...perhaps we should then succeed in diverting the revolutionary energy into lawful channels of an election campaign.[3]

Which would of course provide the bourgeoisie with the vital political breathing space it so desperately needed to begin the rebuilding of its badly mauled state machine and the refurbishing of its tarnished image in the eyes of its millions of petty-bourgeois supporters.* The SPD leaders had been allotted a role in this strategy which, by virtue of their party's history and roots in the masses, could be fulfilled by no other political group. It was the task of the reformists to emasculate the workers' and soldiers' councils which were then springing up all over Germany by securing their agreement to parliamentary elections, thus in effect committing suicide as potential organs of proletarian state power. Contacts between the two partners in the conspiracy were soon made at every level, paralleling the secret pact between Ebert and the High Command. On November 15, after several days of

---

* Even Oswald Spengler, that die-hard enemy of the German workers' movement, saw the need to temporise with the SPD 'Marxists', in order later to prepare a counter-blow against the revolutionary section of the proletariat and finally the entire working class. In a letter written in December 1918, he predicted that 'the old Prussian element with its incalculable treasures of discipline, organising power and energy will take the lead and that the respectable part of the working population will be at its disposal against anarchism in which the Spartacus group has a remarkable relationship with left liberalism of the Jewish newspapers [the 'Jewish conspiracy' yet again] ...Germany has first to suffer for its sins ...until finally ...the Terror has brought to a head such a degree of excitement and despair that a dictatorship, resembling that of Napoleon will be regarded universally as a salvation. But then blood must flow, the more the better. First of all force, the reconstruction, not through the agency of the dilettantism of political majorities, but by the superior tactics of the few who are born for and destined to politics? And these lines were written more than fourteen years before Spengler's 'Napoleon' (or Caesar) acted out this scenario!

private talks, the leaders of the ADGB concluded an agreement with the major employers' organisations.* If abstracted from the time and place where they were formulated, the demands secured by the leaders of the trade unions seemed highly commendable. Indeed, after a half century of stubborn resistance, the 'hard-line' bosses conceded the right of unions to freely organize in their plants, while withdrawing their former support for company 'unions'. The November agreement also provided for the workers' right to be consulted on conditions of work, and the establishment of freely elected works' councils to represent the interests of the workers in their dealing with the employers. Finally, in this ostensibly impressive list of concessions extracted from the employers, the limit of the working day was fixed at eight hours — a demand for which the Second International had fought since its foundation in 1889. Now the leaders of German industry were falling over themselves to grant it — and a lot more besides.

The reasons for this sudden about turn are not hard to find. In November 1918 Germany's employers were faced with something far more radical — and final — than conceeding the eight hour day or the right of workers to organise. They were faced point blank with expropriation, and only the blindest in their ranks failed to see that unless they bent to the pressure of the masses, the authority of the trade union bureaucracy would be undermined and the road cleared for the Spartacists and their allies in the shop stewards movement. And this was not denied by one of their most important spokesmen, J. Reichert, the secretary of the Association of German Iron and Steel Industrialists, who with the super-tycoon Hugo Stinnes was instrumental in winning over fellow employers to the pact:

> The question [facing us in the talks] was how can we save industry? How can we spare capitalism from the threatening socialisation? Unfortunately, the bourgeoisie as it is in Germany could not be relied upon in things economic-political. We concluded that in the midst of the general great insecurity and in view of the tottering of the power of the state and the [imperial] government there were strong allies of industry only among the working class, and these allies were the trade unions. Moreover, there was a revolutionary government that consisted entirely of workers' representatives, and it was to be feared that the eight hour day would become law if the employers did not compromise.

Thus did a leader of German heavy industry justify his pact with the once-despised ADGB. And there were few employers who would have at this time — early 1919 — disagreed with him. The workers had the eight hour day, their works' councils and the right to organise, but the bourgeoisie still had its property. And the time would come when what had been conceded under

* The 'Working Alliance Agreement.'

duress would be taken back — with interest.

Having recorded two impressive victories — the undertaking by Ebert to fight the revolution, and binding the trade union leaders to an agreement which implicitly recognised the right of the employers to continue exploiting the working class, even if for one or two hours a day less than previously, the ruling class turned its attention to the pressing task of winding up the council movement. Here they acted only through the social democrats, for by their very nature, the councils excluded the open, as opposed to disguised representatives of the bourgeoisie. From the very beginning, Ebert's strategy was to commit the councils to the creation of a parliamentary — and hence bourgeois — republic, as opposed to a workers' republic based upon the council system. The SPD was assured of a majority in the councils not only by virtue of the infancy of the movement itself — the Mensheviks and Social Revolutionaries swamped the Bolsheviks at a similar stage of the Russian Revolution — but due to the delayed nature of the split in German social democracy. The USPD broke from Ebert's party only in April 1917 — and even then the rupture was precipitated by mass expulsions — and the KPD in its turn severed its links from the centrists as late as December 30, 1918 — two weeks *after* the opening of the First Congress of Workers' and Soldiers' Councils in Berlin.

The choice facing the 488 delegates* was very clear, and one that had faced a similarly momentous congress in Petrograd little more than a year earlier — council ('soviet') power, or the continued rule of the bourgeoisie, however democratic its guise. Yet the USPD centrists, like the compromisers Zinoviev, Kamenev and Stalin on the very eve of the October Revolution, sought to blur over the fundamental and absolute contradiction between these two opposites. When the time came at the Congress to vote on resolutions calling for the mutually exclusive policies of vesting all state power in the workers' and soldiers' councils and the holding of elections to a constitutent assembly, a sizable group of USPD delegates voted 'yes' to both resolutions.** Yet there was no such confusion — if confusion it was — in the minds of the SPD delegates. They took their line from Ebert's opening address, which after demagogically lauding the heroism and discipline of the working class in the revolution, proceeded to spell out his plan for the new Germany:

* The relative strength of the parties was SPD 289 delegates (60%), USPD 90 (20%), delegates without party affiliation 74 (15%) and smaller groups 25 (5%). There were but ten Spartacists in the USPD delegation.

** Voting on the two resolutions was as follows: to hold elections to a Constituent National Assembly on January 19: 400 for, 50 against. To vest all power in the councils: 98 for, 344 against. Thus 48 delegates voted for both resolutions!

...the victors [of the revolution] had to seize power and establish the provisional government, which until the meeting of the National Assembly is confronted with the task of regulating and strengthening the new regime ...On the basis of victorious revolution you shall erect the new legal state. For ...in Germany there can be permanently only one source of law: the will of the entire German people. This was the meaning of the Revolution. The rule of force hurled us to destruction, we will not suffer any sort of rule by force in the future, no matter from whom it may come. [sic!] The sooner we succeed in placing our new German people's state upon the firm foundation of the will of the entire nation, just so soon will it realise its great socialist goals. The victorious proletariat does not establish any class rule. It conquers the old class rule — first politically, then economically — and establishes the equality of all who bear a human countenance.[4]

Ebert was carrying out the instructions of Prince Max — and Gröner — to the letter: i.e. 'stifling the revolution' with parliamentary elections, one of the most tried and trusted cards in the bourgeoisie's pack. Ernst Daumig, speaking in support of the council system of government, was tragically prophetic when he declared to a largely hostile audience:

> When the history of these revolutionary weeks in Germany is written, people will smile and say: "Were they so blind as not to see that they were putting ropes around their own necks?" For anyone who thinks clearly must perceive that the jubilant approval of the National Assembly is equivalent to the death sentence of the system of which they now form a part, the council system.[5]

Daumig pleaded to no avail. Not even the sharp lash of the tongue of a Lenin or a Trotsky, a Liebknecht or a Luxemburg* could have undone in a few minutes what had accumulated over years and decades. In a solid phalanx, Ebert's men raised their hands in support of political suicide. And, as subsequent history has shown, it led not only to the self-destruction of the councils — the national congress met but once more to hand over its powers to the Constituent Assembly — but the suicide of the entire German labour movement. Failure to overthrow the bourgeoisie and destroy its state when the class enemy was at its weakest and most demoralised led inexorably — with the aid of the Stalinists — to the triumph of national socialism fourteen years later. And even some of Ebert's closest collaborators in this monumental act of betrayal paid for it with their lives.

Even as Ebert spoke in condemnatory tones about the 'rule of force' preparations were being made to assemble the counterrevolutionary units which were destined to play such a crucial role in the history of Weimar — Gustav Noske's 'Free Corps'. The first step had already been taken when Ebert undertook — on the insistence of the High Command — to subordinate the soldiers'

---

* A request to admit the Spartacist leaders to the congress — they were not elected as delegates — was turned down by a large majority.

councils to the discipline of the old officer corps. With the revolution in the army contained, and socialist 'contamination' of its troops stemmed, the High Command felt more secure. It at once began to apply pressure not only on the left wing of the workers' movement, but even the Ebert government itself whenever it felt the social democrats to be making too many concessions to the workers. Troops loyal to their officers were brought back into Berlin, the centre of the council movement, and at once there were bloody clashes with armed workers and sailors. Gröner subsequently said of this stage of the counter-revolution:

> At first it was a question of wrenching power from the workers and soldiers' Councils in Berlin, an operation was planned for this purpose, the military entry of ten divisions into Berlin, the People's Commissar Ebert was completely in agreement with this ...there were a number of difficulties ...some Independent members of the Government, but also I think some soldiers' councillors ...demanded that the troops move in without live ammunition.* We naturally opposed this at once, and Herr Ebert naturally agreed that the troops should move into Berlin with live ammunition. For this entry by the troops which was to afford us at the same time an opportunity to re-establish a firm government in Berlin ...a day-by-day military plan had been elaborated. This plan set out what was to happen: the disarming of Berlin i.e. the Berlin workers clearing Berlin of Spartacists, etc.

In conclusion Gröner (who was giving evidence at the official inquiry into the so called 'stab in the back' legend held in 1925) lauded the 'socialist' Ebert to the skies:

> I am especially grateful to Herr Ebert for this and have defended him against all attacks for his absolute love of the Fatherland and his complete dedication to the cause. This plan had been formed throughout with Herr Ebert's knowledge and agreement.**

The formation and brief flourishing of the November bloc was faithfully echoed in the ruling class press. Thus the extreme right-wing *Berliner Lokalanzeiger* conceded: 'We must face realities. We therefore subscribe to the Government's programme'. That was, until the ruling class was strong enough to change it. The Junker *Deutsche Tageszeitung* was even enthusiastic about the virtues of democracy: 'Only a government chosen by impeccable methods, ensuring the triumph of the people's will can have any authority ...We repeat that there must be no disagreements among the German bourgeoisie, and that it must strongly support

---

* The USPD wanted a parliamentary republic with workers councils, and now counter-revolutionary troops without any ammunition!

** This plan provided for the most draconian punishments against revolutionary workers: "Whoever is found in possession of arms without a licence is to be shot ...Whoever assumes an official function without authorisation is to be shot ...etc.etc." It was implemented in the wholesale repressions of workers during the 'Spartacist Uprising' of January 1919.

the Socialist government'.

And yet only a few weeks earlier, this same paper had denounced in the most scathing terms Ebert's government for seeking peace with the allies:

> Words cannot suffice to express the indignation and the grief ...Germany, yesterday still unconquered, now left at the mercy of her enemies by men bearing the name of German, forced to her knees in ignominious disgrace by felony in her own ranks ...This is perfidy that can never and shall never be forgiven. It is an act of treason, not only towards the monarch and the army, but towards the German people...

Paul Becker — the journalist who wrote the article — meant every word, and his paper's apparent *volte-face* a matter of weeks later in no way involved a retraction of anything he had said about the social democrats. The old imperialist circles simply had to bide their time, making the necessary purely tactical adjustments to the new political situation.

But it was only on the extreme left flank of the bourgeoisie that a readiness to permit social democracy anything approaching a permanent say in the affairs of state could be discerned. And predictably, the spokesmen of this trend were to be found not in heavy industry, where the Ruhr barons still gravitated to the monarchist right, but in commerce, the professions and intellectual strata. Such was the German Democratic Party, whose strategy of collaborating with the SPD against the threat of revolution while seeking to whittle down the party's programme to one acceptable to German capitalism, was devised by Max Weber, the pre-war pioneer of this policy, and the prominent banker Hjalmar Schacht. It is indeed ironic that the man who not only helped smooth Hitler's path to power but served him for eight years as Director of the Reichsbank and Minister of Economics should have begun his Weimar political career as an outspoken partisan of parliamentary democracy and close collaboration and even coalition with the 'Marxists'. Yet if we look closely at what he himself says about this period, we will discover that the contradiction is only a formal one. In each case, Schacht the democrat and Schacht the Nazi pursued a clear class line devised for vastly different circumstances.

Schacht's account of the formation of the DDP is most revealing for the insight it provides into the thinking of the liberal wing of the German bourgeoisie at that parlous period of its history.*

---

* It is all the more significant in that in his earlier career as a director of the Dresdner Bank (which he left in 1915 to join the smaller but highly influential Nationalbank fur Deutschland) Schacht had built up a highly confidential network of contacts both formal and informal with leaders of German industry, among them Karl Friedrich von Siemens (Electric Trust) August Thyssen and Hugo Stinnes (heavy industry) and Herr Schlitter, manager of the Deutsche Bank. And his more discreet

My reasons for engaging in political activity were very simple. Throughout the whole of the last year of the war Germany was already in a state of invisible revolution only restrained by the discipline of war. Strikes, heated arguments in factories and Parliament, protest marches — all these were signs which could no longer be ignored. We cudgelled our brains as to what the new Germany would be like which was destined to emerge from this process of revolution. There was no doubt that there would be a swing to the Left. But would it be as definite as in Russia where, after a brief struggle, the extremists had prevailed against the moderate groups? Would Germany, in short, turn Bolshevik; would Lenin — as he had already intimated — establish his ultimate headquarters not in Moscow but in Berlin?[6]

We can see that on this question — the possibility of Germany taking the Soviet road — there was almost total agreement between Schacht the banker and Scheidemann the social democrat, even though they formulated their views entirely independently of each other. So quite naturally, the social democrats became the rallying point for Schacht and his capitalist co-thinkers. In the storm of revolution, the Ebert government was to serve as their life-line. Let it prattle away about 'socialisation' and the end of 'class rule'. The central task before both the bourgeoisie and the reformist bureaucracy was to smash German Bolshevism and murder the German Lenins:

> The danger [of proletarian revolution] was there. No one could fortell how matters would develop once the bonds were broken. Since August 1914 too much political dynamite had accumulated in cellars, back yards and tenement houses. I asked myself and my friends: what was to be done? ...I met kindred spirits — solicitors, journalists, business-men, bankers, all were filled with the same anxiety: What was one to do? My reply was: 'We must prevent the moderates in Germany from falling victim to the extremists. We must endeavour to form a mighty reservoir of all those elements who, without being extremist, are dis-satisfied with present conditions. We need a middle class Left which will throw in its lot with the organised workers in the coming coalition government.' These deliberations led soon afterwards to the founding of the German Democratic Party.[7]

This extremely class conscious banker also gives a superb picture of the disarray and despondency in the highest level of the bourgeoisie on November 9, 1918, the day the Kaiser fell and Ebert's government was hoisted into power by Berlin workers. It

operations as an adviser to members of the royal houses enabled Schacht to enjoy intimate relations with among others the Princes Hohenlohe-Orhingen and Fursten-berg, both of whom had badly burned their fingers in highly speculative under-takings. All in all, Schacht was admirably suited to be entrusted with the onerous task of launching a party whose prime aim was to ensnare the SPD in a reformist-liberal coalition. With such a background and class pedigree, there was little chance of Schacht being sucked into a policy of 'socialisation'. Schacht's business and social connections were equally valuable a decade later when he turned towards his new allies — the Nazis.

underlines once more the perfidy of the social democrats in rescuing the ruling class at the precise moment in history when it had lost not only the means to rule, but even in some quarters, the will:

> Meanwhile there were increasing signs that the end might come at any moment. On November 3, 1918 the sailors of the main fleet started to mutiny. Spartacists elements had infiltrated the lower decks and hoisted the Red Flag. The revolution began to spread through Germany like wildfire. Workers' and Soldiers' Councils sprang up from nowhere and took over local authorities ...During the early days of November 1918 Berlin prepared for civil war. Barbed wire entanglements appeared in the streets, barricades were erected from overturned vehicles. Shots whistled through the streets in the centre of the town and sent citizens scuttling indoors. No one appeared to have any authority: an armed mob stood ready to seize the helm...* Towards midday on November 9 I came out of the Hotel Esplanade-Platz with a friend and saw the first lorries drive across the Potsdamer-Platz filled with heavily-armed Red troops. It was a curious sight. People passed by the lorries looking depressed and indifferent — they did not even glance at them. The Red revolution shouted, brandished their rifles and generally threw their weight about ...A very curious, significant scene, expressive of Germany's disrupted condition — revolution in lorries, apathy in the streets. [In other words, the 'citizens' i.e. middle class of Berlin, had accepted the revolution as a *fait accompli*. And lacking arms, there was little they could do except look depressed and apathetic. Schacht's narrative continues:] In the face of this incident we changed our direction and made for the Reichstag with the object of finding a member who would enlighten us as to the situation. The great government building was deserted and lifeless ...At last we reached the abode of the Liberal Group i.e. the National Liberals, the main party of heavy industry ...Inside the room a quavering voice asked: 'Who is it?' I recognised it at once — it was Stresemann's voice. At that time he was the leader of the National Liberal Group in the Reichstag ...Have you any recent news? I asked ...Revolution,' was Stresemann's terse reply with a weary gesture. 'And the Emperor — our Army — the Government — the Police?' 'I don't know' said Stresemann. 'I'm the last remaining man in the Reichstag.' ...Stresemann's face was grey his eyes tired, his mouth pinched ...'And what will happen?' I asked. He shrugged his shoulders. 'Ebert will probably do something' he said. 'Now is his chance, His party is the strongest. If he doesn't succeed...'[8]

---

* Hitler's scorn for bourgeois political leaders in this period knew no bounds: 'After the revolution, when the bourgeois parties suddenly reappeared, though with modified firm names, and their brave leaders crawled out of the concealment of dark cellars and airy storerooms, like all the representatives of such formations, they had not forgotten their mistakes and likewise they had learned nothing new. Their political programme lay in the past, in so far as they had not reconciled themselves at heart with the new state of affairs; their aim however, was to participate if possible in the new state of affairs, and their sole weapons remained, as they had always been, words. Even after the revolution, the bourgeois parties at all times miserably capitulated to the streets.' (A. Hitler: *Mein Kampf*, p.531)

Yet more ironies! Until August 1914, Stresemann and his class had measured their political fortunes in inverse proportion to the rise of the SPD vote. Now with the old bourgeois party system in ruins — only the confessional Catholic Centre party was to survive the November Revolution — Stresemann pinned his hopes for capitalist survival on the *strength* and *success* of social democracy. In 1878, Stresemann's National Liberals had voted to outlaw social democracy. Now it looked to the SPD as a saviour.*

Schacht proceeded to outline his political strategy to the demoralised Stresemann:

> We must do something, Herr Stresemann. If the Left gets the upper hand, well and good [i.e. the SPD] But we must start a middle class Left Party so that the Socialist majority don't have everything their own way. A middle class Party with left-wing tendencies, he said. Yes — that might be the way out. We left him. At the time I knew as well as anyone that the great hour for the socialist parties had struck. Their persistent efforts for a negotiated peace, the workers' tremendous contribution to Germany's blood-sacrifice and last, but not least, their promises of social improvements would attract masses of electors to their ranks. That would lead to an extreme opposition from the Right — as in Russia, which might well develop into a war between 'Red' and 'White'. We must act quickly if we were to achieve anything.[9]

Schacht sought to retard the polarisation of the classes by erecting a middle class buffer between them, a 'third force' which on crucial issues would throw its weight on the side of social democracy where and when its leaders were under attack from the left. Likewise, it would counsel caution, restraint and patience to the monarchist-inclined forces in the landlord and big bourgeois camp lest ill-prepared and insufficiently supported attempts to overturn the rule of the reformists resulted in a violent proletarian backlash, a consequent diminishing of the stabilising influence of the much-needed social democrats and a corresponding growth in the revolutionary forces. There was also the added danger that without a radical middle class party to attract the democratic petty-bourgeoisie — and their ranks had swelled enormously as a direct result of their disillusionment with the old regime — they would turn to the SPD in their millions, giving the Ebert leadership an absolute majority in Parliament which would have been as much an embarrassment to them as to their bourgeois opponents. For such a majority would have stripped away the last excuse the reformists in fact employed to justify their refusal to proceed with the SPD's programme of socialisation — that such measures would be undemocratic in that they lacked the support

---

* And to anticipate the completion of this cycle: before going into voluntary liquidation under the Third Reich, its successor the DVP (German People's Party) had its two surviving Reichstag deputies cast their votes for Hitler's Enabling Act, under which the social democrats, squeezed dry of the last drop of treachery, were outlawed once again.

of a majority of the Reichstag.*

In normal times, parties can take years to gestate and formulate their programmes. But in the white heat of revolution, men accomplish in hours what would otherwise take decades. On November 9, the Kaiser fell, and with it, the constellation of Junker and bourgeois parties which had revolved around the throne of the Hohenzollerns for nearly half a century. On November 11, the first of the Republic's new bourgeois parties was born, displaying a countenance that if not exactly republican, was at least committed to the formal supremacy of parliament.

That the new party equivocated on this issue was largely due to Schacht's own intervention in the discussion on the DDP's declaration of principles. As he himself relates:

> Theodor Wolff [of the liberal *Berliner Tageblatt*] read out his proclamation which began with the words: 'We are republicans...' 'Stop!' I interrupted. 'I can't sign that. I'm a monarchist.' General astonishment. How, the others demanded, could a monarchist be a co-founder of a Democratic Party? ...There are quite a few constitutional monarchies in the world which are democratically governed ...' Theodor Wolff gave in and began again. This time the sentence ran: 'We base our standpoint on republican principles.' I signified my agreement.[10]

And so the would-be German bourgeois democrats, like so many of their ancestors, still recoiled in horror from the prospect of a total and final rupture with the feudal institution of hereditary monarchy.** This farcical scene took place at the founding meeting of the DDP, among whose most prominent early supporters, were, apart from Schacht and Wolff, the proprietors of the liberal *Frankfurter Zeitung,* the industrialist Walther Rathenau, Max Weber the sociologist and Hugo Preuss, the legal authority and historian. Although their views differed widely on a range of questions, they were all united on the need to pursue a policy of rapprochement with the leaders of social democracy. Thus Preuss (who was soon to be charged with the task of drawing up the new republic's constitution) wrote in the *Berliner Tageblatt* on November 14, 1918:

* The elections to the Constituent National Assembly on January 19, 1919, gave the two workers parties — the SPD and the USPD — a combined vote of 13,826,400, which amounted to 45.5% of the total poll. Schacht's DDP, on a programme that approached closely that of the SPD, secured 5,641,800 votes — 18.6 of the total. Thus it would have required only a minority of the democratic middle class vote to have gone to the SPD (or even the USPD) to give the workers' parties an *absolute* majority in Parliament. Schacht's strategy had worked brilliantly since the reformists could now claim that they had no alternative but to form a 'centre-left' coalition with the DDP and the Catholic Centre Party. This alliance became known as the 'Great Coalition' even though it later included the solidly big-bourgeois DVP of Stresemann.
** Even though the deposed Kaiser had already fled Germany to seek exile in Holland.

We have the hope of escaping the dreadful shift from Red Terror to White only if a strong, energetic movement is formed within the German middle class, based candidly on events that have occurred, but not docile in the face of new authorities, and ...only if these new authorities welcome the collaboration of this movement and tender it full equality of responsibility.

Again one cannot help but comment on the contrast between this strategy, so successful in the period during and immediately after the November Revolution, and that pursued by the Nazis in the last years of the Weimar Republic (in the case of Schacht, he actively participated in both).German fascism also sought to build 'a strong, energetic movement within the middle class' not, however, to *buttress* the social democrats, but to *crush* them, and with the SPD, the entire organised power of the German proletariat. In both cases, the social basis of these movements was the petty-bourgeoisie, emphasising the truth of the contention that despite differences in policy and ideology, *liberalism and fascism arise on the same class foundation.**

Nevertheless Schacht had good reason to commend himself on

---

* The DDP vote, which in 1919 made it Germany's third largest party after the SPD and the Centre, declined in direct proportion to the growth of middle class disillusionment with the Republic. Former DDP voters steadily moved to the right, often through the DVP, then the openly monarchist DNVP and finally, after the onset of the economic and political crisis in 1929, into the ranks of national socialism. This dramatic shift of the German petty-bourgeoisie through the entire spectrum of German bourgeois politics, marking as it did the break up of the so-called 'middle ground', the foundation of class collaboration and compromise, can be depicted graphically: (The Economic Party appealed specifically to small businessmen. It was bitterly hostile to the Republic, and not averse to employing anti-semitic propaganda).

Votes (in millions)

Election year	DDP	DVP	DNVP	Economic Party	NSDAP	Total
1919	5.6	1.3	3.1	0.3	0.0	10.3
1920	2.3	3.9	4.2	0.2	0.0	10.6
1924 (May)	1.7	2.7	5.7	0.7	1.9	12.7
1924 (Dec.)	1.9	3.0	6.2	1.0	0.9	13.0
1928	1.5	2.7	4.4	1.4	0.8	10.8
1930	1.3	1.6	2.5	1.4	6.4	13.2
1932 (July)	0.4	0.4	2.1	0.1	13.8	16.8
1932 (Nov.)	0.3	0.7	3.0	0.1	11.8	15.9
1933	0.3	0.4	3.1	0.0	17.3	21.1

the success of his counter-revolutionary manoeuvrings when he wrote many years later:

> The surmises we had entertained in connection with the formation of the DDP came to pass. The Social Democrats failed to obtain a majority in the National Assembly. The DDP secured 74 seats, and at a critical juncture ensured that socialist theories were not applied in too one-sided a fashion. The Social Democrats were compelled to form a Coalition Government with the middle class Left.* The DDP produced two ministers who were invaluable in helping to establish a gradual and continuous political development in place of an extremist upheaval [Preuss and Rathenau][11]

Schacht wrote these lines some ten years after the end of the war. They differ little from the judgement made much closer to the events in question, in his book *The Stabilisation of the Mark*, published in 1927:

> The spectre of Bolshevism, more menacing then ever, suddenly raised its head. The bourgeois element was entirely excluded by the revolutionary government from power; and the only question was whether the extremist form of socialism in more or less Bolshevik shape, or the more moderate form of socialism which clung to democratic forms of government, would prevail ...It may be said that it was primarily the efforts of the DDP which gave the non-socialist elements (and especially the parties standing further to the right whose leaders completely disappeared from view in the first moments of the collapse) the courage once more to assert themselves, and in the elections to the National Assembly left the Social Democrats and other elements still further to the left in a minority.[12]

And Schacht was not exaggerating when he said the leaders of the old right-wing parties were nowhere to be seen in the first days of the revolution.** Hence their temporary, if reluctant acceptance of the Ebert government. Only after some weeks had passed did the leaders of the pre-1914 'cartel' — the National Liberals and the Conservatives — begin to pull themselves together. The blunting of the council movement meant that Germany was due to pass through a phase, however short and insecure, of parliamentary government, and that necessitated, if the centre and Left parties were not to carry all before them, a new approach to the problem of seeking support amongst the masses for reactionary policies. For a short time it seemed as if Stresemann and his National Liberals might throw in their lot with Schacht's DDP (which was in fact an updated version of the old Progressive Party), but at the last moment he baulked at what he regarded as being its over-eagerness to collaborate with the SPD.

---

* Schacht retired from active politics after the elections of January 19, only to surface again in the midst of the economic crisis which erupted in the United States and rapidly sent industry and banking spiralling downwards towards disaster. Now Schacht appeared in a new role — contact man between big business and the Nazis.

** Stresemann's paralysis and abject despair was typical of the old monarchist Right.

Stresemann's party was, we should bear in mind, the main party of heavy industry, and as such, it still looked on the 'Marxists' with grave misgivings.*

Stresemann himself was inhibited from following Schacht's policy not only by the interests of heavy industry, but his own subjective attitudes, which had been shaped in the pre-1914 period when throne, sword and altar were the holy trinity of all decent 'national' Germans. He therefore regarded the revolution of November 9 as an act of monumental betrayal, or as he put it some months afterwards, 'the death day of Germany's greatness in the world'. In fact Stresemann had been subjected to the crowning humiliation of being marched out of the Reichstag building on that day by a squad of armed workers. A week later, he agreed to take his tottering party, the National Liberals, into a merger with Progressives to fight on a united platform against the social democrats. But Schacht had meanwhile succeeded in winning them over to his line of guarded collaboration with reformists. This left Stresemann with little alternative but to launch his old party under a new label more suited to the nature of the times — the German People's Party (DVP), which he did on November 22. But Stresemann's problems were far from over. Seeing that he had broken off negotiations with the DDP, leaders of the Junker Conservatives, who were even more isolated from the masses than the DVP, approached Stresemann with a view to forming a monarchist, anti-parliamentary and openly counter-revolutionary right-wing party. But again, Stresemann found himself unable to undertake such a fusion.

Although a monarchist,** he realised more clearly than the old Conservative leaders that restoration of the Hohenzollerns was a

---

* Some captains of industry were however, more adventurous. As early as October 17, 1918, Carl Duisberg of the Chemical Trust wrote to a friend to tell him that 'from that day when I saw that the cabinet system was bankrupt, I greeted the change to a parliamentary system with joy ...where it is possible I work hand-in-hand with the trade unions and seek in this way to save what can be saved ...I am an opportunist and I adjust to things as they are. 'But Duisberg cannot be regarded as typical of industry, since he supported the DDP and helped to finance its most sympathetic voice in the newspaper world, the *Frankfurter Zeitung*, which on November 14, 1918 had excelled all other bourgeois democrats in declaring: 'The new Germany must be radical and socialist to the core ...Only with a radical programme can the middle class dare to engage in politics with a prospect of success ...The bourgeoisie must be radical or it will cease to be.' And Duisberg, like Schacht, was soon to change his tune. In a speech to the 1925 Conference of the Federation of German Industry, he stated: 'Be united, united, united. This should be the uninterrupted call to the parties in the Reichstag. We hope that our words of today will work, and will find the strong man who will finally bring everyone under one umbrella, for he is always necessary for us Germans, as we have seen in the case of Bismarck.'

** In a letter dated January 6, 1919, Stresemann declared: 'I have emphasised in almost every one of my campaign meetings that I was a monarchist, am a monarchist and shall remain a monarchist.' And on the 27th of the same month, he sent, together

lost cause for the foreseeable future, and that the only realistic policy was to win as much popular support as was possible for the banner of moderate — moderate that is in terms of German bourgeois politics — conservatism. Right from the beginning, the new party was plagued with constant conflicts and periodic splits. And this was scarcely surprising, since under Stresemann's leadership it sought to reconcile not only sections of the big bourgeoisie which were fundamentally opposed to each other over political strategy and tactics, but the big bourgeoisie as a whole with the party's main mass of voters — the propertied middle and small bourgeoisie. And yet few could have been better suited for such a thankless task, since Stresemann, although a man of impeccable bourgeois pedigree, stood midway between the Ruhr industrialists of his party who provided it with most of its funds — the Vöglers and the Stinnes — and the small and medium employers in light industry who provided it with the majority of its votes. Stresemann was himself the owner of a medium-sized light manufacturing enterprise, and sat on several boards of other small firms in the Berlin area. But in the course of his business and political career he had succeeded in becoming the spokesman for wider economic interests, and even while leader of the DVP, still sat on the boards of two of Germany's most influential employers organisations — the Association of Saxon Industrialists and the national League of Industry. His balancing act on the tight rope that was the internal politics of German big business typified the dilemmas confronting those bourgeois politicians and statesmen who sought to defend the interests of all property owners without either becoming ensnared in the embrace of organised heavy industry, or stoking up the fires of a petty-bourgeois revolt against the entire Weimar political structure.

We have already noted that Stresemann was a monarchist by tradition and by conviction, and yet despite all previous protestations to the contrary, by the time of the DVP's founding Congress in April 1919 he was prepared to accept republicanism as a permanent feature of German politics, telling delegates that 'we must be clear about one thing, that Greater Germany can only be reconstructed on a republican basis.' This apparant change of heart was almost certainly due to the DVP's poor showing at the January elections. It managed, despite its hastily assumed

with other DVP leaders, a birthday greetings telegram to ex-Kaiser Wilhelm which ended: 'Millions of Germans, even under new circumstances and on a new foundation of political life, join us in acknowledging the monarchist principle and will oppose any unworthy renunciation of the high ideals of the German Empire and the Prussian Kingdom.' Less than four years later Stresemann became Chancellor of a Cabinet which included not only his own DVP, but four members of the SPD and two representatives of the DDP!

populist nomenclature, to assemble a mere 4.4% of the total poll, while the more strident monarchism of the DNVP — which Stresemann had no intention of emulating — had gained just over twice that amount. Even taken together, the two sole survivors and representatives of the *ancien regime* cut a sorry figure, winning between them a paltry 4.5 million votes, less than 15% of the total cast. How far the cause of monarchy and traditionalist nationalism had lost ground in Germany can be appreciated by comparing these results with the returns for the last pre-war election to the Reichstag, when together the National Liberals, Conservatives, Free Conservatives and Anti-semites secured very nearly twice that proportion. However unpalatable it might have been to Stresemann and his DVP colleagues, the truth had to be faced that there was no political force visible on the horizon that could dislodge the social democrats and their bourgeois radical allies from their preponderant position either in the National Assembly, where they exercised an absolute majority over all the other parties combined, or indeed at the lower and local echelons of the machinery of government. Neither was there a sign as yet of that ground swell of petty-bourgeois disillusionment with Weimar democracy which would soon begin to disrupt the precarious compromise effected between the reformists and the leaders of bourgeois liberalism at the time of the Revolution. A year after the elections, when sections of the DNVP leadership were already heavily committed to supporting the abortive military coup of Wolfgang Kapp, Stresemann rejected an offer from DNVP leader Albrecht von Grafe to form a united front of their two parties against the 'Weimar bloc' of the SPD, DDP and Centre:

> It seems to me that the immediate task at hand in our political development is to eliminate the Social Democrats' present overwhelming influence and to reduce it to more modest proportions. A government without the Social Democrats during the next two to three years seems to me to be quite impossible since otherwise [i.e. if it is forced into opposition] we shall stagger along from general strike to general strike. There is a very real danger that the two Peoples parties [i.e. the DVP and DNVP] will withdraw into the sulking corner for many years if they do not at once receive a voice in government proportionate to their numerical strength ...The danger is great that the [state] bureaucracy will be progressively alienated from us or replaced by persons from hostile parties, and that the people will become accustomed on a permanent basis to the rule of the present day majority parties.

Stresemann's refusal to join with the DNVP in an anti-Weimar united front — a bloc principally directed against the SPD — caused much trouble in the leadership and ranks of his own party. Albert Vögler, a director of the steel trust* and a future supporter

---

* Vögler regarded his position as one of the DVP's 19 deputies in the National

of the Nazis, was especially vocal in opposing Stresemann's moderate policies, and called for the united front offer to be taken up. In fact Vögler's views — and those of several other heavy industrialists in the DVP — were in many ways far closer to the hard-line policies of the DNVP, and in fact some of them defected to it as they became progressively more critical of Stresemann's middle-of-the-road orientation, which year by year brought the DVP closer and closer to open collaboration with the social democrats.

Moving even further to the right we do indeed come to the DNVP, the revived corpse — and sometimes a pretty virulent one at that — of that old pillar of Bismarckian and Hohenzollern Prussia, the Conservatives. And we shall see that even this party could not ignore the magnetic attraction exerted on its more plebeian supporters by the power of the proletarian movement in the early weeks of the Republic. Moves anticipating the foundation of a more populist-oriented version of the old party were made several days before the fall of the Empire. On November 7 the inner executive of the largely defunct Conservative Party met under the Chairmanship of Count Westarp to draft a statement of principles for the proposed new organisation. It too like the DDP and the DVP manifestos and proclamations, paid lip-service to the new spirit abroad amongst even those who had previously been the most politically backward of Germany's population. The DNVP appeal, issued on November 22, 1918, declared that the new party was 'ready to co-operate with all parties that share our aim: to heal the wounds inflicted by the war on our sorely tried fatherland, and to restore law and order.' But whose law and order? Certainly not that of the Junkers, whose military- bureaucratic machine was at that time patently unable to exercise it. So making the painful but inescapable adjustment to the demands of political reality, the appeal demanded, in the most unJunker-like fashion; a 'return from the dictatorship of a single class to the parliamentary form of government which alone is possible after recent events.' Only the rule of the 'single class' was not the Junkers, who had enjoyed a virtual monopoly in the exercise of political power under the empire for nearly half a century, but the proletariat, whose council system threatened to sweep them away.

The East Elbian barons and landlords had not given up hope of restoring their old privileges in the exercise of state power, but

Assembly as an opportunity to represent not so much his party, even less those who voted for him, but the interests of his own industrial undertakings, which were admittedly considerable. In his maiden speech to the Reichstag he abashed even the most venal of his parliamentary colleagues with his opening words: 'I speak here as a representative of an industry.' When the opportunity came to make an end with parliamentary democracy, tycoons like Vögler obviously had no regrets.

they had sense enough to realise — at least some of them — that until the Ebert government had performed its initial allotted role of smothering and beating back the revolution, even they had to resort to the language of democracy. The DNVP was also compelled to present itself, as its name suggests, as a 'people's' party, much as its more moderate monarchist rival, the DVP had done. But beneath the hastily revamped image of a party sympathetic to parliamentary democracy there remained the class features of the old chauvinist, anti-semitic right. Sometimes the two faces of the party were combined in a single policy statement, as in the case of a DNVP leaflet issued in Berlin for the elections to the National Assembly:

> No class domination ought to decide the future of our people. All classes must be represented in the National Assembly. No wealthy foreign race should continue to abuse its power behind the scenes. Germany must be governed by us Germans. [And for good measure, the leaflet rounded off this diatribe against proletarian rule and the Jews — combined, it should be noted, with support for the National Assembly — with a thrust at that other Junker whipping boy, the Catholic Church] No Romanist intrigues are going to rob us of our heritage of the reformation. Protestant spirit must remain strong in the fatherland.*

* The Lutheran Protestant Church had for centuries been a most faithful supporter of the Prussian Monarchy enjoying in its turn the special patronage and protection of the state as against the Catholic Church, traditionally regarded as an arm of 'Roman' influence inside Germany. The authority of God was frequently invoked at moments of great crisis for the Reich, both in wars and revolutions. In March 1918, the Lutheran journal *Allgemeine Evangelisch Lutherische* justified the rapacious Treaty of Brest Litovsk in the following terms: 'Russia had to yield up booty in inconceivable quantities. We needed guns and ammunition for the last assault on the enemy in the west. God knew that we needed it. So He gave it to us freely, for God is munificent ...If there were still clear-sighted Christians in England they would now have to rise up and cry to their government in fear:"We have had enough, God is fighting for Germany". ' Understandably the revolution loomed in the thinking of such men as the work of the devil himself. The 1848 revolution had already been roundly condemned by a Lutheran theologian as 'a breach of loyalty and the graveyard of respect, bringing with it the end of morality and therefore of the freedom and salvation of the people.' November 1918 therefore found the Protestants in a state of apoplexy, their feelings being summed up some years later by one of their number, who declared that 'our chief misfortune has been the social democrats, who have made this unecessary and unbelievably stupid revolution, who have deprived Germany of the fruits of its glorious struggles over four years, who have betrayed our country solely in order to bring their party to power'. Marxism was of course the scourge of all decent, God-fearing Germans. Another theologian stated in 1923 'Our political downfall, our entire misery has its roots in Marx's theory, and this in turn, in Rousseau's delusion about the nobility of man'. There was much in Luther's writings to bolster this line: 'Because the sword is a very great benefit and necessary to the whole world, to preserve peace, to punish sin and to prevent evil, he [a true Christian] submits most willingly to the rule of the sword, pays taxes, honours those in authority, serves, helps and does all he can to further the government that it may be sustained and held in honour and fear ...you are under obligation to serve and further the sword by whatever means you can, with body, soul, honour or goods ...Therefore, should you see that there is a lack of hangman, beadles, judges, lords or

But the DNVP's attempt to recapture its old following among the small propertied classes — artisans and peasants in the main — necessitated a more radical social policy than the old Conservatives (with the exception of those who leaned towards Stöcker's brand of 'social' Christianity), had been prepared to risk. The self-styled 'Christian Socialist' wing of the new party, led by Siegfried von Kardorff, soon antagonised Westarp and the DNVP's chairman, Oskar Hergt, with their insistence on the need to attune the nationalist movement to at least some of the social and economic demands of the petty-bourgeoisie and peasantry. Westarp and Hergt, nationalists of the old school, were far more intent on representing the interests of the big agrarians and heavy industrialists than emulating or outdoing their rivals in social demagogy. They could not at that stage see that the one by no means excluded the other. Here the influence of the press magnate and former Krupps director Alfred Hugenberg was decisive. This future ally of Hitler, together with Gustav Rosicke, head of the highly influential agrarian organisation, the *Bund der Landwirte,* were the chief contributors to the party's coffers, and saw to it that they and the big-propertied interests they represented called the tune. Those elements in the party allied with the Christian Socialist movement and the white-collar workers organisation, the *Deutschenationaler Handlungsgehilfen Verband,* were viewed by the majority of its leadership as vote-catchers without any right to a say in shaping DNVP policy. As a result, many of these plebeian supporters of the party turned elsewhere after the crisis of 1929 when it became clear that under the Hugenberg leadership, the nationalists were functioning purely as a mouthpiece for the interests of heavy industry and the big landowners. From a peak of 6.2 million in December 1924, the DNVP vote slumped to 2.6 million in the crisis elections of September 1930. The bulk of these losses had, without the least shadow of doubt, accrued to the Nazis, who not only equalled them in nationalist fervour, but completely outclassed them in the use of social demagogy aimed at the DNVP's main source of support — the artisans, small traders, clerks and peasants.

This is not to say that there existed no points of contact between the DNVP and the 'social' ultra-right. The Pan-Germans and old monarchists shared the Nazis hatred of Weimar and the parties which dominated it in the republic's early years. Thus the Pan-German congress held at Bamburg in February, 1919,

princes, and find that you are qualified, you should offer your services and seek the place, that necessary government may by no means be despised and become inefficient or perish. For the world cannot and dare not dispense with it.' (M. Luther: *Secular Authority: To What Extent Should It Be Obeyed?,* 1523. In *Martin Luther: Selections From His Writings,* pp.373-375, New York, 1961.

declared its undying loyalty to the overthrown regime and political system:

> The events after the 9th November proved unmistakably that a nation like ours, which so obviously lacks political instincts, is not made for the republican form of government. It should entrust its fate to a firm leadership, such as a monarchy can supply much more effectively than a republic ...we shall always propagate the Kaiser sentiment.* [The manifesto also, very much on lines that the Nazis were later to follow called for a] planned racial superiority of the German nation by selection of, and help for, all those persons who are gifted in the good old German manner. [We will] fight against all those powers which hamper and harm the racial development of our nation, especially the predominance of the Jews in all cultural and economic fields.

It was not surprising therefore that this manifesto, drafted in a spirit of raging hatred for the most elementary forms of bourgeois democracy, declared that the Pan-German League had 'no confidence in the present government nor does it consider the present state as adequate for the German nation.' And to develop a counter-weight to the new state which they so despised, the Pan-Germans together with the DNVP and smaller monarchist associations, formed the ultra right-wing, para-military veterans organisation, the Steel Helmet or *Stahlhelm,* founded at the end of 1918 under the leadership of Franz Seldte (Seldte became Minister of Labour in the Nazi-Nationalist coalition of January 1933, a post he held to the fall of the Third Reich in 1945.). Though never becoming a battering ram against the workers movement in the way that the more plebeian-based Nazi Storm Troops did, the *Stahlhelm* certainly served as a breeding and training ground for many former officers who subsequently passed over into the ranks of national socialism.

Continuing this review of the parties and movements which comprised the German body politic at the time of the foundation of the Weimar Republic, we must turn to that enigmatic organisation, the Catholic Centre Party. This party's commitment to the Weimar Republic was at best equivocal,** even though it

* Though monarchist circles were by no means united in their tactical appreciation of the Ebert government. The *Norddeutsche Allgemeine Zeitung* was more astute than most when it wrote or November 9, 1918, that 'the development in the Reich, which threatened to lead to anarchy, could — in the belief of the SPD — be controlled only by certain ultimative demands which would acquiesce the people and lead them back to order. The demand foremost was the abdication of the Emperor. One may grant that the social democrats wanted this not only to realise the aims and ambitions of their party, but also to serve the fatherland, which they saw as heading towards perdition [i.e. revolution]; only the future can prove whether their decisions will bring the salvation which they themselves — and now all the other parties — expect ...It has, for the time being helped us to get out of a critical situation.'

** 'In our opinion, every government enjoys God's blessing, whether it be monarchic or republican.' (Centre Party statement of principles, read to the National Assembly on February 13, 1919) This highly ambiguous declaration, derived as it was from

provided a minister for every cabinet until the formation of von Papen's 'non-party' administration in May 1932. (Ironically, the man who ended the Centre Party's unbroken run was himself a Catholic!) And the reasons are not hard to find. Although founded in 1870 as a defensive measure by the Catholic bourgeoisie and hierarchy to ward off Bismarck's offensive against 'Roman' influences (the so-called *Kulturkampf)* the party never embraced consistently democratic views. It fought only for its own sectional, confessional interests, even though in so doing it found it convenient on occasions to make common cause with others oppressed by Protestant-Junker Berlin.

By very virtue of its being a confessional party, the Centre found it necessary to project a 'social' image towards the catholic working class and, to a lesser extent, the artisans and poorer sections of the peasantry. Catholic workers were for some time insulated from social democratic influence through their organisation into Christian 'trade unions', which while claiming to represent the special interests of the workers, in fact spent much of their time attacking Marxist socialism, class-based trade unionism and defending the rights of private property. But at the same time, the Centre was not averse to indulging in a little of what Marx and Engels had termed in the *Communist Manifesto* feudal or clerical socialism. The founding Centre Party pro-gramme declared that one of its aims would be to 'maintain this middle class in the midst of perils created by the doctrines of political economy, by industrialism, by complete occupational freedom and by the power of capital...' And by middle class the manifesto of course meant the hundreds of thousands — indeed millions — of artisans, peasants and other independent small producers who were already beginning to feel the pressure of Germany's industrial growth. Thus there evolved a 'guild socialist' wing to the Centre which its leaders not only tolerated but encouraged as an indispensable counterpoise to the rapidly expanding social democratic political and trade union movement. Its targets were liberalism both political and economic, Marxism, and large-scale industry and banking. Thus Franz Hitze, an early pioneer of Centre Party guild socialism, wrote in 1880:

> The guild is to absorb all associations having any connection with handicraft, and the whole social life of the craftsman is to be concen-trated in the guild. [The guild would] overcome the anarchy of

Thomist teaching on the state, left the door ajar for future Centre Party adjustments to anti-republican movements and regimes. In this declaration, which heralded the Centre's collaboration with the 'atheistic' SPD, was the germ of the opportunist strategy which permitted the political arm of the hierarchy to vote its unanimous support for Hitler's Enabling Act on March 23, 1933, which in turn became the con-stitutional foundation stone for the tyranny of the Third Reich. 'Render unto Caesar ...'

production [and create] a new society of social responsibility through the conquest of egotism.

Such a guild socialism was not therefore unlike the 'people's community' — the community interest before self-interest — of national socialism and indeed, there is much evidence to suggest that the former helped to shape the latter. And as also with national socialist economic and social theory, capitalism was not so much to be abolished as regulated in accordance with a — spurious — harmony of class interests. Instead of a 'labour movement [which] is a tearing loose, a secession from the rest of society, [trade unionism] would be a joining on, it would be only one organisation among many. The other, more conservative estates would show the workers the path ...*and the state would compel the workers to set themselves common goals and to put their own house in order alongside the ordered regiment of capital'.* (emphasis added)

With the aid of this social as well as clerical 'cement', the Centre succeeded remarkably well in smoothing over the many class and sectional divisions within the party. And of course, the bitterly anti-Catholic attitude of the state Lutheran Church greatly assisted its leaders in this work. The solidity of the 'vertical' Catholic bloc is evident from the steady vote the Centre Party received in all the elections under the Empire. In 1871, barely a year after its formation, it secured 0.7 million votes and 63 deputies. In 1874, its vote had doubled and its Reichstag representation had been raised to 93. From then until the last elections of 1912, the Centre party vote and Reichstag strength remained almost constant, the latter varying between a low of 91 and a peak of 106. Unlike the Conservatives, National Liberals, and Progressives, the party survived the upheavals of November 1918 and in the elections of January 1919, polled 5.9 million votes with 91 Reichstag deputies, thus becoming the second largest party to the SPD. And as such, it could not but avoid taking some sort of stand on the new political system ushered in by the November Revolution. Naturally, a party that functioned as the political arm of an immensely powerful, rich and entrenched caste* commanding widespread support in all classes of the

---

* In the middle 1920s the German Catholic Church employed more than 20,000 priests — one for every 2,000 German Catholics. Its youth organisations, instrumental in indoctrinating young workers against Marxism, had a membership of 1.5 million. There were also associations for a whole host of occupational groups and catering for sports, cultural and other activities. At every level it sought to both duplicate and counter the organisational methods and influence of social democracy. The historian of the Centre Party, Karl Bachem, was entirely justified when he claimed in 1931 that 'never yet has a Catholic country possessed such a developed system of all conceivable Catholic associations as today's Germany'. We should add to them the many and richly endowed Catholic publishing houses, which catered for every class and type of reader from the traditionalist devout Bavarian peasant to the more modern thinking and class conscious Ruhr miner or steel worker.

population could not but look on the events of November 1918 and the rise to political power of the atheistic 'Marxists' with some trepidation. Indeed, Cardinal Faulhaber regarded the November revolution as 'perjury and high treason', a view shared by the majority of the German hierarchy. Yet the Centre could not afford to adopt an openly hostile or abstentionist attitude to the system that had issued out of this 'crime'.

If the Centre set itself squarely against collaboration with the SPD, it ran the very real danger of losing much of its proletarian support in the Ruhr, where Catholic workers had joined with their socialist and communist class brothers in a united struggle against the old regime. And in fact this process had already begun. With each passing year, the Centre increasingly became a party depending upon female support, roughly 60% of its vote coming from women once they were enfranchised under the Weimar Constitution (they also voted in the elections to the Constituent National Assembly). A confidential report submitted to the Vatican after the 1928 Reichstag elections by Cardinal Eugenio Pacelli, Papal Secretary of State, and after 1939, the pro-fascist Pope Pius XII, revealed the alarming situation for the hierarchy that from a high of 85% in 1875, the proportion of Catholic males voting for the Centre had dropped to 65% by 1907, 55% in 1912, 48% in 1919 and a calamitous 39% in 1928. Confronted with this steady erosion of Catholic political influence amongst the proletariat — for in rural regions the situation was understandably very different — the leaders of the Centre opted for a policy of support for the new regime, exploiting their strong bargaining position in the Reichstag (they held the balance between left and right) to secure the protection of their own sectional interests in educational and other matters.

Far better to enter the Cabinet with the godless Marxists, many reasoned, and to temper their reforming zeal, than to permit them to function alone or with their equally secular-minded DDP allies. So in the first Weimar cabinet under SPD Chancellor Scheidemann (Ebert had meanwhile been voted President by the National Assembly), the Centre joined with the DDP as the social democrats' partners in the 'great coalition'. But all was far from sweetness and light in the Catholic camp. We have already noted the attitude of Cardinal Faulhaber, a hard-line opponent of Weimar. Even more significant, in view of his subsequent role as stirrup-holder for the Nazis, was the Catholic Westphalian aristocrat, Franz von Papen. This odious bootlicker of Hitler — he even continued to serve him after his private staff had been butchered by Nazi thugs in the purge of June 30, 1934 — never made any secret of his detestation of all things democratic and tinged with even the pinkest hues of socialism. It was an attitude he maintained up to his death — mourned incidentally by the pro-Tory British press — in 1969. His autobiography provides us with a clear picture of the utterly reactionary mentality of the man who cleared the road to power for Hitler in the summer of 1932.

First, the revolution:

> Instead of the thousand-year-old monarchy, the Red Flag had been planted in the centre of Germany. It was the end of everything we had believed in for generations, the disappearance of all we had loved and fought for ...Berlin and every other German city was torn by revolution. Liebknecht, Rosa Luxemburg, Eisner and their followers were fighting a bitter battle, setting up 'soviets' everywhere, against the more reasonable wing of the SPD led by Ebert and Noske.* The world I had known and understood had disappeared. The whole system of values into which I had integrated myself and for which my generation had fought and died had become meaningless.[13]

But not quite, for like many of his class and outlook, Papen did not give up all hopes of a monarchist restoration, certainly not of eventually driving the SPD back into opposition and so subverting the Republic in preparation for a more authoritarian type of regime. For while the social democrats and their bourgeois radical allies ruled the roost, there was simply no room in the new Germany for dyed-in-the-wool traditionalists. Neither was it a question of attitudes of mind only. Many like Papen realised that the social and economic concessions, made to the workers as the price for staving off revolution, were not only galling in themselves, but seen as establishing dangerous inroads into the hallowed rights of private property. It was his class consciousness, conceived though it was in romantically-flavoured and aristocratic catholicism, and not a psychologically-grounded inability to 'adjust' to Weimar Germany that took Papen all the way along the road of opposition to parliamentary democracy and the German Labour movement:

> The position of trust which we held under the Crown meant that we became conservative by nature. Now everything had changed. All these traditions had been swept away by the Republic, and we were all free to adopt an independent attitude. By background and upbringing I could hardly help being conservative, but even before the war I had found myself out of sympathy with the political development of the Conservative Party ...A conservative must always be progressive. Tradition and principles are basic values, but conservatism implies their application to changing circumstances.[14]

Papen represented that section of the west German aristocracy

---

* Even Papen was forced to concede that there were some who wore the 'Marxist' label who could be regarded as at least temporary allies. Nevertheless, it was Papen who ousted the 'reasonable' SPD leaders from the Prussian State Government in July 1932 on the grounds that they were preparing to form a revolutionary united front with the Communist Party.

which had successfully branched out or married into industry or allied itself with it. He was therefore critical of the Junker Conservative party for failing to adjust to the rise of this new centre of economic power in the Reich, and to see that the massive proletariat which had been created by this industrial upsurge could not be countered by the traditional weapons of reaction. Papen's answer was yet another variant on the old 'social' christianity theme, in the name of which he eventually threw in his lot with the Nazis:

> Since the beginning of the Industrial Revolution, and at an ever increasing speed in the first half of our century, we have witnessed a gigantic and fundamental conflict ...The threat to the body politic has increased with the conversion of individuals into 'the masses' — a Marxist weapon in the struggle to overturn the capitalist system.* Collectivist philosophies, combined with the materialist conception of history, proclaim the overthrow of those Christian principles which have provided for two thousand years the basis of the Western world's growth ...The problem has been to find some means of combatting these forces. In the tumult of the post-war period, the duty of all conservative forces was to rally under the banner of Christianity, in order to sustain in the new Republic the basic conceptions of continuing tradition. The Constitution approved at Weimar in 1919 seemed to many a perfect synthesis of Western democratic ideas. Yet the second paragraph [quoted at the beginning of this chapter] of its first article proclaimed the false philosophy of Jean-Jacques Rousseau — 'all power derives from the people'. This thesis is diametrically opposed to the teachings and traditions of the Roman Catholic Church. Over the centuries, the monarchy had represented the highest form of temporal authority in the State, but above it stood the still higher authority of

---

* Not all 'Marxists' were villains however, as Papen explains: 'As in all times of revolutionary change, the radical parties were in the ascendant, and the various forms of Marxism attracted the largest measure of support. Fortunately for Germany, there were, amongst the social democrats, a number of civic-minded leaders like Ebert and Noske, who stood firm against the Bolshevist storm'. The only problem was that 'in spite of their statesmanlike attitude, the basic programme of their party still exalted class warfare and the fight against religious influences. The cry for the 'Dictatorship of the proletariat' was heard from all shades of Marxist opinion even though more moderate policies were actually put into practice.' Papen was for this reason critical of the Centre Party for remaining in the coalition with the 'Marxist' SPD longer than the exigencies of revolutionary upheaval demanded: 'When our institutions seemed likely to collapse at the end of the war the Zentrum [Centre] undoubtedly did right to combine with the Socialists ...They were able to block measures of a too radical nature and prevented Germany from becoming a field for too many socialist experiments. This was a signal contribution to the conduct of our affairs. But the Weimar Coalition of Socialists, Democrats and Zentrum held obstinately to office once the first shock had been countered. In the Central Government, feeble attempts were made from time to time to incorporate representatives of the right-wing parties. In Prussia, however, the Weimar Coalition remained in power without a break from 1918 [until Papen became Chancellor]. The Zentrum could never make up its mind to break with the socialists in order to rescue the right-wing parties from the torpidity of endless opposition. This was one of the major reasons for the collapse of the Weimar brand of democracy [which Papen eagerly helped to bring about] and the growth of Hitler's party'. (F. von Papen: *Memoirs*, pp.104-106.)

spiritual teachings and Christianity ...Ever since the French Revolution and the *Contract Social* [how the German reaction loathed Rousseau] and its bastard offspring the *Communist Manifesto,* the transfer from faith to reason has acquired increasing momentum. The philosophy of naked force has replaced the old relationship between power and authority, between reverence and piety on the one hand, and force on the other ...Marxism in all its forms has now set force against force, and the power of the masses against the authority of the rulers. [Papen now unveils his own, corporatist, solution, to the 'social question']. My father-in-law Privy Councillor von Boch-Galhau, was one of a small group of enlightened industrialists who recognised the inherent evils of the capitalist system. He tried to establish a relationship of mutual confidence between capital and labour, while yet retaining the traditions of a family enterprise [sic!]. The shadow of class warfare was already on the horizon. The socialists were propagating the principles of Marxism, and, in spite of the social reforms carried out under Kaiser Wilhelm II, were trying to organise the 'proletariat' on an international basis and detach the workers as a 'class' from the bourgeoisie. Only a few industrialists had grasped the fact that the best way of countering these methods was to assume that besides his wages, the worker should have a share in the prosperity of the enterprise and a dignified and satisfying existence. My father-in-law had been a leader in the provision of well-built modern houses, hostels and holiday estates for his workers, as well as medical care and pension and insurance rights. The results [i.e. the weakening of trade union and Marxist influence] proved a striking example of what could be accomplished by applying the principles laid down by Pope Leo XIII in his Encyclical *Rerum Novarum.*[15]

In fact the Encyclical nowhere attacked the foundation of capitalist exploitation — private ownership of the means of production. Such attacks on capital that it did make — and they came well from the world's richest private organisation — were of a backward-looking, guild type, with the predictable criticisms of 'usury' (though the Vatican was discreet enough not to link this with the Jews):

It is no easy matter to define the relative rights and mutual duties of the rich and the poor, of capital and labour. And the danger lies in this, that crafty agitators are intent on making use of these differences of opinion to pervert men's judgements and to stir up the people to revolt ...the ancient workingmen's guilds were abolished in the last century, and no other organisation took their place ...Hence by degrees it has come to pass that workingmen have been surrendered ...to the hardheartedness of employers and the greed of unchecked competition. The mischief has been increased by rapacious usury, which, although more than once condemned by the Church, is nevertheless ...still practised by covetous and grasping men. To this must be added the custom of working by contract, and the concentration of so many branches of trade in the hands of a few individuals ...To remedy these wrongs, the Socialists, working on the poor man's envy of the rich, are striving to do away with private property, and contend that individual possessions should become the com-

mon property of all ...But their contentions are so clearly powerless to
end the controversy that were they carried into effect the workingman
himself would be among the first to suffer. They are, moreover,
emphatically unjust, because they would rob the lawful possessor,
bring State action into a sphere not within its competence, and create
utter confusion in the community ...Socialists ...by endeavouring to
transfer the possessions of individuals to the community at large,
strike at the interests of every wage earner, since they would deprive
him of the liberty of disposing of his wages, and thereby of all hope
and possibility of increasing his stock and of bettering his condition in
life.*[16]

Papen was therefore treading on safe ground when he cited
Rerum Novarum, to bolster his own reactionary political views,
all the more so since the encyclical stated quite bluntly what was
to be done with those who continued to propagate the socialist
doctrines of class struggle and the nationalisation of the means of
production:

The great mistake ...is to take up with the notion that class is hostile to
class, and that the wealthy and the workingmen are intended by nature
to live in mutual conflict ...Capital cannot do without Labour, nor
Labour without Capital ...Thus religion teaches the labouring man
and the artisan to carry out honestly and fairly all equitable agreements freely entered into; never to injure the property, nor to outrage
the person, of an employer, never to resort to violence in defending
their own cause, nor to engage in riot or disorder; and to have nothing
to do with men of evil principles ...It should ever be borne in mind that
*the chief thing to be realised is the safeguarding of private property by
legal enactment and public policy.* Most of all it is essential, amid such
a fever of excitement, *to keep the multitude within the line of duty;* for
if all may justly strive to better their conditions, neither justice nor the
common good allows any individual to seize upon that which belongs
to another, or, under the futile and shallow pretext of equality, *to lay
violent hands on other people's possessions* ['Thou shalt not steal' —
from thy exploiter!] ...there are not a few [workers] who are imbued
with evil principles and eager for a revolutionary change, whose main
purpose is to stir up tumult and bring about measures of violence. *The
authority of the State should intervene to put restraint on such*

---

* The *canard* also used by fascism that socialists seek to collectivise the personal
possessions of the worker as well as the productive property of the bourgeoisie and
big landowners, is answered by Marx in *Capital*, where he writes: 'The capitalist
mode of appropriation is the first negation of individual private property, as founded
on the labour of the proprietor. But capitalist production begets ...its own negation
...This does not re-establish private property for the producer but gives him
individual property based on the acquisitions of the capitalist era: i.e. on co-
operation and the possession in common of the land and the means of production.
The transformation of scattered private property, arising from individual labour into
capitalist private property is, naturally, a process incomparably more protracted,
violent and difficult, than the transformation of capitalistic private property, already
practically resting on socialised production, into socialised property. In the former
case, we had the expropriation of the mass of the people by a few usurpers in the
latter we have the expropriation of a few usurpers by the mass of the people'. (K.
Marx: *Capital*, Vol. I, pp.764-765.)

firebrands, to save the working classes from their seditious arts, and
protect lawful owners from spoliation.[17]*(emphasis added)*

Guided by this obscurantist outlook, Papen opted to join the
Centre party, even though he did not share the willingness of
many of its leaders to partake in the running of the new Republic.
It was their 'social' policy which appealed to him:

> As a party of the centre it was essentially one devoted to compromise,
> and had always pledged itself to interpret the social precepts of Pope
> Leo XIII.[18]

And if we are to believe Papen's own testimony, it was this
same 'social' Catholicism which convinced him of the moral
justice of Hitler's early policies:

> Hitler sought to put an end to class warfare by granting the working
> class equal rights in the community [sic!]. It was the best point in his
> programme ...Class warfare was a Marxist tool and the socialist Trade
> Unions were its principle protagonists. The employers federations
> manned the opposing front. If class warfare was to be abolished, then
> the opposing forces would have to be disbanded. Neither in moral law
> nor in Christian doctrine is it laid down that the interests of the
> working class may be represented only by the Trade Unions [both the
> Bible and the Roman Catholic Church certainly predate the formation
> of the first trade unions]. The Trade Union organisations have made
> an overwhelming contribution to raising the standards of the workers,
> but their purely economic functions had been transmuted by the
> Marxist parties into a weapon of class warfare.* The coalition govern-
> ment of which I was a member went to great pains to build up a new
> relationship between worker and employer [sic] and between both and
> the state. Our principle concern was to eliminate class warfare. To
> achieve this we were prepared to approve the dissolution of the
> Trade Unions. There was much in this National Socialist conception
> which ran parallel to principles familiar to Catholics and enunciated in
> the Papal Encyclical *Quadragisimo Anno*** ...The time may yet come
> when the principles involved, if put into practice by more moderate
> and sensible regimes, will prove to contain the germs of a solution.[19]

---

* Papen's views were identical to Hitler's on this question — see Chapters Eight and
Nine.

** This Encyclical, *On Reconstructing the Social Order,* dates from 1931, and was
promulgated by Pius XI. It updates and expands on *Rerum Novarum,* criticising
certain 'excesses' of capitalist exploitation while intransigently upholding the sacred
rights of private property. It went further in that it proposed a thoroughly fascist
solution to the problem of the class struggle: 'The complete cure will not come until
this opposition [of the classes] has been abolished and well-ordered members of the
social body — industries and professions — are constituted in which men may have
their place, not according to the position each has in the labour market but
according to the respective social functions which each performs.' In other words,
the corporate state, which, had Pope Pius XI cared to look out of his Vatican
windows, he would have seen being put into brutal practice by the atheist Mussolini's
fascist regime. Papen, who enjoyed the most intimate relations with the Vatican — it
was he who more than any other member of Hitler's government smoothed the way
for the Concordat between Rome and the Third Reich — leaves no room for doubt
on this issue: 'Once the parties had disappeared [sic!] it became necessary to organise

So much then for Papen, the 'gentleman horserider'* as he liked to regard himself.

How were these contradictory, and in some cases mortally hostile forces, to be reconciled? Excluding the Nazis, who were yet to become a force in German politics — in fact Hitler only joined the German Workers Party towards the end of 1919 — ranged against the Weimar system on the right were die-hard monarchists, DNVP Junkers, militarist and jew-baiting Pan-Germans, profit-hungry and labour-hating industrialists, anti-democratic Catholics like Papen and Faulhaber, Prussian officers either still on the army pay roll or fighting as freelance counter-revolutionaries in the Free Corps, and — and this was to be a most important factor throughout the Republic's history — a state bureaucracy which from top to bottom remained, both as regards ideas and personnel, the identical state and judicial machine which had served so loyally under the Imperial regime. These men — almost without exception convinced monarchists and opponents of democracy — were now to be called upon to administer 'the most democratic constitution in the world'. How they saw their role in the new Germany can be illustrated by comparing their partisan reactions to political crimes committed by Left and Right respectively. Between 1919 and 1922, the Judges of Weimar handed down the following sentences for alleged political murders:

	Right	Left
Not Convicted	326	4
Convicted	1	17
Partly Convicted	27	1
Self-confessed murderers acquitted	23	0
Average length of jail term	4 months	15 years
Fine per murder in marks	2	(no fines)
Number of executions	0	10

the democratic system on another basis, founded on the groups of trades and professions which formed the backbone of the nation. *The corporate state has long been an element in Catholic social philosophy,* and in many ways represents an improvement on the party system' (F. von Papen: *Memoirs*, p.259 - emphasis added)

* Let be noted here that like that other man of breeding, the banker Schacht, Papen escaped scot free at the Nuremberg war crimes trials, despite a mountain of evidence, documentary, as well as oral, of their both having not only been complicit in aiding Hitler's rise to power, but ready to share in the spoils of victory. Inveterate enemies

No comment is surely needed on these figures. They speak for themselves, far more loudly and plainly than Article 109 of the Weimar Constitution, which proudly proclaimed that 'all Germans are equal before the law.'

The same can indeed be said for the entire document. It promised much, yet could allow so little. Thus after beginning with the classic bourgeois-democratic proposition that 'political authority emanates from the people', the Weimar Constitution incorporated an escape clause which ensured that in moments of political crisis and decision, it would rest in the hands of — in theory at least — a single man. Bonapartism, the classic form of rule for Germany for so many of the pre-war years, was now officially enshrined within a constitution supposedly the last word in modern democracy! To be specific, the whole Article in question, the notorious number 48, declared:

> If any state [of the German Reich] does not fulfill the duties imposed upon it by the Constitution or the laws of the Reich, the Reich President may enforce such duties with the aid of the armed forces. In the event that the public order and security are seriously disturbed, the Reich President may take the measures necessary for their restoration, intervening if necessary, with the aid of the armed forces. For this purpose he may abrogate temporarily, wholly or in part, the fundamental principles laid down in Articles 114, 115, 117, 118, 123, 124 and 135.

Fundamental indeed, for the rights covered by these articles were respectively personal liberty, the inviolability of the home, secrecy of letters and telephone communications, freedom of the press, the right of assembly, the right of association and the right to own private property.*

Thus with a stroke of a President's pen — for that was all that was needed to revoke these basic rights and liberties of the German people — the ground work could be laid for the erection of a Bonapartist system of rule, as indeed it was under the regimes of Chancellors Brüning, von Papen and Schleicher, each of whom repeatedly by-passed a deadlocked Reichstag by the use of Article 48; not only as a means of enacting political legislation, but in order to drive down the living standards and wages of the working class. And it should not be forgotten for one moment

of Marxism and labour both, their responsibility for the hideous crimes of German fascism was not one wit less than those who paid with their lives. Like convicted war criminal Alfred Krupp, whose company grew rich on the profits extracted from Soviet and Jewish slave labour, and who conducted board meetings in his own cell, they were doubtless thankful that class justice, which Papen demagogically decried in his Nazi days, applied even to the most monumental crime committed in the history of mankind.

* Article 48 was never once in all the times it was employed, invoked to violate the property rights of the bourgeoisie. It was used, however, to seize and impound the property of the workers' movement — i.e. newspapers, membership lists and the like.

that the social democrats — whose constitution this was — finally
found themselves driven out of office in the state of Prussia,
under this very Article 48, which, they fondly believed, would be
invoked only against the enemies, Right as well as Left, of the
Weimar Republic.

Article 48 was included, it is generally believed, on the insistence of Max Weber, one of those charged by the Ebert government with drafting the new constitution. He was determined to
have a strong executive authority standing over the legislature, a
political structure that had its authoritarian potential multiplied
by Article 41, which — again on Weber's insistence — provided
for the President to be elected directly by the population as a
whole, thus once more by-passing both parties and parliament.*

Finally there were the Weimar constitution's social and
economic clauses, which in many cases, due to the intransigent
resistance of the employers, remained little more than dead
letters. And those that were implemented had to be fought for and
defended in the teeth of bitter resistance by both the right-wing
parties and the heavy industrialists, who regarded them as an
outrage against the rights of private property. The articles which
aroused so much hostility amongst the bourgeoisie were numbers
159, which proclaimed 'freedom of association for the
preservation and promotion of labour and economic conditions';
161, which established a 'comprehensive system of [social]
insurance'; and 165, which provided for the setting up of works'
councils to make possible the 'co-operating on an equal footing'
of 'workers and employees' with employers 'in the regulation of
wages and of the conditions of labour, as well as in the general
development of the productive forces.' This last proved to be the
bitterest pill for the employers to swallow, for even though it was
but a liberal-reformist sop to workers who had been demanding

* Although chosen to assist Preuss in drawing up the constitution Weber can hardly
be termed a consistent democrat. An unrepentant chauvinist and militarist, he
declared in the November of 1918: 'For the resurrection of Germany in its old
splendour I would certainly ally myself with every power on earth and even with the
very devil himself...' And early in 1919, in frank discussion with General Ludendorff,
he remarked in reply to the question 'What do you understand by democracy?', that
'In a democracy the people elects the leader whom it trusts. Then the elected one
says: "Now shut up and obey. People and parties must no longer butt in"', to which
Ludendorff, who lent his considerable military prestige and personal presence to
Hitler's ill-starred Munich putsch, responded: 'Such "democracy" is alright with me'.
Weber's notion of democracy differs but little from Hitler's, whose definition we
have already quoted. Hitler favoured a 'truly Germanic democracy, characterised by
the free election of a leader and his obligation to assume all responsiblity for his
actions and omissions: in it there is no majority vote, but only the decision of an
individual who must answer with his fortune and his life for his choice'. (A. Hitler:
Mein Kampf, p.91.) Even on this last point there is similarity with Weber's
definition, for he told Ludendorff that 'afterwards the people can judge — if the
leader has made mistakes, to the gallows with him'. Only the leader was in the case of
Hitler at least, also chief hangman!

the nationalisation of the major industrial concerns — this had after all been part of the SPD's programme — it offended against heavy industry's slogan of 'master in the house'. No jumped-up trade union official or seditious shop steward was going to pry into the affairs of a Krupp or a Thyssen if German industry was to have any say in the matter. One can appreciate their horror at Article 165. Part of it ran:

> Workers and employees shall, for the purposes of looking after their economic and social interests, be given legal representation in factory workers' councils, as well as in district workers' councils and in a workers' council of the Reich district. Workers councils of the Reich shall meet with the representatives of the employers ...as district economic councils and as economic councils of the Reich for the purpose of performing economic functions and for co-operation in the execution of the laws of socialisation...

Big business never reconciled itself to Article 165, and it was steadily eroded after 1929, finally to be dispatched, along with all other laws and institutions which pre-supposed independent working class organisations, after the Nazis came to power.

And what of opposition to Weimar from the Left, the proletarian flank? True, it could be argued that in its early days, this was negligible, since the 'Spartacist Uprising' (wrongly so called, for the Spartacist leaders Liebknecht and Luxemburg both opposed it) only actively involved a small fraction of the Berlin working class, as did a similar revolt two months later. But while it is true that mass working class hostility to the Republic was slow to crystallise and articulate itself — after all, the workers had been instrumental in creating the Republic, so they could hardly be expected to revolt against it *en masse* when their own leaders stood at its head — organised and widespread opposition to the bourgeois republic did begin to emerge quite early in the new year, as the Ebert government came to rely more and more readily and openly on Noske's Free Corps scum. In fact it was under their protection that the Constituent Assembly held its first session at Weimar, a small Thuringian town selected by virtue of its relative isolation from the main areas of proletarian strength and militancy.*

In fact, working class disillusionment with Weimar can be measured much in the same fashion as the shift towards the anti-democratic right in the middle class — by voting returns for the

---

* But around Weimar things were not quite normal. General Märcker, in charge of the Free Corps units detailed to protect the tender shoots of German parliamentarianism, later recalled that 'Weimar was encircled at ten kilometers distance; all roads situated in this circle were secured by groups of officers and non-commissioned officers with full equipment ...Villages and industrial hamlets in Thuringia were unfriendly to our troops ...' (General Ludwig Märcker: *Vom Kaiserhof zur Reichswehr Geschichte des frei willeigen Landesjagerkorps,* p.91, Leipzig, 1927.)

pro- and anti- Weimar workers parties. The USPD voted against the Weimar Constitution when it was put to the vote in the National Assembly at Weimar, as did, for opposite reasons, the DVP and the DNVP. Thus workers who voted USPD and, after 1920, in increasing numbers, for the KPD, did so fully aware that these two parties were as utterly opposed to the Weimar system as the SPD was in support of it. Thus we arrive at the following picture:

	Pro-Weimar SPD	Anti-Weimar USPD & KPD
Jan 1919	11.5	2.3
June 1920	6.1	5.0

And if we turn to the balance of forces in the right-wing camp, the same trend emerges:

	Pro-Weimar DDP + Centre	Anti-Weimar DVP + DNVP
1919	11.6	4.5
1920	6.2	8.2

Thus a year after the National Assembly voted by 262 to 75 to adopt the proposed new constitution, the Weimar majority which had seemed so stable had melted away to be replaced by an anti-Weimar majority in the Reichstag of three, and if the Catholic Bavarian People's Party is excluded from the Weimar bloc, of 24. Weimar was built on quicksands: economically, socially and politically. In the end only the social democrats remained faithful to it as one by one, the SPD's bourgeois allies, their mass following almost completely eroded by the magnetic pull of Nazi counter-revolutionary dynamism, threw in their lot with Hitler. DDP, Centre and DVP — all voted for Hitler's Enabling Act, which authorised him to outlaw the SPD and the trade unions fully within limits prescribed by the Weimar Constitution. No doubt the leaders of social democracy thought they were scaling the heights of tactical subtlety when, acting as accomplices of the bourgeoisie, they derailed the German revolution by counter-posing trade union recognition against expropriation, parliamentary democracy against council rule and social welfare against the dictatorship of the proletariat. But their bourgeois allies of 1918 had the final word, since the reformists not only succeeded in strangling the revolution, but in so doing, opened the door for the reaction that was to sweep away the very concessions which they had used to camouflage their treachery.

REFERENCES FOR CHAPTER TEN

[1] K. Marx and F. Engels: *The Manifesto of the Communist Party* in *Selected Works,* Vol. I, p.54.
[2] F. Engels: Letter to J. Bloch, London, September 21-22, 1890, in *Selected Correspondence,* p.498.
[3] Prince Max of Baden: *Memoirs,* Vol. II, p.351.
[4] *Political Institutions of the German Revolution,* p.214, New York, 1966.
[5] Ibid, p.223.
[6] H. Schacht: *My First Seventy Six Years,* p.148, London, 1955.
[7] Ibid, pp.148-149.
[8] Ibid, pp.149-150.
[9] Ibid, p.150.
[10] Ibid, pp.151-152.
[11] Ibid. p.152-153.
[12] H. Schacht: *The Stabilisation of the Mark,* pp.36-38, London, 1927.
[13] F. von Papen: *Memoirs,* pp.84-90, London, 1952.
[14] Ibid, pp.90-91.
[15] Ibid, pp.91-93.
[16] *Rerum Novarum: The Condition of the Working Classes* (May 15, 1891) in *The Papal Encyclicals,* pp.167-168, New York, 1963. (Nihil Obstat John. A. Goodwine, J.C.D., Censor Librorum, Imprimatur Cardinal Francis Spellman, Archbishop of New York)
[17] Ibid, pp.174-184.
[18] F. Von Papen: Ibid, p.97.
[19] Ibid, pp.283-284.

Chapter Eleven

NSDAP

> The Revolution's greatest piece of stupidity was to leave us all alive. If
> ever I come to power again there will be no pardons. With a good
> conscience I would have Ebert, Scheidemann and company strung up
> and dangling. (General Erich Ludendorff, February, 1919)

It is almost a truism to say that as a political 'theorist', Hitler
invented nothing. Neither did he found the party that under his
leadership, and with an amended name, rose from its Munich
obscurity to seize the levers of state power in little more than 13
years. And in fact even as regards nomenclature, the National
Socialist German Workers' Party (NSDAP) was not the first
organisation to bear this thoroughly undeserved title. As we have
already noted in Chapter Nine, the Bohemian-based 'German
Workers' Party', founded in 1904 to defend the privileges of
German-speaking highly-skilled workers and artisans against an
imagined threat from their Czech fellow-workers, rapidly evolved
in a chauvinist, anti-Marxist direction. At its Vienna conference
in August 1918 the Party not only adopted a new name,
(NSDAP) but a new programme which foreshadowed many of
the demands soon to be put forward by the Hitler movement in its
bid to win support from the middle class masses:

> The NSDAP aims at the elevation and liberation of the German
> working population from economic, political and intellectual
> suppression and at a complete equality of rights for it in all fields of
> *volkisch* and political life ...It rejects, therefore, as unnatural a com-
> bination on the basis of supra-nationalism. An improvement of the
> economic and social conditions can, on the contrary, only be achieved
> by bringing together all those engaged in work on the basis of the
> individual nationality ...[therefore] the NSDAP is not a narrow class
> party, but defends the interests of all those engaged in honest
> productive work. The party is libertarian and strictly *volkisch,* and it
> opposes all reactionary tendencies, the privileges of the Church,
> nobility and capitalists, and all alien influences, but above all the over-
> whelming power of the Jewish trading spirit in all spheres of public life.

The programme, in line with the party's already established tactic
of indulging in entirely spurious anti-capitalist rhetoric, called for
the nationalisation of all enterprises which were working against

the 'common interest', and specifically for the rooting out of so-called 'Jewish' finance from the national economy. Like Feder, whose ideas were cast in the same petty-bourgeois *volkisch* mould, the programme took pains to distinguish between what one of its leading publicists, Rudolf Jung, called 'disintegrating finance capital' and the highly desirable 'productive national capital'. Jung also coined a well-worn slogan of the Nazi era, 'the common weal comes before private interests', one which Ley's Labour Front constantly employed to drive workers to even greater sacrifice on behalf of their employers, who always chose to appear in the self-effacing guise of the 'people's community'. The reader can judge for his or herself to what degree the original NSDAP contributed towards the Hitler movement's programme by comparing these demands with the 25 point programme adopted in January 1920, which is reproduced at the end of this chapter.

One thing is certain. Neither the birth of the Nazi movement, nor its initial growth, can in any sense be considered accidental. Firstly, there is the role of Hitler himself. He did not join the Munich GWP as a free agent, but as a political officer of the German army. Nor was it purely by chance that Hitler rather than some other right-wing fanatic came to be chosen for the task of establishing contact with the various anti-Marxist organisations that had sprung up in the Bavarian capital after the defeat of the Soviet Republic in May 1919. In fact Hitler's emergence as an army 'politico' dates from the Munich Bavarian revolution, when he served as an army stool-pigeon, informing on those among the regular troops who became sympathetic to the workers' move-ment in the course of the Bavarian Soviet Republic's brief life. When counter-revolutionary troops under the command of the future Nazi, Lt. General Franz Xavier Ritter von Epp, took Munich on May 1, Hitler added to the ensuing blood-letting by volunteering evidence that led to the decimation of supposedly 'disloyal' units.* This Hitler subsequently termed — with some justification — as his 'first more or less purely political activity.'[1]

Not only in Bavaria, but throughout Germany the reaction was on the offensive, emboldened by the treachery of the reformists and the vacillations of the USPD centrists. The swing to the extreme right was more marked in Munich for a variety of reasons, historical as well as political. The Bavarian capital had long been a centre of anti-semitic flavoured *volkisch* nationalism, a tradition to which the Catholic church had not been slow in

---

* Hitler only makes the vaguest of allusions to this episode in his autobiographical *Mein Kampf*: 'A few days after the liberation of Munich, I was ordered to report to the examining commission concerned with revolutionary occurrences in the Second Infantry Regiment.' (P.208).

accomodating in its efforts to deflect charges that the 'Romanists' were lacking in German patriotism. Neither was there that liberal bourgeois tradition which we encounter in the equally Catholic Rhineland, one which owed it origins to the spread of democratic ideas and institutions from neighbouring revolutionary France. 1789 and 1848 passed Bavaria by, just as in the Bismarckian period, the rise of heavy industry and large scale capitalist farming were least in evidence in this, the most rural of all Germany's states. Social democracy in Bavaria was from the very beginning prone to seek opportunist solutions to the problems posed by the class and political structure of the region. Faced by an intransigently hostile clerical movement, which drew its main strength from a pious peasantry and small town artisans, the Bavarian SPD leadership began to cast around for anti-clerical allies in the ranks of the bourgeoisie. And so was conceived and born that forerunner of the Stalinist 'popular front', the SPD-Progressive electoral alliance, in which the two parties mutually agreed to support each other in run-off ballots against the clericals and monarchists. It is evident from the evolution of Bavarian social democracy before 1914 that its leaders (notably Kurt Eisner and Erhard Auer) did not even conceive of the struggle for socialism on a national, let alone international plane, but rather viewed it through the double lenses of Bernsteinian revisionism and Bavarian particularism. All major principled and strategic questions were reduced to the small change of regional peculiarities and tactical combinations, a method which had not only utterly reformist consequences, but could — and in fact did — lead in a period of revolutionary upsurge, to the most ill-conceived and ineptly-led adventures. Here too, social democracy proved to be the midwife of the most extreme reaction, for undoubtedly the defeat of the Bavarian soviet republic created the most favourable political conditions for the birth and rise of movements such as Hitler's. His political career dates, as he himself acknowledged, *from the crushing of the Munich proletariat.* To ensure a secure base for the new military regime in the still-seething city, and to root out and counter 'subversive' ideas in the army itself (many rank and file soldiers had been influenced by the workers' movement, and had themselves participated in the revolution as members of soldiers' councils) a bureau was set up (*Abteilung I b/P*) to carry out political work in the army. The bureau's head, staff officer Karl Mayr, drew up a list of possible candidates for his staff of spies and informers, one of the the first to be drawn to his attention being ...Adolf Hitler.

To prime him for his new role, Hitler was sent on a course of lectures at Munich University, and it was here that he first heard Feder extolling the merits of 'national capital'. Feder's selection

by the army as one of the 'lecturers' in this induction course
indicates just how reactionary was the political climate prevailing
in post revolutionary Munich. But there were already present
elements that could not be directly identified with either militarist
or monarchist reaction. The harrowing experience of the soviet
republic had strengthened Hitler's conviction (and also many
others of a similar *volkisch* outlook) that the old style 'dynastic'
nationalism had had its day, even in Bavaria, where it had proved
most impervious to the passage of time and the rise of the
workers' movement.

Still as yet largely independently of the main *volkisch* groups
in Munich, Hitler in his new post of political officer began to
grope his way towards the notion of a plebeian-based counter-
revolutionary movement which could achieve what the old
bourgeois parties had so abysmally failed to accomplish — the
extirpation of Marxism:

> For the value of the whole affair [the lecture course at Munich
> University] was that I now obtained an opportunity of meeting a few
> like-minded comrades with whom I could discuss the situation of the
> moment. All of us were more or less firmly convinced that Germany
> could no longer be saved from the impending collapse by the parties of
> the November crime, the Centre and the social democracy, *and the so-
> called 'bourgeois-national' formations, even with the best of
> intentions, could never repair what had happened.* A whole series of
> pre-conditions were lacking, without which such a task simply could
> not succeed. The following period confirmed the opinion we then held.
> Thus, in our own circle we discussed the foundation of a new party.
> The basic ideas which we had in mind were the same as those realised
> in the 'German Workers' Party'. The name of the movement to be
> founded would from the very beginning *have to offer the possibility of
> approaching the broad masses; for without this quality the whole task
> seemed aimless and superfluous.* Thus we arrived at the name of
> 'Social Revolutionary Party'; this because the social views of the new
> organisation did indeed mean a revolution.[2] (emphasis added)

The nature of this 'revolution' we have already discussed at
some length. Hitler himself took great care to distinguish his use
of the term from the sense in which the word had been traditionally understood not only by the workers' movement, but by its
class enemies. It was a political 'revolution' — counter-revolution
to be precise — that Hitler sought, the forging of a cadre and
movement which while usurping the political prerogatives of the
old ruling elites — the so-called 'political bourgeoisie' and its
supplementary literary agencies — would create a new state
structure resting on and defending the same capitalist property relations. This is why Hitler so eagerly seized on Feder's theory of
'productive capital' as it enabled him to reconcile his aim of a
'popular' national movement with his utterly conservative views
on private property. As Hitler himself commented:

Previously I had been unable to recognise with the desired clarity the difference between this pure capital as the end result of productive labour and a capital whose existence and essence rests exclusively on speculation. For this I lacked the initial inspiration [sic], which had simply not come my way. But now this was provided most amply by one of the various gentlemen lecturing in the above mentioned course [at Munich University]: Gottfried Feder.[3]

Thus the struggle against 'Jewish' Marxism became, by virtue of this theory, synonomous with the fight against an equally hebraic 'finance capitalism':

...it was the conclusions of Gottfried Feder that caused me to delve into the fundamentals of this field with which I had previously not been very familiar. I began to study again, and now for the first time really achieved an understanding of the content of the Jew Karl Marx's life effort. Only now did his *Kapital* become really intelligible to me, and also the struggle of the social democracy against the national economy, which aims only to prepare the ground for the domination of truly international finance and stock exchange capital.[4]

Stripped of its wilder moments of rhetoric, there was in fact very little even in Hitler's public utterances on economics to give the big bourgeoisie cause for concern about their property rights. On the contrary, those that took the trouble to read chapter four of Volume Two of *Mein Kampf, Personality and the Conception of the Folkish State,* would have found Hitler's main quarrel with the capitalist class to be over its failure to apply consistently what he called the principle of 'personality'. The bourgeoisie upheld it in economics by — in Hitler's declared opinion quite rightly — refusing to countenance any interference by the trade unions or works councils in the running of their enterprises. But by their toleration of, or even collaboration with, the Weimar system, they denied this same principle of 'personality' in politics and the affairs of state. And in so doing, they were sinning against what Hitler termed the 'aristocratic principle of nature'.

In such a 'Folkish State' founded on this principle, there would be room for neither trade unions nor parliamentary democracy, for they both were its pure negation:

A philosophy of life which endeavours to reject the democratic mass idea and gives this earth to the best people, must logically obey the same aristocratic principle within this people and make sure that the leadership and the highest influence in this people fall to the best minds. Thus it builds ...upon the idea of personality ...Even purely theoretical intellectual work ...appears as the exclusive product of the individual person. It is not the mass that invents and not the majority that organises or thinks, but in all things only and always the individual person ...organisation ...must itself be an embodiment of the endeavour to place thinking individuals above the masses, thus subordinating the latter to the former ...it must proceed from the principle that the salvation of mankind has never lain in the masses, but in its creative minds, which must therefore be regarded as benefactors of the human race ...the selection of these minds ...is primarily accomplished by the hard struggle for existence. Many break and perish, this showing that they are not destined for the ultimate, and in the end only a few appear to be chosen. In the fields of thought, artistic creation, even, in fact, of economic life, this selective process is still going on today, though especially in the latter field, it faces a grave obstacle...[5]

And what is this 'grave obstacle' that defies nature by standing in the way of the unfettered functioning of the aristocratic or 'personality' principle? Hitler's answer to this question is at the same time an exposition of the historical role of fascism:

Only political life has today turned completely away from this most natural principle. While all human culture is solely the result of the individual's creative activity, everywhere, and particularly in the highest leadership of the national community, the principle of the value of the majority appears decisive, and from that high place begins to gradually dissolve it ...Marxism presents itself as the perfection of the Jew's attempt to exclude the pre-eminence of personality in all fields of human life and replace it by the numbers of the mass.[6]

At this point, Hitler draws a direct parallel between the threat posed to 'personality' in political affairs by bourgeois democracy and the subverting of 'personality' in economics by the workers' movement, specifically its trade unions:

To this [i.e. the rule of the masses], in the political sphere, corresponds the parliamentary form of government,* which, from the smallest germ cells of the municipality up to the supreme leadership of the

---

* For all his attempts to equate bourgeois parliamentary democracy and Marxism (on the grounds that both upheld the right of the 'masses' to rule), Hitler was well aware that there were important differences between the two, and that the Marxist defence of what were essentially bourgeois democratic freedoms and rights was a subordinate part of its overall revolutionary strategy: 'The Marxist will march with democracy until they succeed in indirectly obtaining for their criminal aims the support of even the national intellectual world. [But if today] they came to the conviction that from the witches' cauldron of our parliamentary democracy a majority could be brewed which ...would seriously attack Marxism, the parliamentary jugglery would come to an end at once. The banner bearers of the Red International would then, instead of addressing an appeal to the democratic conscience, emit a fiery call to the proletarian masses, and the struggle at one stroke would be removed from the stuffy air of our parliamentary meeting halls to the factories and the streets. Democracy would be done for immediately; what the mental dexterity of those people's apostles in the parliaments had failed to do, the crowbar and sledgehammer of incited proletarian masses would instantly succeed in doing, as in the autumn of 1918...' It was from this fanatically anti-Marxist, anti-proletarian viewpoint that Hitler rejected and attacked parliamentary democracy. Not so much for what it was or seemed to represent in itself, but because it was, by virtue of its formal commitment to the principle of popular rule, unable to take the extreme measures necessary to defeat the revolutionary Marxist movement: 'They [the 'incited proletarian masses'] would drive it home to the bourgeois world how insane it is to imagine that they can oppose Jewish world domination with the methods of Western democracy.' (A. Hitler: *Mein Kampf,* p.377)

Reich, we see in such disastrous operation, and in the economic sphere, the system of a trade union movement which does not serve the real interests of the workers, but exclusively the destructive [i.e. revolutionary] purposes of the international world Jew. *In precisely the measure in which the economy is withdrawn from the influence of the personality principle and instead exposed to the influences and effects of the masses, it must lose its efficacy in serving all and benefitting all, and gradually succumb to a sure regression. All the shop organisations which, instead of taking into account the interests of their employees, strive to gain influence on production, serve the same purpose. They injure collective achievement, and thus in reality injure individual achievement...* The folkish philosophy is basically distinguished from the Marxist philosophy by the fact that it not only recognises the value of race, but with it the importance of the personality, which it therefore makes one of the pillars of its entire edifice.[7] (emphasis added)

That fascism has been the instrument for the crushing of the individual's personality, and his total subordination to the imperialist drive for profit and to war, and that Marxism seeks as its goal the liberation of the individual from this same oppression, is really not the main point here. What has to be stressed is that these conceptions were maturing in Hitler's mind at precisely the point when he launched himself on his chosen career as a 'socialist' and 'revolutionary', as an aspiring leader of the very masses he despised as ignorant, inferior and totally unable to guide their own destinies. As we have repeatedly contended, Hitler's sole strategic orientation was towards a counter-revolutionary alliance with the big bourgeoisie, a bloc in which the Nazi leadership would defend its allies against the threat of revolution in return for its being ceded the dominant positions for its main cadres (drawn almost exclusively from the petty-bourgeoisie) in the government. *The quarrel was over politics, not economics.* Hence Hitler's lack of interest in this most vital branch of human activity, and the relatively small importance he placed on it as a determinant of historical development. It was as if Hitler was saying to the bourgeoisie:

> You have been selected by nature, through the ruthless working out of its aristocratic principle of the survival of the fittest,* to own and dispose of the nation's wealth, and you rightly cherish and defend this nature-given right against those who seek to subvert it. But by your

* This is no exaggeration. In the same chapter of *Mein Kampf* Hitler declares: '...as in economic life, the able men cannot be appointed from above, but must struggle through for themselves, and just as the endless schooling, ranging from the smallest business to the largest enterprise, occurs spontaneously, with life alone giving the examinations, obviously political minds cannot be discovered.' (Ibid, p.449) And, in another even more explicit comment on the allegedly 'natural' rights and origins of business tycoons, Hitler once said: 'The capitalists have worked their way to the top through their capacity, and on the basis of this selection, which again only proves their higher race, they have a right to lead.' (Hitler to Otto Strasser, May 22, 1930, cited in O. Strasser: *Hitler and I*, p.113.)

failure to apply this same principle to the administering of the affairs of state, the selection of those who stand guard over your own property, you place your prized possessions and rights in the gravest jeopardy, for you delegate the running of the state to those who not only do not recognise this aristocratic principle, but are dedicated to eliminating it from every walk of life from culture and government to the army and above all, the running of the economy. In other words, it would lead, step by step, through the gradual encroachment by the trade unions and works councils on your property rights — for which provision has been made in Article 165 of the Weimar Constitution, and against which your parties voted in the Reichstag — to final and total expropriation. The destruction of the national economy — the long term goal of Jewish Marxism and Jewish loan capital — would have been achieved, and entirely because of your criminal refusal to apply consistently the very principle to which you owe your present position of leadership in the economy. And so there is only one answer. If you wish to remain leaders of the economy, you must break your compact with the Weimar system and strike out on an entirely new course. You must smash parliament, and above all, you must smash the workers' movement, for until that has been done, you will never be safe, never be free from the pressure of the masses.

This was the message Hitler hammered home over and over again in a series of meetings and secret conversations with business leaders between 1920 and 1933, and it was one which only began to make sense to those who counted, when all other methods had been tried and found wanting.

Yet such an outcome seemed utterly improbable as Hitler commenced his duties as political officer in Captain Mayr's Abteiling I b/P, even when by dint of his undoubted prowess as an orator, he found himself entrusted with the task of 'decontaminating' soldiers infected with socialist ideas during their stay in the Soviet Union as prisoners-of-war. In this capacity he penned what is believed to be his first political document, a reply to a letter written to Captain Mayr by one of his former agents, one Adolf Gemlich, who expressed alarm that the 'Jewish' Marxists were appearing to gain the upper hand in the new Germany. Hitler's reply, dated September 16, 1919, indicates that he had indeed by this date arrived at the conceptions which were to shape his political strategy for the remainder of his life. Anti-semitism by itself was not enough, he explained. The final goal must be the creation of a ruthless dictatorship that could carry through not merely the removal of the Jews from public life, but their physical elimination, what Hitler prophetically termed the 'final solution'.

Four days before writing this letter, Hitler had, in the course of his work as an army political agent, attended a meeting of the tiny 'German Workers' Party' where none other than Feder happened to be one of the speakers. Small though this group was — when

Hitler joined it he was presented with a membership card numbered seven — it nevertheless had origins and associations which
linked it with far more elevated circles of Munich society than its
humble meeting place and modest means would suggest.

As we have already pointed out, the DAP first saw the light of
day as a 'plebeian' offshoot of the Fatherland Front, an ultra-
chauvinist breakaway from the Conservatives, which with
support from several important industrialists and military
leaders, stridently opposed a negotiated peace with the allies when
this idea began to gain ground in more liberal sections of the
bourgeoisie after 1916. These intransigent Pan-Germans dimly
perceived the need to win a degree of popular support for their
policies, and to this end looked benignly on the formation of
patriotic 'workers' groups which espoused and propagated their
imperialistic views to a proletarian audience, however small it
might be. And so was born the Munich 'Free Labour Committee
for a Good Peace', founded by the engineer Anton Drexler on
March 7, 1918. Horrified by the growth of anti-war sentiments in
the working class — they had even begun to take hold of a section
of the traditionally backward Munich proletariat — he gathered
around himself a small group of skilled artisans and craftsmen in
the city's railway workshops on a programme of all-out support
for the Kaiser's war and an equally uncompromising opposition
to all and any manifestations of democracy and Marxism in the
German body politic. Drexler's support dwindled as the war grew
more and more unpopular with the workers, till in October 1918
he was almost totally isolated even in his own former stronghold.
The overthrow of the Wittelsbach dynasty was a further body-
blow to Bavarian and Munich ultra-rightists and it seemed to
many that it was only a matter of time before the rising workers'
movement would make a clean sweep of them all. But here events
moved directly — and tragically — parallel to those in Berlin.
True, the Eisner regime veered further to the left, but like its
counterpart, the Ebert Provisional Government, it never settled
accounts with those who sought its downfall at the first
opportunity. How else can we explain the survival of out-and-out
racialist organisations such as the Thule Society, which despite its
cultural pretensions, functioned as a meeting place for counter-
revolutionaries and would-be assassins.* Apart from organising
the infiltration of the Eisner government's security forces, the
society also attempted to establish links with more popularly-
based *volkisch* groups in the city, and for this purpose one of their

---

* The Thule Society, whose emblem was the Swastika, was the Bavarian branch of
the Pan-German Teutonic Order, and at its peak had a membership of 1,500, nearly
all of whom were drawn from the 'cream' of Munich society — aristocrats, army
officers, professors, publicists, etc.

number, Karl Harrer, formed a so-called 'Political Workers' Circle' to spread the anti-semitic gospel amongst the more backward elements of the Munich proletariat. Harrer's circle lacked one essential however — workers. The search for a genuine 'national-minded' proletarians eventually brought the Thule Society, through the intermediary of Harrer's empty 'Circle', into contact with Drexler and his tiny following of railway workshop engineers.' At Harrer's instigation, Drexler took the step — momentous as it proved for history — of launching the German Workers' Party, a title which, as we have already suggested, was in all probability derived from the Bohemian organisation of the same name. The founding meeting of the new party, on January 5, 1919, was held quite openly under the benevolent protection of the Eisner government. No doubt the Munich social democracy believed such seemingly absurd grouplets — there were fewer than forty present at this inaugural meeting — were as much beneath its contempt as were the new party's pretensions to speak on behalf of the German worker. Yet if we examine the DAP's programme, we will find contained in it all that was essential to national socialism: rejection of the class struggle, opposition to 'Jewish' stock exchange capital, support for 'creative' 'national' capital and a call for solidarity between all workers of 'hand and brain' in a struggle against international Marxism.

And so we can establish a direct lineage, organisational as well as political, from the highest levels of German bourgeois and Junker society down to the formation of the Hitler movement; from the Junker Conservatives, through the Fatherland Front and the Thule Society to Drexler's DAP on the one side of the 'family tree', and on the other, Hitler as a professional army political agent of this same bourgeios-Junker class. The two lines intersected in Munich on the night of September 12, 1919, when Hitler attended his first meeting of the DAP. But before continuing with the genealogy of the NSDAP, we should look again at the political forces and individuals which were gathering in Munich under the very nose of the Eisner government. The most notorious of these was without doubt Alfred Rosenberg, the author of that preposterous essay in national socialist 'philosophy' and historical demonology, *The Myth of the Twentieth Century*. The entry of Rosenberg into German *volkisch* politics, (via his membership of the Thule Society) and thence into the Nazi party, had a truly symbolic significance, for it represented the unification of two allied, but until then, disparate movements of extreme reaction: the Russian and the German. For Rosenberg was a German Balt who fled the Russian Revolution whilst an art student in Moscow. Before departing, he was introduced to the phantasies of the *Protocols* by a Russian anti-semite, and he brought to Munich their message of a world Jewish conspiracy which set as its final goal the destruction of the 'gentiles' by means of a Marxist-led proletarian revolution.* This unbelievably clumsy forgery belongs to that species of 'anti-capitalism' which Marx and Engels denoted in the *Communist Manifesto* as 'Feudal Socialism'. It portrays the aristocracy as the true friend and defender of the proletariat, and the Jew, both in his usurious and revolutionary guises, as its sworn enemy. Thus the *Protocols* not only declared the workers' movement to be under the control of the mythical 'Elders of Zion', but even claimed credit for all the great bourgeois-democratic revolutions. Each and every forward stride of the peoples was but another move in the secret chess game being played by the Elders. The proletariat was nothing but a pawn in their hands, just as, in its time, had been the revolutionary bourgeoisie. For all its lunacy, this view of history gained widespread support in Russia,** where

* The following words are put into the mouths of the 'Elders of Zion': 'We appear on the scene as the alleged saviours of the worker from this [capitalist] oppression when we propose to him to enter the ranks of our fighting forces — Socialists, Anarchists, Communists ...By want and the envy and hatred which it engenders we shall move the mobs and with their hands we shall wipe out all those who hinder us on our way ...We shall create by aid of gold, which is all in our hands, a universal economic crisis whereby we shall throw upon the streets whole mobs of workers simultaneously in all the countries of Europe ...Remember the French Revolution, to which it was we who gave the name 'Great': the secrets of its preparations are well known to us for it was wholly the work of our hands. Ever since that time we have been leading the peoples from one disenchantment to another, so that in the end they should turn also from us in favour of that King-Despot of the blood of Zion, whom we are preparing for the world.' (*Protocols*, pp.24-26.)

** And not only Russia. While *The Times* equivocated over the genuineness of the Protocols when they first appeared — in 1920 — in English translation, the staunchly Conservative *Morning Post* (the forerunner of the equally reactionary *Daily Telegraph*) was quite certain. The paper published no fewer than 18 articles in the summer of that year on the theme of the world-Jewish conspiracy, which was unfolding in the Soviet Union before the eyes of the paper's horrified readers. (So enthusiastic was the response to this anti-semitic filth amongst the *Morning Post's* upper and middle class readers, the articles were republished in book form with a preface by the paper's editor). The right-wing London weekly review, *The Spectator* did not venture to declare the *Protocols* to be genuine, but neither did it expose them as the obvious forgery they were: 'Upon that much vexed subject of the authenticity of the Protocols of Zion we shall not enter, except to say that if the document is a forgery, as is alleged, then it is one of the most remarkable in the history of literature.' (*The Spectator*, October 16, 1920). Henry Ford, as notorious an anti-semite as he was an enemy of trade unionism and socialism, had no doubts, his private daily paper, the *Dearborn Independent*, proclaimed to the citizens of Detroit on July 10, 1920: 'It is too terribly real for fiction, too well sustained for speculation, too deep in its knowledge of the secret springs of life for forgery.' Ford himself endorsed the authenticity of the *Protocols* in the classic language of American pragmatism: 'The only statement I care to make about the *Protocols* is that they fit in with what is going on. They are sixteen years old and they have fitted the world situation up to this time. They fit it now.' (*New York World*, February 17, 1921.) But it was in Germany that the *Protocols* found their most avid audience. First published in German in 1920, they were destined to become the gospel of the entire *volkisch*

the aristocracy felt itself threatened both by the rise of large-scale capitalism and its inevitable polar opposite, an industrial proletariat. Its slanderous legends were retailed in the highest court circles, and, after 1905, provided the counter-revolutionary 'Union of the Russian People' (the 'Black Hundreds') with all that it required in the way of 'ideology' and programme. Based largely on the town petty-bourgeoisie — small shopkeepers, artisans etc. — and the criminal underworld, it was led by a motley assortment of clergymen, ultra-right wing politicians, police agents and aristocrats. The rallying cry of the Black Hundreds was brutally simple — 'Beat the Yids and save Russia.' Founded like the Nazi party to beat back the rising tide of revolution, it very quickly developed the strategy of mobilising the more backward middle class and proletarian elements against the revolutionary movement, using the age-old ruse of anti-semitism to incite mass hatred against bourgeois liberalism and Marxism alike. Typical of Black Hundred propaganda at this time, and providing an instance of how it borrowed from the forged *Protocols*, was the following proclamation:

> The efforts to replace the autocracy of the divinely appointed Tsar by a constitution and a parliament are inspired by those bloodsuckers, the Jews, the Armenians and the Poles. Beware of the Jews! All the evil, all the misfortune of our country comes from the Jews, Down with the traitors, down with the constitution!

Such raging anti-semitism, not one iota less murderous than that later employed by the Nazis, enjoyed the support of none other than the head of the Romanov dynasty, Nicholas II, even though certain of his politicians looked askance at the 'plebeian' methods and following of the Black Hundred movement itself.*

movement, going through no less than 33 editions, before Hitler's accession to power in 1933. Perhaps this statistic, more than any other, measures the degree to which the German bourgeoisie and wide sections of the middle class had become saturated with fanatical chauvinist hatred for the Jews. As Norman Cohn, in his excellent book on the history of the *Protocols* makes clear, this most infamous of all forgeries became the Third Reich's 'warrant for genocide'. And when the time came, years of anti-semitic indoctrination ensured there would be no shortage of executioners.

* Thus Prime Minister Witte wrote of the Russian anti-semitic movement that it was 'patriotic to the depths of its soul ...but its patriotism is primitive ...Most of its leaders are upstarts [they] concentrate all their efforts on unleashing the lowest possible impulses in the benighted, savage masses ...its leaders are political villains, it has secret sympathisers in court circles and amongst nobles with all kinds of titles — people who seek their salvation in lawlessness and have as their slogan: "Not we for the people, but the people for the good of our stomachs" ...And the Tsar dreams of restoring greatness to Russia with the help of this party. Poor Tsar...' (quoted in N. Cohn: *Warrant for Genocide,* p.111, London, 1967) The similarity between Witte's reaction to 'plebeian' counter-revolution and the repugnance felt towards the Nazis by his German counterparts is quite remarkable. But it did not prevent either from resorting to the services of the 'lawless' and 'savage' plebeians when the only alternative seemed to be defeat at the hands of the Marxist-led proletariat. Nevertheless, there are also important differences between the two movements,

When the revolutionary threat was at its greatest, the Tsar's government poured funds into the coffers of the Black Hundreds to finance its counter-revolutionary activities, which embraced not only the wide dissemination of anti-Marxist and anti-Jewish propaganda, but organised pogroms. In one year alone, 2.5 million roubles found their way from the royal exchequer into the hands of this gang of murderers and Jew-baiters. It was this tradition of virulent anti-semitism, allied with a hatred of communism, that Rosenberg brought with him to Munich in the winter of 1918-1919, and which drew him irresistibly towards the city's most reactionary political circles.

Rosenberg's first acquaintance of note was the playwright and translator Dietrich Eckart. This kindred Jew-baiter and anti-Marxist was preparing to publish an anti-communist journal inspired by all the usual *volkisch* garbage about a world Jewish conspiracy of Marxism and high finance, and Rosenberg soon became involved in the venture. As it turned out, they did not found a new magazine but took over the *Munchener Beobachter* of Rudolf von Sebettendorff, who had himself bought it in July 1918 to publicise the theories of the Thule Society, of which he was the founder. Once under Eckart's proprietorship, the organ changed its name to the *Volkischer Beobachter* (the 'Racist' Observer). Eckart and Rosenberg may well have differed in terms of genuine intellectual powers, but they shared a common passion for the most reactionary strands of German idealist philosophy — notably Schopenhauer — and they were soon engaged in the common task of doling out a weekly dose of anti-semitic poison to the more gullible of the Munich petty-bourgeoisie. Eckart's *volkisch* views had already brought him into the ranks of the German Workers' Party before Hitler joined it, and it was through his good offices that the latter met not only Rosenberg, but a far wider and more influential circle of white Russian emigres, who saw in the young movement a possible source of support for their campaign to regain their lost positions and possessions in the Soviet Union. Eckart also introduced Hitler into German 'society', one of his first converts being Frau Helene

which relate not so much to their social composition, combat methods or ideology but their historical juxtaposition to the major classes in Germany and Russia. The Black Hundreds sought to mobilise 'the people' in defence of the monarchy against what was essentially, despite its proletarian vanguard, a bourgeois democratic revolution, even though the bourgeoisie in its majority recoiled from the implications of its 'own' revolution. The national socialists did not come out as defenders of throne or altar, though they were not averse, when the opportunity presented itself or the tactical situation demanded it, to aligning themselves with supporters of both. Although combatting and finally destroying bourgeois democracy, the Nazis' main — in fact only — target was the organisations of the German proletariat. Fascism is therefore, contrary to the claims of popular front Stalinism, the plebeian instrument of *bourgeois* and not *feudal*, counter-revolution.

Bechstein, the richly endowed wife of the famous piano manufacturer. In turn, through the Bechsteins, who held pseudo-cult-
ural *soirees* in Berlin and Munich to round up fresh support for
the Nazi cause, and Eckart's influential position in the Thule
Society, Hitler gained access to people whom he would otherwise
never have met, and without whose aid the young Nazi movement
would have barely kept its head above water. Cash was found
from these circles to keep the newly-acquired organ, the
Volkischer Beobachter, running first as a weekly, and then, after
March 1923, and with Rosenberg now its editor, as a daily.* The
'Russian' element in the formative years of the Nazi party was
important — and in some ways decisive — for its subsequent
evolution. Up until 1919, Hitler knew and cared little about
political developments outside the German-speaking world.
When he spoke of Marxism, it was the German social democratic
movement that he had in mind, and not the Marxism of the
Russian Bolsheviks. His horizons began to broaden only with the
arrival in Munich of emigres such as Rosenberg and the even
more influential Balt, Max Erwin von Scheubner-Richter. They
had witnessed — and in the latter's case, actually fought against
— Marxism in its most militantly revolutionary form, by which
the 'Marxism' of Ebert and Noske paled in comparison. They
provided the *volkisch* movement with an internationalist
perspective which it had previously lacked — internationalist that
is in the sense that Rosenberg and his co-thinkers saw the need to
combat Marxism on a continental and indeed global scale.** At

* 'Angels' contributing to the struggling paper's finances included Captain Mayr's
political department, which donated a large sum in December 1920 to help secure
Nazi ownership of the *Volkischer Beobachter*. Army influence was also reflected in
Hitler's choice of business manager for what had become the Nazi Party's official
organ — Max Amman, who had been a close friend of Hitler's during his period of
political service in *Abteilung I b/p*. Other donations came from Kurt Lüdecke, the
big business broker and buying agent who on the testimony of Alfred Rosenberg
'had money, foreign money ...and placed some of it at the disposal of the Party. He
even outfitted, at his own expense, a troop of the SA.' (A. Rosenberg: *Memoirs*,
p.60.)

** This Rosenberg did in an official state capacity after the Nazi victory in 1933,
heading the *Amt Osten* (Eastern Department) of the Foreign Political Office of the
NSDAP. In this capacity he was also involved in the propaganda and activity of the
Anti-Komintern, the anti-Soviet alliance concluded between Germany, Italy and
Japan, although this organisation was initially a sub-department of Göbbels'
Ministry of Propaganda. Preparatory to the invasion of the USSR in June 1941,
Rosenberg was appointed by Hitler (on April 20) as 'Commissioner for the Central
Control of Questions Connected with the Eastern European Region'. Proudly
sporting this grandiose title, Rosenberg now planned the plunder of the country
whose revolution he fled in 1918, and the physical extermination of its population by
mass murder and slow death by systematic starvation: 'The job of feeding the
German people stands this year without doubt, on top of the list of Germany's claims
on the East, and here the southern territories and the northern Caucasus will have to

the very centre of this outlook was an all-embracing hatred for the
Soviet Union, depicted in the writings of Rosenberg as the rule of
evil on earth. Eckart was a rapid convert to Rosenberg's anti-Bolshevik crusade, and soon they were publishing a spate of pamphlets and articles on the Soviet menace to aryan culture and civilisation. Naturally, their anti-Bolshevism had to be given a
'populist' flavour if it was to find favour amongst the broader public, and so we find Rosenberg writing, very much after the style he
had gleaned from his reading of the *Protocols:* 'The Black, the
Red and the Gold Internationals represent the dreams of Jewish
philosophers from Ezra, Ezekiel and Nehemia to Marx, Rothschild and Trotsky'. (The three 'internationals' were that of the
Roman Catholic Church, the Communist International, and international Jewry respectively. It was not to prove the last occasion
on which trotsky found his name linked with a mythical
conspiracy!)

It took Hitler some time to find his bearings in these — for him
— rather sophisticated political surroundings. Ebert.
Scheidemann, Noske, Luxemburg, Lenin — all were Marxists,
and there was nothing more to be said about it. But under the
influence of the two Balts, and also as a result of their success in
arousing interest in the Nazi movement amongst richer white
Russian emigres and even pretenders to the vacant Russian
throne itself, Hitler began to evolve a foreign policy to
supplement his already well-defined political strategy for winning
power in Germany. Among the more prominent and generous of
Hitler's white-Russian backers were the pretender Prince Kyrill of
Coberg, and the Russian industrialists Gukassov, Nobel and
Lenissov. For Scheubner-Richter was not only active in the Nazi
party (he first met Hitler in October 1920) but a front rank
organiser of contacts between the various and often rival Russian
emigre groupings. It was he who served for a brief period as
liaison officer between the emigration and General Wrangel, and
when this mission proved abortive as a result of Wrangel's defeat
in south Russia towards the end of 1920, he convened the
monarchist 'unity' conference held at Bad Reichenall in May
1921. His goal transcended that of its main participants in that he
not only desired the restoration of the old regime in Russia, but a
union of the two counter-revolutionary movements — 'brown'
and 'white' — as the foundation for an anti-Marxist bloc
dominating the entire European continent. The struggle for this
goal, Scheubner-Richter wrote two weeks before the Munich

serve as a balance for the feeding of the German people. We see absolutely no reason
for any obligation on our part to feed also the Russian people with the products of
that surplus'. (A. Rosenberg: speech to his staff, June 20, 1941, *N.D. 1058-PS.*)
Rosenberg, Hitler's mentor in Soviet affairs, was now carrying out his Fuhrer's
'eastern policy', as enunciated in *Mein Kampf,* to the letter.

Putsch (he was one of its 16 fatal Nazi casualties) 'will be waged under the slogan Soviet Star against Swastika. And the Swastika will prevail!'

It should not be overlooked that at this time (1920-23) right-wing and even *volkisch* circles were by no means agreed on the future direction that German foreign policy should follow. In the general staff, there were some — Hans von Seeckt was perhaps their most articulate and brilliant spokesman — who saw in the Soviet Union a valuable counter-weight to the Versailles powers' military and economic supremacy in Europe. For the military it was simply a matter of tactical and strategical expediency, though there was also a very genuine admiration for the way in which the Red Army had defended the revolution against what seemed to be impossible military odds. But there were others on the far right, more 'ideologically' inclined, who sought to construct an amal-gam of Bolshevism and German nationalism, of the armed forces and the organised German proletariat. A war of revenge would then be waged against the west — a 'revolutionary' war, for it would not be fought in the interests of the decadent bourgeoisie, but for the greatness of the entire German nation. Von Seeckt referred to this tendency — utterly utopian, where it was not a conscious stratagem to trap the war-weary German working class into yet another blood bath on behalf of its class enemies — in a secret report to Presdient Ebert on June 26, 1920 entitled *Germany's immediate political tasks:*

> The ideas of the Russian Revolution exert a powerful attraction for our epoch. Such [revolutionary] developments in the midst of a great crisis in world history cannot in the long run be held down by armed force. It is therefore essential to take the initiative and harness them to the service of the people's future. Wide sectors of the German people would regard any fight against Russia as a fight against their own ideals ...It would swing the broad masses sharply against us and in the end probably bring Bolshevism in its worst form to Germany ...The Entente fears the pan-Russian movement ...because, in the sphere of foreign policy it is directed against the system which won this war, against Anglo-Saxon capitalism and imperialism ...A Russian defeat by the entente seems out of the question because that vast land mass and its peoples is inconceivable. The future belongs to Russia ...This must be said publicly and with the greatest frankness — for in this period of extraordinary difficulty for German internal politics we must win over the broad masses for our policy and lead the German people to ideas of unity ...At the same time we ought to give assurances that we wish to live in friendship with Russia ...and we ought to set our hopes on Russia, fully respecting the 1914 frontiers ...In this way we should have found a few words to draw everyone together, including the German nationalist circles, thereby laying the foundation for ways of overcoming disunity. State power ...needs ...a politically intact, well-disciplined army with leaders who understand the modern age and the people's plight. But it is even more important for the government to

deal with the present troubles by internal reforms.

Hitler entirely rejected this 'eastern orientation.' That he came to do so was to a large degree attributable to the ideological influence of Rosenberg and Scheubner-Richter and — though in a different fashion — to the strategic requirements of the white-Russian emigre circles into which Hitler was introduced by these same two fanatically anti-communist Balts. The fight against advocates of an eastern orientation occupied Hitler for many years, and was only finally resolved on June 22, 1941, the day the Nazis launched their fateful invasion of the Soviet Union. And it was a dispute whose origins dated back to well before the First World War, when German imperialist strategy oscillated between what Hitler termed a 'colonial' and 'continental' policy. Successive chancellors associated with them rose and fell as these two strategic options gained or lost support in military and bourgeois circles. By the time Hitler came to write *Mein Kampf*, he had irrevocably decided where the destiny of German imperialism lay:

> For Germany ...the only possibility for carrying out a healthy territorial policy lay in the acquisition of new land in Europe itself. Colonies cannot serve this purpose unless they seem in large part suited for settlement by Europeans. But in the 19th century such colonial territories were no longer obtainable by peaceful means. Consequently, such a colonial policy could only have been carried out by means of a hard struggle which, however, would have been carried on to a much better purpose, not for territories outside Europe, but for the land on the home continent itself.[8]

The historical basis for Hitler's repudiation of a 'colonial' policy was therefore Germany's retarded development as a major capitalist power, and its consequent debilitating effect on the struggle of German imperialism for a colonial position commensurate with its French and British rivals. And by the same token, if Germany was to seek its colonies in the European land mass itself, then it could only turn eastwards, thus parting company with the Bismarckian strategy of securing the German rear by a political and military understanding with the rulers of Russia. The Romanovs, for centuries the 'gendarmes of Europe' had gone. Now Russia was ruled by a party and ideology which proclaimed as its final aim the establishment of world-wide socialism. This change was to weigh more heavily in Nazi strategic thinking than the prospect of a tactical alliance with the Red Army against the Entente powers:

> If land was desired in Europe, it could only be obtained by and large at the expense of Russia, and this meant that the new Reich must again set itself on the march along the road of the Teutonic Knights of old to obtain by the German sword sod for the German plough and daily bread for the nation.[9]

It is obvious that for all his archaic imagery and precedents,

Hitler approached foreign policy from the standpoint of creating
an autarchic unit in central Europe, one in which German
industry and technique would be supplemented by the rich
agricultural and raw material regions of the Soviet Union,
notably the Ukraine, traditionally the 'bread basket of Europe'.
Now the entire USSR was to serve as the larder of the Third
Reich, a strategy whose wisdom and efficacy was doubted by
many who were otherwise in sympathy with Hitler's counter-
revolutionary goals:

> Since these very circles are beginning to divert the tendency of our
> foreign policy in the most catastrophic way from any real defence of
> the folkish interests of our people, placing it instead in the service of
> their fantastic ideology. I feel it incumbent upon me to discuss for my
> supporters the most important question in the field of foreign affairs,
> our relation to Russia ...The foreign policy of the folkish state must
> safeguard the existence on this planet embodied in the state, by
> creating a healthy, viable natural relation between the nation's
> population and growth on the one hand and the quantity and quality
> of its soil on the other hand ...Only an adequately large space on this
> earth assures a nation of freedom of existence ...If the National
> Socialist movement really wants to be consecrated by history with a
> great mission for our nation, it must be permeated by knowledge and
> filled with pain at our true situation in the world; boldly and conscious
> of its goal, it must take up the struggle against the aimlessness and
> incompetence which have hitherto guided our German nation in the
> line of foreign affairs. Then, without consideration of 'traditions' and
> prejudices, it must find the courage to gather our people and their
> strength for an advance along the road that will lead this people from
> its present restricted living space to new land and soil ...The National
> Socialist movement must strive to eliminate the disproportion between
> our population and our area — viewing this latter as a source of food
> as well as a basis for power politics — between our historical past and
> the hopelessness of our present impotence ...Land and soil as the goal
> of our foreign policy, and a philosophically established, uniform
> foundation as the aim of political activity at home.[10]

And to achieve these intimately linked and mutually
conditioning goals — those of fascist dictatorship at home and a
war of conquest against the Soviet Union — Hitler was even
prepared to relegate in strategic importance the longed-for war of
revenge against France:

> [Such a war] can and will achieve meaning only if it offers the rear
> cover for an enlargement of our people's living space in Europe. For it
> is not in colonial acquisitions that we must see the solution of this
> problem, but exclusively in the acquisition of a territory for settlement
> ...And so we National Socialists consciously draw a line beneath the
> foreign policy tendency of our pre-war period. We take up where we
> left off six hundred years ago. We stop the endless German movement
> to the south and west, and turn our gaze towards the land in the east.
> At long last we break off the colonial and commercial policy of the pre-
> war period and shift to the soil policy of the future.

> If we speak of soil in Europe today, we can primarily have in mind
> only Russia and her vassal border states.[11]

Nor was it simply a question of 'soil', as Hitler's quasi-mystical
language and romanticised view of earlier penetrations of the east
would seem to suggest. The invasion, colonisation and
'Germanisation' of the Soviet Union was also a political task, the
international projection of national socialism's war to the death
against Marxism in Germany. To those nationalists who still contemplated an alliance with the USSR, Hitler replied:

> Never forget that the rulers of present-day Russia are common blood-
> stained criminals, that they are the scum of humanity which, favoured
> by circumstances, overran a great state in a tragic hour, slaughtered
> and wiped out thousands of her leading intellectuals in wild bloodlust,
> and now for almost ten years have been carrying on the most cruel
> tyrannical regime of all time ...Do not forget that the international Jew
> who completely dominates Russia today regards Germany, not as an
> ally, *but as a state destined to the same fate.* And you do not make
> pacts with anyone whose sole interest is the destruction of his partner
> ...*The danger to which Russia succumbed* [i.e. proletarian revolution]
> *is always present for Germany.* Only a bourgeois simpleton is capable
> of imagining that Bolshevism has been exorcised ...In Russian
> Bolshevism we must see the attempt undertaken by the Jews in the
> 20th century to achieve world domination ...*Germany is today the
> great next war aim of Bolshevism.*[12] (emphasis added)

Tragically, due to the rise of Stalinism in the Soviet Union,
which resulted in the reactionary, nationalist policy of 'socialism
in one country' being foisted on the parties of the Communist
International, (of which the KPD was numerically the largest and
strategically the most important) Germany was not to become the
'next great war aim' of what began as Bolshevism, but under
Stalin's leadership, became transformed into its counter-
revolutionary opposite. Nevertheless, this does not negate the
validity from a German imperialist standpoint of Hitler's contention that any alliance, however fleeting or grounded in 'real
politik' with the Soviet Union — at least while its rulers pursued
the Bolshevik goal of world revolution — could only undermine
not just the strategic aims of German imperialism, which Hitler
insisted should lie in the conquest of the Soviet east, *but the
prosecution of the struggle against communism at home.* Hitler's
great merit as far as the bourgeoisie was concerned — and this
was something they only came to realise in the last year of the
Weimar Republic — was that he offered them — at a price — *a
unified counter-revolutionary plan of action on a continental, and
not merely national scale.* This is where national socialism scored
over its competitors among the 'national' parties of the
bourgeoisie. And it was also why Trotsky warned, in the months
preceding Hitler's victory, and especially against the criminal
policies of the Stalinists that were clearing the road for such a

Nazi triumph, that if Hitler was permitted by the leaders of the the German proletariat to come to power, he would 'become the super-Wrangel of the world bourgeoisie.'[13]* Hitler was still conducting much the same polemical war three years later in a work that remained unpublished for many years and has passed down to posterity under the title *Hitler's Secret Book*. The extent and obduracy of the resistance to his 'continental' imperialist strategy amongst *volkisch* circles, not to speak of the bourgeoisie itself, is evidenced by the amount of space Hitler devotes to the question of foreign policy in this work. And once again, there emerges the same fundamental critique of the 'political bourgeisie' that was so evident in Hitler's attack on the domestic policies of the main nationalist parties of Weimar Germany:

> In terms of foreign policy the national socialist movement is distinguished from previous parties by, for example, the following: the foreign policy of the national bourgeoisie has in truth always been only a border policy; as against that, the policy of the National Socialist movement will always be a territorial one. In its boldest plans ...the German bourgeoisie will aspire to the unification of the German nation, but in reality it will finish with a botched up refutation of the borders. The National Socialist movement, on the contrary, will always let its foreign policy be determined by the necessity to secure the space necessary to the life of our people ...Thus the point of departure of its thinking is wholly different from that of the bourgeois world ...Nevertheless, a part of German youth, *especially from bourgeois circles,* will be able to understand me. Neither I nor the National Socialist movement expect to find any support whatsoever in the circles of the *political* national bourgeoisie active at present, but we certainly know that at least a part of the youth will find its way into our ranks.[14] (emphasis added)

Hitler was perfectly content to remain a voice in the *volkisch*

---

* At the very time when Stalin was beginning to look towards an ultra-nationalistic regime in Germany as a counterweight to what he wrongly considered to be an interventionist threat from French imperialism (presumably mounted through its semi-vassal state, Poland) Trotsky wrote: None of the 'normal' bourgeois parliamentary governments can risk a war at the present time [1931] of immense internal complications [Precisely the point made by von Seeckt in his report to President Ebert!] But if Hitler comes to power and proceeds to crush the vanguard of the German workers, pulverising and demoralising the whole proletariat, the fascist government will be the only government capable of waging war against the USSR ...The crushing of the German proletariat by the fascists would already comprise at least half of the collapse of the Soviet republic.' (L. Trotsky: *Germany, the Key to the International Situation,* November 26, 1931, in L. Trotsky: *The Struggle Against Fascism in Germany,* pp.126-127.) And Hitler's armies did occupy roughly this proportion of European Russia, to be driven out, not by the genius of Stalin's military leadership, as the official Soviet history textbooks are once again claiming, but by the heroism and avoidable sacrifice of the Soviet working class and peasantry. Their German comrades having been defeated in the battle for power in Berlin, the Soviet proletariat was only able to check the brown onslaught, which began in 1933, at the very gates of Moscow and Leningrad, and in the shattered tractor factories of Stalingrad.

wilderness seemingly isolated from and even opposed to the main policy trends in the German ruling class. And this was just as true of foreign as domestic issues. He was convinced that time and events — accelerated by the bursting of the Weimar bubble — would prove him right:

> I'm afraid ...that I will never be understood by my bourgeois critics, at least as long as success does not prove to them the soundness of our action...Just as the National Socialist movement not only criticises democratic policy, but possesses its own philosophically grounded programme, likewise in the sphere of foreign policy, it must not only recognise what others have done wrongly, but deduce its own action on the basis of this knowledge.[15]

In this respect, Hitler was far ahead of all but the most astute bourgeois circles. Even before the war, he had already drawn the main lesson of Bismarck's failure to crush social democracy, and in the immediate post-1918 period, he arrived at similarly critical conclusions concerning what he considered to be the false international strategy of the German ruling class. Deprived of arms by the Versailles Treaty (its military clauses forbade arms manufacture in Germany, and limited the army to 100,000 officers and men) the bourgeoisie, so Hitler claimed, thought it could restore Germany's 'greatness' by purely economic means. This, he argued with great passion, was tantamount to committing national suicide. His alternative strategy was brutally simple, and proceeded in three stages: first, utterly destroy the 'pacifists' and the internationalists as a force in German politics; next re-arm the German nation, only this time for an onslaught on the Soviet east. Finally, and only then, the conditions would have been created for an economic flourishing, the goal so fervently sought by the German bourgeoisie:

> Blood values, the idea of personality, and the instinct for self-preservation slowly threatened to be lost to the German people. Internationalism triumphs in its stead and destroys our folk value, democracy spreads by stifling the idea of personality and in the end an evil pacifist liquid manure poisons the mentality favoring self-preservation ...*The great domestic task of the future lies in the elimination of these general symptoms of decay of our people. This is the mission of the National Socialist movement.* A new nation must arise from this work which overcomes even the worst evils of the present, the cleavage between the classes, for which the bourgeoisie and Marxism are equally guilty.* The aim of this reform work of a domestic political kind, must finally be the regaining of our people's strength to represent its vital interests abroad ...Whoever wants to act

---

* A typical demagogic turn of phrase, for elsewhere in the same work, Hitler writes: 'The German national bourgeosie, which alone is under discussion here — since international Marxism as such has no other aim but Germany's destruction — even today has learned nothing from the past ...' (*Hitler's Secret Book* 1928, pp.110-111, New York, 1961) Far from condemning them equally, Hitler finds fault with the

in the name of German honour today must first launch a merciless war against the internal defiling of German honour. They are not the enemies of yore, but they are the representatives of the November crime [i.e. November Revolution] that collection of Marxist demo-pacifists, destructive traitors of our country who pushed our people into its present state of powerlessness. To revile former enemies in the name of national honour and recognise the shameless allies of this enemy as the rulers within their own country — that suits the national dignity of this present day so-called national bourgeoisie.[16] (emphasis added)

Hitler was far more charitable towards the Pan-Germans, who at least had the virtue in his eyes of refusing to acknowledge the 'November criminals' as the legitimate rulers of Germany. But here too there was a fatal weakness, precisely that which he detected in the policies of the Schonerer movement in pre-1914 Vienna:

> ,...the foreign policy of the Wilhelmian period was in many ways viewed by not a few people as catastrophic and characterised accordingly. Innumerable warnings came, especially from the circles of the Pan-German League of that time, which were justified in the highest sense of the word ...[When the revolution came] what they had foretold for decades had now come to pass. We cannot think of these men [the Pan-German League pioneers]* without a deep compassion, men condemned by fate to foresee a collapse for 20 years, and who now, having not been heeded, and hence in no position to help, had to live to see their people's most tragic catastrophe ...[and] when the revolution shattered the Imperial sceptre and raised democracy to the throne, the critics of that time were as far from the possession of a weapon with which to overthrow democracy as formerly they had been from being able to influence the imperial government. In their decades of activity they had been geared so much to a purely literary treatment of these problems that they not only lacked the real means of power to express their opinion on a situation which was only a reaction to shouting in the streets [sic!] they had also lost the capacity to try to organise a manifestation of power which was to be more than a wave of written protests if it were to be really effective ...they could carry out their view in practice only if a large number of them have the opportunity of representing it. *And even if they wanted a thousand times to smash the political parties, they still indeed first had to form a political party which viewed as its task that of smashing the other parties.*[17] (emphasis added)

Although these strategic conceptions were set down in written form between 1924 and 1928, they in fact originated in the months

---

bourgeoisie only in so far as it has proved itself unable either to learn from the past or pursue a consistent national policy in the present and future, while Marxism is rejected out of hand as internationalist, and therefore by its very nature incapable of serving the 'national' cause.

* Among whom was numbered Max Weber, a co-author of the Weimar Con-stitution!

which followed Hitler's entry into the DAP, the precise period when he began to come under the influence of Rosenberg.

> *Since the year 1920* I have with all means and most persistently had to accustom the National Socialist movement to the idea of an alliance among Germany, Italy and England.* This was very difficult, since the 'God punish England' standpoint, first and foremost, still robbed our people of any capacity for clear and sober thinking in the sphere of foreign policy, and continued to hold it prisoner.[18] (emphasis added)

So before returning to Hitler's early activities in the DAP, it would be appropriate to look briefly at a representative sample of Rosenberg's literary excrement. Not to engage in a useless 'refutation' — fascism is least of all a tendency vulnerable to intellectual persuasion — but to glean both an insight into the mind of the man who was — justly or otherwise — regarded as the high priest of national socialism, and to see to what degree Rosenberg's brand of racial mysticism was related to the main stream of German subjective idealist philosophy. Despite his ponderous pseudo-erudition and, verbose rambling and at times only semi-coherent style, there is indeed a common thread running through all his writings; an *intuitionism* which we also encountered on a far higher intellectual and cultural plane in the writings of Schopenhauer, Nietzsche and also, though from a contrasting line of approach, Bergson. A reading of the following key extracts makes this clearer.

> The actions of history and the future no longer signify class struggle or warfare between Church dogmas, but rather the conflict between blood and blood, race and race, people and people. And this means conflict between spiritual values ...the values of race-soul, which stand behind the new world-picture as driving forces, still have not been brought to living consciousness. Soul means race viewed from within. And, vice-versa, race is the externalisation of soul.[19]

Thus the age-old German 'inwardness' — the religious expression of which was Lutheranism — now found a new and even more mystical language — that of Rosenberg's 'race-soul'. All human history must be viewed through its prism until, like Rosenberg,

---

* As in the earlier *Mein Kampf* Hitler still found it necessary to warn against the implications of a possible German-Soviet alliance: 'The belief in a German-Russia understanding is in itself fantastic as long as a regime rules in Russia which is permeated by one aim only: to carry over the Bolshevist poisoning to Germany. It is natural, therefore, for communist elements to agitate for a German Russian alliance. They thereby hope, rightfully, to be able to lead Germany her self to Bolshevism. It is incomprehensible, however, if national Germans believe that it is possible to achieve an understanding with a state whose great interest is the destruction of this very national Germany.' (*Hitler's Secret Book*, p.132.) Hitler actually only felt free to make tactical adjustments to this line when the Stalinist counter-revolution had, through the Moscow Trials and the mass purges that accompanied them, crushed Soviet supporters of a genuine internationlist perspective for the European working class. This became the basis for the Stalin-Hitler pact of August 1939, a treaty which in turn enabled German imperialism to defeat its enemies in the west before launching the long-awaited and prepared invasion of the USSR.

we discover such earth-shattering truths as 'at the latest excavation of the pyramid of Cheops at Mastabas, it was discovered that the princes and Queen Meres-Anah were depicted as having blond hair' or that 'in all the sagas, the legendary, myth-enshrouded Queen Nitokris is described as being blonde.'[19]

In all movements that undermined the rule of aristocracy Rosenberg detected the hidden hand of 'racial polluters'. Thus:

> By the middle of the fifth century the first steps towards chaos had been taken; mixed marriages between patricians and plebeians were legalised. For Rome, as for Persia and Hellas, mixed marriages signified the collapse of *Volk* and state. In AD 336, the first plebeians had already pushed their way into the Roman Assembly and around the year AD 300 there were reports of plebeian priests. In AD 287 the plebeian public assembly had been elevated to the position of being a state institution. Tradesmen and money changers hawked their wares [an early manifestation of the conspiracy between the 'money power' and democracy perhaps?]; ambitious apostate priests like Gracchi, driven perhaps by a generous but falsely presented sense of benevolence, displayed democratic tendencies. Others, such as Publius Claudius, openly placed themselves at the head of Roman city mobs.[20]

The frightening thing is not the lunacy of such notions, nor even that their author came to wield the power of life and death over millions of human beings, but that others took them seriously and actually embraced Rosenberg's phantasies as a guiding world outlook.*

Entirely in the German subjectivist tradition was Rosenberg's total rejection of reason and logic as a means of learning about and changing the world. And he shared Bergson's substitution of the intuitive method of cognition for that of the materialist world outlook developed by the natural scientists of the 18th and 19th centuries.

> In one forward-striving advance towards self, the solutions necessitated by atomism, mechanism, individualism and universalism, solutions to pedantically posited problems of existence, were transformed and nullified. Through this ...a new morality was established: the soul does not adhere to abstract rules imposed from the outside; neither does it move toward a goal posited from without; in no case does it go outside itself, but rather, comes to itself. With this, however, a rather different conception of truth is outlined: for us, truth does not mean that which is logical and that which is false; rather

---

* Despite his proclaimed hostility towards Christianity, Rosenberg was at pains to exonerate its founder from slanderous charges concerning his ethnic origins: 'As far as Jesus' ancestry is concerned, there is not the slightest reason to believe ...that Jesus was of Jewish ancestry, even if it be admitted that He had grown up in Jewish intellectual circles ...The thoroughly un-Jewish teachings of the 'Kingdom of heaven within us' strengthen this realisation.' (A. Rosenberg: *The Myth of the 20th Century*, in Alfred Rosenberg: *Selected Political Writings*, p.70.) It is significant that Rosenberg's proof of Christ's 'un-Jewishness' is the latter's Germanic 'inwardness' — in political terms a passive acceptance of the status quo.

it demands an organic answer to the question: fruitful or unfruitful, self-governed or unfree.[21]

This mystically-conceived pragmatism was derived from Nietzsche's notion of truth — namely that it was the prerogative of the powerful, the few, the elite. And Rosenberg invoked Nietzsche's authority — and it was great indeed with the more intellectually-inclined German middle and upper classes — to bolster his attacks on Marxism:

> He offered a thorough critique of the whole social structure, a critique of the Marxist movement, which at that time had already been falsely dubbed socialist — a critique which in logic [sic!] and detestation, is unthinkable even today. For him, Marxism is the tyranny of the least and the dumbest, i.e. of the superfluous, the envious and the hack-actor, carried to its final conclusion ...Nietzsche, above all, opposed the attempt to overthrow the property concept, because the overthrow of the property concept would encourage a destructive struggle for existence.[22]

In fact Rosenberg's own views on property allied him with Hitler and the rest of the Nazi 'conservatives', as he himself made clear in his own memoirs, written while awaiting execution at Nuremberg. His remarks on this question also underline with extra emphasis the nature and purpose of Hitler's polemic against the leaders of the bourgeois parties in Weimar Germany. The dispute was not about whether they should rule, but how:

> Hitler had come to the conclusion [in the immediate post-war period] that a just socialism had, *per se,* nothing to do with class war and inter-nationalism. To perpetuate class war was wrong. It would have to be eliminated. Thus he became an opponent of Marxism in all its mani-festations, and characterised it as a philosophy of government inimical to both the state and the working class. *As far as the workers were con-cerned, it was therefore a question of renouncing this doctrine as well as their opposition to both the farmer and the property owner.* The middle class [i.e. bourgeoisie] too had every reason to revise their attitude, they had failed to provide the working classes in their hour of dire need with leaders conversant with their requirements and had left them to the tender mercy of international propagandists. German nationalism, Hitler believed, was hemmed in by the nobility, while an entirely false conceit separated the middle class from the broad mass of the productive population. *The bourgeoisie would have to shed its prejudices before it would once again be entitled to leadership.*[23]
> (emphasis added)

Such was the truly abysmal intellectual level and thoroughly bourgeois outlook of the man who not only posed as the philosopher of national socialism, but in the formative years of the Nazi party, probably exerted more political influence over its leader on questions relating to the Soviet Union (and of course the 'Jewish conspiracy') than any other member of the NSDAP's inner circle.

By 1920 therefore, the various strands which came to comprise German fascism had been fused in the DAP: imperialist Pan-Germanism, and belligerent anti-Sovietism in the field of foreign policy, and at home, a murderous anti-Marxism which cloaked its hostility towards the proletariat in spurious anti-capitalism and an unbridled appeal to all the traditional anti-semitic prejudices and political backwardness of the German petty-bourgeoisie; and finally, demarcating national socialism from all those earlier and contemporary movements which contributed to its ideology and aims, there was Hitler's truly epoch-making contribution to the counter-revolutionary armoury of the bourgeoisie — the 'brown terror'. The Pan-Germans had merely written about the destruction of Marxism and democracy — Hitler intended to carry it out:

> The German state is gravely attacked by Marxism. In its struggle of 70 years it has not been able to prevent the victory of this philosophy of life, but, despite a sum total of thousands of years in prison and jail sentences and the bloodiest measures which in inumerable cases it applied to the warriors of the menacing Marxist philosophy, has nevertheless been forced to almost total capitulation ...The state which on November 9, 1918, unconditionally crawled on its belly before Marxism will not suddenly arise tomorrow as its conqueror: even today feeble-minded bourgeois in ministerial chairs are beginning to rave about the necessity of not governing against the workers ...But in view of this fact — that is, the complete subjection of the present state to Marxism — the National Socialist movement really acquires the duty, not only of preparing the victory of its idea, *but of taking over its defence against the terror of an International drunk with victory.*[24] (emphasis added)

Past experiences had taught Hitler that such a counter-revolutionary overturn could not be accomplished merely by fiery oratory or vitriolic press campaigns, nor even the sheer weight of state repression. Bismarck had attempted such a solution, and as Hitler frequently observed, failed miserably. For Hitler had set himself the task that had not even been achieved — in France, it is true — with the massacre of tens of thousands of communards. The political preconditions for a new imperialist war being waged by Germany demanded the extirpation of the last vestiges of socialist internationalism from the German proletariat, and the physical destruction of each and every one of its organisations:

> Historically it is just not conceivable that the German people could recover its former position without settling accounts with those who were the cause and occasion of the unprecedented collapse which struck our state. [in 1918] ...any possibility of regaining outward German independence is bound up first and foremost with the recovery of the inner unity of our people's will. But regarded even from the purely technical point of view, *the idea of an outward German liberation seems senseless as long as the broad masses are not*

also prepared to enter the service of this liberating idea ...a foreign struggle cannot be carried on with student battalions, that in addition to the brains of a people, the fists are also needed ...[Yet] unconquerable ...seem the millions who oppose the national resurrection out of political conviction — *unconquerable as long as the inner cause of their opposition, the international Marxist philosophy of life, is not combatted and torn out of their hearts and brains.*[25] (emphasis added)

Summed up in these incredibly hate-laden, savage lines is the historical role of fascism. German monopoly capital could only be rendered secure from revolution, and its wars of conquest waged, over the battered corpse of the German labour movement, and the embers of its Marxist literature. But tearing requires claws, and when Hitler joined the DAP, he possessed none. Once again, and however involuntarily, the SPD leadership was to come to his aid. The Free Corps, which under Noske's supervision had swollen to an army of 400,000 officers and men, contained just the material the young fascist movement needed to stiffen its ranks in the coming war which its leader had pledged himself to wage against Marxism. They had returned from the trenches thirsting for revenge against the 'November criminals' who had, so the right-wing legend ran, 'stabbed in the back' a Germany on the verge of victory over the Entente powers. Their sacred war decorations and emblems ripped off their uniforms by revolutionary workers and war-weary soldiers as they made their way home from the front-line, these future warriors of national socialism found to their horror and intense frustration that their trusted officers, instead of leading them into battle against the 'Marxist traitors', were actually negotiating with them, and even more monstrous, calling upon the old imperial army to lend its moral and material support to the Ebert regime! Some, like Hermann Göring, could not stomach such a humiliation even if it was deemed by the High Command to be necessary to present a united front of armed forces and social democrats against the socialist revolution.* But the vast majority of right-wing officers

---

* At a meeting of officers, held in the Berlin Philharmonic Hall in December 1918, Göring denounced attempts being made by the leaders of the armed forces to win their support for the Ebert government of 'November criminals'. Minister of War General Reinhardt had told the rally that officers would have to discard their treasured epaulettes and other insignia of imperial caste and rank for the colours of the new republican regime. This was too much for Göring: 'We officers did our duty for four long years [Göring had been a fighter pilot in the crack Richtofen Squadron] and we risked our bodies for the Fatherland. Now we come home — and how do they treat us? They spit on us and deprive us of what we gloried in wearing ...Those alone are to blame who have goaded on the people — those men who stabbed our glorious army in the back and who thought of nothing but attaining power and of enriching themselves at the expense of the people [sic! Göring, the greatest Nazi predator of them all, looted the art galleries and museums of all Europe to decorate and furnish his lavish palaces built at the expense of the German people.] And therefore, I implore you to cherish hatred — a profound abiding hatred of those animals who have outraged the German people!' And before striding out of the hall

and men decided that it had, at that stage, to be a choice between the lesser of two evils. First, with arms provided by the social democrats, crush the communists, and then, with these same arms, turn on Ebert, Scheidemann and company, and settle accounts with the remainder of the 'November criminals'. Thus reasoned some of the politically more aware members of the Free Corps. The Kapp Putsch of March 1920, which will be treated in some detail in Chapter Thirteen (*From Kapp to Munich. The Genesis of a Strategy*), represented the first serious attempt by extreme right-wing military circles to put this plan into practice. Its failure, though initially an enormous blow to the counter-revolutionary camp, in fact accrued to the advantage of the young Nazi movement, for literally thousands of Kapp putschists swarmed from all over Germany to Munich, where the right-wing government installed during the coup remained in power after its collapse, and was therefore able — and only too willing — to offer these rebels against the legal government of Germany a haven from Weimar justice.* Here too, the reformists were responsible for this regrouping of the forces of counter-revolution, for they, as the major partners in the Berlin coalition, could have insisted on their 'extradition' to face charges of overthrowing the legally elected government of Germany. Afraid of antagonising their bourgeois coalition partners, and even more fearful of the consequences of appealing to the working class for support should the military come out in defence of the Kapp putschists, the SPD leadership continued their step-by-step retreat before the forces of reaction that from the spring of 1920 were gathering in Munich around the national socialist movement. Their arrival not only co-incided with Hitler's determined bid for leadership within

in protest against what he regarded as General Rheinhardt's treachery, he ended his speech with the following pledge, one which those who were arming the Free Corps to allegedly defend democracy from the 'dictatorship of the councils' would have done well to heed: 'The day will come when we will drive them [the social democrats] away out of our Germany. Prepare for that day. Arm yourselves for that day. Work for that day!'

* Two who were particularly zealous in their protection of the Nazi party at this time were Ernst Pöhner, a former Bavarian police president, who became a justice of the Bavarian Supreme Court in 1921. At the trial of the Munich Putschists he proudly declared 'For five years I did nothing but treason'. Sentenced to a ludicrously short sentence of a few months by his court cronies, he in fact never went to jail, his election as a *volkisch* deputy in the Bavarian Diet conveniently providing this self-confessed traitor with immunity from arrest. The other benefactor of the Nazis was Wilhelm Frick, Bavarian police deputy president, who in 1933 became Hitler's Minister of the Interior. This appointment was in part at least a reward for service rendered. When Pöhner was asked, in the period preceeding the Munich Putsch, whether he knew of the existence of right-wing killer squads operating openly on his 'patch', he replied: 'Yes, but there aren't enough of them'. Of these two Hitler wrote that they were in his eyes 'the only men in a state position who possess the right to be called co-creators of a national Bavaria'. (A. Hitler, *Mein Kampf*, p.368.)

the DAP, but supplemented it in a most direct and concrete way. Hitler, despite his agreement with the 'theoretical' and programmatic postulates of the party founded by Drexler and directed politically by Feder, saw that it had to develop an entirely new style of agitation and combat if it was to avoid the fate suffered by numerous other similar *volkisch* and nationalist formations in the past — i.e. their total isolation from the masses. The new movement, Hitler insisted, had to be a *combat* party, had to take the offensive against the workers' organisations by carrying the battle onto their own territory — the streets* — and above all, if the entire undertaking was not to go the way of all other *volkisch* movements, the new party had to be 'anti-bourgeois', had to demarcate itself as clearly and demonstratively as possible from even the most chauvinist and reactionary of the parties of the 'national bourgeoisie'.** For only in this way could the 'national classes' break out of the relative political isolation that had been forced on them by the November revolution, and the rise of the Weimar coalition based on the bloc between the bourgeois radicals, the Centre and the social democrats:

> In purely political terms, the following picture presented itself in 1918: a people torn into two parts. The one, by far the smaller, includes the strata of the national intelligentsia, excluding the physically active. It is outwardly national, yet under this word can conceive of nothing but a very insipid and weak-kneed defence of so-called state interests, which in turn seem identical with dynastic interests. They attempt to fight for their ideas and aims with spiritual weapons which are as frag-mentary as they are superficial, and which fail completely in the face of

* What we needed and still need were and are not a hundred or two hundred reckless conspirators, but, a hundred thousand, and a second hundred thousand fighters for our philosophy of life. We should not work in secret conventicles, but in mighty mass demonstrations, and it is not by dagger and poison or pistol that the road can be cleared for the movement, *but by the conquest of the streets*. We must teach the Marxists that the future master of the streets is National Socialism, just as it will some day be the master of the state'. (A. Hitler: *Mein Kampf*, p.543, emphasis added)
**'The red colour of our posters in itself drew them [our opponents] to our meeting halls. The run-of-the-mill bourgeoisie were horrified that we had seized upon the red of the Bolsheviks and they regarded this as all very ambiguous. The German national souls kept privately whispering to each other the suspicion [entirely unjustified, as they later found out] that basically we were nothing but a species of Marxism, perhaps Marxists, or rather, socialists in disguise. For to this day these scatterbrains have not understood the difference between socialism and Marxism. Especially when they discovered that, as a matter of principle we greeted in our meetings no "ladies and gentlemen", but only "national comrades" and among ourselves spoke only of party comrades, the Marxist spook seemed demonstrated for many of our enemies. How often we shook with laughter at these simple bourgeoisie scare-cats, at the sight of their ingenious witty guessing games about our origin, our intentions, and our goal'. (Ibid p.483) Such confusion and suspicion in the less politically aware elements of the bourgeoisie was but a small price to pay for the enormous advantage these tactics gave the Nazis in the fight for influence in the masses. Hence also Hitler's injunction: 'Any meeting which is protected exclusively by the police discredits its organisers in the eyes of the broad masses'. (Ibid, p.487.)

the enemy's brutality. With a single frightful blow, this class, which only a short time before was still governing, is stretched on the ground and with trembling cowardice suffers every humiliation at the hands of a ruthless victory.[26]

So much for Hitler's opinion of the 'national classes' — principally the Junkers and the big bourgeoisie. If left to their own devices, these classes were doomed to perpetual humiliation at the hands of the 'victors' of November 1918, for they faced a far more formidable enemy — the proletariat:

> Confronting it is a second class, the broad mass of the labouring population. It is organised in more or less radical Marxist movements, determined to break all spiritual resistance by the power of violence. It does not want to be national but consciously rejects any promotion of national interests, just as, conversely, it aids and abets all foreign oppression. It is numerically the stronger and above all comprises all those elements of the nation without which a national resurrection is unthinkable and impossible.[27]

This then was the balance of forces as Hitler saw them in the immediate post-war period. How could the deadlock be broken? For all his vehement polemicising against the bourgeoisie, Hitler acknowledged that the natural allies of his aggressive imperialist policies were to be found within its ranks:

> Wretched as our so-called 'national bourgeoisie' is on the whole, inadequate as its national attitude seems, *certainly from this side no serious resistance is to be expected against a powerful domestic and foreign policy in the future.** Even if the German bourgeoisie, for their well-known narrow-minded and short-sighted reasons, should, as they once did toward Bismarck, maintain an obstinate attitude of passive resistance in the hour of coming liberation — an active resistance, in view of their recognised and proverbial cowardice, is never to be feared.[28] (emphasis added)

This 'socialist' and 'workers' party had to fight and crush the socialist workers in order to achieve its aims, which were precisely those of the German bourgeoisie:

> It is different with the masses of our internationally-minded comrades [sic!] In their natural primitiveness, they are more inclined to the idea of violence, and, moreover, their Jewish leadership is more brutal and ruthless. They will crush any German resurrection just as they once broke the backbone of the German army. But above all: in this state with its parliamentary government they will, thanks to their majority

---

* 'The characteristic thing about our bourgeois world is precisely that it can no longer deny the ailments as such. It must admit that much is rotten and bad, but it no longer finds the determination to rebel against the evil, to muster the force of sixty to seventy millions with embittered energy, and oppose it to the danger ...our present bourgeoisie has become worthless for every exalted task of mankind, simply because it is without quality and no good; and what makes it no good is not so much in my opinion any *deliberate* malice as an incredible indolence and everything that springs from it'. (A. Hitler: *Mein Kampf,* pp.406-407) Hence the need for a 'plebeian' solution to — for the bourgeoisie — the seemingly intractable problem of the class struggle.

in numbers, not only obstruct any national foreign policy, but also make impossible any higher estimation of the German strength, thus making us seem undesirable as an ally. For not only are we ourselves aware of the element of weakness lying in our fifteen million Marxists, democrats, pacifists and Centrists; it is recognised even more by foreign countries, which measure the value of a possible alliance with us according to the weight of this burden.[29]

And so was begun what Hitler termed the battle for the 'nationalisation of the masses', a war that cold never be won by

> half measures, but only by a ruthless and fanatically one-sided orientation toward the goal to be achieved. ...a people cannot be made 'national' in the sense understood by our present-day bourgeoisie, meaning with so and so many limitations, but only nationalistic with the entire vehemence that is inherent in the extreme. *Poison is countered only by an antidote, and only the shallowness of a bourgeois mind can regard the middle course as the road to heaven.*[30] (emphasis added)

It might appear from this analysis undertaken by Hitler that he had left out of account the many-millioned German petty-bourgeoisie, since he speaks here only of the bourgeoisie and the 'broad mass of the labouring population'. Viewed statistically, the middle class of town and country seemed a formidable force, numbering, according to the various methods of classification, between roughly a quarter and a half of the total German population. But never at any time in the history of modern Germany had it proved itself capable of pursuing an independent political line, and this characteristic it of course shared with every other petty-bourgeoisie in Europe. Hitler too acknowledged this by excluding it in his calculations from both the main class formations, for he writes specifically of the 'labouring population', which in reality includes the lowest layers of the petty-bourgeoisie — i.e. working peasantry, artisans, self-employed tradesmen etc. — as being 'organised in more or less radical Marxist movements'. Now Hitler was well aware that only a tiny fraction of the working petty-bourgeoisie either identified itself with or was organised in these 'more or less radical Marxist movements' — meaning of course the SPD, KPD and ADGB.

And we also know, from Hitler's own account of his Vienna experiences as a petty-bourgeois 'drop out', that he was fully aware of the important distinctions between even the most humble lower reaches of the middle class and the industrial proletariat, distinctions which under certain economic conditions and with the involuntary aid of the leaders of the workers organisations, could become transformed into an almost unbridgeable gulf of anti-Marxist hatred. Yet Hitler never valued the middle class highly as a political force.* It had all the vices,

*In one of his many scornful references to the lack of fighting power exhibited by the

and none of the virtues, of the German bourgeoisie it at the same time aped and envied. Alone, it could never provide the forces needed to destroy the workers' movement. It could only carry out its counter-revolutionary task of a battering ram against the proletariat, as a subordinate partner in the anti-Marxist front:

> Every national body can be divided into three great classes: into an extreme of the best humanity on the one hand, good in the sense of possessing all virtues, especially distinguished by courage and self-sacrifice; on the other hand, an extreme of the worst human scum ...Between the two extremes there lies a third class, the great, broad, middle stratum, in which neither brilliant heroism nor the basest criminal mentality is embodied. Times when a nation is rising are distinguished, in fact exist only, by the absolute leadership of the best extreme part. Times of a normal, even or of a stable development of affairs are distinguished and exist by the obvious domination of the elements of the middle, in which the two extremes mutually balance one another ...Times when a nation is collapsing are determined by the dominant activity of the worst elements.[31]

And here Hitler reaches the nub of his argument, which relates intimately to his entire political strategy:

> ...the class of the middle only manifests [itself] perceptibly when the two extremes are locked in mutual struggle, but that in the case of the victory of one of the extremes, they complaisantly submit to the victor. In case the best people dominate, the broad masses will follow them; in case the worst element rises up, they will at least offer them no resistance; for the masses of the middle themselves will never fight.[32]

In a general sense this was true, just as Hitler's description of the balance of forces in the Weimar republic was, despite its *volk-isch* conceptions and language, nearer the mark than estimations made by the leaders of bourgeois liberalism or social democracy. The many and violent oscillations within the German petty-bourgeoisie after 1918 were basically determined not by its own highly subjective impressions of Weimar politics, but the objective conflict between the two polar opposites, the bourgeoisie and the proletariat — or to employ Hitler's ill-assumed moralistic terminology, between the 'good' and the 'bad'. But what if the bourgeoisie — for a whole constellation of historical, economic and political reasons — proved itself unable to win the support of the 'elements of the middle', and by its political impotence, drove them into the arms of the 'internationally minded' proletariat? Here the Free corps, or rather their most ruthlessly disposed elements — became integral to Hitler's strategy. As rootless cut-throats, they could never accomplish

bourgeois parties in the early years of the Weimar Republic, Hitler writes: 'It is obvious that such a "bourgeois" guild is good for anything sooner than struggle; especially if the opposing side does not consist of cautious pepper sacks [German slang for small traders] but proletarian masses, incited to extremes and determined to do their worst.' (A. Hitler: *Mein Kampf*, p.407)

their proclaimed goal of destroying Marxism.* But as the spear-head of a terrorist movement attracting to its side the avowedly anti-Marxist and duping the more gullible with Hitler's 'socialist' demagogy, they could — and indeed did — serve as the officer corps of the fascist counter-revolutionary army. As we have already noted, the Kappist Free Corps officers and men began to arrive in Munich in the spring of 1920. By the summer of that same year, Hitler had not only succeeded in attracting many of them into the Nazi movement, but was already laying the foundations of what was to become the 'plebeian' shock force of German fascism — the SA:

> At the very beginning of our big meetings, I began the organisation of a house guard in the form of a monitor service, which as a matter of principle included only young fellows. These were in part *comrades whom I knew from military service;* others were newly-won comrades who from the very outset *were instructed and trained in the viewpoint that terror can only be broken by terror* ...They were imbued with the doctrine that, as long as reason [sic!] was silent and violence had the last word, the best weapon of defence lay in attack; and that our monitor troop must be preceeded by the reputation of not being a debating club, *but a combat group determined to go any length.* And how this youth had longed for such a slogan! *How disillusioned and outraged was this front-line generation, how full of disgust and revulsion at bourgeois cowardice and shilly-shallying.* Thus, it became fully clear that the revolution had been possible thanks only to the disastrous bourgeois leadership of the people. Thus fists to protect the German people would have been available even then at the time of the November revolution, *but the heads to play the game were lacking.*[33] (emphasis added)

* While eager to enrole these ultra-right class warriors into the ranks of the young Nazi movement, Hitler had no illusions about their political immaturity, which he saw confirmed by their readiness to serve under the Ebert government. Even though they shouldered arms for the Republic to fight Bolshevism, it was in Hitler's judgment, a monumental political error: 'As volunteer soldiers they banded together into free corps and began, though grimly hating the revolution, to protect and thus for practical purposes, to secure, this same revolution. This they did in the best good faith ...Gradually the Spartacist barricade fighters on the one hand and the nationalist fanatics and idealists on the other were bled white, and in exact proportion as the two extremes wore each other out [i.e. the 'best elements' and the 'scum'] as always the mass of the middle was victorious. The bourgeoisie and Marxism [i.e. social democracy] met on a 'realistic basis' and the Republic began to be consolidated ...The sole organisations which at this time would have had the courage and strength to oppose the Marxists and their incited masses, were for the present the free corps, and later the self-defence organisations, citizens' guards, etc. and finally the tradition leagues i.e. the *Stahlhelm.* [But] just as the so-called national parties could exert no sort of influence for lack of any threatening power on the streets, likewise the so-called defence organisations, in turn, could exert no sort of influence for lack of any political idea, and above all of any real goal. What had given Marxism its success was its complete combination of political will and activistic brutality. What excluded national Germany from any practical activity in shaping the German development *was the lack of a unified collaboration of brutal force with brilliant political will.'* (A. Hitler: *Mein Kampf,* pp.523-532, emphasis added)

More accurately, the 'heads' who did their thinking for them belonged to Ebert, Noske and company. Given a leadership and organisation which proceeded from mercilessly counter-revolutionary conceptions and strategy, the Free Corps could serve as the military arm and defender of what Hitler termed the 'national idea'. The so-called 'red terror' would now be answered by an even more remorseless 'brown terror':

> How many times the eyes of my lads glittered when I explained to them the necessity of their mission and assured them over and over again that all the wisdom of this earth remains without success if force does not enter into its service ...How much more vividly the idea of military service now dawned on them! ...And how these lads did fight! Like a swarm of hornets they swooped down on the disturbers of our meetings, without regard for their superior power, no matter how great it might be ...As early as midsummer 1920, the organisation of the monitor troop gradually assumed definite forms, and in the spring of 1921 little by little divided into hundreds, which themselves in turn were split up into groups.[34]

Standing at the head of these first Storm Troop units were the veterans of more than a year of almost ceaseless civil war against the revolutionary German workers. These exponents of what was often called 'trench socialism' (the term employed by Free Corps officers for the regime which reigned in the trenches of the First World War!) were greatly enboldened by their hero Ludendorff's open espousal of the Nazi cause. Following the collapse of the Kapp putsch, he moved his headquarters to Munich and there became at once involved in the counter-revolutionary intrigues of *volkisch* groupings and Free Corps officers alike. Hitler soon visited the war-time dictator of Germany and at once reached agreement with him over the need to fuse the 'political' wing of the *volkisch* movement with the growing band of anti-Marxist war veterans now gathering in the Bavarian capital. The Rossbach,* Epp and Ehrhardt Brigades, together with their commanders, placed themselves under the banner of the young

---

* To take only three of the more notorious Free Corps brigades — the von Epp, Rossbach and Ehrhardt. The following officers served the Nazi movement in the positions specified: *von Epp Brigade,* (which, as the unit which overthrew the Bavarian Soviet Republic, had the deepest roots in Munich) Hans Baumann, Battalion commander of Epp Brigade, founder member of DAP, later NSDAP Reichstag deputy; Robert Bergmann, SS *Standführer,* Reichstag member Friedrich Eichinger, joined NSDAP 1921, in Third Reich, adjutant to Bavarian Minister of Interior; Otto Engelbrecht, Munich putschist, appointed to SA leadership, 1933; Hans Hoffmann, leader of SA *gruppe* Bavaria 1931, inspector of SA and police chief of Regensberg, 1932, Reichstag member; Franz Krausser, co-founder with Röhm of the SA on supreme SA leadership, purged with Röhm in 1934; Otto Lancelle, secretary of von Epp, on staff of SA leadership, 1931; Johann Malsen-Ponickau, on SS chief Himmler's personal staff: Wilhelm Stuckart, NSDAP 1922, director in Prussian Ministry of Culture [sic!] under Third Reich; Gerhard Wagner, founder of NSDAP medical association, adviser to Hess on 'medical questions'; Wilhelm Weiss, SA *gruppenführer,* on staff of *Volkischer Beobachter,* Reichstag member 1936; Karl

Nazi movement, and, as we have seen, comprised the nucleus of
the first SA units. There was also, of course the swashbuckling
Captain Ernst Röhm, main organiser of the Storm Troops and,
moreover, one of the first members of the original DAP (He
joined even before Hitler).

It is difficult to over-estimate the importance of the Free Corps
movement in securing the victory of national socialism. For even
though — as in the famous case of Captain Röhm — many of its
more demagogic officers proved to be an embarassment to the
Hitler leadership once ensconced in the government, they were
absolutely indispensable in the years of bitter fighting with the
workers' organisations which blasted Hitler's road to power.

The skeletal structure of the movement was now complete. It
had a programme — jointly drafted by Hitler and Feder and
presented to the first mass meeting of the party in Munich on
February 4, 1920 — it had a leader, and the embryo of a fighting
force that could put his new strategic and tactical conceptions to
the test in battle against the workers movement. But these were by
no means sufficient to guarantee the party a mass following, let
alone the opportunity to stake its claim to state power. Such a
course of development lay entirely outside Hitler's control. The
'national classes' would turn decisively to the Nazi party only
when all other means of combatting democracy and the workers'
movement had been exhausted, and even then, with great anxiety
as to the repercussions of such a strategic shift inside the working
class. And even this would not necessarily mean that the petty-
bourgeois masses would follow them. As Hitler well understood,
the middle class would submit to the side that proved itself the
stronger. Only the calibre of proletarian leadership would

Wolff, adjutant to von Epp, SS brigade leader, Himmler's adjutant, Reichstag
member. *Rossbach:* Kurt Dalueg, joined NSDAP 1922, founded Berlin SA, Lt.
General of Prussian State Police; Edmund Heines, Rossbach chief in Silesia,
Reichstag 1932, purged 1934; *Ehrhardt* Heinz Hauenstein, NSDAP 1922, editor of
Nazi paper, Hanover 'North German Observer'; Wilhelm Heinz, Munich putschist,
SA chief for west Germany, 1933; director of Reich Union of German Writers [sic!];
Manfred von Killinger, organised murders of Rathenau and Erzberger, SA
Obergruppenführer, Reichstag member, Nazi Minister President of Saxony, Nazi
'ambassador' to Slovakia, 1940, and to Romania, 1941; Helmut Nicolai, fellow
assassin of above (as members of 'Organisation Consul') 1931, chief of NSDAP
domestic policy departments, 1933, director in Ministry of Interior; Carl Eduard,
Duke of Saxe-Coberg-Gotha, supreme staff of SA, President of German Red Cross
[sic!] And these are but a sample of the far longer list to be found in Robert Waite's
study of the Free Corps movement in his *Vanguard of Nazism* (Cambridge, Mass.,
1952.)

And in Daniel Lerner's study of the social and occupational origins of the Nazi
leadership in the Third Reich, it emerges that 25% of the top Nazi administrators
served at some time in the Free Corps. The Bavarian basis of the NSDAP is
evidenced by 20.5% of its administrative officials being born in that state — precisely
double the proportion warranted by Bavaria's population, which at that time stood
at 10.1% of the total Reich. (D. Lerner: *The Nazi Elite,* Standford, 1951)

determine which side that would be.

REFERENCES FOR CHAPTER ELEVEN

[1] A. Hitler: *Mein Kampf,* p.208.
[2] Ibid, p.208.
[3] Ibid, p.209.
[4] Ibid, p.215.
[5] Ibid, pp.446-447.
[6] Ibid, p.447.
[7] Ibid, p.448.
[8] Ibid, p.139.
[9] Ibid, p.140.
[10] Ibid, pp.642-649.
[11] Ibid, pp.653-654.
[12] Ibid, pp.660-662.
[13] L. Trotsky: *Germany, the Key to the International Situation,* in L. Trotsky, *The Struggle Against Fascism in Germany,* p.126.
[14] A. Hitler: *Hitler's Secret Book* (being the sequel to *Mein Kampf,* written in 1928, but unpublished until after the war) pp.44-45, New York, 1961.
[15] Ibid, p.42.
[16] Ibid, pp.79-90.
[17] Ibid, pp.38-39.
[18] Ibid, pp.166-167.
[19] A. Rosenberg: *The Myth of the 20th Century,* in Alfred Rosenberg: *Selected Political Writings,* p.34.
[20] Ibid, p.40.
[21] Ibid, p.87-88.
[22] A. Rosenberg: *Address on the 100th anniversary of Nietzsche's birth,* October 14, 1944, in ibid, p.143.
[23] A. Rosenberg: *Memoirs,* p.56.
[24] A. Hitler: *Mein Kampf,* p.535.
[25] Ibid, pp.334-335.
[26] Ibid, p.331.
[27] Ibid, p.331.
[28] Ibid, p.333.
[29] Ibid, pp.333-334.
[30] Ibid, p.337.
[31] Ibid, pp.519-520.
[32] Ibid, p.520.
[33] Ibid, pp.490-491.
[34] Ibid, p.491.

The Founding Programme of the NSDAP

1. We demand the union of all Germans, on the basis of the right of the self-determination of peoples, to form a Great Germany.
2. We demand equality of right for the German People in its dealings with other nations, and the abolition of the Peace Treaties of Versailles and St. Germain.
3. We demand land and territory for the nourishment of our people and for settling our surplus population.
4. None but members of the nation may be citizens of the State. None but those of German blood, whatever their creed, may be members of the nation. No Jew, therefore, may be a member of the nation.
5. Anyone who is not a citizen of the state may live in Germany only as a guest and must be regarded as being subject to the Alien laws.
6. The right of voting on the leadership and legislation is to be enjoyed by the citizens of the State alone. We demand, therefore, that all official appointments, of whatever kind, whether in the Reich, the provinces, or the small communities, shall be granted to citizens of the State alone. We oppose the corrupt Parliamentary custom of the State of filling posts merely with a view to Party considerations, and without reference to character or capacity.
7. We demand that the state shall make it its first duty to promote the industry and livelihood of the citizens of the State, foreign nationals must be excluded from the Reich.
8. All further non-German immigration must be prevented. We demand that all non-Germans who entered Germany subsequently to August 2, 1914 shall be required forthwith to depart from the Reich.
9. All citizens of the State shall possess equal rights and duties.
10. It must be the first duty of every citizen of the State to perform mental or physical work. The activities of the individual must not clash with the interests of the whole, but must proceed within the framework of the community and must therefore be for the general good.
We demand therefore:
11. Abolition of incomes unearned by work. Abolition of the thraldom of interest.
12. In view of the enormous sacrifice of life and property demanded of a nation by every war, personal enrichment through war must be regarded as a crime against the nation. We demand therefore the ruthless confiscation of all war profits.
13. We demand the nationalisation of all businesses which have been amalgamated.
14. We demand that there shall be profit sharing in the great industries.
15. We demand a generous development of provision for old age.
16. We demand the creation and maintenance of a healthy middle class, immediate communalisation of wholesale warehouses and their lease at a low rate to small traders, and that the most careful consideration shall be shown to all small purveyors to the State, the provinces, or smaller communities.
17. We demand a land reform suitable to our national requirements, the passing of a law for the confiscation without compensation of land for communal purposes, the abolition of interest on mortgages, and prohibition of all speculation in land.
18. We demand ruthless war upon all those whose activities are injurious to the common interest. Common criminals against the nation, usurers, profiteers, etc., must be punished with death, whatever their creed or race.
19. We demand that the Roman Law, which serves the materialistic world order, shall be replaced by a German common law.
20. With the aim of opening to every capable and industrious German the possibility of higher education and consequent advancement to leading positions the State must consider a thorough reconstruction of our national system of education. The curriculum of all educational establishments must be brought into line with the requirements of practical life. Directly the mind begins to develop the schools must aim at teaching the pupil to understand the idea of the State. We demand the education of specially gifted children of poor parents, whatever their class or occupation, at the expense of the State.

21. The State must apply itself to raising the standard of health in the nation by protecting mothers and infants, prohibiting child labour, and increasing bodily efficiency by legally obligatory gymnastics and sports, and by extensive support of clubs engaged in the physical training of the young.

22. We demand the abolition of mercenary troops and the formation of a national army.

23. We demand legal warfare against conscious political lies and their dissemination in the press. In order to facilitate the creation of a German national press, we demand:

(a) that all editors and contributors to newspapers employing the German language must be members of the nation:

(b) that special permission from the State shall be necessary before non-German newspapers may appear. These need not necessarily be printed in the German language:

(c) that non-Germans shall be prohibited by law from participating financially in or influencing German newspapers, and that the penalty for the contravention of the law shall be suppression of any such newspaper and the immediate deportation of the non-German involved. It must be forbidden to publish newspapers which do not conduce to the national welfare. We demand the legal prosecution of all tendencies in art and literature of a kind likely to disintegrate our life as a nation, and the suppression of institutions which militate against the above mentioned requirements.

24.   We demand liberty for all religious denominations in the State so far as they are not a danger to it, and do not militate against the morality and moral sense of the German race. The Party, as such, stands for positive Christianity, but does not bind itself in the matter of creed to any particular confession. It combats the Jewish-materialist spirit within and without us, and is convinced that our nation can achieve permanent health from within only on the principle: the common interest before self-interest.

25. That all the foregoing requirements may be realised we demand the creation of a strong central power of the Reich. Unconditional authority of the politically central Parliament over the entire Reich and its organisation in general. The formation of Diets and vocational Chambers for the purpose of executing the general laws promulgated by the Reich in the various States of the Confederation. The leaders of the Party swear to proceed regardless of consequences — if necessary at the sacrifice of their lives — towards the fulfilment of the forgoing points.

On August 31, 1927, Hitler decreed this programme to be immutable, declaring: 'Questions of programme do not concern the Council of Administration; the Programme is fixed, and I shall never suffer changes in the principles of the movement as laid down'. (G. Feder, *Hitler's Official Programme,* p.10) But his alliance with the leaders of industry and banking, which he had begun to forge by 1930, necessitated certain programmatic adjustments, and this delicate task was allotted to the dutiful Feder: On the land question (point No. 17) he said the following: 'No hard and fast rule can be laid down as to the size of agricultural holdings. From the point of view of our population policy large numbers of prosperous small and middle-sized farms are all-important. Farming on a large scale however, has its special and *necessary* part to play ...' (Ibid, p.33 emphasis in original) Feder also made a declaration on behalf of the NSDAP in reply to a series of questions from 'leading circles' of the Brandenburg Landbund, published in *Deutsche Tageszeitung* of January 25, 1930. The questions from this Junker organisation pertained chiefly to private ownership of land, profit sharing (demanded in point 14 of the 1920 programme) inheritance, tariffs, credits etc. To the question 'Is the NSDAP prepared to give guarantees that it will not encroach upon private property?' the author of the clause demanding the nationalisation of the trusts (point 13) and the confiscation of war profits (point 12) replied: 'National Socialism recognises private property ownership in principle, and places it under state protection ...It follows from the spirit of the whole programme, clearly and irrefutably that National socialism, as the most convinced and consistent opponent of Marxism, most decisively repudiates its cardinal doctrine of the 'confiscation of all property' ...and also that National Socialism, as the keenest adversary of the misguided international doctrines of Marxism sees in a class of landowning farmers the best and surest foundation of the national state ...We need a strong, healthy class of farmers, free from interest, slavery and taxation-Bolshevism [sic!]'. And finally on the vexed question of profit sharing, one that perplexed and worried many potential Nazi supporters in the German business community, Feder wrote: 'The present demand for profit sharing springs either from the desire for gain (essentially capitalistic) or from envy (essentially Marxist) ...The lowering of prices is the magic formula which must give every member of the nation a share of the profits of national production.' The industrialists had got the answer they wanted. What did it matter if they had to employ the language of anti-capitalism in order to protect their profits?

This is how the Nazis began to discard their 'socialist' demands under pressure from agrarian and big business interests even before they came to power. The study of Nazi 'socialism' in action we shall reserve to future chapters.

Chapter Twelve
ITALY. THE FIRST WARNING.

The Brown shirt would probably not have existed without the Black shirt. The march on Rome in 1922 was one of the turning points of history. The mere fact that anything of the sort could be attempted and could succeed, gave us impetus ...If Mussolini had been out-distanced by Marxism, I don't know whether we could have succeeded in holding out. At that time National Socialism was a very fragile growth.
(A. Hitler, 1940)
It would be incorrect to conclude that Germany is faced directly with the establishment of a Fascist government a la Mussolini ...The great change that has taken place [since the march on Rome] is the growth of Fascism within social democracy.
(Social Fascism in Germany, Communist International, Vol. VI, No. 11-12-13, May 1929, p.529)
In Italy Mussolini has triumphed. Are we guaranteed against the victory of German Mussolinis in Germany? Not at all.
(L. Trotsky: *Report on the Fourth Congress of the Communist International,* December 28, 1922)

There was one sphere of activity in which the leaders of the German working class cannot be deemed remiss and that was in the manufacture of alibis. Confronted in the spring of 1933 with the ruins of what once had been the world's most powerful labour movement, a movement which they had jointly led to defeat and destruction, Stalinists and social democrats frantically heaped abuse on one another, as the leaders of the two tendencies conspired to conceal from their tormented followers their mutual responsibility for the victory of fascism in Germany. While Comintern and KPD pen prostitutes railed hysterically against the 'social fascists' for their policy of 'tolerating' the 'lesser evil' of the quasi-Bonapartist Brüning regime (a policy which resulted in the victory of the Nazi 'greater evil'), the reformists hit back tellingly by pointing to the several occasions on which the KPD leaders had not merely refused a united front with the 'social fascists', but actually entered into a united front with the so-called 'national fascists' (a 'third period' Stalinist term distinguishing Nazis from 'social fascists') against the SPD! But there was one alibi or diversion that not even the most debauched and case-hardened bureaucratic hireling dared employ. None could claim that Hitler's victory took them by surprise, that the rise of German fascism lacked an historical precedent, that there had not been ample warning of the fate that awaited the German proletariat should its leadership not be equal to the task of carrying through the socialist revolution. For staring the German workers' movement in the face for fully ten years had been the tragic consequences of the fascist 'March on Rome'. By an unprecedented campaign of systematic anti-proletarian terror, Mussolini's black-shirted *Fascisti* had not only succeeded in turning the tide of revolution which had been running high in the summer of 1920, but unlike previous strike-breaking organisations, had at once gone over to the offensive in a determined bid for state power. This was something entirely new in the history of the class struggle under capitalism. Eagerly seizing the initiative presented to him by the Italian Socialist Party (PSI) reformists and centrists after their betrayal of the September factory occupation movement, Mussolini launched an unremitting siege of the Italian proletariat's major citadels. Spearheaded by squads of World War I veterans, blackshirted columns blazed a counter-revolutionary trail through north Italy until one by one, every stronghold of the labour movement had fallen into fascist hands. In every case, the pattern was the same. Armed fascists (often with weapons supplied by the army and police) would bodily eject the constitutionally elected administration from the town hall, and replace it with power-hungry petty-bourgeois, craving for rewards of office. The premises and print-shops of the local workers' organisations would be looted, sacked and frequently closed for good. Workers leaders and labour activists would be publicly humiliated before their comrades by the forcible administration of castor oil, and even on occasions simply shot out of hand. With the proletariat either cowed or divided by the cowardly retreat of its leaders, who, at no stage in the fascist offensive organised any serious resistance to the gathering reaction, Mussolini rapidly convinced important sections of the bourgeoisie — not to speak of key army leaders and the highest circles of the royal family — that the formation of a fascist-dominated government was the logical outcome of his bloody crusade against the Italian labour movement. Four years of fascist rule in Italy were sufficient to root out the last remnants of any independent workers' organisation. The trade unions were outlawed, being superseded by fascist 'corporations' which claimed to harmonise the interests of workers and employers in the interests of production and for the greater glory of the state, while the two workers' parties, the PSI and the

Communist Party of Italy (PCI) were declared illegal and driven underground by the fascist secret police. A movement which at its peak had numbered millions, and enjoyed the devoted support of millions more, had been shattered. Not since the crushing of the Paris Commune had the European proletariat suffered such a terrible reverse. Its theoretical lessons and political implications would be neglected at the peril of every single detachment of the international working class army. And just as had been the case in Germany, the ideological pre-conditions for the emergence of such a movement as Mussolini's had been a long while maturing. In searching for and discovering them, we find ourselves amidst philosophical surroundings that are remarkably similiar to and in some cases identical with those that nurtured the ideologues of national socialism. For Mussolini, although a renegade from the extreme left flank of the pre-1914 PSI, had from his earliest years as a political activist been influenced more by the subjective idealist schools of European thought than the theories of Marx and Engels. Both before as well as after his defection to the counter-revolution, Mussolini bolstered his political conceptions by invoking the very same names that in France, as well as Germany, had helped to stoke up the fires of philosophic reaction: Nietzsche, Max Stirner, Schopenhauer, Bergson and Sorel.*

What unites each of these major figures in the history of European thought is not so much a shared political outlook — Nietzsche, Schopenhauer and Bergson were all in their own fashion avowed opponents of socialism, while Sorel considered himself an uncorrupted champion of the proletariat — as a common theory of knowledge which can be summed up in one word: intuition. And it was in the name of this mystical force that Mussolini struck out along the uncharted path that was to lead

---

* In 1911, Mussolini wrote from prison of his literary journey through the mountain peaks of European culture: 'And of these summits of the spirit are called Stirner, Nietzsche, Goethe, Schiller, Montaigne, Cervantes etc.' On the young Mussolini's desk, so a contemporary of his relates were always to be found volumes of Nietzsche, Stirner and Schopenhauer. In 1919, and now embarked on his new career as a professional enemy of the socialist party he once served so ably as agitator and journalist, we find Mussolini more deeply committed than ever to a defence of his early philosophic mentors: 'leave the way free for the elemental power of the individual' he wrote in his demagogic, pseudo-anarchistic style, 'for there is no other human reality than the individual! Why shouldn't Stirner become significant again?' Mussolini attempted an exposition of Italian fascism's guiding ideology in his maiden speech to the Chamber of Deputies on June 21, 1921, in which he claimed to have 'introduced into Italian socialism something of Bergson mixed with much of Blanqui', while in his definitive essay, *The Political and Social Doctrine of Fascism*, which dates from 1932, he writes that 'in the great stream of Fascism are to be found ideas which began with Sorel, Peguy, with Lagardelle in the "Mouvement Socialiste" and with the Italian trade union movement which throughout the period 1904-1914 was sounding a new note in Italian socialist circles.' Some, but by no means all, of these sources of fascist ideology are discussed in this chapter.

him from the extreme left of the Italian socialist movement to the ultra-right flank of the counter-revolutionary bourgeoisie. His revolt against the supposed rigidities of Marxist theory and principles, and his quest for 'action' at all costs became the ideological hall mark of what passed for the 'philosophy' of fascism: faith and 'deeds' rather than science and action guided by theory:

> I do not believe in the supposed influence of books ...For myself, I have used only one book ...I have had only one great teacher. The book is life lived. The teacher is day-by-day experience. The reality of experience is far more eloquent than all the theories and philosophies in all the tongues and on all the shelves ...my political evolution has been the product of a constant expansion, of a flow of springs always nearer to the realities of living life, and always further away from the rigid structures of sociological theorists.[1]

The intuitionist, or 'integralist' influence of the Bergsonian subjectivist school, especially as distilled through Sorel, is all too obvious in these lines. With Mussolini, the rejection of Marxism was open and brutal in the extreme. However in the case of Sorel's attack on the dialectical materialist foundations of the Marxist theory of knowledge, it was carried out in the name of defending Marx from his traducers and epigones.* This line of approach is most clearly expressed in his two famous essays, *Reflections on Marxism* (1906) and *The Decomposition of Marxism* (1908), written at a time when the French trade union movement was passing through its peak of pre-war militancy. Viewing this combativity of the French proletariat through the eyes of a romantic, anti-rational intellectual, and seeing in it the antidote to the senility, parliamentary cretinism and ministerial opportunism of the official French socialist movement, Sorel raised this class aggression to an absolute, and equated its most developed form — the general strike — with the proletarian revolution itself. Thus was born the Sorelian 'myth' of the general strike, as being a goal for which the proletariat strived for its own sake, and not as a means to an end, the overthrow of capitalism and the establishment of a socialist society. But firstly it is essential to see by what methodological route Sorel arrives at such intensely mystical conclusions, ones which have absolutely

---

* And this, despite Sorel's collaboration in the immediate pre-1914 period with the French ultra monarchist movement, the *Action Francaise*. Sorel co-edited the monarchist journal *l'Independence* with two avowed anti-semites and enemies of socialism, Paul Bourget and Maurice Barres. Sorel also participated in this journal's forerunner, *Cite Francaise*, with the equally reactionary George Valois, who attempted to synthesise anti-semitic monarchism with a Proudhonist anarchism. Valois' *Cahiers du Cercle Proudhon* had a frankly corporatist flavour, a fact which led its editor to claim some fifteen years later, that it was the first journal to espouse the cause of fascism in France. It should be noted that this enterprise enjoyed, even if only for a short period, the support of Mauras, the founder of the *Action Francaise*, and Sorel, the high priest of the myth of the proletarian general strike.

nothing in common with Marxism, even though they can, with some justice, be said to share a common basis with the theoretical postulates of the so-called 'revolutionary syndicalism' of the decade preceding the first world war. Sorel was an avid pupil and follower of Bergson, seeking to apply the latter's 'integral' theory of knowledge, which Bergson had evolved in his critique of mechanist theorists and 'model builders' in the natural sciences, to history and primarily, to the study of the class struggle under modern capitalism.

> ...I put before my readers the working of a mental effort which is continually endeavouring to break through the bonds of what has been previously constructed for common use, in order to discover that which is truly personal and individual. The only things I find it worth while entering in my notebooks are those which I have not met elsewhere; I readily skip the transitions between these things, because they nearly always come under the heading of commonplaces.[2]

Yet such 'commonplaces' are precisely the repositories of all those shadings, the 'skipped transitions', wherein and by whose integral polarity the unique evolves and finally bursts forth as something which to the subjective idealist appears invested with a magical quality of *absolute* uniqueness. Thus 'intuitionism', far from laying bare the secrets of nature and society shrouded by hidebound dogmatic theorists, both obscures the mediations and transitions by which the old is negated into the new and the very inner complexities and further polarities contained within the fruits of this act of negation. What we ironically described as Bergson's 'short cut to infinity' becomes a plunge into an abyss of mysticism and political reaction.* And this was as true in the case

---

* 'The "myth" of the general strike', Sorel writes, 'has all the advantages which "integral" knowledge has over analysis, according to the doctrine of Bergson; and perhaps it would not be possible to cite another example which would so perfectly demonstrate the value of the famous professor's doctrines ...Movement, in Bergson's philosophy, is looked upon as an undivided whole; which leads us precisely to the catastrophic conception of socialism ...' Yet Sorel does not believe that such a 'catastrophe' will come about, nor even that this matters in the least: '...it is even possible that nothing will come to pass — as was the case with the catastrophe expected by the first Christians ...The myth must be judged as a means of acting on the present [i.e. purely from a pragmatic standpoint]; any attempt to discuss how far it can be taken literally as future history is devoid of sense. *It is the myth in its entirety which alone is important* ...we know that the general strike is ...the myth in which socialism is wholly comprised i.e. a body of images capable of evoking *instinctively* all the sentiments which correspond to the different manifestations of the war undertaken by Socialism against modern society ...*We thus obtain that intuition of Socialism which language cannot give us with perfect clearness — and we obtain it as a whole, perceived instantaneously ...This is the "global knowledge" of Bergson's philosophy.*' (G. Sorel: *Reflections on Violence*, pp.123-128, New York, 1961, emphasis added). Another theorist of French syndicalism Hubert Lagardelle, whom Mussolini cites as one of the ancestors of Italian fascism, embraced a similar theory of knowledge: 'No more dogmas or formulas; no more fruitless discussions on the future society; no more compendious plans for social organisations; but a sense of struggle that provides through practice a *philosophy of action which gives first*

of Sorel, the renegade syndicalist, as it was with Mussolini, the renegade socialist. Let us follow through the main progressions of Sorel's argument in favour of a cult of proletarian violence and his propagation of the 'myth' of the general strike. Firstly Sorel frankly concedes that his theory lacks either substantiating objective evidence or any real prospect of fulfilment. And that is precisely its virtue:

> ...men who are participating in a great social movement always picture their coming action as a battle in which their cause is certain to triumph. These constructions, knowledge of which is so important for historians, I propose to call myths, the syndicalist 'general strike' and Marx's catastrophic revolution are such myths... [Like] those which were constructed by primitive Christianity, by the reformation, by the Revolution and by the followers of Mazzini ...we should not attempt to analyse such groups of images in the way that we analyse a thing into its elements, but they must be taken as a whole, as historical forces, ...*we should be especially careful not to make any comparison between accomplished fact and the picture people had formed for themselves before action.*[3] (emphasis added)

In other words, the myth (and here Sorel the would-be Marxist equates the proletarian revolution with the reactionary utopias of the early Christians) must at all costs be preserved intact, must be protected from the inquisitive scrutiny of science, and above all must continue to dominate the thinking of those it holds in thrall:

> In employing the term myth I believed I had made a happy choice, because I thus put myself in a position to refuse any discussion whatever with the people who wish to submit the idea of a general strike to a detailed criticism, and who accumulate objections against its practical ...possibility.[4]

Sorel's refusal to countenance such a critical examination of his theories was re-enforced by the opportunist political position of his opponents in the leadership of the French socialist party, who looked with suspicion on the activities of the syndicalists not so much for fear they might derail the struggle for socialism but actually bring it about by revolutionary, rather than evolutionary means.* It was this cleavage within the French workers movement — a split which found what Trotsky once called the

place to intuition and which indicates that the simplest worker engaged in the class struggle knows more than the most doctrinaire thinkers.' (emphasis added) Lagardelle's evolution is most instructive in this regard. Following the collapse of the Third Republic in 1940, he drifted towards a collaborationist position, and in 1943, entered the Vichy regime as Minister of Labour.

* ...the objections urged by philosophy against the revolutionary myths would have made an impression only on those men who were anxious to find a pretext for abandoning any active role, for remaining revolutionary in words only. ...[those] socialists who are afraid of a revolution ...do all they can to shake the confidence of the workers in the preparations they are making for the revolution; and in order to succeed in this they cast ridicule on the idea of the general strike — the only idea that could have any value as a motive force'. (G. Sorel: *Reflections on Violence*, pp.45-49, New York, 1961)

'healthiest' forces in the ranks of 'revolutionary syndicalism' —
that both nourished and created an audience for Sorel's
theorising. And here there is an important parallel with the pre-
1914 career of Mussolini, whose anarchist-flavoured Marxism
was without doubt a largely intuitive reaction against the class-
collaborationist policies favoured by the majority of the PSI
leadership.

As a fervent anti-rationalist (rationalism being equated. in his
mind with parliamentary democracy, reformist socialism,
bourgeois liberalism and middle class intellectualism) Sorel welcomed any expression of the class struggle which in his view,
would give primacy to the instinct, to the dark forces of intuition,
to violence that knew no limits or predetermined goal (as is the
case in Marxist-led proletarian revolution). Thus in the scenario
devised by Sorel, the proletariat, mobilised by the myth of the
syndicalist (and not political) general strike, did not fight as a
force in its own right and for its own emancipation from the rule
of capital. For if we look more closely at what Sorel is saying, we
see that his aim, far from the expropriation of the bourgeoisie, is
its re-invigoration. Sorel spends much time denouncing the
leaders of French socialism for their 'bourgeoisification', yet it is
to the rescue of this same bourgeoisie that Sorel summons the
proletariat:

> It is here that the role of violence in history appears to us as singularly
> great, for it can ...so operate on the middle class [bourgeoisie] as to
> awaken them to a sense of their own class sentiment ...The day on
> which employers perceive that they have nothing to gain by works
> which promote social peace, or by democracy, they will understand
> that they have been ill-advised by the people who persuaded them to
> abandon their trade of creators of productive forces for the noble
> profession of educators of the proletariat [i.e. bourgeois reformers].
> Then there is some chance that they may get back a part of their
> energy ...proletarian violence not only makes the revolution certain,
> but it seems also to be the only means by which the European nations
> — at present stupified by humanitarianism — can recover their former
> energy. This kind of violence compels capitalism to restrict its
> attentions solely to its material role and tends to restore to it the
> warlike qualities which it formerly possessed. A growing and solidly
> organised, working class can compel the capitalist class to remain firm
> in the industrial war; if a united and revolutionary proletariat
> confronts a rich middle class, eager for conquest, capitalist society will
> have reached its historical perfection ...Everything may be saved if the
> proletariat, by their use of violence, manage to re-establish the division
> into classes, and so restore to the middle class something of its former
> energy; that is the great aim towards which the whole thought of men
> ...must be directed. Proletarian violence, carried on as a pure and
> simple manifestation of the sentiment of the class war, appears thus as
> a very fine and very heroic thing; it is at the service of the immemorial
> interests of civilisation ...[5]

For all their invocation of 'proletarian violence', these are ideas pregnant with a whole range of the most reactionary conceptions. For it transpires that Sorel is by no means a partisan of the proletariat in the class struggle. If he summons it into battle, it is to bestir a reformist and democratic bourgeoisie to take up its old ways (exemplified by the 'June days' of the 1848 revolution, and the massacre of the Communards in 1871) by regaining its former lust for power and counter-revolutionary violence. In this gladiatorial fashion, the nation can purge itself of its 'weaker' elements, and thus regain its lost virility. Shades of Nietzsche, whom incidentally, Sorel greatly admired, despite the former's well-known aversion for all forms of socialism and trade unionism.* Sorel's position therefore seems to straddle the

---

* Sorel shared Nietzsche's cult of the 'superman', finding him not in the ranks of the proletariat, which he viewed as an elemental mass devoid of individual personality whose only valid contribution to 'civilisation' was the unleashing of periodic salvos of therapeutic violence, but the so-called 'captain of industry' (a reverence he shared with Carlyle and Spengler, not to speak of Feder): 'We know with what force Nietzsche praised the values constructed by the masters, by a superior class of warriors who, in their expeditions, enjoying to the full freedom from all social restraint, return to the simplicity of mind of a wild beast ...I believe that if the professor of philology had not been continually cropping up in Nietzsche he would have perceived that the master type still exists under our own eyes, and that it is this type which, at the present time, has created the extraordinary greatness of the United States. This type is still found today in all its purity in the United States: there are found the indomitable energy, the audacity based on a just appreciation of its strength, the cold calculation of interests, which are the qualities of great capitalists.' (Ibid, pp.230-231, p.89) Sorel tries to establish a common bond between the ruthless tycoons of his day (exemplars of Nietzsche's 'wild beasts' freed from 'all social restraint') and his conception of 'revolutionary syndicalism' which, he asserted, 'would be impossible if the world of the workers were under the influence of such a morality of the weak'. (Ibid, p.236) Sorel's was a 'warrior socialism', a 'socialism' of the 'strong', of the 'violent' and the pitiless. And as such, it had absolutely nothing in common with the socialism of Marx. Also to be noted here, and of special significance not only for Sorel's pre-1914 flirtation with the pioneers of French corporatism, but for Mussolini's subsequent use of the syndicalist vocabulary to conceal the class basis of his own fascist 'corporate' state, is the former's use of the term 'producers'. It was a word freely used in the syndicalist movements of France and Italy to distinguish the workers from those who parasitically exploited them as mere owners or 'non- producers.' Both Sorel — and following him Mussolini in his fascist career — distorted this admittedly vague term to include what Feder called 'productive' bourgeoisie. 'Proletarian violence' writes Sorel, 'confines employers to their role of producers, and tends to restore the separation of classes just when they seemed on the point of intermingling in the democratic marsh.' (Ibid, p.92) And Mussolini, while like Hitler denouncing the political leadership of the bourgeoisie for its lack of resolve in combatting Marxism, allots to it the leading role in the organisation of the so-called 'corporative' economy. In his pronouncement published on the eve of the 'March on Rome', Mussolini wrote: 'Fascism does not march against the police, but against a *political* class both cowardly and imbecile, which in four long years has not been able to give a government to the nation. Those who form the *productive class* must know that Fascism wants to impose nothing more than order and discipline upon the Nation and to help raise the strength which will renew progress and prosperity.' (emphasis added)

embattled classes. He urges both to fight with the maximum vigour and ruthlessness, to cast aside all democratic and reformist subterfuges, to scorn the parliamentary process and by-pass the various mechanisms which a reformist labour movement and a liberal bourgeoisie has evolved to regulate the social conflicts and mitigate their repercussions in the political sphere. So for all tne scorn Sorel displays for the middle class intelligentsia, which he sees as the main agency in this muffling process, he adopts the classic pose of the politicised, but disoriented petty-bourgeois thrown hither and thither in a period of violent class conflict (France was in this period the battleground for a series of monumental clashes between the syndicalist-led workers and an intransigent industrial bourgeoisie and capitalist state). His attacks on the 'middle class' were not so much a critique of its pernicious influence on the proletarian movement, as a total repudiation of theory, a position which he found fortified by the writings of his mentor Bergson.* Sorel saw as his mission the liberation of the workers from their intellectual seducers, for only in this way could they be led back to their pristine 'trade union' purity. Here too, Sorel was no innovator, since an almost identical line of attack on Marxist leadership had been launched less than a decade previously inside the Russian workers' movement, by the tendency which came to be known by the name 'Economist'. Its advocates argued that socialist students and intellectuals were diverting the working class from its trade union struggles by seeking to harness the power of the proletariat to the struggle to

---

* Thus in the thundering tones of the French petty-bourgeois *enfant terrible,* (epitomised by the anti-militarist rhetoric of a Gustav Herve who at his bourgeoisie's hour of need, rallied to the flag he once declared to be fit only for planting on a dung-heap) Sorel pours scorn on 'our parliamentary socialists, who spring from the middle classes and who know nothing outside the ideology of the state [and who] are so bewildered when they are confronted with working class violence ...If revolutionary syndicalism triumphs, there will be no more brilliant speeches on imminent justice, and the parliamentary regime, so dear to the intellectuals, will be finished with!' (Ibid, p.40) Very much in the Economist fashion, Sorel claims that 'a new culture might spring from the struggle of the revolutionary trade unions against the employers and the state: our greatest claim to originality [sic!] consists in our having maintained that the proletariat can emancipate itself without being compelled to seek the guidance of that section of the middle classes which concerns itself professionally with matters of the intellect'. (Ibid, p.53) Here Sorel finds himself totally opposed to Lenin, who in his polemic against the Russian 'Sorelians', the Economists, wrote that 'there could not have been Social Democratic consciousness among the workers. It would have to be brought to them from without. The history of all countries shows that the working class, exclusively by its own effort, is able to develop only trade union consciousness ...The theory of socialism ...grew out of the philosophic, historical, and economic theories elaborated by educated representatives of the propertied classes, by intellectuals.' (V. Lenin: *What is to be Done?,* in *Collected Works,* Vol. 5, p.375) Events both in France as well as Russia proved Lenin, not Sorel, to be right. The French proletariat certainly lacked nothing in combativity as its history shows. But what it lacked in Sorel's day — and lacks still — was a revolutionary party guided by what Lenin called 'the most up-to-date revolutionary theory'.

overthrow the autocracy, an aim that transcended trade union goals and methods of combat, even though it would necessarily embrace them. Economist agitators exploited the mistrust felt by the more backward workers towards middle class intellectuals, and incited them to 'wrest their fate from their leaders'. Politics —i.e., the struggle for the destruction of tsardom — was seen as a corrupting influence on the Russian proletariat which, the Economists insisted, was perfectly capable of devising its own theory, tactics and strategy for socialism without the assistance of Marxist intellectuals. Their job was not to interfere in the workers' movement, but to win over the liberal bourgeoisie.

Now Sorel by no means shared all these essentially revisionist* notions — we cannot even be certain that he knew of them. But this much is sure. Sorel was part of that process of theoretical degeneration within the pre-war international workers movement which in the summer of 1914 reached its treacherous nadir with the collapse into rampant chauvinism and collaboration with the capitalist state. And this collapse became the starting point for Mussolini's defection from the ranks of the PSI and his rapid transition towards the extreme counter-revolutionary right.

If we view the origins of German and Italian fascism from the standpoint of the personal biographies of their founders, there is much that separates the two movements. Hitler, as we have noted, was never a supporter, let alone member or activist, of the Austrian workers' movement, while Mussolini was from his youth until his defection from the PSI in the autumn of 1914 a passionate advocate of revolutionary socialism, suffering repeated police victimisation and persecution for his convictions. Nor can we detect in the younger Mussolini any trace of the national hatreds that dominated the thinking of Hitler from the dawn of his social and political consciousness. Indeed, the future butcher of Ethiopia was famed (or feared) in the PSI and the Second International for his seemingly intransigent opposition to militarism and chauvinism in all their forms, just as he was regarded as the leading antagonist of those PSI leaders who

* Sorel the super-revolutionary was deeply sympathetic towards Bernstein the evolutionary. Both denied the importance of the goal of the workers' movement, regarding the latter as sufficient unto itself. Despite differences of terminology and emphasis, their method was closely similar, as was their counter-posing of the 'practical' aspects of the trade union struggle to what they both declared to be the utopian goal of a socialist society: 'Bernstein's ideas were received most favourably by those who wanted to see Marxism escape the rigid mould in which Kautsky wanted to keep it ...thus life was introduced into a doctrine which was, until then, condemned to sterility ...Bernstein asserted ...that the final aim is nothing and that the movement is everything. *He thus penetrated the true spirit of contemporary i.e. 'integralist' or Bergsonian philosophy, in that he does not trouble himself with a point of departure, or with a starting point, but rather with the forces which, at each instant, are able to generate the movement in the sense that he conceives it.'* (G. Sorel, *The Decomposition of Marxism*, in I. Horowitz: *Radicalism and the Revolt against reason*, pp.118-119, London, 1961, emphasis added)

sought to enter the portals of the government ministries in coalition with the 'reformist' wing of the bourgeoisie headed by Giovanni Giolitti, leader of the Liberals.* Yet the historical, political and economic soil which nurtured the two movements and fertilized their early growth was in many ways strikingly similar. Firstly there is the oft-stated fact of the retarded national unity of Germany and Italy, a delay which in both countries led to the 'national question' predominating in the political, social and cultural life of both countries. In Germany, it tended to take the form — for deep seated historical reasons — of militant anti-semitism mingled with an almost equal hatred for France and Poland; while in the case of Italy, imperialist sentiment was directed primarily against Austria in the north, and only later southwards towards Africa, where the still-unconquered expanses of Libya beckoned on protagonists of an aggressive colonialist policy. Looking more closely at the class and political structure of the two nations, we can also detect similarities as well as differences. Rapid industrialisation of north Italy, though by no means as tempestuous and massive as in the German Ruhr, had hewn a militant proletariat out of what had been up to the last decades of the nineteenth century a primitive and God- (or rather priest) fearing peasantry. Consequently the 'social question' loomed as large as the national question in every quarter of the bourgeoisie and aristocracy just as the two issues had become fused during the Bismarckian era in Germany. And so the ideological antecedents of Italian fascism are to be found amongst those organisations and individuals which, as in Imperial Germany, saw the solution to these twin dilemmas as residing in a political counter-revolution sweeping away bourgeois democracy and independent workers' movements alike, and the creation of a regime which would harness the energies of the working class in a struggle for empire. Such was the Nationalist Party, which played the ideological role in Italy performed for national socialism in Germany by the Pan-German League. Its contribution to Italian fascism was in fact greater in

---

* The anarchist flavour of Mussolini's anti-parliamentarianism distinguished his critique of bourgeois democracy from that of Marx and Lenin, revealing an indifference towards democratic rights and freedoms which subsequently became one of the hallmarks of fascist anti-parliamentarianism. 'I take an absolutely negative view of the value of parliamentary suffrage ...The uses to which it has been put should prove to the workers that it is not the weapon which will enable them to win complete emancipation [the former assertion does not at all flow logically from the latter statement]. We hold that Italy needs a strong, homogeneous socialist, incohesive democracy ...Bissolati, Cabrini, Bonomi [all leaders of the PSI 'coalitionist' wing] can go to the Quirinal [the king's residence] to the Vatican too, if they wish; but the Socialist party must declare that it will not follow them today, tomorrow, or ever.' (B. Mussolini: *Speech to the PSI Congress, Reggio Emilia, July 8, 1911*). Little more than ten years later, Mussolini did follow them, smashing on the way not only 'Italy's chaotic, incohesive democracy', but his own Socialist party.

that it not only helped to shape Mussolini's aggressive foreign policy, but also pioneered many of the conceptions which were later to reappear in the official fascist theory of the corporate state. Founded in 1910, a time when clamour for empire had reached a crescendo, the Nationalist Party fused Catholic social doctrines (see Chapter Ten) with a militant anti-parliament-arianism and a bellicose nationalism. The party's principle ideologist, and one who exerted a considerable influence on later fascist thinking, was the high school teacher Enrico Corradini. It was he who evolved the notion of an Italy condemned to poverty and backwardness by its being denied its rightful share of colonies. Italy, he claimed, was a 'proletarian nation', and it would only end its servitude to the sated capitalist powers when the energy-sapping fratricidal struggle of classes within Italy was brought to an end.*

The Nationalists, like their counterparts in the Pan-German League, never secured a mass following, though they were ahead of them in seeing the need to acquire one. Their 'social' and even 'proletarian' phraseology did however succeed in attracting into their ranks a small group of renegade socialists and more significantly for the future development of Italian fascism, defectors from the syndicalist movement. These latter comprised the embryo of that counter-revolutionary tendency which assumed the title 'national syndicalism' and after 1914, gravitated rapidly into the orbit of fascism. We should recall that in Germany, the forerunner of the Nazi movement, Drexler's DAP (not to speak of the Bohemian organisation of the same name), advocated a national 'trade unionism', as indeed did Hitler, and that the DAP served as a bridgehead for the Pan-German Father-land Front and the Munich-based Thule Society into masses, which they themselves could never hope to reach. So it was with the Italian Nationalists. The foundation of the party had been anticipated and to some extend prepared by the publication of Corradini's nationalist review, *Il Regno,* which first appeared in November 1903. Right from the beginning, he struck a new note in ruling class politics, scolding the bourgeoisie for its 'decadence' and summoning it, very much in terms that Sorel employed in his *Reflections on Violence,* to regain its lost virility and ruthlessness.

* Corradini even coined the term *socialismo nazionale* to delineate his social and foreign policies from those of the labour movement and the bourgeois liberals. In his *Italian Nationalism* (Milan, 1914) he bitterly assails the 'plutocratic nations' (France, Britain and Germany) for denying Italy its place in the imperialist sun. Imperialism divided nations into the 'haves', the plutocrats, and the 'have-nots', the proletarians, for whom pacifism and democracy were not only luxuries they could ill-afford, but downright obstacles to their emancipation: 'Nationalism ...is the socialism of the Italian nation in the world'. Similar reactionary ideas were also peddled in Germany at this time, not only by the traditional right, but by extreme nationalist elements of the SPD (see Chapter Seven).

This was also the theme of his address to the founding Nationalist Congress, where he called upon the government to throw caution to the winds and carve out an empire in north Africa before Italy's imperialist rivals choked the 'proletarian nation' to death:

> As socialism teaches the proletariat the value of the class struggle, so we [the Nationalists] must teach Italy the value of the international struggle ...But if the international struggle means war, well then, let there be war!

And when war against Libya did come only a few months later, Corradini's chauvinist rantings were being echoed by voices which had till then been strident in their opposition to imperialist war and national hatreds. Arturo Labriola, militant syndicalist leader and theoretician, hailed the invasion and conquest of Libya in terms both reminiscent of Sorel and foreshadowing the glorification of war indulged in by Mussolini:

> [War is] a school of character, virility and courage ...A people that does not know how to make war, will never make a revolution ...Behind Turkey [whom Italy was fighting to annexe Libya] is the Europe of money, which desires its prey ...We are really combatting Mammon ...* [shades of Carlyle and Feder]

With the approach of the world war, Italy and Germany presented what was in many ways a similar picture — an imperialist-oriented bourgeoisie confronted by an increasingly powerful labour movement, a polarisation which was itself mirrored at each pole by deep divisions over strategy and tactics. The liberals, encouraged by openly reformist and national trends in the workers' movement, sought a *rapprochement* with the more 'moderate' of their former enemies (thus Weber and certain of the Progressives in Germany, and Giolitti in Italy), while the extreme chauvinists demanded a policy of all-out war on every shade of socialism (in Germany, the Pan-German Junkers and

---

* 'War may be considered from its noble side ...the idea that the profession of arms cannot compare to any other profession — that it puts the man who adopts this profession in a class which is superior to the ordinary conditions of life, that history is based entirely on the adventures of warriors, so that the economic life only existed to maintain them.(2). The sentiment of glory which Renan [a Catholic 'integralist' admired by Sorel] so justly looked upon as one of the most singular and the most powerful creations of human genius, and which has been of such incomparable value in history. (3). The ardent desire to try one's strength in great battles, to submit to the test which gives the military calling its claim to superiority, and to conquer glory at the peril of one's life ...The Syndicalist general strike presents a very great number of analogies with [this] conception of war'. (G. Sorel: *Reflections on Violence,* pp.166-167) 'Fascism ...believes neither in the possibility nor the utility of perpetual peace. It thus repudiates the doctrine of Pacifism, born of a renunciation of the struggle and as an act of cowardice in the face of sacrifice. War alone brings up the highest tension all human energy and puts the stamp of nobility upon the peoples who have the courage to meet it. All other trials are substitutes, which never really put men into the position where they have to make the great decision — the alternative of life or death. Thus a doctrine which is founded upon this harmful postulate of peace is hostile to Fascism'. (B. Mussolini: *The Political and Social Doctrine of Fascism*)

industrialists, in Italy, the Nationalists). In both countries, the outbreak of the imperialist war threw these conflicting tendencies into flux. All except the most intransigent enemies of the German workers' movement welcomed its leaders' collaboration in prosecuting the war, while within the SPD and the trade unions, chauvinist degeneration proceeded at such a tempo that the voice of internationalism was all but stifled.

In Italy, events took a different turn. Waverings and divisions among the bourgeoisie and the military over which side to support enabled the leadership to take a seemingly firm stand against the war. Since the government was officially neutral, it did not require the courage of a Liebknecht to call on the workers' movement to be neutral also. Yet this stand did not satisfy all of the PSI leadership, no more than did the Italian government's neutrality please the militantly imperialist Nationalists, who were demanding a crusade to 'liberate' the Italian-speaking population of the Austrian Tyrol. For Mussolini, the editor of the PSI daily *Avanti*, a more 'active' policy was called for, even if it involved support for one or other of the two imperialist camps. This blind quest for action for its own sake, which had been a feature of his thinking both as a party activist and journalist, led Mussolini to challenge every single basic principle of Marxism. If adherence to such 'rigid' and abstract 'dogmas' as internationalism and anti-militarism stood in the way of action, then Mussolini the pragmatist decided they had to be jettisoned, as ideas condemning the movement to passivity in the face of great events. The crisis came on October 18, 1914, when Mussolini broke party discipline by publishing in *Avanti* his notorious article calling on the PSI to revise its policy on the war. In it he combined eclectically the terminology of Marxism with the intuitive philosophy of Sorel and Bergson:

Many indications support the inference that the PSI is not at ease on the cushions of so comfortable a formula as 'absolute neutrality'. Comfortable because it is negative, *allowing one to abstain from thought and to do nothing but wait*. A party that wants to live in history, to shape history, cannot accept a rule that has been made into a sacred dogma or eternal law independent of the inexorable exigencies of space and time ...We have condemned war, but this condemnation of the phenomenon itself, viewed in its 'universality', has not prevented us from distinguishing — logically, historically, socialistically — between wars. The war forced upon Belgium and Serbia and in a certain sense upon France is quite different in character from the war waged by the Austro-German combination ...Marx believed that 'whoever formulates a programme for the future is a reactionary'. Paradox! In our case, however, it is true: a programme of 'absolute' neutrality for the future is reactionary. Such a programme made sense once. *Today it is dangerous because it immobilises us. Formulas are accomodations to events; to accomodate*

*events to formulas is sterile ...If tomorrow ...it should become evident
that Italy's intervention can hasten the end of the terrible slaughter,
who among us Socialists would favour a 'general strike' to prevent a
descent into hostilities which, by saving hundreds of thousands of
proletarian lives in France, Germany, Austria, etc. would constitute a
supreme attestation of international solidarity?* Under pressure from
the Socialists, could not Italy become tomorrow the armed mediator
of a peace based on a limitation of armaments and respect for the
rights of all nationalities? *...unless we are prepared to condemn
ourselves to immobility, we cannot remain bound by any formula
...Do we wish to be — as men and Socialists — inert spectators of this
grandiose drama ...sometimes the 'letter' destroys the 'spirit'. Let us
beware of saving the 'letter' of the party if by so doing we destroy the
'spirit' of socialism.*[16] (emphasis added)

As so often has been the case both before and after Mussolini,
the attack on Marxism began with a passionate invocation of its
founder's name. This particular onslaught was all the more
pernicious in that it sought to defend the revolutionary, or
rather activist 'spirit' of Marxism from the allegedly passive
exponents of its 'letter'. Neither was Mussolini alone. Others also
previously identified with the extreme left-wing of the PSI and
the main trade union organisation, the CGL (General
Confederation of Labour) began to talk in the same highly
ambiguous terms, among them the syndicalist Fillippo Corridoni
(not to be confused with the Nationalist Enrico Corradini) who
had been jailed for his part in the violent struggles of the so-called
'Red Week' in June 1914, when workers and land labourers took
over entire townships in Emilia and the Marche and defied police
and army efforts to dislodge them for nearly a week. It is therefore too simple an argument to explain his and Mussolini's
renegacy in terms of material corruption. Mussolini lost his post
as editor of *Avanti*, while Corridoni proclaimed his support for
Nationalist interventionist policy from the gloom of an Italian
prison! And this line of reasoning is not only vulgar, it is
dangerous, for it obscures the profoundly idealist philosophical
roots of the movement that rapidly crystallised out of the fusion
between the PSI and syndicalist renegades from the left and the
Nationalists on the far right. If all treachery to the working class
can be explained purely — or even largely — in tems of material
corruption, or — and this is but a more sophisticated version of
the same theory — that such renegades, whether they pass over to
fascism or stop short at an opportunist position within the
workers' movement — are pursuing a course they have already
clearly mapped out in their heads, then this is merely another
variant of idealist philosophy, which views the behaviour of
individuals in moral terms or as a part of a larger 'conspiracy'. In
the case of Mussolini, the intuitionist *par excellence*, we can see
that this method of analysis is patently unable to explain his

ITALY. THE FIRST WARNING

work than 'bad faith' or some other moral deficiency.* Following
Mussolini and Corridoni into the interventionist camp were small
fractions from the PSI and the CGL. Among defectors from the
latter were Michele Bianchi, Edmondo Rossini, Alceste
Ambrisi and Giusseppe Giulietti, and they wasted no time in
founding their own nationalist organisation which took the name
Italian Labour Union (UIL). The 'national syndicalism' of Arturo
Labriola, first expounded in the heat of the Libyan war, was now
on the verge of becoming a vital ingredient in fascist demagogy
and after 1922, an organisational prop of the corporate state. But
by its very act of separation from the main body of the Italian
syndicalist movement, the UIL surrendered all claims to being a
genuine trade union. It denounced both the class struggle and the
international solidarity of the working class, and called upon the
proletariat to wage war, not on the Italian bourgeoisie, but its
class brothers in uniform, the cannon fodder of the Austrian
imperial army.

Meanwhile, Mussolini's career as a PSI journalist was coming
to a bitter and fateful end. Outraged militants demanded his
removal from the editorship of *Avanti* and his expulsion from the
party, both being carried out before the end of November 1914.
One career had ended, and a new one was about to begin. On
November 15, Mussolini launched his new interventionist daily
paper, the *Popolo d'Italia,* which carried on its masthead the
legend 'A socialist daily', suggesting that its editor had not parted
company with socialism, rather he was seeking a more national
interpretation of it. Describing the outlook and background of his
first supporters in this new journalist venture, Mussolini writes:

> They were composed of revolutionary spirits who believed in inter-
> vention. They were youths — the students of the universities, the
> socialist syndicalists, destroying faith in Karl Marx by their ideas.
> There were professional men too, and working men who could still

---

* Thus Trotsky writes of the leader of the Soviet Thermidor that 'if Stalin could have
forseen at the very beginning where his fight against Trotskyism would lead, he
undoubtedly would have stopped short, in spite of the prospect of victory over all his
opponents. But he did not forsee anything ...He did not have the slightest understanding of the historical function he was fulfilling'. (L. Trotsky: *Stalin,* p.393,
London, 1947) Mussolini's defection from the PSI was also governed by social
processes and objective forces that he at first had little or no comprehension of. He
later told Hitler that 'at the moment when he undertook the struggle against
Bolshevism, he didn't exactly know where he was going.' (*Hitler's Secret
Conversations,* p.118) But this did not prevent either Stalinism or Italian fascism
from emerging as consciously counter-revolutionary movements (the former as a
corrupted bureaucratic tendency *within* the workers movement, the later as a direct
instrument of monopoly capitalism *against* it) at a certain critical stage in their
development. As for Hitler, he began as and remained until the end of his days an
avowed and fanatical enemy of proletarian socialism, and in this sense his political
make-up and evolution differs from that of Mussolini.

hear the real voice of the country.[7]

In December 1914, this group founded the germ-cell of the future Fascist Party, the Fascio d'Azione Rivoluzionara, the Fascio of Revolutionary Action (the word *Fascio* or Fascist being derived from the symbol of authority carried before the rulers of ancient Rome — an axe surrounded by a bundle of rods). At this stage, as the name of both his group and the sub-title of his paper implied, he was still posing as a revolutionary socialist albeit of a highly unorthodox kind. Still groping for a new programme to replace the rejected internationalism of the PSI, Mussolini was at first motivated mainly by blind hatred for the movement which had expelled him from its ranks as a class traitor, and by a desire for violent action no matter what the cause or cost. Nevertheless, his subjectivism and intuitionism served as a vehicle for the most reactionary and consciously anti-working class forces in Italian and international politics. The Nationalists and other interventionists began to look with favour upon Mussolini's patriotic drum beatings, especially since his 'national syndicalist' allies could prove invaluable in lending substance to Nationalist propaganda concerning the 'proletarian' and 'revolutionary' nature of Italian imperialism's struggle for new land and markets. Support of a more tangible kind was forthcoming from another and at first sight more unlikely source. Acting with the full approval of the French government, Marcel Cachin, a pro-war leader of the French Socialist Party (and subsequently of French Stalinism) visited Italy in the December of 1914 with funds for the financing of interventionist groups in and around the Italian workers' movement. And among the beneficiaries of Cachin's largesse was Mussolini's new daily paper, *Popolo d'Italia.* With the fall of the neutralist Giolitti government on May 12, 1915, Mussolini's Fascio seemed to be left high and dry without a programme, since the pro-war administration of Antonio Salandra proceeded to carry it out by invading Austria on the 25th of the same month. Yet it rapidly became clear that Mussolini was not merely seeking war to regain the Italian-speaking regions of the Tyrol. His Fascio (who by now had been joined in their pro-war clamour by a motley band of Futurist literati and bohemians) also desired an entirely new political system where there would be little or no room for either parliamentary democracy or independent workers organisations. 'Parliament' wrote Mussolini on the eve of Giolitti's fall 'is Italy's

---

* The aptly-named Cachin, who acted as go-between for the French government in its dealings with Italian socialist and syndicalist 'interventionists', negotiated an initial cash grant of 1,000,000 lire for Mussolini's struggling new daily, a sum that was compounded by further monthly payments of 10,000 lire. After a brief flirtation with Bolshevism, Cachin became a Stalinist stalwart, and after the adoption of the Popular Front policy of alliances with bourgeois liberals in 1934, was able once more to give his suppressed patriotic sentiments full vent.

bubonic plague which poisons the blood of a nation. It mut be extirpated.'[8]

Along with several others of his group, Mussolini volunteered for front line service, leaving the day-to-day running of his paper to his closest co-thinkers. As working class opposition to the war hardened (by 1917 real wages had dropped 27% from their pre-war level), so *Popolo d'Italia* became more strident in its demands for a war on two fronts — against Austria and against the socialist movement at home. The campaign came to a head with the cataclysmic rout of the Italian army at Caporetto in October 1917. All pretence at being a socialist movement was discarded. The imperialist fatherland was in danger, and all those who hampered its struggle for survival were traitors to be shown no mercy. The paper then dropped its old sub-title of a 'socialist daily' and now claimed to speak for the 'combatants and producers', a change which Mussolini himself later regarded as marking a watershed in the history of Fascism.* The tone of the paper's articles also hardened:

> With a fiery style I demanded on the part of the government severe action against slackers and whosoever undermined the spirit of the War. I called for the organisation of a volunteer army. I asked for military rule in the north of Italy, insisted on the supression of socialist newspapers.[9]

Unlike Hitler, who totally lacking in original political thought, took over ready-made the programme of the Pan-German and *volkisch* right, Mussolini was groping his way into unmapped territory, feeling his way step by step towards the rounded-out strategy and ideology that was to become Italian fascism. And all the time Mussolini the ex-socialist and former editor of *Avanti* was applying his considerable knowledge of mass movements and agitation to the task of breaking up, and not building the movement he had served with no little skill and devotion for more than a decade.** Business circles most closely linked to the war

---

* '...the word 'producers' was already [in the summer of 1918] the expression of a mental attitude', wrote Mussolini in his *The Political and Social Doctrine of Fascism*. By 'producers' he meant not the proletariat alone, but all those classes and individuals whom corporatist doctrine declared to be 'productive'. This included not only the working class and the rural proletariat, but 'productive' capitalists and landowners. This misuse of syndicalist terminology — a salient characteristic of Italian fascism — had already been forshadowed more than a decade before by Sorel in *Reflections on Violence,* which Mussolini is known to have received with great enthusiasm. The admiration was mutual, Sorel remarking that Mussolini (who by this time was a fully blown fascist) was 'the only energetic man capable of redressing the feebleness of the government'.

** Comparing the fascist dictators of Germany and Italy, Trotsky considered Mussolini to be far more original: 'Mussolini from the very beginning reacted more consciously to social materials than Hitler ...Mussolini is mentally bolder and more cynical ...the Roman atheist only utilises religion as he does the police and courts, while his Berlin colleague really believes in the infallibility of the Church of Rome'.

industries — notably the Ligurian shipbuilding firm Ansaldo — soon overcame their inhibitions at collaborating with a former notorious enemy of Italian capitalism, and began to subsidise Mussolini's paper and the activities of his group. The company was a classic example of a medium size firm which mushroomed to enormous wealth and importance. Ansaldo shared Mussolini's enthusiasm for war, even though not for the same reasons. Government contracts increased its capital from 30 million lire in 1914 to 500 million by 1918, and its labour force over the same four year period from 4,000 to 56,000. By the war's end Ansaldo was producing not only warships, but guns, ammunition and even aeroplanes. Ansaldo's owners, the brothers Pio and Mario Perrone, also had a controlling interest in the big Banca Italiana di Sconto, so their decision in the summer of 1918 to subsidise Mussolini's movement possessed a significance far beyond the actual sums of money involved. It indicated that for the first time, Mussolini was being taken seriously not only as a patriotic drum-boy for imperialist wars, but a potential candidate for the role of strikebreaker and counter-revolutionist once the war came to its inevitable conclusion amidst a wave of working class radicalism.

Though events never went as far as the formation of workers' and soldiers' councils — partly at least because unlike Germany, Italy was a member of a victorious, and not defeated imperialist coalition — Mussolini found no response to his nationalist anti-socialist and anti-democratic propaganda amongst the working class. They had had enough of war, and they detested Mussolini as a traitor to socialism. Like Hitler, he rapidly discovered that middle class ex-servicemen were far more sympathetic to his ideas:

A war of the masses ends with the triumph of the masses ...The

And while Hitler denied the class struggle in theory only to wage it the more viciously in practice, Mussolini never forgot that which he learned in the PSI, namely 'the theory which sees in the life of contemporary society first of all the reciprocal action of two classes, the bourgeoisie and the proletariat.' And, Trotsky went on, 'just as scientific medicine equips one with the possibility not only of curing the sick but of sending the healthy to meet their forefathers by the shortest route, so if scientific analysis of class relations, predestined by its creator for the mobilisation of the proletariat, enabled Mussolini, after he had jumped into the opposing camp, to mobilise the middle classes against the proletariat. Hitler accomplished the same feat in translating the methodology of fascism into the language of German mysticism.' (L. Trotsky: *What is National Socialism,* in *The Struggle against Fascism in Germany,* pp.401-401) And in his biography of Stalin, Trotsky writes of Mussolini's intuitionism, that the leader of Italian fascism was '...Agile and inordinately ambitious, he smashed his socialist career in his greedy quest for success. His anger at the party became a moving force. He created and destroyed theory along his way. He is the very personification of cynical egotism ...Hitler exhibits traits of monomania and messianism. Personal hurt played a tremendous role in his development. He was a declassed petty-bourgeois who refused to be a working man ...He achieved a vicarious social elevation by execrating Jews and social democrats. He was desperately determined to rise higher...' (L. Trotsky: *Stalin,* p.413.)

bourgeois revolution of 1789 — which was revolution and war in one — opened the gates of the world to the bourgeoisie ...The present revolution, which is also war, seems to open the gates of the future to the masses, who have served their hard apprenticeship of blood and death in the trenches.[10]

And though separated by victory and defeat, the political conditions which compelled Hitler and Mussolini to turn towards the 'trench socialist' for their firmest cadres were remarkably similar. In Italy too, the bulk of the middle class of town and country were pulled to the left by the pre-revolutionary upsurge within the working class movement. This profound shift away from the old parties of order* drove the Vatican to the unprecedented and momentous decision of sanctioning the formation of a Catholic 'social' party, the Populari, or populists, and the creation of a parallel trade union organisation to counter the rising influence of the CGL amongst the more backward Catholic workers. (In fact the Catholic union, the Italian Confederation of Labour — CIL — was founded in March 1918, some ten months before the official launching of the Populari). Another indication of the crisis in extreme right-wing circles was the rout of the Nationalists, who lost all three of their seats in the November 1919 elections, and the decline of the right-wing Liberals, Italy's main bourgeois party (analogous to Stresemann's DVP) who also lost support in the middle class. In all, the outlook for a movement of Mussolini's type looked grim, no more promising than that which confronted Hitler when he decided with all his doubts about its future prospects of success to become member number seven of the Munich German Workers' Party. That Mussolini was able to break out of his group's post-war isolation, and blaze a counter-revolutionary trail which inspired Hitler to follow him was due entirely to a series of fatal tactical and strategical errors committed by the leadership of the Italian workers movement, not excluding that section of it, organised after 1920, in the Communist Party. And here too, there is a common bond with Germany, where the treachery of the reformists and mistakes of the centrists permitted the counter-revolution to regroup and strike back at the proletariat with deadly consequences.

And Mussolini's political prospects at the end of 1918 were black indeed. A movement which proclaimed harmony between

* The degree of this shift can be partially measured by comparing the election results for 1913 with those for 1919. In the last pre-war election, the bourgeois parties with a middle class following — the liberals, democrats, radicals, republicans and nationalists — won 417 of the 508 seats in the Italian parliament, while the PSI secured but 51. In the first post-war election (November 1919), the bourgeois bloc had been cut down to a total of 151 seats, while the PSI had tripled its representation to 156. The Populari accounted for the remaining 100 seats.

classes and preached the mystical doctrines of nation and race could expect precious little support from the proletariat, now surging into the trade unions and the ranks of the PSI like a torrent.* While this movement maintained its forward impetus, Mussolini could only bend to it, even mimicking its radicalism and outbidding the socialist leaders with shameless demagogy.

That his pseudo-anarchist rantings** of this early post war period were pure camouflage for his sinister counter-revolutionary aims is evident from his later recollections:

> Everything was discussed again. We Italians opened the box of political problems and took apart the social clockwork. We pawed over everything from the Crown to Parliament, from the Army to our Colonies, from capitalistic property to the communistic soviet proposal for the federation of the regions of Italy, from schools to the Papacy. The lovely structure of concord and harmony that we combatants and the wounded had dreamed that we would build after the luminous victory of October 1918 was coming to pieces.[11]

And as in Germany, nationalist war-veterans returned from the 'harmony' of the trenches and the barracks thirsting for revenge against those who had snatched from them the rewards they believed their courage and sacrifices had merited. They did not relish the Italy they saw — a battlefield of classes, not of nations. Unity therefore had to be imposed on the nation, and by military means if needs be. The following passage from Mussolini's autobiography describes the circumstances which brought about the formation of the Italian fascist movement:

> ...I knew very well that a strong government would quickly put in order the socialists and anarchists, the decadents and wreckers and the instigators of disorder ...And thus ...one Sunday, the 26th of

---

* CGL membership rose from 300,000 in 1914 to 1,375,000 in 1919 and to a peak of 1,300,000 in 1920, the year of the September factory occupations. From this date, there was nothing but decline. PSI membership also followed the same curve — 100,000 in 1920 as against 50,000 before the outbreak of war.

** 'I start with the individual and strike at the state ...Down with the state in all its forms and incarnations: the state of yesterday, and of today and of tomorrow, the bourgeois state and the socialist state. To us, there remains during the present gloom and dark tomorrow, only the religion, at present absurd, but always consoling, of Anarchy!' This was how Mussolini wrote in the April of 1920. Within a year, he was denouncing the 'bourgeois state' for its liberalism! And in his first speech to the Italian Chamber of Deputies after the march on Rome on November 16, 1922, this former enemy of the state declared: 'The state is strong and will prove its strength against everyone ...Whoever defies the state will be punished.' Finally, this champion of the individual against all authority wrote, in his *The Political and Social Doctrine of Fascism* (1931): '[being] anti-individualistic, the Fascist conception of life stresses the importance of the state and accepts the individual only in so far as his interests coincide with those of the state ...The Fascist concept of the State is all-embracing; outside of it no human or spiritual values can exist ...The State is not only the present, it is also the past and above all the future ...The Fascist State expresses the will to exercise power and to command.'

> February, 1919, I saw at Milan a fact more disquieting and more important than I thought possible. I saw a socialist procession — with an endless·number of flags ...with banners cursing the War. I saw a river in the street made of women, children, Russian, German and Austrians [sic!] flowing through the town ...They had numerous meetings. They clamoured amnesty for the deserters. They demanded the division of the land![12]

And equally disturbing for Mussolini was the same cowardice or indifference in the propertied classes which drove Hitler to conclude that only mass terror could combat the menace of Marxism:

> As the procession passed through the streets the bourgeois closed hastily their windows and doors. They pulled down their roller blinds. 'There', said I, 'are eyes closing with the weariness of anxiety and fear ...Not a single force *interventista* (i.e. nationalist) or any other put their feet on to the street to stop the irresponsibles'.[13]

The very next day, Mussolini thundered against the socialist 'beast' in *Il Popolo d'Italia:*

> If the opposition to war that is not only finished, but was victorious, is now a pretext for an ignoble doubt, then we, who are not ashamed to have been interventisti, but feel the glory of our position, will shout to the heavens — 'Stand back — you jackals!' No one shall separate the dead ...We shall defend the dead ...even though we put dug-outs in the public squares and trenches in the streets of the city.[14]

It was a declaration of war against the Italian proletariat. Less than a month later, on March 23, 1919, the Fasci di Combattimento held its historic meeting (in a hall fittingly offered to Mussolini by the Milan Association of Merchants and Shop-keepers) which saw the adoption of the founding fascist programme.*

Taken at its face value, the programme was distinctly 'left' in flavour demanding not only a republic but the 'suppression of all forms of speculation' and 'confiscation of unproductive revenues'. But there was much that was deliberately ambiguous and even mystifying, especially point 12, which called for the 'reorganisation of production according to the cooperative principle, including the workers' direct share of profits' Mussolini's speech to the Milan meeting helped to resolve at least some of these uncertainties. His new movement might appeal to the proletariat, but not in the name of socialism. Socialism was 'reactionary', 'national syndicalism' revolutionary:

> Unquestionably, Bolshevism has ruined the economic life of Russia ...For our part, we declare war on socialism ...because it has aligned itself against the nation ...The official socialist party has been obviously reactionary ...It cannot lead a movement of renovation and reconstruction ...Majorities are inevitably static, minorities dynamic.

---

* Reproduced at the end of this chapter.

We wish to be an active minority, to separate the proletariat from the Socialist party. [Then in a typical display of demagogy, Mussolini continued] But if the middle classes think that we shall be their lightning conductors, they are mistaken. We must go toward the workers ...and accept their premises. Do they want an eight hour day? Will miners and night workers insist on a six hour day, invalidity and old age insurance, control over industry? We will support these demands, partly because we want the workers to become accustomed to the responsibilities of management and to learn in consequence that it is not easy to operate a business successfully ...as for economic democracy, we favour national syndicalism and oppose intervention by the state whenever it is aimed at throttling the creation of wealth ...There are industrialists who shun technical and moral innovations. Should they prove incapable of changing, they will be swept aside. However, we must impress on the workers that it is one thing to destroy, another to build ...We are strongly opposed to all forms of dictatorship, whether of the sword or the cocked hat, of wealth or of numbers. The only dictatorship we do acknowledge is that of will and intelligence.[15]

This is the classic 'supra class' programme of fascism. The workers are to be rewarded with a voice in the running of industry — and backward employers are to be 'swept away'. Yet the state will not tamper with the economy while wealth is being created. Socialism is to be fought, but not for the benefit of the bourgeoisie ...and so on. Each point balances out the next, the end result being a policy which promises everything to everybody yet commits the movement to nothing.

Both Hitler and Mussolini began their careers as professional counter-revolutionaries hoping to win over a sizable segment of the proletariat to fascism. Early experiences taught them that this was impossible, and that the potential mass reserves of their movements lay elsewhere, namely in the petty-bourgeoisie. Proletarians were conspicuous by their absence from the cadre of the early national socialist movement, and so it was in the case of its Italian counterpart. True, Mussolini enjoyed the support of a handful of renegade socialists, (as did Hitler: i.e. Esser and Otto Strasser) and syndicalists, but they brought precious few workers with them into the infant fascist movement. Fifty-four persons attended the Milan rally — 'syndicalists, old interventionists, demobilised officers still in uniform, and many *Arditi*, those brave grenade and knife-shock troops of the war'.[16] These last, and not the renegades from socialism and syndicalism, were to comprise the fighting forces of Italian fascism, just as in Germany, the commanding staff of the SA was recruited largely from the ranks and leadership of the Free Corps brigades:

This typically Italian formation [the *Arditi*] lived on after the War. The first fighting Fascisti were formed mostly of decided men. They were full of will and courage. In the first years of the anti-Socialist, anti-Communist struggle the *Arditi* war veterans played an important role.[1]

Their baptism of fire on the home front came the next month, when a general strike in the Milan industrial region provided the pretext for a fascist attack on the offices of Mussolini's old paper, *Avanti*. Though massively outnumbered by thousands of demonstrating workers, the *Arditi* veterans of hand-to-hand trench fighting in the alpine north, routed the hastily assembled forces guarding the *Avanti* offices. The premises were sacked and burned with the Arditi escaping unharmed, much to the delight of the Milanese bourgeoisie, who were beginning to despair of the red tide ever receding.*

Even so, only a small trickle of anti-socialist fanatics found their way into the new movement's ranks in its first few months of activity. The bulk of its future middle class supporters were still either putting their trust in bourgeois liberalism or watching — full of a mixture of hope and apprehension — the struggle of the proletariat to re-fashion Italy along socialist lines. Only when this bid had been decisively betrayed by the PSI reformists and centrists, and the bureaucrats of the CGL, did Mussolini find the courage to launch his massive onslaught on the proletariat, and only then did the middle class begin its violent plunge to-wards the extreme right. The great tragedy was that in Italy as well as in Germany, the revolutionary crisis matured more rapidly than the assembling and steeling of the leadership necessary to exploit it. In Germany, the Spartacists split from the USPD centrists at the end of 1918. Though long-delayed, the formation of the KPD at least enabled the most advanced sections of the working class to enter the massive class battles of the next months and years behind a clear and distinct communist banner.

Not so in Italy, where the genuinely Bolshevik elements in the party, headed by Antonio Gramsci and Amadeo Bordiga, only succeeded in demarcating themselves from the centrist 'Maximalists' in January 1921; that is, *after* the working class had passed through its most momentous offensive battles against the bourgeoisie. The PCI was founded in conditions of political re-action, and this too, redounded to the tactical and strategic advan-tage of the fascists.** The revolutionary energies squandered

---

* Like Hitler, Mussolini took care not to become closely identified with the old bourgeois parties. Anxious to deflect charges by his former comrades that he had gone over to reaction, Mussolini demonstratively supported an 'occupation' organised by the 'national syndicalist' UIL at the Dalmine engineering works near Milan. By not striking, and by raising the Italian tricolour rather than the red flag, these workers were acting 'creatively' by 'not forgetting the nation'. It was a 'strike' with a difference.

** Addressing the Third Congress of the Communist International on this problem, Trotsky warned against the adoption of a 'leftist' line by the newly formed PCI in the wake of the historic September reverse: 'I might have said "Here is a country ruined

by the PSI and trade union leadership in the first two post-war years were truly prodigious. In 1913, a year of violent class conflict, 385,000 workers engaged in strike action. In 1919, this total had soared to 1.5 million, and was itself surpassed in the fateful year of 1920, when 2.3 million proletarians struck work. If, as the syndicalists and worshippers of spontaneity claimed, militancy were enough to overturn capitalism, then it should surely have done so in these two years. Yet it did not. The high point was reached in the September of 1920, when what began as a trade union struggle turned into an occupation of the major industrial concentrations of north Italy. Spreading from that hot-bed of proletarian radicalism in the Fiat works at Turin, the factory seizures rapidly embraced Milan, Florence, Bologna and all the other industrial centres of the so-called 'iron triangle'; while in the countryside, from the fertile Po valley in the north to poverty-stricken Sicily in the extreme south, poor peasants and land labourers were also on strike for the right of their 'leagues' to negotiate their own working conditions with the employers and landlords. For the first time in the history of modern Italy, the whole nation was aflame with struggles of revolutionary dimensions and implications. But the one factor required to fuse these two still distinct, yet parallel streams into a single torrent was lacking.

by war where the workers have seized the factories, where the Fascists are sacking labour printing plants and setting fire to working class institutions. And if this party does not raise the cry: 'With All Our Forces Forward Against the Enemy', then it is a cowardly party which will be condemned by world history". But if we look at things not from the standpoint of weighing the situation cold-bloodedly, we would have to say what comrade Zinoviev did, namely: they must gain anew the confidence of the working class since the workers have become much more cautious precisely owing to this treachery. They will say to themselves: "We heard the same phrases from Serrati [leader of the PSI centrists]. He said virtually the same thing and then he betrayed us. Where is the guarantee that the new party will not betray us, too?" The working class wants to see the party in action before going into the decisive battle under its leadership.' (L. Trotsky: *Speech on Comrade Radek's Report on Tactics of the Comintern*, July 1, 1911, in L. Trotsky: *The First Five Years of the Communist International*, Vol. I, p.178, New York, 1945) Trotsky's advice was not heeded by all the leaders of the new party. The group headed by Amadeo Bordiga stubbornly refused to adopt a united front tactic with the centrists and reformists workers' organisations and leaders, arguing that such a policy involved a surrender of revolutionary principles. Neither did Bordiga distinguish between the parliamentary and Fascist forms of capitalist state power. 'If the fascists destroy parliament, we shall be delighted,' declared Bordiga to the PCI Congress, held at Rome in October 1911, with the fascist coup only a matter of days away. And continuing a line of reasoning that the Stalinist KPD leadership developed to its ultra-leftist nadir in the period of Hitler's rise to power, Bordiga claimed that no distinctions existed between the various non-communist parties in Italy. He termed them the 'socialist-Populist Fascist ruling class' while their respective leaders, Turati, Sturzo and Mussolini, were three names for a single 'grim tyrant', Bordiga and his leftist comrades were soon to discover that there was a very great difference between the 'grim tyrants' of the PSI and those of Italian Fascism, for within a matter of months, PSI and CPI militants — and even leaders — were sharing the same cells and prison compounds!

For two weeks, the revolutionary situation ripened as the government, headed by the wily old Liberal Giolitti, stood back, powerless to intervene. It was a situation analogous in many ways to that of Germany in November 1918. The Italian bourgeoisie lacked both the will and the material reserves to crush the advancing proletariat by sheer brute force. And as in Germany, the most astute elements of this fearful bourgeoisie, guided by a Giolitti who knew the PSI and CGL reformists like the back of his hand, staked the fate of Italian capitalism on this bureaucracy's sure conservative instincts. With the agreement of the PSI centre and right, the trade union leaders were permitted to shift the struggle away from the issue of state power to a more familiar and less explosive terrain, and naturally, like their German counterparts in November 1918, the Italian employers, organised in the recently-founded General Confederation of Industry (*Confindustria*) were only too pleased to sign on the dotted line. Anything rather than expropriation! But it was an agreement which only one side intended to keep. While the CGL leaders prided themselves on their 'moderation',* the big industrialists began to consider ways and means of taking back what had been extracted from them under duress. In this too there was a direct parallel with Germany, where the big employers reneged on the November 1918 accords with the ADGB by opposing the social and economic clauses of the Weimar Constitution; but in Italy, the most reactionary employers (and landlords) wasted little time experimenting with the various parties of the traditional right. The defeat of the September occupation movement almost at once reflected itself in a rapid shift of the middle class towards the far right. The socialist movement having failed in its hour of great opportunity to give the clear lead the petty-bourgeoisie requires in periods of crisis, the treachery of the trade union bureaucracy and PSI reformists and centrists now created the conditions for a counter-revolutionary movement in the middle class which the big bourgeoisie could exploit to take the offensive against a working class thrown into disarray by the September defeat.

Yet this new situation was partially masked by the communal

---

* Just prior to the march on Rome, CGL secretary Ludovico D'Aragona declared with obvious sincerity that 'it is our glory and pride that we prevented the outbreak of the revolution which the extremists desired.' One can understand why Mussolini wrote in August 1921: 'If the three secretaries of the Labour Alliance [the alliance of Italy's three main trade union bodies] had been three of the most fanatical fascists, they really could not have rendered a greater service to the cause of Italian fascism.' (B. Mussolini: *Il Popolo d'Italia,* August 5, 1921) The socialist reformists were no better. Following the ignominious collapse of a poorly organised anti-fascist general strike at the beginning of August 1921, Turati wrote: 'The general strike has been our Caporetto ...We must have the courage to recognise that today the fascists are masters of the field.' Giacomo Matteotti, the reformist deputy murdered by fascist assassins in June 1924, adopted a similar defeatist line, advising workers to 'stay at home ...Even silence and cowardice are sometimes heroic'.

election results of October 31, 1920. Held little more than a month after the end of the factory occupations, they more reflected the level of political consciousness which produced that great movement than the period of political decline which set in during the following months, and which culminated in the victory of Fascism two years later. The PSI won 25 of the 69 provinces, and more than a quarter of Italy's 8,300 communes, thereby maintaining its position as the country's largest party. But there was a shadow on the horizon. A resurgent bourgeoisie had combined its political forces to form the so-called 'National Bloc', and under its anti-socialist banner they rallied the middle classes to such good effect that not only in the backward south, where the PSI had but a small following, and Rome, where the population was predominately petty-bourgeois, but even in industrial Florence, Genoa and Turin, the birthplace of Italian communism, Giolitti's bloc (with Fascist support in Milan) took control of the local administration. The Catholic Populists also lost ground — heavily — on their performance in November 1919, reflecting a shift in the rural poor and more conservative workers back towards the right. Fascism itself also underwent a change in this period. Many of those misguided workers who had been dragged in its tow (while rarely becoming members of the party) through their membership of the UIL began to drift away as the middle class donned the black shirt of the *squadristi* and armed itself with knives, pistols and castor oil for the crusade against the 'reds'.

Bologna was Mussolini's first target. A stronghold of the workers' movement, it had returned a socialist administration in the elections of November 1920, and was still celebrating the PSI's great ballot box triumph when a motorised fascist assault column roared into the city armed to the teeth on November 21 and set about teaching the local socialist officials some basic lessons of class warfare — lessons which they were tragically slow to learn. The arrival of the black-shirted army heralded an orgy of anti-proletarian terror which did not abate until every socialist had been driven from office, the local labour press and premises sacked, looted and burned, and the city's working class driven to distraction and despair by the utter inability of their leaders to organise any resistance.

Mussolini's march on Rome began on that black day in the history of Italian and European labour, signposted by the reformist and centrists of the PSI. For none had heeded the prophetic warning of Gramsci, made at a time when the Italian working class was still in the ascendent and Fascism regarded by most PSI militants as little more than a minor political irritant:

> The present phase of the class struggle in Italy is the phase that precedes either the conquest of political power by the revolutionary

proletariat ...or a tremendous reaction by the propertied classes and the government caste. No violence will be spared in this subjection of the industrial and agricultural proletariat to servile labour: a bid will be made to smash inexorably the working class's institutions of political struggle (the socialist party) and to incorporate its institutions of economic resistance (unions and co-operatives) into the machinery of the bourgeois state.[18]

Gramsci only erred in assuming that the reaction would stop short at the smashing of the unions and co-operatives. Once in power, Fascism, despite its demagogic pledges to preserve the 'economic' organisations of the workers, made no distinction between the PSI, the CPI and the CGL. Being independent class organisations, all stood condemned by the corporatist principles of class harmony and 'national syndicalism'. There was to be no 'incorporation', as Gramsci had predicted, (indeed the very nature of the corporate state precludes it) but total obliteration.*

Rich landowners as well as industrialists began to subsidise the fascists once it became evident that Italian labour, while still

---

* Gramsci was of course speaking at a time (spring 1920) when there were no concrete historical precedents to work from. His premonition of fascism — for such it was, even though he does not refer to Mussolini specifically — cannot be faulted simply because it failed to predict with complete accuracy the course of the fascist regime. But when, more than half a century later, and 47 years after the official liquidation of the Italian trade union movement with the promulgation of the Rocco Labour Law (April 3, 1926), we still encounter Marxist publications which refer to corporatism as if the March on Rome had never happened, let alone Hitler's liquidation of the German trade unions in May 1933 or Franco's merciless extermination of the Spanish UGT and CNT, we can only be amazed at such theoretical slovenliness. Repeatedly *Workers Press* treats what it calls 'corporatism' as a species of 'collaboration' between the trade union leaders and the employers and capitalist state. Thus in *Workers Press* of August 3, 1973, we read that 'in answer to the demand that a labour government is returned to power by revolutionary working class action, committed to nationalising big capital, they [the TUC] hold out the sop that unions would be allowed to nominate their own men to help organise the counter-revolution. And in opposition to the demand for full workers' control of both former private and former state-run industry, they suggest politely that officials of the new, corporatist unions could sit in the boardrooms of the corporate state too'. (*Scanlon Praises TUC's Corporatist Report, Workers Press,* August 3, 1973, p.9.) Here the TUC figures not merely as an essential element of a future corporatist regime, but as its *pace maker,* as the following extract from the same article bears out: 'Thus Scanlon becomes an essential prop for the bureaucratic corporatist machinery with which the trade union leaders *want* to divert the growing support in the working class movement for immediate policies of socialist nationalisation and workers control.' (emphasis added) So, *Workers Press* tells us, the TUC actually *wants* to institute a corporatist regime. And since, in the Trotskyist book, corporatism is the ideology of the fascist state (after all, the corporatist Mussolini was also a fascist), we arrive at the proposition that far from being an obstacle — however feeble — to the establishment of a fascist dictatorship by the monopolies, as Trotsky repeatedly insisted against 'third period' Stalinist claims that the reformist unions had turned 'social fascist', the trade unions will become one of the main agencies in the institution and maintenance of such a regime. This dangerous line of thinking is a mockery of Trotskyism, and, moreover, it flies in the face of history. Corporatist Italy was the graveyard of trade unions — and a prison for even their most collaborationist leaders.

capable of fighting heroic defensive battles, was in full-scale
retreat before the gathering reaction. During September 1920,
Mussolini had not dared to come out openly against the factory
occupations. He even criticised the employers for not accepting
some of the CGL's demands. But by the summer of 1921, and
with his black shirted *Arditi* blazing a trail of burned-out trade
union, and socialist, communist and co-operative buildings
throughout north Italy,* he was speaking with a rather different
voice:

> ...let me warn you at once that we shall resist with all our strength any
> attempt at socialisation, collectivisation and state socialism ...we assert
> that the real history of capitalism is only now beginning, because
> capitalism is not just a system of oppression, it also represents a choice
> of values, a co-ordination of hierarchies, a more developed sense of
> industrial responsibility.[19]

In this, his first speech to the Italian Parliament following his
election — on a Giolittian National Bloc ticket — he also revised
his previously anti-clerical views on Church-state relations:

> Fascism does not preach and does not practice anti-clericalism ...I
> affirm here and now that today the Latin and imperial tradition of
> Rome is represented by Catholicism. I believe and affirm that the
> universal idea that exists in Rome today is that which radiates from
> the Vatican ...I believe that if the Vatican were to renounce once and
> for all its dreams of temporal power — and I think it is going to —
> profane or lay Italy would furnish the Vatican with material aid for its
> schools, churches and hospitals.[20]

And so the first foundation stone was laid for the Lateran
Accords of February 11, 1929, which established Catholicism as
the Italian State religion and as 'the basis and apex of public
education'. (The drafters of Italy's post-war constitution
—headed by the Stalinist Minister of Justice Palmiro Togliatti!
— were obviously delighted by Mussolini's handiwork, since the
Lateran Accords were incorporated into the republican constitution which went into effect on January 1, 1948.)
The elections of May 1921 which brought 35 Fascist deputies
into the Italian Parliament marked a further shift to the right by
the middle class. The bourgeois democrats and radicals lost 60
seats, dropping to 108, while the National Bloc and right-wing
liberals totalled 148 seats. The Republican non-socialist left, like
the democrats lost heavily (43 down to 22), while the Populists
made a good showing, increasing their representation to 108. But
now the workers' parties could not escape the consequences of the
September defeat. Whereas in 1919, the PSI had won 156 seats,

* This was the tally of fascist destruction visited on the workers' movement during
the first six months of 1911: 17 newspaper offices and printshops, 59 'People's
Houses', 119 chambers of labour, 107 co-operatives, 83 peasant leagues offices, 141
socialist and communist clubs and offices.

the PSI and CPI combined could now only claim 131 (PSI 108), CPI 15). The writing was on the wall, and written in language that even the most cretinous parliamentarian could decipher. Yet what was the reaction of *Avanti*? 'The Italian proletariat has buried the Fascist reaction under an avalanche of red ballot papers'. Other — and more real — burials and cremations were soon underway. Emboldened by his enemies' total lack of a fighting strategy and tactical plan, and greatly strengthened by tacit and often open support from the organs of state, Mussolini's offensive against what remained of the Italian labour movement now gathered momentum. His middle class army waged a truly ferocious war of revenge on the proletariat, which it saw as the cause of all its political frustrations and economic problems. An official break-down of Fascist Party membership made at its congress at Rome in November 1921 revealed that of the movement's 320,000 members, many were workers dragooned into the fascist party by virtue of their forcible enrolment into the UIL after the destruction of their own local trade union organisation. By contrast, landowners (36,000) tradesmen (7,000) manufacturers (8,000) and learned professions (20,000) comprised a percentage of Fascist Party membership far above the proportion warranted by their representation in Italy's total population. In other words, Mussolini's movement recruited its main forces from the propertied upper and middle classes and those strata and groups most closely associated with them either occupationally, materially or ideologically. As one fascist squad leader — U. Banchelli — himself once stated in his memoirs with remarkable frankness, the black-shirted onslaught on Italian labour was unleashed by those who did not consider themselves so much fascists as 'sons of lawyers, doctors, tradesmen ...for long these gangs had only to meet people who looked like workers to attack them without pity'.*

* Italo Balbo, one of the top four fascist leaders (quadrumvirs) described in his diary one such onslaught — that on the working class stronghold of Ravenna in July 1921: 'We undertook this task in the same spirit as when we demolished the enemy's stores in war-time. The flames from the great burning building [the socialist headquarters] rose ominously into the night. The whole town was illuminated by the glare, we had to strike terror into the heart of our enemies ...I announced to him [the Ravenna police chief] that I would burn down and destroy the houses of all the socialists in Ravenna if he did not give me within half an hour the means required for sending the Fascists elsewhere ...I demanded a whole fleet of lorries ...after half an hour they told me where I could find lorries already supplied with petrol. Some of them actually belonged to the office of the chief of police ... We went through Rimini, Sant'Arcangelo, Savignano, Cesena, Bertinoro, all the towns and centres in the provinces of Forli and Ravenna, and destroyed and burnt all the red buildings, the seats of the Socialist and Communist organisations. It was a terrible night. Our passage was marked by huge columns of fire and smoke. The whole plain of the Romagna was given up to the reprisals of the outraged Fascists determined to break for ever the red terror'. (I. Balbo, *1922 Diaries*, pp.103-109)

Hitler's assumption of power was preceded and to a great extent prepared for by a period when the polarisation of class forces produced a parliamentary stalemate in which no party or coalition of parties could 'form a majority government. This became the political basis for the semi-Bonapartist government of Brüning, and the fully Bonapartist regimes of Papen and Schleicher. So it was in Italy, where Populist disaffection with the Giolitti regime, which had adopted a harsh attitude towards the Catholic trade unions, brought about its fall after the May elections and its replacement by the administration of Ivanoe Bonomi, which sought to adopt a more compromising attitude towards the moderate left. These waverings in the political circles of the bourgeoisie only redoubled Fascist determination to brush aside the liberals and step up the war against Italian labour. In the last months of the Weimar Republic, decisive sections of heavy industry and finance broke with their traditional parties — the DVP and DNVP — in calling for the formation of a Hitler-led government. By the beginning of 1922, this trend was under way in Italy. Sufficient numbers of rich landowners, bankers and industrialists had switched their allegiance from the old bourgeois parties and leaders to the fascists to make a Mussolini government a distinct possibility if the workers' movement found itself so tied by the reformists that it could not offer any serious resistance to a fascist coup. Bonomi fell in February 1922, to be replaced by the even more ineffective Luigi Facta. His government did little more than hold the ring while the black shirts moved with impunity from town to town crushing the last centres of working class resistance to fascism. Thus the stage was set for the final act in this tragedy — the so-called 'march on Rome'. This theatrical affair was carefully stage-managed by Mussolini and his closest aides to deck out the fascist seizure of power in a revolutionary garb, for *Il Duce* had been under heavy pressure from the fascist militants not to compromise with the old rulers of Italy. The trek from Naples — where the Fascists had been holding their congress — to Rome was certainly not undertaken with a view to toppling the Facta government by force, nor to intimidate the big bourgeoisie. A series of important speeches made throughout the previous year had banished the last lingering doubts in the minds of the propertied classes about Mussolini's intentions as to private property, the monarchy and religion. In November 1921, at the Rome party congress, he had declared:

> Our aim is not to introduce socialism but to leave it far behind. We are economic liberals because we maintain that the national economy cannot be entrusted to collective, bureaucratic agencies. In view of the Russian experiment, the time has come to put a stop to all that. I would return the railways and the telegraph lines to private ownership

because the present arrangement is monstrous and vulnerable in every
way ...We oppose the economic state. Socialist theories have been
disproved; internationalist myths have crumbled. The class struggle is
a fairy tale, mankind cannot be divided. Instead of being separated the
proletariat and the bourgeoisie are integral parts of a single whole
...One hears it said that the masses must be won over ...We do indeed
wish to serve them, to educate them, but we also intend to flog them
when they make mistakes ...we are hereby warning them that when the
interests of the nation are at stake, the egoism of everyone, of the
proletariat as well as the bourgeoisie, must take a back seat.

Ten months later, Mussolini made another speech which was
nothing less than a demand to be handed the reins of state power.
Only Fascism could quell the rebellious masses and set them to
work:

You know very well that I do not worship the masses, that new
divinity created by democracy and socialism. [According to them the
masses] are necessarily in the right solely because of their numbers.
Nothing of the sort is true ...history proves that it is always minorities
...that produce profound changes in human society. We refuse to
worship the masses even if they come endowed with all the sacrosanct
calluses on hands and brain ...

He then went on to explain why fascism had to resort to
'social' demagogy and employ some of the language of
syndicalism:

We have had to practice syndicalism and are continuing to do so.
Some say 'Your syndicalism will end up by becoming entirely
indistinguishable from socialist syndicalism; you will be forced by the
necessary logic of events to wage the class struggle' ...In actuality, our
syndicalism differs from that of others because we absolutely deny the
right to strike in the public services. We particularly favour class
collaboration and are therefore trying to imbue our syndicates with
this ...idea.

On the vexed question of the monarchy (Mussolini had continued to favour a republic even after his defection from the PSI),
Mussolini stated:

I really believe that the regime can be renovated in depth even if the
monarchy is left untouched. We shall leave the monarchy alone
because we believe a large part of the country would view with suspicion any transformation of the regime which went as far as that ...I
am basically of the opinion that the monarchy has no reason whatever
to oppose the Fascist revolution.

Mussolini was right. After a conference in Milan with the
Confindustria leaders, who were pressing Rome to appoint him
Prime Minister in place of the demoralised Facta, Mussolini
arrived at the Naples party congress, where after once again
stressing to assembled bourgeois, aristocratic and military
dignitaries that fascist syndicalism was not really syndicalism at
all, he made his most significant ploy of all. Fearing a possible

clash with the army en route to Rome, he declared to the rally that 'the army should know that we defended it at a time when the ministers were advising its officers to go about in civilian dress in order to avoid clashes.' Mussolini now hoped the army leaders would repay this loyalty by refusing to defend these ministers should they give the order to fire on the black-shirted army when it arrived at the gates of Rome.

There was talk of such an order being given, but King Emmanuel III, who had grown increasingly sympathetic to fascism as it steadily shed its republican hue, refused to sign the order proclaiming a state of siege in the capital. Now back in Milan, Mussolini awaited the call to the once scorned and despised Quirinal. Whilst there, he held a series of last-minute conferences with the leaders of Italian industry, notably Crespi, Conti, Pirelli and Olivetti (the last being head of the all-powerful *Confindustria*). He made it clear to them that the aim of his government would be 'the restoration of discipline especially in the factories.' So when Mussolini did finally enter Rome on October 30th as its new Caesar, it was with the full approval of Italy's leading men of industry and in response to a summons from the king. And he arrived, not on a white horse at the head of his black-shirted legionaries, but in a first class sleeper from Milan wearing that symbol of bourgeois rectitude, a bowler hat. The reactions of his business backers were predictable enough. Three days after the formation of the Mussolini coalition* the *Confindustria* organ, *L'Organizzazione Industriale,* gleefully heralded the advent of the first fascist dictatorship in human history:

> We look to it with great hopes. We will support the programme of this regime with all our strength, for in it, for the first time after long years, protection of property rights, the general obligation to work, a full valuation of the energy of the individual and of national sentiment are energetically proclaimed.

In making this triumphant declaration, the leaders of Italian

---

* The composition, as well as origin, of Mussolini's first government was similar to that of Hitler's (both also shared the official designation of governments of 'national concentration'), though it included representatives of parties whose German counterparts were excluded from the smallest share in the exercise of power in the early months of the Third Reich. Mussolini headed a coalition of, besides himself, three Fascists, two Populists, two rightist Liberals, three 'Democrats' a Nationalist and two 'non-political' appointments as heads of the army and navy. Though excluded from power, Germany's liberals, democratic and Catholic leaders were not one whit less anxious to lick the fascist boots than their Italian predecessors. Both Hitler and Mussolini received unanimous votes of confidence from the old bourgeois parties, Hitler's enabling act of March 23, 1933, being opposed only by the SPD — the KPD was already banned — while in Italy, the confidence vote of November 16, 1922 was carried 306-116, with once again only the deputies of the two workers parties — the PSI and CPI — voting against. At the death, the bourgeois liberals, democrats and radicals preferred fascism when the alternative appeared to be a victory of socialism.

monopoly capitalism were running true to form, as were the reformist leaders of the trade unions, who rather than continue to resist the fascist menace, sought to come to terms with it. In doing so they foreshadowed the miserable capitulation to fascism carried out by their opposite numbers in Germany, who in the first weeks of the Nazi regime, grovelled on their knees before Hitler in the vain hope that he would spare them and their organisations.

Oblivious to the fact that unlike previous governments, fascism had no need of their services, the CGL leadership curried favour with Mussolini by announcing their separation from the PSI, a move which elicited from Mussolini the ironic remark 'at last'. Though the CGL unions were destined for eventual liquidation, it suited Mussolini to play along with the right-wing bureaucracy as a counterweight to the left-wing of the workers' movement. The CGL leaders lent themselves to this manoeuvre shamelessly participating in talks with Mussolini in December 1922, just as the ADGB parleyed with NSBO officials in April 1933, at the very time when Hitler was already putting the final touches to his plans for winding up the entire trade union movement and putting its leaders in jail.

The pay-off for Mussolini was immediate. The CGL unleashed a furious witch-hunt against PCI and other trade union militants, many of whom were summarily expelled over the next few weeks. Nor was this all. The CGL bureaucracy issued a statement 'fingering' those workers who despite intimidation refused to accept its collaborationist policy, and warning others of the dire consequences of resisting the new regime, a 'struggle from which they must absolutely remain aloof'. Non-political trade unionism, one of the hall-marks of syndicalism, had reached its nadir. But even though the CGL grovelled on its belly before Mussolini, it was all to no avail. Having performed their function of choking off the revolutionary militancy of the working class in the September 1920 occupations, and then of damping down their burning desire to hit back at the fascists when the black counter-attack began later that same year, the bureaucrats of the CGL found the new regime had no more use for them. What big business demanded of fascism was not a new era of compromise in which the union leaders would be permitted to 'win' a series of reforms for their members, but a long period of reaction, of naked dictatorship, in which the proletariat would have torn from its grasp everything that it had won — despite and even against its own leaders — in the period when the employers had been in retreat before the onrushing workers' movement. Much to their dismay, there was to be no 'tying of the unions to the state', nor were Ludovico D'Aragona and the other leaders of the CGL bureaucracy permitted to 'sit in the boardrooms of the corporate state'. In fact some were soon to find themselves sitting in far less salubrious surroundings, as step by step, the functions of the CGL were usurped by the bogus fascist 'unions', which, because of their non-proletarian character and open adherence to the corporatist conception of 'national syndicalism' rapidly secured exclusive 'bargaining rights' with employers in all the major industrial centres of Italy. By 1926, Italy's once-powerful trade union movement, which had struck fear into the heart of many an employer and landowner, had been reduced to rubble. Under fascist corporative legislation (samples of which are reproduced at the end of this chapter) strikes were banned, militants jailed, wages cut, hours lengthened and working conditions worsened as big business reclaimed all that it had been compelled to surrender in the period of upsurge in the first two post-war years.* Little wonder that Mussolini's triumph gladdened the heart of reactionaries the world over.

The Nazis were no exception. Even though Hitler made the initial mistake of believing he could mechanically reproduce on German soil and from his Munich base the teutonic equivalent of a march on Rome — i.e. the 'march on Berlin' — he gleaned a

---

* Italian labour succeeded in forcing a wide range of concessions from the bourgeoisie in the period of its greatest militancy between the end of the war and the autumn of 1920. By 1921, industrial wages had increased by 557% on their pre-war monetary value, while prices had risen over the same period by 501%. This marked an increased share for the proletariat of the total national product, and a considerable diminution in the rate of profit of the industrial and banking bourgeoisie. With the defeat of September 1920 capital once more took the offensive, and aided by the onslaught of Mussolini's black shirts on the nerve centres of the labour movement, began to restore the dominant position it held before and during the war. While retail prices rose to an index of 517 by the end of 1922 (base year being 1913) industrial wages were, with the tacit acceptance of the trade union bureaucracy, pushed back from their 1921 peak of 557 to 503 two months after the march on Rome. And the bosses counter-attack had only just begun. With their fascist allies holding the reins of government, and the fascist-dominated 'syndicates' increasingly becoming the only organisations permitted to 'represent' Italian labour, wage cuts, price increases and the lengthening of the working day continued apace. Retail prices soared to 633 by the first half of 1926, while wages now limped along 38 points behind. And this was in a period of industrial expansion, when had it been free to organise in independent trade unions, the proletariat would have been able to exploit the increased demand for its labour power by demanding higher wages. Instead, they were in real terms, progressively cut. Meanwhile company profits rose from 1.7% on total capital in 1922 to 8% in 1925 and 7% in 1926. Other measures which gladdened the hearts — and helped replenish the coffers — of Italian big business included the restoration of the telephone system to private enterprise, the ending of the state monopoly in life insurance created by Giolitti in 1921, the winding up of the Ministry of Labour, and the abolition of rent controls. The *Confindustria*, whose support for Mussolini had been crucial in the days prior to his appointment as Prime Minister, was rewarded by being recognised as the sole spokesman for industrial interests, much to the chagrin of the fascist 'national syndicalists' and the small businessmen who had provided many of the activists and funds for fascism in its early days of struggle. Fascism in power was, despite its 'national' and 'social' claims, the most ruthless champion of big business, and by the same token, a merciless enemy of the proletariat.

great deal more from the Italian experience than did those whose task it was to wring the last drop of political wisdom from this tragic defeat lest fascism be unleashed on any other section of the international working class. That the lessons of the Italian disaster were drawn by only a handful of Marxists, and not by the entire vanguard of the European workers' movement, is almost entirely due to the rise of Stalinism in the Soviet Union, and its malignant effects on the political life of the other sections of the Communist International. Only the most thorough-going and unrestricted discussion inside the communist parties on the origins, nature and role of fascism, the mistakes committed in the fight against it in Italy (and in Germany, where the Nazis were already becoming a menace to the labour movement), and the correct policy to be adopted in the workers' movement to defeat it, could arm the International in what was its very struggle for existence. Such a discussion was indeed begun after the march on Rome and the rise in the early months of 1923 of the Nazis in Germany, but it had barely got under way when the bureaucratic hand of Stalinism, first in the CPSU, then in all the other parties of the CI, stifled all genuine discussion and polemic on this as on all other questions germane to the struggle for socialism. This is not the place to discuss the consequences for Germany of the rise of the Stalinist bureaucracy in the USSR — this will be dealt with in far greater detail in later chapters — but it must be stressed here that the Italian defeat had a dialectical relationship with events both in Germany and the Soviet Union. Mussolini's triumph, because it marked a decisive set back for the Bolshevik strategy of extending the revolution from backward Russia to the more economically advanced regions of central and western Europe, by the same token greatly strengthened the forces of conservatism both outside and within the Soviet state and party.* Likewise Mussolini's victory over Italian labour emboldened his Nazi emulators in Germany who now had living proof that the hated Marxist enemy could be crushed.

In this period [between the march on Rome and the Munich Putsch] — I openly admit — I conceived the profoundest admiration for the great man south of the Alps, who, full of ardent love for his people, made no pacts with the enemies of Italy, but strove for their annihilation by all ways and means. What will rank Mussolini among the great men of this earth is his desire not to share Italy with the

---

* '...Russia could not isolate itself from the profound reaction that swept over post-war Europe in the early twenties ...the coincidence of such dates as the organisation of the first Fascist coup under Mussolini on October 30, 1922 in Italy, the coup in Spain of September 13, 1923, which placed Primo de Rivera in power, the condemnation of the Declaration of the 46 Bolsheviks by the joint plenum of the Central Committee and the Central Control Commission of October 15, 1923 are not fortuitous. Such signs of the times will bear serious consideration'. (L. Trotsky: *Stalin*, pp.411-413.)

Marxists, but to destroy internationalism and save the fatherland from
it. How miserable and dwarfish our German would-be statesmen seem
by comparison ...[20]

The impact of Mussolini's victory on the Nazi movement was
immediate. In Munich only days after the march on Rome,
Hermann Esser told an ecstatic Nazi rally that 'what has been
done in Italy by a handful of courageous men is not impossible. In
Bavaria too we have [our] Mussolini. His name is Adolf Hitler.'
Volkisch as well as Nazi circles began to talk of a 'march on
Berlin' with Munich serving as their Naples — or rather Milan —
as Munich police reports recorded that the Nazis had received 'a
special force of gravity' following Mussolini's victory in Italy.
Hitler later recalled that 'the mere fact that anything of the sort
could be attempted, and could succeed, gave us impetus. A few
weeks after the march on Rome, I was received by the [Bavarian]
Minister Schweyer. That wouldn't have happened otherwise.'[21]
And a former close colleague of Hitler's, Ernst Hanfstangl
relates that in a speech to another Nazi rally in Munich, Hitler
'quoted approvingly the role of Kemal Ataturk and the example
of Mussolini who had marched on Rome three weeks earlier'.[22]

Neither was it a question of inspiration alone. Just prior to
Mussolini's victory, Kurt Lüdecke, a Nazi businessman who
enjoyed wide political connections abroad as well as in Germany
by virtue of his activities as a buying agent for large companies,
visited the fascist leader in Milan for a discussion on the joint
aims of their two movements. To Lüdecke (whose mission had the
personal approval of Ludendorff and the north German *volkisch*
leader Count Ernst zu Reventlow, 'it seemed apparent that the
Italian fascist movement, like the Nazis, was strongly nationalist
and directed against Marxism and Bolshevism, and that it might
develop into an attack on the whole parliamentary system'.[23]

Mussolini's victory continued to be a model and source of
strength for national socialism right up to its assumption of
power in 1933. Hitler's future Minister of the Interior Frick told a
Young Plan referendum rally in Pyritz on October 18, 1929 that
the Nazis 'were determined to promulgate by force that which we
preach. Just as Mussolini exterminated the Marxists in Italy, so
we must succeed in accomplishing the same thorough dictatorship
and terror'. And finally Göbbels wrote shortly after his own
'march on Berlin' had ended in victory that

> the march on Rome was a signal, a signal of storm for liberal
> democracy. It is the first attempt to destroy the world of the liberal-
> democratic spirit which started in 1789 with the storming of the
> Bastille and conquered one country after another in violent
> revolutionary upheavals, to let the nations go under in Marxism,
> democracy, anarchy and class struggle.

That German capitalism did not 'go under' in the same way was due in no small degree to the fact that unlike the Stalinists and social democrats, the Nazis proved themselves to be capable of learning from history.

REFERENCES FOR CHAPTER TWELVE

[1] B. Mussolini: *My Autobiography*, pp.34-35, London, 1939.
[2] G. Sorel: *Reflections on Violence*, p.28, New York, 1961.
[3] Ibid, pp.41-42.
[4] Ibid, p.43.
[5] Ibid, pp.90-98.
[6] B. Mussolini: *From Absolute Neutrality to Active and Operative Neutrality*, *Avanti*, October 18, 1914.
[7] B. Mussolini: *My Autobiography*, p.49.
[8] B. Mussolini: *Il Popolo d'Italia*, May 11, 1915.
[9] B. Mussolini: *My Autobiography*, p.59.
[10] B. Mussolini: *Il Popolo d'Italia*, March 5, 1919.
[11] B. Mussolini: *My Autobiography*, p.65.
[12] Ibid, p.69.
[13] Ibid, pp.69-70.
[14] B. Mussolini: *Il Popolo d'Italia*, February 28, 1919.
[15] B. Mussolini; March 23, 1919.
[16] B. Mussolini: *My Autobiography*, p.74.
[17] Ibid, p.75.
[18] A. Gramsci: Speech to the PSI National Council, published in *L'Ordine Nuovo*, May 8, 1920.
[19] B. Mussolini: Speech to Chamber of Deputies, June 21, 1921.
[20] A. Hitler: *Mein Kampf*, p.681.
[21] *Hitler's Secret Conversations*, p.9.
[22] E. Hanfstangl: *Hitler: The Missing Years*, p.34, London, 1937.
[23] K. Lüdecke: *I Knew Hitler*, p.58, New York, 1937.

The Founding Programme of the Italian Fascist Movement, Adopted March 23, 1919.

1. A national Constituent Assembly, Italian section of the international Constituent Assembly of nations, which will proceed to a radical transformation of the political and economic foundations of collective life.
2. Proclamation of the Italian Republic. Decentralisation of executive power; autonomous administration of regions and municipalities by their own legislative bodies. Sovereignty of the people exercised by means of universal, equal and direct suffrage, by all citizens of both sexes, the people keeping the right of initiative for referendum and veto.
3. Abolition of the Senate. Suppression of political police. Election of magistrates independently of the executive power.
4. Suppression of all titles of nobility and orders of knighthood.
5. Suppression of compulsory military service.
6. Freedom of opinion, of conscience and of belief, freedom of association and of the press.
7. An educational system, general and professional, open to all.
8. A maximum of public health measures.
9. Suppression of limited liability companies and shareholding companies; suppression of all forms of speculation, suppression of Banks and Stock Exchanges.
10. Census and taxation of private wealth. Confiscation of unproductive revenues.
11. Prohibition of child labour under the age of 16. Eight hour day.
12. Reorganisation of production according to the cooperative principle, including the workers' direct share of profits.
13. Abolition of secret diplomacy.
14. Foreign policy inspired by international solidarity and national independence within a Confederation of States.

Postulates of the Fascist Programme (May 1920)

'...the broad lines of the immediate tasks that confront the *Fascio di Combattimento* can be sketched under the following major headings: support for our recent war, winning the peace. Resistance to the theoretical and practical degenerations of politically oriented socialism. Against political parasitism ...With the hope of mobilising all our national energies to win the peace, the *Fascio di Combattimento* express their disgust for those men and agencies of the political bourgeoisie who have shown that they are incapable of handling domestic and foreign problems, that they are hostile to every profound renovation and to every spontaneous recognition of popular rights and that they are inclined to make those concessions that are dictated by calculations of parliamentary advantage.
For a bourgeoisie of Labour.
The Fascists recognise the very great value of the 'bourgeoisie of labour', which in all fields of human endeavour (from that of industry and agriculture to that of science and the professions) constitutes a precious and indispensable element for bringing out progressive development and the triumph of national aspirations.
Against the degeneration of the Labour struggle.
The *Fascio di Combattimento,* which are anxious to support the moral improvement of the proletariat and to help the establishment of syndical organisations that will increase the self-confidence of labour, feel that it is their duty to maintain an attitude of staunch opposition to those labour struggles in which strictly economic goals are submerged by considerations of pure demagogy...
The Fasci and the Labour organisations.
The *Fasci* express their sympathy with and intention of supporting every initiative of those minority groups of the proletariat who seek to harmonize the safeguarding of their class interests with the interests of the nation. With respect to syndical tactics, they advise the proletariat to make use of whatever forms of struggle assure the development of the whole and the well-being of the various producers, without any special prejudices and without dogmatic exclusiveness...'

This was the first clear exposition of 'national syndicalism', since the founding Fascist Programme of March 1919 said nothing about 'harmonizing' the interests of the proletariat 'with the interests of the nation', nor indeed of assuring the 'well-being of the various producers', by which last term Mussolini meant not only the working class, but the so-called 'bourgeoisie of labour', the 'productive' bourgeoisie. These notions were subsequently codified in the various social, economic and labour legislation of the Fascist regime, from which selections are reproduced below.

Excerpts from the *Rocco Labour Law,* April 3, 1926, drafted by Alfredo Rocco, Minister of Justice and former leader of the Nationalists.

1. Associations of employers and of workers ...may obtain legal recognition when they can prove that they comply with the following requirements ...in the case of associations of workers that the workers who have voluntarily registered as members number not less than one-tenth of those of the class for which the association has been formed ...that besides the protection of the economic and moral interests the association proposes to promote, and does actually promote, the assistance, instruction and moral and patriotic education of its members ...that the director of the association affords guarantees of ability, morality, and sound national loyalty...

5. ...Only legally recognised associations can appoint representatives of employers or workers to sit on councils, guilds, or other bodies on which such representation is provided by law ...

6. ...In no case can associations be recognised which, without the preliminary consent of the Government, have contracted any ties of discipline or dependence with associations of an international character.

18. The lock-out and the strike are forbidden ...Three or more workers who, by concerted agreement, leave their work or perform it in suchwise as to interfere with its continuity or regularity, with a view to obtaining from their employers different labour conditions, render themselves liable to a fine of not less than 100 and not to exceed 1,000 lire ...When the persons guilty of the offences forseen under the above paragraph are more numerous, the leaders, promoters, and organisers are liable to detention for not less than one year and not to exceed two years, besides the fine provided ...[More stringent punishments are stipulated in Articles 19 and 21 for the same offences committed by workers in the state and public services, and for striking for the purposes of 'coercing the will or influencing the decisions of a department or organ of the state', i.e. for political strikes. The former offence merited a maximum sentence of two years, and the latter, of three years.]

Excerpts from the *Decree on Corporations,* July 1, 1926. [These derived from Article three of the *Rocco Labour Law,* which made provision for the merging of 'associations of employers and workers ...by means of central liaison organs ...']

42. The liaison organs provided for by Article 3 of the Act of 3rd April 1926 are of a national character. They bring together the national syndical organisations of the several factors of production, employers, intellectual and manual workers connected with a given branch of production, or with one or more given classes of enterprise. Organisations thus linked up form a corporation...

43. The corporation is ...an organ of the state Administration...

44. ...Corporative organs are endowed ...with the following powers ...to promote, encourage and subsidise all initiatives aiming at the co-ordination and improvement of production...

56. ...corporate organs shall be guided by the considerations of equity and endeavour to conciliate the interests of the employers and workers, and both these interests with the higher interests of production...'

Charter of Labour, April 21, 1927.

III. There is complete freedom, of professional or syndical organisation. But syndicates legally recognised and subject to State control alone have the right of legal representation of the whole category of employers and workers for which they are constituted...
IV. Solidarity between the various factors of production is concretely expressed by the Collective Labour Contract, which conciliates the opposing interests of employers and workers, subordinating them to the higher interests of production.
VII. The corporate state considers that private enterprise in the sphere of production is the most effective and useful instrument in the interests of the nation ...The worker ...is an active collaborator in the economic enterprise, the direction of which rests with the employer, who is responsible for it...
IX. State intervention in economic production arises only when the private initiative is lacking or insufficient, or when the political interests of the State are involved. The intervention may take the form of control, assistance or direct management.
XII. The action of the Syndicate, the conciliatory efforts of the corporative organs, and the decisions of the Labour Court guarantee that wages correspond to the normal demands of life, to the possibilities of production, and the output of labour. Wages shall be determined without reference to any general rule, by agreement between the parties to the collective contracts.
XIX. Breaches of discipline or the performance of acts which disturb the normal working of the concern on the part of the workers shall be punished, according to the gravity of the offence, by fine, suspension from work, or in very serious cases, by immediate discharge without indemnity...'

These three key laws make it abundantly clear that the fascist corporate state as practised in Italy did not rest in any sense on 'collaboration' between trade unions and the state, or between trade unions and employers. The very definition of what constituted a *bona fide* 'workers' association' (articles one and six of the *Rocco Labour Law*) excluded the CGL from participating in the machinery of the corporate state, however much the trade union bureaucracy might have desired to do so. The 'corporations' were formed out of the fusion of an entirely bogus 'workers' syndicate' (staffed by hard-core fascists and run on the explicitly anti- proletarian principles of 'national syndicalism') and employers' 'syndicates' that represented their members in practice as well as in theory. Once again then we see how false is the claim made by *Workers Press* that corporatism is a form of class collaboration practised between reformist trade union leaders and the capitalist state. It is not. It is, on the contrary, the *supersession* of the methods of class collaboration by the systematic dismemberment of all those mechanisms and agencies by which this collaboration has in the past been carried out. Fascism is not a form of collaboration between the classes, as its ideologists demagogically claim. For all its talk of social harmony, Fascism wages the most brutal class war — even on those whom the *Workers Press* so wrongly terms 'corporatists'.

Corporatism and 'national syndicalism' in Spain, France and Portugal.

Fascism almost always attempts to establish a base — however temporary or precarious — among the masses by stealing some of the slogans, vocabulary and even programmes of its proletarian enemies. Thus in Germany, Hitler — despite his own misgivings about the use of the term — stood before the German petty-bourgeoisie and backward workers as a 'socialist', while in Italy, fascism bedecked itself out in the garb of 'national syndicalism'. In both cases, fascism worked up its own counter-revolutionary ideology and propaganda from materials stolen from the dominant tendencies in the workers' movement and perverted by the reactionary doctrines of nationalism and racialism. (In Britain today, we can see a similar tactic being employed by various shades of reaction from the Tory government, through Powell to the fully-blown fascist groups on the far right. They all speak of 'fair play', 'justice', the 'rights' of the 'individual', and claim to stand for the protection of the 'small man' against the 'faceless' bureaucracies of big business and the trade unions. This last is, of course also a ploy of the Liberal Party). The three other European countries which witnessed the growth of fascist movements — Spain, France and Portugal — were also strongholds of syndicalism, and it is no surprise therefore that in each case once in power the movements attempted to conceal the capitalist bases of their regimes with a veneer of 'syndicalist' demagogy. In Spain, the founder of 'national syndicalism' was Ramiro Ledesma Ramos, whose journal 'The Conquest of the State' began publication in 1931. Influenced by Mussolini's corporatism and pseudo-syndicalist demagogy, Ledesma wrote that the 'syndication of economic forces will be obligatory and in each instance bound to the highest ends of the state. The State will discipline and will guarantee production at all times ...Our primary goal is revolutionary efficiency. There we do not seek votes but audacious and valiant minorities ...Our organisation will be founded on the basis of syndical cells and political cells.'

The other, and more well-known pioneer of Spanish fascism, Jose Antonio Primo de Rivera, also employed much of the vocabulary of syndicalism to conceal his reactionary aims. Yet few workers were deceived by his noisy rhetoric, of which the following is a sample: 'If anything truly deserves to be called a workers' state, it is the fascist state. Therefore, in the fascist state — and the workers will come to realise this, no matter what — the workers syndicates will be elevated to the dignity of organs of the state.' In fact, the fascist state of General Franco ground them to pulp. And since the army, and not a fascisied petty-bourgeoisie provided the main support of the new regime, Franco had little need of a pseudo-radical doctrine to justify his rule. Spanish 'national syndicalism' was accordingly given a more conservative flavour than in Italy, where even for a period after Mussolini's seizure of power, the fascist 'syndicates' had to compete against the genuine workers' unions of the CGL (See Chapter Eight, *The Political Economy of National Socialism*).

In Portugal, Salazar's rise to total power was accompanied by the growth of a 'national syndicalist' movement under the leadership of Dr Rolao Preto. In 1934, one year after the Salazar regime instituted its corporative *National Statute of Labour*, the movement's national executive voted to join the pro-government National Union against the wishes of Preto, who went into opposition and was eventually deported to Spain. Salazar's corporatism like that of his close ally Franco, eschewed the excesses of pseudo-syndicalist demagogy: 'We are opposed to all forms of internationalism, Communism, Socialism, syndicalism and everything which may divide or minimize or break up the family. We are against class warfare, irreligion and disloyalty to one's country ...'

No renegades from the trade union or socialist movement ever held high office in Salazar Portugal or Franco Spain. This was not true of Vichy France however, where two former syndicalists, Rene Belin and Hubert Lagardelle (the old Sorelian 'integralist') served Petain and Laval respectively as Ministers of Labour. Like Mussolini, Belin certainly did not begin his career as a trade unionist with the intention of ending up as an oppressor of the French proletariat. After a militant record as a leader of the postal and telegraph workers in Lyon (where he organised a stubborn strike against the government) Belin climbed rapidly up the trade union hierarchy, and in 1935 was appointed Deputy General Secretary of the main trade union federation, the CGT. His anti-political approach to trade union questions drove him sharply towards the right when in 1938, he founded a weekly journal, *Syndicate*, which campaigned against Communist Party influence in the CGT (The Stalinist-led minority trade union federation, the CGTU, after denouncing the CGT as a 'social fascist' organisation throughout the 'third period', had unified with the 'social fascists' following the adoption of the popular front strategy in 1934). His anti-communism (an extension of his anti-political syndicalism) led him even further to the right two years later when with the formation of the Vichy regime of Marshal Philippe Petain, he agreed to serve it as Minister of Labour. In this capacity he helped draft the thoroughly corporatist *Charter for Labour,* which became law in 1941 after gaining the approval of the Nazi authorities in Paris. Belin also presided over the liquidation of his old trade union federation, the CGT, which was officially outlawed by government decree on November 9, 1940 (Like their counterparts in Italy and Germany the CGT bureaucrats had sought to evade this fate by disavowing any intention of waging the class struggle, but to no avail). The Vichy 'national revolution', with its slogans of 'work, family, country,' was badly in need of ideological embellishment and a social doctrine, and Belin helped to provide both. The preamble to the programme of the Vichy 'national revolution' declared: 'only one aristocracy will be recognised: the aristocracy of intelligence; one sole merit: work ...Work and talent alone will be the foundation of the French hierarchy ...The class struggle, so fatal to the nation, can only be done away with by doing away with the causes that formed those classes and set them against one another. Thus there will be born again the true elites that the superseded regime spent years in destroying ...the economic life of our country is about to have a new orientation ...It will ....be necessary to put an end to the present economic order by a rational organisation of production by corporative institutions.

In each of the cases cited — and this cannot be emphasised too often or too strongly — the establishment of a 'corporative' system was only possible after the total destruction of the independent workers' organisations, economic as well as political. Belin had to resign from the CGT, and Vichy had to liquidate it, before this syndicalist renegade could concoct his corporatist phantasies about termination of the class struggle. Those who recklessly talk of reformist trade union leaders or social democrats being transformed into corporatists (*Workers Press* of Monday, September 3, 1973 refers to Transport Workers' leader Jack Jones as a 'devoted disciple' of corporatism' — Stephen Johns: *Stewards Keen on Merseyside collaboration scheme,* ibid, p.11) have simply learned nothing from the immensely rich history of the workers' movement in its fight against fascism. If Belin, Lagardelle and the Italian syndicalist renegades were corporatists when they entered the service of Vichy France and Italian fascism — and they undoubtedly were — then on what political grounds, and with what historical and theoretical justification, is it correct to describe a leader of a *bona fide* workers' union also as a 'corporatist' — and a 'devoted' one at that? To do so is to equate, or closely relate *reformist* class collaborationism as advocated and practised by Jones and the rest of the TUC leadership, left as well as right, with the entirely bogus claim of fascist corporatism that it too, stands for 'collaboration' between the classes. Formalist thinking has led the *Workers Press* into the trap of taking the claims of corporatist propaganda seriously.Corporatism in Italy, Spain, Vichy France and Portugal, and the Nazi variety in Germany, with its demagogic talk of a 'people's or 'works' community', had nothing to do with class collaboration. *It was all-out class war,* masked by an ideology that preached social harmony and justice. By detecting a fully-blown 'corporatism' in the words and deeds of British trade union and Labour Party leaders, *Workers Press* has mistaken myth for reality.

Chapter Thirteen

FROM KAPP TO MUNICH:
GENESIS OF A STRATEGY

The more highly developed a democracy is, the more imminent are pogroms or civil war in connection with any profound divergence which is dangerous to the bourgeoisie.
(V. Lenin: *The Proletarian Revolution and the Renegade Kautsky)*

When in 1923 for the first time we determined to act we already had behind us a big history of preparations for a putsch. I can confess quite calmly that from 1919 to 1923 I thought of nothing else than a coup d'etat.
(A. Hitler, 1936.)

The historical role of fascism can only be assessed within the context of the reciprocal relationships which have evolved between the three classes of modern capitalist society: the monopoly bourgeoisie, the proletariat and the petty-bourgeoisie. Fascism mobilises the middle class masses to crush the organised proletariat on behalf of monopoly capital. This, reduced to its most brutal essentials, is the historical task of fascism, performed in Italy by Mussolini, in Germany by Hitler, in Spain by Franco* and most recently by the military dictatorship in Chile. In other words, fascism is the 'plebeian' method of resolving the bourgeoisie's 'social problem' — what to do with the organised proletariat when all other solutions based on a degree of compromise, or on the exclusive use of bureaucratic-police methods, have failed. At this point, elements within the ruling class will begin to turn towards a solution which can perhaps be described as 'counter revolution from below', involving the mobilisation of

---

* Spain differed from Germany and Italy in that a mass fascist movement amongst the urban petty-bourgeoisie was completely lacking in the period prior to the military uprising of July 1936. However, the more traditionalist wing of the Franco camp — Carlists and pro-fascist clergy — did undoubtedly succeed in drumming up sizeable support for the revolt amongst strongly monarchist and Catholic peasants, many of whom could by no means be described as wealthy.

millions of middle class and even backward proletarian forces against the labour movement. Thus the bourgeoisie fights its class enemies by calling in the demagogues, the rabble rousers and the street warriors. It cuts adrift from its own parties, whose leaders have failed, either through a lack of material forces or a sufficiently ruthless strategy, to implement the anti-working class policies demanded by big business. With great trepidation, the big bourgeoisie places its destinies in the hands of men drawn for the most part not from the higher ranks of the propertied classes, nor from the traditional governing and bureaucratic castes, but from the middle and nether regions of the despised petty-bourgeoisie, and even the gutter itself in the persons of the SA gangsters. This 'plebeian' character distinguishes fascism in its classic German and Italian forms from all other movements of anti-socialist reaction, and a fascist dictatorship from all other right-wing governments which to one degree or another, persecute or repress the organised workers' movement.*

But fascism does not provide us with the only instance of the bourgeoisie resorting to 'plebeian' methods to fight and crush its class enemies. In its struggle to overthrow a deeply entrenched absolute monarchy, nobility and clergy, the rising bourgeoisie of the 17th and 18th centuries was finally compelled, however reluctantly or hesitatingly, to summon the plebeians of its day to arms, and to permit all but their most radical spokesmen to partake in the formulation of government policy. And when the fate of the revolution demanded the most extreme terroristic measures against the feudal reaction and its allies, the higher echelons of the bourgeoisie found itself thrust aside as the plebeians seized entire sections of the machinery of state, or created new organs of coercion and mass mobilisation where the need arose. Such was the plebeian-based revolutionary dictatorship of the Jacobin Committee of Public Safety, which ruled France from April 1793 to July 1794, when the anti-Jacobin bourgeoisie succeeded in securing the arrest and execution of four of its twelve members — the brothers Robespierre, Couthon and Saint Just. Thermidor marked the temporary exit of the plebeian masses from the stage of French history, just as the formation of the 'sections' and the rise of the *sans culotte* agitator or *enrage* signified their explosive entry.

So often in the literature of Marxism has revolutionary — and reactionary — France served as a source of theoretical inspiration

---

* Thus it would be inaccurate to describe the Greek military junta as a fully-blown fascist regime, likewise the racialist regimes in Rhodesia and South Africa. The presence of a highly privileged white settler minority, with its own racialist-based parliamentary system and 'opposition' parties and press, further complicates matters and renders the label 'fascist' almost meaningless if applied indiscriminately to such regimes.

for the unravelling of the complexities of the class struggle in modern Europe.* And because Jacobinism provides us with a classic instance of the bourgeoisie fighting its class enemies by plebeian, terrorist methods (even though those enemies were feudal in origin, and therefore stood to the right of the bourgeoisie) its rise — and fall — can furnish us with valuable insights into what for formal thinkers often appears to be an insoluble contradiction between fascism as a counter-revolutionary buttress of capitalist rule and fascism as a mass movement mobilising literally millions of 'plebeians' behind a programme of radical action against capitalism and the 'political bourgeoisie'.

Trotsky certainly considered the example of Jacobinism valuable in this respect. In a speech to the Comintern Executive in July 1926 (convened to discuss the opportunist conduct of the Polish Communist Party during the coup of Marshal Josef Pilsudski in May 1926) he pointed out to a largely hostile audience the similarities as well as differences between petty-bourgeois Jacobinism and fascism:

> The movement he [Pilsudski] headed was petty-bourgeois, a plebeian means of solving the pressing problems of capitalist society in process of decline and destruction. Here there is a direct parallel with Italian fascism ...These two currents undoubtedly have common features: their shock troops are recruited ...among the petty-bourgeoisie; both Pilsudski and Mussolini operated by extra-parliamentary, nakedly violent means, by the methods of civil war; both of them aimed not at overthrowing bourgeois society, but at saving it. Having raised the petty-bourgeois masses to their feet, they both clashed openly with the big bourgeoisie after coming to power** ...one is forced to recall Marx's definition of Jacobinism as a plebeian means of dealing with the feudal enemies of the bourgeoisie. That was in the period of the *rise* of the bourgeoisie ...now, in the epoch of *decline* of bourgeois society, the bourgeoisie once again has need of a 'plebeian' means of solving its problems — which are not progressive but, rather, thoroughly reactionary. In this sense, then, fascism contains a reactionary caricature of Jacobinism ...The bourgeoisie in decline is incapable of maintaining itself in power with the methods of its own creation — the parliamentary state. It needs fascism as a weapon of self-defence, at least at the most critical moments.[1]

---

* Examples of this are the coup d'etat of Louis Bonaparte, the Bismarck regime in Germany, and the rise of the Stalinist bureaucracy in the Soviet Union.

** As in his turn did Hitler, who after the formation of the Nazi-Nationalist coalition in 1933, began to demand the whole power for his party, to the exclusion of 'dynastic' nationalists like Hugenberg and Papen, who believed they could use Hitler to crush the proletariat and then squeeze him out of office. In the end, it was Hugenberg and Papen who found themselves dispensable. Hitler was also successful in securing the liquidation — voluntary or otherwise — of all the bourgeois political parties, together with their various allied associations such as youth movements, confessional trade unions and para-military and veterans leagues. The Nazis demanded a total monopoly of political power — and they got it.

This takes us far away from the vulgar explanation of fascism so often encountered in the labour movement and radical circles that it is 'cooked up' by the ruling class and used and discarded just as one switches on or off a water tap. Precisely because of the plebeian basis of fascist movements, and the demagogic social programme which its leaders employ to mobilise the petty-bourgeois masses against the organised proletariat, they generate an internal impetus and volatile 'lumpen' radicalism that threatens, once the fascist leaders are installed in power, to bring it into collision with its big-bourgeois paymasters. Indeed, the German monopolists, bankers, agrarians and military leaders had to wait more than a year for their 'Thermidor' before Hitler offered them the heads of the 'brown Jacobins' on the sacrificial platter, and even then (unlike the period of bourgeois con-solidation which followed the fall of Robespierre) the bourgeois and Junkers were not permitted to insert themselves into the political vacuum created by the purge of the SA 'plebeians'. Himmler's SS, and not the monarchist clubs or the Junker officer corps, was to be the supreme political arbiter in the Third Reich. For Hitler, despite the delusions of the old monarchist right, was no tame second edition of Bismarck. He was a counter-revolutionary of the twentieth century, not of the nineteenth.

Trotsky characterised this ever-present and fluctuating tension between the big bourgeoisie and the fascist 'plebeians' in the following manner:

> The bourgeoisie does not like the 'plebeian' means of solving its problem. The bourgeoisie had an extremely hostile attitude towards Jacobinism, which [nevertheless] cleared a path for the development of bourgeois society. The fascists are immeasurably closer to the bourgeoisie in decline than the Jacobins were to the bourgeoisie on the rise. But the established bourgeoisie does not like the fascist means of solving its problems either, for the shocks and disturbances, although in the interests of bourgeois society, involve dangers for it as well. This is the source of antagonism* between fascism and the traditional parties of the bourgeoisie.[2]

The bourgeoisie therefore resorts to the 'plebeian' solution only when all other available methods of combatting or con-taining the proletariat have failed, and more specifically, when class compromises which are tolerable in conditions of capitalist

---

* Even though Trotsky made these remarks with the experiences of Italy and Poland fresh in his mind, they anticipated with rare accuracy the relations that developed between the big bourgeoisie and the Nazis in the last year of the Weimar Republic. And in fact he returned to his analogy between fascism and Jacobinism in *The Only Road*, written — in September 1932 — at the precise moment when the German ruling class was waging a furious and quite open polemic within its ranks as to whether to continue supporting von Papen's Bonapartist 'cabinet of barons', which conducted its war against the proletariat with 'legal' means, or to summon to power Hitler's plebeian hordes. Papen and Hitler conducted their debate by means of 'open letters' in their respective house organs!

expansion and periods of world peace become insufferable in conditions of capitalist crisis, declining world trade, falling profit rates, inter-imperialist rivalries, potential military conflicts and a proletariat which obstinately refuses to yield what it has won in the boom in order to rescue its hard-pressed employers. The momentous decision to call in and arm the fascist plebeians therefore necessarily marks the end of a political era of class compromise and class collaboration in which differences are settled (or settlements postponed) through the peaceful alternation of various parliamentary combinations, and by the regulation of the class struggle through the mechanism of the political and trade union wings of the reformist bureaucracy. Fascism puts a brutal end to bourgeois democracy as well as all the organisations of the proletariat, and for this very reason, its assumption of power generates considerable, if secondary, tensions between the propertied, exploiting bourgeoisie, whose only concern is the extraction of surplus value from the labour power of the proletariat, and the former political and literary representatives of the bourgeoisie and the democratic — or rather non fascist — middle class. The bonds which tie these two segments of the bourgeoisie are strong, even though not unbreakable, and it is with the greatest reluctance that the leaders of the economy (who comprise only a tiny fraction of the ruling class as a whole) part company with those who have represented and defended its interests in the past. But when as in Weimar Germany the terrain of the struggle shifts from parliament, the editorial office and the salons of high society to the streets of the proletarian quarters of industrial Germany, other qualities and skills than those of debate, syntax and social respectability are called for. The bourgeoisie's old politicans and 'literati' are thrown to the wolves as into the seats of power clamber brownshirted gangsters who only yesterday were fraternising with the underworld. Small wonder that in Germany, the big bourgeoisie resolved to secure the appointment of a Hitler administration only after it had run through a gamut of governmental forms and combinations ranging from intimate collaboration with social democracy, guarded support for bourgeois liberalism, reluctant acquiescence in bourgeois republicanism, a brief flirtation with military dictatorship to finally, in the last two years of Weimar, a critical endorsement of Bonapartism.* The German bourgeoisie came to fascism unevenly and with many inner reservations and

---

* The French bourgeoisie also came to its 'plebeian' solution via a series of experiments and alignments with more moderate leaderships, beginning with the 'Patriot Party' and Lafayette, who sought to reconcile a reformed monarchy with a conservative bourgeoisie, through the bourgeois republican Girondins to the petty-bourgeois Jacobins, who alone proved capable of consummating the struggle begun in 1789.

misgivings, and only after a rich and protracted period of experimentation with almost every other form of rule encountered in the history of modern capitalism convinced it that the continued toleration of parliamentary democracy and existence of independent workers' organisations were incompatible with the restoration of capitalist economy and the resurgence of German imperialism. It was on these two fundamental issues that the decisive sections of the monopoly bourgeoisie finally found common ground with the Nazis, and thus made possible the formation of the Hitler government of 'national concentration' in January 1933. Yet Hitler had been striving towards this goal for a full thirteen years, and on more than one occasion, the ruling class had denied it to him.*

So while it is correct to say that in 1933 the paths of 'plebeian' fascism and big bourgeois reaction converged on a single point — the annihilation of the workers' movement — this convergence must be placed in a perspective of time, and viewed as a product not only of the strategic requirements of a ruling class in its most profound crisis, but of the failings of leadership on the part of the two parties of the German working class, the SPD and the KPD. We can see from a study of the turbulent period between the November revolution and the Munich putsch that while important sections of the big bourgeoisie and agrarians were prepared to sanction or even initiate repressive measures against the entire German workers' movement, the conditions had by no means matured sufficiently either in their own ranks or that of the petty-bourgeoisie to make a fascist solution necessary and possible. Nor had the workers movement, for all the mistakes and treachery of its leadership, been forced back onto the defensive and its fighting capacities gravely undermined.

Capitalists and military leaders there certainly were who looked to Hitler to provide a solution to the 'social problem', but they proved, when the time came, to be in a small minority. The Munich putsch failed not only because it lacked sufficient support in the nationalist petty-bourgeoisie, but because a majority of the monopolist bourgeosie still considered it possible to resolve their economic and political problems within the framework of Weimar parliamentary democracy, and without a decisive break from social democracy. And even when its thinking turned towards open dictatorship, it still rejected the Nazi 'plebeian' solution, as the events leading up to and surrounding the Kapp putsch indicate.**

---

* Not only in his abortive Munich putsch of November 1923, but in the several unsuccessful bids for the Chancellorship Hitler made between his first election triumph in September 1930 and his eventual appointment by President Hindenburg little more than two years later.
** We must also remember that since the German bourgeoisie divided itself politic-

The Kapp Putsch.

The Kapp putsch of March 1920 represented the first serious attempt by right-wing forces to overturn the Weimar Republic, and as such it merits serious study, not only for the immediate impact which it had on German politics, which was indeed explosive, but its longer term effects, which without doubt turned more astute ruling class minds away from traditional notions of reaction towards the strategy of a counter-revolution not, *a la* Kapp, from 'above', but on plebeian lines, from 'below'. Kapp's military coup flowed from the aborted nature of the November Revolution. The old ruling classes had been forced to retreat, but had not, thanks to the duplicity of the reformists, been decisively defeated. Even as the republic's founders were celebrating the triumph of democracy over 'despotisms of Left and Right', the ground swell of counter-revolution was already gathering impetus. Firstly, the big industrialists were preparing to fight against the implementation of the concessions extracted from them by the ADGB under the November 1918 'Working Agreement'. Hugo Stinnes, himself the employers' chief spokesman in the negotiations with the trade union leaders, bluntly declared some three months later that 'big business and all those who rule over industry will some day recover their influence and power. They will be recalled by a disillusioned people, half dead with hunger, who will need bread and not phrases'.

A former government minister closely associated with heavy industry — Dernberg — denounced the eight-hour day conceded by the employers in the 'Working Agreement' as 'a nail in Germany's coffin',* a sure indication that a significant group of

ally into no fewer than four parties — the Catholic Centre, the DDP, the DVP and DNVP — it is impossible to speak of a single ruling class policy being pursued at any time in the history of the Weimar Republic. At best, we can pin-point factions which coalesced around certain important policy questions, and which on occasions could cut across party frontiers. Thus the Chemical Trust and Rathenau's electrical combine, AEG, tended in their early years at least to support the Republic and its democratic parties, along with that section of the Catholic bourgeoisie which identified itself with the Centre (other Catholic bourgeois like Thyssen were bitterly hostile to Weimar) while heavy industrialists grouped around the DVP and DNVP, were more often than not, ranged against the bourgeois democrats on important questions such as social welfare, collective bargaining, reparations etc. The internal divisions were accentuated in every great political crisis, and found their reflection at every level of the state apparatus from the High Command to the judiciary and police.

* Politically necessary though these concessions undoubtedly were, German monopoly capitalism was in no economic position to make them. The war had drained the nation's resources to an unprecedented extent, and without the compensation of the spoils of victory. In 1913, Germany's national wealth was calculated at 225 billion gold marks. The war had seen this sum more than halved, while the national debt soared to 250 billion gold marks. Even before the entente powers began their plunder of the German economy, it was in the red to the tune of

big employers was about to renege on the deal concluded with the ADGB in November 1918. But they must have been well aware that to do so while the social democrats remained the main government party would court the most violent political repercussions, for not even the reformists, with their Communist and USPD rivals daily gaining ground on them, could afford to sanction such a brutal breach of trust. The Stinneses and the Thyssens therefore had no alternative but to grudgingly honour the November Working Agreement until such time as political forces came to hand capable of overturning the government coalition, which rested on the class compromise embodied not only in the Working Agreement, but the entire legislative social, economic and political system created by the November Revolution.*

The big employers and agrarians made their feelings known not only through their own organisations and press, but in the National Assembly, where DVP and DNVP deputies daily denounced the republic and all its works in the most scathing terms. It was a depressing spectacle for Hugo Preuss, who had spent so many laborious hours devising a constitutional system acceptable to all reasonable men. The problem was, so many of Germany's old rulers refused to accept reason as the governing principle in human affairs:

> How foreign a parliamentary system seems to even the most enlightened Germans. I have often listened to debates with real concern, glancing often rather timidly to the gentlemen of the Right fearful lest they say to me: 'Do you hope to give a parliamentary system to a nation like this, one that resists it with every sinew of its body?' One

nearly 150 billion gold marks. Apart from its colonial empire, the German bourgeoisie was compelled by the terms of the Versailles Treaty to surrender 13.1% of its own European territory, which accounted for 75% of its iron ore production, 68% of its zinc, and 26% of its coal. When reparation terms were finally fixed, they involved Germany paying out three times its annual national product. Naturally, the German ruling class did not envisage paying this gigantic tribute out of its own pocket, payment would be made by squeezing more surplus value out of the working class. Hence the constant pressure brought to bear by the bourgeoisie on the eight hour day and the various social and economic articles of the Weimar Constitution.

* The newly-formed Federation of German Industry, the main employers organisation, rapidly became a battleground for the factional struggle between the 'hard-line' heavy industrialists and the more liberal, pro-Weimar medium and light industrialists, who were more oriented towards the consumer market. Stinnes, Hugenberg and Krupp were regarded as spokesmen for the former faction, while Duisberg (Chemical Trust), Rathenau (AEG) and Ernst von Borsig (engineering) were prominent as representatives of the second group. Both factions were, however, generally agreed, in the early post-war period, that Germany's inflation should be used to regain its lost positions on the world market, a policy strongly opposed by the banks. Thus Stinnes declared to a steel producers meeting in Dusseldorf on July 16, 1919: 'If we have the coal we need, our country will be the land of quality production, on the one hand, because of our exchange situation, and on the other, because of our wages, which in view of our exchange situation, are the lowest in the world'.

finds suspicion everywhere; Germans cannot shake off their old political timidity and their deference to the authoritarian state. They do not understand that the new government must be blood of their blood, flesh of their flesh, that their trusted representatives will have to be an integral part of it. Their constant worry is only: how can we best keep our constituted representatives so shackled that they will be unable to do anything?

But once again, like the big employers and landowners for whom these 'gentlemen of the Right' spoke, there was little they could do to translate their anti-democratic invective and class arrogance into deeds. Together with the USPD (who opposed Weimar for opposite reasons to the extreme right) the DVP and DNVP could only muster 75 votes against the new constitution when it was finally presented for approval to the National Assembly at the end of July 1919. What these would-be counter-revolutionaries so desperately lacked were arms and men to wield them. So where else could they turn but to the units formed *by the Ebert Government* to combat the revolution: the Free Corps Brigades of Gustav Noske? Quite early in the new year, it was becoming evident even to the most hardened reformist that many Free Corps officers and men were becoming disgruntled with having to fight under an alien political leadership for a republic they openly despised as 'Jewish' and 'Marxist'.* Little time was lost in establishing contact with more political elements in the Free Corps such as the *Nationale Vereinigung* of Captain Pabst (it was Pabst who ordered and supervised the murder of Rosa Luxemburg and Karl Liebknecht) and the *Baltikum,* which waged its own private war in the east against German proletarians, Poles and Baltic communists alike. As the SPD leaders gradually disengaged themselves from the more extreme anti-socialist Free Corps commanders and brigades, the latter readily turned towards other and more amenable forces prepared to finance their counter-revolutionary activities.**

* The right-wing social democrat Max Cohen Reuss described a visit to one such Free Corps unit in January 1919: 'I felt a chill down my spine. There are a lot of officers there who will have nothing to do with socialism [not even of the Noske variety!] and are looking forward to beating people up again. I must say what happens horrifies me. These people have learnt nothing at all'. This was an under-statement. Colonel Reinhard, the 'butcher of Berlin', openly referred to the Ebert government as 'riff-raff', while Captain Gengler of the 'Iron Host' corps wrote in his diary on January 21, 1919, that 'the day will come when I shall get my own back on this government and unmask the whole pitiful pack'. Finally another Free Corps officer, Lt. Col. Heinz, wrote in an ultra-rightist journal that 'this state, born of revolt, will always be our enemy, never mind what sort of constitution it endows itself with and who is at its head ...Fight against the government! Death to the Democratic government'.
** Eduard Stadtler, an ideologue of 'revolutionary conservatism', was instrumental in channelling funds from big business into the cash boxes of the main anti-communist fighting units. For a short time he headed the *Antibolschewistische Bewegung,* which with the support of Stinnes and other industrialists, was to the fore in com-

Finally, there was the old High Command itself, banned by the allies from functioning under its old name, and so now masquerading as the 'Preparatory Commission for the Peace Army'. Thirsting for revenge, and fearing that the prevailing pacifist political climate would become institutionalised in the shape of the SPD-dominated coalition, at least some of its more influential officers could be expected to look with sympathy on moves to install a regime that would restore German arms to their former glory — and of course, put the social democratic upstarts and 'November criminals' in their rightful places. The predatory terms forced on Germany by the victorious Entente powers only served to feed nationalist sentiments and provide imperialist circles with a splendid opportunity and pretext to intensify their plottings against the republic and the organised workers' movement, whose leaders were always depicted as tools of Germany's enemies.*

Thus there were four main streams of right-wing opposition to Weimar — the Junker and industrialist 'intransigents', elements in both the DVP and DNVP, a section of the officer corps, and the more political leaders of the Free Corps — which given a favourable conjuncture could converge to form a single counter-revolutionary front. And this is precisely what did happen. Already by the summer of 1919, a section of the old High Command, headed by General von Lüttwitz, had begun to depart from the old Prussian Officer corps tradition of non-intervention in politics by calling for the establishment of a military regime

batting the two 'Spartacist uprisings' of January and March 1919. Stadtler later addressed a meeting of industrialists on the need to maintain an independent combat organisation to fight the left flank of the workers' movement, after which Stinnes offered to set up an 'anti-Bolshevik fund' of 500,000 marks. This sum, together with donations from other wealthy industrialists, was subsequently distributed to various nationalist organisations, including several Free Corps brigades. Contributors to Stadtler's 'Anti-Bolshevik Movement' included some of the most illustrious names of German industry and banking, who despite their tactical differences over their approach to the new republic, were united in their desire to avoid a repetition of the Russian disaster in Germany: the steel producers Vögler, August Thyssen (father of the Nazi supporter Fritz) Paul Reusch of the Haniel group, Fritz Springorum of the Hoesch group and of course Kirdorf. The electrical industry was represented by Carl von Siemens and Felix Deutsch from the rival and reputedly more liberal AEG, and financed by Mankewitz of the Deutsche Bank and Salomonsohn from the Diskonto-gesellschaft. This anti-communist alliance fell apart once the initial 'Spartacist' menace had been overcome, many of its members edging their way back to a policy of toleration of Weimar and its social democratic architects.

* On the day of the signing of the Versailles Treaty, the Pan-German *Deutsche Zeitung* shrieked: 'Vengeance! German nation! Today in the Hall of Mirrors at Versailles a disgraceful treaty is being signed. Never forget it! On that spot where, in the glorious year of 1871, the German Empire in all its glory began, today, German honour is dragged to the grave. Never forget it! The German people, with unceasing labour, will push forward to reconquer that place among the nations of the world to which they are entitled. There will be vengeance for the shame of 1919'. (*Deutsche Zeitung*, June 28, 1919.)

which would combat 'Bolshevism' at home and defy attempts by Germany's enemies abroad to further weaken its military power. Divisions within the ruling class over policy towards the new republic were inevitably mirrored in the army leadership. Lüttwitz found his proposals opposed by General Märcker and Col. General von Hammerstein, who in linking their more recently-begun military careers with the new republic, feared a conflict between army and government that would end in defeat for the Reichswehr and a consequent debacle for their policy of winning over the SPD and its liberal coalition allies to a position of supporting the rebuilding of German military strength. Opposition from these 'moderates' did not deter Lüttwitz from proceeding with his plottings. On August 21, 1919, he held his first meeting with Wolfgang Kapp, an old Pan German, founder member of the ultra-chauvinist Fatherland Front (whose lineal connection with national socialism we have already discussed) and now employed by the Weimar Republic as a rather minor civil servant in that redoubt of Junker reaction, East Prussia. Their discussion resulted in the formulation of a programme which apart from the customary military and nationalist demands, called for the abolition of the right to strike, the ending of dole payments to the unemployed, and the scrapping of the Weimar Republic's quite substantial social welfare legislation. Clearly the views of influential industrialists were making themselves felt among the growing circle of conspirators, who now included not only Lüttwitz and his circle of fellow officers, but Captain Pabst, who provided a valuable link with the Free Corps, Count Westarp of the DNVP, the former Police President of Berlin Traugott von Jagow and, representing the 'spiritual' arm of the movement, the Lutheran Pastor Gottfreid Traub, who had been court Chaplain to William II in the last years of the Empire. While the bourgeois wing of the anti-Weimar opposition preferred for the most part to adopt a circumspect attitude towards the conspirators, a significant section of the Junker-dominated DNVP leadership readily endorsed the aims of the Lüttwitz-Kapp circle. Apart from Westarp, not only Kapp but Traub and von Jagow were prominent DNVP members, and they were joined in their preparations for the putsch of March 1920 by party colleagues Kurt von Kessel and Hans Freiherr von Waggenheim (Traub served the short-lived Kapp regime as its Minister of Church and Cultural Affairs).

Kapp and Lüttwitz knew they could rely on a sizable proportion of the Free Corps commanders and brigades to support their planned coup, and provide it with the fighting forces necessary to combat the inevitable resistance which it would encounter from the working class. But what of the attitude of big

business? Represented mainly, but not exclusively by
Stresemann's DVP, the leaders of heavy industry were as divided
over their attitude towards the anti-Weimar movement as was
every other segment of the ruling class. They wavered between a
policy of 'critical support' for the republic (i.e. Duisberg) and one
of open hostility (Thyssen, Kirdorf and, to a lesser degree,
Stinnes). But once the conspiracy — whose progress was discussed daily in the German press — began to gather impetus, a
group of business leaders began to abandon their waiting attitude
and decided to lend the counter-revolutionary movement
financial and well as political aid. Contact with Kapp was
established by Vögler (of the Gelsenkirchen Mining Co.)
Stinnes, Borsig (a future Nazi supporter) and Kirdorf through the
medium of the ultra-reactionary National Club, an exclusive
association established after the war as a venue for anti-Weimar
politicians, aristocrats, military leaders, landowners and businessmen. At the beginning of 1920, with the Kapp putsch now little
more than two months away, Stinnes stated in a letter to government leaders that the time had come to dispense with
parliamentary democracy in Germany, that 'it is a sign of a true
democracy that in times of mortal peril, it finds its dictator'. At
the same time, he placed at the disposal of Kapp a sum of 1.5
million marks, paid into the latter's account at the Königsberg
(East Prussia) branch of the Mid-German Credit Bank at the
monthly rate of 125,000 marks.*

The attitude of 'hard-line' industrialists was summed up by
Thyssen:

> During an entire year — 1918-1919 — I felt that Germany was going
> to sink into anarchy ...It was then that I realised the necessity — if
> Germany was not to sink into anarchy — of fighting all this radical
> agitation [of the USPD and KPD] ...The SPD endeavoured to main-
> tain order, but it was too weak. The memory of those days** did
> much to dispose me, later on, to offer my help to National Socialism...[3]

---

* A letter to Kapp from the director of the bank branch in question, dated January 8,
1920, stated that 'the Berlin Handelsgesellschaft, the Dresdner Bank, the Mid-German Credit Bank and the Deutsche Bank are very well disposed towards our efforts'.
Financial support was also forthcoming from Carl Duisberg, who in October 1918
was looking forward to a long period of peaceful and fruitful collaboration with the
labour movement.
** The violent class battles of this period left deep scars on the memories of other
industrialists too. Otto Steinbrinck, private secretary to Freidrich Flick of the giant
steel trust *Vereinigte Stahlwerke* (United Steel Works), handled most of his boss's
dealings with the Nazis in the year prior to the formation of the first Hitler
government. The Flick concern turned towards the Nazi movement in 1932, he
explained at the Nuremberg trial of Nazi industrialists, because it feared a resurgence
of the proletarian radicalism experienced in 1923: 'One has to consider that our
plants were situated in the most radical territories of the Reich; that is, Saxony,
where Riesa, Goeditz and Lauchhammer were situated. This district has always been
one of the reddest parts of Germany and the plants Brandenburg and Hennigsdorf,
very close to Berlin, were almost on the same level as this Red Saxony. That's why

But in those early months of the republic, there was no Nazi Party, nor any other comparable movement capable of rousing the petty-bourgeois masses against Weimar and the 'November criminals'. Nor was there a significant body of opinion inside the ruling class considering such a 'plebeian' solution to its problems. Such opposition that there was to Weimar flowed for the most part through the already existing parties and institutions of the ruling class, subjecting them to such tremendous strains that at the time of the Kapp putsch open rifts were precipitated within them.

1920 began with a renewed eruption of crises on both the domestic and international fronts. The imminent passage through the Reichstag of the Works Council bill (see Chapter Ten) precipitated an even more intense polarisation of the classes, creating a situation where the social democrats found themselves simultaneously attacked from Left and Right. The bill, derived to a large extent from the class collaborationist principles enshrined in the November Working Agreement, had aroused bitter hostility not only among reactionary employers, but wide sections of the working class, who rightly considered it to be a betrayal of the socialist goals for which they had fought in the revolution of November 1918. The already harrassed Weimar coalition now headed by the former trade union bureaucrat Otto Bauer (Scheidemann had resigned the Chancellorship in June 1919) lashed out against the Left flank of the workers' movement, rounding up 400 USPD and KPD activists in the Ruhr region alone and banning rallies and demonstrations by both parties throughout Germany. And on January 13, while SPD deputies and their bourgeois allies were voicing their approval of legislation which purportedly ushered in a new era of class peace in the factories and mines of Germany, outside on the steps of the Reichstag building, the Weimar police were pumping lead into a vast crowd of workers demonstrating against the passage of this self-same bill. Dozens of workers were slaughtered, and many more wounded in this show of brute force against the revolutionary wing of the proletariat.

But as has so often been the case in such situations, the January 13 massacre did not placate the anti-Weimar alliance of Junkers, officers and industrialists. On the contrary they saw this sharp shift to the right on the part of the government as an

our plant managements in these plants ...were rather worried because the same troubles which we had experienced eight years previously might revive again. Then ...we had seen fairly heavy fighting with the revolutionary Red Army in the Vogtland, and in Saxony, and Riesa, and ...the memory was still fresh'. (*The Flick Case, U.S. Military Tribunal,* Vol. 6, p.346.) Punishment for the mistakes of leadership committed in 1923 may have been long delayed, but was all the more merciless when it came.

opportunity to press even more extreme policies on its leaders, as a prelude to driving the SPD out of the coalition entirely and forming a new 'national' cabinet firmly anchored on the hitherto oppositional parties, the DVP and DNVP. Such a policy was in fact mooted by DVP treasurer and steel tycoon Albert Vögler* at a meeting of his party's managing committee on March 3, but was successfully opposed by Stresemann, who by this time had opted for a tactic of gradual reduction of social democratic influence in the government and state.

Stresemann considered the wisest plan to be to force the holding of new elections, and to this end he joined with the DNVP leadership in pressing the government for an immediate dissolution of the Reichstag. This step had been taken mainly as a response to demands by the Entente powers that the German government deliver up to the Allies for trial as 'war criminals' nearly 900 military leaders, some of whom were among the most illustrious names in the Prussian officer corps. The other demand which incensed all German nationalists and militarists, and seriously concerned those bourgeois seeking to maintain an armed counter-weight against the increasingly radicalised workers' movement, was the Allied insistence that the two strongest and most political Free Corps brigades, the Marine, under Commander Captain Erhardt, and the Baltikum, led by General Count von der Goltz, should be immediately disbanded.**

Now the group of plotters around Kapp and Lüttwitz decided that the time had come to strike, since if they delayed any longer their chief combat forces could well be dispersed when the government complied with the Allied demand. On March 4, Lüttwitz conferred with Rudolf Heinze and Oskar Hergt, chairmen of the DVP and DNVP Reichstag fractions respectively, suggesting that they swing their parties behind Kapp's proposed bid to unseat the government. Though eager to effect a shift towards the right in government policy, both party leaders baulked at Lüttwitz's proposal that they present the Bauer cabinet with an ultimatum, for they realised that its probable rejection would precipitate a

---

* Vögler was of course just one among many of the big business contingent in the DVP Reichstag fraction who along with their co-thinkers in the DNVP, voted against the Works Council bill. Others included Hugo Stinnes, Kurt Sorge, a director of the Krupp concern (Krupp himself was a member of the DNVP) and President of the Federation of German Industries, Reinhold Quaatz, a leading officer of the influential Essen-Mulheim-Oberhausen Chamber of Commerce (his divorced wife Magda later married Göbbels), Hans von Raumer, regarded as a spokesman for the electrical industry, and Helmuth von Raumer of the Potash industry.

** In his March 4 meeting with the DVP and DNVP leaders, Lüttwitz declared quite bluntly that 'if the Free Corps are dissolved, and in addition, half the regular army is disbanded, the country will be left defenceless in the face of the threat from Bolshevism.'

military revolt.

News of these manoeuvrings soon leaked out, yet the government still hesitated to move decisively against the military-monarchist Right for fear that in so doing, it would be compelled to rely on the strength of the working class and thus unleash a wave of militancy which would break out of the defensive limits imposed on it by the social democrats.* And that is in fact precisely what did happen.

On March 12, after several days of bargaining with the Lüttwitz faction, the Bauer government found itself confronted with a mutiny by a section of its 'own' army leadership. Refusing to comply with a government order (ironically issued by Defence Minister Noske, founder of the Free Corps) to disband the two offending brigades. Luttwitz ordered one of them, the Marine, which was stationed a short distance outside Berlin at Doberitz, to march on the German capital. With swastikas on their steel helmets, and chanting the refrain which had echoed throughout Germany, Erhardt's men entered Berlin in the early hours of March 13 as Kapp and his monarchist entourage made ready to pronounce themselves the new rulers of Germany.

Kapp's brief reign dramatised the enormous gulf that separated the aims of the counter-revolutionary Right from its ability to achieve them. Proclaiming all strikes to be 'treason' and 'sabotage',** the new regime looked on helplessly as its grip on Berlin and the rest of Germany was progressively undermined by the largest general strike in the history of world capitalism.

Literally nothing moved in Berlin as its entire labour force, clerical and professional as well as manual, refused to lift a finger

---

* Even Scheidemann had his doubts about the wisdom of government policy towards the rightists. In a letter to President Ebert, dated February 20, 1920, he wrote: 'The German nationalists are now raging against the government worse than the Spartacists ...People do not understand ...why the USPD papers are shut down for attacking the government ...Much closer attention than hitherto must be given to the activities of the German nationalists if we do not want to have very sad experiences. Steps should most certainly have been taken against the DNVP newspapers before [sic!] proceeding against those of the extreme left.' (P. Scheidemann: *Memoirs of a Social Democrat*, Vol. II, pp.646-647)

** The proclamation of the Kapp regime, issued on March 13, was not couched in the language of the traditionalist monarchist Right. It employed social demagogy which foreshadowed a dictatorship which while not lasting for the predicted thousand years, proved far more durable than that of Kapp and Luttwitz: 'The government stands for economic freedom. It will ruthlessly suppress strikes and sabotage. Strikes mean treason to the people, the Fatherland and the future. *This will not be a government of one-sided capitalism, but will defend German labour against the harsh fate of international slavery under finance capitalism* ...We shall govern not with theories but through the pracitical needs of the state and the people. *The government will be an objective judge in the current battle between capital and labour. We decline to favour any party, whether Right or Left.* We recognise only German citizens. Every person must do his duty. Today work is the most important duty for any person. *Germany must be a moral working community*.' (emphasis added)

for the illegal regime. For the first — and in all probability last — time, top ranking civil servants ignored ministers' instructions, lost safe keys, and hid rubber stamps for official documents. Chancellor Kapp's writ did not even run within the confines of the government buildings, let alone the capital or the rest of Germany. As in the early days of the November Revolution, wide sections of the middle class were drawn towards the side of the proletariat as the latter proved in action its ability and determination to act decisively against the reaction, once again giving the lie to the reformist (and after 1934, Stalinist) claim that militant action by the proletariat drives the petty-bourgeoisie into the arms of the enemies of the working class and socialism. The Kapp putsch also proved something else that was to have an enormous bearing on the outcome of the working class struggle to defeat fascism between 1930 and 1933. Between those two dates (in fact, to be strictly accurate, from 1929 to the middle of 1934) the Stalinist leadership of the Communist International instructed the KPD not to have any dealings at any level with either the SPD or the ADGB. All anti-fascist actions were to be conducted under the exclusive leadership of the KPD and its various affiliated organisations — the so-called 'united front from below' — on the utterly false premise that social democracy had turned fascist and that its leaders would under no circumstances sanction, let alone initiate, any action by its members and supporters against fascism. In forcing such a suicidal line on the KPD, the Stalinists were obliged to either distort or ignore one of the most important chapters in the history of the German workers' movement. If we were to project this Stalinist schema back from 1928, when it was first conceived, to 1920, the year of the Kapp putsch,* we would then have to ask ourselves; who initiated the anti-Kapp general strike? And if we were to take this same Stalinist theory of 'social fascism' seriously, we would have to conclude that it either arose spontaneously, or in response to a call made by the KPD.

Reality was far more complex and from the standpoints of theory and political tactics and strategy, infinitely richer. The anti-Kapp general strike was not in fact called by the KPD, nor the USPD (which by this time enjoyed the support of several million workers) but by that backbone of conservatism in the labour movement, the ADGB! The same trade union bureaucracy that prior to 1914 had, in the words of its leader Karl Legien scorned the weapon of the general strike as 'general nonsense',** and

---

* An important article in the Comintern organ did in fact attempt to detect 'social fascism' in the war-time policy of the SPD (*Decaying Capitalism and the Fascisation of the Bourgeois State, Communist International,* Vol. VII, No. 2-3, April 1, 1930.)

** This sensational reversal of ADGB policy even aroused comment in the international trade union press. One such journal observed that 'the attempt of the mili-

throughout the imperialist war served the ruling class as the custodian of social peace in the factories and mines, the very same bureaucracy which, once again under the leadership of Legien, had done so much to divert the working class away from the struggle for state power and the expropriation of the bourgeoisie by concluding the November Working Agreement with Hugo Stinnes, now became, under the immense pressure of a thoroughly roused and politicised proletariat, the initiator of strike action for exclusively political goals.

Neither did the conduct of the social democrats conform to the arid schemas of 'third period' Stalinism.* The SPD executive jointly supported the ADGB's strike call together with the social democratic ministers in the cabinet. Even President Ebert permitted his name to appear on the official SPD proclamation which announced the strike call. It was evident that when it was a question of preserving their own bureaucratic privileges inside the labour movement, and positions within the government and state apparatus (both of which hinged on the continued existence of a

tarists in March last to overthrow the German republic has forced the trade union movement of Germany, always so careful in the past to have nothing to do with politics, into the political arena ...It was only the organised working class of Germany that formed the defence of the republic ...[they] were the organisers and leaders of the opposition to the action'. (*International Trades Union Review,* No. 5, June 1920, p.16) The official historian of the ADGB also acknowledged that Kapp had compelled the conservative trade union leadership to adopt tactics which it had until March 1920 stoutly opposed as adventurist and disruptive: 'The method of the general strike, so long a point of contention between party and trade unions, was here applied for the first time. The trade union leaders, who had formerly regarded the use of the general strike with great uneasiness as a reckless playing with fire, did not hesitate to resort to it when the right moment for it had come.' (Richard Seidel: *The Trade Union Movement of Germany,* p.100, Amsterdam, 1928.)

* And not only third period Stalinism. Thus in the notes to the most recent edition of Lenin's *Collected Works,* we can read the following legend: '...the Social Democratic government offered no resistance [to the Kapp putsch]. On March 13, 1920, army units were moved to Berlin and meeting with no resistance from the government declared it dissolved and set up a military junta. The German working class responded with a general strike and on March 17, under pressure from the working class, Kapp's government fell and state power again passed into the hands of the Social Democrats, who by deceit succeeded in frustrating the general strike.' (Notes to Vol. 30 of Lenin's *Collected Works,* p.567) This account of the Kapp putsch leaves out one small detail: that the general strike which brought Kapp down was called by the Social Democrats! The text of the SPD strike call ran thus: 'Workers, Comrades! The military putsch is under way. The Ehrhardt marine brigade is marching on Berlin to force a change of government. These mercenaries who fear disbandment, want to put reactionaries in the various government posts. We refuse to bow to this military pressure. We did not make the revolution in order to acknowledge once again the bloody rule of mercenaries. We will make no deal with the Baltic criminals. Workers, Comrades! Use every means to prevent this return of bloody reaction. Strike, stop working, strangle this military dictatorship, fight ...for the preservation of the republic, forget all dissension! There is only one way to block the return of William II; to cripple the country's economic life. Not a hand must move, not a single worker must help the military dictatorship. General strike all along the line! Workers, unite!'

parliamentary system and an independent workers' movement) the reformist leadership could be driven to fight for its survival, even to the extent of sanctioning or initiating mass actions by the working class. True, in the case of the social democratic leadership, the reformists' main concern was to restore Germany to the political situation that existed prior to March 13, but it proved to be a policy which brought them into sharp conflict with the trade union leadership.

Sustained and driven forwards by the sheer power of the strike movement against Kapp, the ADGB executive for the first time in the history of the German labour movement found itself putting forward demands which placed it to the Left of the SPD. While the social democrats contented themselves with issuing directives which simply called for the restoration of 'democracy' (the very same democracy that had permitted Kapp to prepare and spring his putsch) Legien, as the leader of the central strike committee, drafted a programme which if fully implemented, would have precipitated a head on clash with not only monarchist intransigents, but the entire ruling class. When Kapp fled Berlin on March 17, the ADGB proposed the following nine point programme, pending the acceptance of which the general strike would continue:

1. 'Decisive influence' of the trade unions in the formation of a new government, and in the shaping of more radical social and economic policy.
2. Drastic and prompt punishment of all those who participated in any way in the Kapp putsch.
3. The dismissal of Defence Minister Noske, whose Free Corps had provided the armed units for Kapp's take-over on March 13.
4. A purge of all monarchists in the civil service and public administration.
5. 'Democratisation' of the machinery of government, giving a decisive voice to trade unions representing clerical as well as manual workers in its employ.
6. Extension of social legislation.
7. Immediate nationalisation of the mining, potash and electrical industries.
8. Expropriation of large land owners who either failed to deliver foodstuffs or did not cultivate their land intensively.
9. The dissolution of all counter-revolutionary para-military formations, and the establishment of a workers' militia to maintain security.*

---

* Sensing its newly acquired bargaining power, and also fearing that unless it adopted a radical stance, the leadership of the general strike would pass over to the USPD and the KPD, the ADGB executive declared in its official journal that the trade unions 'must intervene as a new factor in political life, with which the government and the parliament must come to terms before all decisive steps. There

Naturally the social democrats rejected the more radical of the demands put forward by their trade union colleagues, not merely for fear that acceptance would drive a wedge between the SPD and its bourgeois cabinet partners, but because reports were flooding from every major industrial region that the working class had gone over to the offensive after the fall of Kapp, and in the Ruhr and Saxony had succeeded in forming its own rudimentary organs of administration. In a situation of imminent dual power, the reformists swung over hard to the right, and immediately began to mobilise against the working class the very forces which had overturned the legal government on March 13. Once again, as in the early days of the November Revolution, the army emerged as the supreme arbiter in the balance of power between the classes and parties of Germany, and for the second time, it was the social democrats who permitted and even invited it to perform this reactionary role. With workers defecting in droves from social democracy, the SPD leadership eagerly clasped the proffered hand of the chief of staff, Hans von Seeckt. Reichswehr might not fire on Reichswehr, but it was only too willing to butcher the flower of the German working class.* Seeckt's order of the day to his troops declared that the German army took its stand 'in defence of peace and order against any Bolshevik and Spartacist attempt to seize power in Germany and thus strike a fatal blow at our people.'

When the gunsmoke finally cleared from the battlefields of the Ruhr and Saxony, and thousands of bereaved proletarian families had buried their dead — women, children and babies as

may be doctrinaire democrats who view such a settlement as incompatible with the constitutional rights of the people's representative bodies. To them we can only say: a parliamentarianism that hardens in external forms without caring for the vital productive power of the people is a danger to the commonweal. The Monarchist Putsch has shown how easily democratic governments and parliaments can be dispossessed. But what cannot be dispossessed, and cannot abdicate or be dissolved, the one remaining power, the source of all the forces sustaining the state, is the working nation, whose economic unions have fearlessly taken up the challenge of the political and military traitors and have defeated them'. (*Correspondenzblatt,* March 27, 1920)

* The savagery of the fighting far surpassed anything experienced in previous repressions of revolutionary workers by army and Free Corps forces. One saviour of Weimar democracy in the von Epp Brigade, the student Max Ziller, described his exhilarating experiences in a letter: 'If I were to write to you everything, you would say these were lies. No mercy is shown. We shoot down even the wounded. The enthusiasm is marvellous, almost incredible...Anyone who falls into our hands gets first the gun butt and then the bullett ...we also shot dead instantly ten Red nurses, each of whom was carrying a pistol. We shot these abominations with joy, and how they cried and pleaded with us for their lives. Nothing doing! *We were much more humane against the French!'* (emphasis added) Of such human material were the extermination units in Hitler's war against the USSR made. Creatures like Ziller, who two decades later were to be found equally joyously gassing Jews by the million, and herding untold numbers of women and children into mass graves across the war-ravaged expanses of eastern Europe, were blooded and trained for this task in Weimar's counter-revolutionary war against the workers of the Ruhr.

well as men — one political fact of life became clear for millions of German workers. Social democracy had bought the 'loyalty' of the High Command by the wanton sacrifice of the most heroic and class conscious elements of the German proletariat. From March 1920 onwards, no government could expect to 'rule' Germany without the support of the officer corps. In periods and moments of great crisis, beneath the skin of Weimar democracy would become visible the Bonapartist outlines of the sinew, muscle and bones of the same Junker caste that stood guard over the throne of the Hohenzollerns. The events of March 1920 provided an object lesson in the class nature of even the most 'advanced' capitalist democracy.

A Balance Sheet of Kapp

The Kapp putsch, brief and ill-conceived though it was, marked a watershed in the history of Weimar Germany.* The convulsions it unleashed within an already crisis-wracked German capitalism subjected every party leadership and political programme to the severest possible test, with the political pendulum swinging at times almost hourly from right to left and back again to the right. We have already touched on the Kapp crisis as it affected the reformist wing of the workers' movement and observed how the trade union bureaucracy by virtue of its position of leadership in the general strike, found itself violently at odds with the SPD leadership once the Kapp regime fell on March 17. What of the conduct of the left flank of the movement, led by the USPD and the small but rapidly growing KPD? Once again, we find that reality confronts the schematist and formalist with all manner of unpleasant surprises.

On March 13, the day the ADGB proclaimed a general strike to bring down the Kapp regime, the KPD Central Committee published and circulated in Berlin and elsewhere a leaflet which far from endorsing and giving a revolutionary perspective to the strike movement, actually opposed the ADGB's strike call, warning the working class 'not to lift a finger for the democratic republic', which the KPD statement deemed to be 'only a thin mask for the bourgeois dictatorship'. But that was hardly the point at issue. Kapp's putsch not only overturned the rickety edifice of Weimar parliamentary democracy, but directly and

* The Kapp putsch tends to be dismissed as an episode of little significance for the subsequent history of the Weimar Republic and the rise of national socialism. Thus the liberal historian, Erich Eyck, writes in his two volume study of Weimar that 'from its very beginnings the Kapp putsch was nothing but the work of overgrown juvenile delinquents' (*A History of the Weimar Republic*, Vol. I, p.150, New York, 1967), overlooking the impact that the coup's failure had on rightist thinking after 1920.

immediately threatened the very existence of all the organisations of the German proletariat, from the SPD and trade unions through the centrist USPD to the revolutionary KPD. That was the meaning of the Kapp regime's declaration banning strikes, and of its intention to transform Germany into what it called a 'working moral community'. In their justifiable anxiety to demarcate their party as sharply as possible from reformist and centrist tendencies in the workers' movement, the KPD leaders overlooked the basic fact that the struggle against bourgeois influences in the proletariat is best waged when there is the maximum freedom for political discussion, polemic and action between and inside the various groupings of the working class, and that with the curtailment or abolition of these conditions, the political and theoretical clarification of the proletariat and its vanguard is gravely impaired.

The KPD leadership, which to a large extent had still to free itself from putschist and sectarian concepts of struggle and leadership, believed that Kapp's putsch, by instituting a regime of naked bourgeois repression, would actively assist in this process of political clarification, and that therefore the sooner the hated Weimar republic was overthrown, the better:

> The Ebert-Republic, the bourgeois democracy, can no longer be saved; it is merely an empty pretence, merely a cracked mask for the capitalist dictatorship ...The revolutionary proletariat remains in chains. Thousands of revolutionary leaders are in protective custody ...The situation is crystal clear. The watchword is evident: all revolutionary workers must rally around the flag of the proletarian dictatorship.[4]

Crystal clear to the KPD perhaps, but not to those millions of workers who were either still loyal supporters of the SPD, or were making their way to the left through the centrist-dominated USPD. The KPD offered no fighting programme to combat the very real menace posed by Kapp's regime, but merely noisy propaganda for the dictatorship of the proletariat. Its leaders failed to devise a tactical bridge between the struggle against Kapp and the final battle for state power. But this sectarian line could not be sustained for more than a day. On March 14, with 12 million strikers defying Kapp, the KPD performed a rapid about turn.

The party's opposition to the strike ran completely counter to the unprecedented upsurge of united militancy that the putsch had unleashed in the entire working class, and was resulting in the KPD being subjected to calculated attacks by social democracy for its refusal to join the battle to defend the basic democratic rights of the proletariat. Partly because of its initial mistake (and also of course due to its relative numerical smallness) the KPD was unable to wrest the political initiative from the

ADGB and the USPD centrists. Serious attempts were however made to rectify the blunder of March 13, and to this end the KPD declared eight days later (that is, *after* the fall of Kapp) that it would function as a 'loyal opposition' to a 'workers' government' of the type proposed by the ADGB in its nine-point programme.*

---

* This statement provoked much controversy inside the leadership of the Communist International, the Hungarian Bela Kun joining with Karl Radek of the Soviet Party in attacking the KPD proposal as opportunist. Lenin thought differently. In his *Left Wing Communism,* Lenin devoted some considerable attention to the tactics of the KPD in the Kapp putsch, upholding the 'loyal opposition' statement of the party as 'quite correct both in its basic premise and its practical conclusions', while insisting that the KPD was theoretically wrong in terming the proposed SPD-USPD 'workers' goverment' a socialist one, and pointing out that the statement displayed illusions in bourgeois democracy when it said that '...a state of affairs in which political freedom can be enjoyed without restriction, and bourgeois democracy cannot operate as the dictatorship of capital is, from the viewpoint of the development of the proletarian dictatorship, of the utmost importance in further winning the proletarian masses over to the side of communism ...' It was enough to say, wrote Lenin, that 'as long as the majority of the urban workers follow the Independents we Communists must do nothing to prevent those workers from getting rid of their last philistine democratic illusions by going through the experience of having a goverment of their 'own'. That is sufficient ground for a compromise, which is really necessary and should consist in renouncing for a certain period, all attempts at the forcible overthrow of a government which enjoys the confidence of a majority of the urban workers'. (V. Lenin: *Left Wing Communism — An Infantile Disorder.* In *Selected Works,* Vol. 31, pp.109-110). These tactics were of course pioneered by the Bolsheviks in the struggle to overturn the Provisional Government thrown up by the first Russian Revolution of February 1917. While the Bolsheviks remained in a minority in the Soviets, they submitted to Soviet discipline and on one famous occasion (the 'July days' in Petrograd) actively restrained the advanced workers and sailors from attempting what would have been a premature and therefore disastrous overthrow of the Kerensky regime, which, because of the support given to it by the majority soviet parties (Mensheviks and Social Revolutionaries) would have been able to mobilise a considerable proportion of the more conservative sections of the proletariat against the Bolshevik vanguard. Lenin was now availing the leaders of German communism of this priceless experience. More than a decade later, Trotsky employed precisely the same tactical concept in seeking a political road to those millions of social democratic workers in Europe menaced by the rise of Fascism: 'Make your party open up a real struggle for a strong democratic government ...We Bolsheviks would retain the right to explain to the workers the insufficiency of democratic slogans; we could not take upon ourselves the political responsibility for such a government but we would honestly help you in the struggle for such a government; together with you we would repel all attacks of bourgeois reaction. More than that, we would bind ourselves before you not to undertake any revolutionary actions that go beyond the limits of democracy (*real* democracy) so long as the majority of the workers has not consciously placed itself on the side of revolutionary dictatorship'. (L. Trotsky: *Our Present Tasks* [November 7, 1933] in *Writings of Leon Trotsky, 1933-34,* pp.138-139, New York, 1972) This declaration elicited a furious outcry from the Stalinists, who were still clinging, nearly a year after Hitler's victory in Germany and the Nazis' destruction of the entire social democratic movement, to Stalin's theory that fascism and social democracy were 'twins'. British Stalinist Andrew Rothstein wrote (under his pen name of 'R.F. Andrews') that Trotsky's proposal to the social democratic workers had 'only one meaning, the abandonment of the struggle against capitalist exploitation and war, class collaboration preparing the way for fascism.' (R.F. Andrews: *The Truth About Trotsky,* p.69, CPGB, London, 1934). Self-styled followers of Trotsky such as Robin Blackburn of the International Marxist Group

Taken together with the early KPD's other leftist deviations — the refusal of certain of its leaders to take part in parliamentary elections and work in the reformist trade unions — the Kapp experience was destined to acquire enormous political significance after 1928, when under the Stalinist leadership of Ernst Thälmann, ultimatism and abstentionism were raised from episodic errors into an entire system of tactics and strategy. Stalin's theory of 'social fascism', forced on what was by far the largest section of the Comintern outside of the CPSU, prevented those millions of workers in and close to the KPD learning the political lessons of the leftist mistakes committed at the outset of the Kapp putsch, since 'third period' Stalinism had now made these false tactics mandatory for the entire international movement.

Stalinism thus acted — and still does — as a political and theoretical chloroform, dulling the sensitivities of the proletariat, preventing it from assimilating the lessons of its past struggles in order to betray those of the present and future.

The same cannot be said of the more politically aware elements in the ruling class and the extreme counter-revolutionary right. But before turning to their assessment of the Kapp putsch, and the changes in their tactical and strategic thinking that were occasioned by its demise, it will be necessary to look briefly at the rise and fall of the Kapp regime as it affected relations between the various factions inside Germany's main bourgeois party, the DVP. As late as March 4, 1920 (nine days before the Kapp putsch) Stresemann had written to a party colleague that he rejected the policy advocated by some of the DVP's heavy industrialists, which was to drive the social democrats out of the government coalition. This would, he wrote, 'force them over into the camp of the Independents and the Bolsheviks.' Stresemann said he favoured 'the elimination of the dominant influence of the social democrats, if possible through a cabinet in which the middle class parties predominate.' At this stage, he certainly did not desire or envisage a head-on, least of all violent, clash with the SPD. Yet the Kapp putsch, whose goals if not methods were shared by Stresemann's right-wing industrialist critics in the DVP, found this apostle of moderation adapting to the military dictatorship with remarkable suppleness.

On the day of the putsch, Stresemann and other DVP leaders met in Berlin to determine their party's attitude to Kapp's regime. The consensus proved to be that though Kapp's methods were questionable from a constitutional point of view, his goals were

(to name the most notorious example) would be hard put to it to explain in what sense their opposition to the demand for a Labour government (with or without socialist policies) differs from Rothstein's denunciation of Trotsky.

admirable.*

Stresemann hoped that his party, while having reservations about certain of Kapp's measures, could exploit the initial success of the putsch to extract concessions from the ejected government on the composition of a future, more constitutional cabinet. This tactic necessitated the DVP performing the role of intermediary between the Kapp regime and the deposed government leaders, who after a brief sojourn in hostile Dresden (army leaders there were openly sympathetic to Kapp) set up their 'exile' headquarters in Stuttgart. The meeting of March 13 agreed to dispatch a three-man deputation to Kapp, to sound out the new 'Chancellor' on his policies. On hearing their favourable reports, Stresemann declared:

> We must seek a line which on the one hand will make no difficulties for the new government but which will leave open the possibility of our acting as an intermediary between Dresden and Berlin ...The *faits accomplis* are recognised, but we demand that the present illegal situation be promptly brought into accord with the law.

This was how things stood on the evening of March 13. But by the next morning, unanimity within the DVP leadership was shattered by the impact of the workers' general strike, which to all but the most obtuse bourgeois, was clearly capable of bringing Kapp to his knees in a matter of days. What Stresemann had predicted in his letter of March 4 — that any attempt to force the SPD out of the government would drive its supporters into a united front with the USPD and KPD workers — had indeed come about.

Two main groups emerged; one favouring a rapprochement with the deposed government (which if the general strike were successful, would soon become the effective ruler of Germany again), the other, 'hard line' faction advocating continued support

---

* The text of the statement issued after the March 13 meeting read: 'The previous government was unable to gain the confidence of the people. It opposed every attempt to set up a new government through the constitutional means of new elections and, beyond that, it sought to violate the hitherto existing constitution in order to insure its own power. It therefore bears the responsibility for the fact that the path of organic development, which we endorse, has been departed from. Now a new government has been formed [sic!]. All of those who want to see the reconstruction of our Fatherland in a peaceful, orderly fashion must now demand that the new government give guarantees for the preservation of order, property and freedom to work. The liberal principles of the DVP remain unaffected by the upheaval. We therefore demand the quickest possible transformation of the present provisional government into a constitutional one. We expect the government to conduct without delay new elections to the legislative bodies on the basis of the present free electoral law and so insure the formation of a constitutional government into which all of those parties will be drawn which are serious about the re-establishment of our economy and the preservation of our national honour. Until that time we must make it our duty, through the co-operation of all Germans, to keep internal strife from bringing about a collapse of our political and economic situation.'

for Kapp. The latter group was led by Oskar Maretzky, who had
been offered the post of Berlin Police Commissioner by Kapp as
an inducement to swing the rest of the DVP leadership behind the
putsch. Not for the last time, Stresemann found himself holding
the balance within his party between the pro-Weimar
'collaborationists' and the anti-republican extremists. Should the
putsch fail (as now seemed likely) and the DVP not detach itself
from Kapp in good time, then the prospects of cobbling together
a Weimar coalition dominated by the bourgeois parties and
depending on the toleration of the social democrats were ruined
for years, if not for good. He therefore despatched Reichstag
fraction chairman Heinze to Dresden, who reported that the
Saxon Landtag (State parliament) fraction of the DVP had
decided to support the legal government temporarily in residence
there. Stresemann himself meanwhile met government party
leaders still in Berlin, and proposed to them a compromise
solution whereby a provisional government nominated by
President Ebert would replace both the Kapp regime and the
deposed cabinet of Chancellor Bauer. Consistent with his tactics
of using the Kapp regime as a lever to shift the political centre of
gravity rightwards, Stresemann proposed that this provisional
government should award the strategic post of Economics
Minister, which until March 1920 had been in the hands of parties
who sought to curb the power and influence of the Ruhr tycoons,
to the DVP.

But before Stresemann's plan could be properly considered
(and it should be remembered that those who were negotiating
with him were not empowered to do so by their respective parties)
the crisis took another turn for the worse so far as the bourgeois
of the DVP were concerned. The general strike, now in its third
day, was developing a momentum and aim of its own which far
transcended the limited political goals of those in the deposed
government who had either called or supported it. It was no
longer a question for Stresemann of facilitating the smoothest
possible transition back towards 'constitutional' rule with a
minimum of damage to the prestige of his party and the maximum of political concessions extracted from a revamped Weimar
coalition. On March 16, and without even consulting any fellow
DVP leaders, Stresemann visited Kapp's Chief of Staff, Col. Max
Bauer, in order to negotiate the withdrawal of the regime in such
a way as to prevent the working class from seizing the political
initiative before the old government could re-establish its
authority and somewhat tarnished reputation. Stresemann's ploy
had the backing of a section of the DDP leadership, who like
Stresemann feared that the anti-Kapp strike movement was now
becoming a danger to the bourgeoisie as a whole, and not merely
that small fraction of it which had either supported or

sympathised with the putsch.

The right-wing social democrats Paul Hirsch and Albert Sudekum, seeing that the general strike had escaped their control, also favoured a graceful exit being arranged for Kapp, Lüttwitz and their chief aides, and only withdrew at the last moment from direct talks with Lüttwitz when instructed to do so by their party executive. The meeting, whose main arrangements had been made by Stresemann, went ahead with representatives present from the DNVP, the DVP, Centre and DDP. Pro and anti-Weimar party leaders alike undertook to work for an anmesty for the Kappists, following which Lüttwitz wrote out his resignation. On March 17, at 3.30 p.m., the Kapp government ceased to exist. Stresemann now hoped that he and his allies in the other bourgeois parties could insert themselves into the vacuum created by its demise. Imagine Stresemann's consternation when the next day, the government on whose behalf he had ostensibly been negotiating repudiated the deal with Lüttwitz. Yet again, the DVP found itself with the necessity of undertaking a sharp tactical manoeuvre, only this time towards the Left.

On March 18, after a party executive meeting called to discuss the crisis (hourly worsening as it became evident that the ADGB would not be able to call off the general strike), the DVP issued another statement on the Kapp events, this time trying to put a constitutional and legalistic gloss on the party's ambivalent, to say the least, attitude and conduct over the previous five days:

> What we had to do in the face of the forcible overthrow of March 13 was prescribed for us by the national and liberal character of the DVP ...it was impossible for us to leave the path of organic, constitutional development. Accordingly, we must condemn decisively any violent undertaking directed against the constitution and any use of our troops ...for an irresponsible undertaking threatening the very existence of the Reich.*

* The resolution was forced through at the insistence of the party's liberal wing, who were anxious to begin collaboration with the pro-Weimar bourgeois parties and the right wing reformists. Stresemann, while sympathising with their objectives, remained unrepentant about his role in the Kapp events, declaring to a DVP leaders meeting on March 28 that he had acted as he did because he felt no obligation to defend the Weimar regime, since it had issued out of a revolution. Neither did it exclude the possibility of the DVP giving its support to a more successful dictatorship in the future: '...if our Lord God and destiny send us a man who, without holding to the paragraphs of Weimar, builds us a great Germany again, then our party would — so I hope — grant him the same indemnity which the fathers of the National Liberal Party [the imperial forerunner of the DVP] granted to Bismarck. Stresemann was to have his wish granted, though he did not live to see it. The DVP Reichstag delegation, whittled down by wholesale defections to the Nazis amongst its middle class supporters, cast its puny two mandates for Hitler's Enabling Act on March 23, 1933, thereby putting its bourgeois seal on the tyranny of the Third Reich. It is hard to reconcile these words of Stresemann, full of yearning for the political 'strong man' so often encountered in even the more liberal representatives of the German bourgeoisie, or indeed his and his party's conduct during the Kapp putsch, with E.H. Carr's comment that 'heavy

(This final act of disengagement from the discredited and defeated rebels was to serve the DVP in good stead some three months later when, after the Reichstag elections of June 6, the old Weimar coalition lost its overall majority and had to make way for a new Cabinet which both excluded the SPD and for the first time in the life of the young republic, allotted two portfolios to the party of Stresemann.)

As we have already suggested, the ways in which the Kapp putsch was evaluated by various elements of the ruling class and the counter-revolutionary Right greatly influenced the contours of bourgeois strategy for the remaining years of the Weimar Republic. Chief of Staff Hans von Seeckt, one of the ablest brains to grace the leadership of the Prussian officer corps, drew the conclusion that a government which relied for support on the armed forces alone was doomed to collapse, a view which he conveyed in his report (quoted in Chapter Eleven) to President Ebert of June 26, 1920. Many other high ranking officers shared the opinions of Seeckt on this question.*

Captain Ehrhardt, whose Free Corps Marine Brigade provided the main military forces for the Kapp regime, also considered that the coup ended in fiasco because those whose duty it had been to support it firmly and openly had conspicuously failed to do so. In an interview given to the London Daily News shortly after the collapse of the Kapp regime, he declared:

> ...the cowardice of the middle class was also responsible for our failure. The German bourgeoisie were delighted with our putsch, but they preferred to remain at home and to act innocent instead of coming to our aid.

Ehrhardt also flayed the Kapp-Lüttwitz regime for its half-heartedness in carrying out its declared policy of crushing all strikes. (Ehrhardt himself had recommended the arrest of the

industry, finding its spokesman in Stresemann ...denounced the putsch and rallied to the restored government.' (*The Bolshevik Revolution,* Vol. III, p.174, London, 1961). Neither is it correct to describe Stresemann as the 'spokesman' of heavy industry, since the DVP leader was constantly battling to prevent his party becoming a tame political mouthpiece for the tycoons of the Ruhr.

* Thus Col. von Wendel of the Supreme High Command under Hitler, wrote of the Kapp putsch that its failure 'proved that recovery required time and had to ripen slowly'. It also taught 'that bayonets may be able to conquer power for a moment but that without approval and consent from at least a large portion of the mass of the people, power cannot be maintained. (von Wendel, in *Wehrmacht und Partei,* p.34, Leipzig.) Similar conclusions had been drawn much earlier by von Seeckt, who wrote in his *Zukunft des Deutsche Reiches* (1930) that 'it is most undesirable that the army be called in to maintain public order: that is beyond the scope of its function which is external, and for this it urgently needs the people's trust and its prompt support, which it risks losing if it is employed as a police force'. And one year earlier, Major H. Foertsch, in the first Nazi pamphlet on military affairs, declared that 'revolutions which are made by the army alone usually destroy the foundations of the army. They do not last long; the confidence of the people has always been a sounder basis for state leadership than guns or bayonets'.

strike leadership, and their shooting, as the only means of forcing the workers to end the general strike):

> The army must maintain order and prevent looting. The government must be ruthless and strong enough to let ten thousand in the North of Berlin starve [North Berlin was the main proletarian quarter of the capital]. With such a lesson in mind the people will refrain for a time from participating in another general strike.

The politically more sophisticated Rossbach* decided after the failure of the putsch to throw in his lot with the Nazis, with whom he established contact on fleeing to Munich. Involved in training and organising the SA he soon became a valuable mediator between the Bavarian Nazis and the north German *volkisch* groups, founding in November 1922 the Berlin-based 'Great Germany Workers Party', with a businessman friend of Hitler's, Bruno Wenzel, as its political director (the new party was to function as a 'front' for the Nazis, who had been banned in Prussia by the state's social democratic government). The Pan Germans, still smarting after their reverse in March 1920, took an interest in Rossbach's party and its Nazi counterpart in Munich, and through Wenzel, offered to make them a gift of one million marks. Wenzel immediately went to Munich to ask Hitler whether he should accept, to which Hitler replied:

> If you can get ten million marks instead of one million, all the better. Politically we all depend on the Pan German League, of which we can only complain that, despite its correct analysis ...up to now it has done no practical work. But now we can make up for this by using its resources.

The Nazis could win the masses, but lacked the 'resources' to do so, while the Pan Germans, never short of ready cash for a 'national' cause, could not hope to secure a popular following. The alliance, as natural as it was mutually beneficial, was to be consumated on a far more devastating scale in the last three years of the Weimar Republic.

Neither were Junker circles satisfied with Kapp's methods and strategy. Hermann Rauschning, the Danzig Nationalist who went over to the Nazis, wrote nearly two decades after the event that the putsch

> was an absolutely perfect model of the way not to organise a modern coup d'etat. It revealed a complete absence of ideas of how the attack should be carried out ...and betrayed an exceedingly inadequate stock

---

* In a speech delivered in Munich on the fourth anniversary of the formation of the Free Corps (November 22, 1922) Rossbach called for unity of all the para-military leagues under a single leadership, obviously that of the Nazis: 'Out of the mass of innumerable separate and competing national groups ...a great unified Power Organisation must be founded which will end this present nonsense for ever. To accomplish that, we must clear the way with black jacks and bayonets ...In Bavaria, you will soon have the opportunity to act. It is to be hoped that we will soon have the same chance in Prussia ...'

of ideas on the subject of the seizure of power ...his idea that the occupation of ministries and the replacement of police by the soldiery were all that was needed for the reorganisation of the State ...shows the incurable weakness of any direct military action in a revolutionary enterprise. The army may instigate a coup d'etat but in order to carry it to completion they need political machinery ...An undisguised military coup remains at all times a mere episode in the political struggle, and throws away the indispensable safeguard of the availability of the army for use in emergency in the day-to-day political struggles.[5]*

It was generally appreciated by Kapp's rightist critics that repressive measures against the working class could only be undertaken by a regime which had extended the basis of its support beyond the state apparatus and the wealthier sections of the propertied classes. And here of course we are returned to the question with which this chapter began: namely that in order to defeat the proletariat and prevent it from re-grouping itself for future defensive or offensive battles, the bourgeoisie must resort to the 'plebeian' or 'Jacobin' solution.** This was precisely the

* The conviction that a lasting political overturn in Germany could and indeed should not be attempted by the armed forces alone went very deep amongst the ruling classes after Kapp, and was certainly shared even by the more politically motivated members of the officer corps. Thus the 'social general' Kurt von Schleicher, strong man behind the von Papen regime and himself the Chancellor whose resignation made way for the appointment of Hitler, issued a statement in the summer of 1932 which exemplified this very real fear of a military-based regime confronted by a hostile population (a prospect which loomed ominously large at the time when the statement was made): '...the support of bayonets is not a sufficient foundation for a government. A government in which popular confidence is steadily diminishing, a government whose parliamentary basis does not correspond to the actual state of popular opinion, would gain nothing from army support. A government can continue usefully in office only if it does not turn against the currents of opinion among the mass of the people, but is able to provide itself with a broad basis of confidence in the vital and productive elements of the people'. Schleicher tried to apply his theories during his brief tenure of office, seeking to widen the narrow basis of his regime (which he had inherited from von Papen's non-party 'Cabinet of Barons') by creating a triangular alliance between the army, the Nazi 'lefts' under the leadership of Gregor Strasser, and the trade union bureaucracy. The project failed to get beyond the exploratory discussion stage, and its collapse cleared the road for the formation of the Nazi-Nationalist coalition.

** Rauschning understood this with remarkable clarity: 'A new phenomenon has emerged, incalculable, menacing like a natural force. Bursting the bounds of all past forms of State and society — the masses. *We must try ...to divide the masses. We must try to hold the masses in check through themselves.* The masses could be contained only through the masses. *Political leadership could only be won and kept through the masses.* The securing of a basis among the masses seemed to us to be the practical teaching of all political wisdom. The non-socialist parties, Liberal and Conservative, and any parties that hope for political survival, must become mass parties ...Disraeli's example was before our eyes when we [i.e. the German ruling class] approached the mass party of Nazism. Not to enrol in it, but to bring it over to us, *and out of it to provide the mass basis that was lacking to the whole of our non-socialist democratic parties* ...What would have become of Germany's democratic liberties if one day the whole of the masses had been brought to a common

factor that was so glaringly lacking in the preparation and execution of the Kapp putsch. Such petty-bourgeois layers as might have been sympathetic to the aims of the coup — and they undoubtedly existed, as the June election results confirmed — never emerged as a tangible counterweight to the organised proletariat during its general strike, and failed even to raise their voices in support of the regime whilst it survived. The behaviour of the nationalist middle class — and here we are referring specifically to the 'old' petty-bourgeoisie, rooted in small property and trading — during the Kapp putsch was in glaring contrast to the role it performed under the leadership of the Nazis more than a decade later, namely that of a human battering ram against the German labour movement.

Movements embracing millions cannot be conjured up overnight simply because the bourgeoisie might find them necessary to combat the working class.

They emerge and develop, not according to the whim or desire of industrial magnates, but in response to profound social crises which shake and shatter the trust which the petty-bourgeois masses have in the efficacy of the methods of parliamentary democracy, and to the extent that the working class fails, by virtue of the inadequacies of its leadership, to convince these exploited and frustrated middle class masses that salvation lies in the revolutionary overthrow of capitalism and the construction of genuine socialism, and not in a fictitious struggle against the 'thraldom of interest' and the creation of a bogus 'people's community' in which monopoly capital, now decked out in its national 'socialist' finery, continues to rule supreme, grinding down the 'small man' and reducing him to pauperism as never before.

Large fascist movements are the outcome of a whole complex of conjunctural events and processes in which the subjective and objective mutually interpenetrate, and this is illustrated perfectly by the development of the Nazi Party between the Kapp putsch and its own abortive bid to seize power in November 1923.

Towards the Munich Putsch

Like those we have already quoted, Hitler regarded the Kapp putsch as a political blunder of the first magnitude, even though he shared the aims of its main perpetrators.* In a conversation

denominator and delivered over to the law of progressive radicalisation? ...*All those years we were under the pressure of the possibility that the Nazi masses would march over to the Communists'.* (H. Rauschning: *Make and Break with the Nazis,* pp.38-39, London, 1941.) (emphasis added)

* Hitler in fact attempted to make contact with the regime, flying to Berlin from Munich with Eckart only to discover on landing that Kapp had just fled the capital

with Otto Strasser (who had, as a former student member of the SPD, been active in the struggle against Kapp) Hitler countered charges that the putsch had been unconstitutional by answering that 'one must not be satisfied with the letter, one must penetrate to the spirit. The Kapp putsch was necessary, though it was ineffectively carried out.'[6] Hitler returned to this question in a speech delivered on the first anniversary of the formation of the Nazi regime, on this occasion stressing the 'bourgeois' inhibitions and cowardice of Kapp's accomplices:

> When the Kapp putsch was at an end and those who were responsible for it were brought before the Republican courts, then each held up his hand and swore that he knew nothing, had intended nothing and wished nothing. That was what destroyed the bourgeois world — that they had not the courage to stand behind their act, that they had not the courage to step before the judge and say: Yes, that is what we wanted to do; we wanted to destroy this state. This courage they lacked and therefore they have suffered shipwreck.

Together with the already-quoted remarks by Hitler on the political shortcomings of those who led and comprised the Free Corps, these judgments on Kapp help us to understand why Hitler was so anxious to build a movement that while ready to accept financial assistance from army sympathisers, and to exploit the army's natural inclination to favour and even protect organisations of a 'national' coloration, would maintain its political independence from any section of the military leadership. National socialists would not be the foot soldiers of another Kapp, but the spearhead of the so-called 'national revolution' in which the Nazi tops, and not the general staff, would wield the supreme political power.

But this did not mean that Hitler had freed himself from the strategy which led Kapp and his allies to disaster. As he himself admitted many years later, Hitler thought of nothing but a putsch — *his own putsch* — between 1919 and 1923, and it was only after the Munich fiasco that he finally arrived at the strategic and tactical conceptions which underlay his successful bid for power in the period between 1930 and 1933. The Nazi counter-revolution could only triumph when supported 'from below' by a mass, predominantly petty-bourgeois, current, profoundly hostile to all forms of proletarian socialism, and 'from above' by an alliance with decisive sectors of the ruling class — i.e. industry, banking, landowners, military etc. Finally — and this was made possible by kind permission of Stalinism and social democracy — the proletariat must be so weakened, divided and disoriented by

---

to his Swedish exile. The mission had been undertaken at the suggestion of Captain Mayr's political department, which still technically employed Hitler (even though by this time the latter was establishing himself as a politician in his own right). Following his return from Berlin, Hitler severed his formal links with the army, though he continued to enjoy the patronage of its more *volkisch*-minded officers.

its own leadership that it cannot offer a co-ordinated defence against national socialism. With these three conditions fulfilled — as they were in the last years of the Weimar Republic — the Nazis had every reason to expect victory. But they were not present to anything like the same degree in the similar period which spanned the putsches of 1920 and 1923.

To be sure, by 1921, the young Nazi party had begun to sink roots into the soil of its Bavarian redoubt, and to attract the interest, if not the committed support, of several business leaders, aristocrats and wealthy Russian emigres; but it was far from enjoying the influence and mass support which it commanded at a comparable stage in its successful struggle for power in the early 1930s.*

Undoubtedly support was growing among layers of the nationalist middle class for the brand of right-wing radicalism offered by the Nazis, and this can be traced through the growing influence the NSDAP exerted in Bavarian politics over the period in question. And it is also true that with the failure of Kapp, certain business leaders began to explore the possibilities of what we have termed after Trotsky, the 'plebeian' solution to the problem of the proletariat. But these trends were only in their infancy. We said at the outset of this chapter that no class travels

---

* Some of Hitler's earliest backers have already been listed in Chapter Eleven. To them we should add the Munich publishing family of Bruckmann, Frau Getrud von Seidilitz, a Balt with shares in a Finnish paper mill, von Borsig the Locomotive manufacturer and prominent member of the Federation of German Industries, and the Augsberg factory owner Grandel. Others from the business world who took an interest in Hitler's movement before the Munich putsch included the Munich industrialist Hermann Aust, who introduced its leader to the august circles of the Bavarian Federation of Industry, as confirmed in the following testimony, given by Aust at Hitler's trial in February 1924: 'In order to discuss Hitler's economic plans a discussion took place in the office of Privy Councillor Kuhlo, a syndic of the Bavarian Federation of Industry. The latter, Dr. Noll, the chairman of the Federation, and myself were present. As a consequence of this discussion another was arranged in the Herren Club ...and later a bigger meeting in the businessmen's Casino. Herr Hitler made a speech on his aims, with much applause. Some gentlemen who were not acquainted with Hitler expressed their satisfaction by handing me donations to pass on to Hitler'. Hitler also spoke at the Berlin National Club in 1922, where he met von Borsig, and from whom he later received a large donation to finance the Nazi party's growing activities. Another business contributor of note was Albert Pietsch, the owner of an electro-chemical plant, who gave Hitler regular cash grants from 1923 onwards. Finally there is of course Fritz Thyssen who claims in his autobiography that he was first introduced to the Nazis by Ludendorff, who told him that Hitler 'was the only man who has any political sense.' Hitler struck Thyssen (this was shortly before the Munich putsch) as a man with the 'ability to lead the masses', and after a meeting with him, Thyssen gave Hitler 'about one thousand gold marks' to aid the coup being prepared in Munich. (F. Thyssen: *I Paid Hitler*, pp.111-114). Among the aristocrats who rallied early to the Nazi cause, Hitler singled out four for special mention: Stransky, Scheubner-Richter, von der Pfordten and 'Prince Ahrenberg, one of our earliest adherents ...the man was a multi-millionaire'. (*Hitler's Secret Conversations*, pp.180, 498).In all, quite an impressive roll call, but nothing approaching the support Hitler drummed up from the big bourgeoisie and aristocracy between 1930 and 1933.

in a straight line towards the solution of the historical problems and crises which confront it. In the case of the German bourgeoisie, repeated attempts were made — some of them enjoying temporary and partial success — to maintain and enhance its social dominance as a ruling and exploiting class by working through existing political parties and institutions, before it came to the conclusion, under conditions of economic crisis which were not to the same extent present in 1923, that its survival as a class was incompatible with the existence of independent workers organisations and parliamentary democracy.

One cannot of course calculate precisely how far to the extreme right the petty-bourgeoisie gravitated between the putsches of Kapp and Hitler, but there are pointers which suggest an underlying trend. Election results for the period between June 1920 and May 1924 indicate that the middle class, while being far more volatile in its behaviour, resembled the bourgeoisie in that it tested out those parties closest to it (both to the left and right before embarking on a more radical course of political action. In the elections to the Constituent National Assembly of January 1919, the petty-bourgeoisie edged to the left, its support for what it hoped would be a more modern and democratic Germany flowing mainly into the channel provided by the DDP, but also towards the SPD. The table below represents in statistical terms how petty-bourgeois disillusionment with Weimar democracy (which proved to be far more unstable and fraught with disasters than Wilhelmian semi-absolutism) expressed itself by a steady shift to the right, away from the DDP and the SPD towards the DVP and then, in 1924, increasingly by support for the DVNP and to a lesser extent, the Nazis.

(votes in millions)

Party	January 19, 1919	June 6, 1920	May 4, 1924
SPD	11.5	6.1	6.0
DDP	5.6	2.3	1.7
DVP	1.3	3.9	2.7
DNVP	3.1	4.2	5.7
NSDAP	—	—	1.9

The collapse of radical liberalism in the middle class, reflected in the catastrophic decline of the DDP vote, was but the obverse side of the equally steady growth of right-wing extremism in this same social layer, as the election returns for 1920 and especially 1924 indicated (The decline in the SPD vote is mainly due to the rise of the USPD, which in 1920 secured five million votes. The bulk of its support went over to the KPD after the two parties fused at the USPD's Halle Congress in October 1920).

But the overwhelming majority of the nationalist petty-bourgeoisie stopped short at the threshold of national socialism. Militant monarchism, or 'dynastic patriotism', was in most cases as far as the bewildered bank clerk, pious peasant or angry artisan was prepared to go in his search for an alternative system to that created by the November Revolution, which he was now being taught to despise as the source of all his ills.*

This rightwards shift can also be traced through election returns for certain key regions of Germany, areas which after 1930 became breeding grounds for national socialism. What also emerges is the remarkable degree to which the SPD's abject failure to act decisively against capital when it held the power in its hands subsequently produced a reaction against social democracy by the middle class. In East Prussia, where the Nazi vote reached 47.1% of the total poll in the Reichstag elections of July 1932, we have the following picture:

(votes in percentages)

Party	1919	May 1924
SPD	43.5	15.3
USPD	6.2	—
KPD	—	11.7
DNVP	12.8	38.9
NSDAP	—	8.6

In Lower Bavaria, another region with a large petty-bourgeois population, a similar pattern emerges, with the middle class moving away from the workers' parties (SPD, USPD and KPD) towards the right, while a section of the Catholic petty-bourgeoisie defects from the confessional BVP (Bavarian People's Party) to the Nazis:

---

* This is not to deny that the Nazis were already learning to adjust their propaganda and agitation to the reactionary 'anti-capitalism' of the propertied middle class, whose origins we have discussed in earlier chapters. A pamphlet from this period, written by the former SPD activist Hermann Esser, skilfully played on the anxieties experienced by the petty-bourgeoisie as the galloping inflation eroded both their incomes and their status: 'Artisans! Civil servants! Artists! Graduates! War pensioners! Officers! Shopkeepers! Small manufacturers! Have you not yet realised that you have already sunk below the so-called proletariat and are the victims of the international stock exchange and currency speculation? Then you must organise yourselves politically. Political neutrality is disastrous. If you want to go on living you must fight. Individually you are nothing; united, a power which no one can resist. The only popular movement which respresents your interest is the NSDAP'. The Nazi Party as a middle class 'trade union'! This was a novel approach, and it was one that obviously appealed to a class which by its very nature was unable to organise in defence of its own variegated and often contradictory interests.

Party	1919	1924
SPD	25.9	9.2
USPD	12.7	—
KPD	—	7.1
BVP	49.7	39.2
NSDAP	—	10.2

In Schleswig-Holstein, one of the few regions where the Nazis actually secured an absolute majority in July 1932 (51%), the first shifts to the right again accrued chiefly to the benefit of the main bourgeois parties, and to the detriment of the SPD and the liberals.

Party	1919	1924
SPD	45.7	24.9
USPD	3.4	—
KPD	—	10.2
DDP	27.2	8.1
DVP	7.8	12.1
DNVP	7.7	31.0
NSDAP	—	7.4

These statistics tell us some, though by no means all of the story of Hitler's failure in November 1923. The observed shift in the petty-bourgeoisie away from liberalism and the reformist flank of the workers' movement towards the extreme right, consummated and exploited by the Nazis with such deadly results for the working class in the last three years of Weimar, had assumed neither an irreversible nor hardened character in the period under review. In its struggle for mastery of the state and total domination of the proletariat, fascism requires a great deal more of its following than passive support at elections. To do its counter-revolutionary work, fascism must organise into compact armies the millions of 'small people', so disoriented by capitalist crisis and the breakdown of parliamentary democracy and so disillusioned with all forms of proletarian socialism, that they will be prepared not only to sanction *but to actively take part in** the

* Ultra-rightist terror was directed, save for a period during the Ruhr crisis of 1923, not against proletarian organisations, meetings or premises, but consisted mainly in the assassinations either of prominent politicians and statesmen identified by the far right with the democratic republic, or individuals who crossed the path of the secret military units which proliferated in the Ruhr region during the first half of 1923. Nor were they carried out by the petty-bourgeois *enrages* who after 1930 swelled the ranks of the SA and the Hitler Youth, but by small squads of Free Corps officers and men banded together in a hideous 'brotherhood' — the *Fehme* — whose origins are traceable back to medieval Germany, when feudal 'justice' was administered by similarly depraved specimens. Thus was Matthias Erzberger done to death on August 26, 1921, as punishment for the signature which he appended to the

violent suppression of the workers' movement and the dismemberment of what remains of bourgeois democracy. All the
available evidence points to the unmistakable conclusion that
while the NSDAP was emerging as the focal point of the counter-
revolutionary, *volkisch* Right in the period which began with the
French occupation of the Ruhr in January 1923 and ended with
the aborted putsch some ten months later, neither in Bavaria,
where the Nazis were strongest, nor in the rest of Germany, had
Hitler gathered sufficient forces to his banner to offer his movement even a remote prospect of success; especially when we
remember that Hitler, while exploiting the particularist prejudices
of the Bavarian clerical Right against Berlin, in fact intended to
use his Munich stronghold as the base camp for the long-awaited
march on the German capital, from where he would then launch,
Mussolini-style, a nation-wide campaign to cleanse Germany of
Marxism (under which heading he of course included the social
democrats).

    Apart from running counter to the policy then being pursued
by Chancellor Stresemann*, who after the collapse of the

Armistice at Compeigne on November 1, 1918. Eleven months later Foreign
Minister Rathenau was laid low by assassins, a deed which precipitated a 24 hour
general strike throughout Germany. Rathenau had not only been associated with a
liberal-democratic domestic policy, but as the country's Foreign Minister, had three
months earlier concluded the Rappallo Treaty with the Soviet Union. Though
delighted at the time by these murders, Hitler also realised that they were counter-
productive so far as his movement was concerned. In *Mein Kampf* he commented
that 'to put any one of these out of the way was completely irrelevant and the chief
result was that a few other blood suckers, just as big and just as threadbare, came
into a job that much sooner ...In those years I kept the national socialist movement
away from experiments [sic!] whose performers for the most part were glorious,
idealistic-minded Germans, whose acts, however, not only made victims of themselves, but were powerless to improve the lot of the fatherland even in the slightest'.
(Ibid, pp.544-546.)

* Shortly after Mussolini's march on Rome, Stresemann had written in his own
journal *Deutsche Stimmen* (December 5, 1922) that 'a great many circles in Germany
have, with an unusual unanimity, already decided in favour of dictatorship.
...Mussolini's victory in Rome ...is acclaimed by them. Herr Hitler holds rallies in
Munich which are allegedly attended by 50,000 persons. The urge toward new things
is unmistakable. They forget one thing, that it has repeatedly been those who stood
farthest right who have, through their policies, brought about the strongest shifts to
the left.' Stresemann's speech to the Reichstag on August 9, four days before his
appointment as Germany's first DVP Chancellor (in a cabinet which, also for the
first time, found the SPD sharing portfolios with the leading party of the German
bourgeoisie), also stressed what he saw as the urgent need to avoid provoking the
working class in view of the fact that the initial attempts at proletarian revolution
had been successfully countered: 'In the period from November 1918 to August 1919,
an important domestic struggle was fought out in Germany ...the issue was whether
we should go the way of the dictatorship of the proletariat or return to the idea of
constitutional government. The victory of the constitutional idea in this struggle
gave us the basis for a possible consolidation of the German situation'. And in the
wake of the Hitler coup, Stresemann declared to the Reichstag (on November 22,
1923) that 'the fascism that has been created under a completely different sun in Italy
by a highly gifted statesman [is not a model] that could suddenly replace this system

revolutionary threat in Saxony and Thuringia, was anxious to return as quickly as possible to conditions of bourgeois normality (which of necessity involved not the suppression of, but collaboration with, social democracy), Hitler's bid for power, if temporarily successful, would have immediately run aground on the same rocks that wrecked the Kapp regime.

Even though the tremendous reverse suffered in the Autumn of 1923 gravely impaired its offensive capacity, there could be no doubting the determination and ability of the German proletariat to wage defensive battles should the extreme right have success-fully defied Stresemann and sought to impose a Mussolini-type regime in Germany. Hitler in fact admits as much in *Mein Kampf,* when in the chapter on 'The Trade Union Question', he states quite candidly that the Nazi movement as it existed in the pre-putsch period lacked both the forces and leadership necessary to challenge, let alone defeat, the German trade unions. The sheer magnitude of the task that confronted the Nazis at that time is accurately reflected in the following passage:

> Anyone who at that time would have really shattered the Marxist unions, and in place of this institution of destructive class struggle, helped the National Socialist trade union idea to victory, was among the very great men of our people, and his bust would some day have had to be dedicated to posterity in the Valhalla at Regensburg. But I did not know of any head that would have fitted such a pedestal ...Today the National Socialist movement must combat a colossal gigantic organisation which has long been in existence, and which is developed down to the slightest detail. The conqueror must always be more astute than the defender if he wants to subdue him. The Marxist trade union fortress can today be administered by ordinary bosses; but it will only be stormed by the wild energy and shining ability of a great man on the other side. If such a man is not found, it is useless to argue with fate and even more useless to attempt forcing the matter with inadequate substitutes. Here we must apply the maxim that in life it is sometimes better to let a thing lie for the present than to begin it badly or by halves for want of suitable forces.[7]*

It would require a decade more of false leadership, the demoralisation brought about by permanent mass unemploy-ment, the backing of important sections of big business, and a middle class driven to despair by the prospect and onset of economic ruin, before Hitler could tackle this task of the destruction of German trade unionism. But having stressed those factors and relationships which militated against a successful Nazi

without tearing Germany to pieces. Our German body politic is feverishly ill and cannot stand the quack treatment of civil war'.

* Hitler's caution was understandable. ADGB membership climbed from 2.8 million in 1918 to an all-time high of 7.8 million in 1922. On the eve of their destruction by the Nazis in May 1933, trade union membership stood at around the four million mark.

bid for power in 1923, we must never neglect that which it undoubtedly contained in embryo — the triumph of ten years later.

The early and last years of the Weimar Republic were similar in that in each period, profound economic crisis propelled the leaders of big business towards openly dictatorial forms of rule. Demands for 'strong government' or a 'strong man' went hand in hand with concerted pressure to liquidate all the social gains of the November Revolution — collective bargaining, works councils, social welfare, the eight hour day, etc. But as we have already pointed out, the ways and means by which this attack on the working class and bourgeois democracy was launched, differed in several vital respects. In 1933, despairing of their own traditional parties being able to carry through the necessary counter-revolutionary measures, heavy industry and finance opted for a Hitler regime, and delegated political power to his armed and unruly 'plebeians'.

No such solution was envisaged in the period preceeding the Munich putsch, *not even by Hitler himself.* With a membership barely reaching 50,000 (mostly concentrated in and around Munich), and an active SA strength of far less, the Nazi Party, when it figured in ruling class strategy at all, could only expect to be allotted the role of auxiliary in any bid to overturn the Republic, with Hitler figuring as the 'drummer boy' for the real wielders of power. Indeed, perhaps 'overturn' is too strong a term, for what the majority of economic and military leaders desired at this stage, was not so much a violent coup *a la* Kapp (for obvious reasons) but a sharp shift to the right inside the Cabinet, allied with a strengthening of Presidential powers through the use of Article 48 of the Weimar Consitution. Matters were also complicated by the rifts continually opening up inside the DVP between Stresemann, who after the Kapp putsch was calling for acceptance of the Republic and collaboration with the SPD, and the heavy industrialists led by Vögler and Quaatz, who proposed a bloc with the DNVP.*

So while on the one hand reactionary industrialists and army

---

* This bitter dispute, which rent the DVP throughout its existence, even spilled over onto the floor of the Reichstag. On July 18, a whole group of DVP deputies led by Vögler defied party policy by either abstaining on, or voting against, the emergency bill for the protection of the republic which was enacted after the assassination of DDP Foreign Minister Rathenau by ultra rightist fanatics. (Three in fact joined with the DNVP in voting against, while another 23 either did not show up for the division or abstained.) The other major split arose after the formation of the Stresemann government on August 13, 1923, following the fall of Chancellor Cuno. For the first time, the DVP and SPD were members of the same cabinet, a state of affairs the industrialists Quaatz and Vögler considered to be little short of a betrayal of their class. In the vote of confidence in the new government on August 14, which was carried 239-76, 19 DVP deputies abstained (as did 53 deputies of the SPD).

officers discreetly encouraged and financed the various *volkisch* and para-military leagues sprouting up all over Germany, they at the same time exploited their growth to exert more pressure on the government and the reformists for even more far-reaching concessions to the monopolies. Already in August 1922, Stinnes and Thyssen had launched a campaign to abolish the eight hour day and to greatly curb the power of trade unions and works councils in the factories and mines. On October 30, the SPD replied that it would never yield on the question of the eight hour day, a pledge that was put to the test and found wanting a year later.

Earlier that month, Thyssen had addressed an open letter to the leftward-leaning Centre Party Chancellor Dr Wirth which in effect called on him to end his policy of collaboration with the reformists, declaring that 'Germany's salvation can only come from a return to the Ten Hour Working Day!' Two weeks later, on the fourth anniversary of the November Revolution, Stinnes also took the offensive in a speech to the National Economic Council of the Republic:

> I do not hesitate to say that I am convinced that the German people will have to work ten hours per day for the next ten to fifteen years ...The preliminary condition for any successful stabilisation is, in my opinion, that wage struggle and strikes be excluded for a long period ...we must have the courage to say to the people: 'For the present and for some time to come you will have to work overtime without overtime payment.'

This trend towards dictatorship, ever present behind the Weimar facade, was greatly accentuated by the onset of the 1923 hyper-inflation.* But at first, the French Occupation of the Ruhr in January 1923 (occasioned by Germany defaulting on its reparation payments to France) revived the moods of August 1914. The social democrats were once again to be found in the embrace of even the most extreme nationalists as patriots all, they rallied to Chancellor Cuno's call for 'passive resistance' in the Ruhr against the army of occupation. A 'general strike' was proclaimed that had official government approval, Cuno even

---

* The trend towards hyper-inflation began in the war, which the government attempted to finance not only by increasing taxes and reducing private consumption, but the printing of vast quantities of paper money. As a result, the national debt rose from 5.4 billion marks in 1913 (costing 230 million marks to service) to 200 billion marks in 1920, its servicing now costing, at 12.5 billion marks, 45% of the total budget! A series of domestic and diplomatic crises, climaxed by the French occupation of the Ruhr, sent the exchange rate of the mark against the dollar spiralling dizzily downwards. On armistice day, November 1, 1918, one mark exchanged for 7.45 dollars. In the Spring of 1922 dollars were exchanging in Berlin at the rate of one to 290 marks. By November of the same year, the dollar rate was 9,150 marks, and the final plunge was about to begin. By the October of 1923, one dollar was exchanging for 12 million marks, on November 1, 120 million marks, and on November 20, 4,200 billion.

going to the extent of paying the striking workers' wages for the duration of the action (thereby greatly exacerbating the already acute inflationary situation.) Only the Nazis on the right, and the KPD on the left, declined to join this so-called 'united front'.

Hitler's position was quite consistent with his overall strategy, which demanded the destruction of the internal foes of the 'German awakening' before starting out on any war of revenge against its foreign enemies:

> Just as in 1918 we paid with our blood for the fact that in 1914 and 1915 we did not proceed to trample the head of the Marxist serpent once and for all, we would have to pay most catastrophically if in the Spring we did not avail ourselves of the opportunity to halt the activity of the Marxist traitors and murderers of the nation for good. Any idea of real resistance to France was utter nonsense if we did not declare war against those forces which five years before had broken German resistance on the battlefields. Only bourgeois minds can arrive at the incredible opinion that Marxism [i.e. social democracy, for it was the SPD that had been enrolled into the national front against France] might now have changed, and that the scoundrelly leaders of 1918, who then coldly trampled two million dead underfoot, the better to climb into the various seats of government, now in 1923 were suddenly ready to render their tribute to the national conscience ...No more than a hyena abandons carrion does a Marxist abandon treason ...Regardless of what type of resistance was decided on, the first requirement was always the elimination of the Marxist poison from our national body ...it was then the very first task of a truly national government to seek and find the forces which were resolved to declare a war of annihilation on Marxism, and then to give these forces a free road; it was not their duty to worship the idiocy of 'law and order' ...No, at that time a really national government should have desired disorder and unrest, provided only that amid the confusion a basic reckoning with Marxism at last became possible and actually took place ...It should have been borne in mind that the bloodiest civil wars have often given rise to a steeled and healthy people ...in the year 1923 the most brutal thrust was required to seize the vipers that were devouring our people. Only if this were successful did the preparation of active resistance have meaning.[8]

Hitler's scorn for the 'political bourgeoisie' (that is, Wirth, Cuno and Stresemann, and those who supported them in their policy of collaboration with social democracy) was limitless as it was impotent:

> At that time I often talked my throat hoarse attempting to make it clear, at least to the so-called national circles, what was now at stake, and that if we made the same blunder as in 1914 and the years that followed, the end would inevitably be the same as in 1918. Again and again I begged them to give free rein to Fate, and to give our move-ment an opportunity for a reckoning with Marxism; but I preached to deaf ears. They all knew better, including the chief of the armed forces [von Seeckt], until at length they faced the most wretched capitulation of all time. Then I realised in my innermost soul that the German

bourgeoisie was at the end of its mission and is destined for no further mission.[9]

But was Hitler opposed to the policies being advocated by these 'national circles', which as we know included men prominent in both business and military affairs? Once again, it is evident that the fierceness of Hitler's polemic was directed not against the goals of the bourgeoisie, which were in essence shared by Hitler (those of a revived German imperialism and a tamed proletariat) but against the means by which they sought to achieve them. Thus we read in *Mein Kampf* that 'if Herr Cuno, instead of proclaiming his subsidised general strike and setting it up as the foundation of the 'united front', had only demanded two more hours of work from every German, the "united front" swindle would have shown itself up on the third day. Peoples are not freed by doing nothing, but by sacrifices'.[10] So the Nazis stood, like Stinnes, Thyssen, Vögler and the rest, *for the abolition of the eight hour day,* just as they echoed the demand of heavy industry for an end to the 'tyranny of the works councils' and the power of the trade unions.*

Nazi preparations for a coup gained momentum and support at the precise moment when an entire section of heavy industry moved over into opposition to the newly-formed Stresemann government.** When it was learned that no less than four portfolios were to be allotted to the SPD (with Finance going to the hated 'Marxist' Rudolf Hilferding) Vögler and Quaatz staged a walk-out by a group of right-wing DVP deputies from the Reichstag. At the same time, the Stresemann government was bitterly criticised by the DNVP and its ultra-rightist allies outside

---

* By the summer of 1923, Nazi Party branches were offering their services as strike-breakers to local employers.
** Hitler had won the right to lead the *volkisch* movement through a series of victories over rival organisations and leaders. In the summer of 1921, he quelled a revolt against his leadership in the NSDAP, staged by its founder Anton Drexler, a battle from which Hitler emerged as the party's President, a position which in effect made him the movement's absolute dictator. At the same time, Hitler succeeded, after much squalid manoeuvring on both sides, in his bid to absorb the rival *volkisch* group of the fanatical anti-semitic school teacher Julius Streicher, whose 'German Socialist Party', with branches in Augsburg, Nuremberg and Munich, was a serious embarrassment to Hitler's claim to exclusive leadership of the south German *volkisch* movement. Over the next two years, Hitler's novel conceptions of mass mobilisation and his aggressive tactics against the workers' movement (as exemplified by the victory over the 'reds' at a national rally in Coburg in October 1922) so impressed itself on the rest of the *volkisch* movement that in September 25, 1923, at a summit meeting of the leaders of the various 'national' organisations — Hitler, Göring, and Röhm for the Nazis, Friedrich Weber of the Bund Oberland and Captain Heiss of the Reichsflagge, agreed to place the leadership of their alliance, the Kampfbund, in the exclusive hands of Hitler. The date of this meeting coincides almost to the day with the renewed offensive launched by Stinnes, Vögler, Thyssen and Quaatz against the Stresemann government, which had declared its willingness to treat with France and was already collaborating with the social democrats.

parliament for submitting to France by calling off the passive
resistance on September 26. And like so many of its predecessors,
the new administration at once found itself assailed from all sides.
In Saxony and Thuringia, communists joined with left social
democrats to form coalition 'workers' governments' that were
intended by the KPD to serve as a central German base for
launching a revolution throughout the country, while to the
south, Hitler's preparations for a coup were nearing completion.
As at the time of the Kapp putsch, Stresemann's first concern was
to counter the threat from the left before turning to negotiate with
the extreme right. On the same day that passive resistance was
wound up in the Ruhr, the government proclaimed a state of
emergency throughout the Reich, which until further notice was
to be governed under Article 48 by the Minister of Defence Otto
Gessler (who had succeeded Noske in this post after the Kapp
putsch). Seeckt's attitude in this crisis was summed up in his reply
to the Pan German Heinrich Class, who in September 1923,
invited von Seeckt to throw his and the army's authority and
prestige into the scales on the side of the anti-Weimar Right,
whose leaders were at that very moment collaborating with
Hitler's bid to seize power in Bavaria. In a letter to Class, dated
September 24, 1923, Seeckt declared that what Class proposed
was 'a violation of the Constitution, an act of sedition. I tell you I
will fight to the last shot against those of the Left, the role of the
Reichswehr is to maintain the unity of the Reich, and those who
compromise this are its enemies, from whichever side they come'.
(Another illustrious Junker officer was not quite so loyal. The
future President von Hindenburg, when asked to send his
greetings to Hitler on the eve of the Munich putsch, replied: You
may, but tell him also I must warn him against any rash action;
the Fatherland cannot stand another Kapp putsch. Hindenburg,
re-elected as President with SPD support in April 1932, had in
fact visited Munich in August 1922, where he met his old High
Command comrade Ludendorff, together with not only a group
of monarchists, but several leading members of the NSDAP!)
  The sudden deepening of the political crisis in September
together with the accelerated devaluation of the mark served as a
signal for big employers to intensify their pressure on the cabinet
to abolish the eight hour day. The SPD, having pledged itself to
oppose such a measure the previous October, now began to
retreat before the Ruhr barons. The SPD cabinet members would
agree to a temporary suspension of the eight hour day for the
duration of the crisis if the government agreed to the face-saving
formula that it would not be officially included in an economic
enabling act then in preparation (the act was passed with
SPD support on October 13). The wedge had been inserted, and
the bourgeois parties had no intention of withdrawing it.

Meanwhile, headed by Stinnes and Thyssen,* a group of the most intransigent anti-Weimar employers were preparing to support Hitler's counter-revolutionary putsch in Munich. They did not for one moment intend Hitler to emerge from the coup as the leader of a new 'national' government, but rather to exploit the situation created by a successful putsch to force their own terms on Berlin. And in this undertaking, they undoubtedly hoped to secure the active support of the general staff. Stinnes' plan, for such it was, has been recorded for posterity by Alanson B. Houghton, a United States official, who met Stinnes on September 21, 1923, and discussed with the industrialist the political crisis then maturing in Germany. According to Houghton's account, Stinnes said:

> If Germany was to live, production must be increased ...factories and workshops were ready. German labour however, must work longer and harder. He said he believed German workmen were underpaid and he could, he thought, double or even treble their wages if a normal ten hours working day were given in return [precisely the demand made by Hitler!]. He is convinced however that German labour will not yield to the necessity and that therefore it must be forced. Then he said a dictator with power to do whatever is necessary must be found. Such a man must speak the language of the people and be himself a bourgeois, and such a man was ready. A great movement starting from Bavaria and determined to restore the former royalties was imminent ...The movement would be joined by all the right parties and by a considerable group of moderate men in the centre and would mean primarily a fight against communism since the communist wing would lead the workmen in opposition. I asked him if the industrialists would unite with the movement. Stinnes replied that they would. The plan as outlined by Stinnes is briefly this: by the middle of October three or possibly four million men will be out of work. The communists will try to take advantage of this to start a revolutionary outbreak ...Directly the communists begin, Ebert in the name of the Republic will name a man, or possibly a committtee of three as dictator and put the entire military force under the dictator's control. Thenceforward parliamentary government will be at an end. The communists will be put

* Thyssen describes how the 1923 crisis led him to Hitler and the Nazis: 'We were at the worst time of the inflation ...In Berlin the government was in distress. It was ruined financially. Authority was crumbling. In Saxony, a communist government had been formed ...In Hamburg, a communist revolt had broken out. After Saxony, Thuringia had given itself a communist government ...Amidst all this chaos, Bavaria seemed to be the last fortress of order and patriotism ...If Germany should break into pieces, it was said, Bavaria would come to the whole country ...Such was the atmosphere in which my first meeting with Hitler took place ...Ludendorff and Hitler agreed to undertake a military expedition against Saxony in order to depose the communist government of Dr. Zeigner [who in fact was not a communist, but a left social democrat]. The ultimate aim of the proposed expedition was to overthrow the Weimar democracy, whose weakness was leading Germany into anarchy. Funds were lacking. Ludendorff ...had already solicited and obtained the help of several industrialists, particularly that of Herr Minnoux of the Stinnes firm. For my part, I gave him about one thousand gold marks ...'(F. Thyssen: *I Paid Hitler*, pp.111-114.)

down with a savage hand and if a general strike should be called that too will be suppressed by force. Socialism as a politically possible method of national existence in Germany will, it is hoped, be thus definitely eliminated and the laws and enactments which hamper production and serve no useful purpose will be forthwith repealed.[10]

Hitler was to be the 'drummer boy' or the pied piper, but the rhythm and tune were to be called by big business. Mooted for the 'directory' that was to replace a parliamentary-based cabinet were Kahr, the Bavarian General Commissar (subsequently press-ganged by Hitler into supporting his putsch), Otto Wiedfeldt, a former Krupp director and currently German Ambassador to Washington, and Stinnes's own banker, Freidrich Minnoux, who had in fact served as mediator between Stinnes and the Nazis in the pre-putsch period. Pressure from this quarter became so intense that following the collapse of the revolutionary threat in Saxony and Thuringia on October 27, (army units occupied the two states unopposed, and ousted the SPD-KPD coalition governments) the SPD withdrew from the cabinet. Von Seeckt, who was known to favour the Stinnes plan for a *troika*, now asked Ebert to form a new rightist cabinet that would be able to reach agreement with the Bavarians, who were now openly in revolt against Berlin's authority. At this stage it became clear that while the army and big business alike sought to impose what they termed a *Burgherblok* government on a reluctant Ebert and Stresemann, with the ending of the revolutionary crisis in central Germany they no longer had need of Hitler's desperadoes, whose declared aim it was to seize power in Bavaria and then 'invade' Red Saxony and Thuringia to put down the Marxists, Hitler's putsch, when it came, was therefore launched in a political situation that was altogether different from the one in which it had been conceived and in which it had attracted the interests and guarded support of counter-revolutionary circles in industry and the army. While an understanding with the clerical-monarchist Bavarian government undoubtedly had attractions for the Stinnes-Seeckt group (as it did indeed for the more moderate Stresemann) clear-thinking rightists had no use for a Hitler regime whose declared aim of waging bloody civil war on the proletariat could only serve to provoke the working class to rebellion, just as Kapp's putsch had done in March 1920.

Hitler made no attempt to conceal his counter-revolutionary aims and strategy, no doubt calculating that the more openly he proclaimed them, the more support he could hope to attract from the 'national' classes.* Typical of his agitation were two speeches

---

* All available evidence suggests that like the mass Nazi movement of the early 1930s, the early 'National Socialist German Workers' Party' was comprised mainly of petty-bourgeois. A 1920 party membership roll lists the following occupations for members whose names began with the letter 'H': manufacturer, man-servant, lock-smith, directress, cabinet-maker, businessman, doctor, manufacturer, doctor, owner

delivered in the late summer, the first of which, made on August 1, made a direct comparison between the prevailing situation in Germany and that which existed between the two Russian revolutions of February and October 1917:

> We stand at the beginning of the second revolution in Germany. Just as after Kerensky in Russia, so after the lemonade [November] revolution, the real Soviet dictatorship will be set up ...[The choice is between] Swastika or Soviet star: the despotism of the International or the Holy Empire of German nationality ...Today the last decisive struggle rests between the Swastika and the star of the Soviet.

On September 5, Hitler threw down an open challenge to the Stresemann government. Since it had extended the hand of friendship to the SPD 'Marxists', Berlin was now the centre of the anti-German conspiracy:

> Our movement was not formed with any election in view, but in order to spring to the rescue of the people ...at the moment when in fear and despair it sees the approach of the Red Monster ...There will be two possibilities: either Berlin marches and ends up in Munich, or Munich marches and ends up in Berlin. A Bolshevik north Germany and a National Bavaria cannot exist side by side ...On us in Bavaria falls the task to be the cell whence recovery shall come to the rest of the Reich.

Denied at the last moment, due to the changed situation in central Germany, of the support his coup required to stand the least prospect of success, Hitler's brown shirts were defied and routed by a company of a hundred policemen.

So with measures already in hand both at home and internationally to restore value to the mark, and to rebuild an economy torn by class strife and the ravages of reparations, and with the revolutionary left and counter-revolutionary right both temporarily eliminated as important factors in Germany's internal political development, the road was clear for the German bourgeoisie to enjoy a period of stability it had not experienced since the birth of the republic four years previously.

Yet for those who followed closely the trial of Hitler and his

of iron works, electrician, author, soldier, businessman, senior secretary, roofer, businessman, bank filing clerk, owner of business school, newspaper representative, deputy sergeant, wife of businessman, pharmacist, businessman, wife of artist, bank official, engineer, clerk, mechanic, medical student, apprentice, doctor's wife. The largest single group is that of 'businessman', which together with manufacturers and owners, makes up no less than 28% of the total sample! A similar picture of the class composition of the NSDAP emerges from the roll call of those killed in the Munich putsch (Hitler was obliging enough to list their occupations when dedicating *Mein Kampf* to their memory.) Of the sixteen who fell on November 9, 1923, no fewer than four were businessmen, while three more were 'bank clerks', another three 'engineers' while the remainder consisted of a retired cavalry captain, a civil servant and a headwaiter, with the 'workers' being represented by a valet, a hatter and a locksmith. Like the previous random sample, this list contains not a single industrial proletarian. Such manual occupations as are represented are of the artisan type, a factor of enormous political significance for the subsequent development of the Nazi Party.

accomplices — and in retrospect there seems to have been precious few who did — there were ample warnings that as far as the leader of German fascism was concerned, the failure of the Munich putsch was merely a temporary setback for a movement destined to seize power and purge the nation of Marxism. The trial, which began in Munich on February 26, 1924, was converted with the tacit agreement of the court, into a flaming indictment of the Berlin government and the 'November criminals' whose creation the hated republic was. Who would guess that the following words were uttered not by Hitler's defence council. *but by the State Prosecutor?:*

> Hitler came of a simple background; in the great war as a brave soldier he showed a German spirit, and afterward, beginning from scratch and working hard, he created a great party, the NSDAP, which is pledged to fighting international Marxism and Jewry, to settle accounts with the November criminals, and to disseminating the national idea among all layers of the population, in particular the workers. I am not called upon to pass judgment on his party programme, but his honest endeavour to reawaken the belief in the German cause among an oppressed and disarmed people is certainly to his credit ...Hitler is a highly gifted man who, coming of simple background has, through serious and hard work, won for himself a respected place in public life. He dedicated himself to the ideas which inspired him to the point of self-sacrifice, and as a soldier he fulfilled his duty in the highest measure. He cannot be blamed for exploiting the position which he created for himself to his own purposes.

It came as no surprise when Hitler, found guilty of treason, received the shortest possible prison sentence for the crime that the law permitted — five years — of which he served less than one, leaving the fortress of Landsberg on December 20, 1924 free to resume his war on the Weimar Republic and the German workers' movement. But it is with Hitler's valedictory speech to the Munich court that we end this chapter, a speech full of foreboding for the German proletariat and indeed, for workers throughout Europe:

> I believe that the hour will come when the masses, who stand today in the street with our Swastika banner, will unite with those who fired upon them ...I aimed from the first at something a thousand times higher than being a minister. I wanted to become the destroyer of Marxism. I am going to achieve this task, and if I do, the title of minister will be an absurdity as far as I am concerned ...At one time I believed that perhaps this battle against Marxism could be carried on with the help of the government. In January 1923 I learned for the first time that that was just not possible. The hypothesis for the victory over Marxism is not that Germany must be free, but rather Germany will only be free when Marxism is broken. At that time I did not dream that our movement would become great and cover Germany like a flood. The army that we are building grows from day to day, from hour to hour. Right at this moment I have the proud hope that

once the hour strikes these wild troops will merge into battalions, battalions into regiments, regiments into divisions.

The 'destroyer of Marxism' ...Yet of the countless thousands who were destined to be exterminated by national socialism, how many heeded this dire warning? And of those who did, how many had even begun to assimilate the lessons of the tumultuous years and months which ended with the failure of Hitler's putsch, a period of missed revolutionary opportunities, of social democratic treachery, of determined attempts to drive the German proletariat back to the conditions of repression that it had endured under Bismarck?

The next decade was to give its answer.

REFERENCES FOR CHAPTER THIRTEEN

[1] L. Trotsky: Speech to the Polish Commission of the ECCI, July 2, 1926, reproduced in L. Trotsky, *The Only Road,* September 14, 1932, in *The Struggle Against Fascism in Germany,* p.282.
[2] Ibid, pp.282-283.
[3] F. Thyssen, I Paid Hitler, pp.86-87, New York, 1941.
[4] *Rote Fahne* (Daily organ of the KPD), March 14, 1920.
[5] H. Rauschning: *Germany's Revolution of Destruction,* pp.4-5, London, 1939.
[6] A. Hitler quoted in O. Strasser: *Hitler and I,* pp.7-8.
[7] A. Hitler: *Mein Kampf,* pp.603-604.
[8] Ibid, pp.678-680.
[9] Ibid, pp.680-681.
[10] Ibid, p.683.
[11] *State Department Documents,* Decimal File 1910-29; 462.00 R. 29, Vol. 68.

The German Communist Party

It is impossible to over-estimate the historical consequences of the defeat suffered by the German working class in the autumn of 1923, when the economic crisis and the political disarray of the ruling class presented the KPD with an unprecedented opportunity for mobilising the proletariat for the conquest of power. Had the German Communist Party pursued an aggressive audacious policy directed towards the seizure of power in the latter half of 1923, there is little doubt that its careful preparatory work over the previous two years would have been crowned by success. National socialism would have been nipped in the bud, and the road cleared for the triumph of the socialist revolution throughout central and western Europe. It was for this purpose, that of world revolution, that the Communist International had been founded in March 1919. Its leadership, comprised of the most advanced cadres of all the world's communist parties, was intended to function as the general staff of the international working class in its life or death battle with the forces of international capital and their counter-revolutionary agencies. All the Bolshevik leadership, Stalin not excluded, recognised and repeatedly emphasised that upon the outcome of this international struggle between the classes hinged the fate of the Soviet Union itself. And Germany, the foremost economic power in Europe, occupying a strategic central position between the victorious imperialist allies and the USSR, and possessing the politically most mature and best organised detachment of this world proletarian army, inevitably became the main battleground for this titanic conflict.

Utterly false is the assertion made by the veteran British Stalinist R. Palme Dutt that 'it was not Lenin, but Trotsky, who clung to the supposedly "Marxist" axiom that the survival of the Soviet Revolution would depend on the speedy extension of the socialist revolution to Western Europe' and that it is a 'grand distortion and fallacy' to say the 'next stage [of the Russian Revolution] according to the supposed "pure" principles of Marxism should have been its extension to Western Europe [and] that this was the universal expectation of the Bolshevik Party and pivot of Lenin's policy ...' (R. Palme Dutt: *Problems of Contemporary History,* pp.78-91, London, 1963). In the same work, Dutt insists that it was a 'vulgar' and 'Trotskyist' distortion of Marxism which 'insisted that the Russian Revolution would be doomed unless the superior enlightened West European socialist revolution came to its rescue'. (Ibid, p.89.)

By this token, Lenin must be included amongst those Dutt describes as vulgar and Trotskyist, for in his report to the Extraordinary Seventh Congress of the Russian Communist Party, on March 7, 1918, Lenin declared quite categorically, as if he had Dutt's allegations in mind, that 'it is the absolute truth that without a German revolution we are doomed ...At all events, under all conceivable circumstances, if the German revolution does not come, we are doomed.' (V. Lenin, *Collected Works,* Vol. 27, p.98) Neither was Lenin given to cynical references to the 'superior enlightened West European socialist revolution'. Lenin, again in common with the entire Bolshevik leadership, understood only too well the immense obstacle that Russia's cultural and economic backwardness presented to the development of socialism in the Soviet Union. It was precisely to the 'enlightened' and culturally 'superior' German proletariat that the Soviet leadership turned for comradely assistance in their struggle to defeat the counter-revolution and lay the foundations of a socialist economy and culture. Four days later, in his short pamphlet *The Chief Task of the Day,* Lenin reminds those still influenced by anti-German prejudices acquired in the imperialist war that the German worker was the ally of the Soviet people: 'Learn from the Germans! Remain true to the brotherly alliance with the German workers ...they will come to our aid. Yes, learn from the Germans! History is moving in zig-zags and by roundabout ways. It so happens that it is the Germans who now personify, besides a brutal imperialism, the principle of discipline, organisation, harmonious co-operation on the basis of modern machine industry, and strict accounting and control. And that is just what we are lacking. That is just what we must learn. That is just what our great revolution needs in order to pass from a triumphant beginning, through a succession of severe trials, to its triumphant goal. That is just what the Russian Soviet Socialist Republic requires in order to cease being wretched and impotent and become mighty and abundant for all time.' (Ibid, p.163)

There was no evading the question of Germany, since the delay of the revolution — the direct consequence of the chauvinist, class-collaborationisht policies being pursued by the social democrats — had compelled the Soviets to make the most far-reaching concessions to German imperialism in the peace treaty of Brest Litovsk. Long term, as well as immediate, Bolshevik strategy therefore took as its starting point the necessity of aiding in every possible way the rapid development of the revolution in Germany, even to the extent of being prepared to sacrifice power in Russia should the triumph of the revolution in Germany demand such a risk being taken. For Germany, not Russia, was the European nation most suited to pioneering the road to world-wide socialism: 'Here [in Germany] we have 'the last word' in modern large-scale capitalist engineering and planned organisation, *subordinated to Junker-bourgeois imperialism*. Cross out the words in italics, and in place of the militarist, Junker, bourgeois imperialist *state* put *also a state,* but of a different social type, of a different class content — a *Soviet* state ...and you will have the *sum total* of the conditions necessary for socialism. Socialism is inconceivable without large-scale capitalist engineering based on the latest discoveries of modern science. It is inconceivable without planned state organisation which keeps tens of millions of people to the strictest observance of a unified standard in production and distribution ...At the same time socialism is inconceivable unless the proletariat is the ruler of the state ...history ...has taken such a peculiar course that it *has given birth* in 1918 to unconnected halves of socialism standing side by side like two chickens in the single shell of international imperialism. In 1918 Germany and Russia have become the most striking embodiment of the material realisation of the economic, the productive and the socio-economic conditions of the other. A successful proletarian revolution in Germany would immediately and very easily smash the shell of imperialism (which unfortunately is made of the best steel, and hence cannot be *broken by the efforts of any* ...chicken and would bring about the victory of world socialism for certain, without any difficulty ...' (V. Lenin: *'Left Wing' Childishness and the Petty-bourgeois Mentality,* [May 1918] in *Collected Works,* Vol. 27, pp.339-340.)

The Bolsheviks were not the only Marxists to appreciate this dialectical relationship between Germany and the Soviet Union. Rosa Luxemburg repeatedly stressed that the German working class held the key not only to its own future, but that of the revolution throughout Europe. Even before the October Revolution, she insisted on the international nature of the struggle being waged in Russia between the proletariat and the counter-revolution, emphasising that there was 'only one serious guarantee against these natural concerns for the future of the Russian Revolution [of February 1917]: the awakening of the German proletariat, the attainment of a position of power by the German 'workers and soldiers' in their own country, a revolutionary struggle for peace by the German people' (*The Old Mole, Spartacus* No. 5, May 1917, in R. Luxemburg, *Selected Political Writings,* p.233, London, 1972). And in September 1918, she sought to defend charges against the Bolsheviks that they had collaborated with German imperialism in concluding the treaty of Brest Litovsk by pointing out that the treaty had been signed in order to buy time for the workers of Germany to make their own revolution: 'There is only one solution to the tragedy in which Russia is caught up: uprising at the rear of German imperialism, the German mass rising [which was in fact less than two months away], which can signal the international revolution to put an end to this genocide. At this fateful moment, preserving the honour of the Russian Revolution is identical with vindicating that of the German proletariat and of international socialism'. (R. Luxemburg: *The Russian Tragedy, Spartacus,* No. 11, September 1918, in ibid, p.243.)

Hence the strategic importance and urgency of securing a revolutionary breakthrough in Germany, the most advanced and best organised stronghold of world imperialism, an imperialism moreover which by virtue of its geographic proximity to the USSR, and an ever-increasing need for certain essential raw materials which Russia possessed in abundance, posed a perpetual interventionist threat to the security of the Soviet Union. And hence, by the same token, the painstaking care with which Lenin and Trotsky especially, despite all their other pressing political and administrative tasks, followed the development of the class struggle in Germany, and the patient way in which they attempted to acquaint leaders of the young and relatively inexperienced German/Communist Party with the priceless experiences acquired by Bolshevism during its preparations and struggle for power in Russia. And this strategic importance of the German proletariat was as clearly perceived on the other side of the class divide, as can be seen from deliberations between the main representatives of the victorious imperialist powers which preceded the foundation of the League of Nations in 1919. Lloyd George, that most astute of all British bourgeois statesmen and political leaders (he was greatly admired by Hitler for his ability to ensnare the masses) declared to the Allied Supreme Council in March 1919 that 'as long as order was maintained in Germany, a breakwater would exist between the countries of the Allies, and the waters of revolution beyond [i.e. the Soviet Union and Hungary]. But once that breakwater was swept away, he could not speak for France, and he trembled for his own country ...[if] the people of Germany were allowed to run riot, a state of revolution among the working classes of all countries would ensue with which it would be impossible to cope.' These fears were expanded upon in Lloyd George's confidential memorandum submitted to the Allied 'Big Four, entitled *Some Considerations for the Peace Conference before they finally draft their terms,* in which, contrary to the rapacious demands of the French imperialists, he advocated a policy of leniency towards the new rulers of Germany, lest harsher peace terms drive the masses to revolt:

'The whole of Europe is filled with the spirit of revolution. There is a deep sense not only of discontent, but of anger and revolt amongst the workmen against pre-war conditions. The whole existing order in its political, social and economic aspects is questioned by the masses of the population, from one end of Europe to the other ...there is a danger that we may throw the masses of the population throughout Europe into the arms of the extremists whose only idea for regenerating mankind is to destroy utterly the whole existing fabric of society. These men have triumphed in Russia ..The greatest danger that I see in the present situation is that Germany may throw her lot in with Bolshevism and place her resources, her brains, her vast organising power at the disposal of the revolutionary fanatics whose dream is to conquer the world for Bolshevism by force of arms. The danger is no chimera. The present [social democratic] government in Germany is weak; it has no prestige; its authority is challenged; it lingers merely because there is no alternative but the Spartacists, and Germany is not ready for Spartacism, as yet ...If Germany goes over to the Spartacists it is inevitable that she should throw in her lot with the Russian Bolsheviks. Once that happens all Eastern Europe will be swept into the orbit of the Bolshevik revolution and within a year we may witness the spectacle of nearly 300 million people organised into a vast red army under German instructors and German generals equipped with German cannon and German machine guns and prepared for a renewal of the attack on Western Europe ...If we are wise, we shall offer to Germany a peace which, while just, will be preferable for all sensible men to the alternative of Bolshevism.'

We find Lloyd George returning to this theme more than a decade later, at a time when a new crisis in Germany had raised once more the spectre of a revolutionary alliance between Europe's major economic power and the USSR:

'The recent growth of Communism in Germany is of the greatest danger to the whole of Europe ...Germany will be much more dangerous to the world than a Communist Russia. Germany possesses the best educated and the most highly skilled working class of the whole world ...I can conceive of no greater danger for Europe, yes, for the whole world, than for such a mighty Communist state to come into being in the centre of Europe — a state that will be led and supported by one of the most intelligent and disciplined people of the world. Hand in hand with Germany and under the skilled and clever leadership of the German people the significance of the Russian revolution would be multiplied a hundred fold. These two countries would provide a mighty combination. Accordingly it is advisable for all countries to make the greatest sacrifices to prevent such a catastrophic alliance from taking place.' (Quoted in the Vienna *Neue Freie Presse,* July 17, 1931.)

And even when the threat of revolution had receded following the victory of the Nazis, Lloyd George (of whom Lenin said that he 'is not only a very intelligent man, but one who has also learned something from the Marxists') was still warning against the consequences of a socialist revolution in Germany. On September 22, 1933, this Liberal, warning as he did in 1919 against a belligerently anti-German policy, declared that 'if the powers succeeded in overthrowing Nazism in Germany, what would follow? Not a Conservative Socialist, [SPD] or Liberal regime, but extreme Communism ...A Communist Germany would be infinitely more formidable than a Communist Russia. The Germans would know how to run their Communism effectively.' Lloyd George's appreciation of the decisive importance of Germany in the world-wide struggle between socialism and capitalism, formulated though it was from the standpoint of imperialism, differs but little from that of Lenin in 1918 and Trotsky in 1930 (We should also recall Hitler's statement that 'Germany is today the next great war aim of Bolshevism').

While, for obvious reasons, a detailed history of the KPD lies beyond the scope of this work, it will be necessary to assess the long-term as well as immediate significance of the errors and weaknesses of the German Communist Party, deficiencies which while having their origins in the characteristics and history of the German working class movement, not only remained uncorrected, but became transformed after 1923 under the leadership of the Stalinised Comintern into an entire system of non-Bolshevik tactics and strategy, a system which finally produced the debacle of 1933.

While it is correct to say that ultra-leftism predominated in the KPD between the party's May 1929 congress and the victory of Hitler four years later (in fact the KPD continued to label the SPD as a 'social fascist' party for more than a year after its destruction at the hands of the Nazis), it is by no means the case that the Stalinist leadership of the C.I. in this period (Molotov, Kun, Piatnitsky, Kuusinen, Manuilsky, Knorin, Lozovsky being among the most important of its members) battened only on the leftist errors committed by the leaders of German communism. Thus the one-sided and mechanical application of the united front by the Brandler leadership in the later summer of 1923, at a time when with the maturing of the revolutionary crisis, the break with left social democracy and the preparations for the insurrection were called for, was after 1928 seized upon by the KPD and Moscow Stalinists to discredit entirely the tactic of the united front between revolutionary and reformist workers' organisations. Yet the error of the KPD leadership in 1923 did not lie in its employment of this tactic, which forms an essential weapon in the armoury of the workers' movement in its struggle against reaction. It resided in the Brandler leadership's failure to accomplish in good time the transition from the period of preparation, carried out through the united front under the slogan, issued by the 1921 CI congress, 'to the masses', to tactics which correspond to the objective revolutionary situation which matured after the fall of the Cuno government on August 9. What Stalinist critics of the so-called 'Saxon mistake' (Saxony, with Thuringia, was the state where communists joined with left social democrats to form a 'workers' government', a manoeuvre which predominated over the arming and political preparation of the proletariat) deliberately obscured was that this centrist orientation itself arose as an 'over-correction' of the thoroughly adventurist tactics pursued during the 'March Action' in March 1921, when on the basis of its theory of the 'revolutionary offensive', the KPD leadership (or rather a large proportion of it) attempted by artificial means to convert a partial struggle by the miners of central Germany into a national insurrection. It was only after a prolonged and at the time heated debate at the third congress of the C.I. in June 1921 that a majority of delegates rejected the theory of the 'revolutionary offensive', and the KPD leadership became convinced of the need to win the leadership of the majority of the proletariat before attempting an overturn.

The relationship between the leftist errors of 1921 and the centrist vacillations of

1923 are well described by Trotsky in his speech to the 5th All-Union Congress of Soviet Medical and Veterinary Workers, made on June 21, 1924, where he deals in some detail with the failure of the revolution in Germany: 'What was the fundamental cause of the defeat of the KPD? This, that it did not appreciate in good time the onset of the revolutionary crisis from the moment of the occupation of the Ruhr ...It missed the crucial moment ...It is very difficult for a revolutionary party to make the transition from a period of agitation and propaganda, prolonged over many years, to the direct struggle for power through the organisation of armed insurrection. This turn inevitably gives rise to an inner-party crisis. Every responsible Communist must be prepared for this. One of the ways of being prepared is to make a thorough study of the entire factual history of the October revolution [a theme to which Trotsky returned — in far more polemical vein — in his *Lessons of October,* whose publication later the same year precipitated what became known as the 'literary discussion', a euphemism for the factional struggle between Trotsky and the *troika* of Stalin, Zinoviev and Kamenev]. Up to now extremely little has been done in this connection, and the experience of October was most inadequately utilised by the German party ...It continued even after the onset of the Ruhr crisis to carry on its agitational and propagandist work on the basis of the united front formula — at the same tempo and in the same forms as before the crisis. Meanwhile, this tactic had already become radically insufficient. A growth in the party's political influence was taking place automatically. A sharp tactical turn was needed *in good time* the decisive tactical turn towards the seizure of power. And this was not done. This was the chief and fatal omission. On the one hand, the party expected a revolution, while on the other hand, because it had burned its fingers in the March events, it avoided, until the last months of 1923, the very idea of organising a revolution ...' (L. Trotsky: *Through What Stage are we Passing?* pp.32-34, London, 1965)

The consequences of the German defeat, for the Soviet Union as well as for the workers of Germany and the rest of the capitalist world, will be discussed later on in this work. But it must be stressed here that one of its effects was to instill into not only the new KPD leadership which replaced that of Heinrich Brandler (with the blessing of Comintern chairman Zinoviev, the KPD central committee was brought under the control of the leftist faction headed by Arkadi Maslow and Ruth Fischer) but among the party's proletarian rank and file, a mistrust not only of unprincipled manoeuvres with the leaders of reformism, but a disregard for the tactic of the united front itself. And of course, this rejection of what was — and remains — an essential component of revolutionary tactics became reinforced by the treacherous policies which the SPD leadership pursued throughout the remaining years of the Weimar Republic. This basically healthy and potentially revolutionary hostility towards social democracy was quite cynically exploited and perverted by the Kremlin bureaucracy, and in particular by Stalin himself, to bolster a political course in Germany that not only helped preserve social democracy at a time when its proletarian supporters should have been deserting it wholesale for the KPD, but actively assisted the victory of the Nazis, thereby condemning the KPD itself to annihilation.

Nor is this all. The period of the high tide of Stalinist leftism, while it battened on all the KPD's opportunist errors, prevented a critical examination of its previous sectarian mistakes, since almost without exception they had been magnified a hundredfold under the sign of Stalin's theory of 'social fascism'. In its early days, the KPD refused either to work in the reformist trade unions or contest parliamentary elections, on the grounds that both tactics involved a compromise with social democracy and the class enemy (Lenin answers these and other leftist arguments in his *Left Wing Communism,* much of which is devoted to the problems of the KPD). While the Stalinist KPD did contest elections, it compounded the party's other early leftist error by not only neglecting to enter and work consistently in the reformist (ADGB) unions, but by setting up its own 'red' breakaway unions, organised by the Revolutionary Trade Union opposition (RGO) which at its peak embraced a membership of fewer than 400,000 workers — that is, barely 50,000 more than the maximum membership of the KPD itself. Then there is the vital experience of the March Action, with its utterly false adventurist theory that a determined minority of the proletariat, by provoking a violent clash with the employers and the capitalist state, can 'galvanise' the previously passive majority into revolutionary action. While the KPD never officially endorsed this tactic during the 'third period', it gave ample evidence that it had compeltely failed to glean anything from either the March Action itself, or the discussion on tactics which ensued as a result of the KPD's policy at the Third Congress of the CI. To take but one example; the 1929 May Day 'confrontation' with the Berlin Police, who were under the control of the Prussian social democratic government and the SPD Berlin police President, Karl Zorgiebel. Until 1929, communist and social democratic workers had marched on the same May Day demonstration behind their own party banners. Proletarian unity was established without any mixing of slogans, banners or programmes. Third period Stalinism however dictated an entirely different and far more 'revolutionary' and 'intransigent' course. The KPD central committee, acting under orders from Moscow, announced that it would not march with the 'social fascists' on May Day (neglecting to explain how it had managed to do so on every previous occasion) and that it would hold its own march and rally through Berlin in direct rivalry and opposition to the 'social fascist' demonstration.

This decision, heralded by the Stalinist press as a master stroke of revolutionary tactics, and evidence of the KPD's resolute opposition to social democracy, proved to be a disaster for not only the KPD, but the entire German working class. Seizing on the golden opportunity presented to them by the new Stalinist course, the SPD administration in Berlin banned the march. Previously, the reformist leaders had had to endure communist workers fraternising on May Day with their own members. Now Stalin's theory of 'social fascism' saved them from that discomfort, and, even more fortuitously, enabled them to set a bloody trap for the communist workers of Berlin. The KPD leadership declared it would defy the police ban, and proceeded to march its thousands of unarmed workers into a hail of police gunfire. Instead of immediately ordering the demonstrators to disperse (the only possible way of avoiding further useless and demoralising bloodshed), the KPD leadership pressed ahead with its 'confrontation', organising the setting up of barricades in the proletarian district of Wedding, where the KPD enjoyed more support than the social democrats. Armoured cars were brought in, and in a matter of hours, the backbone of the uprising had been crushed. The criminal role of the reformists in employing police and armoured cars to settle their differences with the communists workers, a deed no less counter-revolutionary than their use of the Free Corps to crush the Spartacists in 1919, should not be permitted (as the Stalinists indeed hoped it would) to blind us to the fact that at no time in this second version of the March Action did those heroic workers engaged in the street and barricade fighting number more than a few thousand, and at no time did they enjoy the support or sympathy of anything like the majority of the Berlin proletariat, let alone the workers in the rest of the country.

While the May Day clashes provided the Stalinists with good propaganda material to hurl at the 'social fascists' (at least 40 workers were killed and many more injured) their consequences were calamitous so far as the German working class was concerned. Millions of social democratic workers, the very force the KPD should have been seeking to win to its revolutionary programme through the tactic of the united front, were either perplexed or alienated from communism by the May Day adventure, since it was in their eyes directed not against the ruling class, but against another wing of the workers' movement and against a Berlin administration which had been elected with their votes. Instead of helping them, by fraternal discussion and through united action on specific issues, these workers, whose support was indispensible if the revolution was to succeed, were repelled by tactics they could neither understand nor endorse, and were driven back into the arms of the very reformists who had ordered the May Day massacre. Thus did the Stalinists trample on all the traditions of Leninism, and either pervert or negate the perspectives, tactics and strategy hammered out in the first four congresses of the Communist

International.

Finally, there is the question of 'national Bolshevism', which reappeared in 1930 in the guise of the KPD's programme for 'National and Social Liberation'. This turn of the KPD towards the language (and even policies) of national socialism, climaxed by the infamous alliance between the NSDAP and the KPD in the Prussian 'Red Referendum' of August 1931 was like so many other aspects of the party's policy at this time, not a unique creation of Stalinism. The notion that German communism could exploit the antagonism between the German bourgeoisie and the western imperialists by allying the KPD with the anti-French Right was first conceived by the Hamburg communists Heinrich Laufenburg and Fritz Wolffheim. They went so far as to suggest opening the ranks of the anti-western front to officers and men of the Free Corps, who at that very time (1919) were waging their murderous war against the revolutionary workers of Germany (Laufenburg and Wolffheim also belonged to the leftist faction opposing parliamentary and trade union work). The advocates of 'national Bolshevism' argued that a defeated, dismembered and disarmed Germany could only hope to regain its old strength by forming an alliance with the Soviet Union, and that therefore this re-alignment would create the conditions inside Germany for a bloc between the workers, led by the KPD, and a general staff thirsting for a war of revenge against the West.

This line evoked a distorted echo on the extreme right, where *volkisch* intellectuals (some of whom, like Count Ernst zu Reventlow, later became active in the 'radical' wing of the NSDAP) took up Laufenburg's proposal and began to call for an alliance between the general staff and the proletariat for a struggle against the 'decadent' and 'plutocratic' western democracies. The mere fact that 'national Bolshevism' could win the approval of such mortal enemies of communism should have served to doom the project at birth, but in fact, such was the political confusion rife among the working class and radical intellectuals at this time that Lenin found it necessary to polemicise against Laufenburg's theories in *Left Wing Communism:*

'...one of the undoubted errors of the German "Lefts" lies in their downright refusal to recognise the Treaty of Versailles ...It is not enough, under the present conditions of the international proletarian revolution to repudiate the preposterous absurdities of "National Bolshevism" (Laufenburg and others), which has gone to the length of advocating a bloc with the German bourgeoisie against the Entente. One must realise that it is utterly false tactics to refuse to admit that a Soviet Germany (if a German Soviet republic were soon to arise) would have to recognise the Treaty of Versailles for a time, and to submit to it ...To give absolute, categorical and immediate precedence to liberation from the Treaty of Versailles and to give it precedence over the question of liberating other countries oppressed by imperialism, from the yoke of imperialism, is philistine nationalism'. (Ibid, pp.75-76.) What then would Lenin have said about the KPD's 1930 programme of 'national and social liberation', which vied with the demagogy of the Nazis in its strident chauvinism, a programme which declared, following the example of Laufenburg's 'national Bolsheviks', that 'we communists will tear in pieces the robber treaty of Versailles and the Young Plan and repudiate all the international debts and repayments which enslave Germany workers'?

Once again, it is a question of an initial and genuine error, committed in the search for a revolutionary solution to the problems confronting the German working class (and Lenin never doubted the *integrity* of the national Bolshevik innovators) reappearing in a new guise and in a new political situation, and no longer representing a mistake made 'in good faith', *but a deliberate falsification of communist tactics, designed not to develop the revolutionary movement in Germany but to further the foreign policy of the Stalinist bureaucracy in the Soviet Union.* Only a formalist would therefore seek to equate the deviations towards nationalism that can be detected in the activity of the KPD in the Ruhr crisis of 1923 and the quite conscious alignment of the KPD with the Nazis in the Prussian Referendum eight years later.

This does not mean that these errors of 1923 can be ignored because they did not flow from a consciously anti-Bolshevik policy. Indeed, they were mistakes of orientation which can be committed by a revolutionary party in any country where the bourgeoisie, however fleetingly or partially, finds itself in conflict with the imperialist bourgeoisie of another nation. In this category must be placed the famous speech of Karl Radek on the death of the German nationalist and Free Corps officer, Albert Leo Schlageter, executed by the French army on May 26, 1923 for sabotaging industrial installations in the Ruhr. Radek's speech was delivered at a session of the Executive Committee of the CI, which met in Moscow from June 12 to 23. Its theme was that the depth of the crisis in Germany, coupled with elements of national oppression that he saw in the French occupation of the Ruhr, was driving wide sections of the petty-bourgeoisie previously hostile to communism towards an alliance with the proletariat. The Free Corps officer Schlageter typified for Radek these new forces that could be won for communism, given a new orientation on the part of the KPD that would take into account the national sentiment of the petty-bourgeoisie. Radek's speech, in the opinion of the author, went beyond the bounds of what is permissible in undertaking this manoeuvre.

'Schlageter, a courageous soldier of the counter-revolution, deserves to be sincerely honoured by us, the soldiers of the revolution ...If those German Fascisti, who honestly thought to serve the German people, failed to understand the significance of Schlageter's fate, Schlageter died in vain ...against whom did the German people wish to fight: against the Entente capitalists, or against the Russian people? With whom did they wish to ally themselves: with the Russian workers and peasants in order to throw off the yoke of Entente capital or for the enslavement of the German and Russian peoples? Schlageter is dead. He cannot supply the answer. His comrades in arms [i.e. his companions in the Free Corps] swore there at his grave to carry on his fight. They must supply the answer: Against whom and on whose side?

We ask the honest, patriotic masses who are anxious to fight against the French invasion: How will you fight, on whose support will you rely? ...If the patriotic circles of Germany do not make up their minds to make the cause of the majority of the nation their own, and so create a front against both Entente and German capital, then the path of Schlageter was a path into the void ...Germany ...will be transformed into a field of bloody internal conflict, and it will be easy for the enemy to defeat and destroy her ...The powerful nation cannot endure without friends, all the more so must the nation which is defeated and surrounded by enemies ...If the cause of the people is made the cause of the nation, then the cause of the nation will become the cause of the people ...This is what the KPD and the CI have to say at Schlageter's graveside ...The KPD must say openly to the nationalist petty-bourgeois masses: ...we believe that the great majority of the national-minded masses belong not to the camp of the capitalists, but the camp of the workers ...We are convinced that there are hundreds of Schlageters who will hear and who will understand it ...' (*International Press Correspondence*, Vol. III, No. 47, June 28, 1923, pp.460-461)

Chasing after the most viciously anti-communist elements of the middle class in this fashion could only alienate those workers who had experienced at first hand the patriotic handiwork of the Schlageters. It cut clean across the struggle to win the reformist-influenced workers for a united front against the armed fascist gangs that were in the Ruhr especially, terrorising workers and staging provocations that led, as in the case of the massacre at Krupps in Essen, to French troops opening fire on unarmed workers. Neither was the KPD leadership immune from such errors. August Thalheimer, writing in *Die Kommunistisch Internationale* No. 26, declared that 'at least temporarily, and against its own will, the German bourgeoisie is revolutionary in its foreign policy, as it was at the time of Bismarck', a judgment which occasioned a sharp retort from Alois Neurath of the Czechoslovak Communist Party, who took Thalheimer's reasoning to its logical — and chauvinist — conclusion: 'It is clear to what consequences such theses must lead. The German proletariat must first of all support the fight of the German bourgeoisie against "French imperialism". It must "temporarily" conclude a pact for civil peace with Cuno, Stinnes and Co, perhaps not explicitly but in fact ...'

Also impermissible was the tactic of KPD speakers appearing at rallies organised jointly with chauvinists and on one occasion at least, even fascists. *Rote Fahne* No.

183 of August 10, 1923, carried a report of Hermann Remmele speaking at one such meeting in Stuttgart, where he was greeted by 'enthusiastic applause from fascists and workers'. And no wonder! According to the same report in the official KPD organ, Remmele had attempted to parry anti-semitic barrackers by retorting:

'How such anti-semitism arises I can easily understand. One merely needs to go down to the Stuttgart cattle market in order to see how the cattle dealers, most of who belong to Jewry, buy up cattle at any price, while the Stuttgart butchers have to go home again, empty-handed because they just don't have enough money to buy cattle. (Quite right! from the Fascists)'.

These exchanges went on as throughout Germany, communist workers were running the gauntlet of armed attacks by nationalist terrorist gangs. Finally, there were glimpses of another opportunist device employed by the KPD Stalinists in the third period, namely that of permitting party members to write in the counter-revolutionary press, and of encouraging unreconstructed chauvinists and even anti-semites to sully the columns of communist journals. Thus in July, *Die Rote Fahne*, in an issue entitled *Germany's Way*, published not only Radek's Schlageter speech, but articles by Reventlow and the 'revolutionary conservative' and author of *The Third Reich*, Moller van den Bruck. On August 22, 1923, the same paper printed another article by Reventlow with the title *One Part of the Way*, which was answered by Paul Frölich, who wrote that 'whoever comes to us without intrigue will find us ready to march at his side'.

While these tactics failed to win any significant section of the *volkisch* movement to communism (not even its 'national Bolshevik' version), they certainly were counter-productive so far as the KPD's policy of undermining the grip of the reformists on the working class was concerned. The SPD made merry with its exposures of KPD flirtations with the extreme right, and it was this policy which caused serious unrest among rank and file communist party workers, who had to bear the daily brunt of the struggle against the counter-revolutionary gangs whose leaders their party was seeking to convince of the virtues of communism.

Opportunist in its dealings with the social democratic lefts, the KPD leadership displayed similar, though not identical vacillations in its struggle, absolutely essential for the victory of the revolution, to win over or neutralise the middle class masses.

We must bear both these weaknesses of the early, pre-Stalinist KPD in mind when we come to examine its crucial — and catastrophic — role in the later years of the Weimar Republic, when the party leadership degenerated into a loyal outpost of the Kremlin bureaucracy within the German workers' movement, a brake on its revolutionary development not one whit less pernicious than social democracy. We can indeed concur with Trotsky when he writes, in his first great work on the German crisis of 1930-33. *(The Turn in the Communist International and the Situation in Germany)* that 'one of the necessary conditions for the liberation of the party from bureaucratic bondage is a general examination of the "general line" of the German leadership, beginning with 1923, and even with the March Days of 1921 ...The party will not rise to the height of its great tasks if it does not freely evaluate its present in the light of its past'.

Chapter Fourteen
BIG BUSINESS RATIONALISES

Such economic stability as was enjoyed by German monopoly capitalism between 1924 and the onset of the world crisis five years later had its origins in the enormous political reverse suffered by the working class in the autumn of 1923. Entirely involuntarily (and in complete contrast to the social democrats, who consciously worked to preserve the rule of the bourgeoisie) the KPD leadership had, by its vacillations at the moment when the necessity of preparing the revolutionary insurrection was posed point-blank, given a new lease of life to a class that had begun to doubt its own prospects of survival. Even the normally sanguine Schacht wrote, some four years after the crisis, that

> ...not since the spring of 1919 had Germany been so close to the peril of Bolshevisation as in these weeks. It is hard for foreigners to form a conception of the excitement within the country at this time. Germany was then completely isolated. All who held any leading position in the business or public life of the country tortured their brains, day out, to find a remedy for the position.[1]

This was the judgment he adhered to in later years, stating in his autobiography that the September of 1923

> found Germany in the grip of a fever that threatened to undermine her last vestige of strength. In Saxony, Thuringia and Bavaria riots broke out everywhere. Hitler was tub-thumping in the south. The Communist-Social Democratic Zeigner Government in Saxony gave the Red terror a free hand. In Hamburg street fights raged all day and fifteen policemen and sixty-five civilians were killed. The danger of a Communist upheaval was imminent. I felt it my duty to evacuate my family from this hell's kitchen and packed them off to Switzerland so that I myself might not be hindered by personal considerations were I to be drawn into the whirlpool.[2]

Papen was no more optimistic, as he confesses in his autobiography:

> I became conscious at a very early stage of the hopeless inability of the National and State Parliaments to take decisive steps to deal with this social disaster [of inflation] ...Without a firm backbone of authority Germany was gradually sinking into the depths. As early as September 1923 I wrote a pamphlet with the title *Dictatorship or Parliament?* My

thesis was that Germany was on the brink of collapse* and that salvation would not be forthcoming through mechanical parliamentary methods or the sterile clash of rigid party doctrines. I called for a Government of independent, responsible people ...who would use the last remnants of State authority to impose solutions designed to meet the emergency of the times ...It is only too easy to forget the desperate German internal situation at the time. The currency had collapsed, a Communist government had been set up in Saxony, the Socialists were engaged in violent political warfare against the hundred thousand-man *Reichswehr* and the Communists were making a renewed attempt to seize power by illegal means...[3]

And finally there is the estimation made of the 1923 crisis by the SPD Berlin Police Chief Albert Grzesinski that 'in October of 1923, the Communists planned another uprising which,' due to the economic crisis, had a fair chance of success because conditions were desperate'.[4] And as a reformist, Grzesinki would have been more sensitive than most to those shifts in the consciousness of the proletariat away from the politics of compromise and class collaboration which herald every great revolutionary crisis.

All the conditions which for Lenin constituted a revolutionary situation** were present in Germany in the late summer of 1923. Already beset by a profound crisis in its relations with France, the German ruling class was also deeply divided as to how to cope with the hourly accelerating inflation and the political upheavals which accompanied it, a conflict which in the cases of Bavaria and

* In common with leading non-Marxist historians (the most important being Werner T. Angress *(Stillborn Revolution,* Princeton, 1963) and E.H. Carr *(The Interregnum,* London, 1954) the latest Stalinist history of the Communist International denies that a revolutionary situation existed in Germany in 1923: 'The Party's leadership overestimated the degree of readiness of the masses for the decisive battles and the rate at which the revolutionary crisis was building up'. *(Outline History of the Communist International,* p.195, Moscow, 1971.) This volume was produced by a group of Soviet authors headed by A.I.Sobolev, and with the assistance of a team of former Comintern officials and journalists, among them the British Stalinists Andrew Rothstein and Palme Dutt. As we have already noted, Palme Dutt has a vested interest in proving that Germany was not ripe for revolution in the early 1920s. Admitting this would be tantamount to a confession of harbouring 'vulgar Marxist' and 'Trotskyist' views. Yet such heresies succeeded in infiltrating the columns of *Pravda,* which on May 25, 1924, declared 'It is clear that in October 1923, during the unprecedented economic crisis, during the complete disintegration of the middle classes, during a frightful confusion in the ranks of the social democracy resulting from the powerful and sharp contradiction within the bourgeoisie itself and an unprecedented militant mood of the proletarian masses in the industrial centres, the communist party had the majority of the population on its side. It could and should have fought and had all the chances of success.'

** Lenin listed these as follows: '...for a revolution to take place, it is essential, first, that a majority of workers (or at least a majority of the class-conscious, thinking and politically active workers) should fully realise that revolution is necessary, and that they should be prepared to die for it; second, that the ruling classes should be going through a government crisis, which draws even the most backward masses into politics ...weakens the government, and makes it possible for the revolutionaries rapidly to overthrow it'. (V. Lenin, *Left Wing Communism,. Collected Works,* Vol. 31, p.85.)

the Rhineland, expressed itself through the politics of particularism and even separatism. And just as at the time of the Kapp putsch, but now at a far greater pitch of intensity, the factional struggle within the ruling class reverberated throughout the state machine, even disrupting relations within that normally highly homogenous caste, the German general staff. Wide layers of the petty-bourgeoisie, whose savings and fixed incomes were losing value by the minute as the mark plunged towards its November nadir, no longer trusted the old bourgeois and 'national' parties to defend their interests. Many in their despair turned towards the bogus anti-capitalism of the *volkisch* and Nazi Right, but such was the ferment in this highly volatile social layer that it would have in all probability been possible to either win over or neutralise the bulk of the working petty-bourgeoisie to the side of the working class (as had been proved at the time of the Kapp putsch) if the KPD had established itself in the heat of the crisis as a party whose revolutionary propaganda and agitation was matched by deeds.

Finally there was the active, 'negating' force in the crisis, the German proletariat itself. Over the previous five years it had provided ample testimony of not only its political maturity and organisational capacities, but its readiness to fight, and if necessary, risk death, to defend its past gains and go forward to win state power. In the space of these five years, the German working class had passed through more phases of struggle than previous generation had experienced in a life time. From the establishment of councils in November 1918 its most advanced layers attempted to seize power in a series of bitter armed clashes with troops under the leadership of the 'government socialists'. There then ensued a period of bitter disillusionment with the SPD on the part of millions of workers who had been amongst its most loyal supporters over previous years and decades. The treachery of the reformists after the Kapp putsch accelerated this leftwards impulse within the proletariat, a current which did not for the most part flow directly into the KPD, but indirectly, through the USPD, whose centrist leaders, after the party's unification with the KPD in October 1920, then made their way back into the womb of social democracy, taking with them a sizable minority of the UPSD's more conservative-minded workers. After the adventure of March 1921, the KPD then set about winning the majority of the proletariat to its banner, a task which, greatly facilitated by the onset of the Ruhr crisis, was on the verge of completion when paralysis gripped the Brandler-Thalheimer leadership after the formation of the KPD-SPD coalitions in Saxony and Thuringia.

This truly tragic squandering of the resources and energies of the German proletariat cast its shadow across the future path of the revolutionary struggle not only in Germany but throughout Europe from Britain in the west to the Soviet Union in the east. And by the same token, it marked a turning point in the fortunes of the German and European bourgeoisie. Now free to dispense with the services of the Nazis and their para-military allies, the bourgeoisie began to feel firm ground under its feet for the first time in many months, and in a broader sense, since the summer of 1914. Such was the dialectic of revolution and counter-revolution. The economic crisis of 1923 had created all the conditions necessary for the overthrow of the bourgeoise save that of the sub-jective factor — revolutionary leadership. Now the latter's absence — more accurately deficiencies — in turn created the political conditions which enabled this same bourgeoisie not mere-ly to salvage what had only weeks before seemed irrevocably lost, but over the next three years, to so consolidate and restructure its economy that industry reached a level of output that despite Germany's post-war territorial losses, in most departments more than matched its performance in the immediate pre-war period. Lenin had hoped that this restoration of German industrial might would take place on the basis of socialist property relations, thus making possible the creation of the politico-economic union which he had envisaged in early 1918, and which Lloyd George had so feared following the end of the war. But since it unfolded on the foundations of *capitalist* property relations, this revival of the German economy inevitably generated once again, though of course in a greatly changed context, the same tensions between the main imperialist powers and combinations that had precipitated the war of 1914-18. They flowed from the potentially explosive antagonism between the productive forces developed by capitalism on the one hand, and on the other, the barriers erected against their further expansion by not only the capitalist mode of production, *but the bourgeois nation state.* Germany's defeat in 1918, since it had not led to a victorious proletarian revolution, only postponed a violent renewal of these contradictions.   In contrast however with the tempestuous industrial growth which took place under Bismarck and Wilhelm II, the post-1923 boom did not derive so much from any great internal economic strength possessed by German capitalism as from the massive intervention by United States imperialism in the affairs of the European continent. Within weeks of the passing of the revolutionary crisis, moves were afoot both in Germany and internationally to place the economy on a stable footing. Three days after the collapse of the Hitler Putsch, Stresemann's Finance Minister Dr. Hans Luther invited Schact (who was then a director of the big *Danatbank*) to devote all his considerable skill and energies to the task of stabilising Germany's chaotic currency situation. The next day, November 13, Schact assumed the new post of Commissioner for National Currency, with a brief to employ whatever methods he saw fit 'in all matters touching the question of money and credit'.[5]

Meanwhile, Stresemann's government, deprived of the support of the social democrats on the left and the Nationalists on the right, fell on November 23 after losing a vote of confidence (the SPD found itself unable to remain in a cabinet that had sanctioned the removal by military means of legally elected social democratic governments in Saxony and Thuringia, while the DNVP was still opposed to Stresemann over his refusal to join their proposed right-wing bloc against the centre and left parties, also bitterly condemning him for his policy of seeking a *detente* with France). The result was a more rightist government under Dr Wilhelm Marx of the Catholic Centre Party, being a coalition of Ministers from the DDP, the Centre, the DVP and the BVP (Bavarian People's Party).*

After an initial attempt by the Junker DNVP financial expert Karl Helfferich to introduce a stopgap mark whose value would be tied to the price of rye (blocked by the social democrats, who quite rightly saw it as a move to enhance the power of the agrarians) Stresemann had secured the introduction of the so-called *Rentenmark,* which while theoretically equal to the value of the gold mark (which had remained unaffected by the inflation) would be covered by a mortgage on all German landed property. This meant that the new mark could be exchanged on demand for an identical amount in mortgage bonds, thus restoring much-needed confidence to the currency. Schact however, was anxious to place the mark on a more stable footing (even land values were subject to wide variations), his goal being the restoration of the old gold mark. The death of the Reichsbank President, Havenstein, on November 20, led somewhat fortuitously to Schact's appointment to this enormously influential post two days later, and it was in this new capacity that Schact travelled to London to secure Bank of England backing from Montagu Norman for his projected *Golddiskontobank.* which would be entirely based on gold. The bank's main function would be to finance the heavy industries of the Ruhr, which had been hard-hit by the French occupation and the consequent economic and political unrest.

---

* Exclusion from the new cabinet did not prevent the SPD voting for an enabling act which empowered the Marx government to implement, without the consent of the Reichstag, any and all measures 'which it deemed necessary and useful in alleviating the distress of people and Reich'. It was a formulation almost identical to that of Hitler's enabling act which, with only the SPD voting against, ushered in the Third Reich on March 23, 1933. Once again, an instance of the social democrats making a rod for their own backs.

Norman agreed to make available for the proposed bank a sum of 100 million marks, to be paid in sterling, and at an interest of only five per cent (the going rate in Germany was twice that amount). The deal between the Presidents of the English and German central banks, concluded on January 2, 1924, marked another turning point in the recovery of German big business.

Norman's decision to aid his former imperialist rivals was taken with one eye on the conference shortly to convene in Paris under the chairmanship of the US banker general Charles Dawes. The abject failure of military methods to secure the prompt payment of reparations, and the disastrous repercussions such strong-arm tactics had on German economic and political life, had led to a re-consideration of allied policy towards Germany. Reparations were still to be paid, but there was now a realisation that Germany could only pay insofar as its resources and capacities were harnessed to the full. Hence the adoption of the Dawes scheme, whereby credits would be granted by foreign bankers to Germany in order to revitalise its economy and so make possible the payment of reparations. Far-sighted statesmen also saw the urgent need, after the recent revolutionary events in Germany and elsewhere in Europe, to mitigate class tensions throughout the continent by aiding a policy of industrial expansion and concessions to the working class. In the words of the US Secretary of State Hughes, 'there can be no economic recuperation in Europe unless Germany recuperates', and the first consideration of the Dawes Plan (as it became known) was to end the period of turmoil and uncertainty that had characterised Germany's first five post-war years.

This dramatic turn in the relationship between Europe and the United States, one which profoundly influenced the subsequent course and forms of the class struggle in Germany, had been predicted by Trotsky in a series of articles and speeches developing the slogan of the 'United Socialist States of Europe', as the revolutionary solution to the economic, political, national and cultural problems besetting the continent that had cradled both capitalism and its Marxist polar opposite. Trotsky warned all communists that they ignored the might of American imperialism at their peril. The trans-Atlantic colossus could only be confronted by a Europe united by proletarian revolution:

> ...until recently we have failed to differentiate adequately between Europe and America. And the slow development of Communism in America might have inspired some pessimistic ideas to the effect that so far as the revolution is concerned Europe must wait for America. Not at all! Europe cannot wait... if the revolution in Europe is post-poned for many decades, it would signify the elimination of Europe generally as a cultural force. It is nowhere written that the European proletariat must keep waiting until the American proletariat learns not

to succumb to the lies of its triply depraved bourgeoisie ...At the present time the American bourgeoisie is deliberately keeping Europe in a condition of decay. Glutted with European blood and gold the American bourgeoisie issues orders to the whole world, sends its plenipotentiaries to conferences who are bound by no commitments ...The European bourgeoisie, not only of Germany and France but also Britain, begs on its hind legs before the American bourgeoisie which drained Europe in wartime by its support, by its loans, by its gold, and which now keeps Europe in the throes of death-agony.[6]

And if the European proletariat found its most mortal enemies in Washington and New York, then its most loyal and self-sacrificing allies lay to the east, in Moscow.

Two courses are possible: either the European proletariat remains terrorized by the American boot, or the European proletariat is backed by the Russian workers and peasants, and thus assured of grain during the difficult days and months of revolution. That is why each economic success in agriculture is a revolutionary deed.[7]

But should this struggle to establish the unity of Europe by means of proletarian revolution and with the aid of the Soviet workers and peasants fail, then the way would be clear for American Imperialism to dictate its terms to an exhausted bourgeoisie and a defeated proletariat alike:

America is standing aloof from Europe, tranquilly biding her time until Europe's economic agony has reached such a pitch as will make it easy to step in and buy up Europe.[8]

Hence the urgent need, argued Trotsky in the summer of 1923, to impress on the consciousness of the advanced workers the necessity of fixing as their revolutionary goal not merely the defeat of capitalism in their 'own' country, but the creation of a federation of socialist states that would ultimately embrace and unite all Europe. 'Socialism in one country' was as unreal and reactionary a programme in Germany as it became under Stalin in the USSR:

...France cannot stand apart from Germany, nor can Germany stand aloof from France ...The European continent in the present state of the development of the productive forces is an economic unit ...as was proved in the terrible catastrophe of the world war, and again by the mad paroxysm of the Ruhr occupation. Europe is not a geographical term, Europe is an economic term ...Just as federation was long ago recognised as essential for the Balkan peninsula, so now the time has arrived for stating definitely and clearly that federation is essential for Balkanised Europe ...the very danger arising from the USA (which is spurring the destruction of Europe, and is ready to step in as Europe's master) furnishes a very substantial bond for uniting the peoples of Europe who are ruining one another, into a 'European United States of Workers and Peasants.'[9]

It was with this slogan that Trotsky concretised programmatically the perspectives flowing from the uneven development of the class struggle in the Old and New Worlds, at the same time making it abundantly clear that 'this opposition between Europe and the United States stems organically from the differences in the objective situations in the European countries and of the mighty trans-Atlantic republic, and is not in any way directed against the international solidarity of the proletariat, or against the interests of the revolution in America.'[10] (It therefore had nothing in common with the Stalinist-inspired anti-Americanism of the 'cold war' period.)

The American intervention in Europe followed almost exactly the itinerary mapped out by Trotsky. It did not suffice for fascism to triumph in Italy, nor bloody counter-revolution in Hungary and Bulgaria. These defeats, important though they were for both imperialism and the international working class, had been inflicted on the proletariat at the extremities of the continent. US finance capital continued to 'stand aloof' from Europe until the outcome of the strategic struggle in its German heartland had been decided for the foreseeable future. But when the time came to intervene, the operation was carried out on a truly gargantuan and typically American scale. Through such agencies as the Dawes Plan, and by exploiting the political leverage of war debts and reparations payments, United States monopoly capitalism sought to transform its role of *arbiter* between Europe's main imperialist rivals (a role it assumed in the last year of the world war) into that of banker and policeman of the entire continent.*

Under the Dawes Plan, Germany's reparations were re-scheduled, and largely American loans made available to aid their payment, the terms of both being finalised in the London Agreement of August 30, 1924. Germany was to make annual payments

---

* Again it was Trotsky who payed the closest attention to this new factor in European and world politics, devoting many articles and speeches to the problem of the relations between Europe and America in the period between 1924 and 1926. In July 1924 he pin-pointed the main aims of US strategy in Europe; aims that the more they were realised, undermined the very political and economic stability that the US was seeking: 'What does American capitalism want? ...It is seeking, we are told, stability; it wants to restore the European market; it wants to make Europe solvent. How? ...After all, American capitalism is compelled not to render Europe capable of competition; it cannot allow England, and all the more so France and Germany, particularly Germany, to regain the world markets inasmuch as American capitalism finds itself hemmed in, because it is now an exporting capitalism — exporting both commodities and capital. American capitalism is seeking the position of world domination; it wants to establish an American imperialist autocracy over our planet. ...What will it do with Europe? It must, they say, pacify Europe. How? Under its hegemony ...This means that Europe will be permitted to rise again, but within limits set in advance, with certain restricted sections of the world market allotted to it ...This is its aim. It will slice up the markets; it will regulate the activity of the European financiers and industrialists ...*It wants to put capitalist Europe on rations'.* (L. Trotsky: *Perspectives of Development*, a speech to workers, July 28, 1924, printed in *Isvestia*, August 5, 1924, reprinted in L. Trotsky: *Europe and America*, p. 16, Ceylon, 1951.)

starting at 1,000 million gold marks and rising by the fifth year to 2,500 million marks. From then onwards until their intended completion some forty to fifty years later, payments would vary from this sum when the world price of gold either fell or rose by more than 10%. Onerous though these terms were, what irked the nationalist middle classes and the big bourgeoisie most, and later provided excellent grist for the Nazi propaganda mill, was the Allied decision to take over the control of Germany's State railway system, and to seize all its profits as additional tribute. (This naked plunder went hand-in-hand with enforced mortgages on private industrial undertakings with a working capital of more than 50,000 marks).

With practically the entire Germany economy now pledged as security against the proposed loans, there was no shortage of subscribers to what a year previously would have been regarded as a suicidal financial undertaking. Of the initial Dawes Plan loan of 800 million marks, 110 million was raised in New York, being oversubscribed to the tune of 1,000%! And the loan was underwritten by the titan of American finance, J.P. Morgan. Carried forward on the crest of its internal industrial boom,* US capitalism poured its dollars into Germany at an incredible rate, the flood reaching its high point in 1928, when 153.8 million dollars made the journey from Wall Street to the Berlin Bourse. In the five years between 1924 and 1928, of the 15,000 million marks borrowed by Germany from foreign investors, *over half was raised on the US capital market* (Ironically, in view of their original purpose, Germany's loans were almost double the sum paid in reparations to the Allies!)

Into whose accounts were these vast quantities of money paid? Only a portion of the loans went to the German government to enable it to meet its reparations and other foreign commitments, which of course included the servicing of debts already contracted. There were two other major borrowers, destined, when the American well ran dry, to confront each other as bitter enemies. From the outset of the Dawes Plan, the biggest German monopolies** saw US credits as a quick and easy means of raising

* The US gross national product rose from 73.3 billion dollars in 1920 to 104.4 billion in 1929, while its foreign debt of nearly 4 billion dollars in 1914 had, by 1929 been transformed into a credit of twice that amount.

** Among firms taking up US loans, chiefly through the mediation of the house of Morgan, were Krupp AG (which obtained three), Thyssen and the Flick combine which borrowed for a single concern the gigantic sum of 124 million dollars, which at the prevailing rate of exchanges, amounted to roughly four times that amount in marks. US monopolies were quick to exploit their new position as Germany's creditors, to secure a footing in the country's economy. Thus Westinghouse acquired an interest in Siemens, and its powerful rival the General Electric Company one in AEG. Opel, Germany's largest car firm, was purchased by General Motors (whose banker just happened to be ...Morgan). The Dawes Plan became the instrument

the funds necessary to renew and modernise their plant, which because of the war and the ensuing economic and political crises, had either become obsolescent or run down. As for the third main borrower, the social democratic municipal authorities and State governments, American loans were employed to finance a whole series of social reforms and undertakings that would otherwise have proved impossible to carry through on a capitalist basis with revenues raised from purely domestic sources. German social democracy proceeded to build its 'socialism in one municipality' by permission of General Dawes, the blessings of J.P. Morgan and with the dollars of Wall Street financiers!

The hyper-inflation of 1923 temporarily impoverished wide layers of the middle class whose wealth consisted mainly of savings, or income on fixed pensions or dividends. But for a far smaller number, it was a boon, even if one that proved to be short-lived. Owners of large industrial concerns found that their fortunes — since they were mostly tied up in property and not liquid cash — increased in inverse proportion to the decline in the value of the mark, while their debts fell in direct proportion to the rate of inflation. Tycoons such as the insatiable Stinnes, while in no way being responsible for the inflation, exploited it to extend the range and size of their holdings. The shaky nature of these ventures became obvious however, once the currency was stabilised, since debts contracted during the inflation now had to be honoured in gold marks. The Stinnes empire,* the prime

whereby a small but immensely powerful group of corporations linked up with their opposite numbers in Germany, forging trade, technical and even political links that endured up to and even beyond the outbreak of war between the Third Reich and the United States.

* The Stinnes Empire, which in modern economic parlance would be termed a 'conglomerate' was founded by Hugo's grandfather, Matthias Stinnes, the owner of a Rhine shipping firm. By 1914, his grandson had branched out from shipping into iron and coal mining, steel production and electric power supply, controlling by a network of interlocking share blocs the Deutsch-Luxemburgische Bergwerks-gesell-schaft and the Rheinisch-Westfalische Elektrizitats Gesellschaft. In 1918, Stinnes broke into ocean shipping, previously the monopoly of the two Hamburg-based lines, the North German Lloyd and the Hamburg-America Line. Government compensation for losses incurred as a result of war reparations and the seizure of Alsace and Lorraine by France enabled him to widen his interests even further, buying a holding in the iron and steel concern, the *Gelsenkirchener Bergwerksgesellschaft*, and the Siemens-Shuckert electrical engineering firm. Stinnes extended his monopolies both vertically and horizontally, buying entire forests in East Prussia for pit-prop timber for his coal mines, and at the same time enabling him to move into the paper production industry and so on to printing and then newspaper publication, eventually controlling an immense propaganda machine of no fewer than 150 newspapers and periodicals ranging from the semi-official *Deutsche Allgemeine Zeitung* through the more 'popular' mass press to the satirical *Kladeradatsch*. In 1920, Stinnes joined with a group of equally reactionary tycoons — Vögler, Kirdorf and Siemens being the most prominent — to found the Siemens-Rheinelbe-Shuckert Union, a trust whose vertical and horizontal tentacles reached out into virtually every sector of the German economy. At its peak, the Stinnes empire accounted for one eighth of Germany's industrial production.

example of this type of debt-financed undertaking, only outlived its owner by a year, collapsing in June 1925.

Its failure, together with the collapse of a series of similarly unsound and artificially assembled concerns, precipitated a new crisis in German industry, which over the previous year had been enjoying its first real post-war period of prosperity. Demand had been greatly stimulated by the sudden influx of foreign credits, and swelled by government compensation paid to those who had lost their savings during the 1923 inflation, and the majority of firms found that in this market situation they could make reasonable profits without investing in new plant and machinery. Heavy demand ensured that prices remained high, thus masking grave structural and capital deficiencies of many large monopolies. The short boom gave way to a sharp down-turn of production in September 1925 as domestic demand fell away, exposing the high unit costs of firms that had previously been enjoying record post-war profits and sales. From this crisis came the initial impetus towards the rationalisation and further monopolisation of entire branches of the German economy.

Reichsbank President Schact had long seen the need for such measures, though he by no means approved of the means by which they were financed.* As early as October 1902, he had advocated the development of vertical monopolies or trusts in order to reduce by as much as possible the production costs of German industry, thereby rendering it more competitive on the world's markets. The disadvantage of a cartel was its deliberate policy of maintaining high prices, which in turn dispensed with the need to cut costs and maximise the exploitation of the labour force. By the same token, small or medium firms had to be liquidated since their inability to produce at the same low unit costs as their larger cartel partners forced up overall prices. In 1908, Schact cited the example of the electricity generating industry to show how the old cartel system was beginning to act as a brake on the further development of the German economy, and

> ...pointed out the colossal waste among the concerns engaged in electricity generation, whereby the innumerable little local electric

---

* 'Industry was in desperate need not only of money for the purchase of raw materials; it cried out for capital to invest in the restoration and improvement of its means of production. To expect this capital to accrue from even the most economical management and from the thriftiness of the population was a waste of time. A much quicker result could be achieved from the proceeds of a foreign loan. In the course of the next few years a considerable proportion of business firms had incurred debts on foreign loans'. (H. Schacht: *My First Seventy Six Years*, p.217). Schact's continual campaigning against what amounted to a policy of economic and social concessions to the working class (financed largely by US loans) led him after 1929 to seek an alliance with the Nazis against the labour movement, which stubbornly refused to be reduced to conditions of 'thriftiness' in order that big business should continue to prosper.

works have the last word ...By contrast I advocated a concentration of production in large generating stations with the aim of cheapening consumption, bringing electric policy under a single state leadership and combining public control with private enterprise.[11]

The cartel system therefore generated tensions between the primary and power producers and the manufacturers of finished goods, who were being compelled to pay exorbitant prices for their raw materials and power supplies. As a banker standing outside, or rather above, this struggle, Schact was possibly better placed to formulate a policy representing the long-term interests of the monopoly bourgeoisie as a whole. But it was only in 1925 that the first serious attempts were made to cut away the dead wood that had accumulated under the protective umbrella of the cartel system. In that year, the Chemical Trust, I G Farben, was formed out of no fewer than six separate concerns, a merger which gave the new company a 100% monopoly in synthetic dyes, and a near-total monopoly in other products ranging from rayon to fertilizers, synthetic nitrogen, dynamite, photography, potash, aluminium, jute, and even pottery. During the First World War, Germany's chronic lack of certain basic raw materials — the most important being oil — had led to direct government support for the chemical industry in its attempts to develop synthetic substitutes. This tradition was continued under the Weimar Republic, and raised to its hideous apogee in the murderous partnership between I G Farben and the Third Reich, symbolised by the employment of Jewish slave labour at the firm's Buna plant in the shadow of the chimneys of the Auschwitz death camp.

1925 also saw the beginning of a series of mergers in shipping. The Roland, Hamburg-Bremen-Afrika and Horn lines fused with the North German Lloyd, while the following year, the Deutsche-Australische and Kosmos lines were absorbed by North German Lloyd's main rival, Hamburg America. Finally in 1927, all the Mediterranean lines merged into a single group, with the result that Germany's merchant fleet of nearly two million tons was now organised by no more than five shipping companies. At the same time, air travel was rationalised under the government-backed company Lufthansa.

In the Ruhr, steps were also taken to achieve economies of scale and modernisation of plant through the creation in 1926 of the *Vereinigte Stahlwerke* (United Steel Works) under the aegis of Friedrich Flick, who rivalled Stinnes both in his predilection for stock market manipulations and hatred for organised labour. (He was a contributor to Nazi Party funds in 1932, and later shared in the plunder of occupied territories from the USSR to France). Fused in the new concern were the interests of the Thyssen, Stinnes, Phoenix AG and Otto Wolff groups. Members ceded their interests to the company and in return received a proportional amount of its shares. Thus the old Rhein-Elbe-Union, which in December 1926 fused into the *Gelsenkirchner Bergwerksgesellschaft,* received 39.5% of the new share issue, with 26% going to the Phoenix group, where Wolff was prominent, another 26% to Thyssen, and 8.5% to the *Rheinische Stahlwerke,* also partly owned by Otto Wolff (I G Farben also acquired an interest in the new concern by virtue of its 51% holding in the last named firm). Flick exercised control over this iron and steel empire by means of a hierarchy of minority share-holdings in its constituent groups. Flick's original firm, the Charlottenhutte AG, in which he had a 44% controlling interest, also exercised control over the *Gelsenkirchner.* In its turn, the *Gelsenkirchner* dominated, by virtue of its 39.5% share holding and a series of complex financial maneouvres within its other member companies, the entire steel trust. The extent of the *Vereinigte Stahlwerke's* grip on German heavy industry is illustrated by the following figures, which give the proportions of national production accounted for by the newly-formed monopoly: coal: 36%; pig iron: 48%; hoop iron: 49%; bar iron: 42%; semi-finished steel: 56%; thick plates: 47%; tubes: 50%; wire rods: 39%.

Coal mining was even more tightly organised, with the Rhine-Westphalian syndicate increasing its share of total German coal production from 66.7% in 1920 to 77.9% by 1925, and coke production from 61.3% in 1913 to 90% by 1930.

Electrical engineering was already highly monopolised prior to 1914, with two firms — AEG and Siemens-Schukert — accounting for 80% production in this sphere. There was therefore little scope for further concentration, though both concerns did move into the radio and film industries after the end of the war. Banking however presented an altogether different picture, with a steady reduction in the number of big banks and an equally steady increase in their size and deposits. Through a series of mergers, the pre-war Berlin 'big nine' shrunk to seven in 1924, five in 1929, and four in 1931. In 1913, the 'big nine' accounted for just under 50% of the 10 billion marks held by all German banks, while in 1929, the five biggest banks held 11.4 billion of a total deposit of 17.5 billion marks — that is, 67.5%.

Rationalisation and monopolisation were not confined to heavy industry and banking. For example, four syndicates in the cement industry shared by agreement between 85 to 90% of Germany's cement output, while a similar process of concentration was under way in other medium and light industries. These newly amalgamated economic units not only commanded enormous material resources, but dominated whole armies of workers. Thus by 1929, the Flick concern employed 177,000 workers, AEG 60,000, Krupps 90,000 and I G Farben 148,000 (in

1936). Immense power also became concentrated in the hands of a tiny group of industrial and banking magnates, even more than had been the case in the pre-war period of monopolisation. In the basic industries (coal, iron, steel and potassium) 19 persons or families owned fortunes amounting to 810 million marks, while in manufacturing, eleven persons or families owned 210 million marks. Taking industry as a whole, 42 persons and families aggregated 1.25 billion marks, and in finance, 110 owned 3.4 billion marks.* Also greatly enhanced was the role of the major banks in industry. As we have seen, centralisation of the banking system accompanied rationalisation and monopolisation in industry, and these twin processes inevitably led to an even greater representation by the big banks on the boards of industrial companies. The number of big bank directors sitting on the supervisory boards of industrial firms almost doubled from 751 in 1903 to 1,484 by 1932.

Rationalisation consisted of a great deal more than simply the merging of banks or industrial concerns. It also involved the planned reduction in the amount of productive units, the least efficient being closed-down and production concentrated in the most advanced. With largely foreign loans and funds realised as a result of the sale of unwanted assets, technological innovations and improvements were then carried out in line with the latest theories on plant and labour utilisation. Rationalisation became an industrial philosophy bent towards one aim — the maximisation of profit on capital employed by the most ruthless reduction of costs. A German writer on rationalisation, J. Gerhardt, considered that

> the productive process in the factory must be organised, having due regard to the configuration of demand, to lower costs, and all rationalisation consists singly and solely in the elimination of costs ...the immediate purpose of rationalisation in a competitive economy *is not to increase the production of goods, to produce them cheaper and to better their quality, but to increase profit.* (emphasis added)

R.V. Holzer, another authority on rationalisation, echoed these sentiments when he wrote in 1928 that

> the purpose of every private undertaking is profit, and every action undertaken, and every step forward which the employer will make, has the sole purpose of maintaining or increasing profits. If here and there social and ethical considerations appear as the basis for decision and policies [as they did in Nazi ideology], so these must drop into the background ...Singly and solely to increase dividends should be the purpose of every larger measure, and consequently must be the basis

---

* Krupp topped the wealth league in heavy industry, with a personal fortune of 200 million marks, followed by Petscheck, 150 million, Thyssen, Haniel Wolff and Ottmar Strauss, each with 50 million. In manufacturing, von Opel (of the car firm of the same name,) headed the list with 120 million marks, while Siemens followed him with 20 million.

for the rationalisation of every enterprise.*

And since German industry was engaged in a bitter trade war to recover overseas markets lost during and after the war, greater emphasis was placed on cost reduction than price maintenance. A Ruhr mine owner summed up the central aim of rationalisation when he declared it to be 'the increase of productivity and profitability by the reduction of working costs, with prices remaining at the same level, *or actually falling.'* (emphasis added)

To see how rationalisation worked out in practice, it is necessary to study the impact its application made on a specific branch of industry. On the eve of rationalisation, in 1925, the bituminous coal industry employed 557,087 workers in 343 concerns, at an average of 1,624 workers per firm. When the world crisis brought it to a sudden end in 1929, 266 firms employed 517,401 workers, an average of 1,945 per concern. So much for concentration, which proceeded at a far greater pace during these five years than in any other comparable period. But did monopolisation, and its attendant emphasis on cost reduction and optimum utilisation of labour power, succeed in its aim of increasing output per worker and the value created per worker? With production rising from 150 million tons in 1925 to 163 million tons in 1929, and with a declining labour force due to rationalisation, output per worker did indeed increase — from 238 tons annually in 1925 to 315 tons in 1929. Likewise value created per worker increased over the same period from 3,416 marks annually to 4,794.

Larger firms were, of course, better placed to exploit the advantages of rationalisation through economies of scale, and cost-cutting as a result of vertical integration. Thus the Flick

---

* Which brings to mind a guiding principle of the founder of modern 'work study' methods, Frederick Taylor, who in his *Shop Management* (London, 1919) wrote that 'all employers should bear in mind that each shop exists first and last and all of the time for the pupose of paying dividends to its owners'. (Ibid, p.143.) Taylor, and even more, Henry Ford, were taken as models for emulation by modernising and rationalising German employers. Nor were trade union leaders immune from the work study contagion. ADGB Chairman Theodore Leipart sat on the board of the Kaiser Wilhelm Institute for Labour Physiology in Dortmund, presided over by Dr Edgar Aler, a leading researcher into the new science of labour physiology, while in 1920, a 17-man ADGB delegation visited the USA to study mass production techniques, returning home convinced that Henry Ford was pioneering a new economic order. The German Metal Workers Union declared that the unions 'do not oppose the conscious merging of similar industrial establishments, under the stress of technical progress, into concerns and superstate organisations, since these are preparatory steps to the coming socialist communal economy'. The SPD *Vorwärts* was no less opportunist in adapting to the growing power of the big monopolies, saying of Stinnes that he brought 'capitalism into the chrysalis stage, from which one day the socialist economy will emerge as a full grown butterfly. Let us not disturb him in his work. Socialists may yet acclaim him as one of their greatest men'. It was not socialism, but its counter-revolutionary opposite, fascism, that emerged from the monopoly capitalist 'chrysalis', as *Vorwärts* was later to discover.

combine, in the financial year 1926-1927, aggregated an output of 26 million tons for its various products ranging from coal to crude and rolled steel, while employing a labour force of 183,000 wage workers. By 1929-1930, with production slightly down to 25.7 million tons, the labour force had been cut to 144,000. *Labour productivity had therefore increased from 148 tons per worker annually to nearly 192 tons.*

Such drastic reductions in the labour force of the major industries had an immediate effect on the unemployment rate. The number of workers employed in industry actually fell from 9.4 million in 1925 (the peak of the pre-rationalisation boom) to 8.7 million in 1928, the year in which industrial output in the Weimar Republic reached its maximum. And since redundancies tended to occur in those industries and plants where labour was strongly organised, the trade unions were particularly hard-hit by rationalisation. 1926 was an especially lean year, with the proportion of trade unionists out of work increasing from 6.7% to 18%.*

These then were the major advantages accruing to German big business as a direct result of its rationalisation and concentration of industry and banking between 1925 and 1928. But these measures were far from ensuring a prolonged period of stability and prosperity for German capitalism. Firstly it should be pointed out that quite apart from their excessive reliance on foreign (mainly US) credits to finance their modernisation programmes,** the trusts depended on a steadily rising demand for their products to keep their plant utilisation at or near the optimum point, and therefore their costs at a minimum. Heavy industry in particular found its fortunes directly linked to the state of the world market, since its produce was either directly exported, or was purchased by the equally export-oriented German manufacturing industry.

So while world trade, sustained by the roaring US boom, continued to expand, the basically precarious position of the German economy remained masked. Exports in finished manufactures (an industry which enjoyed the full advantages of rationalisation

---

* Total unemployment figures for the period were: 1924: 0.4 million: 1925: 0.2 million; 1926: 2 million; 1927: 0.35 million; 1928: 0.6 million. Not surprisingly, the year of the most intense rationalisation and monopoly concentration was also one in which the jobless rate climbed to its highest point before the onset of the great crisis in 1929-1930.

** Of the 1.8 milliard marks loaned up to 1928 by overseas investors to private industrial undertakings in Germany, 0.8 milliards was borrowed by the mining and steels combines, and another 0.4 milliards by the electrical engineering industry. And overall, the German economy was dependent on foreign loans to a remarkable degree for its capital accumulation. In 1927, an especially good year for domestic investment, German-owned accumulated capital was less than twice that imported from abroad, 7.6 milliard marks as against 4.4. Once again we can see that the foreign capital market — principally that of the USA — was a prime factor in not only stabilising the German economy, but in sustaining its growth.

since the latter not only cut manufacturers' costs, but those of their raw materials suppliers) exceeded the best pre-war levels, rising from 6,630 million marks in 1925 to 7,550 million 1927. The strategic importance of manufacturing for the German economy is self-evident when we note that in 1927, the total value of all German exports was 10,224 million marks! A contraction in demand either in Europe or the USA on the one hand, or a drying up of the sources of foreign credit on the other, would obviously plunge German industry into a profound organic crisis.

There were however, other tendencies towards crisis that emerged even prior to the world slump of 1929. Rationalisation and concentration inevitably led to what Marx termed the increased organic composition of capital,* a process whereby money expended on labour power (variable capital) declines proportionally to that laid out on the means of production, raw materials etc. (constant capital). The never-ending quest of the employer for lower costs drives him to seek ways of increasing the productivity of labour by more efficient work-organisation and technical innovation. In turn, this means that less living labour power is poured into each newly-created commodity, or conversely, that the same amount of labour power now spreads itself over a greater number of commodities. This is indeed one of the aims of all rationalisation procedures. But herein lies the great contradiction of the capitalist mode of production. In seeking to produce as cheaply as possible, the employer of necessity tends to reduce the amount of surplus value contained in the individual commodity, and realised upon its sale. Unless the rate of surplus value is increased (either in relative terms by shortening that portion of the working day in which the worker reproduces the value of his own labour power — i.e. wages — or absolutely, by lengthening the working day) the rate of profit will tend to fall (the rate of profit being the percentage return on capital employed). In fact, it may continue to fall even if the rate of surplus value is increased.

While Marx speaks of the tendency for different rates of profit (this being the result of varying organic composition of capitals) to equalize themselves around the average rate of profit for the aggregate of capitals, it is important to remember that this is a *tendency,* and can be counteracted for considerable periods of time by other factors. Different rates of profit tend to become equal *as a result of a struggle between capitals,* in which those with the lower rate of profit (i.e. where the organic composition of capital is highest, the rate of surplus value being the same) seek to appropriate a portion of the surplus value accruing to capitals

* The relevant sections of Marx's *Capital* are to be found in Volume III, Parts II and III *(Conversion of Profit into Average Profit, the Law of the Tendency of the Rate of Profit to Fall,* pp.140-261, Moscow, 1962.)

where the rate of profit is above the average. This can be done by the owners of capitals with a low profit rate raising their prices above the value embodied within them in human labour time, thereby increasing the return on their invested capital. But since no new real values are created by mere price manipulations, the net result of this practice (which today would be called inflationary) is simply to increase the prices paid by the purchasers of this capitalist's commodities, whether they be means of production, in which case they become part of the costs of another capitalist, or consumption goods, thereby necessitating greater expenditure on the part of the workers.

Though rationalisation cut the production costs of German industry, enabling it to compete more effectively on the world market, it simultaneously reduced the proportion of capital expenditure which created its profits. With a lending rate of about 7% on its loans from the United States, industry therefore came under severe pressure to defend its profit margins, as can be gathered from the average rates of profit in the following branches of industry in the period 1924-27: coal and iron: 3.8%; chemicals: 4.3%; machine production: 6.2%; electrical engineering: 6.7%; artificial silk: 9.9%; breweries: 11.6%. (The average for industry as a whole was 7.6% while dividends between 1925 and 1927 averaged 5%, compared with 8.4% in the last pre-war year). What surely stands out is the precarious position of Germany's two primary producing industries, coal and iron, for any disruption of production here would clearly have immediate repercussions throughout the entire economy, as indeed proved to be the case after 1929. Mining and steel production were also the two industries whose organic composition of capital was highest, reflected in its exceedingly low rate of profit, so that in turn, this low rate of profit inhibited capital accumulation, and threw the trusts into even greater dependence on the banks and foreign loans for new investment.

Since as the figures already quoted suggest, it is in heavy industry where the lowest rates of profit are normally found, and, where, therefore, the pressures will be most compelling to force them up* by raising the prices of the final product, it also follows

* Marx also refers to another means of equalising the profit rate, namely the migration of capitals away from areas where the rate of profit is low to those where it is higher. Yet here too, the capitalist can encounter a series of pitfalls. Firstly capital tied up in heavy industries such as mining or steel does not lend itself to employment elsewhere. The capitalist must therefore either find a buyer (unlikely in view of its low rate of profit, unless the state is prepared to nationalise his firm with good compensation, as in the case of the British Labour government of 1945-50) or as in a period of acute depression, sell it off as scrap. Then there is a further difficulty, concerning not so much the individual capitalist as the entire class of employers. If capital migrates from industries producing the means of production (department I) to those producing consumption goods (department II) in the search for a higher rate

that if, as in the case of the Ruhr coal, iron and steel industry, the producers are organised in trusts and monopolies, buyers will either have to accept these increased prices or cease or curtail production through a lack of raw materials, fuel and means of production. If such capitalists producing consumer goods absorb these price increases charged by the capitalists with a lower rate of profit, then it must necessarily lead to a reduction in their mass profit, and hence rate of profit. Or they can pass the increased cost on in the form of higher prices, which will then have to be met by the consumer, who will, more often than not, be a worker. In his turn, if he is organised in a trade union, and the political regime of the country concerned permits such action, the worker will then seek to protect his own standard of living (which is at once threatened. if not undermined, by such price increases in the necessities of life) by securing a higher price for the sale of his own labour power, either through collective bargaining or, if this proves unsuccessful, strike action. And so, unless the second capitalist does indeed absorb the price increase charged by the first, the wheel has turned full circle. Our original capitalist, after securing an increase in the mass and rate of his profit by the device of raising the prices of his products above their value, now discovers the rate declining again as his mounting wages bill erodes his mass of profit. He must either put up his prices once again, thus making his product less competitive, or he must absorb the increase in wages which he has conceded (on pain of strike action or loss of some of his labour force to higher paid firms) to his workers. We can therefore see that attempts to maintain or increase profit rates by the expedient of price increases are counter-productive and therefore inflationary where capitalists producing consumer goods are able to recoup the portion of surplus value appropriated by the heavy industrialist through the simple device of charging higher prices to the consumer, and where the workers respond in kind by demanding and winning higher wages. Nazi Germany provides us with the classic case of heavy industry seeking, and for a time successfully, to overcome the problem of low profit rates by ensuring, through the intervention of the state, that neither light industry nor the working class is able to take the measures outlined above in order to defend their profit rates and real wages respectively. Trade unions had to be destroyed, and with them the bargaining power of the proletariat, before serious inroads could be made on this most pressing problem of German heavy industry. Likewise the consumer-oriented capitalists had to be expropriated politically

of profit, then this will tend to disrupt the equilibrium between these two intimately inter-related spheres of production, causing a famine in the means of production, and an over-production of consumption goods.

and allotted a far more humble share in the total surplus value extracted from the working class. Nor must we overlook the strategic imperialist considerations of such a policy. The Third Reich valued iron smelters, coal producers, and the makers of tanks far more than it did artificial silk manufacturers.

And even should the capitalist class succeed, either by improved technology which cheapens the price of the necessities of life (and therefore of labour power) or by depressing the wages and living standards of the masses, in raising the rate of surplus value (i.e. in shortening the portion of the working day during which the worker reproduces the value equivalent of his own wages), then this by no means removes the basis of this antagonism. If technology is improved, then this means that more constant capital and less living human labour will be required to produce the same, or even more commodities. Therefore the organic composition of capital rises, while the mass of surplus value may fall, even though the rate has risen. The final result will be a decline in the rate of profit. Likewise with a cut in the consumption of the masses. This will, as the experience of Nazi Germany has shown, produce a sharp increase in the accumulation fund of the capitalists, which will return to them in the form of increased profits (since the wages fund has now been reduced). However in the next cycle of production, this extra revenue reappears, no longer as additional profit increasing the capitalists' rate of profit (as it did on the previous cycle) but as *capital* only a small portion of which, if any, will be variable capital, and therefore capable of expanding rather than reproducing its value. Thus yet again, the basic tendency of the rate of profit to fall reasserts itself, and the capitalist is once more driven to seek fresh measures to arrest its decline. And there is in fact no long-term solution that can overcome this contradiction on the basis of the capitalist mode of production, since the latter's driving force is not the creation of use values for human needs, but exchange values for profit.

We must say at this juncture that the foregoing is by no means a digression from our central investigation, which is to unravel those social, political and economic forces and processes which culminated in the victory of national socialism. These 'chemically pure' abstractions, derived from the labour theory of value, assume a living, concrete character when employed to illuminate the problems confronting German heavy industry in the Weimar Republic, and help to establish on a rigorous scientific basis the reasons why its leaders were finally compelled to turn towards fascism in an attempt to overcome them.

Profitability and the formation of new capital were also undermined from another quarter. As we have stressed on many occasions, the German bourgeoisie was only able to cling onto the state power in the winter of 1918-1919 through making a series of concessions which while not renouncing the principle of private property in the means of production (it was in fact implicitly upheld by Article 153 of the Weimar Constitution), imposed severe financial burdens on employers by compelling them to contribute heavily to state social welfare schemes for their workers. Government, state and communal (municipal) expenditure on social welfare had, by 1926, increased nearly four-fold on the last pre-war year, an indication of the degree to which even the most reactionary employers had been forced to retreat — temporarily — from their stand of intransigent opposition to 'Marxist'-inspired social legislation. Differences frequently came to light in the leadership of the Federation of German industries as to what policy to adopt towards the trade unions. Paul Silverberg, an advocate of collaboration with the reformist leaders — on very well-defined terms — outlined his views on this question to a meeting of the Federation on September, 4, 1926:

> ...it must be fully and gratefully recognised that the old trade unions ...have earned great credit by their cooperation in leading back to constitutionalism that revolutionary movement of workers and soldiers ...We would hope that the present so-called clearing up will not stop here. One should recognise that the overwhelming majority of the German working class give their political allegiance to the SPD and a minority to the Centre Party ...It is intolerable and shameful that such a large party as the SPD should remain more or less in irresponsible opposition. It has been said that one cannot govern against the workers. If this is so, one must face up to the consequences — one cannot govern without the social democrats, they must be brought into responsible cooperation. And they will perish as a party if they do not make up their minds to this effect. We say this on the assumption that the social democrats have the courage to learn the lesson of history — they have neither the power, the vigour nor the capability to rule and lead the state. It is not done by filling the streets with muscle and shouting. We live in a world organised on capitalist economics and culture. If the SPD will abandon its radical doctrines and the disruptive politics of the streets, they will be able to join with the employers in leading Germany and the German economy once again to success.

And this, remember, was a speech made in the middle of a boom by a relative liberal! Silverberg was something of a lone wolf amongst the big industrialists, who were bitterly critical of the then ruling all-bourgeois coalition under Dr. Marx. They passed a resolution at the same meeting condemning the government for its failure to respond

> even to those suggestions which had almost unanimous approval in economic circles and authoritative quarters. [The Federation, obviously troubled by the continued lack of funds for investment, also renewed] its demand for a final settlement of the question of financial

compensation with a view to the reduction of the burden of taxation nationally and locally to facilitate the essential creation of new capital and restore the profitability of the economy. The Federation [the resolution went on] recognising the necessity of making provision for those not able to work, is nevertheless apprehensive about too generous distribution of social benefits. It warns against the premature repeal of a labour law and for premature restriction of hours of work. This could make our country, heavily burdened as it is with reparation payments, uncompetitive in world markets.

To what extent Weimar's social legislation further eroded the already slender profit margins of heavy industry can be seen from the examples of three Ruhr combines. In 1926, the following companies paid these proportions of their total profits to the government in the form of either taxes or social welfare contributions: *Vereinigte Stahlwerke:* 55% Klöckner: 46% Krupp AG: 77%.*

Bearing in mind that in addition to the burdens imposed on industrialists and agrarians by the republic's welfare programmes, social democratic administrations in the states and communes were borrowing heavily from abroad to finance their own social reforms for the working class, we can appreciate why Schact, as President of the *Reichsbank* and therefore responsible for Germany's solvency, openly doubted, from a capitalist point of view, the wisdom of this policy being pursued by the SPD. The truth of the matter was that German capitalism was in no position to make such far-reaching concessions to the proletariat:

> While every effort must be made ...not to allow a setback of civilisation ...there is at the same time an absolute necessity for the very greatest economy in public expenditure. If public institutions are to be financed at all with foreign capital, *it must only be those which contribute in the first instance to increasing the level of production of the country, and not such as serve mere luxury or avoidable increases of consumption.* [sic!] The Reichsbank has been continuously at pains to diffuse such views and to make them effective ...It goes without saying that borrowed capital, which is invested in the improvement of production, can only be paid off in the course of time by annual payments out of regular profits. *Herein lies the need for differentiation in the manner of employment of the capital.* Only capital which is productively invested will yield the required payments. *Foreign loans contracted for unproductive consumption or luxury purposes will only be tolerable if the general increase in production is large enough to make it possible to finance this amortization out of the surplus and savings of the national product as a whole.*[12] (emphasis added)

We should bear in mind that by 'luxuries' and 'avoidable con-

---

* Landed property-owners found Weimar's social welfare legislation no less irksome. A survey of nine Westphalian farms showed that whereas in 1913-1914, taxes and social contributions amounted to but 20.36% of their income, in 1925-1926 this ratio had tripled to 64.57%. Here indeed was common economic and political ground for an alliance between agrarians and industrialists against the Weimar Republic.

sumption' Schact (who three years after he wrote these lines, went over to the Nazis) meant social democratic expenditure on clinics, nurseries, cultural facilities, adult workers' education, welfare for the poor and unemployed etc. All these projects had either to be severely curtailed or scrapped, Schact argued, if German big business was to regain its lost European supremacy and former colonies.*

Finally, there was the highly controversial issue of wages. Here too, the legacy of the November Revolution continued to plague agrarian and industrialist alike. The enhanced bargaining power of the trade unions (codified both in the November 1918 Working Agreement and Articles 159 and 165 of the constitution), together with a policy of government support for the maintenance of wage rates, prevented heavy industry indulging in the kind of wage cutting necessary to combat declining profit margins and compensate for greatly increased expenditures on loan repayments, taxes and welfare contributions, not to speak of the national levies imposed by reparations. With wages now subject, in the event of a dispute, to the veto of a referee appointed by the Labour Ministry, and most cabinets dependent for their survival on the toleration, if not open support, of social democracy, the practice of awarding what were known in industrialist circles as 'political wages' became an established one for the duration of the boom.

Wage rates were subject to the upwards pressure of trade union militancy, but not to the reverse pressure of unemployment, as can be seen from the following table:

Real Wages (% of 1913)

Year	Skilled	Unskilled	Unemployed
1913	100	100	—
1922	64	86	150,000
1923	58	72	140,000 (summer)
1924	76	87	400,000
1925	92	102	200,000
1926	91	101	2,000,000
1927	93	105	350,000

* Not that Schact failed to appreciate the force of circumstances that led to such a policy being adopted by the social democrats. 'The end of the war had been attended in Germany itself by revolutionary portents and had raised revolutionary [i.e. social democratic] politicians to posts of responsibility. Revolutionaries, however, are only kept within bounds if the masses can perceive some outward advantages to themselves. Instead of making up their minds, after their defeat, to live and manage on the most modest and economical basis, everyone succumbed to the demands for increased standards of living and a good time in general. At the head and front were

The cumulative effect of all these factors was to divert that proportion of the national income which would have otherwise accrued to capital in the form of new investment, into public expenditure on social services and increased private consumption (especially by the lower income groups who gained from the rise in real wages) on the one hand, and repayment and servicing of foreign loans on the other.* Only under the rule of the Nazis, whose destruction of the trade unions removed wage rates from the realm of collective bargaining and market demand, did this trend become reversed. From a peak of 64% in 1932, the share of wages and salaries in the national income declined, after five years of Nazi tyranny over the working class, to 57% in 1938. Gross investment (which hinged to a large extent on the ratio of distribution of the national income between labour and capital) meanwhile rose from 18% in 1928, and after a record low of 9% in 1932, to 23% by 1937.

Since all these contradictions were concentrated most acutely at the heavy industrial core of the German economy, it was from here that the greatest pressures were mounted to break the resistance of organised labour as a necessary prelude to wage cutting, increased exploitation of labour and the severe curtailment of expenditure on welfare schemes. Certainly, the balance of forces both within the Reichstag and successive cabinets between 1924 and 1928 favoured such an aggressive policy by the leaders of heavy indusry. The elections of May 1924 gave a clear majority to the main bourgeois-agrarian parties, placing further strains on the already fragile Weimar alliance of the SPD, Centre and DDP. Deputies in the new Reichstag were distributed as follows: SPD 100; KPD 62; Centre 64; BVP 21; DDP 28; DVP 45; DNVP 95; Landbund (a purely agrarian splinter from the DNVP which by this time was coming more under the influence of ultra-reactionary industrialists led by Hugenberg, a director of Krupp AG) 10; Economic Party 10; Racist Bloc (dominated by the

the municipal corporations with a preponderance of social democratic circles and those with similiar tendencies'. (H. Schact: *My First Seventy-Five Years*, pp.217-218.)

Elsewhere Schact recalled that 'the battle for votes impelled all parties without exception, but especially those of the left, to let as much foreign money as possible into the country in order to create cultural and social comforts for the people' (H. Schact: *The Magic of Money*, p.47, London, 1967.)

* At the peak of the post-war boom, in 1928, 67.7% of the national income was distributed in the form of wages, salaries and pensions, while of the remainder, 30.4% accrued to the owners of property. This marked a drastic diminution of capital's share in the national product, which in 1913, had been 49.7% as against 48.3% to wages, salaries and pensions. In the crisis which began in 1929, big business found such a division of the spoils of labour intolerable. National socialism was the means it used to restore the return on capital which it enjoyed in the last years of Imperial Germany.

NSDAP) 32. Despite the record vote for the KPD — 3.7 million
— and the impressive electoral debut of the Nazis — 1.8 million
votes — the underlying trend was towards the bourgeois centre.
Had the elections been held six months earlier in the wake of the
1923 autumn crisis, support for the poles of revolution and
counter-revolution would have been appreciably greater, and by
the same token, markedly smaller for the SPD on the left and the
main bourgeois parties on the right. This movement away from
the extremes towards the centre continued at the elections held
seven months later on December 7. The KPD vote fell away by
900,000, while that of the social democrats rose by 1.8 million to
give the SPD 131 Reichstag deputies. On the right, this process of
stabilisation appears at first sight to be contradicted by the
increased vote for the DNVP (up by 0.5 million), a party which
had still to declare its loyalty to the Republic (even though certain
of its leaders were prepared to enter an all-bourgeois cabinet that
leaned firmly to the right.) In contrast to the elections of June
1920, when the DNVP gained at the expense of parties to its left
(i.e. the DDP and the DVP) on May 4, 1924, the main source of
its increment was former Nazi voters edging their way back to the
main stream of nationalist politics (not all the Nazi party's lost 0.9
million votes accrued to the DNVP however, since the Economic
Party, only slightly less strident in its anti-semitic and anti-
capitalist demagogy than the NSDAP, increased its vote by more
than 300,000). At the same time, and as part of this trend towards
bourgeois consolidation, the DVP also gained votes, as did even
the DDP, confirming the point made in Chapter Thirteen that for
most of the lifetime of the Weimar Republic, even the more
conservative and nationalist layers of the petty-bourgeoisie were
by no means irrevocably committed to militant anti-Marxism.*

As a result of these two election victories for the bourgeois
centre and right, Germany between 1924 and 1928 was ruled by a
series of coalitions which completely excluded the representatives
of the SPD. The policy of Schacht and Stresemann had been
vindicated. Moreover, with the Centre Party and the DDP discreetly disengaging themselves from their weakened social
democratic partner, the road was now clear for the entry of the
DNVP into a rightwards-oriented bourgeois-Junker cabinet.
First under Dr Hans Luther in 1925, and then under Wilhelm

---

* This steady movement away from right-wing extremism continued right up to the
onset of the 1929 crisis. In the Reichstag elections of May 20, 1928, in which the two
workers parties polled 39.4% of the total vote (SPD 9.1 million, KPD 3.3 million)
the DNVP voted declined by nearly 1.9 million, while the Nazis slipped yet again to
810,000. It was only due to the failure of the KPD leadership to unite the working
class behind a policy of revolutionary struggle against monopoly capitalism that
drove the petty-bourgeois masses back towards the right and into the eager embrace
of the Nazis.

Marx of the Centre Party throughout 1927 and until the appointment of the social democrat Hermann Müller as chancellor in
June 1928, the ultra-reactionaries of the DNVP exercised a
powerful grip on the conduct of government affairs.

Yet when armed with what must have seemed to them to be a
clear mandate from the electorate to redress the balance of class
and political forces within the republic, the spokesmen of heavy
industry and the agrarians found themselves unable to convert
their undoubted parliamentary supremacy into the degree of
domination over the proletariat which they had exercised and
enjoyed under the Empire. In other words, they encountered precisely the same apparently intractable obstacle that had thwarted
Kapp's attempt to undo all the modest gains of the November
Revolution — the power of the organised labour movement.
Frustration with Stresemann's moderate policy had already led
early in 1924 to the defection of a sizable group of rightists
(including the Ruhr industrialists Klonne, Sorge, Becker and, of
course, the ubiquitous Quaatz and Vögler) to the DNVP, where
under the aggressive leadership of press magnate and former
Ruhr industrialist Alfred Hugenberg, the party was progressively
weakening its exclusive ties with the big agrarians and transforming itself primarily into an ultra-reactionary mouthpiece of
heavy industry. Nor was this all. While the Vögler group made its
way towards or into the DNVP, another faction within the
DVP made a determined bid to take over the leadership of the
party, which they deemed to be heading for ruin under
Stresemann's chairmanship. Flick, and until his death on April
10, 1924, Stinnes, attempted to blackmail Stresemann by
threatening to cut off heavy industry's much needed financial
contributions to the party's treasury, a move which Stresemann
only narrowly averted at the DVP congress in March.

There were other pointers as to the direction of thinking
among leaders of industry. Dr Carl Duisberg, whom we first saw
in 1918 advocating a policy of uninhibited collaboration with the
social democrats, spoke in very different terms when he addressed
the 1925 conference of the Federation of Germany Industry, the
republic's most influential business organisation:

> Be united, united, united. This should be the uninterrupted call to the
> parties in the Reichstag. We hope that our words of today will work,
> and will find the strong man who will finally bring everyone under one
> umbrella, for he is always necessary for us Germans as we have seen in
> the case of Bismarck.

But the only Bismarck on the horizon was the ageing former
Field Marshal Paul von Hindenburg, who in the same year was
elected successor to the deceased Ebert as President of the
republic. While his undisguised monarchist sympathies rendered

him a potentially pliant tool in the hands of the extreme right, Hindenburg was obviously incapable of introducing under his own auspices the reforms desired by industrialists like Duisberg:

> If Germany is again to be great, all classes of our people must come to the realisation that leaders are necessary who can act without concern for the caprices of the masses ...it is to be hoped that there will be found in Germany the necessary number of such personalites who will be the leaders of that nation. Only then will she rise from the deepest misery to her former greatness ...There is no doubt that the German economy can only exist and fulfill its duties, if the burden of salaries, wages, taxes, freights, and — not least — impositions for social security, which it must carry, are limited. German trade unions must from now on hold as their primary duty giving consideration, together with employers, to increasing production. The wage and salary question [will no longer be] of exclusive importance as it unfortunately still is today.

We can recognise here not only the language of political reaction, *but of rationalisation*, which in the case of Duisberg, as with many fellow monopoly capitalists, and bankers such as Schacht, became fused with the former into a single bitterly anti-working class doctrine. Still lacking however, were the political forces willing and able to make these reactionary plans of dictatorship and increased exploitation of the proletariat a reality. The political problems of heavy industry were highlighted in 1927 by the enactment of legislation guaranteeing regular weekly benefits to the unemployed. Ironically, this measure, which angered wide circles of the German business world because of its violation of the bourgeois principle of 'self help', was approved by a cabinet which contained no fewer than four representatives of the DNVP, and another two from the DVP. Between them, they outnumbered their Catholic and non-party cabinet partners, and could have, theoretically, blocked the proposed legislation by threatening to either vote it down or withdraw from the cabinet. In the event they did neither, and the bill became law on July 16, 1927. Already smarting under the burdens imposed by existing social welfare payments, the new act convinced a group of heavy industrialists that continued retreats before the power of organised labour were placing the profitability of the whole economy at risk. Under the leadership of Vögler of the Flick Steel Combine and Paul Reusch of *Gute Hoffnungshutte* steel works, they took control of the highly influential North West Group of the Association of German Iron and Steel Industries, and proceeded to use it as a base from which to launch their offensive against the workers of the Ruhr. At the 1927 conference of the Federation of German Industry, this same faction blocked a proposal by the liberal Jewish banker Paul Silverberg, speaking for the 'moderates', to resume the long-since abandoned collaboration with the ADGB. That same year, in August,

Reusch and Vögler formed their *Ruhrlade,* a circle of twelve Ruhr industrialists who met monthly on an informal basis to discuss common economic and political problems, and to prepare for what they considered to be a decisive battle with the Ruhr workers over the renewal of their 1928 wage contracts. And a year earlier, Reusch, together with industrialist Robert Bosch, had founded his 'League for the Renewal of the Reich', which had as its aim the 'reform' of the Weimar Consitution along more authoritarian lines. In its inaugural manifesto, the League declared:

> In the hour of danger, there can be no other slogan but that of strengthening the state. The imperial government must have decision-making powers in relation to all the general important questions. Apart from foreign policy, law and military affairs, it is concerned with finance and all other determinative economic issues. Such an empire must have the power that once built the old empire and that should now serve the common cause.

Here we have the beginnings not only of a move towards the subversion of the existing Weimar Constitution, which upheld the right of the state and communal authorities to undertake a wide range of social and economic reforms (something that obviously provoked opposition from industrial and financial circles) but of a renewal of imperialist-colonialist tendencies within the monopoly bourgeoisie. These were succinctly summarised by Schacht when he wrote in 1927 that

> It must be possible to make some colonial territory available for settlement and exploitation by the German people, so as to provide Germany with the possibility of regular emigration and to facilitate the solution of the problem of her food supply.[13]

But once again, the question was — how? Just as the monopolist bourgeoisie lacked the internal political reserves to impose a crushing defeat on its domestic foes, so it lacked the military means with which to regain what it had lost in the world war. Fears concerning the durability of the boom (which began to gain currency after 1927)* and an increasing awareness that the time was drawing near when the leaders of the economy would have to claim back from the working class what it had been compelled, on pain of expropriation, to yield in 1918 and 1919, now became allied with a growing restiveness about German capitalism's subordinate position in European politics, an inferiority which was in potentially explosive contradiction with Germany's economic and especially industrial preponderance in

---

* In November 1928, at a time when reformists were still sunning themselves in the boom, and SPD theoreticians such as Rudolf Hilferding were writing about the merits of a crisis-free 'organised capitalism', Stresemann warned: 'I must ask you all to remember that during the past years we have been living on borrowed money. If a crisis were to arise and the Americans call in their short-term loans we should be faced with bankruptcy'. Which is exactly what did happen a year later.

the continent.

This chronic imbalance can be depicted graphically, measuring Germany against its main imperialist rival, France. (All figures are for 1929 unless otherwise stated)

Factor	Unit	Germany	France
Population	mill. inhab.	64.0	41.2
Motive Power in Industry	mill. h.p.	18.1 (1925)	11.7 (1926)
Share of World Industrial Production	per cent	12.6	7.6
Steel Output	mill. tons	16.2	9.7
Export of Manufactured Goods	bill. dollars	2.34	1.23
Foreign Investments	bill. francs	5.0 (1930)	31.4 (1930)
Merchant Fleet	mill. tons	4.1	3.4
Armed Forces: Navy, total tonnage	thous. tons	99.6	552.3
Army	thous. men	100.5	563.0
Population of Colonies	mill. inhab.	—	65 1

Thus Germany had either re-established or maintained its pre-war supremacy over France in every sphere except that of foreign investment, which showed a catastrophic decline from its pre-1914 peak of 44.0 billion francs. And this related directly to those factors in which France now towered over Germany — namely in the military and colonial spheres. Defeat in 1918 led inexorably to German capital being driven out of regions where it had already established itself, and exclusion from others where Allied capital was already supreme. Disarmed and diplomatically isolated, post-1918 German imperialism again found itself hemmed in on all sides, very much as it had done towards the close of the Bismarck era, only now the terms forced on the country's leaders at Versailles denied it the means to clear a new road in Europe and overseas for German capital. To break this deadlock, German imperialism required a regime which while relentlessly pursuing a policy of militarisation of the population and re-armament, switched its strategic orientation away from yet another debilitating collision with the Entente powers, and towards the Soviet east, where far from meeting with their opposition, a German offensive could justifiably expect to win the approval of the Allied imperialists.

The acuteness of this contradiction could not but imprint itself on the consciousness of the heavy industrialists; one of whom, Gustav Krupp, declared:

We need markets, but the markets of the world are closed to us. Great

Britain has erected tariff walls. In France, Italy, Sweden, the Balkans, in fact everywhere, German trade is up against barriers which little by little are becoming insuperable.

Which was precisely the point being hammered home by Hitler in a series of speeches to right wing business and political leaders during the rationalisation period (e.g. his address to the Hamburg National Club in February 1926) and in the sequel to *Mein Kampf,* written in 1928, which is largely devoted to foreign policy questions:

The more market difficulties increase, the more bitterly will the struggle for the remaining ones be waged. Although the primary weapons of this struggle lie in pricing and in the quality of the goods with which the nations competitively try to undersell each other, in the end the ultimate weapons even here lie in the sword ...If a really vigorous people believes that it cannot conquer another with peaceful means, or if an economically weak people does not wish to let itself be killed off by an economically stronger one ...then in both cases the vapours of economic phraseology will be suddenly torn asunder and war, that is, the continuation of politics by other means, steps into its place [Those who do not understand this] open the way to decay in which the inner strength of such a people swiftly disappears, all racial and moral and folk values are earmarked for destruction, ideals are undermined, and in the end the pre-requisites which a people urgently needs in order to take upon itself the ultimate consequences of the struggle for world markets is eliminated. Weakened by a vicious pacifism, peoples will no longer be ready to fight for markets for their [sic!] good with the shedding of their blood ...The sword had to stand before the plough and an army before economics.[14]

As the reader will readily appreciate, this is a purely imperialist programme, arrived at on the basis of what was, given Hitler's quasi-mystical political conceptions, a basically correct estimation of the economic dilemmas confronting German industry in the post-war era.

All save one of the conditions necessary for the forging of an alliance between big business and the Nazis were therefore maturing in Germany at the precise moment when the boom was at its peak. All conditions save one. And Wall Street was to provide it.

REFERENCES FOR CHAPTER FOURTEEN

[1] H. Schact: *The Stabilisation of the Mark*, p.76, London, 1927.
[2] H. Schact: *My First Seventy Six Years*, p.177.
[3] F. von Papen: *Memoirs*, pp.102-120.
[4] A. Grzesinski: *Inside Germany*, p.106, New York, 1939.
[5] H. Schact: Ibid, p.180.
[6] L. Trotsky: *Report on the Fourth World Congress [of the CI]*, December 28, 1922, delivered to a meeting of the communist fraction of the Tenth All-Union Congress of the Soviets, with non-party delegates attending. Re-printed in L. Trotsky: *The First Five Years of the Comintern*, Vol. II, pp.317-328, New York, 1953.
[7] L. Trotsky: Ibid, p.329.
[8] L. Trotsky: *Is the Time Ripe for the Slogan: The United States of Europe?* First Published in *Pravda*, June 30, 1923, reprinted in ibid, p.342.
[9] L. Trotsky: ibid, pp.342-343.
[10] L. Trotsky: ibid, p.344.
[11] H. Schact: ibid, p.95.
[12] H. Schact: *The Stabilisation of the Mark*, pp.220-228.
[13] H. Schact: ibid, p.244.
[14] *Hitler's Secret Book*, pp.22-99.

Two Crises: The Election of Hindenburg and the Princes Referendum.

Two episodes which occurred in the period of — for Weimar Germany — relative political stability between 1924 and 1928 serve to indicate how little the ruling class had succeeded in resolving the internal political differences which had manifested themselves so starkly in the Kapp Putsch and again in the great crisis of 1923. And they also provided ample evidence that temporary economic prosperity and the abatement of the revolutionary threat had done little or nothing to reconcile the hard core of Junkers and heavy industrialists to the political system established by the November Revolution, nor to the prominent role that the workers' movement played within it. The death of President Ebert on February 28, 1925, brought both of these questions to the fore, since the ruling class was neither able to agree on a single candidate to oppose those of the workers' parties, nor to formulate a common political programme on which such a candidate could campaign.

This disunity had indeed already evidenced itself before Ebert's death, since with a new Presidential election pending in the summer of 1925, representatives of the right-wing parties (DVP, DNVP, BVP and Economic Party) had met on February 12 to agree on a joint 'national' candidate. The rift was reflected first of all in the three names put forward at the meeting. Only one could be properly termed a 'civilian' — the DVP Mayor of the Ruhr town of Duisberg, Dr Karl Jarres. The other two were Army Chief of Staff von Seeckt and Defence Minister Otto Gessler. So even in a period of relative tranquility, the General Staff sought to sustain and protect its role of arbiter, even to the extent of running its own candidate for President of the Reich. But such a move was sure to cause great unease not only among the working class, which had bitter memories of the role of the military at the time of the Kapp crisis, and again in 1923, but liberal-democratic circles of the middle and ruling class. The choice of candidate was further complicated by the religious question, since even the ultra-right wing Bavarian Catholics of the BVP could not bring themselves to endorse a protestant nomination for the Presidency. The national bloc therefore began to disintegrate as the elections, scheduled for March 29, approached. Consequently, the ruling class, or rather its various warring factions, presented to the electorate no less than four candidates: Jarres (who emerged, after protracted negotiations between the DVP and DNVP, as the main 'national' candidate), Wilhelm Marx of the Centre Party, Dr Heinrich Held, Minister President of Bavaria and a leader of the BVP, and Dr Willy Hellpach of the DDP. And for good measure, the Nazis and their *volkisch* allies ran General Ludendorff.

For the working class the choice was much less complicated. They could vote for either Otto Braun, the social democratic Minister President of Prussia, or the Communist Party leader Ernst Thälmann. With such fragmentation on the right, it was scarcely surprising that no candidate secured a clear majority at the first ballot. Jarres, as expected, won the votes that in a Reichstag election would have gone to his two main sponsors, the DVP and the DNVP (he in fact secured 10.7 million). Party loyalties also prevailed in the cases of Marx, Hellpech and Held, with 3.8, 1.5 and 1 million votes respectively. The further decline in the fortunes of the Nazis was reflected in the paltry 200,000 votes cast for their candidate, Ludendorff.

On the left, the temporary consolidation of social democracy at the expense of the KPD, which first became visible in the Reichstag elections of December 1924, gathered pace, with Braun receiving 7.8 million votes against Thälmann's 1.8 (less than half the vote won by the KPD in the Reichstag elections a year previously). Under the provisions laid down by an act of 1920, new Presidential elections had to be held, in which the winner did not require an absolute majority. At once, a regroupment took place in both the social democratic left, and the bourgeois centre and right. A popular front-style Weimar coalition was hastily assembled between the reformists and the bourgeois democrats and Catholics, with Marx as its candidate. In theory, if the voting preferences of the first election were reproduced at the second, then Marx could expect to garner at least 13 million votes, enough to give him a clear lead of several millions over the best candidate of a splintered right. The 'Reich bloc' obviously required a more commanding figure than the nondescript and relatively unknown Jarres to rally the middle class masses to the national banner and the good fight against godless Marxism and the alien spirit of parliamentary democracy. For this was precisely the intention of those who prevailed upon Hindenburg to emerge from military retirement, at the age of 78, to run for Presidency of Europe's most crisis-prone state. Now, the Reich bloc hoped (with some justification) party labels and programmes would be cast aside by all 'national' Germans. In electing the victor of Tannenberg, they would not be voting for a party, nor even a man, but a symbol of a lost imperial past that under his leadership, could be recaptured. The popular front Republican bloc proved itself utterly impotent in the face of such a mobilisation of all that was backward, mystical and reactionary in the petty-bourgeoise. All they could offer the middle class was the same souped-up version of parliamentary democracy that had alienated wide layers of the middle class from social democracy and liberalism in the first years of the republic. Bourgeois and social democratic 'moderation' proved itself powerless to prevent the election of the man who eight years later presided over the liquidation of both bourgeois democracy and the SPD. In the second ballot, held on April 26, Marx succeeded in slightly increasing the vote of the Republican bloc to 13.7 million. But it was not enough. Hindenburg trumped him by just under one million votes, and even though this did not give him an overall majority (Thälmann on this occasion receiving 1.9 million) it was enough to place the enormously powerful office of President in the hands of the national right. But he remained a symbol, rather than an instrument of its unity, for even amongst the parties which had endorsed his candidature, there was unease that Hindenburg's election would irrevocably drive the social democrats into opposition, possibly attracting to them a section of the bourgeois democrats and Catholics. Stresemann, for one, reasoned thus, only becoming reconciled, in the best traditions of German liberalism, to the new President when it became clear that the social democrats were in fact contemplating no such drastic action. And Hindenburg was adroit enough in his early months of office not to give the SPD and its bourgeois allies any grounds for abandoning their policy of 'toleration' of the centre-right coalitions that ruled Germany between 1924 and 1928. Stresemann noted in his diary that the new President 'makes a powerful impression ...For the time being I don't have the feeling that Hindenburg will be under the influence of any political camarilla, at least not consciously.' The significance of Hindenburg's election was given an altogether different evaluation by an aspiring member of the 'political camarilla', von Papen. Very much in keeping with his own rigidly authoritarian views, he had dissociated himself from his party's own candidate, the Catholic Marx, and had come out openly in support of Hindenburg the protestant: 'With some friends I issued a declaration in the middle of April 1925 ...we pointed out that important sections of the population had lost faith in the type of society sought by the Weimar Coalition [here Papen is quite right], based as it was, to too great an extent, on rationalistic and atheistic premises ...Calling for a return to the old Christian conception of government, we proclaimed once again Germany's historical duty to act as the watchman and bulwark of the western tradition in the heart of Europe. We felt that the election of such a God-fearing and devout personality as Hindenburg would provide the best guarantee for a return to this fundamental policy'. (F. von Papen: *Memoirs*, p.108.)

Papen had also entertained high hopes of von Seeckt, who on several occasions before his resignation as chief of staff in 1926, had exerted a decisive influence on the course of German politics: 'I have always regretted that at this critical point in our history [Papen refers here to the crisis of Autumn 1923, when the army assumed emergency powers to deal with the revolutionary threat in central Germany] Seeckt did not make up his mind to bring order and authority into the chaotic state of our affairs ...how much better it would have been if the task of organising [sic! — an obvious euphemism for destroying] a working democracy had been entrusted to a man whose whole nature was opposed to dictatorship and war'. (Ibid, p.121.) But we know from Seeckt's expressed views on the role of the army in politics that while he considered it to be an indispensable support to established authority, it should never seek to initiate a drastic change of regime. (We must always remember that this principle does not apply to countries such as Chile and Greece — to cite but two recent examples — where the organised proletariat comprises a small proportion of the population, and where, therefore, a truly nazi-style mass mobilisation of the petty-bourgeoisie against the labour movement is not absolutely essential for the overturn of bourgeois democratic or popular front-type governments; though in Chile, wide sections of the middle class alienated from the Allende government did provide invaluable support for the military during the first days and weeks of their coup).

But many among the ruling class were slow to learn this axiom of counter-revolutionary strategy, as the crisis precipitated by the referendum on the expropriation of the former royal houses a year later revealed.

Ironically, this second crisis arose in part as a result of the frustration felt by extreme right-wing Junker and industrialist circles with the first year of Hindenburg's rule. We should remember that his election had been preceded by the formation of the first truly 'national' cabinet, containing five DNVP ministers, two each from the Centre and the DVP, and for the first time since the short-lived Müller government, which held office from the fall of Kapp to August 1920, no representatives of the bourgeois radicals, the DDP. But, as we have already noted, this cabinet, even when enjoying the obvious advantage of working under a President who made no attempt to conceal his ultra-reactionary, monarchist views, could make very litte headway in its proclaimed task of eroding the more objectionable political features of the Weimar system, and redressing the balance of power against the workers' movement. Sharp divergences over foregin policy, with the DNVP opposing closer relations with France, and Foreign Minister Stresemann's DVP generally favouring them, strained relations between the two main coalition partners, who parted company on October 26, 1925, following the Locarno Conference with the Allied powers. The DNVP, after less than a year of sharing office, went over to their accustomed position once more, thus greatly adding to the crisis already maturing over the controversial question of the Princes' property.

While the November Revolution — contrary to the wishes of Ebert — ended the reign of the Hohenzollerns, successive republican governments, even when they contained social democratic ministers, did nothing to challenge the privileges of the royal houses, whose enormous wealth had been filched from the German people over centuries of absolutist rule. Only in a few instances did state governments expropriate the Princes without compensation, a measure which was later declared to be illegal as it violated article 153 of the Weimar (republican) Constitution. Partly because it involved the still-vexed question of the monarch, but also because it challenged the right of private property in land (the main form of the Princes' wealth) the Communist Party campaign to secure a national referendum on the issue aroused intense feelings on both sides of the class divide, finally precipitating a crisis of near-Kapp proportions. The government crisis began in January 1926, when following a period of nearly two months without a Chancellor (Luther had resigned after the withdrawal of the DNVP from the cabinet the previous October, and no successor to him had been found) a group of Junkers and industrialists formulated a plan to fill the void created by Luther's departure with an extra-parliamentary dictatorship resting only on the authority of the President. Hindenburg, however, pre-empted such a move by re-appointing Luther Chancellor on January 20, 1926, who then proceeded to form a cabinet which leaned back to the centre, excluding the DNVP and including three representatives of the DDP. Over the next few days Hindenburg was subjected to considerable pressure from the usual ultra-rightist circles, for whom the influential and arch-reactionary Junker Oldenburg-Januschau, a close friend of the President, acted as chief spokesman. But to no avail. Hindenburg was not prepared to overturn the constitution and risk plunging Germany once more into civil war. The reaction from the far right was immediate and harsh. The *Berliner Börsen Zeitung* a semi-official organ of finance capital, closely linked with the army leadership was especially biting. It declared, on January 23, that 'the hope that our venerable President would succeed in unifying the multitude of centrifugal elements in our people, as he so ardently wishes, has not been fulfilled...' The President's failure to provide Germany with the leadership it required called for drastic action, since by parliamentary methods, 'one cannot force 60 million individuals into one direction, the individualistic German needs strong government'. (Precisely the message being hammered home by industrial leaders such as Duisberg, Vögler and company.) So if the President was unwilling or unable to act as those who had secured his election desired, then other ways had to be found. It was at this point that the KPD referendum campaign, which had been initiated in November 1925, began to play the central part in the gathering crisis. Such was the support it won amongst non-party and social democratic workers that the SPD leadership found it impossible to oppose the referendum. By March 17, more than 12.5 million signatures had been collected in support of the proposed referendum on the expropriation of the princes, and many must have been from people who had not voted for either the KPD or the SPD in the December 1924 Reichstag elections, since on that occasion, the two workers' parties aggregated only 10.6 million votes. Clearly, a section of the middle class were being drawn into the campaign, one in which, significantly, the KPD and the SPD were collaborating quite closely. Many on the right sensed the danger implicit in the success of the KPD's agitation against the princes. Hindenburg's old general staff comrades petitioned him to assume dictatorial powers, with or without the sanction of article 48, while on May 14, 1926, the ex-emperor's son, the crown prince Wilhelm (later to become a fervent Nazi and storm trooper) wrote to the President that the 'attacks on our Hohenzollern family against the judiciary and landed property, ultimately against all property, are but a systematic preparation for the Bolshevisation of Germany. There is still time for a determined government ready to apply its power ruthlessly to fight these destructive tendencies. But time is running out. If nothing is done, I see us being plunged into a bloody civil war, *whose outcome is quite unpredictable.'* (emphasis added)

The crown prince's frantic tone, and his anguished call for a 'determined government', were quite understandable. How could the new Luther cabinet 'apply its power ruthlessly' when three members of a party — the DDP — that was supporting the expropriation of the princes sat in it? The letter was a clear hint to the President that moves were afoot to unseat what the far right considered to be a weak-kneed government, and replace it by one not dependent for its survival on parliamentary majorities or the approval of the electorate. And such indeed was the case.

As an unrepentant monarchist, Hindenburg also had strong feelings about the referendum, declaring in a letter that it was 'a great injustice, and also an exhibition of a regrettable lack of traditional sentiment ...The legal recognition of property is the very foundation of a constitutional state, and the proposal of expropriation offends the principle of morality and justice'. Count Westarp, the DNVP leader, also stressed the connection between the campaign against monarchy and the property question: 'Beyond the proper issue of a fight against private property, the agitation was primarily directed against the cause of monarchism, to tear the monarchic idea firmly and irrevocably out of the hearts of our people'. Hindenburg also made his sympathies known on another highly controversial and emotionally-charged issue which flared up at this time — that of the naval flag. The Weimar Constitution had already compromised on this issue — one of enormous symbolical and indeed mystical significance for the monarchist right — by specifying a merchant ensign in the old imperial colours of red, white and black, with the Republic's colours — red—black—gold — tucked away in one corner of the flag. But even this did not satisfy the die-hard monarchists. They prevailed upon Luther to sanction and submit to the President a decree instructing all German embassies and consulates outside Europe to display the merchant ensign alongside the flag of the Republic, as well as on German ships in European seaports. When the decree became law on May 5, the storm that at once erupted around Luther's head quickly forced him to resign, after losing a vote of confidence by the narrow margin of 176 to 146, with the SPD and their DDP allies voting against, and the DNVP abstaining. Thus Germany once again found itself without a government, not only for lack of a unified bourgeois policy and leadership, but because for the first time in more than two years, the working class was now beginning to take the offensive again, albeit on a seemingly secondary question. It was at this moment that the ultra-right, led by among others, Hugenberg of the DNVP (who in the same year had denounced universal suffrage as a 'crime'), the Pan German League Chairman Class, and Vögler of the Steel Trust, decided to strike their blow. Many of the details of what followed remain obscure to this day, but the general shape of the plan seems to have been a more discreet version of the Kapp putsch, in which on this occasion, the plotters hoped to exploit both the President's undoubted good will and the paralysis endemic in government quarters. In the event, the coup never got off the ground. Counter-measures were already in hand in Prussia, which came under the control of the social democratic state administration and its Interior Minister, Carl Severing. Otto Braun authorised a series of raids on the homes of leading Ruhr industrialists including that of Vögler, and much incriminating material was in fact discovered, including plans for the dissolution of parliament (the pretext for which would have been the unearthing of a fictitious communist plot to stage a revolution). Death sentences were to be handed out to all those who resisted the new regime or attempted to revive the overthrown one, and there were proposals for co-ordinating army action with that of right-wing para-military groups (such as the *Stahlhelm*) to suppress the anticipated working class resistance to the coup. Stresemann (against whom the intended putsch was in part directed) leaves us a tantalisingly incomplete account of the events surrounding its preparation and detection.

The initial moves in the direction of a right-wing coup seem to have been made towards the end of 1925. An entry in Stresemann's diary for December 16 records that 'at the present meeting of the Association of German Iron and Steel Manufacturers, Herr Dr. Reichart [a DNVP Reichstag deputy and business manager of the Association who together with Stinnes in November 1918 negotiated the

Working Agreement with the ADGB] after the servants had left the room, made the following statement about the formation of the government: the great coalition would not succeed [i.e. it would prove impossible to form a Weimar coalition of social democrats, the Centre, DDP and DVP]. The central government to follow would possess neither a majority nor sufficient authority. Nothing else remained but to govern on the basis of article 48 and not to summón the Reichstag again until there were 13 months in the year. Borsig and Grobler agreed with R's remarks. R insisted it was necessary to get the President's [i.e. Hindenburg's] support for this view. A series of deputations must, therefore, be sent to Hindenburg to put these considerations before him. Baumer was to represent the Association of German Iron and Steel Manufacturers, because he could exercise most influence on Hindenburg, and was the best speaker.' (G. Stresemann: *Diaries, Letters and Papers,* Vol. II, pp.364-365, London, 1935-1940) It also appears possible, though the evidence is far more circumstantial, that the Prussian social democrats were taking their own counter-measures to pre-empt such a rightist coup:

'Von Campe [DVP fraction leader in the Prussian Landtag(state parliament)] gave me the following information: A German Nationalist [DNVP] deputy had told him that in the Prussian Ministry of State all preparations had been made for a Prussian dictatorship. In the Reich there was nothing for it but to govern on the basis of article 48, Prussia was for this development. In the Prussian Ministry of the Interior all preparations had been made for concentrating the entire political power on [SPD Interior Minister Carl] Severing. The deputy in question had expressed the hope that the DVP would not in that case stand on the side of the social democrats. I told Herr von Campe that the whole statement seemed to be very improbable in that form. But I could very well imagine that having regard to the extraordinary increase in the numbers of the Communists these preparations had been made in Prussia so as to be able to take measures in case of any serious unrest arising from intensified unemployment [now standing at around the 2 million mark].' (Ibid, p.365)

The next specific reference Stresemann makes to the activities of this right-wing group of industrialists is on May 11, when he notes that raids carried out by the Prussian police in Berlin on the homes of known ultra-rightists had unearthed plans for the installation of an open dictatorship. The houses of prominent Ruhr industrialists were obviously among those searched, since on June 3, at a meeting of the Reich Committee for Trade and Industry of the DVP, held at Erfurt, charges were made against Stresemann that he had either approved or supported the Prussian social democrats' moves to bloc the proposed coup, and had even connived at the visits paid to the industrialists' homes which had been authorised by Dr Abbeg, a leading official in the Prussian Ministry of the Interior. Naturally, these immensely rich and powerful capitalists were enraged, not only by the frustration of their coup, but the humiliation they had been made to endure at the hands of the social democrats, who remained in their eyes plebeian upstarts and traitors. And therefore we can also appreciate Stresemann's eagerness to refute this accusation, since it seemed to accord with the long-standing grievance of the Ruhr industrialists that the DVP chairman was 'soft' on the 'Marxists'. Stresemann replied that in a telephone conversation on the day of the raids with the Berlin Police Vicepresident, Dr Friedensburg, 'there was no mention of forthcoming domiciliary visits to the leading magnates of the Rhenish-Westphalian industry...' (Ibid, p.384)

Although Stresemann was not privy to the counter-measures of the Prussian social democrats, he was better informed of the activities of the Ruhr rightists. A memo, dated June 3, 1926, records that a 'Herr Dr F... explained in some detail that a large coup had been contemplated, the ultimate aim of which was to remove the President [who had by this time, because of his reluctance to violate the constitution, become an obstacle to the projected overturn] and appoint a Reich Commissar, who should in his turn appoint Commissars in all the constituent states and rule as a dictator, with his directory and without a parliament. As regards methods, Dr F said that the intention was, when the occasion arose, to capture Berlin, in conjunction with sections of the Reichswehr, and he referred to the so-called emergency decree, and the measures therein contemplated against those who opposed the new regime.' 'F' did not name the proposed new Chancellor, 'but ...merely remarked that I

[Stresemann] would be surprised if I knew who was contemplated for the post. However, he gave me the names of the other members of the directory: Hugenberg, Mohl, Luning, etc... I assumed from the very detailed information given me by Dr F ...that we had been directly confronted with a catastrophe...' (Ibid, p.385) Needless to say, Hugenberg had claimed for himself the ministry of Economics. Stresemann speaks of a 'catastrophe', and by this he clearly means a repeat version of the Kapp putsch, whose near-certain failure could have driven the social democrats into opposition. This thought had been uppermost in his mind throughout the last six or more years of his life (he died in 1929), and determined the course of his relations with not only the Ruhr industrialists, who never became reconciled to the SPD's influential role in the Weimar Republic, but representatives of the military opposition. For examply, an entry of February 28 records a visit paid on Stresemann by Captain Erhardt, who, ostensibly, came to thank him for his efforts in securing an amnesty for the participants in the Kapp putsch. The former Free Corps officer and ex-Nazi (he had broken with Hitler after the Munich putsch, when the latter opted for a legal struggle against Weimar) said to Stresemann that 'at the next elections we must combine under the watchword: United nationals against the non-nationals', to which Stresemann, who correctly understood this slogan to mean a renewed offensive against not only the KPD but the SPD, replied that the social democrats 'had done wholly national work ...' (Ibid, p.390)

Stresemann's account is interesting for two reasons. It indicates how deep were the divisions within the German ruling class between some of its leading political representatives, of whom Stresemann was among the most gifted and experienced, and the big employers, who were demanding and even actively preparing a more openly dictatorial form of government; and at the same time, the even more sharp antagonisms between the big bourgeoisie and the social democrats, the latter even being compelled to employ police and emergency measures to protect themselves from a rightist coup (though never for one moment seeking to rally their millions of working class supporters to defend the gains of the November Revolution).

The final vote for the referendum held on June 20, 1926, confirmed the trend detectable in the signature-collecting campaign of three months before. Then, the proposal to expropriate the princes without any compensation had secured the support of 12.5 million people. By June 20, another three million had joined them, proving that the measure had attracted, in the face of a non-stop propaganda barrage from practically the entire bourgeois press, the backing of layers of the petty-bourgeoisie who had not associated themselves with the workers' movement in any way since the earliest days of the November Revolution and the Weimar Republic. In little more than a year, the middle class masses who rallied in their millions to Hindenburg had been split, and a sizable proportion of them won to support a measure which was known to be strongly opposed by the President himself. Although failing to win the required number of votes (more than half the total German electorate), in a straightforward choice between republic and monarchy, and on the even more fundamental issue of the rights of private property, the workers' movement had, despite its deep principled divisions, succeeded in rallying more support for its campaign against the princes than had Hindenburg in the Presidential election of April 1925. This is a factor of some historical significance, and one that not even Trotsky gives its due weight. Of Hindenburg's election he says the following: 'Conservatives, Nationalists, Monarchists, all the enemies of the November Revolution, put Hindenburg in the post of *Reichspräsident* the first time in 1925. Not only the workers but also the parties of the bourgeoisie voted against the Hohenzollern marshal. But Hindenburg won. He was supported by the masses of the petty bourgeoisie moving towards Hitler.' (L. Trotsky: *The German Puzzle,* August 1932, in *The Struggle against Fascism in Germany,* p.269) Neither of these statements is accurate. Hindenburg, as we have seen, was the candidate of the anti-Weimar bourgeoisie as well as of the Junker monarchists. His candidature was endorsed by the heavy industrialists of the DVP and DNVP, and opposed by the Catholic centre (but not by Papen's group) and the bourgeois democrats. In other words, the ruling class *divided* over the Presidency. Nor can one simply say that the millions of petty-bourgeois who voted for Hindenburg in April

1925 were 'moving towards Hitler'. In 1926, a not insignificant proportion of those who had voted for Hindenburg the previous year, (and for Hitler between 1930 and 1933) move perceptibly leftwards, a trend that continued up to and in the Reichstag elections of 1928. The votes of 1925 and 1926 therefore must not be taken in isolation from one another. Between them, they indicated the alternative routes along which the middle class masses can travel —with the monopolies as an anti-labour militia, or with the proletariat against their monopolist exploiters and fascist deceivers.

Surely one could not desire better proof that the German middle class need not have become the foot soldiers of the Nazi counter-revolution, and that under a genuine communist leadership that fought to establish a principled unity of the working class against fascism and all forms of reaction, its best elements could have been won to revolutionary socialism? This is the main historical lesson that has to be distilled from the election of Hindenburg and the crisis of the princes' referendum.

Chapter Fifteen

HITLER REBUILDS

> Only one thing could have broken our movement — if the adversary had understood its principle and from the first day had smashed with extreme brutality, the nucleus of our new movement.
> (A. Hitler at the 1933 Nuremberg Nazi Party rally.)

> If our opponents had been clever, considering that political weapons were so unevenly distributed, they could have undoubtedly found ways and opportunities to make our success impossible.
> (J. Göbbels, 1934.)

> If the enemy had known how weak we were, it would probably have reduced us to jelly. It would have crushed in blood the very beginning of our work.
> (J. Göbbels, 1934.)

Released in December 1924 from his luxurious confinement in Landsberg prison (having served less than a quarter of his original sentence) Hitler was confronted by a Nazi movement in headlong decline, rent by countless political and personal feuds. The latter need not concern us except in so far as they either coincided with or affected genuine political differences. For the most important dispute Hitler found himself called upon to resolve was that concerning strategy. How was the movement to win power — through yet another putsch, in direct conflict with the existing state authorities and the majority of the ruling class; or 'legally', through an alliance with decisive sections of the bourgeoisie, army and agrarians? It was to this question that Hitler primarily addressed himself when he spoke for two hours to a rally of the Nazi faithful in Munich on February 27, 1925.

The movement's great error had been, he explained, to fight on two or even more fronts when it should have been concentrating all its propaganda and energies against the main foe — Marxism. By allowing itself to be drawn into conflicts with secondary opponents, as did the hard-line protestants and pagans, with their polemics against the Catholic church and the Christian religion in general, the Nazi Party unnecessarily alienated sections of the population and the ruling class who would otherwise sympathise with its struggle against Marxism; likewise with the police, the army and even the bourgeois parties. In each case, the movement had to learn to subordinate its secondary and *tactical* differences with these institutions to the long term, *strategical* goal of destroying Marxism, which in Hitler's vocabulary always meant the organised workers' movement:

> To make a struggle intelligible to the broad masses, it must always be carried on against two things: against a person and a cause ...Against whom do the Jews fight with their Marxist power? Against the bourgeoisie as a person, and against capitalism as its cause. Against whom, therefore, must our movement fight? *Against the Jew as a person, and against Marxism as its cause... The success of our movement shall not be measured in votes obtained in the Reichstag or Landtag, but in the degree of annihilation of Marxism and the exposure of its creatures, the Jews.** (emphasis added)

Lüdecke, who had been well-informed of Hitler's change of tactics, endorsed his Führer's speech in an article for the February 1925 number of Rosenberg's journal *Weltkampf:*

> ...we must cease fighting against all fronts at the same time. Our main enemy ...is Marxism. A one-sided fight against Marxism in Bavaria would be a wasted effort, because there is no longer a serious danger. Hence the field of attack aims to be transferred as early as possible to the Protestant north, where the religious question will not divide our strength, where the Centre Party is almost identical with Marxism [presumably a reference to the Centre's support of the SPD in the Prussian State Parliament, where the two parties formed the ruling coalition], and the concentration against Marxism will become a logical step.

Hitler had indeed learned the bitter lesson of the Munich fiasco. After a year's reflection in Landsberg, where he had been engaged for the most part in writing his autobiographical treatise on fascism, *Mein Kampf,* Hitler had come to realise that for all its

---

* Hitler also applied this principle to international questions. Seeing fascist Italy as a natural ally of a future national socialist Germany, he was prepared to forego nationalist claims to the German-speaking Tyrol in order to cement such an alliance: 'Whatever you do, do it completely. By beefing against five or ten states, we neglect the concentration of all our will power and physical force, for the thrust to the heart of our infamous [Marxist and Soviet] enemy, and sacrifice the possibility of strengthening ourselves by an alliance for this conflict ...the National Socialist movement ...must teach our people to look beyond trifles and see the biggest things, not to split up over irrelevant things, and never to forget that the aim for which we must fight today is bare existence of our people, and the sole enemy which we must strike is and remains the power which is robbing us of this existence ...The struggle that Fascist Italy is waging ...against the three main weapons of the Jews is the best indication that ...the poison fangs of this supra-state hydra are being torn out. The prohibition of Masonic secret societies, the persecution of the supra-national press, as well as the continuous demolition of international Marxism, and conversely, the steady reinforcement of the Fascist state conception, will in the course of the years, cause the Italian government to serve the interests of the Italian people more and more, without regard for the hissing of the Jewish world hydra'. (A. Hitler: *Mein Kampf,* pp.635-637). Which rendered it an excellent ally of a Fascist Germany.

pretensions to being a socialist movement of the exploited and oppressed, the Nazi Party could only become a serious contender for power through an alliance with the bourgeoisie (or at least, an important section of it), and that it could only hold this power as its protector.

By declaring that henceforth, national socialism would fight only Marxism, and that this same 'Jewish' Marxism was engaged in an equally bitter war against the bourgeoisie and capitalism, Hitler was in effect saying to the bourgeoisie: the enemies of our enemies are our friends. It remained Hitler's task to convince the leaders of this class that they stood to gain by such a friendship. Here he frankly admitted that a long struggle faced the movement:

> I most solemnly confess: I regret that German industry does not support us ...these men who were so big, support the Marxists [i.e. the social democrats] out of cowardice while they don't even know their German national comrades ...I would take every penny and every million without strings too if from a German ...

But no such largesse was forthcoming from Hitler's future 'national comrades' in heavy industry, save for Thyssen, who loyally soldiered on in the Ruhr as the lonely standard bearer of the Nazi cause. And the reasons for this isolation are not hard to find. Only a matter of days before Hitler delivered this speech, the DNVP entered a Reich cabinet for the first time in the republic's history, raising hopes in industry, army and agrarian circles alike that a new era of reaction and right-wing political consolidation had set in. And these expectations were at once further aroused and apparently given justification by the election of Hindenburg to the Presidency only three months later. Neither could the ruling class be expected to respond enthusiastically to Hitler's clarion call for a war to the death against social democracy, in view of the latter's tacit, and on occasions even explicit collaboration in the bourgeois consolidation of the republic and the rationalisation of industry. Such ruling class elements that were in this period (1925) seeking to eliminate the influence of social democracy in political and economic affairs still vainly looked towards action from the armed forces, as the events surrounding the princes' referendum and leading to the abortive coup of May 1926 would seem to suggest. Besides which scepticism there were also the confusion and anxieties rife in business and landed circles concerning the social and economic objectives of the NSDAP. We can readily understand why they approached with reservations and caution a movement calling itself 'socialist' and addressing itself in wildly demagogic style to the 'workers'. How could they be sure that once in power Hitler would not implement those parts of the 1920 programme calling for the expropriation of profiteers and trusts? And should they

take Hitler's word that he meant something altogether different
from the Marxists when he spoke of 'socialism' and 'workers'?
Outside of rebuilding and reorienting his shattered movement,
Hitler's biggest single task was to convince his chosen future allies
in the capitalist class that Nazi propaganda for the masses was
one thing, and the real aims of the movement's leaders another
— close to the heart's desire of all trade union-hating employers
and war-mongering Junkers.

But before embarking on this task, Hitler and those closest to
him in the party leadership had first to put their own ramshackle
and divided house in order. This was the first pre-requisite for any
future bargaining with the mighty Ruhr industrialists (Kirdorf),
influential bankers (Schacht), political 'fixers' (Papen) and
political generals (Schleicher). And achieving unity in the ranks of
the NSDAP on the strategic and tactical guidelines laid down by
Hitler in his speech of February 27 was no small order. It
occupied him more than a year, and was completed only with the
quelling of the revolt of the self-styled north German 'radicals'
around the Strasser brothers and Joseph Göbbels.

Whilst in prison, Hitler had refrained from lending his name or
support to any of the factions struggling for dominance in the
NSDAP or the broader *volkisch* movement of which it was then
still a part. Quite apart from the fact that he was in the throes of
recasting, in the light of the Munich defeat, many important
aspects of Nazi tactics and strategy, Hitler in all probability felt
that his position of supremacy in the party was best preserved by
ensuring that no single group or leader emerged victorious over
its rivals. The factional conflict first erupted shortly after the
Munich putsch and the trial of Hitler, when differences arose
both within the NSDAP and among its *volkisch* allies in the north
and west Germany over what attitude to adopt to the Reichstag
elections scheduled for May 1924. Rosenberg, nominated by
Hitler as his representative for the duration of his prison term,
favoured participation, even though all the party's previous
agitation had been directed against parliament. Hitler seems to
have fallen out with his deputy, for he lent support to Esser and
Streicher in their opposition to such participation. It was
indicative of Hitler's transitional state of mind at this time that he
rejected a tactical turn that he was to employ to such devastating
effect between 1930 and 1933. A short while later, he had in fact
changed sides in the dispute, commenting to Kurt Lüdecke*
during the latter's visit to Hitler in Landsberg prison that

---

* Lüdecke had been entrusted by Hitler with a mission to the United States in search
of funds for the party's empty coffers. He visited the jew-baiting and anti-union car
king Henry Ford at his Detroit headquarters, but failed to extract anything more
substantial than his platonic support, even though Lüdecke promised Ford that

When I resume active work it will be necessary to pursue a new policy. Instead of working to achieve power by armed coup, we shall have to hold our noses and enter the Reichstag against the Catholic and Marxist deputies. If outvoting them takes longer than outshooting them, at least the result will be guaranteed by their own constitution. Any lawful process is slow ...Sooner or later we will have a majority — and after that, Germany.[1]

Those Nazis favouring the exploitation of the parliamentary tactic found allies in the north German *volkisch* movement of Count Ernst zu Reventlow, whom we earlier encountered debating with the KPD in the columns of its press. The German Racial Freedom Party (DVFP) had broken from the DNVP in 1922 after disagreements over the latter's too-restrained anti-semitism. While sharing the Nazis' understanding for the need to conquer mass support with a pseudo-radical social policy (something the DNVP, whether under the leadership of Count Westarp, or after, 1928, Hugenberg, never fully appreciated), the north German *volkisch* groups remained, like the DNVP from which they had split, oriented towards parliamentary elections and activity. Another weakness (which became more evident in later years when the Nazis began to attract mass support) proved to be the mainly aristocratic background of the movement's leaders. For all their 'national Bolshevik' pretensions, they failed to make inroads into the working class, and won precious little support even from the nationalist petty-bourgeoisie. Nevertheless, since the DVFP represented the most consistently *volkisch* elements within the ruling class, they were useful election allies for the more plebeian-based and led Nazis, and after negotiations, the two parties agreed to run on a single 'Racial-Social Bloc' ticket, polling 1.9 million votes.

Yet scarcely had the 32 Racial-Social deputies ensconced themselves in the unaccustomed comfort of their Reichstag seats

'whoever helped us now would not fare badly from a business standpoint ...a binding agreement could be arranged whereby large concessions would be guaranteed there [Germany] ...from the moment of Hitler's rise to power'. Ford, who could hardly be blamed for his scepticism about the prospects of a movement whose leader was currently in jail for treason, was not tempted even by the offer of a stake in the Russian market, which Lüdecke declared the Nazis would soon open up once they came to power in Germany: 'Pointing to the probability that a Nazi regime in Germany might lead to a change also in the Russian situation, with the re-opening of that vast market, I emphasised the tremendous rewards his initiative would bring, not only in advancing his business interests, but also by furthering his grandiose social policies throughout the world'. (K. Lüdecke: *I Knew Hitler,* p.199, New York, 1937) Lüdecke appears to have had no more success with Hiram Evans, Imperial Grand Wizard of the Klu Klux Klan. In complete contrast with the Nazis, this movement did not lack cash but a strategy for power: 'With such a flood of money pouring in, any man of genius might have been able to anticipate, in America, the work Hitler eventually did in Germany'. (ibid. p.205) Though the KKK may well have been deficient in leadership, its failure to become a serious contender for power was due to objective historical, economic and political factors, and not subjective ones.

than a series of fresh disputes flared up amongst those who had elected them. Nazi 'radicals' schooled in the demagogic propaganda methods and combat techniques of Hitler and Röhm accused their DFVP election allies of ignoring or playing down the social aspects of the *volkisch* doctrine, while in the north, at Hamburg, a group of Nazis not only demonstratively separated themselves from Reventlow's 'parlour Bolsheviks', but committed the unforgivable heresy of proclaiming their independence from the Nazi Vatican in Munich (and by implication, cast doubt on the infallibility of its Pope). North Germany remained an independent preserve of Nazi 'radicals' until Hitler brought them to heel in the spring of 1926.

A third centre of opposition crystallised around Ernst Röhm whom Hitler had appointed leader of the Storm Troops for the duration of his stay in prison. Like the 'radicals' with whom he was in sympathy, Röhm exploited his new found freedom to put his own ideas into practice, founding the *Frontbann,* a bloc of the many para-military and Free Corps formations which had, over the previous four years, aligned themselves with the counter-revolutionary right. In opting for a military organisation independent of the party's political leadership, Röhm was challenging one of the central principles of national socialism as repeatedly enunciated by Hitler, and finally codified in the second volume of *Mein Kampf.* (written during 1925, and there-fore after the first break with Röhm). Hitler insisted that since the SA's purpose was political, 'its training must not proceed from military criteria, but from criteria of expediency for the party'. Nor should it engage in individual terror, such as the assassination of leading politicians or militants of the workers' movement. It should aim at being a movement of the masses,

> fighting for the erection of a new National Socialist folkish state ...The NSDAP ...must neither suffer the SA to degenerate into a kind of combat league nor into a secret organisation; it must, on the contrary, endeavour to train it as a guard, numbering hundreds of thousands of men, for the National Socialist and hence profoundly folkish idea.[2]*

These ideas were anathema to the swashbuckling Captain Röhm. He had attracted to his side men of a similar nihilistic state of mind, trained and hired killers who knew no other profession than murder, and no other ideology than blind activism and destruction. How could they be expected to submit themselves to

* And here Hitler was undoubtedly right. Nothing could have been more intimidating for the waverers within the workers' movement, and inspiring for those who were its enemies, than to see seemingly endless columns of uniformed SA men and youths marching through the working class quarters of Berlin, Hamburg and Germany's other industrial centres, chanting in unison their songs of hate against Marxism, the republic, the Jews — and, in a cunningly demagogic twist, the 'reaction'. Hitler had learned his Vienna lesson well.

the discipline of a political movement, which for all its fanatical hatred of Marxism and democracy, allowed itself to be sucked into the bourgeois game of parliamentary seat-hunting? Rohm took the dispute to the highest authority in the *volkisch* movement — its universally acknowledged patron, Ludendorff. In a letter to the general, Röhm vehemently defended the independence of the counter-revolutionary soldier:

> The political and military movements are entirely independent of each other. Both the political and the military movement are represented in the parliamentary group. As the present leader of the military movement, I demand that the defence leagues be granted appropriate representation in parliament and that they be not hindered in their own particular work ...Germany's liberty — at home and abroad — will never be won by mere chatter and bargaining; it must be fought for.

Detectable in these last lines are the seeds of Rohm's final clash with Hitler., when his insatiable urge to dominate not only the party, but the Reichswehr with his massed columns of SA men — by 1934 no longer a motley collection of Free Corps and world war veterans, but a brown army some four million strong — drove Hitler to unleash the purge of the 'night of the long knives' on June 30. But in the early weeks of 1925, the feud was resolved, not with a mass blood-letting, but by Röhm's resignation as SA leader, and his eventual emigration to Bolivia, where until recalled by Hitler in 1930 to head the SA once more, he served as a military instructor to the army.

The most serious and protracted threat to Hitler's position as supreme party leader and arbiter on questions of national socialist doctrine, tactics and strategy came from the industrial north and west. There, where the NSDAP confronted an immensely powerful and radical workers' movement, party activists were compelled to adopt a 'leftist' stance on most social and economic questions, far more so than was necessary in the predominantly rural and petty-bourgeois Bavaria. It must be stressed at once that their employment of radical phraseology and slogans, in many cases stolen from the KPD and eclectically combined with anti-semitic chauvinism, flowed not from any misguided but genuine socialist convictions, but from a real fear that in its quest for working class support, the party would otherwise be hopelessly outflanked on the left by the KPD and militant elements in the SPD and ADGB.

The emergence of a distinctive north German faction dates from August 1925, when Nazi 'radicals' of various tendencies came together to form the National Socialist Working Association, with its own organ, the *NS Briefe,* edited by a relatively recent convert to Nazism, Joseph Göbbels. The base of the group, significantly, was the Ruhr town of Elberfeld, where radical traditions in the workers' movement were strong, and its leaders were the Strasser brothers Otto and Gregor, Göbbels, Bernard Rust (Hitler's future Minister of Education) Robert Ley (in 1933, appointed head of the Labour Front) and Karl Kaufmann, who afterwards became gauleiter of Hamburg. Of lesser importance in the group's clash with Munich, but destined to hold high office in the Third Reich, were Friedrich Hildebrandt, gauleiter of Mecklenburg, and Erich Koch, East Prussian gauleiter under the Third Reich and after the Nazi invasion of the Soviet Union, butcher and slave driver of the Ukraine.

Reading the speeches, diary entries and articles of the north German Nazis, one gains a new insight into the utter political impotency of the petty-bourgeois *enrage,* the noisy radical who, denied what he thinks is his rightful place in the bourgeois sun, vents his anger on those above and below him. He admires (and fears) the discipline, heroism and dynamism of the revolutionary workers' movement, just as he despises its internationalism and 'class exclusiveness'. He borrows from communism that which he finds useful to intimidate the big bourgeoisie in order to compel it to bestow on him the privileges and power he deserves; while from this same bourgeoisie he takes the poisonous ideology of chauvinism and anti-semitism, using it to divert the proletariat from its revolutionary path, thereby rendering it a passive object under the tutelage of its social and intellectual betters.

The thoroughly petty-bourgeois, eclectic nature of the Working Association's 'socialism' is clear from the account of one of its main practitioners and theoreticians, Otto Strasser:

> Our second step [after founding the group's organ] was to work out an economic, political and cultural programme. In the economic field it was opposed alike to Marxism and capitalism. We foresaw a new equilibrium on the basis of state feudalism. The state was to be the sole owner of the land, which it would lease to private citizens. All were to be free to do as they liked with their own land, but no one could sell or sublet state property. In this way we hoped to combat proletarianisation and to restore a state of liberty to our fellow citizens. No man is free who is not economically independent. We proposed nationalisation only of such wealth as could not be multiplied at will; that is, the country's landed and industrial inheritance. In the political field we rejected the totalitarian idea in favour of federalism. Parliament, instead of consisting of party representatives, would consist of representatives of corporations. These we divided into five groups: workers, peasants, clerks and officials, industrialists, and the liberal professions... The prosperity of the country would be assured by the nationalisation of heavy industry and the distribution of the great estates as state fiefs... Reconstruction, to our minds, could only be brought about on the basis of a new order which could re-establish harmony between labour and capital and between the individual and the community... There would be no dictatorship, either of class or

race.[3]*

No dictatorship of class or race... yet for all his talk of nationalisation (which he clearly learned during his brief career as a student member of the SPD), there remained exploited labour and exploiting capital, and under a regime which denied the worker's right to organise himself in trade unions and political parties. As for Strasser's claim that his 'left' version of national socialism rejected racialism, there is the clear call in his brother Gregor's draft programme (drafted towards the end of 1925 and submitted for discussion to his fellow north German Nazis) for the deportation of all Jews who had entered Germany since August 1, 1914, and for the withdrawal of German citizenship from all those who remained, a demand which was the stock in trade of every German anti-semite throughout the life of the Weimar Republic. Otto Strasser, who broke with Hitler in 1930 on the grounds that the Nazi leader had sold out to big business, for obvious reasons later chose to play down the 'national' aspects of his 'socialism', and to exaggerate the latter. His brother's draft was in fact little more radical than the original Nazi programme of 1920. Apart from its anti-semitic clause, it proposed the nationalisation of the land and the breaking up of all estates larger than 1,000 acres into small peasant holdings, a distinctly less radical measure than Otto Strasser said was demanded by the north Germans. Neither did Gregor's draft demand outright nationalisation. Instead, a form of 'mixed economy' was advocated, with the state owning 51% of the shares in vital industries and 49% in the remainder. 10% of the private stock would then be set aside for distribution among the workers. Finally, and again in contradiction to the account given by Otto Strasser, the draft envisaged, not a European Federation, but a greatly enlarged Germany with its lost colonies restored, and one that would consequently dominate the entire continent: 'The organisation and powerful concentration *on a racial basis* of the German nation in a Greater German Reich: this German Reich to be the centre of gravity for a mid-European customs union and the basis for the United States of Europe'. (emphasis added)

---

* While Otto Strasser gave a medievalist slant to his fascism (in common with so many others) he was ahead of his time in advocating a European economic and trading union some of whose proposed features have been incorporated into the Common Market: 'A European Federation based on the same principles ...would lead to a disarmed Europe, forming a solid bloc in which each country retained its own administration, customs and religion. The abolition of tariff walls would create a kind of European Autarchy, with free trade prevailing throughout the continent'. (O. Strasser: *Hitler and I,* p.83) And autarchy, of course, was Hitler's central economic aim, though he saw it being realised not through a Pan European federation in which all member nations enjoyed (theoretically at least) equal rights, but under the total domination of German arms and industry. In this sense too, Hitler assumed the mantle of Bismarck.

This quotation also raises the other cardinal facet of north German national socialism. Until their capitulation to Hitler early in 1926 (and on occasions, even afterwards), Göbbels and the two Strassers flirted with a *volkisch* version of national Bolshevism. They argued that in order to enable Germany to break out of the isolation imposed on it by the defeat of 1918, it was necessary, despite the unbridgeable ideological chasm that separated communism from national socialism, to solicit Soviet diplomatic and military aid in imperialist Germany's preparation for the war of revenge against the 'plutocratic' and 'decadent' Entente powers. At least, that is how the theory stood until 1925. But with Stalin's rise to power, and his revision of Marxist internationalism with his nationalist theory of socialism in one country, 'left' Nazis began to write more sympathetically on internal developments in the USSR. Stalin's approaching victory over the Trotskyist Left Opposition was quite correctly seen as the triumph of conservative, nationalistic forces over proletarian internationalism (Nazi national Bolsheviks were also quick to draw attention to Stalin's well-known anti-semitism, and the fact that many of the opposition leaders — Trotsky, Zinoviev, Kamenev, Radek to name but four — were of Jewish origin. The pogrom of communists had started, and the Nazi 'lefts' were delighted.) Göbbels developed this theme in an article addressed to KPD members in October 1925, pointing out that Soviet and CI policy under the leadership of Stalin had begun to veer towards a national conception of socialism, and thus it was now necessary for KPD workers to take this development to its logical conclusion: 'never has a suppressed class liberated itself through international protest, but only through nationalistic will for the future...'[5] Göbbels at this time was also conducting a debate with white Russian emigres, explaining why for tactical reasons it was necessary to align Germany diplomatically with the USSR. In one letter to an emigre he wrote:

> We look to Russia because it is the country most likely to take with us the road to socialism, because Russia is an ally which nature has given us against the devilish temptation and corruption of the West. We watch in bitter pain while so-called German statesmen destroy all bridges that lead towards Russia [an obvious reference to Foreign Minister Stresemann's 'western orientation']. Our pain is so strongly felt *not because we love Bolshevism,* but because an alliance with a really national and socialist Russia will strengthen our own national and socialist position and dignity.* (emphasis added)

---

* The Nazi 'left' followed with close interest and not a little sympathy Stalin's campaign against the Left Opposition, with articles appearing on this theme in the *NS Briefe* for October 15, November 15 and December 15, 1927. All were concerned with the expulsion of the Trotskyists from the Bolshevik Party just prior to its 15th Congress, a development which the journal heralded as further confirmation that Stalin was embracing a national and anti-semitic version of socialism. Göbbels, now

We encounter essentially the same pseudo-radicalism in the early writings of Göbbels. For all his noisy rantings against capitalism and its exploitation of the proletariat, this future Nazi Minister of Propaganda's conception of what he terms 'socialism' is that of a petty-bourgeois chauvinist, a typical German middle class *enrage* who wants to solve the 'social problem' not through the abolition of private property, but its wider and more even distribution, thereby abolishing both monopoly capitalism and the proletariat without disturbing the small-propertied foundations of his own existence:

> Socialism can be realised only in the national state... in materialistic terms, socialism is not a question of wages, but a question of indigenousness and therefore of property. The working classes can be made free materially and spiritually by increasing the number of property owners up to the last possible point...[4]

The Working Association, largely because of its close study of the workers' movement, was able to develop a tactic that paid handsome dividends after 1930, when the NSDAP at last began to make serious inroads into the more backward strata of the proletariat. They cunningly exploited all the past betrayals of the social democrats (just as after 1930, they did those of the Stalinists) to confuse workers and to prove to them that in contrast, to the 'Marxists', the Nazis were the real socialists. One typically 'left' Nazi poster of the period, playing upon nationalist opposition to the SPD's acceptance of the Dawes Plan, read:

> The socialist railways are now, in the seventh year of the republic, a capitalist undertaking of the American bank and stock exchange Jews. Workers of the hand and brain, you like us are socialists. When are you going to understand? Today your leaders no longer speak of the

writing in his own Berlin daily, *Der Angriff*, commented (on January 16 and February 6 1928) that Stalin's victory over the Left Opposition represented the ascendency of agrarian, nationalist and non-proletarian forces in the USSR over 'Jewish' internationalism as represented by Trotsky. Earlier, on November 21, Göbbels had denounced the Trotskyist opposition and warned German workers against adhering to a 'Fourth International' (which Soviet and other Stalinists were also slanderously asserting Trotsky was about to found). On March 12, 1928, Göbbels waxed sarcastic on the prospects of building a genuine communist leadership in opposition to the Stalinist faction in the USSR and the CI, as well as the reformists of the Second International: 'Four "Internationals" and still no solidarity: on the contrary, only new fissures and establishments! This ought to make clear, finally, to the thinking German worker that all internationalism is a swindle and that he can achieve a betterment of his situation only through a national organisation of labour'. Even Rosenberg's *Weltkampf*, normally a mouthpiece for the most vitriolic attacks on the USSR, began to revise its opinion on the post-Lenin regime, with approving articles on Stalin's anti-semitism and nationalism appearing in its issues for February and April 1929. The Hitler-Stalin pact of August 1939 flowed directly from the Nazi leadership's appreciation of how far the Kremlin leadership had departed from proletarian internationalism. All of which renders even more piquant the charge trumped up at the second and third Moscow Show Trials against Trotsky and other leading Soviet oppositionists that they were agents of German fascism.

socialist republic ...You don't want alms. You want nothing more and nothing less than your rights, than to live in the Republic a life fit for human beings.

Gregor Strasser, ever anxious to prove himself more left than the reformists (a task that was made all too easy by their supine collaboration with the class enemies of the proletariat and the non-exploiting layers of the petty-bourgeoisie) wrote in a special 'May Day' number of his organ, *Der Nationale Sozialist,* that the SPD had only functionaries, not a single leader, and that the reformist bureaucracy had lost all contact with the workers, being 'narrow minded, petty-bourgeois, ambitious intriguers, dull after-dinner speakers'. In a word, the social democrats had become bourgeoisified. Thus did the Nazi 'lefts' borrow from and then per-vert for counter-revolutionary purposes the revolutionary Marxist analysis and critique of the reformist bureaucracy.*

And very much in the same vein, the article complained that because of the SPD's retreat from its pledge to expropriate the giant trusts, 'marching socialisation has become stuck in the mud, in the mire of corruption of parliamentary democracy... This is the way the Marxist social democracy leads us, this is its great sin'. And this from a party that once in power, was fanatical in its defence of the monopolies!

But such 'leftism' also had its dangers for the Nazi leadership in Munich. With one eye on a future alliance with big business and the agrarians, and the other on the nationalist petty-bourgeoisie who were to provide the bulk of the Nazis mass support, Hitler utterly rejected the north Germans' wild talk about founding *volkisch* 'trade unions' and their attempts to outbid the SPD and KPD in radicalism. While he was not opposed to winning workers to the NSDAP, this had to be done only on the basis of his own firmly held convictions on the defence of private property. Hitler was in the process of finalising his views on the trade union question during 1925, when the north Germans first raised the demand that the NSDAP should either found itself, or lend its support to, *volkisch* organisations of workers. His con-clusions are set down in the second Volume of *Mein Kampf,* and they show that by the end of 1925, he had opted for a policy that would later win the Party the enthusiastic support of the big employers who looked forward to a Germany without independent trade unions. Hitler begins by addressing four questions to his readers (and, we suspect, especially to those who

*'Third Period' Stalinism, instead of taking a principled stand against such cunning demagogy, and defending the social democrats, *leaders as well as rank and file,* from all Nazi attacks, whether verbal, written or physical, (while at all times demarcating itself from reformism, and pointing out that these Nazi manoeuvres were only possible because of social democratic treachery) actually lent credence to such demagogy by aligning itself, as on the occasion of the Prussian Referendum of 1931, with the Nazis against the SPD.

were pushing for a more 'left' trade union line in the NSDAP):

1. Are trade unions necessary?
2. Should the NSDAP itself engage in trade union activity, or direct its members to such activity in any form?
3. What must be the nature of a National Socialist trade union? What are our tasks and aims?
4. How shall we arrive at such unions?[6]

He answers these question in the following way. Since the Nazi Party claimed, for purely demagogic purposes, to be a party of the 'workers' (though the Nazi definition of this term was, as we have already seen, highly elastic, and could even, when the occasion demanded, embrace big industrialists!) and since it was seeking to detach at least a portion of the proletariat from its allegiance to its traditional organisations, then Hitler could not avoid making a verbal commitment to the need for trade unions. To proclaim publicly in advance his intention of destroying them would have been tantamount to committing political suicide. This is where the Nazis scored so heavily and frequently over their rivals in the bourgeois nationalist parties and the monarchist leagues. He is however at pains to give his affirmative answer a nationalistic twist; and conditional on the continued existence of the Weimar system:

> As things stand today, the trade unions ...cannot be dispensed with. On the contrary, they are among the most important institutions of the nation's economic life. Their significance lies not only in the social and political field, but even more in the general field of national politics. A people whose broad masses, through a sound trade union movement, obtain the satisfaction of their living requirements and at the same time an education, will be tremendously strengthened in its power of resistance in the struggle for existence.[7] (emphasis added)

What Hitler means by a 'sound trade union movement' becomes clear in the passage which follows. We learn that 'trade unions are necessary as foundation stones of the future economic parliament or chamber of estates'.[8] Can it be that Hitler was proposing to allot a place in his corporate state (for this is what he means by 'economic parliament' and 'chamber of estates') *to the existing class trade unions of the ADGB?* A superficial reading might indeed suggest this, lending credence to the utterly false theory which sometimes masquerades as Trotskyism that the fascist corporate state is created by the merging of employers and workers organisations, and by the incorporation of the latter into the capitalist state. We have already established that Fascism in Italy did not take this form, and that its corporative state structure not only in practice but in theory specifically excluded the class-based trade unions from any participation in the new regime. And we find that it was also the case with the NSDAP. When Hitler refers to 'trade unions', he has something entirely different in mind from the Marxist, social democrat, Stalinist, centrist, or any other tendency in the workers movement:

> The trade union in the National Socialist sense does not have the function of grouping certain people within a national body and thus gradually transforming them into a class, to take up the fight against other similarly organised [employers] formations. We can absolutely not impute this function to the trade union as such; it became so only in the moment when the trade union became the instrument of Marxist struggle. Not that the trade union is characterised by class struggle; Marxism has made it an instrument for the Marxist class struggle. Marxism created the economic weapon which the international world Jew uses for shattering the economic base of the free, independent national states, for the destruction [i.e. nationalisation] of their national industry and their national commerce, the enslavement of free peoples in the service of supra-state world finance Jewry. In the face of this, the National Socialist trade union must, by organisationally embracing certain groups of participants in the national economic process, increase the security of the national economy itself... Hence for the National Socialist union the strike is not a means for shattering and shaking national production, but for enhancing it and making it run smoothly by combatting all those abuses which due to their unsocial character, interfere with the efficiency of the economy and hence the existence of the totality.[9]

There are visible here elements of the 'national syndicalism' which emerged on the 'radical' wing of fascist movements in France, Spain and Italy. The proposed 'unions' were to embrace not only workers, but their employers, a conception which the Strasser group at first found difficult to accept, since they were in direct competition with trade unions based firmly on the class principle. Hitler saw the dangers implicit in such rivalry:*

> Real benefit for the movement as well as for our people can only arise from a trade union movement, if philosophically this movement is already so strongly filled with our National Socialist ideas that it no longer runs the risk of falling into Marxist tracks. For a trade union

---

* How anxious Hitler was to prevent the development of a 'proletarian' wing to the Party paying lip service to class trade unionism is clear from the following passage: '...the germ cells for the economic chambers will have to reside in bodies representing the most varied occupations, hence above all in the [Nazi] trade unions. And if this future body representing the estates and the central economic parliament are to constitute a National Socialist institution, these important germ cells must also embody a National Socialist attitude and conception ...Upon the economic chambers themselves it will be incumbent to keep the national economy functioning and eliminate the deficiencies and errors which damage it. The things for which millions fight and struggle today must in time be settled in the chamber of estates and the central economic parliament. Then employers and workers will not rage against one another in a struggle over pay and wage scales, damaging the economic existence of both, but solve these problems together, in a higher instance, which must above all constantly envision the welfare of the people as a whole and of the state...' And consequently, the right to strike, which Hitler demagogically upheld under the Weimar Republic, has no place in a regime which has 'abolished' the class struggle: 'For the National Socialist union ...the strike is an instrument which may and actually must be applied only so long as a National Socialist folkish state does not exist'. (A. Hitler: *Mein Kampf*, pp.599-602.)

movement which sees its mission only in competition with the Marxist [i.e. ADGB-social democratic] unions would be worse than none at all. It must declare war on the Marxist union, not only as an organisation, but above all as an idea. In the Marxist union it must strike down the herald of the class struggle and the class idea and in its stead must become the protector of the occupational interests of German citizens.[10]

This answered question number three — what must be the nature of Nazi 'trade unions' — but it did not resolve question number four — how would the NSDAP arrive at such unions. Here Hitler posed two alternative lines of attack:

(1) We could found a trade union and then gradually take up the struggle against the international [i.e. class] Marxist unions; or we could (2) penetrate the Marxist unions and try to fill them with the new spirit; in other words, transform them into instruments of the new ideology.[11]

Hitler ruled out the first line of action. The Party simply lacked the resources to launch a Nazi 'union' which could defeat the reformist unions in open combat. Hitler also undoubtedly realised that his 'national trade unionism' stood very little chance of winning large numbers of workers away from the class unions, at least until a really historic defeat had been inflicted on the proletariat. And by the same token, the second alternative offered little better prospects of success while the fighting capacities of the working class remained unimpaired. A turning towards the forms of organisation and ideology advocated by the Nazis could only gather pace in conditions of profound demoralisation — or at the point of a gun. And this is in fact the solution which Hitler finally hints at:

Today the National Socialist movement must combat a colossal gigantic organisation which has long been in existence, and which is developed down to the slightest detail. The conqueror must always be more astute than the defender if he wants to subdue him... Here [therefore] we must apply the maxim that in life it is sometimes better to let a thing lie for the present than to begin it badly or by halves for want of suitable forces.... The more we muster the entire strength of our movement for the political struggle, the sooner we may count on success all along the line; but the more we prematurely burden ourselves with trade union... and similar problems, the smaller will be the benefit for our cause as a whole. For important as these matters may be, *their fulfilment will only occur on a large scale when we are in a position to put the state power into the service of these ideas.*[12] (emphasis added)

In other words, only when the Nazis actually wielded state power, and with it, the entire machinery of class repression augmented by their own fanatical hordes, could the 'trade union' question be tackled with any hopes of success. And this is precisely the course that events followed, with the destruction of the class trade unions on May 2, 1933, and their replacement by the Labour Front of Dr Ley which embraced not only the members of the former free trade unions, but also the employers. The ADGB was not 'tied to the state', its leaders did not, despite all their pleadings, become 'policemen' of the employers and the capitalist state, nor instruments of exploitation and repression. They ended up in jail.

Shrewd tactician that he was, Hitler sought neither an immediate nor head-on clash with the north Germans. Instead, he devoted most of his energies to consolidating his Munich base, where he continued, despite the events of November 1923, to enjoy the indulgence of leading Bavarian government and state officials. The issue which finally brought the dispute between the two factions into the open towards a final resolution on Hitler's terms was the same as had precipitated a full-scale crisis in the ruling class — namely the referendum on the compensation of the princes. The Working Association, in keeping with their more 'left' interpretation of the Nazi programme (and also, no doubt, because of the widespread and enthusiastic support the demand for expropriation without compensation had aroused among the workers of north and west Germany) came out against the princes.

Hitler, who had opted more than a year previously for a thoroughly conservative economic policy, would not hear of the NSDAP becoming involved in a campaign, initiated by the KPD, against the sacred rights of private property. But before the issue was finally resolved at the well-known meeting in Bamberg on February 14, 1926, the north Germans, although divided between themselves on certain issues, had made a bid to supplant the 'old guard' in Munich as Hitler's political confidants (for never was there any question of their seeking to depose the Führer himself). The intention seems to have been to persuade Hitler that he was surrounded in Munich by 'reactionaries' such as Streicher and Feder, and that he should instead bring to the forefront of the party the leaders of the Working Association. But a series of meetings held by the north Germans and their allies failed to achieve the political unity they had been counting on in their challenge to Munich. Gregor Strasser's draft programme was attacked from all sides, some deeming it too radical, others lacking in sufficient anti-semitic venom. There were also disagreements in the group on the questions of Pan-Europeanism and policy towards the USSR. In the last conference held by the 'radicals', in Hanover on January 25, 1926, the main item on the agenda was the princes referendum. Pfeffer von Salomon, whom in November 1926 Hitler appointed as commander of the SA, later frankly admitted that the question 'was extremely embarassing for everybody and they would much rather have avoided taking up a position on it'. But they could not, since it was the number one issue of German politics, and every political leader and party was being compelled to take sides for or against the princes. The Nazi 'lefts' could not retreat from their previous position of support for the campaign against compensation for the princes, but neither could they unequivocally endorse it. In order to differentiate the NSDAP from the KPD and SPD, they proposed, in the event of the referendum succeeding, to move an amendment in the Reichstag calling for the confiscation of all the property of Jews who had entered Germany since 1914, together with the confiscation of all bank and stock exchange profits (i.e. the gains of 'speculative capital') made since the beginning of the war. The meeting — held in the presence of Feder, who had been sent by Hitler to report on the proceedings — also discussed critically the party's 1920 programme, which had been drawn up by none other than Hitler and Feder. Finally, the gathering drew up a slate of 'lefts' whom they hoped Hitler would agree to promote onto his central staff at Munich. Taken together, these three acts of insubordination confirmed Hitler's fears that the Strasser-Göbbels group were seeking to supplant him as the supreme authority on questions of programme, policy, doctrine and organisation — in fact the entire gamut of Nazi theory and practice, tactics and strategy. On hearing Feder's report of the Hanover meeting of rebels, he convened the confrontation at Bamberg. Hitler went to the meeting knowing just what he wanted, and aware of the utterly opportunist nature of the opposition, who were, as subsequent developments proved, craving for high office and power. In contrast, the north Germans went to Bamberg divided amongst themselves and full of envy for Hitler's entourage, who were already beginning to live the lives of rising politicians and party bureaucrats. Otto Strasser summed up Hitler's reasons for opposing the referendum campaign when he wrote, many years after the Bamberg meeting, that

> ...to have understood Hitler's fury [against the north Germans] it was necessary to have followed his recent change of front. Hitler had become [sic!] conservative. He needed money for his party, and this could only come from the capitalists. The expropriation of the princes would obviously alarm the big industrialists, the financiers, and the landowners who would naturally regard the breaking up of the property of the former reigning houses as as the first step towards similar measures directed against themselves... [At the Bamberg meeting] Adolf made a brilliant plea for the princes and the claims of the aristocratic families.[13]

Even if Hitler had wished to make a demagogic switch of line, as the north Germans were suggesting, he could not have done so, since he was already receiving subsidies from at least one of the former royal houses now threatened with expropriation without compensation. For at this time (early 1926) he had not succeeded in convincing the big capitalists that his party could further their interests. Such links that the NSDAP had established with the ruling class, Hitler clung on to tenaciously. They were his life line to wealth, political influence and eventually power, and therefore could not be endangered on any account, least of all to indulge the pseudo-radical whims of the Strassers and Göbbels. The referendum campaign, he told the meeting, was nothing but a 'Jewish swindle' and the Nazis must therefore back the princes' fight to defend their property to the hilt.*

But while rejecting their demands for a more radical orientation for the party, Hitler was quick to see that the north German faction contained leaders who could serve him ably in Munich. He skilfully disintegrated their group by offering its spokesmen plum posts in the party apparatus. The stages and political convolutions through which Göbbels passed *en route* from his blustering national Bolshevism to complete agreement with Hitler are well traced in his private diary entries of the period, as indeed is the utterly eclectic nature of his radicalism. For example on January 31, 1926, we find him regretting the fact that Nazis and communists have to 'bash each other's heads in', and asking 'where can we meet leading communists', while only three days later, he delightedly records that 'at last' he has had the good fortune to meet 'a prominent businessman'; and then that same evening, a 'discussion ...[with] a follower of the Communist Workers' Party'. (The Communist. Workers' Party — KAPD — was a syndicalist offshoot from the KPD, breaking away after the Kapp putsch.)

> *September 11:* National and Socialist! What comes first and what second? For us in the West [i.e. Ruhr] there can be no doubt. First the socialist redemption, then, like a hurricane, national liberation. Prof. Vahlen disagrees. First, make the workers national minded. But how? Please talk to our people. Hitler stands half-way in between. But he is about to come over to our side. [Neither statement was true. Hitler, as he makes clear in *Mein Kampf*, aimed at the 'nationalisation of the masses', a perspective from which he had no intention of shifting — as Göbbels was soon to discover.]

---

* Hitler was currently receiving a monthly subsidy of 1,500 marks from one of the royal houses threatened with expropriation — that of von Sachsen-Anhalt, via the divorced Duchess Eduard. The Rhineland Prince Eulenburg had also shown an interest in Hitler's movement, though it is not known whether this went to the extent of giving its leader money. At any rate, he and his fellow aristocratic parasites must have been flattered by Hitler's description of the referendum. Apart from being a 'Jewish swindle', it represented the revolt of the 'subhuman' against the 'elite'. Alfred Rosenberg, who entirely shared Hitler's orthodox bourgeois views on private property, recalled Hitler 'declared that as long as private property was recognised as one of the foundations of national life, he would not yield, irrespective of how bad the rulers of the various states had been. The NSDAP adopted this point of view'. (A. Rosenberg: *Memoirs*, p.204.)

September 30: Strasser is a dear fellow. He still has a lot to learn. But he will accept anything that adds radical content to the idea. He is to be our battering ram against the Munich bosses. Perhaps the battle will flare up very soon.

October 2: Long drawn-out negotiations with Strasser. We have reached complete agreement ...Munich seems really to be a big pigsty ...we shall launch a big offensive. National Socialism is at stake.

October 12: Letter from Strasser. Hitler does not trust me. He has abused me. How that hurts ...In Munich, cads are at work.

October 14: I am finishing Hitler's book [*Mein Kampf*]. Thrilled to bits! Who is this man? Half plebeian, half god!

October 16: Locarno: the same old fraud. Germany gives in and sells out to the capitalist west. A horrible prospect! Germany's sons will be bled to death on the battlefields of Europe as the mercenaries of capitalism. Perhaps, probably, in a 'holy war against Moscow!' [An accurate prediction — and Göbbels was to be one of its high priests] Can there be anything politically more infamous?

October 19: Hitler will be in Hammand Dortmund on Saturday and Sunday, and Streicher will be there to protect him. That damned idiot Hermann Esser. I shall not be a party to this Byzantianism for long. We must get close to Hitler. The programme, the spiritual and economic fundamentals, all of that is vague ...That is not the way to start a revolution.

October 23: We shall be the mercenaries against Russia on the battlefields of capitalism. We have been sold ....in the last analysis better go down with Bolshevism than live in eternal capitalist servitude.

October 24: In Essen with Kaufmann last night. Julius Streicher was there, the 'hero' of Nuremberg. A typical Bavarian bum-brusher. ...Poor Hitler! Woe betide National Socialism!...Strasser reports from Munich. We have cleared up matters with Hitler. Hitler also wants to employ me more.

November 14: Osnabruck ...Speech in the evening. To bourgeois. About 2,000. Raging applause.

November 28: To the Bechstein family [one of Hitler's first capitalist benefactors]. Hitler's saloon. I am received like an old friend.

December 23: Every day at work on a comprehensive programme for National Socialism. I am beginning to see how difficult it all is. [sic!]

January 25: Arrival, Hanover [for meeting of north Germans] ...Gottfried Feder turns up, the servant of capital and interest [a sarcastic reference to Feder's phoney anti-capitalism].

[The meeting] begins at eight o'clock ...Feder speaks. Intelligently but obstinately dogmatic. And then a confused debate without end ...What is a social distress? asks Ley ...Then Russia. I am attacked without restraint ...Then I go for it. Russia, Germany, Western capital, Bolshevism ...Everyone listens in hushed silence. Then stormy agreement! We have won [another delusion. This speech proved to be Göbbels' swan song as a radical oppositionist]. Strasser shakes my hand. Feder very small and self-effacing.

January 31: I think it is horrible that we and the communists bash each other's heads in ...Where can we meet leading communists?

February 3: Monday afternoon with Herr von Bruck, a leading Rhenish industrialist. A prominent businessman at last. He gave us a political-economic lecture of astounding breadth. That is a man with whom we can collaborate. Knew Chicherin [a leading Soviet diplomat, succeeded Trotsky in the spring of 1918 as Commissar for Foreign Affairs] Confirmed the last tittle of our views about Bolshevism. We are following the right trail. In the evening a discussion in Elberfeld. A follower of the Communist Workers' Party. Interesting debate.

February 6: Hitler is in a rage about the programme [in all probability, Gregor Strasser's draft]. The Bechsteins. Old lady. Property must be preserved [the Bechsteins were obviously becoming agitated about the forthcoming referendum]. Next Sunday, Bamberg. Invitation from Hitler. Stand up and fight! That will decide.

February 15: Hitler speaks for two hours. I am almost beaten. What kind of Hitler? A reactionary? Amazingly clumsy and uncertain. Italy and Britain the natural allies. Horrible! ...It is our job to smash Bolshevism. Bolshevism is a Jewish creation! ... Compensation for princes! Question of not weakening private property. Horrible! Programme will do! Happy with it. Feder nods. Ley nods. Streicher nods. Esser nods. It hurts me in my soul to see you in that company. Short discussion. Strasser speaks. Hesitant, trembling, clumsy ...Lord, what a poor match we are for those pigs down there ...I can no longer believe in Hitler absolutely.

February 22: Fobke told me more hair-raising stories from Bamberg. Streicher waffled. Called me literally dangerous. That swine ...Let the men of Munich enjoy their Pyrrhic victory. Work, get strong, then the fight for socialism.

February 26: Letter from Rudolf Hess. They are trying to whitewash Julius Streicher. I shall not let go until this matter is settled.

March 12: To Hitler: 'It hurts my soul to see you in this company'.

March 13: Reading: Adolf Hitler, The South Tyrol Question and the Problem of German Alliances. An amazingly lucid pamphlet with a grand perspective. What a man he is ...the chief! Once again he has removed many a doubt from my mind. [And indeed, the turning point appears to have been reached. The entry for *March 21* reads:] Via Wurzburg ...to Nuremberg ...Julius Streicher [the 'Bavarian bum brusher' and 'swine'] expects me. Long talk. Reconciliation. At least Julius [sic!] is honest.

And reconciliation it was. On March 29, Göbbels records with evident relish that he had 'lunched with the Thyssens' and that he had that morning received a letter from Hitler. 'I am to speak in Munich on April 8th'. There follows a glowing account of Hitler's speech to a gathering of party leaders in Munich on April 13, to which, significantly, Göbbels had been invited:

Matters of principle: Eastern affairs ...The social question. The Bamberg evidence. He speaks for three hours. Brilliant ...Italy and Britain our allies. Russia wants to devour us ...We are moving closer. We ask. He gives brilliant replies. I love him. Social question. Quite new perspectives. He has thought it all out. His idea: Blend of collectivism and individualism. The land: all that is on it and below it for the people. Production, individualistic [i.e. capitalistic] for those who create. Combines, trusts, production of finished articles, transport, etc. to be socialised ...He has thought it all out. I am reassured all round ...with this sparkling mind he can be my leader.

June 10: Still don't know where I am. Now Hitler is to decide next week. He [Strasser] suspects that I am compromising.

June 12: I would like Hitler to draft me to Munich. There I would be away from the muck [eight months previously, Göbbels had declared that *Munich* was a pig sty!].

June 19: Yesterday Hitler addressed industrialists in Essen. Fabulous!

August 25: The latest story, in the eyes of the movement I have met my Damascus.* Bowed to Hitler and Munich. The hawker of this story: the two Strassers.

Göbbels had indeed seen the light. The one-time terror of the landed aristocracy, we find him entering in his diary on October 2, 1926, shortly before assuming his post as *Gauleiter* of Berlin: 'Brunswick. I stay with Herr von Wedel-Parlow. Genuine old nobility.'[14]

Hitler's rout of the radicals began to pay immediate dividends in more ways than one. Set against themselves by their defeat at the Bamberg conference, Hitler felt free to offer them the jobs they wanted on his terms. In August 1926, Göbbels announced his final defection from the Strassers in the *Volkischer Beobachter,* disparaging them as 'revolutionaries in speech but not in deed ...' Three months later Göbbels was heading for Berlin as the city's newly appointed *Gauleiter.* Other posts were also doled out as the 'lefts' came to heel, von Pfeffer** taking over the leadership of the refounded SA, and Otto Strasser, after a spell as propaganda chief, assuming the responsibilities of party organiser. Hitler was

---

* Of Göbbel's defection to Hitler, Otto Strasser writes that in the course of his visit to Munich in April, 'Göbbels had time to make contact with the officials of the Bavarian party [who were, for the first time receiving a steady salary]. The number of cars at the disposal of Hitler's associates did not fail to impress him, and he compared his own modest way of living with the luxury already enjoyed by the Streichers, the Essers, the Webers. His choice was made even before the meeting [at which Hitler won Göbbels over] started. (O. Strasser: *Hitler and I,* p.89). Shortly prior to this sudden 'conversion' — in February 1926 — Göbbels had written to Hitler suggesting that he take on the leaders of the north German 'lefts' as a new 'general staff', hinting that their oppositon would melt away if he did so: 'The men are available. Just call them. Or rather, summon them one after another just as in your eyes they seem to deserve it'.

** In a letter to Pfeffer, Hitler made it plain his new SA chief was to make a clean sweep of the Röhm old guard and its methods: 'The training of the SA must be carried out, not according to military principles, but according to the needs of the party ...In order also to divert the SA from any temptation to activism by petty conspiracies, they must from the very beginning be completely initiated into the great idea of the movement and so fully trained in the task of representing this idea that the individual does not see his mission as the eliminating of some petty rogue, but as committing himself to the establishment of a new National Socialist people's state. Thereby the struggle against the present state will be raised out of the atmosphere of petty acts of revenge and conspiracy to the grandeur of a philosophical war of annihilation against Marxism. We shall not work in secret conventicles but in huge mass marches; the way for the movement cannot be opened up by dagger or poison or pistol, but by conquest of the street'.

now in a position to begin the realisation of the plans and strategy he had devised during his stay in Landsberg prison and in the first year of his renewed party activity:

> From this failure of the putsch we drew a great lesson for the future: we recognised that the new state must previously have been built up and practically ready to one's hand ...In 1933 I had behind me by far the greatest organisation which Germany ever possessed, a movement which was built up from the smallest cells until it had become an organisation embracing the whole Reich. This mighty reconstruction of the party contributed to create the most important condition for taking over power in the state and maintained it securely.[15]

The formation of these 'cells' of the Third Reich dated from the period between 1926 and 1928, by which time the party had been divided into three main compartments. The first, under Gregor Strasser's energetic and highly-talented supervision, had as its sole task the destruction of the existing political order, especially the party's main opponents, the SPD, KPD and the trade unions. The second section comprised the skeleton of the Nazi regime of the future, with leaders responsible for security, economics, agriculture, 'race and culture', law and the projected 'labour service' ministry. As the movement grew in size and influence, attracting into its ranks increasing numbers of military, police, civil service, business and other leaders with technical expertise, so the skeleton took on flesh, in 1933 enabling the party to achieve a relatively smooth take-over when it began to usurp and displace the less pliable personnel of the old system. Finally there was the propaganda department, which functioned under the watchful gaze of Hitler himself. Göbbels became chief of this section towards the end of 1928, a post for which his brief career as a psuedo-revolutionary Nazi eminently suited him.

The 'trade union question' was also tackled in a way that had not been previously possible. Now that the 'radicals' had been bought over and tamed, Hitler felt more free to encourage the development of this side of party work, since it ran far less risk of developing in directions that would antagonise his freshly-won supporters in the business world. Hitler's recommended policy towards the trade unions, it will be recalled, was to enter and seek to weaken them as much as possible. To this end, a Berlin Nazi, Johannes Engel, founded a small cell of anti-Marxist workers at the city's Pneumatic Brake Co., a move that was endorsed by Berlin *Gauleiter* Göbbels, who subsequently appointed Engel NSDAP 'Head of Secretariat for Labour Affairs'. Though it met with little success except amongst workers who were either non-political or had previously adhered to one or other of the bourgeois parties, another step towards a national trade union faction was taken in July 1928, when the party launched its National Socialist Shop Organisation, the NSBO. The director was Reinhold Muchow, who had defected to the Nazis from the nationalist white-collar 'trade union', the DHV (Engel served under him as assistant director). However this organisation did not achieve full party status until as late as January 1931, the main reason presumably being that it had signally failed to win anything approaching mass support in the factories, mines and other work places. At the end of 1931, the NSBO claimed a mere 43,000 members, though this figure was to rise sharply over the next two years as unemployed and near-pauperised workers, despairing of any positive and united action by the two workers' parties and the reformist trade unions, turned to the Nazis as their last hope of salvation. All this however lay in the future as Hitler, emerging victorious from his fight with the north Germans, set out to re-establish the links with the business world that had been shattered by the Munich fiasco and his year of enforced political retirement. He now had something to offer the big employers, and he wasted little time in letting them know.

A year and a day after Hitler had instructed his followers to concentrate all the movement's forces against one enemy — a foe that had as its sole aim the destruction of capitalism — the Nazi leader launched himself on a series of speeches to industrialists and bankers that in the course of the next seven years was to raise the Nazi party from the depths of its post-putsch division and depression to the summit of state power. At Bamberg on 14, 1926, Hitler had laid down the Nazi law on private property to his 'leftist' critics, and routed them. On February 28, he travelled north to the 'radicals' own territory in Hamburg to address, not a meeting of backward workers in the style of Gobbels or the Strassers, but an exclusive gathering of big employers, bankers and right-wing political and military figures at the Hamburg 1919 National Club. Founded shortly after the November Revolution to represent and defend the interests of the port city's beleaguered bourgeoisie (the Hamburg proletariat was among the most militant in all Germany), the club regularly invited well-known personalities from the business and political worlds to address them on themes of their own choosing. Among its guests had been Field Marshall von Mackensen, Admiral von Tirpitz, Schacht, Stresemann, Luther, von Seeckt, Gessler and Cuno. This formidable list would seem to suggest that the National Club had assumed more than a parochial role. In fact it had become a forum for the discussion and formulation of bourgeois-Junker political policies and philosophy, and as such, the club's decision to invite Hitler could not have been taken lightly nor, indeed, without some of its members having already displayed some interest in the ideas and activity of their guest's party. And as Hitler's speech progressed, it became evident that others who were not so well acquainted with his views found Hitler's 'socialism' far more acceptable than the brands they had grown to hate and fear in their native Hamburg. For what Hitler outlined in his address was nothing else than a blueprint for the destruction of the German labour movmement; the detailed strategy and tactics of fascist counter-revolution. Hitler at once went to the root of the problems confronting German imperialism. They did not, as so many on the bourgeois right asserted, date from the November Revolution. This disaster was itself only a symptom of a far more deep-seated disease, whose origins Hitler traced back to the formation of the German workers' movement:

> On that day when a Marxist movement was allowed to exist alongside the other political parties the death sentence was passed on the Reich. All else flowed logically and was the political consequence of the activity of a movement which from the first had as its goal the destruction of the Reich...[16]

Hitler then scourged the old bourgeois 'national' parties and leaders for failing to grasp the root of the problem and take the necessary measures as Bismarck had vainly attempted to do with his anti-socialist legislation.

> The parties of the right were powerless. It has always been our tenet that the people can be educated, that politics is a matter which can be fought about with intellectual weapons. That is wrong, as the final objective of politics, now and for the future, is war. We cannot talk about the laws of democracy prevailing, the determination of things to come by a free people, by the majority of the people. This only makes sense if people recognise it and abide by it. In a so-called democratic society, on that day when a minority, however small, says this law does not apply to us, we will build up our own force and we are prepared to achieve whatever we want by the most brutal means regardless of the cost, when we feel strong enough, on that day, the whole democratic lunacy is doomed.[17]

Hitler had struck just the right note, for these were the sentiments of many of those gathered in the audience. They loathed the political system created by the 'November crime', and the consequent prominent role allotted within it to the reformist representatives of the workers' movement. Before November 1918, the worker knew his place. He would not have dreamt of prying into the business affairs of his employer. Now the same worker had the right — on paper at least — to elect representatives from his shop organisation to check on the operations of the company, just as he had secured the right to free collective bargaining. His employer was now compelled by law to negotiate with his trade union's officials. All this to the reactionary employer, bred in the palmy days of Bismarck and Wilhelm II, was nothing short of 'Marxist dictatorship'. Hitler knew how they felt, since this had long been his own opinion. What he had new to tell them, and what they wanted to hear, was how to end this 'red tyranny'*. But first they listened approvingly to Hitler's explanation of why the bourgeoisie had failed to establish its authority in the early years of the Weimar Republic:

> The bourgeoisie had not the power on their own [they shared it with the social democrats], but in practice they governed the state and the power was still embodied in the state. The whole military establishment and the administration still represented power. But our bourgeoisie so little recognised the necessity of possessing power or of the need for a political philosophy, that it did us the most serious harm. The soldier was persuaded: 'politics are not your affair'. The politicians had been brought up in the conviction to use no brutality, only intellectual weapons. The two had been so far separated that they could not now get together.[18]

Thus the bourgeoisie held in its hands the main levers of state power — the army, police, bureaucracy, courts, etc. — but due to its entire tradition of political indecisiveness and lack of schooling in the harsh business of ruling, could not or would not use them to crush its mortal Marxist enemy. Indeed, they sat in the cabinet with its social democratic representatives, the leaders of a movement which Hitler claimed was characterised by the very qualities the bourgeoisie lacked: 'spirit and brute strength.' Hitler understood far more clearly than any theoretician of 'third period' Stalinism that for all its 'bourgeoisification' the social democratic movement had to be utterly destroyed if Germany was to be politically, economically and militarily equipped for its imperialist role in Europe and the Soviet east. After 1928, the CI leadership repeatedly declared that the SPD was taking on the twin tasks of the fascisation of Germany and the preparation of a new war of intervention against the USSR.** Here we have Hitler, two years earlier, insisting the precise opposite; that the agency for enslaving the German proletariat was national socialism, and that to achieve this aim, it had to *annihilate* social democracy:

---

* 'On the one side [against the bourgeois parties] were the social democrats, not as a weapon of reason but as a weapon of terrorism, as brutal force. They did not appeal to the mind nor to democracy. They called the masses into the streets and with these street masses ...this affair [the November Revolution] was carried out by a handful of people. But this handful had a creed to which they were brutally dedicated'. (A. Hitler: *Speech to the Hamburg 1919 National Club,* February 28, 1926, translated from W. Jochman, *Im Kampf um die Macht,* Frankfurt, 1960)

**'One of the features of [the] approach of a new revolutionary rise is the fact that in the leading capitalist countries (Germany and Britain) the bourgeoisie had been compelled to bring into action its last reserve — social democracy. The Müller and Macdonald governments have accepted the task entrusted to them by the bourgeoisie — to break the rising movements of the workers, establish a Fascist dictatorship and prepare for war, war first and foremost on the USSR'. (S. Gusiev: *On the Road to a new Revolutionary Rise, Communist International,* Vol. 6, No. 19, August 15, 1929, p.717). Less than a year later, Hermann Müller and his fellow social democrats had been ejected from the government by the big bourgeoisie, the first

Thus the revolution succeeded and became stabilised in these past seven years. I emphasise 'the revolution' but not 'the republic' because it is not a question of republic or monarchy but of the structure the revolution has fashioned, which still endures even if it appears to have slowed down [Hitler here refers to the greatly enhanced role the reformist labour movement enjoyed under the Weimar regime — a supposition which becomes obvious in the next passage.] The reasons for the perpetuation of this revolution lie in two human weaknesses: one is the cowardice of [the bourgeois] part of the nation and the other in extreme selfishness. For the revolution has understood something. Not only has it torn down the old building but replaced it by their own apparatus. *There are now 60-70,000 of their supporters in government employment posts and they know their existence depends on the con-*

step taken towards the assumption of power by the real fascists and German imperialism's war on the USSR. As Hitler so rightly insisted, the precondition for the fascisation of Germany and the securing of 'living space' in the Soviet east was the *total destruction* of what the Stalinists termed 'social fascism'. Since third period Stalinism denied the existence of any contradiction between the reformist bureaucracy and the Nazis, it was unable to exploit the antagonisms which arose between the bourgeoisie and the SPD when the former began to hound the reformist leaders and their lower functionaries out of the government and state administrations (as in the case of von Papen's removal of the Prussian social democratic government on July 20, 1932, when even the SPD police chief ended up in one of his own prison cells!). Trotsky on the other hand repeatedly insisted that the KPD should discard its adventurist, ultra-leftist policy of rejecting a united front with the social democratic organisations and instead employ the tactic of the united front, exploiting even the smallest and most transitory conflicts which the bourgeois offensive generated between the Nazis and the reformist leaders. Their struggle to cling onto their long-accustomed posts and privileges, which whether they liked it or not, was directed against the fascists who were seeking to displace them, helped to create the conditions for the formation of an anti-Nazi united front between the SPD, the ADGB, and the KPD, the three principal organisations of the German working class: 'The thousands upon thousands of Noskes, Welses and Hilferdings prefer, *in the last analysis*, fascism to Communism. But for that they must once and for all tear themselves loose from the workers. Today this is not yet the case. Today the social democracy as a whole, with all its internal antagonisms, is forced into sharp conflict with the fascists [just as in March 1920, it was forced into sharp conflict with Kapp]. It is our task to take advantage of this conflict and not to unite the antagonists against us ...It is necessary to show by deeds a complete readiness to make a bloc with the social democrats against the fascists in all cases in which they will accept a bloc'. (L. Trotsky: *For a Workers' United Front against Fascism* December 8, 1931 — in *'The Struggle against Fascism in Germany*, p.137). Less than two months later, with the bourgeoisie hourly mounting its pressure on besieged social democrats, Trotsky again insists that the depth of the German crisis is forcing the ruling class towards a total rupture with the reformists that had served it so well in the past: 'Just now their [Hitler's and the social democratic leaders'] interests diverge. At the *given* moment the question that is posed before the Social Democracy is not so much one of defending the foundations of capitalist society against proletarian revolution as of defending the semi-parliamentary bourgeois system against fascism. The refusal to make use of this antagonism would be an act of gross stupidity'. (L. Trotsky: *What Next?*, January 27, 1932, in ibid, p.173). The Stalinist movement only broke from 'social fascism' and turned towards a bloc with the social democrats when the reformist leaders found themselves threatened principally not by fascist counter-revolution, *but proletarian revolution*. This was the genesis of the Stalinist — reformist — bourgeois liberal popular front in France and Spain before the war, and it remains so to this day, as witnessed by Chile.

tinuance of the present situation. Should this edifice collapse, so would their own existence. Just think gentlemen how incompetent and incapable are those at the top who are bound up in such a situation. How can such low grade people be members of state government, how can such worthless people qualify for the office of Reichs President. Also, when things collapse, their own existence shatters into a thousand fragments. When this scum is so incapable that he can hardly make a living as a guttersnipe, but is now elevated to the governing class, surely *he will fight fanatically to preserve this situation.* You see today the consequences of this tragedy, *and each one feels it personally.*[19] (emphasis added)

Thus did Hitler speak of the working class when snugly closeted behind the locked doors of his future big business paymasters. 'Low grade' proletarian 'guttersnipes' and 'scum' had no right to hold office in the German state or any of its subsidiary organs. The bourgeoisie would only be able to concentrate on its main task — making profits — when this alien growth had been expelled from the German body politic. That was the meaning of Hitler's repeated assertion that the question of political power had to be resolved before there could be any question of an economic flowering.

Economically Germany is gradually facing the danger of a take-over by foreign capital ...The object is no longer to give Germany some assistance but to get the German economy under its control. That is what the Dawes Plan is all about. It was originally believed in many quarters that the Dawes Plan would bring about an unending flow of gold into Germany. The experience has been the opposite and Locarno has been the political receipt for it ...I would [therefore] like to touch on an important manifestation of the post-war period ...the quite incomprehensible belief that the German economy would one day recover and be built up again ...It is madness to spread the idea that Germany will one day rise again by economic means [i.e. by means of the Dawes Plan]...because experience shows that a blooming economy cannot safeguard the state, unless accompanied by a vigilant political will to survive, economics can even be the lure to the destruction of a state. Each one is capable of growth, but woe to those who do not back it up with power ...If we ask ourselves the question what have we really been doing all these years for the salvation of Germany, the honest answer is, we have tried to revive the economy ...You know, perhaps better than others, how treacherous this conclusion has proved ...What is depicted as a revival of Germany is in reality only the organisation of Germany as a colony for its colonialist masters [shouts of 'quite so'].[20]

Hitler has now reached the nub of his case. He poses to his bourgeois audience the question he asks in *Mein Kampf*: how can the political deadlock in Weimar Germany be broken? He describes the polarisation of forces between left and right, worker and capitalist with a rare degree of class consciousness:

What has brought about this downfall? Not recognising the Marxist danger. And what is the position today? There are 30 or 34 million people who decide Germany's fate — by their votes. They consist of three sections. One couldn't care less about what happens. Then there is another section who are internationally, or at least only vaguely nationally minded ...it consists not only of the social democrats but also the communists, the pacifist social democrats and reaches into the centre or to the so-called right parties who will not commit themselves to the national interests, but hope for international pacifist support. This gives opposing groups of 14 to 15 millions and 10,12 or 13 millions of nationally minded with temperament, energy and strength ...Why then cannot Germany rise again? Numbers do not count. What does count is the will to power. The international groups combine the most active, powerful and disciplined ...The communists could win by some form of violent attack. Believe me, if they do, in three years, you wouldn't know Germany. Perhaps millions would go to the scaffold. Every theatre, every cinema, everything down to the railway trains would carry communist propaganda ...On the other hand, suppose the DVP won. You would see no change from now. The hoardings would still have communist propaganda, bookshops their manifestos etc. etc...these Left groups, at most 12-14 million strong, *are more deter-mined and ruthless than the millions on the other side.* The broad masses are blind and stupid and don't know what they are doing. *The parties of the right are without the will to grasp power.* It is quite obvious they have become timid inside the walls of their own camp ...Be clear on this — since time began, the freedom of nations has only been won and safeguarded in battle. Germany will be no exception. Germany is disarmed and encircled, *any national policy is thwarted by the presence of these 14 or 15 million negative elements.* Germany cannot today conduct a policy nor can she fight a battle.. If Germany had to fight today, the warriors could only be taken from the universities and from a few patriotic associations ...At the next election the KPD will get five to six million votes. Many do not see the danger. The grave diggers of Germany are at work. *If the communists were to march today, the social democrats would follow them* ...Read the social democratic press and you will find a continuous leftward trend ...It almost exceeds the communist in agitation. *It has to, otherwise their flock would desert them.* Today the social democrats are demanding a people's referendum ...the wind has changed direction ...they can sense coming events and do not want to be left behind.[21] (emphasis added)

So whichever way the German bourgeoisie turned, whether towards the restoration of its lost colonies and territory, or in the search for political stability and economic prosperity at home, it came up hard against the same obstacle — the 14 to 15 million 'negative elements' of the German proletariat. At this point, when no avenue of escape appears either to be visible or possible, the most determined among the ruling class will turn to the fascists for a solution. And Hitler gives it:

Whether the DVP or the DNVP gets an electoral victory today, takes 15 or 20 seats from the rest, has no significance ...That is what people will not face up to, and that is why Germany will not rise again but decline further year by year. I want to state a plain fact. *The matter of Germany's revival is the matter of the destruction of Marxism* ...The recognition of this was the moving cause of my political activity and of the foundation of the movement I represent today. There are 15 million willing and convinced anti-nationals. *Until they are led back into the fold of a collective national feeling, all talk of a German revival is meaningless.* [shouts of 'hear, hear!'] ...It was so in Italy. It has been resolved there, not thanks to the genius of one man, but to the intelligence of a part of the nation [obviously Hitler means here the bourgeois 'part' since it backed fascism to the hilt against the Italian labour movement], *who realised that all the flowering of trade is ridiculous as long as this poison is in the body* [shouts of 'Bravo!'], It is on the recognition of this that my movement was founded. *Its task is single minded: the destruction and elimination of the Marxist philosophy.* The bourgeois parties have no such aim. All they want is electoral activity. The fundamental thing is — *either Marxism exterminates us or we exterminate it, root and branch.* This formula will eventually create a force which alone can govern as in Italy today, *where the political doctrine makes no secret of the fact that it will break the necks of its opponents,* just as Russia has done on its side. This idea is unacceptable to conventional parliaments. When the moment of danger arises, it is much easier to appoint a commission, which in the end does nothing.[22] (emphasis added)

And what does Hitler then propose; since parliamentary methods are powerless to combat and defeat the Marxist enemy, a movement embracing millions? He proposes the 'plebeian solution', or in the apt words of Rauschning, to pit 'mass against mass'. By its very nature, it is a counter-revolutionary task that is beyond the capabilities of even the most gifted bourgeois career politician, steeped as he inevitably must be in the traditions and methods of parliamentary manoeuvrings, and tricky combinations with the leaders of reformist labour. Such men might serve as invaluable fixers and wirepullers for the fascists, but they cannot substitute for them, as Hitler makes clear and as his capitalist audience ecstatically acknowledges:

> If we have grasped the fact that our fate is to be decided by the destruction of Marxism, then *any means are justified to bring it about ...a movement which turns to the broad masses, to those among whom the Marxists themselves work [is essential].* One can only get rid of poison with an antidote. We must be hard-headed, ruthless, sternly resolved and idealistic [thunderous applause from audience]. So such a movement must turn to the masses wherein lies the source of all power.[23] (emphasis added)

This was heady stuff. The Hamburg bourgeois had never heard anything like it before in their lives. For the first time, here was a movement that not only sought the destruction of Marxism, but actually had a plan to carry it into practice. But Hitler also cautioned them. In order to break into the masses the social democrats and communists regarded as their own private preserve, it would be necessary to indulge in frequent bouts of social demagogy, in which the Nazis would have to pledge themselves to a struggle against capitalism on behalf of the exploited workers and petty-bourgeois. This was the price the bourgeoisie had to pay for their salvation. And besides, as Hitler made clear, the eventual winners would be the employers, since the Nazi 'unions' would not press for material gains as the ADGB unions had done, but drive the worker to produce more:

> These broad masses who are deluded into fighting for Marxism are the only weapon the [Nazi] movement can use to destroy it. But they must be convinced of the rightness of our objective and that all means are justified ...the German trade union movement ...was implanted from abroad and had Marxist tendencies ...The Marxists are behind all these demands [for higher pay, shorter hours, etc.] ...They say 'Behold the bourgeoisie, they feast and revel and you get nothing'. But if a new movement arises which genuinely looks after the broad masses, *don't you think it could conduct the struggle differently, that the masses could be won over?* They must be convinced of our intention to create an independent German national state that will satisfy all their reasonable [sic!] demands. They must believe they will share the benefits of increased production. *The objective must no longer be higher wages; but increased production which will benefit all.*[24] (emphasis added)

Hitler had evidently caught the spirit of the rationalisation movement then gathering momentum in Germany industry, a fact which his audience probably noted with approval. A regime which set as its goal the keeping down of wages and the maximisation of production must have been an exciting prospect after seven years of the Republic's 'political wages', and enforced collective bargaining and the eight-hour-day.

Hitler quickly reassured his audience that there was no question of the Nazi movement yielding to the working class simply because national socialism had espoused a radical-sounding programme and a mass-oriented and aggressive propaganda style:

> It is no use saying to them [the masses] 'I invite you to a discussion'. What you must say is: 'fellow Germans, I hereby open the mass assembly. I must point out that we are in charge and anyone daring to interrupt will be flung out and land up with a broken head [tumultuous applause from audience]. Individual workers can often make so-called reasonable and sensible utterances. *But when he undergoes the effect of 200,000 in the Lustgarten, he is only a worm among them, and these 200,000 are not only a symbol of strength, but also the truth of the movement* ...The [Nazi] movement must be intolerant! This is especially important in view of the bourgeois attitude that everyone has the right to express an opinion ...Our movement will not tolerate that kind of thing ...If a movement wants to carry out a struggle against Marxism it must be as intolerant as Marxism itself ...If I succeed in reclaiming the 15 million folk who today cry 'down

with Germany, long live the international, down with the bourgeoisie, long live the proletariat' *who is going to question my means of doing it?*[25] (emphasis added)

Who indeed. Certainly, very few of those gathered in the Hotel Atlantic on the night of February 28, 1926. And to prove his point, he cited the example of his mentor, Mussolini:

> Remember how we said about Mussolini: he suppresses eleven newspapers, sets fire to four trade union headquarters, and that tomorrow he will do this and that and the other [terrible thing]. But this man has freed Italy from its greatest enemy, and restored it as a great power.[26]

And Hitler knew full well that this was the argument which carried most weight with the German bourgeoisie. The close of his speech was greeted, as it had so often been punctuated with 'tumultuous ovations and cheers.'

There then followed in quick succession further meetings with business leaders, mainly industrialists, as Hitler followed up his great triumph in Hamburg. (There was also the added advantage for Hitler of the rightward swing in the bourgeoisie during and after the princes referendum campaign.) On June 18, he addressed industrialists in Essen (Göbbels was present, and described the meeting as 'fabulous'), where he returned again in the December of the same year, this time addressing about 200 industrialists on the evils of Marxism, democracy etc. A new note appears to have been struck by his call for living space in eastern Europe, a topic which he left alone in his Hamburg speech.

Hitler attached a great deal of importance to these meetings with capitalists, as can be seen from a letter by his deputy, Hermann Hess, to a Nazi supporter in London, Walter Hewel:

> You will probably be most interested to learn that last year [1926] he spoke three times before invited industrialists from Rhineland-Westphalia etc. twice in Essen, and once in Königswinter. Each time it was as successful as that time in the Atlantic Hotel in Hamburg. [Hess also makes the revealing admission that the privacy and composition of the meeting meant that] Hitler could speak quite openly about his political and economic aims; because he could attune his speech to a fairly uniform audience, he was able to stick to a consistent line. As in Hamburg, so in this instance the attitude was at first rather cool and negative ...It was a great pleasure for me to be able to observe how the men slowly changed their outlook not without visible signs of their inner resistance. At the end they clapped in a way these men probably rarely clapped. The result was that at the second meeting of industrialists in Essen about 500 gentlemen accepted invitations. Hitler will probably speak to industrialists for the third time on April 27 [1927].

Hitler, after two years in the political wilderness, was on the way back. And the men of the Ruhr were beginning to take interest.

REFERENCES FOR CHAPTER FIFTEEN
[1] K. Lüdecke: *I Knew Hitler,* p.217.
[2] A. Hitler: *Mein Kampf,* pp.546-553.
[3] O. Strasser: *Hitler and I,* p.83.
[4] J. Göbbels: *Volkische Beobachter,* May 24-25, 1925.
[5] J. Göbbels: *NS Briefe,* October 15, 1925.
[6] A. Hitler: ibid, pp.597-598.
[7] A. Hitler: ibid, p.598.
[8] A. Hitler: ibid, p.598.
[9] A. Hitler: ibid, pp.600-601.
[10] A. Hitler: ibid, p.605.
[11] A. Hitler: ibid, p.603.
[12] A. Hitler: ibid, pp.604-605.
[13] O. Strasser: ibid, pp.87-88.
[14] J. Göbbels: *Diaries, 1925-1926,* Passim, London, 1962.
[15] A. Hitler: Speech to NSDAP rally, Nuremberg, 1933.
[16] A. Hitler: Speech to the Hamburg 1919 National Club, February 28, 1926, translated from W. Jochman: *Im Kampf um die Macht,* Frankfurt, 1960.
[17] Ibid.
[18] Ibid.
[19] Ibid.
[20] Ibid.
[21] Ibid.
[22] Ibid.
[23] Ibid.
[24] Ibid.
[25] Ibid.
[26] Ibid.

Chapter Sixteen
UNITED FRONT FROM BELOW

The Müller ...government [has] accepted the task entrusted to [it] by the bourgeoisie: to break up the rising movements of the workers, establish a fascist dictatorship and prepare for war, first and foremost against the Soviet Union.
(S. Gusiev: *On the Road to a New Revolutionary Rise, Communist International,* Vol. 6, No. 19, August 15, 1929, p.717.)

The kicking out of Hermann Müller's coalition Government by finance capital was the first signal for the establishment of a Fascist dictatorship.
(H. Neumann: *The International Significance of the Reichstag Elections, International Press Correspondence,* Vol. 10, No. 69, August 15, 1930.)

The formation of the Hermann Müller government on June 6, 1928, created a radically new political situation in Germany. For the first time since the break-up of the Stresemann 'grand coalition' in November 1923, the SPD was sharing office with its old liberal and Catholic allies. And we must go back to June 1920 for the last occasion on which a social democrat actually held the post of Chancellor (when by coincidence, Müller was then also the leader of the government). Most important of all, the return to office of the social democrats opened up for the KPD the greatest opportunity to weaken and eventually break the grip of reformism and centrism on the German working class since the crisis year of 1923. That it lamentably failed in this task was directly the outcome of the false policies being pursued by the leadership of the Communist International after 1923, and was not in any sense attributable to a lack of militancy, devotion or courage on the part of rank and file members and supporters of the KPD. In the course of the following five years, they were to furnish more than enough proof of their desire to fight the social democrats and so clear the road to the German revolution. We must repeat and insist: *only the zig-zags of Stalinist policy, forced on the KPD by the Moscow leadership of the CI, prevented them from doing so.* For all the long term advantages — and many of

the tactical ones — lay with the Communist Party. The social democrats had not entered the cabinet as a result of backstairs dealings between the party leaders, but had been thrust into the government by an upsurge of working class militancy and radicalisation that the republic had not witnessed since the stormy summer months of 1923. The Reichstag election of May 20, 1928, only confirmed the continued evolution of a revival in the workers' movement that had been evident from the beginning of 1926, when millions of workers threw themselves into the KPD-SPD campaign to confiscate the princes' property:
(The figures in brackets are for the previous Reichstag election in December 1924)

Party	Votes (million)		%		Deputies	
SPD	9.15	(7.9)	29.8	(26.0)	153	(131)
KPD	3.26	(2.7)	10.6	(9.0)	54	(45)
Centre	3.7	(4.1)	12.1	(13.6)	62	(69)
BVP	0.94	(1.13)	3.0	(3.7)	16	(19)
DDP	1.5	(1.9)	4.9	(6.3)	25	(32)
DVP	2.67	(3.04)	8.7	(10.1)	45	(51)
DNVP	4.4	(6.2)	14.2	(20.5)	73	(103)
Econ. Party	1.4	(1.0)	4.5	(3.3)	23	(17)
Agrarians*	1.26	(0.5)	3.9	(1.9)	21	(8)
NSDAP	0.81	(0.9)	2.6	(3.0)	12	(14)

* Combined totals for Landbund, Bauern und Landvolk, Deutsche Bauernpartei.

Therefore the two workers' parties had gained both in absolute and relative terms as against the parties of the bourgeois centre and right. In a reduced poll (74.6 in 1928, 77.7% in December 1924) the KPD and the SPD increased their combined vote by approximately 1.7 million, while their share of the total poll rose from 35.0% to 40.4% — a level only exceeded twice in the entire history of the Republic (January 19, 1919: 45.5%; June 6, 1920: 41.6%). The election returns of May 1928 not only reflected through the parliamentary prism the renewed combativity of the German proletariat, but the contradictory fashion in which this process of radicalisation was unfolding. On all previous occasions, an increase in votes for the KPD (or in 1919-1920, the USPD) had been accompanied by a decline in electoral support for the SPD. Thus in June 1920, the USPD vote rose by 2.7 million in the National Assembly elections of January 1919, while the SPD lost 5.4 million, being divided roughly equally between working class defections to the left, and middle class shifts towards the bourgeois centre and right. A contrary trend was at work during 1924, following the defeat of the previous year. In December, the KPD lost 0.9 million votes on the May elections, while the SPD picked up 1.8 million. Now in 1928, we find *both* parties gaining simultaneously (though at a different tempo), a sure indication that the entire workers' movement was becoming radicalised, attracting to its side previously passive or even hostile layers of the working population. The rates of growth of the two parties also tell us something about the changed political climate after 1928. While the SPD vote had increased by 15%, that of the KPD was 20% above the level recorded in the elections of December 1924. This could only have meant that the KPD was attracting hundreds of thousands of former SPD supporters and voters, while at the same time, the SPD was more than making good its proletarian losses to the left by winning over a considerable section of the democratic petty-bourgeoisie that had deserted the party after the National Assembly elections of January 1919. Both tendencies worked to the advantage of the KPD, since they indicated that the party was becoming a powerful pole of attraction for workers on the left flank of social democracy, while a significant layer of the middle class, by voting for the SPD, had given indications that as in the campaign for the princes' referendum, they were prepared to align themselves with the workers' movement against the parties of the big bourgeoisie and the ultra right. And here it should be noted that the Nazis reached their all-time low, with a wretched 810,000 votes. How that total became multiplied eightfold within the space of 28 months cannot be explained simply in terms of the impact of the 1929 world economic crisis, which hit Germany harder than any other capitalist state. To argue thus is to concede that fascist movements on such a stupendous scale must inevitably arise under similar conditions of economic crisis, and that therefore there is little or nothing the workers' movement can do to prevent the middle class going over *en masse* to the counter-revolution. This was certainly never Trotsky's view. Analysing the Reichstag elections of September 14, 1930, when the Nazis scored their first spectacular triumph (6.4 million votes), he wrote:

> For the social crisis to bring about the proletarian revolution, it is necessary that, besides other conditions a decisive shift of the petty-bourgeois classes occur in the direction of the proletariat. This will give the proletariat a chance to put itself at the head of the nation as its leader. The last election revealed, and this is its principal symptomatic significance, a shift in the opposite direction. Under the impact of the crisis, the petty-bourgeoisie swung, not in the direction of the proletarian revolution, but in the direction of the most extreme imperialist reaction, pulling behind it considerable sections of the proletariat. The gigantic growth of National Socialism is an expression of two factors: a deep social crisis, throwing the petty-bourgeois masses off balance, *and the lack of a revolutionary party that would today be regarded by the popular masses as the*

acknowledged revolutionary leader. If the Communist Party is the party of revolutionary hope, then fascism, as a mass movement, is the party of counter-revolutionary despair. When revolutionary hope embraces the whole proletarian mass, it inevitably pulls behind it on the road of revolution considerable and growing sections of the petty-bourgeoisie. Precisely in this sphere, the election revealed the opposite picture: counter-revolutionary despair embraced the petty-bourgeois mass with such force *that it drew behind it many sections of the proletariat.[1] (emphasis added)*

So what had transformed the cautious optimism of the democratic petty-bourgeoisie in 1928 into the 'counter-revolutionary despair' of 1930 was not only the economic crisis (which should have worked to the even greater advantage of the KPD) but the reciprocal relations between the two parties of the German proletariat. To understand why the KPD failed to exploit the crisis in social democracy unleashed by its assumption of power in 1928, and further aggravated to near-breaking point with the onset of the depression a year later (when the big bourgeoisie launched its campaign to oust the SPD from the government and replace it with a ruthlessly anti-working class alliance of the right wing parties) to understand why almost the entire petty-bourgeoisie, in the space of three years, stampeded into the camp of fascist counter-revolution, and why even at the very nadir of its fortunes, the SPD still clung onto the bulk of its proletarian support, it is necessary to turn our attentions towards the crucial developments within the Soviet Union and the leadership of the CI over the period between the defeat of the German Revolution in October 1923 and the Sixth Congress of the Communist International, held in Moscow in the summer of 1928.

As the leading section of the CI the Soviet Communist Party carried an enormous historical responsibility on its already heavily burdened shoulders. Not only had it to confront daily the gigantic task of organising the proletarian dictatorship and nationalised economy of a vast and culturally backward multi-national state debilitated by eight years of uninterrupted imperialist and then civil war. The international character of the Russian Revolution, a revolution which issued out of the crisis of a world system of capitalist economic and political relations, necessarily meant that the USSR could only be defended and strengthened against the pressures of imperialism by the methods of international revolutionary class struggle, by the revolution's extension to the heartlands of advanced industrial Europe, principally Germany. This, as we have already noted, was the perspective of Lenin from the first days and weeks of Soviet power. And if we study closely the writings and speeches of Lenin and Trotsky in this period, we are immediately struck by their internationalist approach to even the most mundane or routine task confronting the Soviet government or party. Repeatedly they stress the indissoluble yet contradictory unity between the struggle to consolidate Soviet power and the socialist elements of the economy in the USSR, and the fight for proletarian revolution in central and western Europe. The highest expression of this unity of oppo,ites was to be found in the pre-Stalinist activity of the Co:nmunist International, summed up and generalised in its first four congresses between 1919 and 1922.

The history of the CI after 1923 is one of the squandering, perverting and near-liquidation of the immensely rich practical experience and vast theoretical capital accumulated both before its foundation, in the work of the Bolsheviks, and from 1919, in the activity of its national sections. Step by step, the Stalinist faction in the CPSU gained control of the leadership of the International, driving out its most experienced, gifted and devoted cadres, disorienting and corrupting those who remained, and elevating to its supreme leadership those who for the most part owed their promotion to subservience to the ruling clique in the Kremlin, and an uncritical readiness to accept and embellish each and every slanderous attack on the Trotskyist Left Opposition concocted by the Soviet Stalinists. Central to Trotsky's analysis of Stalinism is his theoretical explanation of how and why the main turns in CI policy after 1923 flowed not from an objective Marxist appraisal of the strategic revolutionary requirements of the working class in the country concerned, but from the tactical exigencies of the burgeoning Soviet bureaucracy. Trotsky was able to demonstrate in his many writings on the USSR and the CI that both the period of *right*-opportunism between 1925 and 1927 when Stalin's faction drove key sections of the International into uncritical blocs with trade union and social democratic lefts (Britain) and left bourgeois nationalists (China), and the subsequent phase of *ultra-leftism* (that ended in 1934 with the adoption of the popular front during which these same reformists were now deemed to be transformed from valuable allies of the proletariat into 'social fascists' and with whom no alliance of any description was permissible) the fundamental theoretical and material basis of Stalinist policy was the same. Whether pursuing a policy of the wildest adventurism, as in Germany between 1930 and 1933, and which made possible the victory of fascism, or the crassest opportunism, as was the case in the bloc between the Chinese Communist Party and the Kuo Min Tang of Chiang Kai-shek, which led directly to the massacre of the Shanghai proletariat in April 1927, the Stalinist faction in the CPSU and the leadership of the CI clung firmly to its leader's policy of building 'socialism in one country', independently of the course of the class struggle in either the colonial world to the Soviet Union's south and east, or in the advanced imperialist nations to the west.

The essence of Stalin's nationalist revision of all Marxist teachings on the international nature of the class struggle was this: that provided further imperialist interventions were kept at bay, the USSR could, alone and unaided by socialist revolutions in the west, proceed to construct a fully developed socialist society. The world division of labour, the international nature of economic relations, the need for the backward Soviet economy to avail itself of the technological expertise and material assistance of culturally advanced countries such as Germany — all this was discarded as Stalin's new nationalist doctrine became the official line of the CPSU and then the CI. Those such as Trotsky who continued to uphold the original internationalist perspectives of the Russian Revolution were slandered either as adventurists who wished to carry the revolution to the west by military means (the 'export of revolution', which in Stalinist parlance became identified with Trotsky's theory of the permanent revolution), or alternatively (and sometimes simultaneously) as capitulators who had abdicated the struggle to develop a socialist-type economy in the Soviet Union. These fundamental differences over questions of internationalism and socialist construction in the USSR were to have a profound bearing on the course of the class struggle in the imperialist world, and nowhere more so than in Germany. After the great defeat of October-November 1923,the KPD was confronted with two central tasks. It had first of all to frankly acknowledge that an historic defeat had indeed been inflicted on the party and the working class and secondly, to learn the reasons why. Here the rise of Stalin's bureaucratic clique in the CPSU played an especially pernicious role. Because of a unique conjuncture of political forces in the two parties, it was able to ally itself briefly with a faction on the Central Committee of the KPD which was widely regarded by communist workers as a genuine left alternative to the centrist inclined Brandler group which had so badly and tragically bungled the revolutionary opportunity in the autumn of 1923. In the early months of 1924, it should be remembered, Stalin had aligned himself with two other prominent 'old Bolsheviks, Zinoviev and Kamenev (the so-called 'Troika') to block Trotsky's fight against bureaucratism in the party and state apparatus.* Appearing before the party and the International as the custodians of orthodox Bolshevism — a

---

* Lenin had been the instigator of this campaign, when he proposed to Trotsky a year earlier that they should form a bloc to cleanse the party of the bureaucratic methods personified by Stalin. Lenin's prolonged illness, and then his death in January 1924, rendered their alliance stillborn, and the battle was only joined in earnest towards the end of 1923 with the letter submitted to the CC of the CPSU by 46 prominent party members — the *Platform of the 46* — and Trotsky's series of articles in the party press on the dangers of bureaucratism, subsequently published under the title *The New Course*.

claim that appeared substantiated to the majority of members by their long records in the party — Stalin, Zinoviev and Kamenev succeeded in having Trotsky condemned by the 13th Party Conference in January 1924 as the leader of a 'petty-bourgeois deviation' in the CPSU. At once, the 'Russian question' became an issue for every section of the CI since the *Troika* now had to ensure that their line prevailed not only in the Soviet Union, but throughout the entire Communist movement. This meant that in the KPD, the major party of the CI (where an oppositional movement would prove most damaging to the prestige and position of the Stalin faction in the Soviet Union) a tendency had to be sought out which would uncritically support the ruling group in the CPSU, and Zinoviev's leadership on the Executive Committee of the CI. This task had acquired a double urgency in view of the fact that both Zinoviev and Stalin were directly implicated in the defeat of 1923. Zinoviev had been responsible for the directives sent to the KPD over the preceding months of preparation, and Stalin had dispatched a letter to the KPD Central Committee recommending the continuation of the party's cautious united front policy which the developing crisis demanded should be rapidly terminated.*

A scapegoat was found — Brandler — and a new group brought into the top leadership which owed its promotion more to direct support from Moscow than the democratic decisions of the appropriate German party bodies. Trotsky was completely opposed to such a blatantly administrative and factional 'solution' to what was a far more deep going and complex problem involving the entire history of the German workers' movement. It could not be overcome by the removal of one leadership, however inadequate, and its arbitrary replacement by another, whatever its pretensions to revolutionary intransigence. Even though Trotsky made clear his political differences with Brandler (differences that continued to widen over the years) his principled defence of Brandler led to his name being linked with an alleged centrist, semi-Menshevik tendency in the CI as well as the CPSU (Radek who also opposed the removal of Brandler by Zinoviev's ukase, was indeed in political sympathy with the deposed KPD secretary, an error quickly exploited by the *Troika*

---

* The letter was couched in the most opportunist terms, inveighing against any rupture with the reformists, whose continued support was seen as a pre-requisite for the eventual victory of the revolution: 'Should the communists (at a given stage) strive to seize power without the social democrats? That, in my opinion, is the question ...If today in Germany the power ...falls, and the communists seize hold of it, they will fall with a crash. That in the "best" case. At the worst, they will be smashed to pieces and thrown back ...Of course, the Fascists are not asleep, but it is to our interest that they attack first; that will rally the whole working class around the communists ...In my opinion, the Germans must be curbed and not spurred on.' (Quoted in L. Trotsky: *The Third International After Lenin*, p.322, New York, 1957.)

in its campaign against the entire Opposition, since Radek endorsed many of Trotsky's criticisms of the Soviet party regime and political line). Thus Trotsky became identified as a supporter of the German 'right', while Stalin and Zinoviev formed an episodic alliance with the KPD 'left' of Ruth Fischer, Ernst Thälmann and Arkadi Maslow, whose group was now given an enlarged representation on the CC of the party.* The fruits of this unprincipled bloc were a grotesque parody of Bolshevism, a pseudo-revolutionary intransigence against social democracy that forshadowed, albeit on a very embryonic plane the ultra-leftism of the Stalinist third period.

Having disposed of Brandler, the ruling group in the Soviet party and the CI had to assert that no serious reverse had been suffered under its leadership in Germany, that the revolutionary crisis was continuing to develop, and that the revolutionary opportunity, far from being missed in the autumn of 1923, lay ahead in the near future.** This utterly false assessment of the

* The Ninth KPD Congress was held in Frankfurt in April 1924, when the party had just emerged from the illegality imposed on it by Seeckt's military rule. Out of the 118 delegates, only 11 were committed supporters of Brandler, the party's general secretary. The newly-elected KPD Central Committee was made up of 11 'lefts' (who were in turn divided amongst themselves, as was soon to become clear) and 4 supporters of the 'centre' including Klara Zetkin and the future Stalinist, Wilhelm Pieck. In a letter addressed to the Congress, the ECCI, had openly backed the 'lefts' (Fischer, Maslow, Thälmann) by endorsing its ultra-left rejection of the united front tactic: 'In Germany it is essential for us to use the united front tactic only from below, that is to say, we will have no dealings with the official social democratic leaders. The tactics of the united front from below must, however, be pursued honestly, consistently, and to the end'. The letter also anticipated the decisions of the Congress when it confidently declared that 'the triumph of the left wing of the KPD is of tremendous significance for the fate of the German revolution'. Within a year, when the helm had been swung by the Stalin faction hard over to the right, the German 'left' was to be given an altogether different evaluation, save for a handful around Thälmann who proved their subservience to the ruling faction in the USSR by shifting their political stance in accordance with every twist and turn in the CI line.
** Trotsky had no time for this empty-headed radicalism. He insisted that a defeat be given its correct name, and that a new orientation be worked out for the KPD which took into account the impact of this defeat on the consciousness of the various layers of the German working class. Once again, as so often in the past, it was a question of making a *transition* from one period and phase of struggle to another, in which new opposites had been established and needed to be grasped consciously before the party could begin to make good the losses of the previous reverse. This was the central theme of several speeches made by Trotsky in the wake of the German defeat. Thus in his address to Military Science Society on July 29, 1924, he warned against the blind optimism then still in the ascendent in the CI: 'It is clear that the bourgeois regime which has been restored in Germany, following the abortion of the proletarian revolution, is of durable stability ...But if we close our eyes to the experience of these events, if we do not use this experience to educate ourselves, if we continue passively to make mistakes like those already made, we can expect to see the German catastrophe repeated, and the consequent dangers for the revolutionary movement will be immense'. (L. Trotsky: *Problems of Civil War*, p.21, New York, 1970) And in a speech given a month earlier, he scourged those who denied that the KPD was in temporary decline, and had lost a large proportion of its mass support in the working class, and that a considerable period of recuperation would be

political situation in Germany provided the sounding board to the mounting leftist rantings that reached a crescendo at the Fifth Congress of the CI held in Moscow in July 1924. In January 1924, at a conference of the International Red Aid, Zinoviev stated that 'Germany is apparently marching towards a sharpened civil war', while a month later, the Praesidium of the EC of the CI declared in its resolution on the recent German events that the KPD 'must not remove from the agenda the question of the uprising and the seizure of power. On the contrary this question must stand before us in all its concreteness and urgency.' On March 26, the ECCI advised the KPD that the defeat of October 1923 was 'only an episode' and that 'the fundamental estimate remains the same as before'.

With the working class in headlong political retreat under Seeckt's military dictatorship, and the German bourgeoisie at last beginning to consolidate itself after years of turmoil and crisis, the ECCI, under Zinoviev's direction, made no call for the KPD to change its tactics or policies: 'The KPD must continue as hitherto to exert all its forces in the work to arm the working class'. *Arm the working class!* That this advice could be given to a party driven into illegality under conditions where any attempt at armed resistance to Seeckt's rule would have been met by the most savage repressions imaginable, indicated just how rapidly the ruling clique in the CI was veering away from Leninist strategy and tactics. One need only recall Lenin's tactical retreat at the time of the 'July Days' in Petrograd to see how little Zinoviev's suicidal recipes had in common with Bolshevism. In the summer of 1923, when the maturing of the revolutionary crisis demanded that the KPD sever the united front with the SPD lefts, and begin the preparations for the arming of the proletariat and the insurrection, Stalin and Zinoviev counselled restraint. Now, when the revolutionary opportunity had been missed, they demanded the arming of the proletariat and the rejection of the united front on the grounds that the revolution was still approaching. The question of the united front is the one that concerns us most here, since it had a crucial bearing on the outcome of the conflict between the Nazis and the German proletariat between 1930 and 1933, when the Stalinists — *for the second time* — banned the formation of a united anti-fascist front between the KPD and the SPD. The ECCI statement on the

required before the KPD could once again regain the political initiative: 'It would be absurd to shut one's eyes to this: revolutionary politics are not the politics of the ostrich ...The German proletariat suffered last year a very big defeat. It will need a definite and considerable interval of time in order to digest this defeat, to master its lessons and to recover from it, once more to gather its strength; and the KPD will be able to ensure the victory of the proletariat only if it, too, fully and completely masters the lessons of last year's experience'. (L. Trotsky: *Through What Stage are we Passing*, p.37.)

German events, dated January 19, 1924, had this to say on the united front tactic in Germany:

> The leading strata of German social democracy are at the present moment *nothing but a fraction of German fascism wearing a socialist mask*. They handed State power over to the representatives of the capitalist dictatorship in order to save capitalism from the proletarian revolution ...It is not just now that these leaders of German social democracy have gone over to the side of capital. At bottom they have been always on the side of the class enemies of the proletariat, but it is only now that this has been revealed to the masses in a glaring light,* *by their completing the transition from capitalist democracy to capitalist dictatorship. This circumstance induces us to modify the united front tactics in Germany. There can be no dealings with mercenaries of the white dictatorship.* This must be clearly grasped by all German communists and solemnly and loudly announced to the entire German proletariat. Even more dangerous than the right wing SPD leaders are the left   the last illusion of the deceived workers ... The KPD rejects not only any dealings with the SPD centre, *but also with the 'left' leaders* until they shall have shown at least enough manliness to break openly with the counter-revolutionary gang in the SPD presidium. The slogan of the united front tactic in Germany is now: *Unity from below!* ...The KPD must learn how to put this slogan of the united front from below into operation. (emphasis added)

Thus even while Lenin lived   he died two days after the adoption of this resolution   the revolutionary tactics and strategy, principles and theory which will forever be associated with his name were being quite openly challenged by the Stalin-Zinoviev bloc. Social democracy is no longer characterised as a *bourgeois tendency within the workers' movement*, but as a 'fraction of fascism wearing a socialist mask'. In other words, *social fascism*. The statement that social democracy had completed the transition from capitalist democracy to capitalist dictatorship was not only proved false in the light of subsequent developments in Germany (where far from serving as an instrument of capitalist dictatorship, the SPD found itself excluded from participation in the government for more than four years, and on at least one occasion — the attempted coup of May 1926 — ran the risk of being the victim of capitalist dictatorship itself), but in a general theoretical sense, in that no tendency which has its historical roots in the proletariat and depends for its survival on a measure of working class support,

---

* Glaring for workers who already adhered to the KPD certainly, but not for those many millions who still clung to the SPD, despite its treacherous record since the foundation of the Republic (and indeed, since August 1914) as was proved by the Reichstag Election results of May 1924, which gave 3.7 million votes to the KPD, but six million to a party that according to Zinoviev had not only gone over completely to capitalist dictatorship, but had become a 'fraction of German fascism'. Lenin dealt with this classic leftist-subjectivist error in his *Left Wing Communism*, where he writes: '...we must not regard what is obsolete to us as something obsolete to a class, to the masses'. (V. Lenin, ibid, *Collected Works*, Vol. 31, p.58.)

can merge *completely* and *permanenently* with an open, military or fascist-type bourgeois dictatorship. The false propositions that social democracy had turned fascist (or to employ a term much abused by the *Workers Press*, 'corporatist') and that it had fused totally and irrevocably with the military dictatorship of Seeckt (a dictatorship that terminated barely a month after this resolution was adopted, when Ebert lifted the state of emergency first proclaimed in September 1923) served to justify the abandonment of the united front tactic, and its replacement by the 'united front from below'. Finally, an *ultimatum* was issued to the SPD lefts — break with your party centre and right, *or we will refuse to form a united front with you*. In other words, the KPD was instructed to form a 'united front' only with those workers and leaders outside its ranks who *in advance* gave undertakings to accept *in toto* KPD policy — a complete violation and travesty of the meaning and spirit of the united front as it was conceived by the CI in the years 1921 and 1922.

The Leninist United Front.

Towards the end of 1921, the CI — not without some considerable inner resistance on the part of its sections — turned towards the tactic of a united front with the parties of the Second International, the centrist Vienna Union (the '2½ International') and the reformist Amsterdam International Federation of Trade Unions. What had brought about this tactical change of line was not a reappraisal of social democracy, nor indeed any change of policy within the leadership of the reformist and centrist internationals, but the temporary recession of the post-war revolutionary wave in Europe. Fascism was on the offensive in Italy, and bourgeois reaction in its various forms in Germany, France and Britain. Every worker and every labour organisation, no matter what political tendency, had to bear the brunt of the capitalist attack on wages, working conditions, jobs and democratic rights then gathering speed across the continent. With a view to establishing a united front of *all* workers' organisations against the bourgeoisie, the ECCI sent out to all the sections directives on how the campaign for the united front should be conducted. It stressed the two underlying principles that had to be observed in all united front activity. Firstly, that far from repelling those workers seeking unity with the communist parties, but reluctant to break from their own leaders and organisations,

> The ECCI is of the opinion that the slogan of the Third World Congress of the CI 'To the Masses', and the interests of the communist movement generally, require the communist parties and the CI as a whole to support the slogan of the united front of the workers *and to take the initiative in this matter.*[2] (emphasis added)

The second, and equally important principle, went to the root of all genuine revolutionary activity:

> The principal conditions which are equally categorical for communist parties in all countries are ...the *absolute independence* of every communist party which enters into an agreement with the parties of the Second and Two and a Half Internationals, its *complete freedom to put forward its own views and to criticize the opponents of communism.* While accepting a basis for action, communists must retain the *unconditional* right and the possibility of expressing their opinion of the policy of all working-class organisations without exception, not only before and after action has been taken but also, if necessary, *during its course* [emphasis in original] *In no circumstances can these rights be surrendered.* While supporting the slogan of the greatest possible unity of all workers' organisations in every practical action against the capitalist front, communists may in no circumstances desist from putting forward their views, which are the only consistent expression of the defence of working class interests as a whole.[3] (emphasis added)

The history of Stalinism is one of the violation of these two cardinal communist principles, either through an ultra-leftist rejection of the united front, first in 1924, and then, with far more deadly repercussions, between 1928 and 1934; or an opportunist, uncritical bloc with the reformists, exemplified by Stalin's combination with the TUC General Council during the British Gerneral Strike of 1926, and later by the liquidation of an already existing unprincipled united front into a counter-revolutionary alliance with the liberal wing of the ruling class – the Stalinist policy of the popular front, inaugurated officially by the Seventh Congress of the CI in 1935, and never since abandoned. Nor was the united front in Lenin's day conceived of simply as a manoeuvre to 'expose' the reformists. It was also a response to and acknowledgement of the profound, organic desire of the working masses for unity against the main class enemy.* The Leninist united front devised a form of struggle whereby this unity could be achieved while at the same time, the fundamental differences in the workers' movement could continue to be fought out without any one of its tendencies surrendering either its organisational independence or political principles. 'March

---

* Drawing on the experience of the revolutionary struggle in Russia before the revolution, the directive pointed out that despite their ceaseless fight against the Mensheviks, the Bolsheviks 'often came to an understanding with the Mensheviks ...The formal break with the Mensheviks took place in the spring of 1905, but at the end of 1905, the Bolsheviks formed a common front with the Mensheviks ...and these unifications and semi-unifications happened not only in accordance with changes in the fractional struggle, but also under the direct pressure of the working masses who were awakening to active political life and demanded the opportunity of testing by their own experience whether the Menshevik path really deviated in fundamentals from the road of revolution ...The Russian Bolsheviks did not reply to the desire of the workers for unity with a renunciation of the united front ...' (as did the Stalinist KPD leadership in 1929-1933)

separately strike together', was the slogan under which the CI launched its world campaign for the united front with the centrist and reformist internationals.

The initiative of the ECCI did not fall on stony ground. Under pressure from their millions of proletarian members and voters,who were daily feeling the same lash of the capitalist offensive in the factories and mines, and on the dole queues, as did their communist class brothers, the leaders of the Second and Two-and-a-half Internationals accepted the ECCI invitation and attended a joint conference of the three movements which opened in the Berlin Reichstag building on April 2, 1922. The discussion was always sharp, at times acrimonious and even verged on virtual civil war. Yet at the end of the day, all three delegations were able to put their names to a joint statement committing the reformists and centrists to a united plan of action with the CI against the capitalist offensive and for the defence of the Soviet Union. The agreed resolution called for united demonstrations in every country over the next month on the following demands:

> For the eight-hour day.
> For the struggle against unemployment, which has increased immeasurably on account of the reparations policy of the capitalist powers.
> For the united action of the proletariat against the capitalist offensive.
> For the Russian Revolution, for starving Russia, for the resumption by all countries of political and economic relations with Russia.
> For the re-establishment of the proletarian united front in every country and in the International.[4]

Of course, the reformists immediately attempted to backtrack on these jointly agreed demands once the question arose of putting them into practice, and this retreat obliged the CI to both denounce the reformists for breaking the agreement concluded at the Berlin conference, and to press on independently with such support as the communist parties could muster amongst the rank and file of the reformist movement. The tactic of the united front was never intended, when first conceived, to bind the hands of revolutionaries simply because the leaders of other tendencies either refused to enter into such tactical agreements, or proceeded to break them when confronted with the resoluteness of the class enemy. As the ECCI statement on the Berlin conference made very clear, 'the united front is not and should not be merely a fraternization of party leaders ...With the leaders, if they want it so, without the leaders if they remain indifferently aside, and in defiance of the leaders and against leaders if they sabotage the workers' 'united front.'[5] And for a brief period in the early summer of 1922, following the breakdown of the arrangements to hold a world congress of the three internationals, the ECCI did recommend to the sections that they struggle to build a 'united front from below'. But it should be remembered that this turn followed a period of repeated attempts to secure a united front with the *leaders* of the reformist and centrist internationals, an agreement which when finally reached, was promptly violated.

And it is evident from the text of the document in question that this 'united front from below' had nothing in common with the versions of Zinoviev (1924) and Stalin (1928-1933), as the following extract makes clear:

> The proletariat without distinction of party has had the opportunity of convincing itself who is for the united front and who is against. The resistance of the leaders of the Second International has frustrated the attempt to organise the proletarian united front from above. That makes it a duty to rally all forces to organise the proletariat for the common struggle in opposition to the leaders of the Second International. Communist workers, it is your duty to spread the lesson of this first attempt to establish the united front among the broadest masses of the working class. Workers of the parties of the Second and Two-and-a-half Internationals! After this experience with your leaders it is your duty to do everything, to omit nothing, *to show the leaders of your parties who have forgotten their duty that you will no longer tolerate sabotage of the united front* ...The slogan of the world workers' congress *will be the slogan of further struggle, but the experience of this first* attempt has shown that to be successful *it is necessary to break the resistance of the social democratic leaders* ...Fight the leaders of the Second International who are splitting the working class. Build the united front from below.[6] (emphasis added)

There is not the slightest trace here of ultra-leftism. The workers in the reformist parties are called upon 'from below' to fight their leaders *in order to drive them back into the united front which they had so shamefully deserted.* It was not, as under Zinoviev and then Stalin, an administratively conceived manoeuvre to 'capture' the reformist-led workers from their already sufficiently 'exposed' leaders, but a tactical turn, a necessary prelude to a renewed offensive to force the leaders of the Second International *back into the united front,* thus bringing into struggle against capitalism (and, given a correct tactic and a favourable conjuncture, eventually against their own reformist leaders) millions of workers who would without such a lead from their organisations, have remained on the periphery of the fight.

The CI did indeed return to the united front tactic later that same year, when at its Fourth World Congress, held in the shadow of the victory of Italian fascism, it issued a challenge to the leaders of world reformism:

> The Fourth Comintern Congress puts a plain question to the Second and Vienna Internationals: Are they willing, now that their policy has still further worsened the position of the working class, to offer their hand to establish the common front of the international proletariat for the struggle for the basic rights and interests of the working class. It

asks the Amsterdam International whether it is willing to stop splitting the trade unions, stop excluding communists from the unions, willing to help in a united front of the working class? ...As we said at the Berlin conference, *the CI does not expect the parties of the Second International, the Vienna Labour Union and the Amsterdam trade union leaders to fight for the dictatorship of the proletariat,* which was and is our goal.* But we ask them whether they want to fight against the dictatorship of capital, *whether at least they want to use what remains of democracy to organise resistance to the triumph of that same capital which turned the world into a* mass grave and is now digging new mass graves for our proletarian youth. The CI has spoken ...It is now the turn of the Second International, the Vienna Labour Union, the Amsterdam Trade Union International and its Hague Congress to speak.[7] (emphasis added)

With the leftwards shift in the German proletariat that gathered pace after the eruption of the Ruhr crisis in January 1923, the KPD was especially well placed to develop the united front tactic on a local and national scale, and it was pursued with great energy and success up until the summer of that year when with the general strike and the fall of Cuno, a sharpening of the attack on social democracy called for a new tactical turn. The failure of the Brandler leadership to make such a turn (a failure which was due in no small part to the role played by Zinoviev, and to a lesser degree, Stalin, who sent his letter to the KPD CC at this crucial moment) was used in the early months of 1924 to cast doubt on the validity of the united front tactic generally. The formulation 'united front from below' was given a leftist interpretation, since it now ruled out negotiations with reformist leaders on principle, whereas the formula had originally applied to a situation which arose when the reformists had either *already broken off* or *declined to enter* a united front between the reformists and revolutionary organisations of the working class.

The Fifth Congress of the CI, held in July 1924, should have placed the German defeat right at the top of its agenda, not in order, in the manner of Zinoviev and Stalin, to hunt down, denounce and disgrace scapegoats, but as Trotsky repeatedly insisted at this time, to prevent such a disaster occurring in the future. But the consolidation of the Stalin-led bureaucratic clique in the leadership of the Soviet Party, drawing its strength from the moods of depression in the working class and the party following the defeat in Germany and the decline of the revolutionary wave throughout Europe, conspired to prevent such a discussion from taking place. The result was a Congress conducted as if in a political and historical vacuum, in which Leninist formulas were eclectically interwoven with the leftist

* Unlike the WRP, which has as its main strategic aim the adoption of a full socialist programme of nationalisation by the Labour Party — in other words, the expropriation of the bourgeoisie.

rhetoric in which Zinoviev and his supporters in the CI were so adept at this particular time. For the first time in an official CI Congress resolution, social democracy was designated as a pro-fascist tendency, and not a *reformist* current *within* the workers' movement which served the interests of the bourgeoisie by diverting the proletariat from the revolutionary struggle for power. In the resolution adopted by the Congress on Fascism, we read the following formulation, one that was put into cold storage for the duration of the right turn between 1925 and 1927, and then revived and given an even more leftist emphasis in the six years between 1928 and 1934.

> As bourgeois society continues to decay, *all* bourgeois parties, *particularly social democracy,* take on a more or less fascist character ...Fascism and social democracy are the two sides of the same instrument of capitalist dictatorship. In the fight against fascism, therefore, social democracy can never be a reliable ally of the proletariat.[8] (emphasis added)

This utterly false characterisation of the relationship between fascism and social democracy was rendered all the more dangerous in this instance in that it was combined with an impeccable definition of fascism.*

Once again we can see the same idealist method being employed in the approach to social democracy. First it is dubbed 'more or less' fascist, then for good measure, workers are told in suitably grave tones that it 'can never be a reliable ally of the fighting proletariat'. *But the Communist International was founded in 1919 for this very reason!* Was it therefore necessary to 'prove' it yet again by abusing reformist leaders as fascists? The test of whether social democrats can prove reliable allies of the proletariat in its struggle against capitalism — an issue not in doubt amongst communists — is to repeatedly summon them, through mass pressure *from below,* combined with direct appeals *from above,* to joint struggle on a limited and agreed set of demands, under the condition that neither party demands of the other that it surrenders its right to criticise its united front allies, or its freedom of action on issues where there is not and can never be any such agreement. The Fifth Congress recommended a different united policy from that pursued under the leadership of Lenin and Trotsky — and, incidentally, Zinoviev — in earlier years. The sections of the CI were now summoned to 'fight for the international united front under Comintern leadership'.[9] In other words, participation by other tendencies in this 'united front' was excluded from the outset, since by definition, it was to be under the sole leadership of the CI and therefore no united front at all.

---

* The question of fascism, social democracy and social fascism in the early years of the CI is discussed at greater length in a note at the end of this chapter.

And as if this was not enough to bemuse the delegates and those they represented, another resolution, the *Theses on Tactics,* adopted a mid-way position between the already-quoted formulation on the united front, and that which had been current in the CI in 1921-1923. Here the main purpose of the united front was characterised as a 'struggle against the leaders of counter-revolutionary social democracy and ...emancipating social democratic workers from their influence', a view which was contrasted with a 'right wing tendency' in the CI (a thrust primarily at Brandler) which 'tended to interpret the united front as a political alliance with social democracy'.

Both are wrong. The united front is neither simply a struggle against the leaders of reformism, any more than it is an *alliance* with social democracy. It is a fighting bloc of two or more workers' organisations which come together on certain basic class issues which affect them all and which agree to fight together for a limited time for a limited set of demands. In the course of the struggle for the united front, and during its operation, it will become possible for the communists to convince workers following the reformists that their leaders do indeed fail to defend their class interests, *but only in so far as the communists prove themselves by their wholehearted committment to the united front action that they are fighting for the class as a whole, and not simply in order to expose the reformist leaders.* Along this sectarian path lies certain alienation of the reformist workers, *and the consequent strengthening of social democracy.* The same resolution underlined its eclectic character by then swinging over to the leftist position adopted in the resolution on Fascism: i.e. the 'united front from below':

> The tactics of the united front from below are the most important, that is, a united front under communist leadership concerning communist, social democratic, and non-party workers in factory, factory council, trade union, and extending to an entire industrial centre or area or industry.[10]

All very impressive on paper. But, a naive worker might ask, since you intend to form a 'united front from below' with social democratic and reformist trade union workers at every imaginable place, why not, instead of calling upon these millions of workers *individually* to place themselves under the leadership of the Communist party (something they are obviously not prepared to do, since they have decided to remain with the reformists) why not address this demand to the *organisations* to which these workers belong, or owe their political allegiance? At the Fifth Congress, such a question would have received several answers, according to which resolution it was drawn from. After the Sixth Congress in 1928, there was only one permissible reply: the social democrats have turned social fascists, together with the organisations they lead, even down to their middle and lower officials, cadres, shop stewards and municipal councillors. There-fore, no unity with the social fascist traitors, but only a united front from below under the leadership of the communist party. We can see how — quite unconsciously — the ground was being prepared for this suicidal rejection of the Leninist united front in the period of leftism which followed the defeat of the German revolution and reached its apogee at the Fifth Congress of the CI.

Far more issues were at stake for the *Troika* at the Fifth Con-gress than an examination of the German defeat. Indeed, the fantasy was still sustained in defiance of all the evidence that the proletariat was still advancing towards the revolution!* Neither was there a serious appraisal of the application of the united front tactic in a period when large numbers of workers previously behind the communist parties were drifting back towards the reformists. The central issue at the Congress was the isolation and defeat of Trotsky and his real or suspected supporters in the other sections of the CI. This campaign of necessity had to take the form of a fight against Trotsky's alleged attempts to 'substitute Trotskyism for Leninism'. By a clever series of manoeuvres, the Zinovievists in the ECCI and the national sections were able quite falsely to link Trotsky with genuine centrist elements in the In-ternational, who had indeed been guilty of committing oppor-tunist errors in their dealings with social democracy during the period of the application of the united front tactic in Germany and elsewhere.** Thus the so-called 'Bolshevisation' campaign was a two edged weapon. While it directed justified blows at the centrists, it also served to undermine Trotsky's standing in the Soviet Party and the CI, thereby clearing the ground for the re-vision of Leninist principles and theory that was shortly to be

---

* 'The prospects for the German revolution, as outlined by the ECCI in the autumn of 1923, remain unchanged ...by its very nature the international position of the German bourgeoisie and social democracy remains hopeless ...The internal crisis may come to a head very quickly'. (*Theses on Tactics* adopted by the Fifth Congress of the CI, July, 1924.)

** 'The Congress ...observes that the opposition in the RCP [Russian Communist Party] was supported by groups in other parties, in the Polish, German and French parties, etc; this, like the RCP opposition, is a manifestation of a right (opportunist) deviation in these parties, and was condemned as such by the fifth congress of the CI ...The congress resolves ...to endorse the resolutions of the 13th conference and 13th congress of the RCP, which condemned the platform of the opposition [the '46'] as petty-bourgeois, and its conduct as a threat to the unity of the party and con-sequently to the proletarian dictatorship in the Soviet Union'. (*Resolution of the Fifth CI Congress on the Russian Question*). Thus support for the Soviet Left Opposition was not merely branded as right opportunism, but deemed tantamount to threatening the existence of the Soviet Union itself. And here it should be noted that Zinoviev's leftist course at this time enabled the *Troika* to depict Trotsky (who was arguing for a sober policy that would favour the eventual revolutionary regroup-ment of the shattered ranks of the German proletariat) as a rightist seeking to 'de-Bolshevise' the RCP and the CI and subvert it with his own brand of 'Menshevism'.

undertaken by Stalin with his new nationalist policy of 'socialism in one country', which he first enunciated in October 1924.

In a superficial sense it could be argued that the leftist line prevailing in the CI from January 1924 until a year later did not correspond to the rightwards course being pursued within the Soviet Union by the *Troika* in the field of economic policy and on questions of party democracy and the fight against bureaucracy. But this is to miss the contradictory essence of the Thermidorian reaction then unfolding in the Soviet Union. Its most acute manifestations appeared at the core of the party organisation, and it was consequently against Stalin, the recently appointed party general secretary, that Lenin intended to direct his heaviest blows. But precisely because bureaucratisation was concentrated at the party centre, it assumed a highly contradictory form. The eroding of party democracy was carried through in the name of defending the party rank and file against 'aristocrats' such as Trotsky. The entrenchment of Stalin's bureaucratic clique took place under the sign of a 'Leninist' struggle against bureaucracy. Casting itself — initially quite sincerely — in the role of the defender of Bolshevik tradition, the *Troika* depicted Trotsky as the leading spokesman for a 'social democratic deviation' in the party, in which role Trotsky was fast regressing to his alleged former Menshevik errors.

And this line was carried over into the CI, a manoeuvre greatly faciliated by Zinoviev's chairmanship of the ECCI, from which position he was able to build up anti-Trotsky factions in most of the parties of the International (many of the Zinovievists soon found themselves out of favour when their patron temporarily broke from Stalin in the spring of 1926 to form a bloc with Trotsky — the Joint Opposition). This unity between the lines pursued by the dominant faction in the post Lenin CI and Soviet party also expressed itself in another subtle fashion. Throughout 1924, and even into the early months of 1925, the ECCI tried to sustain the illusion that the working class was still on the offensive. This was in part a factional position directed against Trotsky (the leader of the 'social democratic deviation') who argued that on the contrary, the immediate perspective was not one of a naked clash between the forces of proletarian revolution and fascist counter-revolution (in which the social democrats had been allotted by Zinoviev and Stalin the role of a left cover for fascism), but of the revival of social democracy *on the basis of an easing of tensions between the classes.* As the year drew on, more and more evidence piled up that Trotsky was correct, that the workers' movement was in decline almost everywhere, that the reformists were not only regaining their grip on large sections of the proletariat who had moved towards communism over the previous two to three years, but were even preparing to or had entered coalition governments with the liberal representatives of the bourgeoisie (France and Britain). Yet still Zinoviev, sustained by the Stalin faction in the Soviet party, refused to acknowledge this new situation, one which demanded different tactics towards reformism from those called for in Germany in the autumn of 1923. And if a real mass movement of workers could not be found by the CI, then substitutes for it had to be created. To adopt a long-term perspective that took into account the real level of the working class movement was tantamount to conceding that Trotsky was correct in his estimation of the nature of the period through which the CI was passing, something Zinoviev, for factional reasons, was not prepared to do, no more than were his supporters around Stalin in the Soviet party apparatus. Thus began the search for forces *outside* the proletariat that could fill the vacuum created by the decline in working class militancy after the defeat in Germany, the continued rule of fascism in Italy, and the renewal of social democracy throughout Europe.

Organisations and leaders who briefly flitted across the Comintern stage in this period included the Peasants International (Krestintern) headed by the Pole, Dombal, a movement whose size and influence was exaggerated out of all proportion as the specific weight of the CI declined in the major capitalist countries. In the United States, the Communist Party attempted to create the semblance of a mass movement by throwing its few and precious cadres into a campaign designed to boost and 'capture' the Farmer-Labour Party of the radical petty-bourgeois, LaFollette. None of these opportunist ventures produced any tangible 'results' for the CI except confusion and a shameful mixing of banners and programmes. And what is especially significant is that this liquidationism proceeded at full speed at the precise time when the ECCI was proclaiming from the Kremlin rooftops its undying hostility to a social democracy that was turning fascist, and remonstrating with all those in the sections who still argued for the application of a genuine Leninist united front with the reformist workers' organisations. Leftism, as is so often the case, *provided the screen for a transition to opportunist positions.* For what was the essence of Stalin's CI policy between 1925 and the end of 1927? That in order to prevent an imperialist intervention from disrupting the USSR's gradual progression towards 'socialism in one country', it was necessary to subordinate the parties of the CI to the *strategy* of building a series and network of blocs with reformist and bourgeois nationalist organisations, whose sole task it would be to restrain the imperialists from an invasion of the USSR. In Trotsky's words, Stalin's policy was to transform the parties of the CI from movements fighting for the proletarian revolution into 'frontier guards of the Soviet Union'. The essential groundwork for this right wing turn, one which ruined a pre-revolutionary situation in Britain, and a revolutionary one in China, *had been laid during the period of ultra-leftism in 1924*. In both instances, the CI leadership leaned for support on organisations and leaders whose entire outlook was hostile to the methods and goals of proletarian revolution. In the 1924 phase of *leftism*, this took the form of seeking to artifically and administratively *accelerate* the tempo of the class struggle, a method which had its tragic climax in the suicidal Estonian uprising of December 1924, while in the *rightist* phase of 1925-1927, it was to *restrain* a working class now resuming the offensive by subordinating its communist leadership to an unprincipled alliance with reformists (the TUC General Council in Britain) and bourgeois nationalists (Kuo Min Tang in China). In both cases, the method of organisation and leadership was bureaucratic, and had its social roots in the growth of bureaucracy within the Soviet Union in conditions of economic backwardness, cultural poverty and imperialist encirclement. Trotsky summed up the dialectical relationship between these three crucial phases of the CI — the rightist errors in Germany in 1923, the year of leftism which followed, and the opportunist line of 1925-1927 — in the following way:

> The Left illusions of 1924 rose thanks to the Right leaven. In order to conceal the significance of the mistakes and defeats of 1923 from others as well as from oneself, the process of the swing to the Right that was taking place in the proletariat had to be denied and revolutionary processes within the other classes optimistically exaggerated. That was the beginning of the downsliding from the proletarian line to the centrist ...which in the course of the increasing [capitalist] stabilisation, was to liberate itself from its ultra-left shell and reveal itself as a crude collaborationist line in the USSR. in China, in England, in Germany and everywhere else.[11]

Thus the formation of the Anglo-Soviet Trade Union Committee was *conceived* under the *leftist* schemas in force during the unfettered reign of Zinoviev, but *applied* in a thoroughgoing *right-opportunist* fashion in the period before, during and even after the betrayal of the General Strike by the Soviet trade unions' British TUC partners. What had changed in the course of 1925 was not the method of leadership in the CI but a definite bedding down of the rising bureaucracy on the foundations of the more privileged elements of Soviet society — the technical experts, richer peasants (*Kulaks)* highly skilled workers, party and non-party officials and the like. This layer, like the labour bureaucracy in the capitalist countries, was either in the process of solving its own 'social question', or in the case of the most privileged layers in the party, state and economy, had done so already. And as a satisfied social stratum, it acted as a conservative force within the Soviet Union and its ruling party, eschewing all political or social upheavals that might disrupt its own petty-bourgeois or even bourgeois conditions of life. Here too it began to exhibit, though necessarily in the guise of adherence to Stalin's revisionist version of 'Bolshevism', all the ideological and psychological traits of its counterpart in the trade union and social democratic bureaucracies in the major capitalist countries. Inevitably, this stratum began to exert enormous pressure on the organisation and leading cadres of the CI, since this movement, while it remained true to its revolutionary principles, was a permanent and intolerable challenge to the untramelled rule of the usurping bureaucracy in the Soviet Union. Just as had been the case in the Soviet party, Stalin became the instrument for the exertion of this pressure, for despite his many weaknesses, Zinoviev found himself drawn towards Trotsky on a series of key issues: China, where the communist party had, on the instructions of the ECCI, liquidated itself into the bourgeois Kuo Min Tang; Britain, where the Communist Party and its Minority Movement in the trade unions was functioning as little more than a mouthpiece for the TUC lefts with the slogan of 'All Power to the General Council'; and on economic policy in the Soviet Union, where Stalin, now backed by his new theoretician, Bukharin, was leaning on the *Kulak* and the private trader and opposing Trotsky's repeated demands for a planned policy of rapid industrialisation and *voluntary* collectivisation of private farming. The eclipse and final ousting of Zinoviev from the chairmanship of the ECCI* a post he had held on Lenin's

---

* Zinoviev was removed from the leadership of the CI by decision of the CPSU CC at its session of October 1926, where Trotsky and Kamenev were removed from the party Politburo. Bukharin became the new CI Chairman. The composition of the ruling body of the CI between its congresses, the Presidium of the ECCI, had undergone drastic changes in personnel since the death of Lenin, reflecting the violent oscillations of the factional struggle in the CPSU. At the last congress at which Lenin spoke — the fourth, in December 1922, Lenin and Trotsky were elected to the ECCI, while on the Presidium sat Zinoviev and Bukharin from the Soviet Party. The rise to power of the *Troika* in the USSR greatly influenced the composition of the ruling bodies elected at the fifth Congress less than two years later. Now the Soviet representation on the Presidium was doubled to include not only Kamenev, who had been active in the work of the CI from its early days, but the third member of the *Troika* Stalin, who had never even so much as attended either a CI Congress or written on its problems in any of the party or CI organs. The Soviet fraction in the ECCI was equally dominated by opponents of Trotsky — Zinoviev, Bukharin, Stalin, Kamenev — with Trotsky now relegated on purely factional grounds to the position of candidate. The break-up of the *Troika* was also faithfully reflected in the Presidium and ECCI membership. At the Sixth Plenum of the ECCI in the spring of 1926, Kamenev (now in opposition with Zinoviev, and shortly to form a bloc with Trotsky) was removed and on came Kuusinen and Lozovsky, both firm Stalin men; and from the KPD, Remmele, who joined Thälmann, elected by the ECCI after the Fourth Congress. Then in the Autumn of 1928 there began a purge of Bukharinites, which reached its climax with the removal of their leader from the Chairmanship of the CI on July 3, 1929, by a decision of the ECCI on the 'recommendation' of the CPSU CC. Six years later, at the Seventh and last Congress of the CI (where under Dimitrov's guidance, the line was mapped out that prepared counter-revolution in Spain and France) a squad of utterly depraved and subservient Stalinists was

proposal since its foundation in March 1919, was therefore a treacherous blow struck by the bureaucracy against the international working class and on behalf of the most reactionary anti-Soviet forces in the USSR. This progressive weakening and eventual destruction of the CI as a revolutionary factor in the life of the Soviet and world working classes was absolutely essential for the triumph of the Stalinist bureaucracy, and its leader could not afford to rest until its finest cadres had either been expelled, broken or murdered in the cellars of the Lubianka, along with the victims of Stalin's purges in the CPSU.

Towards the Sixth Congress.

Trotsky makes the theoretically acute observation that beginning with the false leftist line of 1924, each wrong orientation of the CI originated in the mistakes of the previous phase. Thus we have two interpenetrating processes. After 1924, Stalin's bloc with the *Kulak* and the private trader (justified on the basis of Bukharin's theory that the rich peasant could be persuaded to peacefully 'grow into' socialism) provided the national foundations for the CI's international policy of blocs with reformists and bourgeois nationalists. However it was not simply a question of a mechanical or automatic reflex projection of the Soviet line onto the CI, but also of such an opportunist turn being nourished by the leftist errors of 1924. The same process was at work on a national scale three years later, when recoiling at the last moment from the threat of a revolt against the Soviet power by the pampered and appeased *Kulaks*, Stalin swung sharply to the left and demanded what amounted to enforced collectivisation of the peasantry and a crash programme of industrialisation. This leftist zig-zag, just like those that had preceded it in the CI, had been prepared by the previous policy, one of steady retreat before restorationist elements in the town and country, and of continuous and mounting persecution of the Left Opposition, which had developed a programme to counter the crisis and to bring the CI back to its original revolutionary perspective.

What effect did Stalin's abrupt about-turn on domestic economic issues have on the policy of the CI, which from 1925 until the last months of 1927, had been one of the right-opportunist blocs with reformists, bourgeois nationalists and

elevated to the body that in Lenin's day, had been staffed by the finest leadership that had ever stood at the head of the world workers' movement. Of the Presidium elected after the Fourth Congress in 1922, (12 full members, 3 candidates) only two — Kuusinen and the Bulgarian Kolarov — survived the successive waves of purges to serve Stalin after the Seventh. Just as the Stalinist bureaucracy destroyed Bolshevism in the USSR, so it devastated the international movement founded by Lenin, Trotsky and Zinoviev to carry the Russian revolution to every corner of the globe.

petty-bourgeois radicals? Once again, the problem is more complex than might appear at first sight. It has almost become a truism today to say that the line of the CI was after Lenin's death determined by the policies being pursued by the dominant faction in the Soviet bureaucracy. This can indeed be substantiated by referring to the ultra-leftist swing which began in the CI early in 1928 and gathered pace step by step with the increased tempo and ferocity of Stalin's drive to 'liquidate the *Kulaks* as a class'. Likewise with the right turn towards the popular front and entry into the League of Nations (1934), which coincided with the completion of collectivisation, a slackening in the tempo of industrialisation, and the emergence of fresh recruits — several millions strong — to the Soviet 'elite', whose material basis had been created by the enormous economic and social changes wrought over the previous six years. But we have also to consider the CI as a force in its own right, led by cadres whose record of struggle in the workers' movement in many cases went back over more than a quarter of a century. For all their political faults, they were not made of the stuff that lent them readily or willingly to becoming puppets of Stalin's ruling clique. Indeed, not only the leading bodies of the CI, but those of its national sections had to be purged repeatedly before Stalin could trust the International to function as a servile tool of Kremlin diplomacy. Nor should we neglect the millions of workers who over the years joined the parties of the CI in order to make the socialist revolution in their own countries, and not simply to worship and applaud 'socialist construction' in the USSR from afar (as did in the popular front period so many middle class liberals and radicals). The proletarian base of the CI in the major capitalist countries could not be expected by Stalin to submit knowingly to a line that spelt defeat and even physical destruction for themselves and their movement. Then we must also remember that what Trotsky says about the first two zig-zags after 1923 also holds good for the third in 1928, when suddenly and without exception the national sections were found to have been harbouring hordes of right wing deviationists who had unaccountably remained undetected over the previous three years. The opportunist line of that period now bore the same relationship to the ultra leftist one that was to succeed it as did the centrist mistakes of the KPD in 1923 to the Zinoviev-inspired leftism of 1924. The policy of aligning the Communist Parties with the reformists had not only led to serious new defeats (as in Britain) but had generated considerable hostility towards the social democrats among rank and file communist workers. This thoroughly justified hatred for the reformists who had betrayed the general strike of 1926, and crucified the miners right into the winter of that year, was not developed along Leninist lines by the adoption of correct tactics in relation to the reformist movement in Britain and other countries where it was strong; but perverted and exploited through a renewal, in an even more leftist fashion, of the sectarian formulas of 1924, which had been gathering dust in Bukharin's office for the duration of the bloc with the TUC and the Kuo Min Tang. While the basic and decisive impetus for the ultra-left turn towards the 'united front from below' and the theory of 'social fascism' came from the dramatic turn in the Soviet Union at the beginning of 1928, it was without the least doubt anticipated, supplemented and augmented by the dialectical relationship between the manifold stages and phases in the degeneration of the CI that began with the German defeat of 1923.

Nor, finally, should we for one moment underestimate the importance of the theoretical, programmatic and agitational activity of the Left Opposition. Although increasingly denied access to the party press and the right to address meetings of fellow party comrades, the Left Opposition tirelessly warned of the dangers implicit in the Stalinist course both nationally and internationally, which Trotsky described as one of clinging to 'rotten ropes' — the TUC in Britain, the Kuo Min Tang in China, and the *Kulak*, Nepman and bureaucrat in the Soviet Union. On the fate of each of these alliances, the Left Oppositions' warnings were tragically confirmed, and with each reverse suffered by the Stalin faction, the pressure increased within it to execute a manoeuvre towards the left — not in order to return to the Leninist course of the pre-1924 period, which would have demanded the jettisoning of the Stalin-Bukharin theory of 'socialism in one country' — but to cut ground from under the feet of the Left Opposition, and to disarm at least some of their criticisms by paying lip service to the need for a firm proletarian and internationalist line.

Unless we take these secondary, but by no means insignificant factors into account, we are in danger of arriving at a view of the CI which might appear to be formally correct, and in accordance with 'orthodox' Trotskyism, but which in practice tends towards schematicism. Thus we will be unable to explain or understand why, on December 12, 1927 — a full month before Stalin's first report on the grain procurement crisis — two of Stalin's budding henchmen, Heinz Neumann of the KPD, and the fellow Georgian Besso Lominadze, usurped the authority of the Chinese Communist Party Central Committee by launching a disastrous revolt in the south Chinese city of Canton. The 'commune' was drowned in the blood of thousands of workers in a matter of hours, whilst its two chief architects made their way back to Moscow to report to their patron. Stalin's reaction to the episode seems to suggest that by this time (early 1928) he had begun to consider a turn to the left in CI policy as a possible way of both outflanking the expelled Left Opposition and of undermining the position of Zinoviev's successor in the ECCI, Bukharin. For in the bitter arguments that ensued in the unavoidable post mortem on the fate of the Canton Commune, Bukharin received little, if any support from Stalin in his verbal onslaught on the two adventurers.*

Neither is it hard to see why Stalin adopted such a guarded attitude towards the Canton Commune adventure, since elements of his future ultra-leftist line can be detected in his Political Report of the CPSU Central Committee to the 15th Party Congress, delivered on December 3, 1927 — that is, nine days *before* the Canton insurrection. Here we find Stalin repeatedly asserting, in complete defiance of the facts, that 'only the blind and the faint-hearted can doubt that the Chinese workers and peasants are moving towards a new revolutionary upsurge', and that 'whereas a couple of years ago it was possible and necessary to speak of the ebb of the revolutionary tide in Europe, today we have every ground for asserting that Europe is obviously entering a period of new revolutionary upsurge...'[12] What conclusions can be drawn from Stalin's remarks on the situation in Europe and China? Firstly, he dates the ebbing of the post-war revolutionary wave at 1925, two years later than was actually the case — in autumn 1923, with the definitive defeat of the German revolution. But under Zinoviev (with whom Stalin was then allied against Trotsky) the official CI line was that the revolutionary wave was still in the ascendent, a false perspective that was

* One former anonymous CI official relates: 'They had no reason to tremble for their careers when Bukharin, who had learned about the Canton insurrection only from the wires published in the newspapers [thus confirming that the whole suicidal undertaking had been launched behind the back of the leading organ of the CI, a higher authority than either the Chinese Party or even the CPSU.], was shouting at them during the secret session of the Comintern in Moscow. In back of them stood a mightier man who gave the two boys a thorough scolding but did not permit any harm to come to them. [Not at any rate until the onset of the great purge, in which both Neumann and Lominadze — now bitter opponents of their former protector — shared the fate of so many other functionaries and leaders of the CI.] A year later, Bukharin was finished in the Comintern and a new leadership instituted. Heinz Neumann returned to Germany, became a deputy in the German Reichstag, and one of the mighty in the KPD: (Ypsilon: *Pattern for world Revolution*, p.191, New York, 1947). This account, which is corroborated by other independent versions of the Canton Commune episode, bears out Trotsky's own judgement on the motives behind the staging of the insurrection, namely that it 'was an adventure of the leaders in an effort to save their "prestige" '. And he also makes the telling observation that the emergence of putschist moods in the Chinese CP, hypocritically condemned by an ECCI resolution on the Canton commune, were 'a reaction to the entire opportunist policy of 1925-1927, and an inevitable consequence of the purely military command issued from above to 'change the step' without an evaluation of all that had been done, without an open revaluation of the basis of the tactic, and without a clear perspective.' (L. Trotsky: *The Chinese Revolution* — June 1928 — in *The Third International After Lenin*, p.200, New York, 1957). All of which holds good for the leftist turn that was to gather pace throughout the CI during the early part of 1928, and nowhere more so than in Germany.

silently abandoned early in 1925, when under the influence of Stalin's new theory of 'socialism in one country', the CI began to establish 'united fronts at the top' with the reformists of the British TUC and the bourgeois nationalists of the Kuo Min Tang. There then, in accordance with the new CI line, ensued a period of 'stabilisation', just when in Britain and China, the masses began to take the *offensive* against their class enemies, an offensive that clashed with and was finally blunted by the prevailing opportunist line of the CI. Yet precisely at this point, when the British and Chinese masses were still reeling from the blows inflicted on them as a direct result of Stalin's rightist course, the architect of these defeats proclaims that a 'new revolutionary upsurge' has begun and in the very countries where the opposite trend is gathering momentum! This was leftism at its most infantile. Thus as in 1923, 1924, and 1925-1927, the CI orientation was in violent conflict with the real, objective movement of the class struggle and the development of class consciousness in the proletaritat and its communist vanguard. The CI was to the right in 1923, when it should have been driving the KPD on towards the seizure of power, and to the left in 1924, when it should have applied the brakes and digested the lessons of the defeat of the previous autumn. It then swung back to the right during 1925 when in China and Britain especially, historic class battles were in preparation. And finally, at the very close of 1927, Stalin began to push the line back towards and then quite rapidly beyond the Zinovievist leftism of 1924, with his empty chatter about 'new revolutionary upsurges', designed to conceal why the real upsurges of the previous two years had been beaten back and, in China, drowned in blood.

Then there was another aspect of Stalin's report to the 15th Congress, one that has remained unaccountably neglected by those (such as Theodore Draper*) who have hunted high and low

---

* Cf. T. Draper: *The Strange Case of the Comintern, Survey,* Summer 1972, Vol. 18, No. 3. This is a near-exhaustive inquiry into a most important subject, presumably carried out by its author as part of his research into the history of the Communist Party of the United States, which Draper is currently engaged in writing. Nevertheless, Draper's long essay on the origins of 'social fascism' is not without its errors and ommissions. He picks up Stalin's December speech reference to the onset of a 'new revolutionary upsurge' (p.104) but not his associated claim that 'the policy of the bourgeois governments' was gradually becoming 'fascicised' (J. Stalin: *Political Report of the Central Committee,* December 3, 1927, in *Collected Works,* Vol. 10, p.288.) Equally surprising, in view of Draper's otherwise copious textual references, is his categorical assertion, made on two separate occasions, that Stalin 'never used the term [social fascism] himself, still contenting himself with repeated references to social democracy' (ibid, p.128) and that he 'always used the more respectful term 'social democracy' without an intimation that it was becoming something else or something worse'. (Ibid, p.126) In Stalin's *Report to the 16th Congress of the CPSU,* June 27, 1930, we can read the following classic third period formulation: 'Will many workers be found today capable of believing the false

for the origins of the 'third period' in the CI. One of the central propositions of 'third period' Stalinism was the repeated assertion that all governments, whatever their political complexion, were rapidly turning, or had already turned, fascist.

Thus at the Tenth Plenum of the ECCI, held in June 1929 when the 'third period' was in full swing, Kuusinen only developed the line first tentatively advanced by Stalin at the 15th CPSU Congress, when he declared that 'along with the fascisation of the bourgeois class rule there goes on also the process of the fascisation of the reformist trade union bureaucracy and of the parties of the second international. Reformism and social democracy develop into social fascism'.[13] While R. Gerber of the KPD wrote shortly afterwards in the CI organ that the party's 'conciliators' (i.e. those who supported, or refused to fight, Bukharin's right opposition) denied 'the obliteration of all differences within the reaction' and therefore the transformation of reformism into 'social fascism'.[14] These notions, first evolved in the initial leftist phase of the CI in 1924, and obligatory between 1928 and 1933 (and in fact, some way into 1934) were definitely being revived by Stalin as he felt his way towards a left turn in the CI at the end of 1927. When in his 15th Congress report he spoke of a 'brutal pressure of the fascisised governments',[15] he had in mind not only Italy and Poland (the latter being a doubtful case) but Britain, France and Germany, where right centre bourgeois-*parliamentary* coalitions were in office, and where the trade union and political workers' movement, while certainly under pressure from the ruling class, was enjoying full bourgeois legality. This abuse of the term 'fascism' was to become one of the hallmarks of third period Stalinism, when it was applied indiscriminately to social democratic, liberal, conservative and genuinely fascist governments alike. Finally, as another harbinger of the new line that was to emerge in the new year, there was the sharper edge to Stalin's remarks on social democracy,* striking a tone that had not been heard in official CI circles since the winding up of the Zinovievist leftist line more than two years before; and his false optimism about the degree and depth of disenchantment with social democracy that was present in the broad masses of workers:

doctrines of the social fascists? ...the best members of the working class have already turned away from the social fascists'. (J. Stalin, ibid, Vol. 12, p.260.)

*Stalin's speech must have left the scribes of the official CI organ in a quandary since it contained much that was old as well as a little that sounded new. One writer solved the problem thus: 'As earlier so now the central slogan of our party is the united front. But ...in so far as we have a strong rightward movement of the upper ranks of social democracy, all the weight of the struggle for the united front must be transferred below, in which the attacks against the social democratic leaders must be carried on with double and triple energy.' (*The Comintern's Militant Task, The Communist International,* Vol. 5, No. 2, January 15, 1928, p.30) Bukharin, as chairman of the ECCI, could scarcely afford to be either pre-empted or outflanked

Facts like the British general strike ...the obvious differentiation that is taking place in the British working class movement. whereby the workers are moving to the left while the leaders are moving to the right, into the camp of avowed social imperialism, the degeneration of the Second International into a direct appendage ot the imperialist League of Nations [into which Stalin took the USSR in October 1934], the decline of the prestige of the social democratic parties, the universal growth of the influence and prestige of the Comintern and its sections ...all these facts undoubtedly indicate that Europe is entering a new period of revolutionary upsurge ...revolutionary energy has accumulated in the depths of the working class and is seeking ...an occasion ...to break to the surface and hurl itself upon the capitalist regime. We are living on the eve of a new revolutionary upsurge both in the colonies and in the metropolises.[16]

This last reference to an alleged mass radicalisation of the British working class proved to be a broad hint that a new line was already in preparation for that country, where the Communist Party had been faithfully and enthusiastically pursuing the opportunist policy towards reformism that had aided the TUC in its betrayal of the General Strike 18 months previously. For when the Ninth ECCI Plenum began its first session on February 9, 1928, it at once became clear that a gentle, yet unmistakable leftist breeze was blowing through the corridors of the Comintern headquarters. Under the newly proclaimed slogan of 'class against class', the CPGB was launched towards the line that was soon to become mandatory for all sections of the International. Feeding on the previous three year history of adaption to social democracy, and exploiting the monstrous betrayals perpetrated by the TUC General Council, lefts as well as rights, the Plenum's call for a sharper tactic against the Labour Party won the immediate backing of Palme Dutt, who had in fact been agitating for such a turn — quite possibly in the foreknowledge that it was coming — for some time before the Plenum, in his own journal, *Labour Monthly*. Undoubtedly a move to the left was called for (Trotsky had been demanding it two years earlier, and been expelled for his pains) but as was always the case in Stalinist manoeuvres, the shift proceeded on false theoretical premises and largely for factional purposes. Thus in the resolution on the 'English Question' we find the following schematic formulation on the new relationship that was said to be evolving between the capitalist state and the reformist-led organisations of the British working class:

The policy of the British ruling classes is designed to draw the major

by Stalin, and so at the CPSU Congress he took up and even embroidered on the theme of a sharper struggle against social democracy, obviously never guessing for one moment where it would eventually lead him: 'Never before has the gulf between us communists and the social democrats been so great from top to bottom as now. We must attack the social democrats still more resolutely than ever before along the whole line of front'. (*Report of the ECCI to the 15th Congress of the CPSU*)

workers organisations — the Labour Party and the trade unions — into their sphere of influence, despite the resistance of the working class. The leaders of these organisations ...are doing their best to transform them into subsidiary organisations of the bourgeois state and the employers' organisations ...This integration of capitalist bourgeoisie and reformism is accompanied by the development of the struggle between the right wing and the revolutionary workers. [From this analysis that the Labour Party was fast losing its proletarian character, the resolution concluded that the CPGB had] to change its attitude to the Labour Party and Labour government, and consequently to replace the slogan of a Labour Government by the slogan of a revolutionary workers' government.[17]

That the bourgeoise seeks to subordinate to itself the organisations of the proletariat — especially the trade unions — is not in dispute. But the Plenum resolution went further than this. It claimed that the main agencies in this process were the leaders of the labour movement, and that it was not simply a question of a 'sphere of influence', but of the trade unions' actual 'transformation into subsidiary organisations of the bourgeois state', of the 'integration of capitalist bourgeoisie and reformism'. Now the classic and only correct definition for a modern imperialist state where all the independent organisations of the working class have been destroyed (for there can be no other way of achieving this 'integration', as the example of Italy should have already taught the drafters of this resolution) *is the fascist corporate state*. Yet the schema put forward by the Ninth Plenum was one of the reformist leaders actually administering this regime on behalf of the capitalist state and the employers, and that instead of the rise of such a regime driving even the most craven of reformists into opposition (as Trotsky insisted would occur in Germany, where far from accepting the services of the social democrats, the Nazis jailed and murdered them alongside the communists) the Ninth Plenum presented them as 'doing their best' to liquidate the very organisations from which they derived their role as reformist collaborators with the bourgeoisie. Once again, as the examples of Italy and Germany (and now Chile) prove, however good this 'best' might be, it is never good enough to earn reformists an honoured or even subordinate role in the operation of the fascist corporate state. For this exacting task, other social and ideological types are required, absolutely ruthless oppressors of the proletariat who have been trained for their murderous work by years of counter-revolutionary struggle against the entire workers movement and its leaders, reformist no less than revolutionary. How important this theoretical error was for the subsequent development of the class struggle in Germany will become evident when we trace the evolution of the 'new line' from the Ninth Plenum through to the Sixth Congress of the CI.

The formulations employed by Stalin at the 15th Congress were sufficiently tentative to permit a manoeuvre back towards the right should the factional struggle in the Soviet Union or considerations of international diplomacy demand it. But this was less true of the line promulgated just over two months later at the Ninth Plenum, though even here it should be noted that the CPGB had not been unequivocally committed to its policy of 1929, which demanded calling the Labour Party and TUC fascist organisations. Indeed, the door had been left ajar to the reformists, since the *English Resolution,* belying much of its cheerful idiocy about the prospects of a 'revolutionary upsurge' in Britain, declared that as 'large sections of the masses still support the reformist leaders, it is absolutely essential to propose a united front locally *and nationally,* in order once more to expose the Labour Party and trade union leaders who prefer unity with the capitalists to unity with the revolutionary workers.'[18] (emphasis added)

When we bear in mind that these proposals for a sharper line against social democracy were intended initially only for the British Party, then it is almost certainly correct to say that up to and during the Ninth Plenum, Stalin's policy options in the CI were still open. What dramatically solidified this fluid situation, driving Stalin along the road to a break with Bukharin and to the rapid adoption of far more ultra-left policies than could have possibly been anticipated from either the 15th Congress or the Ninth Plenum, was the long festering crisis in Soviet agriculture, which after several years of Stalin's denying its existence, starkly confronted the Soviet regime in the early weeks of 1928.

A report dispatched by Stalin on February 13, 1928 (that is, while the Ninth Plenum was still in session) 'to all organisations of the CPSU', enables us to date with some precision the change of line on agrarian policy. After frankly admitting that as compared with January 1927, the state cereal procurements were down by 128 million poods to 300 million poods — a catastrophic shortfall — Stalin revealed that the CPSU Central Committee

> found it necessary to issue on January 6, 1928, a third directive the first two having failed to produce the required quotas of cereals, one quite exceptional both as to its tone and as to its demands. This directive concluded with a threat to leaders of party organisations in the event of their failing to secure a decisive improvement in grain procurements within a very short time.[19]

The left turn in domestic policy begins from the promulgation of this emergency directive, since it almost at once brought Stalin's centre faction in the party into conflict with the right tendency led by Bukharin and supported by Rykov (Lenin's successor as Chairman of the Council of People's Commissars) and Tomsky, head of the Soviet Trade Unions. Stalin had exploited this rightist group's pro-*Kulak* sympathies in his fight against the Left Opposition, and in doing so, had encouraged openly restorationist tendencies in the countryside. Now he found that in order to continue to defend the bureaucracy which had raised him to supreme power in the party and the state, he had to hit out at the extreme right, whence came a new and sinister threat to overturn the property relations established by the Russian Revolution, and from which the bureaucracy drew its material and political privileges. As events were soon to reveal, Bukharin, and especially at this stage Rykov, favoured a continued policy of full-scale retreat before the *Kulaks*, one which, as the Left Opposition had pointed out, rendered impossible the conversion of the surpluses of the rich peasants into funds for laying the foundations of a modern industrialised Soviet economy. In the early months of 1928, the nature of Stalin's left turn in domestic policy was both empirical and tentative. He also had to cope with the united resistance of Bukharin, Tomsky and Rykov (who reportedly stalked out of a Politburo meeting on hearing Stalin's emergency proposals to deal with the grain crisis) and not least, the embarrassing similarity between his own strictures on the parlous state of Soviet agriculture and the warnings the now expelled Left Opposition had been issuing on this very question for the previous two years. He therefore had to move circumspectly, feeling his way towards a new course as the pressures in the International and the economy for a new line mounted and became fused.

The battle had already been joined in the KPD, where Brandler, who had enjoyed something of a comeback under the discreet patronage of Bukharin, had just published in the CI organ a centrist *Programme of Action for Germany*. It nevertheless managed to say some correct things about certain developments in the SPD that were not at all to the liking of the ECCI, now that it had taken up Stalin's new line on the struggle against social democracy. In relation to the SPD left, Brandler stated it was

> the more or less expressed rejection of the coalition government and the purely parliamentary opposition, and at the same time, the rejection of revolutionary mass action. In the present, when the policy of coalition is becoming more and more difficult [this was of course written when the right wing parties were dominating successive German cabinets to the total exclusion of the SPD] the left wing of the SPD attains an increased importance. It reflects two things: one, the opposition of the masses to the coalition government and secondly, the attempt of a certain section of the party bureaucracy to stifle this opposition by a verbally radical policy ....With regard to the trade unions, it is also necessary to transform the bureaucratically administered central and professional unions into democratic industrial unions, directed by the members and organised on the basis of factories.[20]

Naturally, Brandler's observations on the SPD produced vehement accusations that the exponent of the 'Saxon mistake' was proposing a revamped version of the same centrist manoeuvre with the social democratic left. Nor were his views on trade union tactics welcomed, as they jarred with the new line that the unions were fast becoming instruments of capitalist dictatorship and oppression, and that the time was approaching when fresh 'organs of struggle' would have to be built up — under communist leadership 'from below' — to supersede *and even destroy* the unions led by the reformists. Already implicit in the Ninth Plenum resolution on the *English Question,* this line became explicit in the course of the preparations for the Fourth Congress of the Red International of Labour Unions (RILU), held between March 17 and April 3, 1928. As the head of the RILU (the communist rival to the reformist Amsterdam-based trade union international, the IFTU) Lozovsky had a vested interest in accelerating the disintegration of his rivals, and so he took up with obvious relish the new line that the reformist unions were becoming tools in the hands of the employers and the capitalist state.

> We have now entered into a phase of development of the class struggle in which the reformist trade unions and employers' organisations are not two warring parties *but are one party,* which reaches agreement in the measure that the dissatisfaction of the masses accumulates ...This *assimilation of the trade union apparatus into the bourgeois state* bears an extremely varied character, but in general it indubitably presents a growing alliance between the Amsterdam organisations and the bourgeois state, a continually increasing alliance between the trade unions and the employers' organisations. Before our very eyes is going on a process of *fusion* of the Amsterdam union with the employers organisations and the transformation of those unions into *organisations for strike breaking.*[21] (emphasis added)

Even more ominous, in view of the line that was soon to be forced on all sections of the CI (that the reformist trade unions had turned fascist, and therefore had to be deserted by communists to form new 'red' unions) was Lozovsky's assertion (as early as March 1928, it should be noted) that in the United States, where the trade unions were suffering a substantial loss in membership,

> such a slogan as 'save the unions' is out of place. It does not say anything, it confuses the issue, *it distracts the workers' attention from important questions* [sic!], *it sows the illusion that the present AFL is an advantage for the American workers.* Where did this slogan come from? It is a desperate slogan arising from an overevaluation of the importance of the *fascist AFL* and the misinterpretation of the united front.[22] (emphasis added)

This abstentionist position on the fight to defend trade unionism in the United States marked a definite shift towards the ultra-left line of forming break-away 'revolutionary' unions in countries such as Germany, where in 1931, after a series of reverses in the strike movement, the KPD launched 'red' unions parallel with those of the ADGB. This adventurist tactic flowed from the false analysis of the relationship between the reformist bureaucracy and the capitalist state made by Lozovsky and codified at the RILU Congress:

> The rule of the reformist leaders in the trade unions is leading more and more and more to the destruction of the difference between the organisations which came into being as organs of the class struggle [Lozovsky had in mind here the ADGB unions in Germany] and bourgeois [i.e. company] unions working for industrial peace.[21]

The resolutions and discussions at the RILU Congress shared the same eclectic and schematic character that Trotsky detected in the proceedings of the Comintern Congress which followed it. The cloudiness and ambivalence of many of the formulations could well have concealed deep disagreements within the CI leadership over the questions of the united front, social democracy and fascism, and the degree to which the 'leading lights of the trade union machinery [had become fused with] the apparatus of the bourgeois state', to quote from the main policy resolution of the Congress. This transitional and contradictory nature of the RILU Congress is well illustrated by its observations on the united front:

> The tactics of the united front and unity which have justified themselves during the last few years [sic — the British General strike!] must be continued ...at the same time it is essential to fight most determinedly against the subordination of the class struggle to formal unity [as indeed was done through the bloc between the Soviet and British trade union leaders] ...In view of the evolution undergone by the leaders of the Amsterdam International, the *main slogan should be unity from below* [emphasis in original] at the point of production. This does not exclude the possibility of negotiations, which after the break-up of the Anglo-Russian Committee (which was a model of the united front from above and below) are remoter than ever ...Thus *unity from below* [emphasis in original] must be given first place...[24] (emphasis added)

So that which had been prescribed only for the British Party at the Ninth ECCI plenum back in February now became mandatory for every section of the CI. The 'new line' was taking shape as in the USSR, tensions mounted in the CPSU Politburo between supporters and opponents of Stalin's left turn in agricultural policy. A new leftist *nuance* can also be detected in the Thesis on *Measures for fighting fascism in the trade union movement,* adopted by the RILU Congress on reports by Monmousseau (the leader of the French Communist-dominated trade union federation, the CGTU) Redens and, it should be noted by those who quite wrongly credit him with always having opposed the Stalinist theory of 'social fascism', Georg Dimitrov. As at the Fifth Comintern Congress four years previously, also held in a period when a leftist line predominated in the CI (only on that occasion, it was shortly to be abandoned for the opportunist policy of 1925-27, while the RILU Congress inaugurated a far longer and more devastating period of adventurism), the main characteristics and role of fascism were correctly defined:

> Fascism represents a special system of class domination of the bourgeoisie in the epoch of imperialism and social revolution ...For the class movement of the proletariat of all countries, fascism is a constant and growing danger. For fascism, the possession of the trade unions, *the destruction of the class trade union movement, is a vital necessity,* just as the dictatorship of the proletariat is unthinkable without a class trade union, so, too, *the fascist dictatorship of the bourgeoisie is impossible without the break up of the class trade union movement. Fascist terror is directed against any genuine working class movement, and against any economic struggle.*[25] (emphasis added)

Therefore, one must deduce from this analysis that by its very nature, the fascist offensive against the trade unions and the entire organisations of the proletariat must bring it into conflict with the leaders and cadres of even the most moderate wing of the workers' movement, since as the resolution states, fascism requires the *total destruction* of the trade unions in order to establish its own regime securely. And of course this is what precisely did happen in Italy, where by 1926, all class trade unionism had been driven underground and the reformist union leaders either hounded into exile, jailed or placed under police surveillance. Those responsible for the drafting of this resolution, of vital importance for every trade unionist faced with the threat of fascism and the destruction of his organisations, were fully aware of the experience of Italy, since they called upon workers in that country to 'leave the fascist corporations [and] join the General Confederation of Labour,' even though that reformist body had been long since outlawed by Mussolini and was working in conditions of total illegality. Yet this same resolution, after making the entirely justified observation that 'by their anti-working class policy, the reformist Amsterdam bureaucracy is clearing the way for fascism in the trade union movement' (though even here, there is a certain ambiguity about the word 'in', which is used rather than 'against'), goes on to lump together fascism and reformism after the fashion of Zinoviev and Stalin in 1924:

> ...thus reformism is actually taking up the *same* stand as fascism. The line of demarcartion between its ideology and the ideology of fascism is tending to *disappear more and more, and the reformist bureaucracy is being transformed into the instrument of fascism in the trade union movement ...working in the united front with fascism.* Part of the

leaders of the reformist trade unions *are already in open and full ideological and political union with fascism* (Italy [sic!] Bulgaria, Hungary, etc.). The other part *is on the way to fascism* (Jouhaux, Thomas [with whose social fascist CGT the Stalinist CGTU merged in 1936 during the popular front period] Grossman [ADGB] etc. The more the masses in the reformist unions move to the left and become revolutionised, and the more they resist the treacherous policy of the reformist bureaucracy, *the more ...will the leadership of the trade unions move to the right — towards fascism.*[26] (emphasis added)

The decisive turn had been made on the very eve of the Sixth CI Congress. The trade union bureaucracy had allegedly either already transformed itself into an instrument of fascist repression, or was fast doing so. Given this utterly false analysis, there could obviously be no question of any serious approaches being made to reformist organisations for a united front against fascism when these very bodies were serving as the vehicle for the fascist attack on the working class. The RILU Congress, despite its lip service to the continuation of the old united front policy, therefore forshadowed the decisions of the Sixth Congress on this question, as well as its revival of the 1924 theory of 'social fascism', since it was at the Sixth Congress that the crucial decision was finally made to scrap the united front tactic of the previous three years and to go over exclusively to the 'united front from below'.

The fact that Bukharin, as secretary of the ECCI, gave the main political report to the Congress helped to mask from many of the assembled delegates the violent factional struggle that had only days before, erupted inside the Soviet Politbureau over Stalin's new policy towards the *Kulaks*.* Valiantly mouthing the leftist

---

* The real relationship of forces at the Congress is well depicted by a supporter of Bukharin in the ECCI apparatus: 'The Congress was a comedy worthy of the pen of Gogol, Bukharin acted as president and made the big programmatic speech ...But in the halls and corridors a flood of dirty rumours against Bukharin was spreading, such as I have never experienced in the Comintern. It was really in the halls and corridors that a change of regime was manoeuvred while Bukharin himself was proclaiming the principles of Communism at the meetings'. (*From the Papers of Comrade X:* Ypsilon: *Pattern of World Revolution,* p.118)
Shortly after the close of the Congress, in an unpublished article *Who leads the Comintern?* Trotsky wrote that 'the leadership of the sixth congress seemed Bukharin's. He gave the report, put out the strategic line, put forward and carried through the programme ...and opened and closed the congress ...And yet everybody knows that in fact Bukharin's influence on the congress was virtually nil. Togliatti, who ventured to cast doubts on the new formulas regarding fascism and reformism admitted in a private conversation that 'it is impossible to speak the truth about the most important, the most vital problems. We cannot speak. In this atmosphere, to tell the real truth would have the effect of an exploding bomb'. Even Maurice Thorez, who was soon to begin his climb to the summit of the French Party machine as Stalin's loyal executor, expressed misgivings about the theory of 'socialism in one country'. Five years of increasingly bureaucratic mis-leadership had reduced the once powerful and respected CI to a shambles. No mass revolutionary movement could have withstood the succession of left and right zig zags and changes of

cliches that had recently become the stock-in-trade of Comintern functionaries and journalists, the future leader of the Right Opposition facilitated his own destruction by propagating tactics which a year earlier he would have condemned out of hand as adventurist:

> The change in the objective situation [sic!] compelled us to change our tactics. It was a proper reaction to the altered state of affairs ...The change in the attitude of our British party was determined by the change in the objective situation, by the new organisational methods of the Labour Party, by the new relationships that arose between our party and the Labour Party ...The political pivot of this change is our changed attitude towards the social democratic parties ....United front tactics must, in most cases, now be applied only from *below* [emphasis in original] No appeal to the central committees of the social democratic parties. In rare cases appeals may be made to local social democratic committees. In the main, we must appeal only to the social democratic masses, to the rank and file social democratic workers.[27]

But others were more anxious even than Bukharin to prove their leftist pedigree, especially in the KPD delegation,* where

leadership imposed on the CI from the Kremlin. Trotsky takes up these and allied questions in his classic Marxist analysis and history of the post-Lenin CI *The Draft Programme of the Communist International* (published in *The Third International After Lenin*, New York, 1957.)

* The pro-Stalin faction in the KPD was quicker off the mark than any other section in backing the 'new line' and giving it even more leftist emphasis. On June 1, 1928, there appeared in the KPD theoretical organ *Die Internationale* an article by Josef Lenz which contended, as Zinoviev and Stalin had done four years previously, that social democracy was 'developing tendencies in the direction of social fascism', an opinion which won approval from an unsigned article in the *Communist International* ten weeks later. Also written at this time, and indicating the eagerness with which the KPD 'left' followed — and helped to accelerate — the slide of the CI towards a fully blown theory of social fascism, was an article in the June 15 number of the CI organ, entitled, *The White Terror and the Social Democrats.* Apart from a highly significant reference to the *Volksstaat* as being 'the organ of the Saxon social fascists', the article upbraids the Prussian social democrats for allegedly forming an alliance with an anonymous 'white terror' against the KPD. Yet this harsh line was contradicted by another contributor to the organ a month later, who in analysing the Reichstag elections of May 1928, grouped the SPD together with the KPD as a workers' party. The article was also noteworthy in that unlike so many others being written on Germany at this time, it drew attention to the possibility of a revival in the fortunes of the Nazis: 'It is absurd to regard the German fascists as finished' (*The Lesson of the German Elections, Communist International,* Vol. 5, No. 14, July 15, 1928, p.311.) An altogether different approach was adopted on the same theme by Hermann Remmele, a supporter of the Thälmann faction in the KPD, in the next issue. He grouped the SPD with the 'bourgeois left parties', and reserved for the KPD the distinction of being the sole workers' party in Germany. And he added, in tones that boded ill for the KPD centre and right, that 'the line of battle between Menshevism and Communism is becoming more sharply defined. The task of winning over the workers from the ranks of the social democrats necessitates the use of different methods and conditions from those that were customary years ago. On this account the Communist Parties were obliged to examine their relations to the social democrats and make certain changes.' Remmele obviously had his own party in mind when he said this, for he went on to criticise 'supporters of the right group

Ernst Thälmann was emerging as the leader, if not the most articulate spokesman, of those favouring an even harsher line against social democracy. This became clear in the discussion on Bukharin's report. Fritz Heckert, a future Stalinist henchman, proved how conversant he was with the new line on fascism and social democracy when he told delegates (many of whom had, like Heckert himself, been working closely with left reformists and centrists in their own countries over the previous three years) that

> reformism has ...a strong tendency towards fascism in countries where the situation for capitalism is critical. It is only a small step from reformism which had developed in industrial peace, to fascism, to the defence of an aggressive foreign policy and strict measures against the revolutionary elements of the country. Thus we see that reformism has undergone a change and that we are compelled to accentuate our struggle against it.[28]

This theme was taken up by Dimitrov, the future darling of the popular front liberals and clergymen, who in 1928, far from seeking to build 'broad peoples' alliances' with all manner of opportunist and pro-imperialist elements, was anxious to ingratiate himself with a Stalin faction in the CPSU which was already preparing to ditch Bukharin to clear the way for the development of a far more leftist line in the International. Dimitrov's performance was even more obsequious in that he slanderously linked Trotsky to the activities of the 'social fascists':

> By its role of agent and pace-maker of social fascism among civil servants, it [social democracy] does great harm and the struggle against it must be continued with unabated energy. Trotskyism found no followers in the Communist Parties of the Balkans and among the proletariat. Its champions in the Balkans were the social fascists and the most shameless renegades of the communist movement.[29]

By far the most important and significant contribution came from Ernst Thälmann, leader of the most powerful section of the CI outside the USSR. His formulations on the question of fascism and social democracy were not only far harsher than anything uttered by Bukharin (or any other delegate for that matter), they also gave ample warning of the new leftist line the KPD was about to adopt on the recently-formed government of social democrat Hermann Müller:

> In this government the social democrats are the driving factor in the war preparations against the Soviet Union ...The development of reformism into social fascism is a phenomenon of which one can give various examples in the various countries ...In Germany, reformism is the bourgeoisie's best support, and will continue to be so in the coming years [sic!] if the communist movement does not grow even stronger

within the party, who expect much from an alliance with the "left wing" as a means of winning over the masses'. (H. Remmele: *Communist International,* Vol. 5, No. 15, August 1, 1928, p.353.)

than it is now ...This development of reformism into social fascism* is closely connected with the growing war preparations of the bourgeoisie and the growing war danger. The SPD is not only a fighting organisation working against the revolutionary proletariat and the proletarian revolution, it is engaged in preparing for joint action with the bourgeoisie in the ideological and military sphere. [Then for good measure Thälmann, who led the parade of delegates mounting the speakers' rostrum to voice their approval of the expulsion of Trotsky from the CI at the end of 1927, went on] We can declare at the Sixth Congress that for the first time in three years the KPD is in the pleasant position of being able to say that the renegades of ultra-left [sic!] Trotskyism have been finally beaten. They have been dissolved partly into petty-bourgeois nothingness, and partly they have landed into the ranks of social democracy; we need not waste a single word here about them.[30]

The main event of the Congress was intended to be the presentation and adoption of the Comintern Programme, which Bukharin had been busy drafting for the previous two or three months behind closed doors. However, a conflict flared up over Bukharin's theses on *The international situation and the tasks of the communist parties,* which had failed to reflect the changing line on the struggle against left social democracy.** There also

* Only one delegate seems to have had the temerity to imply that all was not well with the new theory of 'social fascism'. Ercoli (Palmiro Togliatti), while conceding that there was an 'ideological connection between fascism and social democracy' and even in some cases an 'organic connection' where social democracy 'in certain cases and under certain circumstances [used] frankly fascist methods', he warned that 'one must beware of excessive generalisations, because there are [also] serious differences. Fascism as a mass movement is a movement of the petty-bourgeoisie and middle bourgeoisie dominated by the big bourgeoisie and the agrarians; more, it has no basis in a traditional organisation of the working class. On the other hand, social democracy is a movement with a labour and petty bourgeois base, it derives its force mainly from an organisation which is recognised by enormous sections of the workers as the traditional organisation of their class'. (*IPC,* Vol. 8, No. 53, August 23, 1928, p.941). And Togliatti knew this better than almost anyone else present at the Congress, since his own party, together with the entire Italian labour movement, 'social fascist' as well as revolutionary, had been smashed by the genuine fascists. This speech proved to be Togliatti's last as a secret supporter of Bukharin's. His supple spine and elastic principles enabled him to make the transition to the third period — and then back again in 1935 to the right opportunist line he always preferred.

** Stalin gives the following account of this episode, which if true, confirms that differences over domestic policy had already spilled over into the International: 'How did the disagreements in this sphere [that of 'driving the Rights out of the Communist Parties'] begin? They began with Bukharin's theses at the Sixth Congress on the international situation. As a rule, these are first examined by the delegation of the CPSU. In this case however, that condition was not observed. What happened was that the theses, signed by Bukharin, were sent to the delegation of the CPSU at the same time as they were distributed to the foreign delegations at the Sixth Congress. But the theses proved to be unsatisfactory on a number of points. The delegation of the CPSU was obliged to introduce about twenty amendments to the theses ...In order that the fight against social democracy may be waged successfully, stress must be laid on the fight against the "Left" wing of social democracy ...It is obvious that unless the "Left" social democrats are routed it will be impossible to

appears to have been considerable and more open controversy on the vexed question of the relations between social democracy and fascism, which after 1923 was always a barometer of changes in the party and CI line. In the draft programme, fascism and social democracy were, as in 1924, lumped together quite arbitraily. After quite correctly pointing out that fascism and social democracy were two alternative forms of rule for the bourgeoisie, which varied according to circumstances, the programme declared, in complete violation of this view, that 'social democracy itself, particularly at critical moments for capitalism, not infrequently plays a fascist part.'[31] And if that indeed was the case, what need had the bourgeoisie of the other variety of fascism, if the 'social fascist' could do the same job? *In Germany, this became the line of the KPD.* The Müller government was 'introducing the fascist dictatorship', and nobody else. Therefore the 'main enemy' was not the bourgeois parties, nor the para-military monarchist leagues nor even the Nazis (who even as the Congress debated and approved the line that led to the defeat of the German proletariat, were perfecting the tactics and strategy that with the aid of the reformists and Stalinists, were to lift them to power less than five years later).

Thus Ernst Schneller of the KPD, in a speech on the struggle against the danger of imperialist war, listed the following organisations as comprising the 'fascist movement' in Germany: The Red Cross, the Young Christian Organisations, the Christian and Nationalist Women's organisations, and the *Stahlhelm.* Only the Nazis were missing! Commented the suicidally myopic Schneller: 'It is characteristic also for Germany that certain relations between the fascist and reformist movement are becoming even closer because they are marching towards the same goal.'[32] The KPD seems to have been very agitated about the dangers implicit in a joint Red Cross-SPD invasion of the USSR, or of a bloc between the ADGB and Catholic Women against the Red Front Fighters League (the para-military body of the KPD, which was banned after May Day fighting in Berlin in 1929) but it seems to have viewed with remarkable equanimity the prospect of a counter-revolutionary and anti-Soviet alliance between the Nazis, the *Reichswehr,* and the Ruhr industrialists.

As we have said, there was some discussion in the commission on the CI programme about the relationship between fascism and social democracy, and here Bukharin seems to have been forced

overcome social democracy in general [The core of Stalin's policy at the time of the British general strike in 1926 had been an unprincipled bloc with these same lefts on the TUC General Council — Hicks, Cook and Purcell]. Yet in Bukharin's theses the question of "Left" social democracy was entirely ignored'. (J. Stalin: *The Right Deviation in the CPSU,* speech to the Plenum of the CC and Central Control Commission of the CPSU, April, 1929, *Collected Works,* Vol. 12, pp.21-23.)

to give a little more ground to the hard-line leftists:

> First of all there is not the slightest doubt that social democracy
> reveals a social fascist tendency, secondly this is merely a tendency and
> not a complete process, for it would be a mistake to lump social
> democracy and fascism together. Nor must this be done in analysing
> the situation or in laying down communist tactics. Our tactics do not
> exclude the possibility of appealing to social democratic workers and
> even to some minor social democratic organisations, but we cannot
> appeal to the fascist organisations.[33]

But despite Bukharin's desperate attempt to salvage a few fragments of the old line from the wreck it had suffered both before
and at the Congress, it was no good. The helm was over to the
extreme left, and the entire CI boat was heading full speed
towards the still partially submerged rocks of German fascism.

What effect did the new line have on the policy and internal life
of the KPD, which now found itself working in a country ruled by
'social fascism'?

To answer this question, it is necessary to recapitulate briefly
on developments in the German Party since 1924, when the
Zinoviev-backed Left ousted the disgraced Brandler-Thalheimer
Right at the April 1924 Ninth KPD Congress. Both men were
promptly 'exiled' to Moscow and assigned to routine duties in the
Comintern apparatus — a convenient method later frequently
used to silence critics of the CI line or leaders of the national
sections. Even with their main rivals out of the way, all did not go
smoothly for the new Fischer-Maslow-Thälmann leadership. The
collapse of Zinoviev's ultra-leftist perspectives, accelerated in
Germany by the KPD's poor showing at the December 1924
Reichstag elections, brought great pressure to bear on the party
CC for the adoption of a more realistic line, one that took into
account both the obvious consolidation of the bourgeoisie that
had taken place throughout the year, and the equally self-evident
recuperation of the SPD. In fact, the rightwards swing so disturbed Maslow that he departed from his previous radicalism and
started to call for a policy of 'defence of the republic' against the
monarchist right, which in the spring of 1925, grouped itself
behind Hindenburg's presidential candidature. How easily
yesterday's — or today's — super leftists can be transformed into
tomorrow's opportunists is illustrated by the case of Maslow,
since he rapidly went beyond calling for a united front of the two
workers' parties in defence of democratic rights to a demand for
what was in effect a 'popular front' alliance between the KPD, the
SPD ...*and the Catholic Centre* — presumably on the grounds
that this last party, although both bourgeois and clerical, was an
upholder of the Weimar Republic, and could therefore perform a
useful role in an anti-monarchist bloc. Once again, we can see
how a leftist deviation fed its mirror opposite. And the process of

interaction did not end there, for once Maslow's views on this question became known to the party, numerous workers in the militant Ruhr region and the KPD Berlin stronghold of Wedding revolted against this even more opportunist version of Brandlerism, and rapidly provided a base in the party for a new ultra-left consisting of Arthur Rosenberg and Werner Scholem.

Tensions that were just beginning to emerge within the ruling *Troika,* between Stalin on the one hand and principally Zinoviev on the other, led to another intervention by Moscow in the affairs of the KPD (which at no stage since the end of 1923 had been permitted to develop its own internal party life and train its cadres in the way that Lenin and Trotsky had favoured in the early years of the CI.) Differences over tactics for the run-off ballot in the Presidential elections now found Zinoviev ranged with KPD 'moderates' against an ultra-left who argued, like Iwan Katz, that it would be a betrayal of the party to vote for the SPD candidate Braun in the second ballot, rather than split the republican vote and risk letting in Hindenburg. This question was thrashed out in Moscow, on April 2, 1925, at a session of the ECCI Presidium in the presence of both Zinoviev and Stalin. Katz put the position of the German ultra-left, declaring demagogically that 'our comrades see in the Ebert party the worst enemy of the working class, a corrupt group of the bourgeoisie', and that anyway, the monarchist danger had receded since the collapse of the Hitler putsch. It was a reformed Zinoviev who put the case for supporting the SPD candidate. Gone was the bluster of 1924, with its rash talk of an approaching proletarian revolution, and social democrats becoming transformed into fascists:

> We cannot at all accept the point of view that the choice, Republic or Monarchy, is immaterial to us ...Bourgeois democracy is generally more favourable than monarchy for our class struggle even if this democracy is a very poor one...We started with the perspective of an imminent fight of the proletarian revolution against bourgeois democracy [but] the moment the revolutionary wave declines, the difference between bourgeois democracy and monarchy is of great importance ...The situation is like this: the social democrats got 8 million votes, we got 2 million, the Nationalists 11 million, the so-called republican bloc has 13 million, the monarchists 11 to 11.5 million — everything hangs by a thread. If a monarchist candidate is elected, the social democrats and the [liberal] bourgeoisie will try to hang the responsibility on us ...The greatest danger is that the broad strata of the working class will be estranged from us ...I believe that our slogans must be very simple; only the most popular demands should be put forward ...In the first election, we tested out forces; in the run-off, we must take into account the final result ...You can learn these tactics by reading Lenin.[34]

And in reply to Katz's noisy abstentionism, Zinoviev coolly answered:

We live encircled by enemies. We need brains; if we lose, the working class will have to bear the capitalist yoke 25 years longer. In Britain we voted for MacDonald; people like Engels and Lenin had studied the English question for decades to find a road in Britain. *You don't understand what kind of enemies we have.*[35] (emphasis added)

Zinoviev's iron logic did not carry the day, possibly because Stalin, who was already discreetly backing the German ultra-left against Zinoviev's supporters in the KPD refused to commit himself to either side. As a result, the opportunity was missed to make a principled united front proposal to the SPD, who had still to decide whether to run Braun again in the second ballot. Of course, when Braun eventually stood down in favour of the centre Party candidate Marx, the KPD had no alternative but to run Thälmann once again, since there could be no question of voting for an openly bourgeois candidate, however sincere his protestations of democratic and republican loyalties. Hindenburg's narrow victory — by a smaller margin than the votes given to Thälmann — put the KPD in the invidious position against which Zinoviev had warned in the April Plenum. The SPD and the bourgeois democrats — and following their lead, countless historians of the period — have sought to place the blame for Hindenburg's victory, and by implication all that ensued from it, up to and including the Nazi triumph eight years later, on to the KPD. Perhaps if the full truth were known, part of the responsibility should fall on Stalin, not to speak of the German reformists, whose capitulation to their liberal bourgeois allies on the second ballot made it that much easier for the KPD ultra-lefts to maintain their abstentionist position on the defence of democratic rights against the monarchist threat.

A similar, though not identical, dispute errupted over tactics in the Prussian parliament, which was delicately balanced between republicans and monarchists of various hues. Here Thälmann, who had until now been linked with the Maslow-Fischer group, switched over to Rosenberg's new ultra-left faction, voting against a resolution moved at an extended CC meeting in Hamburg on May 9-10, 1925, which stipulated that 'in a situation where our party is arbiter between the right and the so-called left, it is permissible, and even under certain conditions, mandatory, to make a left coalition against a right coalition'. This resolution shows how wrong it can be to schematise on the history of the CI. In the Soviet Union, Stalin was cementing his bloc with the future Right Opposition — Bukharin, Rykov and Tomsky — insuring himself against a possible split with Zinoviev and Kamenev, who were growing restless with Stalin's repeated retreats before restorationist forces in both town and country. Yet in the KPD, we find the roles briefly reversed. Stalin's man, Thälmann, has moved towards, though not fused with, the extreme ultra-left of

the party, while a section of Zinoviev's supporters in the KPD
were now voting for policies which carried with them undoubted
opportunist implications.* Then followed another zig-zag, one
organically aligned with developments in the CPSU. Stalin dispatched his trusted ECCI troubleshooter Manuilsky to straighten
out the affairs of the recalcitrant German party, none of whose
many factions, tendencies and cliques (other than those
congealing around Thälmann, Pieck and Ulbricht) could be relied
upon to obey the ruling groups in the Soviet party without
hesitation or reservation.

The extreme ultra-lefts had served their purpose to apply
pressure to the old leadership of Maslow and Fischer (just as they
in their time had served Zinoviev in his feud with Brandler). Now
the time had come to reconstruct the KPD along lines more
amenable to the Stalin faction in the USSR. (This was the period
when Neumann began to attract Stalin's attention as a future
leader of a 'tamed' German party.) Despite Manuilsky's
intriguings, the KPD proved obdurate. It had deep roots in the
proletariat, and was justly proud of a revolutionary heritage that
reached back through Rosa Luxemburg and Karl Liebknecht,
Bebel, the younger Kautsky and Wilhelm Liebknecht to the
founders of Marxism itself. The bureaucratic pressure being
applied from Moscow only intensified the factional splinterings in
the party as intellectuals and workers alike struggled vainly to
fight their way out of the crisis into which the bureaucratic clique

* The beginning of Zinoviev's fall from grace in the ECCI dates from December
1924, when the putsch he ordered in Estonia — partly it appears to restore sagging
confidence in his leftist line that the revolutionary wave in Europe was still in the
ascendent — ended in fiasco with several hundred communists killed. Working initially through the exiled Hungarian Bela Kun, Stalin began to build up an anti-Zinoviev bloc in the Presidium of the ECCI. The methods employed were the same as
those used to undermine Trotsky's position in the CPSU: 'A Stalin faction is being
organised in the Comintern. They attempt to cut off Zinoviev from his contacts
abroad. Important documents and information are kept from him. His secretaries
are sabotaged ...Much malicious pressure is applied to the "impure" [a term used to
describe former CI leaders currently out of favour]. Stalin has their complete
sympathy. He uses every opportunity to demonstrate to the foreign comrades his
contempt for the Comintern regime of Zinoviev ...He comes out for democracy and
solidarity within the Comintern. He opposes Zinoviev's system of building up and
dismissing leaders ...Bukharin goes along with Stalin on every single question and is
instrumental in creating an atmosphere of confidence in the Comintern for
him'. (*From the Papers of Comrade 'X'* [a former CI official] in Ypsilon: *Pattern for
World Revolution*, p.102). This eye-witness account of the split developing early in
1925, between Stalin and the ECCI chairman helps to explain the complexities of the
factional struggle in the KPD. As in the USSR, Stalin did not select his (what usually
proved be temporary) allies on the basis of principles, but expediency. He was
perfectly capable of making demagogic attacks on bureaucracy if in doing so he
could win over its past victims to a factional bloc against his current opponents. This
was the device he exploited in his campaign against Zinoviev in the ECCI, which in
Germany led to a fleeting alignment with the new, anti-Zinoviev ultra-left against the
pro-Zinoviev group on the party CC of Maslow and Fischer.

in the CPSU had plunged their once powerful and combative movement. At the Essen Party Congress in February 1927, there emerged no less than ten separate groupings, ranging from supporters of the still-exiled Brandler and Thalheimer on the far right, through the bureaucratic centre of Ulbricht and Pieck, and the pro-Stalin clique of Thälmann, Neumann, Schneller, Philip Dengel and Heinrich Susskind, to the Zinovievist wing of the pro-Left Oppositionists, led by Fischer, Maslow and Urbahns, and the ultra-left, worker-based factions of Hans Weber (Palatinate) Paul Kotter (Wedding) Ernst Schwarz (mainly Berlin) and the most ultra-left of them all, the philosopher Karl Korsch. Only after the Essen Congress was Manuilsky able to report to Stalin that his mission had been accomplished — that of expelling from the KPD all those who stood to the left of the official CI line. The cliques of Ulbricht and Thalmann had seen to it that precious few delegates attended the Congress who were not committed to voting for whatever Manuilsky proposed. Stalin's German pupils were learning their lessons in bureaucratic manoeuvring well. But in warding off this powerful challenge from the assorted groups of lefts and ultra-lefts, the KPD centre had been compelled to lean more than it liked on the old right — which of course was precisely the dilemma that confronted Stalin after his break with Kamenev and Zinoviev and during his ensuring bloc with Bukharin. As a result, the KPD CC came under the control of a pro-Bukharin right that was only finally ousted and broken up towards the end of 1928, as similar blows were being landed on their counterparts in the CPSU.

Now we can see how poorly equipped was the KPD to exploit the favourable new political situation created by the formation of the Müller government in June 1928. Not only were its political perspectives false to the core; its best cadres, many being close comrades of the party's martyred founders Rosa Luxemburg and Karl Liebknecht, and pioneers of the Spartacist League, had been hounded from the party or gagged by decree of the ECCI. At the base, the party gathered around itself the finest of the German proletariat; but at the top, all was confusion, theoretical backwardness, rampant bureaucratism, servile fawning on Stalin. Only a drastic change of course, one that not merely repudiated the anti-Leninist tactics and programme adopted at the Sixth CI Congress, but initiated a serious study of the social and theoretical roots of this degeneration in the KPD, the International and the CPSU, could hope to save the party and the entire German proletariat from disaster. This was the moving principle behind the work of the Trotskyist opposition in the USSR, and its truth was to find tragic confirmation in the events of the succeeding five years.

REFERENCES FOR CHAPTER SIXTEEN

[1] L. Trotsky: *The Turn in the Communist International and the Situation in Germany* (September 26, 1930) in *The Struggle against Fascism in Germany*, p.59.

[2] *Directives on the united front of the workers and on the attitude to workers belonging to the Second, Two-and-a-half, and Amsterdam Internationals, and to those who support Anarcho-Syndicalist organisations*, adopted by the ECCI, December 18, 1921.

[3] Ibid.

[4] *The Second and Third Internationals and the Vienna Union. Official Report of the Conference ...* p.85, London, 1922.

[5] *ECCI Statement on the results of the Berlin Conference*, April 1922.

[6] *ECCI Statement on the meeting of the Committee of Nine* [being a body set up by the Berlin conference to organise the united front of the three Internationals] May 24, 1922.

[7] *Open Letter to the Second International and the Vienna Labour Union, to the Trade Unions of all Countries and to the Hague Trade Union and Co-operative Congress.* December 4, 1922.

[8] *Resolution on Fascism*, adopted by the Fifth Congress of the CI, July, 1924.

[9] Ibid.

[10] *Theses on Tactics*, adopted by the Fifth Congress of the CI, July, 1924.

[11] L. Trotsky: *The Third International After Lenin*, p.124.

[12] J. Stalin: *Political Report of the CC of the CPSU, Collected Works*, Vol. 10, p.290-293.

[13] O. Kuusinen: *Report to the Tenth Plenum of the ECCI*, June, 1929, *The International Situation and the Tasks of the Comintern*, in *IPC*, Vol. 9, No. 40, August 20, 1929, p.847.

[14] R. Gerber: *The Face of German Social Fascism, Communist International*, Vol. 6, No. 21, September 15, 1929, p.800.

[15] J. Stalin: ibid, p.289.

[16] J. Stalin: ibid, pp.290-291.

[17] *Resolution on the English Question*, Ninth Plenum, ECCI, February 18, 1928.

[18] Ibid.

[19] J. Stalin: *First Results of the Procurement Campaign and the Further Tasks of the Party*, February 13, 1928, ibid, Vol. 11, p.13.

[20] H. Brandler: *Contribution to a Programme of Action, Communist International*, Vol. 5, No. 3, February 1, 1928, p.68.

[21] A. Lozovsky: *Problems of Strike Strategy, Communist International*, Vol. 5, No. 5, March 1, 1928, p.113.

[22] A. Lozovsky: *Results and Prospects of the United Front (For the 4th RILU Congress)*, ibid, Vol. 5, No. 6, March 15, 1928, p.146.

[23] *Theses on Lozovsky's report, Fourth RILU Congress*, July 1928, p.12, London, 1928.

[24] Ibid, p.20-21.

[25] *Measures for fighting fascism in the trade union movement*, in ibid, p.51.

[26] Ibid, p.52-53.

[27] N. Bukharin: *Report to Sixth CI Congress, IPC*, Vol. 8, No. 41.

[28] F. Heckert, ibid, p.814.

[29] G. Dimitrov, ibid, p.847.

[30] E. Thälmann, ibid, No. 50, August 16, 1928.

[31] *Programme of the Communist International*, September 1, 1928, p.13, London, 1932.

[32] E. Schneller: *IPC*, Vol. 8, No. 58, September 1, 1928, p.1016.

[33] N. Bukharin: Ibid, Vol. 8, No. 59, September 4, 1928, p.1039.

[34] G. Zinoviev: *Die Monarchistische Gefahr und Taktik der KPD*, p.6, Berlin, 1925.

[35] Ibid, p.11.

Fascism and Social Fascism. 1922-1924.

Mussolini's victory over the Italian working class compelled the CI leadership to ask and answer some basic questions concerning the role of fascism, its class basis, and its relationship to the reformist wing of the labour movement. If initial mistakes were made in this respect, then they were attributable not to a false method, but the uniqueness of the problem. Never before in the history of world capitalism had the working class been defeated and crushed by a movement that stole with such facility and to such devastating effect the political, organisational and tactical weapons of its enemy. The plebeian nature of fascism was recognised from the outset. At first, this led to a falsely optimistic perspective of its inevitable internal disintegration, with deluded workers and rural poor 'sobering up' as they began to taste the bitter fruits of fascism in power, as distinct from the demagogy of fascism in opposition. Thus the *Manifesto to the Italian Workers,* passed at the Fourth CI Congress on November 5, 1922, declared that 'these elements will soon realise how deceptive were the promises which attracted them into this counter-revolutionary adventure and turned them into an army of the landlords against their kindred.' Mistaken too was the CI's belief that Italian fascism was 'primarily a weapon in the hands of the large landowners' and the 'industrial and commercial bourgeoisie [were] following with anxiety the experiment of ferocious reaction, which they regard as black Bolshevism', (ibid) The big industrialists of the *Confindustria* were as eager as the agrarians to place Mussolini in power so that he could continue his bloody work of destruction against the workers' movement. These however were errors of emphasis, and flowed in part from a lack of experience in dealing with the phenomenon of a mass-based counter-revolutionary movement. But one error the CI at this stage did not lapse into was that of bracketing together fascism and social democracy. While the communist press throughout the International scourged the reformist leaders of the CGL and the PSI for refusing to wage a resolute fight against fascism, and especially for their betrayal of the September 1920 strike movement, whose defeat cleared the road for the rise and triumph of Mussolini, with two notable exceptions *it never identified capitulation before fascism with fascism itself.* The two instances where this was done (referred to in Draper's long article on the subject in *Survey* No. 84) followed reports (that proved to be false) that the PSI fraction in the Italian Parliament had agreed to support the newly-formed government of Mussolini. The story, which appeared in *Izvestia* of November 12, 1922, was headed 'Social Fascists', and it was used again on December 28 in an article attacking the PSI and CGL leaderships (in the case of the trade union leaders, who were vainly seeking a *modus vivendi* with the fascist regime, one can understand, but not agree, with the use of the term). Draper suggests that this, the first known use of the term, was probably the brain child of a headline writer in the offices of *Izvestia,* and that therefore its employment did not signify a new theory of fascism and social democracy. The first instance of a responsible CI leader equating the two movements occurs after the defeat of the German revolution, when at a session of the ECCI convened to discuss the recent events in Germany, Zinoviev took the fateful step of declaring that Italian social democracy had become a wing of fascism:

'What are Pilsudski and the others? Fascist social democrats. [The future Polish dictator was a renegade from the Polish Socialist Party]. Were they this 10 years ago? No. But they have become fascists precisely because we are living in the epoch of revolution. What is Italian social democracy? It is a wing of the fascists; Turati is a fascist social democrat ...You may hurl insults at [Ramsay] Macdonald: You are a traitor, a servant of the bourgeoisie, but we must understand in what period we are living. International social democracy has now become a wing of fascism'. Which if true, meant that in Britain, the CPGB had just helped to elect a fascist government, since following Lenin's recommendations in *Left Wing Communism* and also the line of the CI up to that time, the British Party had called and worked for the victory of Labour Party candidates at the December 1923 general election, only running its own where they had either won the support of the local Labour Party, or did not jeopardise the victory of the Labour candidate. But Zinoviev never thought the consequences of this new theory through to the end, which would have been to withdraw all electoral support from the Labour Party, abandon the affiliation campaign being conducted by the CPGB, break off all united front relations with the reformist and trade union leaders, and proceed to build a 'united front from below' under the exclusive leadership of the 3,000 strong communist party (these of course did become CPGB tactics for the duration of the 'third period'). Zinoviev's theory was, however, after a delay of some eight months, taken up and developed from another quarter much nearer home. Stalin was just as anxious as his *Troika* ally to prove that under their leadership, no serious reverse had been suffered by the European working class, and that therefore, the decisive revolutionary struggles lay in the future. (Thus in July 1924, Stalin declared quite unequivocably that 'Germany is more pregnant with revolution than any other country in Europe ...If a revolutionary upheaval commences anywhere in Europe it will be in Germany. Only Germany can take the initiative in this matter...' [J. Stalin: *Speech delivered at a meeting of the Polish Commission of the CI,* July 3, 1924, *Collected Works,* Vol. 6, p.279.] It is important to remember that this false analysis not only preceded, but helped to prepare the sharp turn to the right embodied in Stalin's pronouncement, made some four months later, that socialism could be built in 'one country' — i.e. the USSR — without revolutionary breakthroughs in the advanced imperialist West). And as such, this theory of fascisation of reformism was an attack on Trotsky, who in a series of articles and speeches in the spring and summer of 1924, had examined in some detail and breadth the new political situation that emerged in Europe after the German defeat, and the possible consequences this could have for relations between Europe and the United States. Trotsky argues that following the recession of the revolutionary threat, the European bourgeoisie now felt able to lean to the left, on the right flank of the workers' movement, rather than to the extreme right, on the armed fascist gangs, as it had done during the previous years of crisis. In his speech of June 21, 1924 (*Through What Stage are we Passing?*) he takes issue with loose definitions of fascism, and especially, with wrong appraisals of its role: 'On the most casual grounds it is sometimes said that fascism is developing or that fascism is advancing. If some strikers are arrested somewhere, this fact is interpreted quite often as the establishment of a fascist regime, though the bourgeoisie arrested strikers before fascism existed. We have to think this out, comrades: what *is* fascism? How does it differ from a 'normal' regime of bourgeois violence?' Once again, it is necessary to point out that Trotsky's appraisal of fascism at this time was conditioned by its concrete manifestations, first of all in Italy, where even in 1924, Mussolini had not succeeded in destroying the workers' movement (this was done only in 1926) let alone parliament. Consequently Italian fascism displayed some of the characteristics of a transitional regime, which after blunting the offensive of the proletariat, regressed towards more normal forms of bourgeois rule. Thus Trotsky asks: 'Can a fascist regime exist for an indefinitely prolonged period? Fascism is the fighting organisation of the bourgeoisie during and in case of civil war. That's what fascism is. It plays the same role for the bourgeoisie as the organisation of armed uprising plays for the proletariat ...[therefore] can fascism last a long time? No! If the bourgeoise keeps hold of power, as happened in Italy in 1920, as happened in Germany last year, then, having made use of fascism's bloody work, it strives to broaden its base, to lean upon the middle and petty-bourgeoisie, and once again re-establishes reality. The bourgeoisie cannot exist for long in conditions of fascism, as the proletariat cannot exist for years in a state of armed uprising.' We can, with all the advantages that historical hindsight gives us, see that Trotsky was wrong. He saw only one side of fascism — its combat role in the armed struggle against the revolution. *But fascism also became a system of rule.* It did succeed, for a whole variety of reasons, in passing over from the phase Trotsky describes so well to that which he considered to be impossible, namely the consolidation of a fully-blown fascist regime in which the bourgeoisie finds itself allotted a subordinate political role. It may well, as Trotsky says yearn for a return to the saner days of parliamentary democracy, but the fascist plebeians have other plans. And moreover, as the main governing party, they possess the means to implement them. Just as Mussolini's regime was in a state of flux when Trotsky made this speech, so were

Trotsky's views on fascism. And it could not be otherwise, seeing that he was grappling with a process and movement that lacked all historical precedents (Trotsky was to correct and greatly enrich his analysis of fascism over the following ten years, beginning with his speech on the Polish Question to a session of the ECCI in July 1926, where Trotsky paid a great deal of attention to the plebeian aspects of fascism, especially those that bring it into political conflict with the bourgeoisie, and lead to the latter's exclusion from the state). But as in 1922, Trotsky never fell into the trap equating fascism and social democracy (even though the fascist regime in Italy continued to tolerate the activities of the reformists — as it did those of the PCI). He correctly saw the two movements as clear alternative methods of bourgeois rule, and spoke of the 'replacement of the fascist by the Menshevik' as being 'in accordance with the laws of historical development' — though again it must be said that history knows of no case where the bourgeoisie has persuaded a fascist regime to make way for a reformist one, though there are several examples of the reverse process. Stalin never mentioned Trotsky by name, but it is obvious that his article 'Concerning the International Situation' (Stalin's first on this theme since the Revolution seven years previously!) was directed against Trotsky's contention that Europe was passing through a period of bourgeois pacifism in which social democracy, and not fascism, would be brought forward to share the political power with the parties of the ruling class. (The Labour-Liberal coalition in Britain, the 'Left bloc' in France.) Stalin thought differently:

'Some people think ...that while the decisive battles were in progress, the bourgeoisie needed a fighting organisation, needed fascism; but now that the proletariat is defeated, the bourgeoisie no longer needs fascism and can afford to use 'democracy' instead, as a better method of consolidating its victory. Hence the conclusion is drawn that the rule of the bourgeoisie has become consolidated, that the 'era of pacifism' will be a prolonged one, and that the revolution in Europe has been pigeonholed. This assumption is absolutely wrong. Firstly it is not true that fascism is only the fighting organisation of the bourgeoise. Fascism is the bourgeoisie's fighting organisation that relies on the active support of social democracy ...These two organisations do not negate, but supplement each other, they are not antipodes, they are twins. Fascism is an informal political bloc of these two chief organisations, a bloc, which arose in the circumstances of the post-war crisis of imperialism, and which is intended for combatting the proletarian revolution. The bourgeoisie cannot retain power without such a bloc. It would therefore be a mistake to think that 'pacifism' signifies the liquidation of fascism. In the present situation, 'pacifism' is the strengthening of fascism with its moderate, social democratic wing being pushed into the foreground'. (J. Stalin: *Concerning the International Situation*, ibid, pp.294-295. We should note parenthetically that in a report to the CC, of the CPSU delivered on June 17, 1924, Stalin also detected 'open' fascism in the policies of orthodox bourgeois politicians in France and Britain, while in Italy, he saw its approaching collapse: '...during the last year we have had occasion to witness a number of attempts at the open fascisation of internal policy in the West-European countries ...Leaving aside Italy, where fascism is disintegrating, attempts to fascise European policy in the main countries, France and Britain, have miscarried, and the authors of these attempts, Poincare and Curzon, have, to put it plainly, come a cropper...' [J. Stalin: *The Results of the 13th Congress of the CPSU, Collected Works*, Vol. 6, p.247] For Stalin, 'fascism' was a term employed to abuse any government or political leader of whom the Soviet government disapproved. Significantly, in view of the evolution of Stalin's pro-German foreign policy during and even after the Nazi rise to power, he did not apply this abusive epithet to the German government. Instead, while avoiding any characterisation of the Berlin regime, he wrote of the 'superhuman struggle of the German people against Entente oppression'. [J. Stalin: *Concerning the International Situation*, ibid, p.299.])

Under the 1924 Zinoviev-Stalin schema, fascism becomes the product of the fusion of the counter-revolutionary combat unit of the fascists and the organisations of the reformists. In Germany, this would have meant that the SPD or the ADGB had actually joined forces with the Nazi SS or SA in order to fight the KPD! In such a 'bloc' (which existed purely in the minds of those who devised and propagated this

lunatic theory) social democracy merely represented the 'left' or 'moderate' wing or
'face' of fascism. How this 'bloc' of fascism and social democracy worked out in
practice had already been demonstrated in Italy a matter of weeks before Stalin's
article appeared in the CPSU theoretical organ *Bolshevik*. When the Italian
Parliament met on May 30, 1924, the secretary of the PSI, the ultra-right wing social
democrat Giacomo Matteotti, took the floor on behalf of his party and courageously
hurled a torrent of invective at the fascist regime, whose parliamentary
representatives now dominated the chamber. He accused the fascists of rigging the
recent elections and intimidating voters, and called upon the chamber to declare the
results invalid. It was of course a speech couched within the framework of social
democracy, but the manner of its delivery aroused the fury of the fascists and their
allies. Ending his speech, he remarked to fellow socialists amidst the howls of hatred
and abuse: 'Now you can prepare my funeral oration'. If Stalin's theory held any
water at all, then Matteotti was either suffering from morbid depression or delusions
of grandeur. In the event, he proved to have a sounder comprehension of the real
nature of fascism than Stalin, for all the latter's pretensions to Marxist orthodoxy.
The next day, Mussolini wrote in his *Il Popolo d'Italia* that Matteotti should not be
answered with verbal abuse, but something more substantial and permanent. On
June 10, the socialist was kidnapped by five black shirted thugs (with whom,
according to Stalin's theory, he was in a 'bloc') brutally beaten up and then stabbed
to death as he screamed for help. His body was buried in a wood near Rome, and
only found two months later. This story must be told, not in order to idealise either
Matteotti or the political views which he defended both against the fascists on the
right and the communists on the left. It was none other than Matteotti who prior to
Mussolini's victory advised workers attacked by the fascists to 'stay at home; ignore
all provocations. Even silence and cowardice are heroic'. But here lies the irony and
the contradiction which Trotsky grasped, but Stalin either failed to see or chose to
ignore. Matteotti told the workers to stay at home and to hide, yet when the battle
was lost, he found himself driven, by forces he could not properly comprehend, to
risk and lose his life in a genuinely heroic gesture of defiance towards the fascist
regime.

Had the current staff of the *Workers Press* been at hand to comment on
Matteotti's reformist, and indeed treacherous activities before Mussolini's seizure of
power, and after it up to the events of May 30 - June 10 1924, then in all probability
they would have dubbed him a 'corporatist' (Not a tall order, in view of the fact that
Workers Press has applied this adjective, which for a Trotskyist denotes a supporter
of the corporate state and therefore of fascism, to nearly every tendency in the British
workers' movement bar themselves). And this same editorial staff (acting, as the
masthead of their paper indicates, under the direction of the Central Committee of
the Workers Revolutionary Party and its secretary, G. Healy) would also in all likelihood have blacked out all news of Matteotti's murder, as they did the killing of his
modern counterpart in the Six Counties SDLP, Paddy Wilson. He was also hideous-
ly stabbed to death, with thirty thrusts of a knife, on the night of July 26, 1973, by
fascist — or if *Workers Press* will permit — corporatist — minded thugs as part of
their campaign to terrorise the Catholic working class and break the back of their
opposition to the rule of British imperialism in a part of the Irish nation. The news of
such crimes as the murder of Paddy Wilson, and in 1924, of Matteotti, would indeed
have proved highly embarrassing to those who contend then, and do so again, now,
that under the impact of a deepening capitalist crisis and intensified pressure from
the ruling class, social democrats and reformist trade union leaders become transformed into fascists (Zinoviev, Stalin) or 'corporatists' (*Workers Press*). If we wish to
trace the historical and theoretical antecedents of this type of pseudo-revolutionary
ranting, then we need look no further than the January 1924 speech of Zinoviev and
Stalin's article of September the same year. And, it should be remembered by those
who like to pride themselves on their intransigence towards Stalinism, *both
were directed against Trotsky.* Indeed, we can find further evidence that this was so
in the resolution *On Comrade Trotsky's Actions,* approved by a plenary session of
the CC of the CPSU in January 1925, when Zinoviev and Stalin were still in a bloc
against Trotsky. Here we still find Trotsky being presented as *right deviationist,*

since he rejected the *Troïka's* views on the relationship between fascism and reformism, which were of course of an ultra-left nature: 'On basic questions of inter-national politics (the role of fascism and social democracy, the role of the USA, the duration and nature of the 'democratic pacifist era', whose assessment by comrade Trotsky in many ways coincides with that of the social democratic 'centre') comrade Trotsky adopted a stand different from that of the CPSU and the whole Comintern ...' (The same resolution linked Trotsky with 'the Italian social fascists', an indication not only of the depravity of those who drafted and voted for the resolution, but of the stubborness with which the *Troïka* clung to this formula). What practical, tactical conclusions flow from this theoretically illiterate analysis of fascism? Ob-viously that since reformism and the armed squads of fascism (SA, SGS, *Arditi*, etc.) are one, then there can be no question of a bloc with the reformist organisations and their leaders against this same fascism. A more moderate version of this leftist line had indeed been tentatively and inconsistently applied in the CI throughout 1924, only to give way to an openly opportunist united front tactic with the reformists the next year. And of course, it was invoked and applied with far more severity from the Sixth Congress of the CI to a full year after Hitler's victory in Germany. The theoretical and tactical ground work for this monumental defeat had therefore been laid during the months after the previous great reverse of October 1923, and flowed directly from it. Here is a superb confirmation of the Marxist dialectic of history. On its conscious side on both occasions was the fight of Trotsky for theoretical clarity, the only possible basis for a correct revolutionary line in Germany and inter-nationally. In 1924 he was almost alone in declaring frankly to the Soviet party and the entire CI that there had been a defeat in Germany of such proportions as to shape the course of the class struggle in Europe for the next half decade and more. This perspective became an integral political foundation of the work of the Left Opposition, which in its turn, found its highest theoretical expression on the inter-national plane in the years between 1930 and 1933 in the fight to re-orient the CI, and principally the KPD, back towards the revolutionary strategy and tactics of Leninism. The inner unity of these two periods of the Left Opposition, the first in 1924, and the last, in 1933, together with the complementary struggle against Stalinist right-opportunism in China and Britain between 1925 and 1927, and the campaign for the revival of Soviet democracy and a planned industrialisation economy in the USSR, was consumated after the German debacle with Trotsky's call for the foundation of a Fourth International. That is why the 1924 polemics on the nature and role of fascism have to be grasped from this standpoint, one of the never-ending struggles not only to build a revolutionary leadership, but to equip it with the most advanced revolutionary theory.

Stalin and the KPD

The first open indication that Stalin had begun to search for a new leadership in the KPD to support his recently adopted policy of forming blocs with reformists abroad, while creeping towards 'socialism in one country' at home, came with the publication in *Pravda* on February 3, 1925, of a conversation between Stalin and Herzog, of the KPD CC. No longer were the social democrats falsely categorised and abused as the 'moderate wing of fascism'. Instead we have the mild formulation that 'the social democrats must be pilloried not on the basis of planetary questions, but on the basis of the day-to-day struggle of the working class for improving its material and social conditions ...' Stalin was also playing a cunning game in emphasising his devotion to the principles of democratic centralism and the rights of party minorities — something he was busily engaged in repressing in the CPSU. But here, in the KPD, it was a case of undermining the existing Zinovievist, leftist leadership, one that obstructed Stalin's sharp turn towards the right in the CI and its largest non-Soviet section: 'Some comrades think that strengthening the Party and Bolshevising it means expelling all dissenters from it. That is wrong, of course.' Eight months later, when Stalin made his next recorded pronouncement on the affairs of the KPD, we find him striking a different note. True, there is an even greater emphasis on the need to approach the reformists with great sensitivity (in violent contrast to the line of three years later) but now we find Stalin clelebrating the triumph of the bureaucracy over the very principles he demagogically upheld in his talk with Herzog: 'Undoubtedly, the removal of the "ultra-lefts" has improved the position of the KPD. The "ultra lefts" are people alien to the working class. What can Ruth Fischer and Maslow have in common with the working class of Germany? [This was the same group whose assumption of the leadership of the KPD after the 1923 fiasco was hailed by Stalin as representing the 'decisive' victory achieved by the revoluionary wing in the KPD ...' and as 'sealing the victory of the revolutionary wing in the principal sections of the Comintern (J. Stalin: *Concerning the International Situation,* September 20, 1924, *Collected Works,* Vol. 6, pp.304-306']

The result of the removal of the "ultra-lefts" has been that new leaders of the Communist Party have come to the fore from the workers ...(J. Stalin: *Interview with the Participants in the Conference of Agitation and Propaganda Departments,* October 14, 1925, ibid, Vol. 7, p.242).

Stalin's rejection of the KPD Zinovievists (on whose support he had depended in the struggle against Trotsky in 1924) became even more marked in 1926, when the Soviet bureaucracy's turn towards a domestic alliance with the Nepman and *Kulak,* and internationally, with the reformists and bourgeois nationalists, drove their champion, together with Kamenev, towards a bloc with their former enemy Trotsky. Stalin now deemed the main enemy in the KPD to be not the Brandler right (ideologically in sympathy with Stalin's new ally Bukharin, who was soon to become Zinoviev's successor as head of the CI) but the Fischer-Maslow 'ultra left': 'Either the KPD breaks the resistance of the "ultra-lefts" ' Stalin declared in January 1926 '...or ...it will make the present crisis chronic and disastrous for the Party. Hence the fighting against the "ultra-lefts" in the KPD is the immediate task.' (J. Stalin: *The Fight Against the Right and 'Ultra Left' Deviations,* speech to the Presidium of the ECCI, January 22, 1926, ibid, Vol. 8, p.2.) Stalin intervened in the troubled affairs of the KPD yet again some two months later at the German Commission of the Sixth Plenum of the ECCI, when once more his purpose was to protect the Thälmann 'centre' leadership from its left critics. Using the crudest anti-intellectual demagogy, he heaped praise on the ultra-Stalinist Thälmann faction as true representatives of the German proletariat, on the entirely spurious grounds that it was composed largely of former industrial workers. By contrast, there was the left faction, made up of 'conceited' and 'puny intellectuals' who according to Stalin considered it sufficient 'to have read some two or three books, or to have written a couple of pamphlets, to ...lay claim to the right of leading the Party'. Other qualities than interest in Marxist theory were called for, said Stalin — blanket endorsement of the 'general line': 'You may have written whole tomes on philosophy, but if you have not mastered the correct policy of the KPD CC, you cannot be allowed at the helm of the Party.' As for Marxist theory, that was of little consequence. It was a problem that would take care of itself: 'It is said that theoretical knowledge is not a strong point with the present CC [In the case of Thälmann, this was an understatement]. What of it? — if the policy is correct, theoretical knowledge will come in due course. Knowledge is something acquirable; if you haven't got it today, you may get it tomorrow'. (J. Stalin: *Speech delivered in the German Commission of the Sixth Enlarged Plenum of the ECCI,* March 8, 1926, ibid, pp.116-117) The idea that theoretical knowledge might have some bearing on arriving at a 'correct policy' was anathema to the bureaucratic minds of Stalin and his supporters. All wisdom — and theory — began with the 'correct' or 'general line', which issued forth from the infallible brains of the ECCI apparatus and their manipulators in the Kremlin. Where the German 'lefts' sinned was in their continuing to repeat, in 1926, a period of right opportunism, what they had been allowed and even encouraged to say — against Trotsky — in 1924, the year of leftist adventurism. Such independence of spirit had to be ruthlessly squashed, and Stalin cared not how this was done: 'about the Ruth Fischer group ...I consider that of all the undesirable and objectionable groups in the KPD, this group is the most undesirable and the most objectionable' (ibid, p.120) However the defeat of the old KPD left was no easy matter, as it enjoyed considerable prestige amongst the proletarian members and supporters of the party, and was in fact nourished in its leftism by the deep (and justified) hatred for social democracy amongst the most advanced workers of the KPD. The expulsion of the Fischer-Maslow group therefore was not simply a reactionary blow struck by Stalin against an important section of the party leadership, one that with all its failings (and Trotsky, who entered into a bloc with this tendency at a later juncture, was fully aware of them) had an important contribution to make to the struggle for socialism in Germany. Stalin's war on the KPD lefts drove away from the party and into the political wilderness hundreds and indeed thousands of the finest proletarians to have rallied to the banner of communism. First the purge of the Spartacists, now of the lefts — this was the logic of Stalin's bureaucratic regime in the CI, and of the zig-zag centrist course pursued under its leadership.

Chapter Seventeen
THE WORLD CRISIS AND
THE FALL OF MÜLLER

The theory of 'general over-production' is only an apparition conjured up by empty speculation. It is neither theoretically tenable, nor proved by existence. Are we not producing at a fabulous tempo?
(Emil Lederer, SPD 'theoretician', *August, 1929*.)

...social fascism [i.e. social democracy] ...is the weapon bearer of the fascist dictatorship. It is very difficult to maintain the line of separation between the development of a social fascist dictatorship when it has reached the stage, as in Germany, of a social democratic government using the most reactionary weapons of violence, and the methods of fascist dictatorship ...We are [therefore] of the opinion that the present Social Democratic government will remain at the helm for a long time.
(E. Thälmann: *The Problem of the KPD*, report at the enlarged Presidium of the ECCI, *Communist International*, Vol. 7, No. 4, April 15, 1930, pp.112-113.)

For all their mutual hostility, German social democracy and Stalinism embraced an identical principle; namely that it was possible to build 'socialism in one country'. Stalin invented nothing when he first enunciated this anti-communist theory in the autumn of 1924. The notion of 'national roads to socialism' had been implicit in the practice of nearly all the parties of the Second International many years before its reactionary implications were confirmed in the carnage of the First World War, when almost the entire leadership of European social democracy went over to its 'own' bourgeoisie and the defence of the capitalist nation state against rival imperialist powers. In doing so, it claimed that it was not only protecting the national labour movement from its foreign and internal foes, but that in helping the ruling class to wage war, social democracy was defending the sacred frontiers of a fatherland that one day, the worker would claim as his own. For numerous cadres of the Second International, and even a portion of its leaders, this theory was not just a cynical justification for supporting imperialism, but a genuinely held view that had arisen in the course of the movement's adaptation to the most privileged layers of the proletariat within the advanced nations of Europe.

In breaking irrevocably from the theory, programme and organisation of the Second International, Lenin demarcated himself as sharply and demonstratively as possible from all advocates, covert no less than overt, of nationalism within the workers' movement — a tendency he contemptuously dubbed variously as 'social imperialism', 'social chauvinism' or 'social patriotism'. Without this split from the International of Kautsky, there could have been no October Revolution, for the Bolsheviks were only able to win the support of the majority of the proletariat, and a strong base in the poor peasantry, as a direct result of their principled opposition to the imperialist war, an opposition which did not content itself with pacifist yearnings for peace, but strove to transform the imperialist war into a civil war, a policy of revolutionary defeatism. The Bolsheviks owed no loyalty to state frontiers established by the Tsars, but to the international proletariat and the labouring masses oppressed by imperialism. As far as the leaders of the Revolution were concerned (and this included Stalin up to the end of 1924), the seizure of power in Russia was but the prelude to far more serious blows to be inflicted on world imperialism in the centre and west of Europe. This thoroughgoing internationalist perspective underlay all the preparatory work for the Communist International, and was codified in all the main resolutions adopted at its founding Congress in March 1919. The theory of 'socialism in one country' was explicitly condemned in the *Platform of the CI,* (approved on March 4) which declared:

> The International, which subordinates so-called national interests to the interests of the international revolution, will embody the mutual aid of the proletariat of different countries, for without economic and other mutual aid the proletariat will not be in a position to organise the new society. On the other hand in contrast to the yellow social-patriotic international, international proletarian communism will support the exploited colonial peoples in their struggles against imperialism, in order to promote the final downfall of the imperialist world system.

The *Congress Manifesto,* written by Trotsky was even more adamant in rejecting the conception of class struggle and socialism evolved in the period of the Second International:

> ...the centre of gravity of the workers' movement during this period remained wholly on national soil, wholly within the framework of national states, founded upon national industry and confined within the sphere of national parliamentarianism. Decades of reformist organisational activity created a generation of leaders the majority of whom recognised in words the programme of social revolution but denied it by their actions; they were bogged down in reformism and in

adaptation to the bourgeois state.

Therefore world economy and the world division of labour, already established in a distorted and one-sided fashion by the development of imperialism, became the foundation for the construction of socialism in any single nation. Socialism, as a system of production that seeks to harness the resources of the planet, natural as well as human, in a democratic, planned and harmonious way, can only be built on this international basis. Cramped within the confines of a single state (however vast and bountifully endowed by nature) nationalised production and state planning cannot, on the basis of autarchy, raise the productivity of human labour above that of the most advanced capitalist states (which are, by virtue of their relationship to the world market, able to exploit the advantages of the international division of labour), which alone can provide the material basis for the flowering of a genuine socialist society and culture. Stalin's 1924 statement that socialism could, and indeed, had to be built independently of the world economy and therefore without all the enormous advantages that flow from the exploitation of the principle of the international division of labour, was therefore a clear break with the programme of the Leninist Comintern, and a turning back towards the national conceptions of the Second International. The very way in which Stalin posed the question showed that he conceived of internationalism not as a principle which flowed from the nature of world economy, but as acts of solidarity on the part of the workers in the capitalist countries, whose task it would be to protect the USSR from imperialist attacks.

Stalin soon became far more bold in his formulations when he saw how enthusiastically the more conservative elements in the party rallied to his new perspective. Thus in January 1925, we find him writing:

> Let us assume that the soviet system will exist in Russia for five or ten years without a revolution taking place in the West; let us assume that, nevertheless, during that period our Republic goes on existing as a Soviet Republic, building a socialist economy under the conditions of NEP — do you think that during those five or ten years our country will merely spend the time in collecting water with a sieve and not in organising a socialist economy? It is enough to ask this question to realise how very dangerous is the theory that denies the possibility of the victory of socialism in one country. But does that mean that this victory will be complete, final? No, it does not ...for as long as capitalist encirclement exists, there will always be the danger of military intervention.[1]

It was only a matter of time before this reactionary nationalist theory spread into the sections of the CI, finally becoming endorsed as official Comintern policy with the approval of its programme at the Sixth Congress in 1928, which schematically divided up the world economy into two self-sufficient wholes, and deduced from this purely artificial separation that full socialism could be built in the sector dominated by the USSR, provided only that imperialist intervention could be kept at bay.* Stalinist diplomacy, far from supplementing the struggles of the working class for socialism, became an active brake upon them as the ruling Kremlin clique employed the national sections of the CI as bargaining counters in Stalin's dealings with imperialism and those who represented its interests within the workers movement. This tendency was already evident in the right opportunist policy adopted towards the British TUC and the Kuo Min Tang, both being seen as valuable bulwarks of the USSR against a possible imperialist attack on the Soviet West and East respectively. Similar, and even more conscious motives, lay behind Stalin's repeated interventions in the affairs of the KPD during Hitler's rise to power, when Kremlin diplomacy assigned to Germany the role of a counter-weight to imperialist France (until 1934 regarded, with Japan, as the main threat to the USSR) so enabling the USSR, without the aid of further revolutions in the imperialist countries, to build 'socialism in one country'.

Stalin was far too shrewd to challenge openly the entire internationalist doctrine of Marxism, all the more so in view of his April 1924 speech to students of the Moscow Sverdlov University, in which he declared categorically that 'for the final victory of socialism, for the organisation of socialist production, the efforts of one country, particularly of such a peasant country as Russia, are insufficient ...' In the revised edition of the same speech, republished towards the end of 1924 under the title *The Foundations of Leninism'*, this passage now read as follows:

> After consolidating its power and leading the peasantry in its wake the proletariat of the victorious country can and must build a socialist society. But does that mean that it will thereby achieve the complete and final victory of socialism, i.e. does it mean that with the forces of only one country it can finally consolidate socialism *and fully guarantee that country against intervention, and, consequently, also against restoration?* No, it does not. For this, the victory of the revolution in at least several countries is needed.[2] (emphasis added)

Stalin still asserted that the final victory of socialism in one country was impossible. But the grounds he gave for doing so had shifted, in the course of the summer months of 1924, from economics to those relating to military intervention. It was no longer a question of Russia's economic, cultural and techno-

---

* 'The principal manifestation of the profound crisis of the capitalist system, is the division of world economy into capitalist countries on the one hand, and countries building socialism on the other ...[The USSR possesses] in the country the necessary and sufficient prerequisites not only for the overthrow of the landlord and the bourgeoisie, but also for the establishment of complete socialism...' (*The Programme of the CI*, p.44.)

logical backwardness, isolated from the economies of the
advanced capitalist nations, that stood between the Soviet Union
and the construction of a fully socialist society, but simply the
danger of imperialist invasion.

Under the Stalinist regime both in the USSR and the CI, the
communist parties in the capitalist countries were progressively
transformed from movements struggling to lead the working class
of their own countries to power, into submissive tools of Kremlin
foreign and domestic policy. They were repeatedly called upon to
approve both Stalin's latest diplomatic *volte face* and his murder
of Lenin's closest comrades. And through all these twists and
turns abroad, and barbarous repressions at home, the theoretical
foundation of the Stalinist course remained 'socialism in one
country'. And here we have the theoretical point of contact — and
at times of confluence — with the parties of the Second International. In both cases, the class struggle, and the building of
socialism, was viewed through the prism of the capitalist nation
state,while the national-reformist perspectives of both tendencies
led them not to welcome the periodic crises of imperialism as
opportunities to strike powerful blows at a dangerous but now
divided and weakened class enemy, but to view them with dismay and foreboding, as unwelcome intrusions into a smooth
evolutionary process which at some unforeseeable future date,
would lead to the establishment of socialism.* Such was
Bukharin's conception of the construction of socialism in the
USSR, one shared by Stalin until rudely shattered by the grain
strike and near-revolt of the *Kulaks* in the winter of 1928-29.

And thus too did the pundits of German social democracy
reason, as their party prepared to assume office for the first time

---

* Two examples will suffice. Rudolf Hilferding, next to Kautsky the leading
theoretician of German social democracy (though an Austrian by birth), lectured
delegates to the all-German congress of workers' and soldiers' in December 1918 on
the impractibility of 'socialising' the heavy industries. It was a task that would have
to be deferred until calmer times, he argued. It was impossible to legislate a socialist
economic programme in a period of capitalist breakdown. Hilferding was a prominent member of the 'socialisation commission' appointed by the Ebert government
ostensibly to devise a programme for the expropriation of the biggest trusts and
monopolies. Thanks partly to Hilferding's pseudo-Marxist sophistries, the tycoons
who later backed Hitler survived the holocaust of November 1918 with their
property intact. But Hilferding did not. Fleeing from the Nazi terror in 1933, he
sought exile in France, where in 1940, fate finally caught up with him. Deported to
Germany, he died in a concentration camp in 1942, a victim of protracted political
suicide. The second instance concerns the Stalinist, and not social democratic
bureaucracy. Stalin's bloc with the bourgeois-landlord Kuo Min Tang was
threatened from the left throughout 1926 by the upsurge in the peasant movement,
which had gone over to direct seizures of the land, much of which belonged to pro-
Chiang Kai-shek landlords. Stalin attempted to restrain this elemental movement by
sending a telegram to the leaders of the Chinese Communist Party, who were
allotted the thankless task of not only restraining such seizures, but actually
restoring seized property to its former owners.

since the crisis days of November 1923. Like the Stalin-Bukharin utopia of the *Kulak* 'growing into socialism' at a 'snail's pace', the iron logic of world economic reality was to reduce it to tatters.

The Müller government took office at the precise point in time when the fortunes of both social democracy and German capitalism had reached their post-war peak. But as we have already noted, this joint revival was attributable far more to a temporarily favourable conjuncture of the European and United States economies than any vitality that either German capitalism or reformism might still have possessed. It was the dollar that breathed fresh life into the movement Rosa Luxemburg had once described as a 'stinking corpse', just as US credits provided the funds for German monopoly capitalism to rationalise its plant and continue the process of concentration that began with the cartel system under Bismarck. After 1924, when the revival in the economy had become apparent, the leaders of German social democracy quite consciously trimmed their sails to the wind of Wall Street largesse blowing in from across the Atlantic. The citadels of world capitalism were allotted the unaccustomed role of the benefactors of the SPD's experiment in 'socialism in one municipality'. What did the banking houses of Morgan, Chase and the rest care as long as they received their annual 7%?

Wherever the SPD held office, whether in the communes, the city councils or on a state level (as in Prussia) the party undertook vast welfare programmes involving the construction of well-appointed workers' flats, public baths, clinics, maternity homes, theatres, cultural centres, sports facilities, libraries, child care centres and numerous other projects designed to raise the living standards of the working class. But almost without exception, they were financed by funds borrowed from Wall Street brokers. It was one of the most grotesque partnerships in the history of the German or any other labour movement. The reasoning behind this programme of social reform was as clear as it was faulty and utterly opportunist. Why provoke a head-on clash with the business community in Germany by pressing for even higher social taxation and insurance levies when far larger sums were readily forthcoming from another and even more lucrative source? The SPD's Fabian style 'gas and water' socialism could be built, municipality by municipality, city by city, state by state, without waging class war against the bourgeoisie — in fact even with their toleration, since at no time would their property rights be in question, merely their attitude to their social responsibilities. The German worker was to be rescued from the abuses of capitalism not by revolution (only barbaric Russians indulged in such excesses) but by his party's encasing him in a protective cocoon. If he was a paid-up member of the SPD — and through-out the boom year of the republic, more than a million workers were — then nearly all his social needs would be catered for by the party, even more so if he lived in a state, city or commune where his party held office. His wife would shop at the local co-operative, his children spend their holidays and their evenings with the Nest Falcons (6-10 years) Young Falcons (10-12) Red Falcons (12-14) Socialist Workers' Youth (14-20) and the Young Socialists (18-25), while all his own cultural and sporting needs could find their outlets in the numerous SPD-run societies ranging from chess clubs to theatre groups and athletics associations. Unifying this entire structure was of course the party itself, with its gigantic propaganda machine of 187 daily papers and scores of journals devoted to specialist and theoretical questions. Running parallel to the political movement, and to a certain degree merging with it, were the free trade unions of the ADGB, whose resources were even more enormous. Millions of German workers, by no means all labour aristocrats, dyed-in-the-wool anti-communists or hardened reformists, genuinely believed that this all-embracing movement could not only defend them against any attacks by the ruling class on their hard-won political rights, working conditions and living standards, but eventually carry them forward to socialism. The average German worker believed in and desired socialism with a passion and firmness of conviction that found its highest expression in his devotion to the organisations which he and his ancestors had built up at such enormous financial sacrifice in the face of a barbaric and utterly ruthless class enemy. The sheer magnitude of this edifice is a tribute to the noble struggle of an oppressed class for dignity and emancipation. The Müllers, Kautskys, Eberts and Scheidemanns forfeited all right to represent that tradition when they deserted the German proletariat in its hour of greatest need in August 1914, chaining the party of Marx and Engels to the war chariot of Krupp, Thyssen, Stinnes and Hindenburg; and in November 1918, when after the political power dropped into their laps, they handed it back to the ruling class and launched their bloody campaign of extermination against the finest leaders of the German working class. Yet even then, the party leadership could not afford to effect an open break with the Marxism which it had betrayed. Fearing the attractive power of the KPD, the true historical inheritor of the Marxist legacy, the SPD wove around its reformist and in moments of crisis, counter-revolutionary policies, a tapestry of pseudo-Marxist phrases and analyses. Thus at a time when the party's leaders were carrying their begging bowl to the richest bankers in the world, the 1925 SPD Congress at Heidelberg adopted a programme which declared, in the grand style so beloved of the pre-1914 Kautsky:

The number of proletarians is growing; the conflict between exploiters and those who are exploited increases in violence; the class warfare between the capitalist rulers of economy and those whom they oppress becoming fiercer ...The goal of the working class can only be achieved by transforming the capitalist private ownership of the means of production into social ownership. When capitalist production is replaced by socialist production by the people for the people, then the growth and development of productive forces will become the source of great prosperity and universal betterment. Only then will society, in harmony and solidarity, rise from its subjection to blind economic forces and from general disintegration, and achieve free self government.

The revolting hypocrisy of those who drafted this programme almost defies description when one recalls that it would have been redundant had the SPD taken in 1918 the measures against the Junkers and the big capitalists that the proletariat and a sizable minority of the middle class were demanding. And even if we take its socialist pretensions seriously, there immediately arises the question — how was such a programme to be implemented? Rudolf Hilferding, who blandly brushed aside calls for socialisation of heavy industry at the Congress of Workers' and Soldiers' Councils in December 1918, gave the answer at the 1927 SPD Congress in Kiel:

We are now in the midst of a period of transformation, a time of peaceful transition from capitalism to socialism ...the task is set for our generation of organising capitalist economy with the aid of the state, and of transforming the capitalistically organised and conducted economy into an economy conducted by the socialist state. This signifies nothing more nor less than our generation has to solve the problem of socialism.

Hilferding's notion of 'organised capitalism' and a neutral state provided the theoretical gloss for the opportunist, class collaborationist policies of the SPD and ADGB leaderships. They dinned into the heads of millions of workers that capitalism could be gradually abolished through the agencies of the Weimar Constitution (namely the articles pertaining to trade union and works council participation in economic affairs) and through legislating social and economic reforms at a national and local level. The main task of the movement was therefore deemed to be the preservation of the machinery that would make these measures possible — namely bourgeois democracy and its various institutions — against attacks from the counter-revolutionary right and the revolutionary left. Meanwhile, within the shell of Weimar democracy would grow, slowly but surely, the embryo of a future German socialism. Indeed, some claimed that the chicken had already begun to sprout some feathers, like Herr Klemens, who told the August 1928 Congress of the German Transport Workers' Union:

I cnallenge the view that in the German republic we are still justified in talking of a capitalist and bourgeois state. In such a country as Germany, which in so many ways is already organised in accordance with our desires, where we have comrades and colleagues on almost all the government and social organs, it is ignorant nonsense to talk of a capitalist, bourgeois state, which one has to struggle against.

A similar line was taken by ADGB Chairman Leipart, who wrote shortly before the formation of the Müller government:

> Working class property, producing co-operatives, labour banks etc. also exercise considerable influence on economic life today. Representatives of the working class even took part in the negotiations for commercial treaties, workers' representatives have positions on the administration of the councils of the Post, National and State Railways, and on the canal councils, on all the bodies concerned with production and administration of the affairs of the nation and of the state, and are provided for on the supreme national economic council.[3]

As far as the facts went, Leipart was certainly not exaggerating. The deal of November 1918, as we have repeatedly emphasised, involved the big employers in a series of concessions to organised labour that they would never have entertained in any other predicament than a revolutionary crisis. Social democracy exercised the influence that it did in the economic, social and political affairs of Weimar for this reason more than any other. It was the reformist bureaucracy's reward for betraying the November Revolution. But like all social phenomena and processes, the pact of November 1918 contained a contradiction. The entire history of the Republic from the earliest counter-revolutionary blood-lettings of Noske's Free Corps, through the Kapp and Munich putsches, to the abortive coup of May 1926, had testified to the existence of a hard core of industrialist, Junker and military opposition to the Weimar Republic, which since it flowed from a fulminating hatred and fear of the proletariat, could not but direct itself against the largest and historically the most influential wing of the German labour movement. Every Social Democrat, however reformist, however great his detestation of revolution (and we need only recall President Ebert's heartfelt comments on this subject) was for them a red-blooded Marxist, who had merely chosen another than the Communists' road to subvert the integrity of the German nation. Indeed, some looked with even more suspicion on the social democrats, who had succeeded in capturing literally thousands of posts in the central and local government machinery, than the communists, whose threat was easily identifiable. So here the subjective factor, though of course having its objective roots in the history of the German bourgeoisie and its half century battle against German labour, played an important part in shaping relations between the ruling class and the reformist wing of the workers' movement in this period.

In November 1918, the formation of a social democratic government proved to be the salvation of the German ruling class. Yet in 1928, we find this same bourgeoisie now bitterly hostile to an identical social democracy, even though in the course of the intervening ten years, the latter had proved time and again its undying loyalty to capitalism. The reasons are not hard to discover, though they utterly escaped third period Stalinism, ever anxious to prove to doubters that social democracy, far from becoming an obstacle to the strategy of the German bourgeoisie, was functioning as the advanced guard of fascist counter-revolution and dictatorship. At no time during the life-time of the Müller government was the possibility seriously discussed of the bourgeoisie seeking to eject the social democrats from the cabinet. According to the Stalinist theory of social fascism, the reformists were the chosen instrument for the 'fascisation' of the German republic. Thus declared Stalin's protege in the KPD, Heinz Neumann, at the Tenth Plenum of the ECCI in July 1929:

> While Italy is the classic country of fascism, Germany is the classic country of social fascism. There is no country in the world where social fascism has already found such completion, such thorough formation, also ideologically, as it has in Germany. What is one of the most decisive levers for the acceleration of the social fascist tendency? *It is the part played by social democracy in the government* ...[*down to the small local administrations*] All this implies the *coalescence of the SPD apparatus with the state machine, and the police machine,* which has accelerated the development of social fascism.[4] (emphasis added)

Although couched in obligatory 'third period' jargon, Neumann's estimation of the relationship between the SPD and ADGB bureaucracy and the capitalist state was in its essentials identical with that of the 'social fascists' Leipart and Klemens. All three, as is evident from their quoted statements, shared the illusion that the German ruling class had made its peace with social democracy, and had finally accepted the latter's permanent presence in the leading as well as subsidiary organs of state and government. Neumann, like the leaders of German reformism he denounced with such shrill and empty demagogy, depicted the formation of the Müller government as accelerating a process of fusion between the reformist apparatus and the capitalist state, including even its directly repressive organs such as the police. In fact, the basic trend was in the opposite direction. Even before the May 1928 elections which lifted Müller into the chancellorship, issues had arisen which were destined to place enormous strain on the new government from the moment it took office.

Early in 1928, the new Defence Minister Gröner (Ebert's saviour in November 1918) had won — with very little difficulty — the support of President Hindenburg for a warship building programme, which was to commence with the construction of cruiser 'A'. With the evidence that is now available, it is clear that this proposal was part of a far broader plan to prepare German imperialism for a new European war. And as such, it immediately became a central issue in German politics, with the workers' and middle class radical parties ranged against the cruiser plan, and the entire forces of the Junkers and big bourgeoisie in its favour. It was a line-up similar to that which crystallised around the election of Hindenburg and the referendum on the princes' property. As the date for the Reichstag elections approached, the entire social democratic campaign revolved around this single, immensely important issue. Hermann Müller, as SPD Reichstag fraction leader, was well to the fore in denouncing the war-mongering activities of the right-wing parties and their allies in the military. In fact the main SPD slogan, one which earned a truly heartfelt response from a war-weary working class, was 'Cruisers or feeding centres for children?' In the crisis-laden months that followed, Müller and his fellow reformist leaders must have bitterly regretted the employment of that slogan. For President Hindenburg made it a condition of Müller's taking office that he accept into his cabinet Gröner as Defence Minister, and proceed to implement the cruiser programme proposed by the out-going centre-right coalition. Müller, after hesitations that were resolved with the assistance of Scheidemann, capitulated to the general staff just as he and his predecessors had done in August 1914. But in stark contrast to those heady days, when social democracy became elevated overnight to a status undreamt of in peace-time Imperial Germany, the reformists received precious little thanks for their servility. And to add to Müller's troubles, the issue was to provoke a revolt not only among the party's more militant members, but even within the ranks of the predominantly right-wing Reichstag fraction, who when the question finally came before the house on November 17, 1928, voted against the policy being pursued by their party comrades in Müller's cabinet. The decision to begin building cruiser 'A' was carried with the enthusiastic support of all the right wing parties, against the votes of the SPD and KPD, by 225 - 203. But by this time, new and even greater problems confronted the Müller government.

By the end of 1928, the SPD's election programme was in ruins. The Müller government had already agreed to build warships for the imperialists, and now there were to be no more feeding centres for children. The SPD's crawl to 'socialism in one municipality' had ground to a halt not because the cruiser programme had eroded funds previously allocated for social welfare (building did not commence until some time later) but for an altogether different reason, one for which the SPD had made no provision whatsoever in their political and economic planning. Religious faith in United States capitalism proved to be their undoing. June 1928, the month the Müller government took office, was also by coincidence the period of the highest US investment in Germany. In the second quarter of 1928, 153.8 million dollars flowed from the US into the German economy, much of it of course in the form of loans to social democratic administrations to finance their welfare programmes. But the next quarter showed a dramatic drop to barely 14 million dollars, only partially offset by a rise in the last quarter to 62.4 million. This drying-up of US investment, unlike the total famine of a year later, was due to a new upsurge in the boom on Wall Street, where far quicker and higher returns could be secured than by lending money to a German industrialist, municipal council or government authority at a modest 7% interest.

This trend continued into 1929, with 21.0 million dollars in the first quarter, and negligible amounts in the second and third. So a full year before the Wall Street crash of September-October 1929, German capitalism, and with it, social democracy, was beginning to suffer the negative effects of its subordinate relationship to the USA, established after the defeat in 1918 and formalised under the terms of the Dawes Plan. As for the German working class, what would be the consequences of this sharp down-turn in foreign investment? Within months it would mean a rapid rise in the number of jobless workers, as firms starved of new capital and raw materials began to trim their labour force to lower levels of production and an anticipated drop in sales. Deprived of US credits, firms would be forced to accumulate capital almost exclusively either with loans from German banks, or through increased exploitation of their own workers. In the latter case, this would inevitably lead to a sharpening of the wages struggle. The proportion of foreign loans to domestic share issues brings out this trend. Domestic share issues were at their highest between the third quarter of 1926 and the second quarter of 1927, when they reached 395.5 million marks. Over the next three quarters, however, foreign loans ran at 657,566 and 336 million marks. Thus any appreciable fall in foreign investment in German industry, unless compensated by an approximate equal rise in investment from domestic sources, would obviously have a catastrophic effect on the German economy, and consequently on the living standards of the German working class. And here much was indeed at stake. In the five years of boom that followed the crises of the early post-war years, the German working class had succeeded in restoring its pre-1914 level of real wages. With 1913 as the base year of 100, skilled workers' real wages had climbed from a low of 58 in 1923 to 93 by 1927, while unskilled workers, gaining from the Republic's system of collective bargaining, had risen over the same period from 86 to 105. No other working class in Europe had managed to force up its wages at a comparable rate (in fascist Italy, wages had remained stationary over the period, while in France, they had actually fallen). In terms of food consumption, the German worker had also restored much of what he had lost as a result of war-time deprivations and the periodic near-collapses of the economy in the early post-war years:

Consumption per head of population
(kilograms or litres)

	1913	1923	1927
Rye	153	90	97
Wheat and Spelt	96	47	78
Barley	108	29	71
Oats	128	57	95
Potatoes	700	560	381
Meat	50	40	50
Sugar	19	13	22
Coffee	2.4	0.6	2.0
Fruits	4.6	0.7	6.9
Beer	102	45	81

Modest and inadequate though they were, these hard and recently-won improved living standards, together with the eight-hour day and the rest of the social legislation enacted under the Weimar Constitution, became an increasingly intolerable burden for a German employing class starved of capital investment by the sudden decline in loans from the United States, and under growing pressure from its falling profit margins. Far from welcoming the formation of the Müller government (as the Stalinists vainly attempted to claim) the monopoly capitalists saw it as an unmitigated evil, since it would raise hopes amongst millions of workers for a continued improvement in their wages and social conditions, and therefore find it all the more difficult to come out openly on the side of the employers in any big confrontation between the classes. The only consolation for the big industrialists was the presence in the cabinet of two representatives of the DVP whose task it was to veto any measures Müller and his SPD colleagues might propose that did not accord with the interests of big business (the remainder of the Cabinet posts were taken by the DDP(2), BVP and Centre one each, and Gröner, non-party.

But as had so often been the case in previous periods of political and economic crisis, the traditional party of heavy industry found itself bitterly divided over what policy to adopt towards the social democrats, a rift further widened by the DVP's participation after June 1928 in a cabinet headed by a 'Marxist'.

The dwindling band of Ruhr industrialists who still remained loyal to the party were much perturbed by the catastrophic decline in capital accumulation which followed the sharp decline in loans from the USA. The 1929 level of industrial investment was barely 25% of that in 1928, which in its turn was down on the previous year.

Even before the formation of the Müller cabinet — in November 1927 to be precise — heavy industry had begun to exert pressure for a drastic revision of national and local financial policy. On November 23, 1927, the Federation of German Industries Presidium presented a memorandum to Chancellor Wilhelm Marx containing a series of far-reaching economic and by implication, political proposals:

> The most important objective of all financial measures in the immediate future must be a minimum reduction of 10% in the expenditure of national, state and local authorities compared with the 1927 budgets ...We are convinced that this demands a radical change in the constitution. However, circumstances demand such action. As long as reparations responsibility lasts, it cannot be denied that the lack of moderate financial responsibility by the people's representatives at state and local level make it impossible for the Reich government to function on sound economic and financial principles, and at the same time a successful foreign policy is endangered.

In the discussion that ensued the next day (November 24, 1927) between a deputation from the Federation Presidium and the Marx government, the following points were argued for vigorously by Privy Councillor Kastl on behalf of the deputation:

> The need to strengthen cabinet powers in the economic sphere and to combat a) 'The all too great eagerness of the cooperate Reichstag to spend money; b) The opposition of the state governments to cooperate actively [in proposed economies].' Finally, 'German industry must aim to keep to world market prices. It was [therefore] the duty of the Reich government to avoid anything that would raise price levels. That applied specially to wages policy, social taxes and guaranteed working hours.'

If the industrialists stuck to this programme — and they did — then they were certain to collide with the new Müller government, which had pledged itself in SPD pre-election agitation to continue with its policy of expanding social welfare, raising wages and improving working conditions. Particularly ominous in this regard was the remark made in the discussion by the arch-reactionary heavy industrialist Paul Reusch, a co-thinker of Vögler, who said: 'The attitude of foreign countries which in England and America a year ago had been favourable towards Germany, has recently turned rather alarmingly against Germany. *Therefore the struggle against the masses and with the Reichstag must be taken up with the utmost inflexibility.*' (emphasis added)

From the beginning of 1929 — nine full months before the crash on Wall Street made its impact felt in Europe — German heavy industry applied yet greater pressure through its political and propaganda agencies to secure a drastic cut in the social welfare programmes which had been pursued with such vigour by the reformists over the previous five years. And the first step towards their goal of slashing social expenditure, cutting real wages, lengthening hours and so increasing profits and funds for capital accumulation was naturally the removal of the reformists from office and what was even more integral to the success of their strategy, the progressive whittling away of the influence of the SPD and trade unions in the affairs of the national economy and the administration of the machinery of state and government. Stresemann sympathised with the motives behind such belligerent thinking, while rejecting the methods proposed to realise them. He still clung to the hope — vain as events were to demonstrate — that a *modus vivendi* could be preserved beween organised labour and organised big business. It had proved difficult enough during the years of boom. How could such a policy of compromise work when capitalism in crisis offered not reforms, but demanded the clawing back of all that it had conceded in more prosperous days? Not that Stresemann denied the need for economies along the lines proposed by heavy industry. But he looked at them from another and more sophisticated angle, with one eye on the dangerous political situation that could be created by a policy which neglected the economic interests of the millions-strong propertied petty-bourgeoisie, the traditional backbone of the moderate German conservatism personified by Stresemann.

This was the central theme of his remarkable speech to a session of the DVP Central Committee on February 26, 1929. The meeting had been convened to define the party's attitude to the Müller government following the withdrawal of the Centre party from the cabinet two weeks earlier. Stresemann was under strong pressure from the right wing in the DVP to follow the Centre's example,* and indeed, a resolution had been passed in November 1928 by the DVP CC that the party was not irrevocably committed to supporting the Müller government (this decision had been taken in the light of social democratic opposition to the cruiser programme). Stresemann implored the assembled representatives of heavy industry not to pursue a policy of naked class warfare, since its repercussions would be felt far beyond the

---

* The Centre's temporary withdrawal arose as a result of a dispute over the allocation of cabinet posts. The DVP would only accede to the Catholics' demand for three seats in the Müller cabinet if in return, the Centre would make two portfolios available to the DVP in the Prussian cabinet, where the Centre was in a coalition with the SPD. The Centre won out on this occasion, and in April 1929 returned to the government with its three ministerial seats.

confines of the labour movement:

> We are faced by a crisis in the parliamentary system which is more than a crisis of confidence ...One thing must not be forgotten; that the silent reserves of industry are also the silent reserves of the state. If a boom is followed by a slump, these reserves hold the balance ...Unless we encourage the formation of these reserves, we cannot extricate ourselves from the intolerable state of affairs in which the modernisation, and to some extent, the very maintenance of undertakings, is dependent upon foreign capital ...Since the days when I was engaged in industry ...I have always taken the view that *we must take care to maintain what may be called the independent middle class, and especially the independent businessmen* that have not yet assumed the form of a company, and can set a personal initiative and responsibility against the lack of accumulated capital. There is no doubt that this entire branch of independent German industry will meet a speedy death through want of capital backing. We shall be confronted, if matters go on as present, *by trusts on the one side, and millions of employees and workers on the other. Social distinctions will also become intensified.* All this may stimulate the financial forces of German competitive industry, *but the forces of personality and independence will sink to zero.* Nothing can hasten this course of events so much as the continued rise in the expenditures [on unemployment pay, welfare etc.] approved by parliament, which is expressed in the continued rise in taxation ...Our production is suffering from Germany's want of purchasing power, and indeed, nearly the whole of that industry has come to a crisis that amounts to a catastrophe ...*That is the reason why the parties must give up competing in the race for popularity.* The DVP proposed that in the Budget estimates expenditure shall not be raised nor introduced without the consent of the Reich government...[5] (emphasis added)

In order to prevent the rapid erosion of the mass basis of bourgeois rule in Germany, Stresemann was arguing, the big monopolies would have to pursue a more flexible economic as well as political policy towards the middle class. Certainly there had to be drastic cuts in social expenditure. This was not in dispute between Stresemann and the Ruhr tycoons who were increasingly dominating his party. But whereas a capital-hungry and profit-starved heavy industry wanted all the spoils, Stresemann, sensitive as ever to the moods of the petty-bourgeoisie, insisted that the smaller independent producers should be permitted to share in the capital reserves released by a more stringent economic policy. So once again, the struggle for the division of the surplus product became a key factor in German politics.

Stresemann's advice fell on deaf ears. The party he had originally founded to represent the broader stratum of German burgherdom was fast degenerating into an ultra-reactionary mouthpiece of heavy industry,* as he admitted to a close party

---

* On October 2, the DVP Reichstag fraction voted down a proposal by

colleague:

> The discontent within the party is strengthened by the fact that we are
> associated with the social democrats in a government. On the right, the
> word 'traitor' is used in connection with the social democrats ...we are
> no longer a party with a broad view of affairs, we are more and more
> developing into a purely industrial party ...Today the group can no
> longer muster the courage to enter into opposition to the great
> employers' and industrial associations. We are quite concerned that 23
> members [out of a total of 45] of the [Reichstag] Group should be
> directly or indirectly connected with the control of industry, and are
> indignant when a second wage earner is to become a member of the
> group.[6]

The belligerent stand of the 'Ruhr lobby' in the DVP was but a
pale reflection of the class war it had been waging throughout the
Rhine-Westphalian industrial belt since November 1928. A clash
over wages had only narrowly been averted the previous year, but
now, with recession already biting deep into the reserves of even
the biggest concerns, the leaders of Ruhr industry decided it was
time to resist the demands of the trade union leaders for their
customary annual wage increase. The old contracts covering
200,000 workers in the iron industry lapsed on November 1, 1928,
and so well before this date, the ADGB unions put in for a 15
pfennig wage rise; partly on the grounds of the increased cost of
living, but also because the employers had only recently increased
the prices of their products. Naturally, the Ruhr bosses rejected
this classic reformist argument, since prices had been raised not
with a view to paying more wages, but to increasing profits and
so, partially at least, enabling them to offset the decline in capital
accumulation resulting from the dramatic falling off in foreign
credits. The trade union leaders naturally looked to their allies in
the Müller government to lend them support in the forthcoming
conflict with the Ruhr iron masters since the Minister of Labour,
Rudolf Wissell, was himself an old trade unionist with something
of a left reputation (as Minister of Economics in the first SPD
government of 1919, Wissell had resigned when the cabinet
rejected his proposals for the socialisation of industry). With the
negotiations deadlocked, and all the stages of local arbitration
exhausted, the chairman of the Düsseldorf arbitration board
ruled on October 26 (five days before the current contracts lapsed) that the unions should be awarded an increase of 6 pfennigs

Stresemann to accept a new unemployment insurance bill being presented to the
Reichstag the next day by the Müller government. Its proposed cuts in benefits and
eligible categories were not nearly severe enough for the DVP industrialists, who
succeeded in defeating Stresemann's resolution to accept the bill by 17 votes to 10,
with two abstentions. It marked a decisive defeat for the DVP Chairman's avowed
and well-known policy of collaboration with the SPD. On October 3, Stresemann
died of a stroke. The DVP then decided to remain in the Müller government only
until the ratification of the Young Plan, due in March 1930.

an hour. Even though this sum was well under half the original claim, the employers still found it exorbitant, while the union leaders readily snapped it up. Thus on November 1, 1928, began the biggest lock-out in the history of Ruhr heavy industry. In taking this momentous step, the iron masters were not only challenging the unions, but openly defying 'the Müller government and the Weimar Constitution, whose arbitration proceedure had determined the level of the wage award. It was the opening salvo in a war that was to end four and half years later with the total destruction both of German trade unionism and the party of Hermann Müller. The issues involved in the lock-out were indeed of enormous significance. Here were at most a few score employers defying with impunity a government headed by a party that less than a year before, had won the votes of more than nine million German workers, and which enjoyed the backing of the most powerful and richest trade union movement on the continent of Europe. Yet the legally elected government, acting in accordance with the constitution — its own constitution — and armed with a massive Reichstag majority of 208 in support of welfare for the locked-out workers, found itself paralysed when confronted with this challenge to its authority from the arrogant iron masters of the Ruhr; the same men who two years later, would be financing Hitler's Nazis in their final onslaught on German labour. As a last bid to find common ground between the Metal Workers' Union and the employers, Müller appointed the notoriously right-wing social democrat Carl Severing, the Interior Minister of Prussia, as the final arbitrator in the dispute. Both parties agreed in advance to accept his ruling, and when he finally gave it on December 21, 1928, the employers' confidence in him was vindicated. Severing found that the Düsseldorf award had been too generous to the workers, and they had to accept another cut in their original claim, to take effect from January 1, 1929. Thus did the reformists bend to the pressure of organised big business, even when it was in their interests to resist it. For far from reconciling the iron masters to the rule of the reformists, it served as an example to all German industrialists that with a little more firmness, the whole 'Marxist' crew could be driven from office for good.

The victory of the iron masters over Müller and the Metal Workers' Union led on directly and immediately to demands being made in the DVP Central Committee and Reichstag Fraction for a break with its SPD coalition partners. With the Centre Party temporarily outside the cabinet, the DVP held the fate of the Müller government in its hands, and even the more liberal elements in the party were in favour of using this leverage to extort far-reaching concessions from the social democrats. In

view of the dangerous situation for the working class created by
the Ruhr lock-out defeat, how treacherous was the smug
comment of the SPD official organ on the Düsseldorf award of
October 26, which the paper regarded not only as a great victory
for the metal workers, but proof that under social democratic
rule, the capitalist state was in the process of discarding its
repressive functions:

> Ten years ago the conflict over wages would have been settled entirely
> by a social struggle by force only of trade union resources. Ten years
> ago the workers' organisations would have found no protection from
> the state and its organs, they would then have had to be convinced in
> practice of the bitter truth that the state was on the side of the
> employers. But now the state guarantees the collective agreement. The
> great social differences are settled not only by resort to the trade union
> method of struggle, *but simultaneously by the force of the political
> influence which the workers possess in the state.*[7] (emphasis added)

The employers' answer to that utterly opportunist argument
had been given in the course of the Ruhr lock-out. The methods
of 'social struggle' were not so outdated as the SPD leaders fondly
believed. And the contention that under the Müller government,
the workers exercised a political influence on the state invited the
reply — which was not long in coming — that this was an
excellent justification for removing the social democrats from the
government. But first some more softening up had to be done,
and the annual budget, drawn up by Finance Minister Hilferding,
provided the big employers and bankers with their opportunity.
Presenting his budget to the Reichstag on March 14, 1929, Hilferding was at pains to point out that the financial difficulties being encountered by the Müller government were not the
responsibility of the social democrats, but originated from two
sources; the drying-up of foreign loans, and deficits incurred by
previous ministries in 1926 and 1927. The crisis had been further
exacerbated by an unprecedented and totally unexpected increase
in the number of unemployed. The 1927 unemployment insurance
act had been approved on the general understanding that the jobless rate would not go much above the half million mark, and this
seemed a reasonable assumption in the boom conditions then
prevailing. But with unemployment now nearing the three million
mark — and this, it will be remembered, was still six months
before the Wall Street crash — the funds set aside for dole
payments were proving hopelessly insufficient to meet the most
elementary needs of the unemployed. Already 150 million marks
had been borrowed from the Treasury to meet this crisis, and
another 250 million would probably be needed for the next fiscal
year, even on the basis of the prevailing jobless rate. Where then
were the cuts to be made? Hilferding proposed economies and
taxes ammounting to 379 million marks, but since these were to

be mostly made from and imposed at the expense of propertied interests, the Müller government was once again confronted with the same ruling class intransigence that had forced it to retreat in the Ruhr lock-out. After prolonged bargaining, with the social democrats predictably making most of the concessions, the budget was finally approved by the Reichstag on April 10, 1929, only now, the cuts proposed by Hilferding had been whittled down to a mere 110 million marks. Once again, landed and industrial interests had found that concerted pressure, supported from within the coalition by the bourgeois parties, paid off. But still they were not satisfied. The social democrats had not been persuaded to yield on the basic question of unemployment insurance and other welfare benefits, since to do so would open up its entire left flank to the inroads of the KPD. Refusal to budge on this issue produced an angry comment from the highly influential organ of heavy industry and finance, the *Berliner Börsen Zeitung*,* of May 30, 1929:

> [The] regulation of the finances of the Reich ...calls for an immediate rigorous cut in unemployment insurance, particularly in the direction of an exclusion from benefit of the seasonally and permanently unemployed. The rates of unemployment insurance must be reduced all round, while the supervision of unemployment and the exemption of all cases of proved unemployment must be far more severely carried out. Economies can also be effected in other directions in regard to national insurance, which should gradually be divested of its coercive government character and transformed into an optional matter of thrift [sic!].[8]

The article, a clear indication of the dominant trend of thinking in big business circles, also demanded a revision of the tax system, away from direct taxation (a progressive income tax hampers the accumulation of capital) towards taxation on consumption, which always hits the lower income groups hardest. Reductions in death duties, company taxes etc. were also demanded. Finally, the article called for a new wages policy, one which marked a clear break from the established Weimar system of 'political wages':

> The economy of labour within the country must also be subjected to a fundamental change. The coercive regulations governing wages and working hours must be abolished and we must introduce the freedom of employment and a wage system on the basis of the work actually performed.[9]

---

* Walther Funk, later Hitler's Minister of Economics, was the editor-in-chief of this organ of German high finance, taking up his appointment in 1916. With the development of the economic crisis in Germany, a group of reactionary industrialists (Thyssen, Vögler etc.) invited Funk to head an 'Economic and Political Service' to serve as a liaison between heavy industry and the newly-emerging Nazi Party, an offer which Funk readily accepted. He joined the NSDAP in 1931. The *Berliner Börsen Zeitung* was a thermometer for the political temperature of the big concerns and banks throughout the crisis up to and even beyond the formation of the Nazi regime.

Merging with the controversy concerning the Müller government's domestic policies was the equally fierce and emotionally charged debate on the terms of the new reparations agreement being negotiated with the Allies. After nearly four years of operations under the Dawes Plan, it had been proposed that yet another schedule of payments should be devised at a conference in Paris under the chairmanship of the American Owen Young, from whose name the new plan derived its title. The very composition of the German delegation gave a clear indication of who really ruled in Berlin. Arriving in Paris in the February of 1929, ostensibly to represent the Müller government, were the following leaders of German big business: Reichsbank President Hjalmar Schacht, United Steel Works General Manager Albert Vögler, Ludwig Kastl, Privy Councillor and Director of the Federation of German Industries, and Carl Melchior, of the Hamburg bank of Warburg and Co.

No social democrat dared so much as show his face at this summit of international high finance and industry. Schacht, the main spokesman for the German delegation, presented a memorandum which clearly indicated the growing aggressiveness of imperialist-oriented circles of the bourgeoisie. Not only did it propose a drastic reduction in annual reparations payments (which were anyway being met largely out of loans borrowed from the Allies), the memorandum called for Germany's right to acquire colonies to be recognised by the Allies. It rapidly became obvious in the course of the Paris conference — which dragged on until May — that Schacht and Vögler were acting as independent agents, and not as representatives of the German government. Stresemann, Müller's foreign minister, and the entire SPD leadership, were committed to a policy of *detente* with Germany's former western enemies, and Schacht's aggressive stance threatened to disrupt what for the dying Stresemann was now his life's work. Once again, big business had indicated the contempt it felt for the politicians who ruled Germany. Before long, both Schacht and Vögler were to translate their scorn into active support for fascism.

The Reichsbank President had already given a clear indication of the direction of his thinking in April 1929, at a meeting with government leaders in Berlin on the progress of the talks. When Carl Severing warned Schacht that his belligerent behaviour at the Paris conference could endanger Germany's fragile economic stability, and that the withdrawal of allied support credits would immediately precipitate mass unemployment and political upheavals, Schacht replied coolly:: *'Then we will simply have to shoot'*. But who was to do the shooting? True, Severing, as Prussian Interior Minister, had no hesitation only a few days later in ordering the Berlin police to fire on communist workers celebrating May Day, a crime applauded in every bourgeois paper, however hostile their attitude towards the social democrats. But firing on demonstrations of SPD workers was another question altogether, and both Severing and Schacht knew it. The latter's evolution from being a founder of the republican-radical DDP to an open supporter of national socialism was well under way.

Meanwhile, as the controversy raged over the Young Plan, the Müller government became increasingly bogged down by the inability of its constituent parties to agree on economic and social policies. Any prospects of a deal between the reformists and the DVP were killed stone dead by the collapse of the US boom in October 1929. From this date onwards, however much the social democrats desired it, no stable compromise or coalition with the bourgeoisie was possible. Subjectively, the overwhelming majority of the SPD leadership gravitated organically towards a policy of coalition with the left flank of the bourgeoisie, spurning the possibility of a bloc with any party or tendency to its left against the capitalist parties. But such a strategy — the essence of the 'grand coalition' — demanded not only an economic situation which permitted at least a modest programme of reforms to render the exercise palatable to the millions of workers who followed the SPD. *There had also to be a significant fraction of the bourgeoisie itself willing to co-operate in such an undertaking.* The basis for such a collaborationist trend in the bourgeoisie, quite wide in the first months of the republic, had been eroded not only by the steady decline of the DDP, but the rise of an ultra-reactionary tendency in the Centre headed by Monsignor Ludwig Kaas, who replaced Marx as party leader in December 1928, and the increasing isolation of Stresemann in the DVP. As for the largest ruling class party, the DNVP, there had never been any question of its collaboration with representatives of the SPD in a coalition government. From the birth of the republic until the Reichstag elections of September 1930, when the Nazis erupted from obscurity to the position of Germany's second largest party, governments had the choice of anchoring their parliamentary support either on the SPD or the DNVP. As Count Westarp declared at the Nationalists' congress in September 1927: 'We or the socialists'. And in the unlikely event of both parties going over to a policy of all-out opposition, no majority could have been commanded by any other parliamentary combination, since together with the KPD, which rejected the Weimar system as a matter of principle, they comprised a permanent majority of the Reichstag from January 1919 to the eve of the September 1930 elections. Any alliance policy pursued by the SPD was therefore of necessity predicated on a clear preference on the part of the remaining bourgeois groupings for a bloc with reformists, rather than a homogenous 'national' bloc with the DNVP. Schacht's defection to the ultra-nationalist right was immensely significant in this respect, since in the early days of the republic, it was he more than almost any other bourgeois who had initiated a policy of close collaboration with the reformists against the threat of communist revolution. Now, with the crisis* gathering momentum almost hourly, he had only one political aim: the destruction of the Müller government, and its replacement by a regime that could, without hesitation, do the necessary shooting. Within weeks of the slump on Wall Street, and with United States loans now being recalled in a panic bid to meet debts incurred at home as a result of the crash, German big business stepped up its offensive against the social democrats and the trade unions. Carl Duisberg of I.G. Farben told a conference of 3,000 industrialists in Berlin on November 13, 1929, that Paul Silverberg's proposed policy of mass redundancies and intensified exploitation must have the support of all employers. Evidently not having either himself or his audience in mind, he declared that 'the German people must learn to work more and eat less'. Willi Wittke, the spokesman for Saxon industrialists, went even further, and demanded to loud applause that the Müller government should make way for 'tougher men who could stand unpopularity'.

Three weeks later, on December 2, 1929, the all-powerful Federation of German Industries issued a manifesto under the intimidating title *Go ahead or go under*. Although couched in often abstruse phrases and long-winded economic jargon, its message was as clear as it was brutal. The German working class had to be reduced to conditions of near pauperism and servitude such as it had not experienced since the years of oppression and unfettered exploitation under Bismarck:

---

* In terms of share prices, the German boom had reached its peak more than two years before the Wall Street crash, with the share index ascending to 168 in May 1927, as compared with an average of 100 in the years 1924-1926. From June 1927 onwards, it slid slowly downwards to 125 in September 1929. Then followed the headlong plunge to 107 by the end of the year, and a rock bottom of 45 in April 1932. The extreme fragility of the German boom is brought out by the continued upwards swing of the stock market in all the other major capitalist countries until the spring or summer of 1929, when stagnation, and then slump, set in. Measured by the index of production however, the German boom survived until the very eve of the Wall Street crash, the peak being attained in July 1929. Production alone however gives a distorted picture of the health of German capitalism, because for more than a year before this date, its industry had been progressively starved of new capital, which alone provides the basis for continued expanding production. The rapid shrinkage in the number of bankrupted firms brings this last point out well. There were 31,543 business 'deaths' in 1928, but only 26,864 in the following year, and nearly 2,000 less in 1930, suggesting that the capital famine of 1928 had bitten deep into the soft underbelly of the credit-financed firms well before the first reverberations of the US crisis were being felt on the Berlin Bourse.

The German economy is at the parting of the ways. If it is not possible to adjust taxation and to bring about a decisive turnabout of our economic, financial and social policy, then the collapse of the German economy is inevitable. Rationalisation of the economy has undeniably been energetically pursued and has had some success. It would however have had more favourable results had it not been impaired by increased burdens [precisely the point made and illustrated statistically in Chapter Fourteen!]. It has often had disadvantageous consequences for individual concerns and can only benefit industry as a whole if it is relieved of unproductive expenditure, if interest rates are reduced and if private investment is assured of a reliable return [in other words, the problem of the falling rate of profit, also discussed in the same chapter]. The German economy must be made free. It must not be interfered with by experiments and political influence. The process of socialisation leads to the destruction of the economy and the distress of the masses [sic!]. We therefore reject the attempts at industrial democracy [i.e. the system of workers councils and trade union 'participation' in economic affairs] as a means of socialisation and therefore as a precursor of collectivisation. German industry sees this as a great danger, not only for employers and work people, but for the nation as a whole. The democratisation of the economy for which the socialists are striving, stifles initiative and destroys the sense of responsibility without which no progress is possible. [Therefore we demand] the building up of capital. This is a prerequisite for increasing production ...The German economy must be freed from all economic restrictions. Production must be freed from taxation ...There must be a fundamental recognition of the limit to which the state can interfere in the economy. State enterprise must be limited to those areas where individual enterprise cannot or should not operate. Where public enterprise is justified, it must be run on private business lines. It must have no preferential financing [an obvious attack on social democratic welfare financing] or taxation and must work under the same conditions as private enterprise ...The claims of social policy must be limited to what the economy can support. Economic productivity is the source of social achievement. Recognising this, we unanimously demand: As regards the social insurance laws, their present basis may remain, but payment of benefits and their administration must, unlike at present, conform to what the economy can support. Unemployment insurance. The partial reforms of October 3 [wherein the Müller government sanctioned the disqualification of certain categories from benefit, and reduced benefits for others] does not go far enough. Contributions must be sufficient to meet benefits ...Arbitration and compulsory wage regulations. State compulsory regulation of wages and working conditions must be abolished ...Finance and taxation policy. Taxation in recent years has increased so much as to make the return on investment below the customary rate of interest. This will eventually lead to the disappearance of investment capital ...Indirect taxation must be increased, with the abolition of profits tax as soon as possible, at once by at least one half. [There were also demands for drastic economies by public corporations, state and local government authorities etc.].[10]

Schacht was thinking along similar lines, as became evident

when he published his attack on social democratic economic and social policy, *The End of Reparations,* in the year following the fall of the Müller government:

> It cannot be denied that the post-war policy of Germany has through its socialistic system of financial irresponsibility, hidden from the world the exhaustion of Germany's economic and financial life ...since socialism has so extensive an influence upon the conduct of business and finance in Germany, it remains to be seen whether the productive forces of the people will be adequate to pay for the welfare measures, the bad economics and expensive bureaucracy of this Marxism [i.e. social democracy] ...Not less arbitrary and injurious to the national economic system has been the evolution of wage regulations under the Marxist system ...The result is that often enough the profitability of an undertaking depends upon political rather than economic conditions ...The more the political domination of the socialist trade unions succeeded, by the wage agreement system, in equalising wages, the more emphatically the employers demanded that wages should correspond to actual performance. The decisive historical mistake which must be charged against the SPD is that it seized the occasion of a lost war to promise the masses of the population greater comforts than they had enjoyed before the war.[11]

(Schacht penned these incredibly reactionary lines, full of scorn for even the most modest demands of social democracy, shortly after he made his fateful decision to support the Nazis.)

The severity of the economic crisis was further underlined by the Federation at its extraordinary general meeting held ten days after the publication of its document. A succession of employers took the floor to deliver blistering attacks on the Müller government and especially the trade unions, which they quite correctly saw as the first obstacle to the implementation of plans to cut wages, speed up the tempo of work. Wittke was again prominent in the discussion, drawing the remarks of earlier speakers on the need for a new economic policy to their logical political conclusion:

> To carry out what today's speakers have demanded, requires a firm and durable government. Our present party system does not give this. I am not alone in saying that an enabling act can perhaps be the only means to get us out of our predicament ...This of course demands, above all, civic courage, an attribute which unfortunately is in short supply and which brings temporary unpopularity.

Director Eugen Schnaas of Berlin went still further, proposing not only the suspension of parliamentary party government, but by implication, the destruction of the trade unions. The wild shouts of approval which greeted his anti-union diatribe, and even more, the invocation of the name associated throughout Europe with anti-socialist terror and repression, gave more than a hint of the direction in which German big business was moving:

> Those who have had occasion in recent years to sit down at the table with the trade unions in wage negotiations must have realised that they

haven't got a clue about economics ...I echo the words of the late President Ebert that there will be no industrial peace in Germany until 100,000 party officials have been expelled [cries of 'Bravo!' and 'Mussolini!']. I don't have to say that this radical measure is necessary.

And Germany's Mussolini was already waiting in the wings...

Between the publication of the Federation's manifesto and the meeting of December 12 there exploded the biggest anti-Müller bombshell of them all — the Schacht Memorandum. Issued by the Reichsbank President on December 5, it not only announced Schacht's repudiation of the Young Plan agreement he had signed in Paris on June 7, but his total opposition to the domestic, principally economic policies of the government whose servant he supposedly was (the Memorandum was not even shown to the government before its release). Echoing the arguments of heavy industry, Schacht claimed that a

> true balance of the budget has yet to be achieved; no steps have been taken toward an organised settlement of the former deficit; while new, constantly increasing deficits and fresh demands keep appearing, deficits and demands which in the final analysis can only be covered by further taxation, that is, by a still greater financial burden on the nation.

Schacht had succeeded in drawing first blood. For the immediate target of his attack was Finance Minister Rudolf Hilferding, who having lost the confidence of the head of the state bank, decided to resign rather than fight it out.* Hilferding's successor was not a social democrat, but Paul Moldenhauer, a professor of insurance at Cologne University and what was more to the point, a member of the DVP. The SPD government leaders

---

* Hilferding's resignation was celebrated in papers close to industry and finance. But as the organ of the iron and steel industry, the *Deutsche Bergwerkszeitung,* cautioned on December 29, 1929, an alternative regime and policy had to be ready to take over when the final *coup de grace* was administered. Meanwhile, the social democrats still had some useful work to perform:
'...there is much to indicate that the social democrats are thirsting to return to opposition again. The bourgeois parties should by no means render it too easy for social democracy to realise these intentions. The government will only have successes when the prerequisites are established for a radical abandonment of the present methods, for a break with the ruling system, against the destructive economics of socialism in all spheres. We are drawing near to this, but we have not yet arrived at this state. Before that, let all the nation call for salvation from slavery and exploitation as the result of socialisation, arbitrariness, imprudence and corruption'. Hilferding's removal certainly aroused anger in social democratic circles. On January 15, *Vörwarts* headlined a report of the controversy surrounding the finance minister's departure 'Away with Schacht!' while the next day, it declared that his 'disappearance is an urgent political necessity. In what manner that is to be achieved is a matter of secondary importance.'
And also on January 15, the *Berliner Börsenzeitung* declared in confident tones that it 'would not mind at all if the social democrats were to bring about a Parliamentary Schacht crisis. It would at least demonstrate to them that the party of trade union secretaries is not qualified to take part in the discussion of great things and decisions'.

had already retreated over the questions of cruiser 'A', the Ruhr lock-out, the 1929-30 budget, the Young Plan talks in Paris, unemployment insurance, and now Schacht's attack on their own party comrade Hilferding. What followed was even more capitulatory. Although in no sense a member of the government Schacht in effect laid down the guidelines for its future budgets by compelling the government, on pain of being denied credits by the Reichsbank to meet its debts, to establish a 'sinking fund' of 450 million marks. Once this deflationary proposal was acceded to by a thoroughly intimidated Reichstag and Cabinet, Schacht authorised a consortium of German banks to provide the government with the required funds to meet its more pressing obligations (Schacht's financial dictatorship was rendered all the more effective by the drying-up of other sources of loans as a result of the slump in the USA).

Continued differences with the Müller government over the Young Plan (and not, it should be noted, financial policy) eventually precipitated Schacht's resignation from the Reichsbank on March 3, 1930, nine days before the Plan was ratified by the Reichstag by 266 votes to 193. Schacht had gone, much to the relief of many rank and file social democrats and trade unionists (he was to return three years later as Hitler's Reichsbank chief), but his aim — the removal of the SPD from the government — was now only days away. On the day of the Reichstag vote, Heinrich Brüning, leader of the Centre Party Reichstag fraction and a fast ascending protege of Kaas, visited Hindenburg to inform the President of his party's determination to carry out the financial 'reforms' Schacht and the big employers' organisations had been demanding with mounting urgency over the previous year. And like those from whom he took his cue, Brüning declared he would not shrink from by-passing normal parliamentary methods to achieve his goal. The Centre organ Germania, whose editorial policy was directed by von Papen's reactionary Catholic clique, revealed that in the course of the conversation, Hindenburg had promised Brüning that he would 'make use of all constitutional means' to bring about such a reform of German financial policy. And Germania added darkly, in tones clearly inspired by von Papen himself, that 'if the German parliament cannot accomplish this task, then the President will assume whatever powers are appropriate and necessary ...The dissolution of the Reichstag, or Article 48, or both, stand ready for service if the parties fall.' With this Bonapartist injunction, sentence had been pronounced on the Müller government,* all that needed to be done was to carry it

---

* Although Brüning is generally regarded as the pioneer of rule by Presidential decree based on Article 48 of the Weimar Constitution, the idea had first been mooted a year earlier by Carl Severing, who in a speech in Essen on March 3, 1929, declared: 'If it should really come to pass that this country should be governed by

out. The SPD now stood alone, its 'grand coalition' in ruins. The DVP had voted to withdraw its support from Müller at the end of 1929, and now, with Brünings' decision to invoke the authority of the President to force even more reactionary policies on the government, the social democrats were obviously about to lose the support of their other main coalition partner, the Centre Party. The issue on which Müller's government finally fell was that of unemployment insurance. In January 1930, the number of workers without jobs had risen to well over the two million mark, and even with the reduction in categories qualified to receive benefit undertaken by the government in October 1929, there was no hope of their being maintained at subsistence level unless new funds were made available to replenish the exhausted treasury. The SPD proposed that the deficit be made good by a four per cent levy on higher income groups, notably civil servants. The DVP, whose support was drawn from just these privileged layers of the population, rejected the plan point blank. Then Finance Minister Moldenhauer came up with a compromise solution. He proposed on March 24 that unemployment contributions, which currently stood at 3½% for employers and workers alike, should be raised to 4% providing that a majority of the trade union and management representatives on the directorate of the national unemployment service agreed to this. The DVP turned down this plan also, even though the sum involved was the seemingly trifling one of ½% of employers' incomes. Then with the other two government parties, the Centre and the DVP, acting as mediators, a third plan was drawn up. It now involved an increase of a mere ¼% in contributions, and only then in the event of a government subsidy of 150 millions failing to make good the deficit. This version seemed to satisfy both the DVP and the SPD cabinet members until, at the very last moment, Müller's Minister of Labour Rudolf Wissell declared that he could not vote for it. Wissell was not speaking for himself alone. 37% of the SPD Reichstag fraction were trade union officials and leaders, among them being five members of the ADGB executive committee. On March 27, 1930, Wissell informed his other three party colleagues in the Cabinet — Müller, Severing and Schmidt — that the trade union delegation in the Reichstag could under no circumstances vote for the proposed reform of the unemployment insurance scheme. They were in fact unanimous in their opposition to it, and were assured of a majority in the SPD Reichstag fraction by the support of sympathetic party deputies. Outvoted for the second time by his party, Müller had no choice but to hand in his

Article 48 of the Weimar Constitution, I am not afraid of the responsibility. I place myself at the disposal of the Republic'. In July 1932 Severing, as Minister of Interior in the Prussian State government, was deposed along with his fellow SPD Ministers by von Papen, who of course, invoked this same Article 48.

resignation on March 28, 1930. The last 'grand coalition' had collapsed, torn apart by forces that none of its members could properly comprehend. The liberal *Berliner Tagblatt* was utterly bemused by what it called the 'crisis over ¼ per cent', and superficially it must have indeed seemed absurd that a government that had swallowed so many capitalist camels now strained at such a minute gnat. In fact the fall of Müller had proceeded in accordance with a law first enunciated — in an idealist form — by Hegel; namely the dialectical transition, the leap, from quantity into quality.

In his *Science of Logic,* Hegel says that an objectively existing thing, a 'Being-for-self', is not only constituted qualitatively (thus demarcating itself from and setting itself in opposition to other Beings-for-Self), but 'is also essentially a relation of Quanta, and therefore open to externality and variation of Quantum: it has some play, within which it remains indifferent to this change and does not alter its Quality'[12] However this degree of tolerance or 'play' is not infinite. There exist objective, and as Hegel observes, often unpredictable limits beyond which quantitative changes (either negative or positive) become impossible without subverting the Being-in-self, 'a point in this quantitative change at which Quality changes and Quantum shows itself as specifying; so that the altered quantitative relation is turned under our hands into a Measure and thereby into a new quality and a new Something'.[13] The very nature of this process — a protracted period of quantitative change within a seemingly permanent or at least stable framework, culminating in an explosive and often dramatic leap to a new qualitatitive state — leaves all but the most perceptive bewildered. For it appears that the last quantitative addition or subtraction was responsible for the sudden transformation, that, to return to the subject in question, the ADGB's refusal to sanction a reduction one quarter of a per cent in employers' contribution to unemployment insurance was the cause of the rift in the Müller cabinet between its social democratic and bourgeois partners. Hegel explains how this illusion arises:

> Men like to try to make a change conceivable by means of the gradualness of transition; but rather gradualness is precisely the merely indifferent change [i.e. that which is containable within the existing quality], the opposite of quantitative change. Rather, in gradualness the connection of the two realities — whether taken as state or independent things — is suspended; it is posited that neither is limit of the other, but that one is just external to the other; and hereby, precisely that which is needful in order that change may be understood is eliminated, however little may be required to this end.[14]

And after illustrating the working out of this law in the natural world with famous example of liquid water becoming transformed, by quantitative additions and subtractions of heat, into the qualitatively different states of steam and ice (a process which in both cases, culminates in a sudden, and not gradual change of state) Hegel detects it also in human history:

> Thus too do states — other things equal — derive a different qualitative character from magnitudinal difference ...The State has a certain measure of its magnitude, and if forced beyond this it collapses helplessly under that very same constitution which was its blessing and its strength for as long as its extent alone was different.[15]

These lines could well serve as fitting epitaph on the fate of Weimar democracy, and as a judgement by Germany's foremost exponent of objective idealist dialectics on the miserable theoretical degeneration of that same nation's most vulgar evolutionists.

The political relations and institutions established by the November Revolution held together only so long as they were able to absorb the quantitative additions in class tension (that is, between the polar opposites which comprise the quality in question) precipitated by the general crisis of world imperialism as refracted and mediated through the specific and chronic crisis of German capitalism. On one historic occasion, in the summer and autumn of 1923, a historic opportunity presented itself to bring about a qualitative leap in this struggle between the classes. For unlike the transformation of water into steam or ice, historical change, and most of all, the proletarian revolution, requires deep-going transformations in the consciousness of men, a change which reaches its highest theoretical and practical expression in the revolutionary Marxist party. Such a leap in political thinking, in the form of revolutionary tactics, strategy and organisation, did not take place. The opportunity slipped by, the process of addition was replaced by subtraction, and the stabilisation of 1924-1928, supplanted the crisis of 1919-1923. Then, beginning with the formation of the Müller government in June 1928, and the simultaneous onset of the economic crisis, a renewed process of quantitative change began; one however which found the bourgeoisie, and not the working class, on the offensive.

That it was able to retain this initiative beyond the fall of Müller and through the next three years to the triumph of Hitler was not an inevitable outcome of the objective nature of the crisis, but entirely the consequence of the policies pursued by the two main tendencies in the German workers' movement.

REFERENCES FOR CHAPTER SEVENTEEN

[1] J. Stalin: quoted from a letter written in January 1925, in *The Results of the Work of the 14th Conference of the RCP*, May 9, 1925, *Collected Works*, Vol. 7, p.120.
[2] J. Stalin: *Foundations of Leninism*, ibid, Vol. 6, pp.110-111.
[3] T. Leipart: *Leipziger Volkszeitung*, March 10, 1928.
[4] H. Neumann: Discussion at Tenth ECCI Plenum, July 1929, in *IPC* Vol. 9, No. 51, September 17, 1929, p.1082.
[5] G. Stresemann: *Diaries, Letters and Papers*, Vol. 3, pp.459-464.
[6] G. Stresemann: to Geheimrat Kahl. March 13, 1929, in ibid, pp.468-469.
[7] *Vörwarts*, November 3, 1928.
[8] *Berliner Börsen Zeitung*, May 30, 1929.
[9] Ibid.
[10] *Go Ahead or Go Under*. Memorandum of the Presidium of the Federation of German Industries, December 2, 1929.
[11] H. Schacht: *The End of Reparations*, pp.111-202, London, 1931.
[12] W. Hegel: *Science of Logic*, Vol. 1, p.387, London, 1961.
[13] W. Hegel: ibid, p.387.
[14] W. Hegel: ibid, p.388.
[15] W. Hegel: ibid, p.390.

The Comintern, the KPD and the Müller Government

How did the Stalinist leadership of the CI and the KPD analyse and respond to the events and crises discussed in the foregoing chapter? Did the very obvious deepening of the conflict between the SPD and the reformist trade unions on the one side, and the entire bourgeoisie on the other, occasion any revision of the theory that social democracy had now turned fascist, and was in Germany more than any other country, destined to spearhead the bourgeoisie's bid to install a fascist dictatorship over the working class? On the contrary, the more evident these tensions became, the more the Stalinists frantically tried to deny their existence, since to admit that a split was indeed taking place within the Müller cabinet was to concede that the 'new line' ushered in at the Sixth CI Congress was founded on theoretical quicksands. Equally important was the fact that Stalin had openly fallen out with the Bukharin group in the Politburo of the CPSU, and had finally opted for a course of break-neck industrialisation and forced collectivisation as his bureaucratic answer to the deepening crisis of the Soviet economy. On October 19, 1928, Stalin delivered a report to party officials in Moscow in which he spoke of a 'right danger' in the CPSU, though he repudiated suggestions that it had any supporters on the Politburo. Significantly, in view of the holocaust that was about to descend on Bukharin and his followers in the CI, Stalin linked the 'right deviation' in the CPSU to a similar, and equally — at this stage — anonymous tendency in the International: 'Under capitalist conditions, the Right deviation in communism signifies a tendency ...of a section of the Communists to depart from the revolutionary line of Marxism in the direction of social democracy. When certain groups of Communists deny the expediency of the slogan "class against class" in election campaigns (France [where in the elections of 1928, the French CP had, contrary to earlier practice, refused to stand down on the second ballot to support better placed socialist candidates]), or are opposed to the Communist Party nominating its own candidates (Britain [this had been the line of a right-wing group headed by J.R. Campbell and A. Rothstein]) or are disinclined to make a sharp issue of the fight against "Left" social democracy (Germany) etc. it means that there are people in the Communist parties who are striving to adapt communism to social democratism'. (J. Stalin: *The Right Danger in the CPSU*. October 19, 1928, *Collected Works*, Vol. 11, pp.233-234.) This trend, whose supporters in Germany were near to exercising a decisive voice on the KPD CC, Stalin equated with the Right deviation in the Soviet Union, which 'denied the need for an offensive against the capitalist elements in the countryside' and thereby adapted 'to the tastes and requirements of the "Soviet" bourgeoisie'. (Ibid, p.235, Stalin should have known all about these, because while his alliance with Bukharin endured, he had been instrumental in catering for the prejudices and greed of the rich in town and country alike). This speech is important in that in attacking Stalin's rightist opponents in the CPSU, it gave a broad hint that war was shortly to be declared on those in the sections of the CI and its central leadership who, justly or otherwise, were alleged to share their views. From October 1928 onwards, Stalin's onslaught on the *Kulak* — far more severe than anything envisaged by either Trotsky or Lenin, who had both stood for *voluntary* collectivisation of the peasantry — and forced march to an industrialised economy were organically fused with his fight to gain total control of the International, a battle waged under the banner of war to the death against 'social fascism'.

The biggest challenge to Stalin came from the KPD, the largest party of the CI outside of the Soviet Union, and one that even after its series of maulings and decimations at the hands of successive cliques in the ECCI leadership, still retained something of its former independent and critical revolutionary spirit. A new crisis in the KPD forced Stalin's hand, since it threatened to overturn the leadership of his most trusted representative in Germany, Ernst Thälmann, who even before the Sixth CI Congress, had been vociferous in his support for the theory of 'social fascism'.

Throughout the summer of 1928, rumours had been rife in the Hamburg party organisation (where Thälmann began his career) that KPD funds had been embezzled. A commission set up to investigate the charges finally discovered, after an anonymous tip-off over the telephone, that the culprit was none other the secretary of the Hamburg party organisation, Wittorf, and that several leading party members, including two of those serving on the Control Commission that was investigating the affair, had known about it from the beginning, and had done every-thing to cover it up. Then an even deeper scandal broke. The two commisssion members — Presche and Riess — together with Johnny Schehr, KPD Organising Secretary and a close friend of Thälmann, had been ordered by none other than Thäl-mann to protect Wittorf from the consequences of his act. And Wittorf was Thälmann's brother-in-law! If Wittorf had to be expelled — and on this there was no disagreement — then at the very least, Thälmann had to be disciplined as an accessory after the fact. On September 26, 1928, a plenary session of the KPD demanded that Thälmann return to Berlin from Moscow to face the music. On his arrival in Berlin, the party CC carried the following resolution: "The CC sharply disapproves, as a severe political blunder, the attempt on the part of Comrade Thälmann to keep the events in Hamburg secret from the proper authorities within the party. On his own initiative the affair is referred to the ECCI. He is removed from all party functions until a decision by the ECCI has been reached.' When Stalin heard the news of Thälmann's fall from grace, he was enraged, immediately dis-patching a telegram instructing a delegation from the KPD CC to attend a meeting in Moscow to 'discuss' the matter with leading ECCI officials — Piatnitsky, Kuusinen, Molotov (Stalin's new rising star in the ECCI political secretariat) Manuilsky, Kun, and the Swiss supporter of Bukharin, Humbert Droz. Stalin did not deign to break his holiday-making in Sochi to see the KPD delegation, but simply sent a curt telegram which rendered all further discussion superfluous: 'Thälmann to be confirmed in all his functions, the [Right] opposition to be excluded from the CC.' Only Droz, who also had close ties and sympathies with those being excluded so high-handedly from the German party leadership, voted against this ukase. As one who participated in both the investigation and the 'meeting' in Moscow comments, 'what had at first seemed a petty financial scandal in Hamburg became a major turning point. The moral backbone of a great working class party had been broken'. (*Financial Agent of the Comintern: From the Memoirs of Comrade Y,* in Ypsilon: *Pattern of World Revolution,* p.132.)

The official Stalinist stamp of approval was put on Thälmann's leadership on October 6, 1928, when the ECCI Presidium issued its decision on the Wittorf affair.

After mildly rebuking Thälmann for his failing to report the embezzlement as soon as he learnt of it (an oversight put down to his desire to protect the party from 'the class enemies of the proletariat') the resolution unleashed a barrage of invective against those who voted originally for Thälmann's removal from the CC. This 'crass mistake' was part of a conspiracy against Thälmann being organised by his 'political opponents within the CC', and 'an attempt to change the party leadership and so obstruct the execution of the political line adopted by the sixth world congress', a line, the resolution significantly emphasised, that was best represented in the KPD by none other than Thälmann. The resolution ended by expressing the presidium's 'complete political confidence in comrade Thälmann' and called upon him 'to continue to discharge the functions in the party and the ECCI imposed on him by the Essen party congress and the sixth CI congress'. For once, the presidium's confidence was justified. Thälmann never deviated once from the line imposed on his party from Moscow, even when it entailed placing his own head in the Nazi noose.

With his trusty servitor now bound even more closely to him as a result of his inter-vention on Thälmann's behalf in the Wittorf affair, Stalin felt free to move openly against the German supporters of Bukharin. In December 1928, the Stalinised CC of the KPD voted to expel, against the solitary vote of Ernst Meyer, not only Brandler and Thalheimer, but Walcher, Frölich and Enderle, who up until the recent crisis, had been prominent in the party leadership (and even more significantly all five were old Spartacists and comrades of Rosa Luxemburg). The purge went both wide and deep. Ten members of the CC and more than a hundred on the district committees now found themselves outside the party they had devoted their lives to building. And climbing over them to the top were careerists who unlike the disgraced Luxemburgists, found it easy to adjust their bureaucratic phraseology to the latest zig-zag of Stalinist policy. On December 19, 1928, Stalin summed up the results of the purge in the German party in a speech to the Presidium of the ECCI. His main theme was that the Rights (real and alleged alike) denied that the period of capitalist stabilisation was drawing to a close, to be replaced by a 'third period' of the 'sharp accentuation of the general crisis of capitalism'. Singling out Humbert-Droz as the main spokesman for this tendency in the ECCI (Stalin's open break with Bukharin was still two months away) Stalin criticised him for maintaining that the struggles of the working class against the employers were 'in the main only of a defensive character, and that the leadership of this struggle on the part of the communist parties should be carried out only within the framework of the existing reformist unions'. Now Stalin employed this centrist conception to smuggle in an alternative, ultra-left line on the trade unions, one which set the pace throughout the CI, but especially in Germany, for the drive towards parallel 'red' unions that almost without exception lacked real stability and deep roots in the factory proletariat: 'At the time of the Ruhr battles [the lock-out of November 1928] the German Communists noted the fact that the unorganised workers proved to be more revolutionary than the organised workers. Humbert-Droz is outraged by this and declares that it could not have been so. Strange! Why could it not have been so? There are about a million workers in the Ruhr. Of them, about 200,000 are organised in trade unions. The trade unions are directed by reformist bureaucrats who are connected in all manner of ways with the capitalist class. Why is it surprising then that the unorganised workers proved to be more revolutionary than the organised? *Could it indeed have been otherwise? ...a situation is quite conceivable in which it may be necessary to create parallel mass associations of the working class, against the will of the trade union bosses who have sold themselves to the capitalists.* We already have such a situation in America [Lozovsky had, it will be recalled, written off the AFL as a 'fascist' union at the Fourth RILU Congress in July 1928]. *It is quite possible that things are moving in the same direction in Germany too.* (J. Stalin: *The Right Danger in the KPD*, December 19, 1928, ibid, pp.309-315) (emphasis added)

Those such as Lozovsky who were already inclined towards such leftist tactics were strengthened in their desire to foist them on the parties of the International by the open breach between Stalin's faction and the Bukharin group, which came at the end of January 1929. For the first time, Stalin spoke openly of 'a separate Bukharin group ...consisting of Bukharin, Tomsky and Rykov [with] its own separate platform, which it counterposes to the Party's policy. It demands, firstly — in opposition to the existing policy of the Party — a slower rate of development of our industry, asserting that the present rate is "fatal". It demands — also in opposition to the policy of the Party — curtailment of the formation of state farms and collective farms, asserting that they cannot play any serious part in the development of our agriculture. It demands thirdly — also in opposition to the policy of the party — the granting of full freedom to private trade and the renunciation of the regulating function of the state in the sphere of trade, asserting that the regulation of the state renders the development of trade impossible. In other words: Bukharin's group is a group of Right deviators and capitulators who advocate not the elimination, but the free development of the capitalist elements of town and country'. (J. Stalin: *Bukharin's Group and the Right Deviation in our Party,* speech to a joint meeting of the CPSU Politburo and Presidium of the Central Control Commission of the CPSU, end of January 1929, ibid, pp.332-333). On this occasion, Stalin made no reference to the issues in dispute in the CI. But he did so two months later in a long speech to the April 1929 CPSU Plenum, convened to take organisational measures against the Bukharin Right Opposition.

After slanderously linking the Bukharinites with the Left Opposition (who were their bitterest critics) on the strength of a single conversation in the summer of 1928 between the renegade Left Oppositionist Kamenev and Bukharin (a discussion which mooted the formation of an unprincipled anti-Stalin bloc of former Lefts and supporters of Bukharin's rightist course) Stalin answered Bukharin's charge, made in a declaration to the CPSU CC on January 30, that 'the Central Committee is disintegrating the Comintern'. Evidently Bukharin — still nominal head of the CI could no longer acquiesce in the 'new line' which was daily lurching further and further to the ultra-left with its adventurist slogan of new 'red' unions and claims that the entire social democratic movement from top to bottom was turning 'social fascist'. And while in contrast to Trotsky, Bukharin's opposition to the tactics of 'third period' Stalinism was not based on a rejection of the theory of 'socialism in one country', he nevertheless, precisely because of his organic leaning towards centrist tendencies in the CI and the left elements in the reformist parties, grasped more quickly than most the suicidal implications of the Stalin-Molotov line: '...capitalist stabilisation [said Stalin] is being undermined and shaken month by month and day by day ...the swing to the left of the working class in the capitalist countries, the wave of strikes and class conflicts in the European countries ...all these are facts which indicate beyond a doubt that the elements of a new revolutionary upsurge are accumulating in the capitalist countries. Hence the task of intensifying the fight against social democracy, *and above all, against its "Left" wing* [the same "Left" with whose British trade union representatives Stalin had been aligned during their betrayal of the General Strike and the nine month struggle of the miners], as being *the social buttress of capitalism.* Hence the task of intensifying the fight in the Communist Parties against the Right elements, as being the agents of social democratic influence. Hence the task of intensifying the fight against conciliation towards the Right deviation, as being the refuge of opportunism in the Communist Parties. Hence the slogan of purging the Communist Parties of social democratic traditions [a task allegedly accomplished a full four years previously by the Stalin-Zinoviev 'Bolshevisation' campaign, which on that occasion was directed at supporters of Trotsky]. *Hence the so-called new tactics of communism in the trade unions.'* (J. Stalin: *The Right Deviation in the CPSU, speech to the Plenum of the CC and the CCC of the CPSU, April 1929, ibid, Vol. 12, pp.7-15) (emphasis added)*

The German party, destined to serve as the proving ground for the new leftist course, figured most prominently in the clash between Stalin and Bukharin over international policy. According to Stalin, Bukharin had supported the initial move to depose Thälmann over the latter's involvement in the Wittorf affair: '...instead of swinging the tiller over and correcting the situation, instead of restoring the validity of the violated directive of the Sixth Congress [on the 'fight against conciliation towards the right deviation'] and calling the conciliators to order Bukharin proposed in his well-known letter, to sanction the conciliators' coup, to hand over the KPD to the conciliators, and to revile Comrade Thälmann ...If the Sixth Congress decided to declare war on the Right deviation and conciliation towards it by keeping the leader-ship in the hands of the main core of the KPD, headed by Comrade Thälmann, and if it occurred to the conciliators Ewart and Gerhart to upset that decision, it was Bukharin's duty to call the conciliators to order ...' (Ibid, pp.26-27). Bukharin was also taken to task for procrastinating over 'routing the Brandler and Thalheimer faction, and ...expelling the leaders of that faction from the KPD ...At bottom, it was the fate of the KPD that was being decided. Yet Bukharin and his friends [Humbert-Droz], knowing this, nevertheless continually hindered matters by systematically keeping away from the meetings of the bodies which had the question under con-sideration ...presumably for the sake of remaining "clean" in the eyes of both the Comintern and the the Rights in the KPD'. (Ibid, p.27.) Finally, Bukharin had sinned against the new Stalinist code of conduct in the CI by objecting to the intrigues being woven in the KPD on Stalin's behalf by Neumann.

Bukharin, who had good cause to doubt Neumann's motives in the light of the Canton adventure of December 1927, demanded his recall. No other party of the CI was referred to by Stalin in his diatribe against Bukharin, underlining the fact that the battle between the Stalinist 'centre' and the Bukharin Right was being waged not only in Moscow, but Berlin. The Stalinist faction in the CPSU could not tolerate an oppositional tendency — of whatever complexion — gaining ascendancy in the largest party of the International. Therefore the leftist line assumed a more exaggerated form in the KPD than almost any other section in a party which had it pursued a Leninist tactic (and not a Bukharinite adaptation to left social democracy) could have won the leadership of the majority of the German working class and through a determined struggle for power, blocked the road against the advance of national socialism. Stalin's ultra-leftist line cut clean across such a development, isolating the KPD from the social democratic workers in the trade unions and the SPD with its dictum that the reformists were 'social fascists', and that no tactical agreements were permissible between the KPD and the social democratic organ-isations. With the removal of the Brandler faction, the KPD was now ready to implement Stalin's suicidal policy. The Ruhr lock out provided the first opportunity, where the KPD came forward with the line, first propounded at the Fourth RILU Congress in July 1928, that the reformist unions were fast becoming transformed into strike-breaking machines tied to the capitalist state and the employers' organisations (this despite the fact that the lock-out arose as result of the reformist-led Metal Workers' Union's *failure to agree* with the iron masters over a new pay claim!). Stalin's already-quoted reference to the alleged emergence of a revolutionary layer of workers completely outside (and presumably hostile to) the reformist trade unions in this dispute — never substantiated by any evidence — became converted into an entire system of trade union tactics and strategy. Thus in an article on the Ruhr lock-out, S. Gusiev (a Soviet Stalinist) wrote that the old slogan of 'Make the [trade union] leaders fight' now had to be withdrawn. 'The new united front tactic is the direct projection of the former tactics in the face of con-ditions which have changed.' But despite this brave attempt to preserve a semblance of outward continuity between the old and now discarded line of a united front from above and the new line of a united front only 'from below', Gusiev's article marked a clear shift in Comintern, and especially KPD tactics: 'Now we are strong enough to have been able largely to extend our tactics of the united front, *spreading it among the wide mass of unorganised workers*. Our activities have come to depend much less on the conduct of the leaders of social democracy, and that dependency grows weaker every day'. In other words, the KPD was now seeking to anchor itself on the unstable masses outside the unions, and beginning to turn its back on the five million strategically crucial workers organised in the ADGB, and largely still loyal to the SPD. The 'new line', with its brash talk of 'independent leadership' simply became a *left cover* for capitulation to the continued domination of the reformist bureaucracy over millions of German workers without whose support or at the very least, passive sympathy, there could be no question of a successful revolution.

The Stalinist course also rendered impossible inside the KPD a serious discussion of the highly unstable compromise that existed between the reformist leaders and the big employers and their political spokesmen, a compromise that as we have seen, was being rapidly undermined by the gathering crisis of German capitalism. Gusiev would have none of it: 'Class against class connotes the organised capitalist class (*including the social democrats in this category*) attacking the proletariat on the one hand, and on the other, the swiftly organising working class, driving and leading a counter-attack against the capitalists *under the direct leadership of the communist party*. Such are the tendency and prospect in the coming weeks and months'. And if this were so then obviously there could be no question of the big bourgeoisie falling out with the very social democrats with whom it had concluded an organised bloc: 'It is erroneous ...to explain the capitalists' attack [on the Müller government] (as does *Vorwärts* and as certain communists think) by the influence of the DNVP, who are said to be striving to inflict a blow at the existing coalition government ...A number of political differences exist among the various of the *bourgeois* parties (*including the SPD* but none of these differences has any importance in the struggle now unfolding*'. (all quotes from S. Gusiev: *Lesson of the German Lock-Out, Communist International*, Vol. 6, No. 3, January 1, 1929, pp.76-82) (emphasis added) With the SPD now designated as a 'bourgeois party', the Müller government's problems could be depicted — quite wrongly, as subsequent events proved — as normal differences within the ruling class, and having no relation to the struggle between classes, mediated in a highly attenuated form through the SPD's participation in a cabinet which also included the leading party of big business. This false leftist analysis left KPD workers completely unprepared both theoretically and politically for the political crisis which erupted over the issues of cruiser 'A', cuts in wages and unemployment insurance, the Hilferding-Schacht conflict, and finally, the refusal of the trade unions (who were, of course, in a bloc with the employers) to accept the DVP's revised schedule of unemployment insurance contributions. The remoteness from reality of the new CI leadership's analysis is illustrated in this excerpt from an article in the Comintern organ on the 'right danger in the KPD', which declared that the basis of the party's trade union tactics was 'the most recent evolution of the social democrats and the reformist trade unions, their complete assimilation into the bourgeois state machine and trust capital, their new methods of strangling the independent struggles of the proletariat, their social fascist splitting tactics... [hence] the emphasis laid on the necessity for the communist parties and revolutionary trade union opposition of winning the leadership in mass struggles, and on the question of new forms of struggle and new organisations for the greatest possible mobilisation and activating of militant workers'. (*The CI and the Right Danger in the KPD*, ibid, Vol. 6, No. 6, February 15, 1929, p.180.)

The ECCI *May Day Manifesto* dwelt at some length on this theme of the organic fusion of social democracy with the bourgeoisie. First it quite mechanically, without any regard for the uneven development of the capitalist crises and the class struggle in the imperialist world, projected an identical political perspective for every section of the Comintern — one of imminent civil war: 'The accentuation of the class struggle leads with all capitalist governments to civil war methods in their dealings with the toilers'. We find a similar schematic approach to the current crisis being adopted today by *Workers Press*. On November 24, 1973, *Workers Press* carried a headline on page 3: 'Military coup a threat in all major countries'. And indeed, over the previous two months, confident predictions of such imminent coups and civil wars had been made for the USA, Ireland, Japan, West Germany, Mexico, France Italy and Britain. The method which leads the WRP Central Committee to this conclusion bears a remarkable resemblance to the idealist schematicism of third period Stalinism, since this perspective is put forward for 'all major countries irrespective of whether they are already ruled by military or fascist regimes (such as Chile, Spain, Portugal, Greece, Indonesia, Brazil, to name but six cases), a bourgeois parliamentary system with the direct representatives of the capitalist class in office (as in France, Japan, Britain) or a government comprised either wholly on in part of representatives of the Stalinist or social democratic movements. Thus reformists, Stalinists, bourgeois liberals and conservatives, militarists and fascists are lumped together, after the manner of the original draft of the 1891 SPD Erfurt Programme so sharply criticised by Engels, in 'one reactionary mass'. We are told (*Workers Press*, November 20, 1973) that 'the admiration at the top of the Tory cabinet for President

Pompidou's Bonarpartist regime is part of the Europe-wide preparation for civil war against the working class', and that the 'purpose of the Pompidou club is to pool the experience and knowledge of the heads of state in order to organise counter-revolution throughout the Common Market' (ibid). Anyone familiar with Trotsky's writings on Germany, and especially on the policies the Stalinists pursued in that country between 1929 and 1933, will of course know that he took enormous pains to emphasize the differences between the social democratic, Bonapartist, and fascist varieties of reaction. Brandt will not and cannot, without severing all his links with the SPD and the entire German labour movement (and at the moment he does that, he loses all value for the bourgeoisie!) join with Heath and Pompidou to 'organise counter-revolution throughout the Common Market', since the goal of such a counter-revolution can only be to eliminate bourgeois democracy and the existence of independent workers' organisations, and to establish fascism. Yet in *Workers Press* of October 19, 1973, we can read (in an article reprinted from *Der Funke*, the organ of the Socialist Workers League, which at the time of writing is in political solidarity with the WRP) that 'under the Social Democratic government [of Willy Brandt] civil war preparations are being made which have no precedent in the history of the West German republic'. No-one doubts for a moment that the technical preparations being made by the West German police are for use against the working class. But what this article overlooks — in fact studiously avoids mentioning, although the history of Weimar should surely teach its writer not to do so — is that the repressive machine being built up under the rule of Brandt can and in all probability will be turned against Brandt and his fellow social democratic leaders, just as Noske's Free Corps revolted against the Frankenstein that created them. The fact that *Der Funke* does know this is revealed unwittingly by its demand, which in the context of the rest of the article, is absurd, that 'the unions must force this government to reverse all its civil war measures' and that 'the working class must demand that they [the FDP liberals] should be thrown out of the government and force the SPD to carry out socialist policies'. (Ibid.) So there *is* a difference — and a vital one at that — between Pompidou's regime and that of Brandt. For who, unless he is an inveterate opportunist, would consider addressing such demands to the French Gaullists, Heath, the Greek military or the Italian Christian Democrats, all of whom, we are told, are plotting counter-revolution and civil war in cahoots with Brandt? Yet, in other articles published in the *Workers Press,* no distinction is made between Brandt's reformist-liberal coalition and purely bourgeois cabinets on this most vital of all questions — that of the destruction of the workers' movement and the installation of fascism. It is a false perspective that just as surely as in the last years of Weimar Germany, will lead the working class to certain defeat if it it is permitted to gain ascendancy in the workers movement. Such leftism supplements to perfection the open opportunism of the Stalinists, social democrats and centrist revisionist groups, as once again, the example of Weimar Germany, to which we now return, proves.

From its arid, non-dialectical appraisal of the world situation, the conclusion was drawn by the ECCI *Manifesto* that 'in Germany, France, Great Britain, United States, conditions of an open dictatorship are maturing', obliterating not only widely differing degrees of manoeuvre available to the ruling class in these countries on the foundations of bourgeois democracy, but also the actual composition of the governments in the countries concerned. But according to the Stalinist theory of 'social fascism' that did not matter in the least, since all governments and parties (save those of the Soviet Union and the Comintern respectively) were becoming 'fascicised' and therefore capable of serving as the 'instruments' of fascist dictatorship. The class struggle therefore assumed a new form — the working class, led by the communist party, against a bloc of the trade unions the social democratic parties, fascists, all the bourgeois parties and the capitalist state: 'The struggle of the CI against the Second International ...will not be simply an ideological struggle within one class, but a struggle between two classes developing into civil war against the bourgeoisie who the social democrats are now serving'.

A communist-led civil war against the SPD and the ADGB — his was the lunatic perspective foisted on the KPD at the precise moment when the bourgeoisie was preparing to launch its own offensive against the same organisations. Oblivious to the crisis of the Müller government, the anonymous author of the already-quoted article *Social Fascism in Germany* declared with rare conviction that 'it would be incorrect to conclude that Germany is directly faced with the establishment of a fascist government *a la Mussolini* ...The great change that has taken place is the growth of fascism within social democracy, and in German social democracy in particular. The German capitalists have found a strong support with increasingly definite fascist tendencies. And Germany shows, more clearly than elsewhere, how correct our programme was in its description of the relations between the bourgeoisie, social democracy and fascism, and of the openly fascist role of the social democrats. Facts seem to show that the German capitalists are getting ready for a bourgeois social democratic coalition with fascism ...in every respect, a synthesis of social democracy and fascism is provided for the regime in a political form of the dictatorship of finance capital'. (Ibid, Vol. 6, No. 11-12-13, pp.529-530.) Stalinist stalwart Walter Ulbricht developed this theme with two contributions in the same organ, emphasising that the new line determined that 'the policy of the united front becomes exclusively the policy of the united front from below' (ibid, p.498) and that there now existed a 'tendency towards fascism both in the government and in the SPD and trade union reformist leadership'. For good measure, he called for the 'break-up of the *Reichsbanner*', the SPD para-military organisation, and counterpart to the KPD's own Red Front Fighters' League. The ever-vigilant Ulbricht also detected the influence of the Brandler school in the thinking of some party officials, 'who expect to secure tactical victories by mobilising the masses to the call of the reformist leaders in order to prove later to the workers that everything had been done to secure "unity in the struggle" '. (Ibid, Vol. 6, No. 14, June 1, 1929, pp.574-577) These officials had not grasped the new Stalinist truth that the trade union leaders were now 'strike breakers' and that therefore the demand of the hour was no longer to work for a united front within the trade unions both at the top with the leaders and at the base with the workers, but to devise 'new organisational forms' (ibid, p.582) that would create a pole of attraction against the reformist unions.

There must have been many rank-and-file KPD workers whose doubts about the validity of the new line were set to rest by the conduct of the SPD leadership in first banning, and then dispersing by force, the Communist May Day March in Berlin. The actions of the Prussian socal democratic leaders in authorising the use of armoured cars as well as armed police on the marching workers was entirely consistent with their behaviour in the even more tumultuous clashes of January 1919, when Noske's Free Corps were set loose on the Sparticists in the same working class quarters of Berlin that witnessed the barricade fighting of May 1929. But once again it has to be said quite categorically that the KPD leadership deliberately sought such a 'confrontation' with the Berlin reformists, and gloried in the bloody repressions that followed. It will be recalled that the KPD, having dubbed the SPD a fascist party and an instrument of fascist dictatorship, obviously could no longer march jointly with that party in Berlin's traditional May Day celebrations. A separate march was called, one whose purpose could be divined from the appeal published in *Die Rote Fahne* of April 12, 1929, which summoned all workers to demonstrate with the KPD on May Day 'for the united proletarian front against the bourgeoisie and reformism'. Thus the march was explicitly an anti-SPD one, the reference to the 'united front' being purely decorative. The same appeal also spoke of the march as being a protest against the SPD's 'socal fascist coalition politics'. So well before the banned march got under way, communist workers had been quite cynically and demagogically incited to single out as the *main* object of their class hatred the reformist movement, a hatred not confined to its leaders, but the millions of workers who understandably ignored the ultimatistic demand for a 'united front' against their own 'social fascist' organisations. Justly enraged by the murder of their comrades, the KPD workers swung solidly behind the new line at the party's 12th Congress, held in a suitably militant venue at Wedding (the centre of the barricade fighting) between May 5 and 10. If Thälmann, Ulbricht, Remmele and Neumann required 'proof' of their theory of 'social fascism', then henceforth they could — and often did — point to the May Day massacre to silence their critics. Yet shooting workers, as Trotsky pointed out in 1924, does not constitute fascism. On that basis, the Ebert government must be designated a fascist regime! Fascism is the total destruction of all independent workers' organisations, and while the reactionary policies and repressions of the SPD *facilitated* the victory of fascism, they did not *constitute* fascism. To introduce and administer a fascist corporate state, *the SPD and ADGB would have had to destroy themselves!*

Lubricated with the blood of Berlin workers, who lost their lives in a reactionary adventure that had nothing to do with the struggle against either social democracy or German capitalism, the 'social fascist' bandwagon really began to gather pace throughout the CI. A statement issued after a meeting of the West European Bureau of the ECCI on May 16 demanded that 'all parties ...systematically continue the international campaign of enlightenment regarding the bloody terror of German social fascism in the May days ...' and that in their agitation they should expose social democracy 'as organiser of the war against the Soviet Union', with the hardest blows being delivered against left social democracy. How this particular tactic served to strengthen the SPD right wing will become evident when we come to the 1929 Magdeburg Congress of the SPD, held simultaneously with the KPD Congress at Wedding. Grave unrest had been generated in the SPD, and not only in its working class base, concerning the policies of the Müller government, which marked a big retreat even from its modest election programme. The issue which rankled party members most was Müller's reversal of the SPDs official pre-election opposition to the building of cruiser 'A' (it will be remembered that the SPD had fought — and largely won — the May 1928 election on the slogan 'childrens' feeding centres before cruisers'). While by no means adopting a consistent internationalist position on this question, a caucus of left delegates to the congress succeeded, much to the discomfort of the party leadership, in forcing a debate on the SPD's military policy. In three separate votes related to the military budget, the social democratic left secured the following percentages of the total vote of delegates: 35.4 against a motion from the party executive to table resolutions against the building of cruiser 'A', the military budget and — most important of all — further participation in a coalition with the bourgeois parties; 42.5, a resolution to delay the finalising of military policy to the next party congress (in 1931) — this being an unprincipled delaying tactic; and 38.6, the percentage of votes cast against the SPD executive's statement on military policy. Bearing in mind that as at all SPD Congresses, the votes and proceedure were heavily stacked in favour of the established leadership, which did all that it could to ensure that the 'right' delegations were sent to the Congress, this marked a serious setback for the Müller leadership, and confirmed that after less than a year in office, the SPD was undergoing a severe party crisis that contained all the symptoms of leading to an open split. Had KPD pursued the correct Leninist tactic towards the SPD as a whole, and its growing left flank in particular, enormous gains would have been registered for communism in the following months and years. But we already know that in accordance with Stalin's schema of the left social democrats (who were to be dubbed 'left social fascists') being the main enemy of the working class, no such tactic would be employed. No attempt was made to differentiate between the right and left wings of the SPD, despite there being open rifts between them on several important issues. Thus the CI organ, in an editorial on the May Day events, utterly failed to exploit this conflict by appealing to the left elements to dissociate themselves from the massacre ordered by Severing and Zorgiebel, and to wage a struggle inside the SPD to drive them out of its ranks. Instead, the entire party was branded as having 'openly taken the road of fascism', and as having become an 'openly social fascist party'. (*May Day in Berlin,* ibid, Vol. 6, No. 16, June 15 1929, p.620). Hardly conducive to opening up a dialogue with the leftward moving elements in this 'social fascist party'. Even worse was the article on the SPD Congress by Karl Kreibich. Once again, the main task to be accomplished was the justification of the Stalin line that social democracy, left, right and centre, was turning fascist at full speed. Therefore, there could be nothing but ridicule for the challenge mounted by the 'left social fascists' to the executive at Magdeburg: 'The "lefts" are an even more indispensable and dignified part of social democracy. Their task is to play some seemingly radical accompaniment to the SPD's rapid progress to fascism. The most outstanding characteristic of the Magdeburg congress is that it completed not only the transition of social democracy to social fascism, but also the recent capitulation of the "lefts" '. (The obligatory quotes denoting that there could be no question of a genuine left tendency in social democracy — a notion also to be found in circles that on paper at least repudiate third period Stalinism.) Then Kreibich, writing as if a 35.4% vote against continued participation in the coalition had never taken place, drew the predictable conclusion — one on which his job — and possibly neck — depended — that 'never has a social democratic congress so unanimously recognised in principle the policy of coalition'. As if there could be degrees of unanimity! This seemingly blind denial of a reality that was staring the KPD in the face was taken up not only by Trotsky, who roundly denounced the Stalinist ultra-left course from a Leninist standpoint in his *The 'third period' of Comintern errors,* but by the Brandler group in Germany, who in their centrist organ *Against the Current,* made the correct observation that by describing the SPD as a fascist party, the KPD was repelling workers who were moving to the left away from social democracy towards communism. For at this stage, 'the social democratic workers do not understand the policy of their leaders at all as a betrayal'. To which Gusiev replied: 'But if that is so, then one has to admit that the social democratic workers are in favour of a fascist dictatorship'. 'S. Gusiev: *On the Road to a new Revolutionary Rise,* ibid, Vol. 6, No. 19, August 16, 1929. p.720. And that was soon to become the opinion of a considerable section of the CI, RILU and KPD leaderships.

In yet another article on the May Day events, H. Kurella (later purged by Stalin) the editor of *International Press Correspondence,* roundly proclaimed that 'the social democracy *as a whole* has become an inseparable part of capitalist society. Broad cadres of functionaries of the SPD and of the reformist trade unions are firmly bound up with the state apparatus of the bourgeoisie [how firmly Hitler was to prove four years later!]. The party apparatus of the SPD and of the reformist trade unions have themselves become a part of the apparatus of suppression, have become prop and executive organs of the capitalist state in the working class ...The SPD is developing into a social fascist fighting organ of the bourgeoisie' (H. Kurella: *The Bloody First of May, IPC,* Vol. 9, No. 9, April 19, 1929, p.497.)

This even more leftist analysis and perspective was aired at great length at the Tenth ECCI Plenum held in July 1929. Kuusinen's opening report rambled on about the 'fascisation of the bourgeois class rule' and its being accompanied by 'the process of the fascisation of the reformist trade union bureaucracy and of the parties of the Second International', adding that as result of this processs, and 'since German fascism openly declares in favour of bourgeois dictatorship [quite false], since social fascism openly shows itself up as fascism, it will no longer be difficult to win the majority of the working class in Germany for the proletarian revolution'. (Ibid, Vol. 9 No. 40, August 20, 1929, p.848.) This is one of the first instances of that notorious Stalinist theory which found its most malignant expression in the slogan that gained currency in the last months and weeks of Weimar — 'after Hitler — us'. Manuilsky plumbed even murkier depths on the second day of the Plenum in his report on 'the struggle for the majority of the working class'. Far from the bourgeoisie ever seeking to eject the reformists from the German government (already the declared aim of a sizable group in the DVP Reichstag fraction, not to speak of the entire DNVP!) Manuilsky envisaged that the SPD 'will take ever greater initiative from the bourgeoisie in the suppression of the working class. It will become the more savage, it will become the more rapidly fascised, the more its influence on the working class will decline'. (Ibid, p.855) In other words, the SPD was even more reactionary and eager to crush the proletariat than the bourgeoisie itself! How easy then to 'expose' it, and 'capture' the majority of the working class for communist policies: 'it follows that although the power of resistance of social democracy increases, the task of the communist parties of exposing the social fascist nature of contemporary social democracy is being facilitated'. (Ibid, p.856.) Now there could be no room for doubts. Only one form of 'united front' could be pursued — that 'from below': 'The united front is neither a coalition with the social democrats at the top nor a policy of compromise with their officials below. It is a direct appeal of the communist party to the mass of workers, to the social democratic and non-party workers, to the organised and unorganised. The united front tactic could be the easiest thing in the world if it were to consist of the formation of more or less "cordial" agreements of the communist parties with the other lower organisations in the factories for the purpose of common action. [But] the united front tactic means a most irreconcilable struggle against the reformist and social democratic organisations for the mass in the factories [not, as in Lenin's day, for the unity of the class in struggle against the bourgeoisie, be it noted]. We do not idolise the social democratic lower officials in the factories (members of factory committees and delegates etc. [in other words, not 'officials', but social democratic *workers*]) ...The task of the communist party is to press these elements to the wall in the face of the working masses of the factories, to give them no chance to spread illusions to the effect that they, being connected with rank and file, are of a different quality from their leaders, that they are capable of fighting honestly, in the interests of the workers. We must isolate them, advancing commensurate with the degree of our influence, the demand on behalf of the entire mass of the workers, that the social democratic workers should leave their party'. (Ibid, p.860) *And this was called the united front.*

But worse was to follow. There had been a running debate in the CI leadership between partisans and opponents of a policy, favoured by the RILU leadership, of calling on workers to leave the 'social fascist' trade unions and set up CP-dominated 'red' unions. Stalin had encouraged this leftist trade union tactic when he declared, in his already-quoted attack on Humbert-Droz, that workers outside the trade unions were more revolutionary, as a matter of course, than workers organised in the reformist unions. RILU chief Lozovsky declared, at the beginning of 1929: '...where is the most backward, the most reactionary part of the working class today? That part of the working class which is organised in the reformist unions and follows the reformist leadership is the most consciously reactionary part of the working class... the workers following social democracy are sabotaging the movement. [Thus] a split in the unions in Germany is approaching, to fail to see it is to commit a crime against the German proletariat ...During the Ruhr conflict our comrades put forward the slogan "unorganised workers, join the reformist unions" as though the reformist unions were better than the Christian and Hirsch-Duncker [liberal] unions. I consider that slogan unsound. It deludes the workers'. (A. Lozovsky: *Communist International*, Vol. 6, No. 17, July 15, 1929, pp.659-661) Lozovsky then drew the conclusion that since the reformist unions had ceased either to be organs of class struggle or movements where one could find large numbers of class conscious workers, it was necessary to launch new, pure, revolutionary unions, starting in Germany:.'First we must organise the opposition in the metal workers union on an all-German scale, the same in regard to the miners and other industries.' After that, would come the founding of the new 'red' unions. Piatnitsky, while not denying the social fascist nature of the unions, favoured what was by comparison a more moderate course: 'Should we now adopt the slogan for Germany "abandon that work and form mutual aid societies?" I consider that dangerous. Comrade Lozovsky's proposal plays into the hands of the shirkers who do not wish to work in the enterprises and the unions, for them it is easier to organise new unions'. (O. Piatnitsky: *Speech to Trade Union Commission of ECCI*, February 28, 1929, in ibid, p.655.) But he wisely left the door ajar lest the line continue to veer leftwards as it had done throughout 1928: 'I think that at a certain moment the KPD may, with a development of the class struggle and for the purpose of transforming the unions into fighting class organs, create parallel unions from the members of reformist unions — members who at the call of the KPD abandon those unions'. (Ibid, p.655.) How deserting the reformist unions *en masse* was to 'transform [them] into fighting class organs' was understandably left unexplained, but one can appreciate Piatnitsky's dilemma in seeking to combine his own line with that of Lozovsky.

The dispute appears to have remained unresolved until the Tenth Plenum, where Lozovsky found an influential supporter for his new trade union tactic in Thälmann, now the unchallenged leader of the KPD and close *confidant* of Stalin. In the general discussion on the main reports, Lozovsky returned to his argument that the reformist parties and unions were turning fascist from top to bottom: 'It is clear that fascisation cannot only affect the leading cadres. There is ...a very strong pre-conceived notion in communist circles that only the upper stratum is reactionary, whereas the lower cadres are less reactionary ...we will find that reaction is rife not only in the middle and upper strata, but also among the lower functionaries who are dragging with them a certain stratum of demoralised corrupt workers. The development of social democracy into social fascism will take, on the one hand, the fascisation of *all strata* with the exception of a few insignificant groups, and secession in social democratic ranks will take place precisely to the right [sic! — why to thé right, when the party has already turned fascist!] and to the left'. (*IPC*, Vol. 9, No. 47, p.1038) A little later, Thälmann took the floor to deliver his report on *The economic struggle, our tactics and the tasks of the Communist Parties*, whose second section was headed: *The Fascisation of the Trade Unions, their merging with the state apparatus and finance capitalism*. It provided a broad hint of what was to follow: 'Today we no longer advocate indiscriminate entering of all workers into the reformist trade unions. We advocate only entering of class conscious revolutionary workers to strengthen the revolutionary opposition'. (Ibid, Vol. 9, No. 55, October 4, 1929, p.1185) What was to become of non-revolutionary workers who nevertheless wanted to engage in the economic struggle? No answer was forthcoming to this awkward question, since the line was still in transition from the old tactic of 'transforming the unions into organs of class struggle' to that of establishing 'red' unions that would also seek — quite fruitlessly — to enrol reformist as well as revolutionary workers. Lozovsky's report on trade union work brought the new line a little nearer when, in rebutting Brandlerite and Trotskyist criticisms of the breakaway union tactic, he declared, in a remark obviously also directed at his ECCI rival Piatnitsky, that 'it is necessary to abandon the somewhat hackneyed idea so frequently encountered ...that to form a new trade union means to follow the line of least resistance. (Ibid, p.1197) Yet that is precisely what it did mean.

The main theses adopted at the Plenum marked a new stage in the further evolution of the CI line to the adventurist ultra left, since it endorsed Lozovsky's line of setting up, in the not too distant future, 'red' unions; even though it did so in a cautious, ambiguous formulation: 'The rising tide of the labour movement and the growing crisis of the reformist trade unions have brought forth the dangerous tendency of refusing to work in the reformist trade unions. At the same time this rising tide of the labour movement has brought forth the new problem of establishing at certain stages, under certain conditions, *new* revolutionary unions ...communists cannot be opposed on principle to splitting the trade unions ...The growth of the strike movement [a claim, which as Trotsky pointed out at the time, was not born out by any strike statistics] since the Sixth Congress, and the further onslaught of the social fascist bureaucracy, has created in a numer of countries the conditions under which it has beome necessary to establish new revolutionary unions'. (*On the International Situation and the Immediate Tasks of the Communist Parties*, ibid, Vol. 9, No. 46, September 4, 1929, p.985)

A Plenary session of the RILU in December 1929 presented Lozovsky with the opportunity to carry his offensive on the trade union tactic even closer to the point when he could call for the formation of breakaway 'red' unions in most of the capitalist countries. In his closing speech Lozovsky stressed once again that the reformist unions were useless as organs of class struggle: 'The new fact in the situation is that the higher and middle officials and large sections of the lower officials of the reformist trade unions and a great section of the Labour aristocracy are already fascist'. (*IPC*, Vol. 10, No. 1, January 2, 1930, p.15) This theory — false to the core — was inscribed in the final resolution of the Plenary session: 'The reformist trade union bureaucrats have passed over from covert sabotage of strikes to the open recruitment of blacklegs and the direct organising of police-reformist raids on strikers and their strike committees. Today every strike is opposed by the open blackleg machinery of the reformist unions. We find a rapid fascisation of the reformist trade union apparatus taking place . . . our most important task is to intensify the struggle for the trade union masses [such as were not, by Lozovsky's exacting standards, 'consciously reactionary'] and to pit them against this blacklegging trade union machine, to sharpen the struggle against the scab functionaries of social fascism.' (Ibid, Vol. 10, No. 12, March 6, 1930, p.217) How did the ultra-left Stalinist course and the theory of 'social fascism' equip the advanced workers in Germany to strengthen their party in its fight against reformism, and the bourgeoisie which it sought to serve? The brutal fact is that the KPD was unable to make even the slightist impact in the developing crisis, either on the SPD, or the trade unions, where the ADGB leadership had been forced by the sheer pressure of the capitalist offensive to take up a partially oppositional stance on the question of unemployment insurance. Indeed, how could the KPD intervene fruitfully in these favourable situations when its entire analysis led rank-and-file workers of the party to believe — often against their better class judgment — that the ADGB unions had turned fascist, become tied to or fused with the state machine, and were nothing but instruments for exploiting and repressing the working class? The only logical conclusion from such a false premise was that the sooner one left such 'unions', the better, and that any conflict that did arise between the ADGB leadership and the employers was nothing more than a stunt to dupe such class conscious workers into believing that the trade unions were still fighting the boss. In fact these conflicts were being fought out — certainly on the part of the employers — in deadly earnest, as can be seen from the statements of the Federation of German Industries and Reichsbank President Schacht, reproduced in the foregoing chapter. The arguments employed to explain away the bourgeoisie's offensive on the Müller government were tortuous even by Stalinist standards, and produced the most calamitous results. The following extract is from an article that appeared in the CI organ *after* the fall of the Müller government, an article devoted entirely to proving that such an event was impossible: 'As for the monopoly capitalists, they also, in the person of their DNVP, manoeuvre. They pretend that they are now directing their main attack against the "dangerous" social democratic and reformist trade unions, against their "socialist" policy, and against "economic democracy" and state capitalism, with which it was "time to end". This manoeuvre tripped up even certain of our German comrades, who thought that having exploited social democracy, monopolist capitalism was now ready to dismiss it. That was a great mistake. The monopoly bourgeoisie knew very well that modern social fascism is one of the most important instruments for the fascisation of the state, with which social democracy has now organically fused. The outcry raised by the great bourgeoisie against "economic democracy" was a pure comedy [one that ended for many social democrats in the death camps of the Third Reich] ...The German great bourgeoisie had no intention of eliminating the social democrats from participation in the fascist dictatorship.' (*Decaying Capitalism and the Fascisation of the Bourgeois State, Communist International,* Vol. 7, No. 2-3, April 1 [sic!] 1930, p.73) A little earlier, Hermann Jacobs of the Berlin party organisation had written, in similar vein, that the 'social fascists [were] an indispensable instrument of the fascist dictatorship'. (*IPC,* Vol. 10, No. 3, January 23, 1930, p.66) It was hardly surprising therefore when following the removal of the SPD from the government coalition, and the formation of Brüning's all bourgeois-cabinet, neither the KPD nor the ECCI were eager to discuss the reason for Müller's fall. The only coherent — if false — analysis attempted was that by A. Norden of the Berlin organisation, who lamely argued that 'as it is now a question of carrying out the inner Young Plan [i.e. attacks on workers to pay for it] ...it is more advantageous for the big bourgeoisie to have a sham opposition of the SPD than that the latter should remain in the government.' (Ibid, Vol. 10, No. 17, April 3, 1930, p.331) The theory however remained unchanged, since for the KPD leadership, their could still be no question of a genuine (as opposed to 'sham') conflict between the reformist leaders and the bourgeoisie. Every denunciation of the SPD's 'Marxism', its programme of 'economic democracy' (i.e. those articles of the Weimar Constitution which provided for trade union and works' council representation on local and national economic boards etc.) and municipal reforms, was ridiculed as a put-up job to delude workers into remaining loyal to social democracy. For this Stalinist, idealist method could conceive of no other conflict than that between a revolutionary working class struggling for power under the exclusive leadership of the communist party, and a united front of the bourgeoisie reaching from Trotskyists and 'left social fascists' to the main bourgeois parties and the fascists. Everything else was a pure show, or a 'manoeuvre' staged to dupe the less advanced workers. Yet the events of the next three years were to give ample evidence that far from shamming, the monopolies were in deadly earnest when they demanded an end to the reforms of the SPD, and the interference of the trade unions and works councils in the running of their plants and mines. For how else can we explain the enthusiastic support the trusts later gave to Hitler's secret programme of crushing these same 'social fascist' trade unions, which according to the Stalinists, were capable only of conducting a 'sham' fight with the employers'. One would have thought that after the experience of Germany, and especially on the basis of Trotsky's voluminous writings on the subject, no tendency calling itself Trotskyist today would repeat this most crude of all ultra-leftist errors: namely that of denying the existence of a contradiction (not a social, but a political one) between big business and reformist labour. Yet this is precisely what the *Workers Press* did in its analysis of the 1973 Labour Party conference. The entire bourgeois press fulminated against the line being put forward by certain speakers on the need for extensive nationalisation if and when a Labour government was returned to office. Naturally, Labour lefts such as Anthony Wedgwood Benn and Eric Heffer would not be able to implement the type of programme they said was necessary if a Labour Government was to make serious inroads into the power of big business. That is the task of the working class mobilised and led by the revolutionary party. But does that mean that the ruling class and its press see things in the same Marxist light? Was Benn attacked simply because the bourgeoisie and the Tories wanted to build him up as a fake alternative to the WRP, (in other words, was it a 'sham fight' or a 'manoeuvre' such as the KPD Stalinists claimed was being pursued by the German bourgeoisie on the very eve of the fall of the Müller government'? Or is it rather a case (similar to, though by no means identical with the capitalist offensive unleashed against the German reformists in 1929-1930) of the Tories and the big employers *quite genuinely* fearing the impact that the election of a Labour government, committed to a radical-reform programme along the lines proposed by Benn, could have on the millions of workers who voted for it? Is it not the case that in this period of rapidly worsening capitalist crisis, the economic basis for concessions to the working class, concessions mediated through their reformist leaders, is in the last stages of erosion, and that therefore, capitalism will find even the most modest reformist demands of the trade union and Labour leaders intolerable, as the German bourgeoisie did in the last four years of the Weimar Republic? We often encounter analogies in *Workers Press* between the present situation in Britain and that of Germany in the early 1930s. But let us make the analogy a correct one, let us emphasize that just as the reformists sought to betray in Germany, yet were spurned, persecuted and even murdered by the fascist agents of the bourgeoisie, so too in Britain, the ruling class will reach a point in the development of the crisis and the class struggle when it will dispense with the services of the reformist (as it did in Chile) and however strong may be the desire of the latter to continue serving the capitalist master, this ruling class will turn to other, far more brutal forces, uninhibited by any links with the organised workers' movement, to complete the job that the labour and trade union reformists, with their policies of class collaboration, have begun. The capitalist press onslaught on the 1973 Labour Party Conference was the harbinger of just such a strategic turn: 'The doctrines of class conflict and state ownership are Marxist doctrines, and so long as both are preached at their conference, the Labour Party really must not complain at being described as under the influence of Marxist ideas ...[The Labour Party is] increasingly socialist, believing that the working class should use state power in order to enforce an egalitarian society ...' (*The Times*, first leader: *Mr Wilson and the Liberals,* October 4, 1973) How did *Workers Press* respond to this almost unprecedented attack on the Labour Party? Amazingly, in view of the WRP's claims to Trotskyist orthodoxy, the paper saw the attack — for such it was — *through the spectacles of classic third period Stalinism.* The whole thing was a sham: 'There must be two conferences going on at Blackpool this week. There is the one being covered by *Workers Press*, and the other being covered by *The Times*. Take Monday's coverage. On that day the *Workers Press* revealed that the "lefts" had done a deal to sabotage the proposal to nationalise the top 25 companies in Britain. But *The Times* carried the front-page headline "Marxist challenge to party leadersip". The paper's illustrious political editor said that the nub of the conference was the "power struggle between Marxist and non-Marxist" ...By feeding these fraudulent distortions to the capitalist press they [the alleged source of these stories — the Labour Party and Trade union leaders] achieve two ends: The working class knows that the capitalist press is lying — there is no Marxist challenge in the Labour Party nor is there a fight for socialist policies. Cynicism, a plague on political consciousness, results. The middle class is terrified into believing that Labour's half-baked solutions will tax them into pauperism and industry will be brought into chaos ...It is done wilfully by professional confusion mongers who want to keep the Labour Party free of any specific commitment to the rank and file at the next general election.' (Workers Press, Ocotber 5, 1973) In fact, there were three Labour Party conferences, just as in Germany, there were three Magdeburg Congresses of the SPD. The German bourgeoisie, like The Times saw only Marxists on the rampage, seeking to commit the SPD leadership to a policy of total pacifism, all-out socialisation and brutal class war. Supplementing the bourgeois Right analysis was that of the Stalinists, who dismissed out of hand the existence of any conflict, either between the SPD and the trade unions as a whole and the bourgeoisie (an analysis wrecked within a year) or the possibility of a split between the SPD left and the bureaucracy. Here too, events proved the Stalinists wrong, for after a protracted battle lasting more than two years, a sizeable segment of the social democratic lefts, together with a proportionally far smaller number of former party workers, split from the SPD to form the Socialist Workers' Party (SAP), a development predicted and welcomed by Trotsky. And this was the real Magdeburg Congress, a contradictory and many sided reality that could not be forced into the arid schemas of third period Stalinism without doing violence to the Marxist method and disorienting literally millions of German workers. Likewise with The Times and Workers Press. They each caught only one side of the Labour Party Conference, abstracting it from its national and international setting, not to speak of the entire history of British and world social democracy. Where The Times could see only the so-called 'Marxist intellectual base of the Labour Party', and a concerted campaign by its main exponents to drive the party further and further to the left, Workers Press only had eyes for betrayal, deception, confusion-mongering, lying. That these were all present in abundance at Blackpool is not in dispute. But there was much else that should have caught the attention of a trained Marxist journalist, but which escaped Workers Press because the entire orientation of the movement is towards a perspective which has the trade union and Labour Party leaders moving steadily towards their enthusiastic creation of — and participation in — a corporate state. Such also was the perspective of the KPD after the official inauguration of the 'third period' at the Sixth CI Congress, and for that very reason it too could neither detect nor exploit the growing tensions arising between the reformists leaders and the gathering forces of reaction and fascist counter-revolution. We could continue to point to other and related flaws in this article — for example, that the very demand to nationalise the 25 top companies sabotaged by Wilson and the lefts was, when first proposed by the Labour Party National Executive, roundly denounced as 'corporatism' (Workers Press of June 11, 1973, said of the proposal to nationalise 25 top companies that it was 'not socialist nationalisation but its opposite — corporatism ...by implication a clear move to the right ...') But the central question is one of method. The Workers Press treatment of the reformists is based on a rationalist conception of the class struggle. Since every Trotskyist knows that the Labour Party is neither led nor influenced by Marxists, then when The Times says that it is, it must be lying, and that its only motive must therefore be to deceive the working class, who are searching for an alternative to reformism. Let us overlook the rather obvious fact — one that should have immediately occurred to whoever wrote and checked the article in question — that The Times is written for and read by the ruling class, and not ten million trade unionists or 13 million Labour voters (a fact which, when it suits Workers Press, it too is prepared to admit. On April 30, 1973, when commenting on the fact that the more 'popular' daily papers were going out of their way to 'play down the abject capitulation to the Tories uttered by TUC general secretary Victor Feather', Workers Press observed: 'Of all the capitalist newspapers, only The Times, which is not widely *read by workers,* told the real story ...*The Times* has a clear duty — *to tell the truth to the class* it represents' [emphasis added]. Except, it seems, when it violates the ultra-leftist perspectives and schematic analyses of *Workers Press.*)

There still exists the possibility that *The Times* is worried by the repeated, if vague and as the *Workers Press* correctly points out, ineffectual demands for nationalisation heard at the Labour Party Conference. For if we adopt the position that the ruling class and its various agents are always lying when they describe those communists know to be reformist traitors as 'Marxists'; then how are we to either understand or fight fascism? Did not Hitler in his *Mein Kampf,* not speak of his numerous speeches to leaders of big business, everywhere and always refer to the social democrats, the men who permitted the murder of Liebknecht and Luxemburg, who voted for the Kaiser's war credits in August 1914, who betrayed the November Revolution of 1918, who time and again preferred coalition with the bourgeoisie to a fighting united front with the KPD — *did not Hitler without fail refer to these historic traitors to the German and international working class as Marxists?* What then are we to make of fascism? Does it too *consciously* build up the social democrats in this way — by calling them communists and Marxists, agents of Moscow etc. — in order to head off the working class from the real communists? Can those responsible for the production and political line of *Workers Press* really argue this? Yet that is the direction in which their rationalistic method, exemplified by their treatment of the 1973 Labour Party Conference, is leading them. Should a big right-wing movement develop in this country towards fascism, and should its leaders declare war on the 'Marxist' Labour Party and the 'communist' TUC (not to speak of those who merit such labels) what will the *Workers Press* say then? That such fascist leaders are lying? *As if it was just a question of truth or falsehood.* Yes, it is quite correct to say that the reformists are not Marxists, and almost without exception, never will be. Yet that still does not answer the vital question — why does *The Times* say they are? (Just as the KPD never answered the same question in relation to the big business and then Nazi onslaught on the 'Marxists' of the SPD and the ADGB). Every KPD official could repeat by rote all the betrayals — small as well as big — of the German reformists. Yet that did not prevent them suffering the same fate at the hands of the Nazis as the 'social fascists', just as similar recitations by *Workers Press* will not in themselves insure either the WRP or the working class in this country against ending up in the same camps and death cells as those whom it so glibly and recklessly dubs as 'corporatists'. Trotsky gave the answer to this question more than forty years ago, but tragically few were prepared or able to listen. Can it be that the leadership of the WRP is also deaf?: 'Brüning's regime rests upon the cowardly and perfidious support of the social democratic bureaucracy which in its turn depends upon the sullen, half-hearted support of a section of the proletariat. [The SPD policy of 'toleration' adopted by the reformist leaders after the sensational Nazi election triumph of September 1930 on the spurious grounds that Brüning was a 'lesser evil' to Hitler]. The system based on bureaucratic decrees is unstable, unreliable, temporary. Capitalism requires another, more decisive policy. The support of the social democrats, keeping a suspicious watch on their own workers, is not only insufficient for its purposes, but has already become irksome [witness the anti-SPD tirades of Schacht in his *The End of Reparations*]. The period of half-way measures has passed. In order to find a way out, the bourgeoisie must absolutely rid itself of the pressure exerted by the workers' organisations; these must be eliminated, destroyed, utterly crushed. [Please note, not 'tied to', 'fused with' or 'incorporated into' the capitalist state, as third period Stalinism — and now *Workers Press* — tells us] (L. Trotsky: *What Next?* [January 27, 1932] in *The Struggle Against Fascism in Germany,* p.144). Hence the fulminations against 'Marxism' by the bourgeoisie and its fascist agents. For this is the word with which they can best express their hatred of the organisations — and leaders — that bar their way to the goals outlined by Trotsky. Only a political simpleton can reduce this conflict to one of a 'sham' fight, or in the case of *The Times* (though we are far from lapsing into third period Stalinism by identifying this paper with fascism) to a ruse for the deception and demoralisation of workers, the vast majority of whom never read *The Times* from one year to the next. Despite its own monumental record of betrayals, British social democracy can also become an expendable commodity for the British bourgeoisie, should the working class not be broken from it before this point and led towards the direct struggle for state power. Its leftist line and false analysis of social democracy will mean, unless these faults are corrected, *openly* and in good time, that the WRP will be unable to exploit the opportunities presented by such a sharp turn in the political situation, one that will obviously demand, given the growth of the revolutionary party to a serious mass force, the tactic of the united front. And on such a tactical turn could rest the entire fate of the British working class. That was the lesson of Germany. Has the leadership of the WRP forgotten it?